Rokitno-Wolyn and Surroundings; Memorial Book and Testimony (Ukraine)

Translation of:

Rokitno (Volin) Ve-ha-seviva; Sefer Edut Ve-zikaron

Original Yizkor Book Edited by:

Eliezer Leoni

Published in Tel Aviv, by Former Residents of Rokitno in Israel, 1967
(Hebrew and Yiddish)

Published by JewishGen

**An Affiliate of the Museum of Jewish Heritage - A Living Memorial to the Holocaust
New York**

Rokitno-Wolyn and Surroundings; Memorial Book and Testimony
Translation of *Rokitno (Volin) ve-ha-seviva; Sefer Edut ve-Zikaron*

First Printing: August 2015, Av 5775
Second Printing: August 2019, Av 5779

Translation Project Coordinator: Lora Metelits Hull
Photo Editor: Larry Gaum (Toronto, Ontario)
Layout: Sheldon Z. Lipsky (Centerport, NY),
Layout and Publication Assistant Ann Belinsky (Re'ut-Modi'in, Israel)
Cover Design: Rachel Kolokoff Hopper (Ft. Collins, CO)
Publicity: Sandra Hirschhorn (Monroe Township, NJ]
Yiddish and Hebrew Consultant: Josef Rosin *z"l* (Haifa, Israel)
Indexing: Diana Salman

Published by JewishGen, Inc.
An Affiliate of the Museum of Jewish Heritage
A Living Memorial to the Holocaust
36 Battery Place, New York, NY 10280

Printed in the United States of America by Lightning Source, Inc.
Library of Congress Control Number (LCCN): 2014956957
ISBN: 978-1-939561-25-1 (hard cover: 738 pages, alk. paper)

Cover:
Front cover from the original Yizkor Book
Back cover: The marketplace in Rokitno, from the original Yizkor Book.
Background cover photo by Rachel Kolokoff Hopper of the Starvation Cell 21 inside Block 11 at Auschwitz, Poland.

JewishGen and the Yizkor-Books-in-Print Project

This book has been published by the **Yizkor-Books-in-Print Project,** as part of the **Yizkor Book Project** of **JewishGen, Inc**.

JewishGen, Inc. is a non-profit organization founded in 1987 as a resource for Jewish genealogy. Its website [www.jewishgen.org] serves as an international clearinghouse and resource center to assist individuals who are researching the history of their Jewish families and the places where they lived. JewishGen provides databases, facilitates discussion groups, and coordinates projects relating to Jewish genealogy and the history of the Jewish people. In 2003, JewishGen became an affiliate of the **Museum of Jewish Heritage - A Living Memorial to the Holocaust** in New York.

The **JewishGen Yizkor Book Project** was organized to make more widely known the existence of Yizkor (Memorial) Books written by survivors and former residents of various Jewish communities throughout the world. Later, volunteers connected to the different destroyed communities began cooperating to have these books translated from the original language—usually Hebrew or Yiddish—into English, thus enabling a wider audience to have access to the valuable information contained within them. As each chapter of these books was translated, it was posted on the JewishGen website and made available to the general public.

The **Yizkor-Books-in-Print Project** began in 2011 as an initiative to print and publish Yizkor Books that had been fully translated, so that hard copies would be available for purchase by the descendants of these communities and also by scholars, universities, synagogues, libraries, and museums.

These Yizkor books have been produced almost entirely through the volunteer effort of researchers from around the world, assisted by donations from private individuals. The books are printed and sold at near cost, so as to make them as affordable as possible. Our goal is to make this important genre of Jewish literature and history available in English in book form, so that people can have the personal histories of their ancestral towns on their bookshelves for themselves and for their children and grandchildren.

A list of all published translated Yizkor Books along with prices can be found at:
http://www.jewishgen.org/Yizkor/ybip.html

Lance Ackerfeld, Yizkor Book Project Manager

Joel Alpert, Yizkor-Book-in-Print Project Coordinator

This book is presented by the
Yizkor Books in Print Project
Project Coordinator: Joel Alpert

Part of the
Yizkor Books Project of JewishGen, Inc.
Project Manager: Lance Ackerfeld

These books have been produced solely through volunteer effort of individuals from around the world. The books are printed and sold at near cost, so as to make them as affordable as possible.

Our goal is to make this history and important genre of Jewish literature available in English in book form so that people can have the near-personal histories of their ancestral towns on their bookshelves for themselves and for their children and grandchildren.

Any donations to the Yizkor Books Project are appreciated.

Please send donations to:
Yizkor Book Project
JewishGen
36 Battery Place
New York, NY 10280

JewishGen, Inc. is an affiliate of the
Museum of Jewish Heritage
A Living Memorial to the Holocaust

Title Page of Original Yizkor Book

רוקיטנה (וולין) והסביבה

ספר עדות וזכרון

העורך: אליעזר לֶאוֹנִי

הוצאת ארגון יוצאי רוקיטנה והסביבה בישראל
תשכ"ז תל־אביב 1967

Translation of the Hebrew Title page

Rokitno
(Wolyn) and Surroundings

Memorial
Book
and
Testimony

Editor: Eliezer Leoni

Published in Tel Aviv, by Former Residents of Rokitno in Israel, 1967

FOREWORD FOR THE TRANSLATION

Lora Metelits, Translation Project Coordinator
Granddaughter of Avram Gendelman,
Great Granddaughter of Shimon Gendelman, Kisorich

In 1997, my sister, Lynn and I learned that our grandpop originally came from Rokitno. He had come to the US in 1912 and left most of his family in Europe. Our family had a photograph of my grandpop and his family taken on a visit in 1930. This was the last time he saw his family.

My sister and I also learned of the Rokitno Yizkor book and my sister found the book at the UCLA library, one of five US libraries that had the book at the time. We found our Gendelman family throughout the book, including excerpts of pictures from our 1930 family photograph, but we were not able to read the Hebrew or Yiddish. At this point, I searched in my local area for translators and am thankful that Esther Schlesinger and Alia Schneider translated a couple of stories for us. We turned to JewishGen for help and I am grateful that Thia Persoff translated several articles. Soon after, we were very fortunate to get to know Larry and Ala Gamulka. Larry is from Rokitno and has a personal account of his own experience. His wife, Ala was gracious in devoting so much time and effort into translating pretty much the entire book. I am extremely appreciative of their involvement in this project as I was able to learn so much about Rokitno and my own family from both the translation and additional information given by Larry and even some of their friends.

I would like to thank Haim Sidor for his work of translating the names in the Yizkor section. We were fortunate to have Haim Bar Or, also from Rokitno, review the Yizkor list to ensure the translated names were correct specific to the Rokitno area.

During the time that the book was being translated, my family met and contacted cousins that we had not known existed. Many of these relationships were established as a result of this translation, including contact with three first cousins to my mother and cousins in Australia.

I am honored to be the spokesperson for this translation but all I did was to coordinate the translated work of others. This entire translation was a volunteer effort and I thank everyone who provided their help. We are all grateful to JewishGen for assisting in the original translation and for posting it online for anyone to read. I was thrilled when I was told that JewishGen is publishing this translation! It has always been a dream of mine to publish the translated version of the Rokitno Yizkor book so that others who cannot read the original language can also remember the people and their stories.

And you, child of Rokitno,
From the depth of my heart I send this poem to the sound of bitter cries
If no one listens, it will drown in heavy waters
You must promise to remember our dear ones and to never forget the Holocaust
Tell this to your children, from one generation to another, to always remember.

Taken from "Lamentation on the Destruction".
Nathan Gendelman, Page 289

ADDITIONAL FOREWORD FOR THE TRANSLATION

Ann Belinsky
Publication Assistant

It is a pleasure to present below the completely translated Rokitno-Wolyn and Surroundings; Memorial Book and Testimony.

As explained by the executive committee of the Association of Former Residents of Rokitno and its Vicinity in Israel, the project of commemorating the martyrs of the town and its surroundings was their prime concern since the association was founded:

> "We knew the organization served a purpose – to stoke the dying embers and to not allow the flame of our martyrs to go out. Our dearly beloved were always in front of our eyes. We continuously discussed their commemoration at every meeting and assembly. There was no doubt that the only method of commemoration of our dearly beloved was a literary one, a memorial book. This book would serve to relive the way of life of our parents, to keep the cultural heritage of the Jews of Rokitno and surroundings. We were convinced that as long as we did not fulfill our debt to the martyrs there was no purpose to our activities"

In this English translation we have inserted 10 Appendices, mostly of additional photos of Rokitno and its townspeople. Appendix A originated with an album kept by Yosef Golubowitz and found several years ago. In order to try and identify the people appearing in the photos, I participated in the annual Rokitno and Surroundings Memorial meeting in Israel and requested help. Following this meeting I also received copies of photos from several previous residents and their descendants and names of others to speak to. At the beginning of each appendix is a short text explaining the background of the person/family about whom the photos relate. **Since many of the Golubowitz photos show unidentified people, we would be very happy to receive any more information that readers can give. If you identify someone, please send an email with the Figure number and identification**. See "Notes to the Reader, page xxix" below. These photos are being inserted into the JewishGen online translation of the book, and will be updated as new information becomes available.

Lora Metelits, the original Translation Coordinator, sent us a Foreword describing her work and satisfaction that the book is now appearing in a hard cover edition. In addition I contacted the original translator, Ala Gamulka, who sent me a moving description of a trip returning to Rokitno in 2003 with her husband Larry Gamulka, a survivor.

I hope that this memorial book will be read by as many descendants as possible of the townspeople from Rokitno and the surrounding villages and that by the translation appearing below, we have indeed kept alive the memory of the town, villages and families.

Acknowledgements

We gratefully acknowledge the work of the Translation Coordinator, **Lora Metilits**, who worked closely with Ala Gamulka in organizing the translated book for the JewishGen Yizkor Book project. In her Foreword she acknowledges all those who were part of this project.

This book was almost completely translated by **Ala Gamulka** and we especially thank her for her flowing text.

Larry Gamulka, Ala's husband, gave help to Ala in several of the Yiddish translations (Pages 31, 239, 311, 324).

Thia Persoff translated many of the chapters in the "Personalities" Section (Pages 212-229).

Rabbi Avrohom Marmorstein translated the poem by Rabbi Yehudah ben Kolonimus (Page 274)

We thank the **Rokitna Association** in Israel, headed by **Moshe Trossman**, for permission to publish the book of this translation, and **Rafi Shapira** for providing the list of additional names for the Remembrance of *Kedoshim* (martyrs) (Pages 414-450).

APPENDICES:

Photographs in the Appendices:

Most of the photos comprise part of a collection of more than 150 photographs that **Yosef Golubowitz** carried with him during the Holocaust. We consider them to be of historical and genealogical importance and as such are including most in Appendix A. They include historical photos of the town of Rokitno from the late 1930's and of Yosef, his family and friends at this time. The story behind them appears in Appendix A. We thank his daughters **Levava Roiz** and **Ethel Regerman** for donating them and adding in some identifications.

Syoma Klurfein was Yosef Golubowitz's best friend and survived the war. His daughters **Yaffa Bonwitt** and **Zipi Hayisraeli** have written about him and contributed a story about his life as a child in Rokitno.

Zehava Nevo (Zlatka Perl), who escaped to Russia during the war, identified several people in the album of Yosef Golubowitz.

Haim Bar-Or (Svetchnik), a survivor whose story appears in the Yizkor book, has donated photos of his family, all of who died in the Holocaust.

Meir Burd left Rokitno before 1939 and came to Eretz Israel. He carried with him many photographs of family friends from the Hechalutz Youth

Movement and we have included several in Appendix D, donated by his son **Itzik Burd**.

Chana Goldman (nee **Kleiman**) survived with her immediate family by moving to Uzbekistan, and she has donated photos of her family in Rokitno, taken before WWII. Most died in the Holocaust. Her daughter **Tzipi Yoel** has written some notes about her mother.

Prof. Arieh Kochavi, whose parent escaped to Russia during the war, has donated several family photos.

We would like to thank **Esther Gilbert** for giving us permission to publish several photos she took while on a "Roots" visit with her husband, Sir Martin Gilbert, to the area of Volhyn. We are printing some of her photos of the Sarny mass murder graves and trenches and the Rokitno memorial stones.

Lady Gilbert also gave permission to publish the link to all photos © of her trip to Volhyn, which include the towns of Rovno, Mezerich, Alexandria, Kostopol, Berezna, Sarny and Rokitno:

https://picasaweb.google.com/101835228506722847482?authkey=Gv1sRgCNyDt

We thank **Harvey Spitzer** and his friend **Eli Tanis** for help in translating the dedications written in Yiddish on the backs of photographs.

We thank **Ala Gamulka** for contributing an article she wrote on impressions of her journey to Rokitno together with her husband **Larry**, (who was born there) and a group of survivors and their children and grandchildren.

VISITS TO ROKITNO

The almost yearly pilgrimage is organized by the **Association of Former Residents (and their descendants) of Rokitno and Its Surroundings**. Video clips of these visits can be viewed on YouTube as follows:

VIDEO CLIPS:

David Edelman, whose father **Chanan (Hunia)** was a survivor, made videos of a group trip to Rokitno in 2001 and also of an annual meeting of survivors in 2007 who speak about their experiences during the Holocaust. Even if you do not speak Hebrew, they are worthwhile watching.

The links are:

Journey to Rokitno, 2001. Parts 1 and 2:

https://www.youtube.com/watch?v=WRZxnHxHh3g

https://www.youtube.com/watch?v=-gXpusvFyes

Stories of survivors, 2007. Parts 1 and 2:

https://www.youtube.com/watch?v=kFCj-G4AcyA

https://www.youtube.com/watch?v=JJbXm3Gk7Y8

PHOTOS OF ROKITNO AND OF MEETINGS

In addition, photos of meetings on the Annual Remembrance Day and trips in Israel by survivors and their families can be seen on **Facebook** by typing in the FIND window "**Rokitna Organization**". The texts are in Hebrew, but by pressing on PHOTOS you will see many albums. **David Edelman** manages the Facebook page.

BOOKS ABOUT ROKITNO SURVIVORS:

I wish to note that at least 2 books have been written by Rokitno survivors about their experiences during and after the Holocaust:

1. **Jack Israeli**, 1991. The last time I saw Father: a survivor's story. Ginzburg Press, 186 pages. **ISBN 10: 0969490305** (Jack changed his surname from Rosenstein to Israeli)

2. **Milrad Ruth**, 2010.*Yaarot Avoodim* (Lost Forests). Effi Meltzer Inc. 192 pages (in Hebrew). **ISBN: 9657195241, 9789657195246** The story of **Haim Bar Or** (Svecznik).

Thanks to Ms **Chen Oz** (**Kravchik**) who loaned me the original Rokitno Yizkor book, helping me to prepare this translation for publication.

I thank **Lance Ackerfield**, Yizkor Book Project Manager, and his dedicated team for putting the original translation online in the JewishGen Yizkor Books website.

I especially thank **Joel Alpert**, Yizkor Book in Print Project Coordinator, for his guidance and patience with me during preparation of the book text for publication.

Ann Belinsky

Publication Assistant

Map of the Ukraine with Rokitno

Geopolitical Information:

Located at 51°17' North Latitude and 27°13' East Longitude

Alternate names for the town are: Rokytne [Ukrainian], Rokitnoye [Russian], Rokitno [Polish, Yiddish], Rekitne, Rokitino, Rokitna

	Town	District	Province	Country
Before WWI (c. 1900):	Rokitno	Ovruch	Volhynia	Russian Empire
Between the wars (c. 1930):	Rokitno	Sarny	Polesie	Poland
After WWII (c. 1950):	Rokitnoye			Soviet Union
Today (c. 2000):	Rokytne			Ukraine

Jewish Population	105 (in 1897), 663 (in 1921)
Notes:	Ukrainian: Рокитне. Yiddish: רעקיטנע. Russian: Рокитно / Рокитное. Hebrew: רוקיטנה 27 miles E of Sarny, 62 miles NE of Rivne (Rovno), 68 miles W of Ovruch, 76 miles SE of Pinsk. **[Not to be confused with Rokytne, S of Kyyiv.]**

Nearby Jewish Communities:

Snovydovychi 8 miles E
Tomashgorod 8 miles NW
Klesov 13 miles WNW
Olevsk 19 miles ESE
Drozdin 25 miles N
Sarny 27 miles W
Berezne 28 miles SW

A Short History of Jewish Rokitno

Rokitno had only a short Jewish history of about 50 years. Jews settled in the village of Rokitno (located in Ukraine of today) in the 1880's and at the beginning of the twentieth century the population was 4055 - mainly Russians and 105 Jews. The Jews chiefly earned their living from producing pottery and shoes, and leasing properties.

At the beginning of the twentieth century the erection of the glass factory and the building of the railroad from Kiev to Kovel changed the lives of the Jews in the village. As a result, a modern town of Rokitno was built on the other side of the village. The quick capitalization of Rokitno brought many changes in the economic lives of the Jews in the area. The general growth drew many Jews from nearby villages to Rokitno – from Stariky, Osnitzek, Dert, Krapilovka and from nearby towns – Stolin, Dombrovitza, Sarny, Visotzk, etc.

Soon there were 400 Jews in Rokitno. A beautiful synagogue was built in the town. The Jews of Rokitno were progressive Jews, Zionists who educated their children accordingly. The community membership income was used for annual assistance to Rabbis; food and warm milk to all educational institutions; charitable institutions; the Jewish National Fund and *Keren Hayesod*; soup kitchens for the Jewish soldiers in the local army units.

After World War I, Rokitno became part of Poland. Rokitno was a vibrant Zionist town, full of lively interest in everything that was happening in Eretz Israel. The Youth Movements of *HeHalutz, Hashomer Hatzair* and *Betar* were active and many of the youth went to *Hachshara* (training camps) and then made *aliyah* to Eretz Israel.

The Tarbut school was built in 1931. More than 90% of the children of the town and its surroundings were educated there. In addition to the curriculum of the government schools, Hebrew subjects were taught according to the Tarbut program and under its supervision. Except for geography, Polish history and language the language of instruction was Hebrew.

When war broke out between Germany and Poland in 1939, Poland was completely unprepared. On 17 September 1939, the Soviet army crossed the border and invaded Poland. The Russians were sympathetic to the population and promised that from now on they would live beautiful productive lives. Soon the Soviet regime was well established and Rokitno officially became the district capital. The Jewish population adapted to the new regime. The arrest of four Jews and the first public trial of a Jew- a restaurant owner accused of "speculation"-- showed the other side of the coin. All connections between the town Jews and their relatives in other countries, including Eretz Israel, were broken. They were afraid that they would be accused of Zionist or espionage activities. This was the final curtain for the Hebrew Tarbut school. It was forbidden to study Jewish history or Judaism. Yiddish became the official language of teaching in the school. The teachers became a tool for the authorities. They became passive and stopped being pro-active. Thus the Hebrew school in Rokitno was terminated, together with the Jewish population. This was a population who had known freedom of movement, speech and activity. The youth no longer had hopes of fulfilling the promise of *aliyah.* The Zionist parties and the youth movements self-destructed. Here and there, secret meetings still took place. There were some young people who endangered their lives and tried to reach Vilna on their way to Eretz Israel. A few succeeded while others were caught and sent to concentration camps in the far North. The rest pretended to break off any connections to the past and to join the new regime. In their hearts, the yearning and hope never disappeared. Devout Jews continued to pray in secret, although the authorities could not legally touch matters of faith.

This was really the beginning of the destruction of the Rokitno Jewish community. The destruction began with the burning of the body and soul and ended with extinction.

Some families went to Russia. They were certain that the German army would be stopped near the fortified border between Poland and Russia. They hoped to find shelter in one of the nearby Ukrainian villages where they would wait and then return home to their dear ones.

On June 22, 1941, Hitler canceled the non-aggression pact and declared war on Russia. The war between Russia and Germany went on for several weeks. On the morning of July 10, 1941, the last train going east passed through town. The remnants of the Soviet occupation were on it. A few hours later, the street filled with Poles and peasants from nearby villages. When the Soviets left Rokitno, the suffering of the Jews increased and their daily fare consisted of beatings, robberies and lootings.

On the 5th August the Germans took control of the town, and ordered the Jews to form a *Judenrat* who would have the responsibility in all Jewish matters in town and in the area around it. Jews were not permitted to leave town. Anyone who tried would be shot. Jews were not allowed to do any business with non-Jews. Evil orders were given to the community. In mid September 1941 every Jewish home had to be marked with a Jewish blue star and on the eve of *Yom Kippur*, 30th September, all Jews were ordered to wear a yellow star. The community was assessed to pay 30 rubles per person, of which pure gold was to constitute 10% of the total.

On the 15th April 1942, the ghetto for the Jews of Rokitno was established. The enclosed quarter was not a real ghetto because no walls or barbed wire fences were built. It was enough that an order was given forbidding the Jews from leaving the street. Two Jewish policemen stood at the beginning of the street and watched the traffic. Each room was occupied by at least one family. They were forbidden from going out for fresh air or buying food. Hungry people ate grass and wildflowers from the fields bordering the ghetto. Those who had some seeds of grain, ground them secretly in a mill that was hidden underground in the ghetto. In the evenings, people sneaked out of the houses, went to the fences and exchanged clothes for food. There was no contact with the outside world. No newspapers arrived and radio did not exist. The situation of the *Judenrat* worsened daily and with it that of the Jews. The Germans became crueler in their demands and they slowly revealed their true purpose – extermination.

On August 25, 1942, the strict order was given that all Jews were to present themselves on the following day, in the market square for roll call. There was no panic as two previous roll calls had ended with people returning home. The next day, August 26, 1942, 13 *Elul* 5742, at 9:00 A.M, the entire Jewish community – 1631 people – stood in the market square and waited for the verdict. The roll call was done quickly, but then the Jews were told to stand in two lines – men in one, women and children in the other. This time the Germans and their Ukrainian helpers had decided to annihilate the Rokitno community. The shots in the air and at the people were proof enough. Mindel Eisenberg's voice was heard shouting: "Jews! Save yourselves!" Shots were fired from hundreds of automatic guns. People began to run crazed trying to escape the bullets. Terrible screams, groans, "*Shema Israel*" and non-stop shooting were heard. The market square was drenched in Jewish blood. The market square was covered with broken bodies of men, women and young children. 300 Jews were killed in the market square. Many Jews were caught and put into train cars waiting at the station. The next day, they were slaughtered in Sarny together with other Jews from Sarny and other villages. 10,000 Jews were murdered in 3 hours. This is how the Jewish community of Rokitno was annihilated.

Although many Jews managed to escape from the market square and roamed the fields and forests, a large number were then either cruelly murdered by the Ukrainians or caught and handed over to the German murderers in exchange for a kilo of salt per Jewish soul. However, on the contrary, there were some Ukrainians who had pity on the miserable souls and treated them humanely. At night, they took the escapees into their homes and fed them at great personal risk. Sometimes they paid for their generosity with their lives and property. A special honor must be paid to the Shtundist sect who showed special love to the Jews. Thanks to these wonderful people many Jews from Rokitno and the surrounds were saved from certain death.

Some Jews managed to join the Russian partisan groups in the forests. They carried out many audacious operations against the German and Polish policemen, burned the houses of collaborators and administered due justice to many of the Polish and Ukrainian murderers. They continued with these reprisals until the war ended.

On the 4th January 1944, the Germans retreated and the town was liberated by the Soviets. As soon as they heard that it was possible to return, some residents of Rokitno came out of the forests and hiding places and returned to the town. The utter sadness! The streets were deserted. The old synagogue was no longer standing. After trains began to run again, letters arrived from Rokitno residents who had escaped to Russia. They were anxious for news of their families. One survivor who had returned to Rokitno wrote a letter to his sister in Israel detailing all the hardships, suffering, killing and extermination of the community. It was the first terrible pronouncement about the fate of the Jews of Rokitno and Volyn. The letter appeared in the newspapers in Eretz-Israel and even in the Argentinean press. He began to receive letters from various people in Israel begging him to find out the fate of Jews in other villages. Unfortunately, he had to tell all of them there was no trace left of their families.

Other survivors made their way back to Rokitno. It was very dangerous. The *Banderovtzis* (Ukrainian nationalist partisans) terrorized the area, laying in ambush and planning to finish what they had not accomplished during the Nazi occupation.

Some of the former residents living in Israel organized themselves as an association (*landsmanshaft*) and began to send them food and clothing packages. A committee in Rokitno also took care of food and shelter for some orphans and singles that came out of the forests.

The survivors visited Sarny and applied to the authorities for permission to fence the area where 10,000 Jews had been killed and buried, and to put up a proper gravestone. There was also a common mass grave in Rokitno where the three hundred people murdered at the market place and others killed in the forests, were buried.

A group of partisans was active in transporting survivors to Israel. It was an extremely dangerous and secret undertaking.

An order was issued by Stalin that all Polish citizens were permitted to go west to their homeland, and all the Jews remaining in Rokitno registered to leave. Towards evening on June 5, 1945 they joined a train on its way to Poland. This is how all the survivors, two hundred people, left the town. Two families only remained after they returned from Russia.

The majority of the Rokitno residents, who were loyal to Zionism and to Hebrew, went to Israel via Poland and Germany. They were illegally smuggled to Eretz Israel via Italy by the *Hagana* and *Bricha* organizations.

Even then their trials and tribulations were not over. When the ship approached the shores of Palestine, the British boarded and a face-to-face battle took place. Most of the survivors were taken to a detention camp in Cyprus, and only in early 1948, did they reach Eretz Israel as free Jews.

A national executive committee of Former Residents of Rokitno and its Vicinity in Israel was elected in 1950 and a fund for assistance and *Gmilut Hassadim* (charity) was begun in 1951. A grove of trees was planted in memory of the fallen. The stories of Rokitno partisans appeared in the "Book of Partisans" published by Yad Vashem. The above served as a modest prelude to the major commemorative project – publishing the Rokitno and Surroundings Book. This book details the history of Jews living in Rokitno and surrounding villages, with personal accounts of the lives of the people who dwelt there, until the catastrophe which overwhelmed and annihilated almost all. The book is true to everything that once was and is no longer. The fact that the book was written is proof that the cruel enemy did not succeed in annihilating our nation. There is continuity; there is the guarding of the candle, which will not die out. The proof is our attachment to our martyrs and our book.

We will keep watch over this treasure – the Rokitno and Surroundings Book. This is all we have left.

GLOSSARY

Aliyah - Ascent = Immigration to Israel
Artels cooperatives
Banderovtzis - the followers of Stepan Bandera, the anti-Soviet wartime leader of the Ukrainian Insurgent Army (UPA), who also collaborated with the Nazis
Beitar Brith Yosef Trumpeldor - The Revisionist youth organization
Blue Box - blue charity collection boxes for redemption of the Land of Israel
Bulbovtzes - Headed by Taras Borovitz (calling himself Bulboy), an army group, killed and robbed. They were only interested in an independent Ukraine
Bricha - Escape
Bris -circumcision ceremony
Bund- a secular Jewish socialist party in the Russian Empire
Cheder (*pl* = **chaderim**) - elementary schools
Defansiva - secret service
Eretz Yisrael (Eretz Israel) -the Land of Israel
Eruv - border
Eyn Yaakov - a compilation of all the Aggadic material in the Talmud together with commentaries
Feldsher - practical doctor
Folksdeutch - German-Pole
Fuhrer - guide, leader
Gabbay - dues collector, sexton, beadle
Gaon - Honorable Sage
Gemara - part of the **Talmud**
Gmar Hatima Tova - wish for a good final judgment
Goyim - gentiles
Gmilut Hasadim -Free Loan, Charity
Gur Aryeh Yehudah - scout group
Gymnasia - Hebrew High School
Hachshara (Preparatory) Unit - training, pre-*Aliyah* preparatory training farm, preparatory *kibbutz*
Halacha - Legal part of Jewish traditional literature **Hanoar Hatzioni**
Haganah - a Jewish paramilitary organization in the British Mandate of Palestine from 1936 to 1948, which later became the core of the Israel Defense Forces
Haggadah - a book containing the liturgy for the Seder service on the Jewish festival of Passover
Hakafot - the ritual circling of the synagogue pulpit with Torah scrolls on *Simchat Torah*
Hanoar Hatzioni (The Zionist Youth) - Youth Movement
Hanuka gelt - monetary present at the Hanukah festival
Haoved movement - Workers movement

Hashomer HaTza'ir - Young Guard youth movement
Hasid (*pl* = **hasidim**) - pious, devout ones
Hasidic movement - Pietistic and mystical movement in Judaism that originated in 18th-century Poland. It was a reaction against rigid legalism and Talmudic learning in favour of a joyful form of worship that served as a spiritual outlet for the common people.
Hatikvah - The National Anthem of Israel
Havdalah - religious ceremony marking symbolic end of Shabbat and Jewish holidays. It includes lighting a special Havdalah candle with several wicks.
Hechalutz - Pioneers youth movement
Hechalutz HaTzair Young Pioneer youth movement
Hevra Kadisha - Burial Society
Hol Hamoed of Pesach - Intermediate Days of Passover (which lasts 8 days)
HY"D (Hashem yikom damon) - G-d will avenge his blood
Judenrat - Jewish councils set up within the Jewish communities of Nazi-occupied Europe on German orders. The ***Judenraete***(plural) were given the responsibility to implement the Nazis' policies regarding the Jews.
Kabbalah - Jewish mystical school of thought
Kaddish - Liturgical doxology said by the mourner
Kaparot - whirling a chicken above one's head in belief that an individual's sins will be transferred to the chicken
Kashrut - the set of Jewish religious dietary laws
Kedoshim, Kiddush-Hashem - holy martyrs, martyrdom
Keren Hayesod – United Israel Appeal- literally "The Foundation Fund" - the central fundraising organization for Israel.
Keren Kayemeth Le'Yisrael (KKL) - **The Jewish National Fund**. Its goals were buying land, planting groves and other reclamation works in Eretz-Yisrael
Kibbutz (in Europe) - shared apartment of youth planning to make aliya to Eretz Israel
Kibbutz (in Israel) - collective agricultural settlement
Kibbutz Hameuhad - United Kibbutz Movement
Kiddush - a blessing recited over wine or grape juice to sanctify the Shabbat and Jewish holidays
Klezmers - Jewish folk musicians traditionally performing in a small band
Kol Nidrei - an Aramaic declaration recited in the synagogue before the beginning of the evening service on every Yom Kippur, the Day of Atonement.
Komsomol - the youth division of the Communist Party of the Soviet Union
Kreislandwirt - District farmers
Kupat Holim -Medical Clinic
Kurin - underground dugout
Lamed Vavniks -the 36 secret righteous men of lore
Lebede - grass leaves

Landsmanshaft - a benefit society, or hometown society of Jewish immigrants from the same European town or region.
Liachs - slur word against Poles
Leinen - self study
Linat Tzedek - righteous lodging
Matza (*pl*-Matzos/th) - Unleavened bread, traditionally eaten during Passover
Mazuris - Ukrainians converted to Catholicism
Menorah seven-branched candelabra originally used in the Second Temple, symbolizing the Divine light, part of Channukah tradition
Mezuzah - sacred parchment inscribed by hand with two portions of Torah, stored in a protective case and hung on the doorposts of Jewish homes.
Mikve - ritual bathhouse or ritual bath
Mincha - daily afternoon prayer
Minyan - prayer quorum
Mitnagdim - the Enlightenment movement
Mitzvah - good deed, merit
Mogen David - Star of David sign (6 pointed star)
Neila - Closing prayers for Yom Kippur
NKVD -abbreviation for the "People's Commissariat for Internal Affairs", was a law enforcement agency of the Soviet Union
OZN - abbreviation for "Camp of National Unity", was a Polish political party
(Weekly) Parasha - a section of the Torah (Hebrew Bible) read in Jewish prayer services
Pirkei Avot - Ethics of the Fathers
Palestina Amt - Palestine Office
Pinkas Vilna - the Vilna community ledger
Rada - A local government
Rashi - the outstanding Biblical commentator of the Middle Ages
Righteous Gentiles - Non-Jewish individual who risked their lives to save Jews during World War II
Seder - a ritual performed by a community or by multiple generations of a family, involving a retelling the story of the liberation of the Israelites from slavery in ancient Egypt
Selichot - special prayers for forgiveness, said during the period preceding Yom Kippur and also on fast days
ShD"R. = Shliakh de Rabbanan - emissary
Shtundists - Evangelical Protestant religious sect that emerged among Ukrainian peasants in southern regions of the Russian Empire (present day Ukraine) in the second half of the 19th century.
Slawa - freedom
Shabbat Shuvah - the Sabbath between *Rosh Hashana* and *Yom Kippur*
Shabbes Goy- a Gentile who does work forbidden to Jews on the Sabbath, *e.g.* stoked the furnaces of the Jews
Shamess P235

Shacharit - daily morning prayer
Shema Israel - Title of a central prayer in morning and evening services. It is traditional for Jews to say the *Shema* as their last words
Shekalim(pl) - The Zionist shekel is the name of the certificate of membership in the World Zionist Organisation (WZO) from the First Zionist Congress. Purchase gave the right to participate in the elections of the Zionist Congress.
Shekhita - slaughtering of animals according to Jewish law
Shiva - 7 day mourning period in Judaism
Shoah - Holocaust
Shohet and Bodek (SHO"B) - ritual slaughterer and examiner
Shofar - a musical instrument made of a ram horn, used for Jewish religious purposes
Shulkhan Arukh (The prepared table) - authoritative code of Jewish laws, written by Yoseph Caro (1488-1575)
Tahara - ritual cleansing of the dead person
Talit - prayer shawl
Talmud - a central text of Rabbinic Judaism, with 2 components (Mishnah and Gemara)
Talmud Torah - Religious school for young pupils
Tanach - the Bible
Tarbut - Culture. It is also the name of a chain of Jewish schools throughout Poland
Tashlich - symbolic casting off the sins of the previous year by tossing pieces of bread or another food into a body of flowing water.
Tefillin - phyllacteries
Tisha B'Av - Fast of the ninth of Av, a day commemorating the tragedies that have befallen the Jewish people
Torah Learning, teaching, the first five books of the Bible, rabbinical commentaries on them
Tosafot - annotations to the Talmud
Tzedakah box - for collecting charity
Tzadik (*pl*-Tzadikim) - sages
Unetane Tokef - Important prayer read on Rosh Hashanah and Yom Kippur. "Let us proclaim the sacred power of this day; it is awesome and full of dread. Now the divine Judge looks upon our deeds, and determines our destiny..."
Volksdeutsch - German Poles
Yeshivah, Pl. Yeshivoth - rabbinic seminary -Talmudic college
Yizkor - Memorial prayer for the departed
Yom Kippur - also known as Day of Atonement, is the holiest day of the year for the Jewish people. Its central themes are atonement and repentance.
Youth Aliyah - a Jewish organization that rescued thousands of Jewish children from the Nazis during the Third Reich

Zohar - a group of books including commentary on the mystical aspects of the Torah

Abbreviations:
a"h = aleha ha'shalom - of peaceful memory
mvhr'r = morenu ve'rabenu ha'rav - our teacher and Rabbi
n"e = nishmata b'eden may her soul rest in paradise
HY"D = Hashem yikom damon - G-d will avenge his blood
Sho"b - ritual slaughterer and examiner
YM"Sh = yimakh shmam - may their names be erased
z"l = zichrono livracha - of blessed memory
z"zl = zichron tzadik livracha - of blessed memory

Jewish Festivals:
Rosh Hashana - New Year
Yom Kippur - Day of Atonement
Sukkot - Festival of Tabernacles
Shemini Atzeret - Eighth Day of Assembly
Chanukkah - Festival of Lights
Purim - commemorates the deliverance of the Jewish people in the ancient Persian Empire where a plot had been formed to destroy them.
Passover (Pesach)- commemoration of the liberation of the Israelites over 3,300 years ago from slavery in ancient Egypt
Lag B'Omer - a minor festival between Passover and Shavuot
Shavuot - commemorates the giving of the Torah on Mt. Sinai.

Months in the Hebrew calendar:
Nissan, Iyyar, Sivan, Tammuz, Av (or Menachem Av), Elul, Tishri, Heshvan, Kislev, Tevet, Shvat, Adar
Rosh Hodesh - first of the month

Movement newspapers - **Haatid, Davar, Hapoel Hatzair**

Various Prayers:
Aleinu Anim Zemirot
Ashrei"Shmone Esre
El maley rachamim
Hineni
Kadosh
Melave Malka
Neila (see above)
Shema Koleinu - "Hear our voices"
Shmone Esre
Unetane Tokef (see above)
Yavo Adir Bimhera Beyamenu

Youth Movements

Ahdut - Unity youth movement
Agudat Yaldei Zion -Union of Children of Zion
Betar
Brit Hehayal - organized pioneering Zionist youth movement
HaNoar HaTzioni - Zionist Youth
Hapoel Hatzioni - the Zionist Worker movement
Hashomer HaTza'ir - Young Guard youth movement
Hechalutz - Pioneers youth movement
Hechalutz HaTzair Young Pioneer youth movement
Mizrahi
Poalei Zion -Workers of Zion - Socialist workers party
Tseirei Zion - Young Zionists youth movement

Notes to the Reader:

Within the text the reader will note *"[Page 34]"* standing ahead of a paragraph. This indicates that the material translated below was on page 34 of the original book. However, when a paragraph was split between two pages in the original book, the marker is placed in this book after the end of the paragraph for ease of reading.

Also please note that all references within the text of the book to page numbers, refer to the page numbers of the original Yizkor Book.

Please note that not all the photographs in the appendices have been identified. Hopefully people will write to the Yizkor Books Project with identifications. The captions will be updated on the Yizkor books web site for Rokitno

http://www.jewishgen.org/Yizkor/rokitnoye/rokitnoye.html

A list of new captions will be available at

http://www.jewishgen.org/Yizkor/rokitnoye/newcaptions.html

so the book can be updated too.

If you can help with identification of people in the photographs of the appendices, please contact:

Lance Ackerfeld <lance.ackerfeld@gmail.com>
Ann Belinsky <ann.belinsky@gmail.com>
Joel Alpert < joel.alpert@uwalumni.com >

Family Notes

Table of Contents of the Translated Yizkor Book

All articles were originally written in Hebrew except for those marked with [Y] (Yiddish)

CULTURE AND EDUCATION

VILLAGES IN THE VICINITY

ROKITNO AS SHE LIVES IN OUR MEMORIES

PERSONALITIES

DURING THE SOVIET OCCUPATION

THE HOLOCAUST

THE ROAD OF SUFFERING

VENEGEANCE AND REPRISAL

IN THE TOWN OF SLAUGHTER

Original Yizkor Book Table of Contents

All articles were originally written in Hebrew except for those marked with [Y] (Yiddish

CULTURE AND EDUCATION

VILLAGES IN THE VICINITY

ROKITNO AS SHE LIVES IN OUR MEMORIES

PERSONALITIES

DURING THE SOVIET OCCUPATION

THE HOLOCAUST

THE ROAD OF SUFFERING

VENEGEANCE AND REPRISAL

IN THE TOWN OF SLAUGHTER

{Page 3]

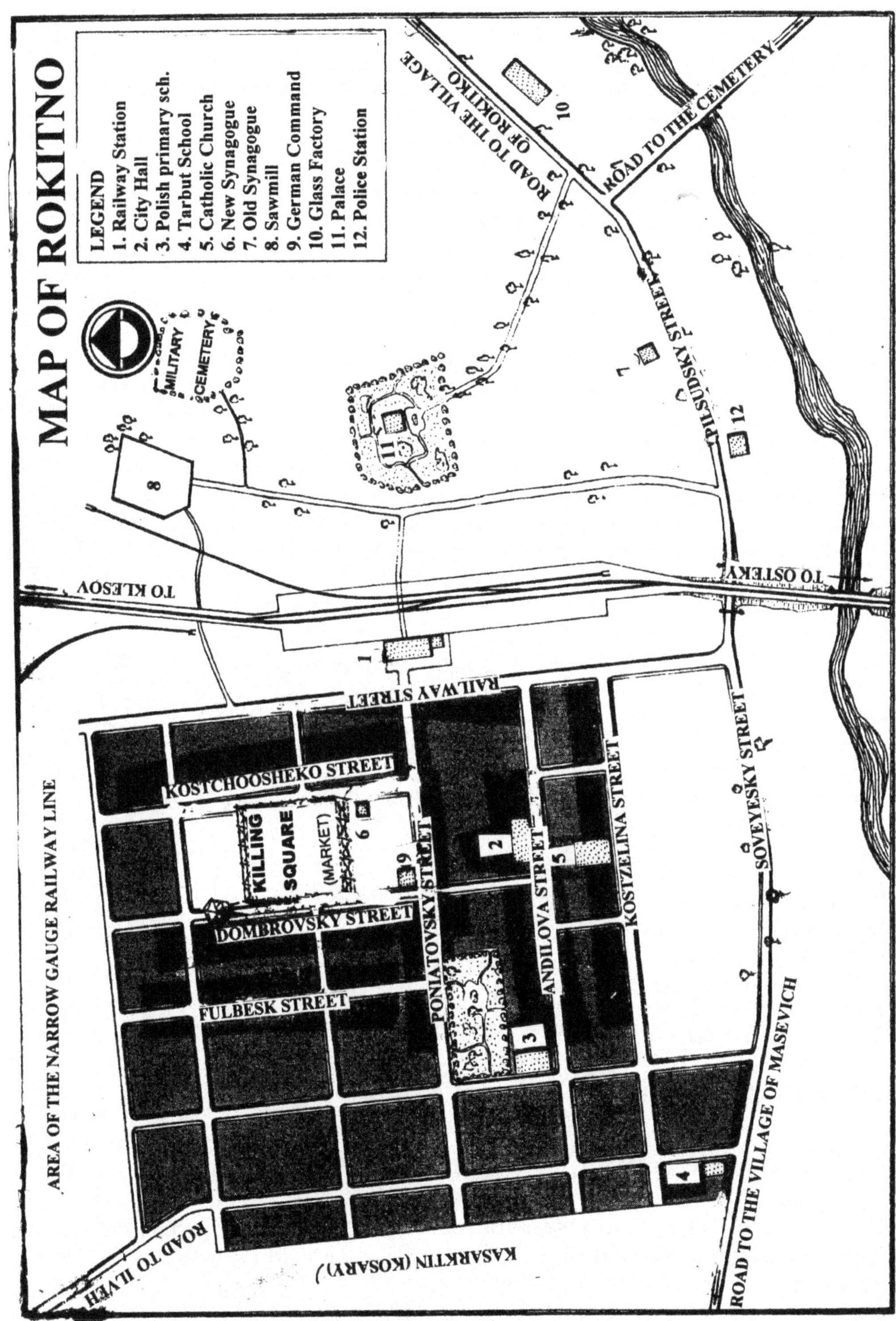
MAP OF ROKITNO
LEGEND
1. Railway Station
2. City Hall
3. Polish primary sch.
4. Tarbut School
5. Catholic Church
6. New Synagogue
7. Old Synagogue
8. Sawmill
9. German Command
10. Glass Factory
11. Palace
12. Police Station
MILITARY CEMETERY
ROAD TO THE VILLAGE OF ROKITKO
ROAD TO THE CEMETERY
PILSUDSKY STREET
TO KLESOV
TO OSTEKY
RAILWAY STREET
KOSTCHOOSHEKO STREET
KILLING SQUARE
(MARKET)
DOMBROVSKY STREET
FULBESK STREET
PONIATOVSKY STREET
ANDILOVA STREET
KOSTZELINA STREET
SOVEYESKY STREET
ROAD TO THE VILLAGE OF MASEVICH
KASARKTIN (KOSARY)
ROAD TO ILVEH
AREA OF THE NARROW GAUGE RAILWAY LINE

Map of Rokitno

[Page 5]

Comments from the Editorial Board

Translated by Ala Gamulka

The Jewish Community of Rokitno lasted for a short time- less than 50 years. However, in this short period a vibrant town was built. A town that produced loyal and traditional Jews, scholars and businessmen, ordinary persons imbued with love for our nation and our people and with a deep esteem for Zion. These people were well-known for their superior qualities. They founded a life full of youthful vigor and a wish to present Rokitno as an example and a spiritual center for the surrounding villages.

Our town was small and modest. It was young and its inhabitants were vibrant. They shaped her personality and entrenched in her Western culture and modern life, as it was then known. This magnificent structure of life was razed during the Holocaust by the Nazi beast of World War II. Our town is destroyed and is no longer here.

With great trepidation we have erected a monument for generations to come. We have told her history with reverence. We described her life-style and her image. Thus we "resurrected" her from her ruins, as she was once - in her shining times and in her decline, in times of bloom and growth and in times of poverty and misery- from her beginnings to her destruction.

The historical tale of our town is short since Rokitno is not ancient. However, it was written accurately and is based on written sources as well as on personal recollections of the town veterans.

The decisive period in the life of the town began in the early twenties of the twentieth century and it is significant in our book. We cannot claim that we were able to tell all. Definitely, there may be certain events or experiences which were not fully described - either because there were no people to tell them or due to oversight.

Most of the events that we brought up and on which we concentrated belong to this era. A second period that is fully discussed in the book is that of the Holocaust where the remnant that was spared was able to recollect. The stories of the survivors in the book have a value which is not only local but belong to the general literature of the Holocaust.

Rokitno served as a center of a large group of villages where there were a small number of Jews who were closely tied to our town. The life story of these villages is well represented in our book.

An important section of our book is the *Yizkor* (Remembrance) pages in which we list all our dearly departed. As well, we included eulogies to several people whose lives and deeds helped to shape our town. We also dedicated a prominent section to members of our town who fell during the War of Independence and to those from our town and its vicinity who died in Israel.

This book of Rokitno and its vicinity shall serve as an eternal monument to the memory of one of the most interesting towns in the Diaspora where we were born, where we grew up and were educated. For us Rokitno is not just of historical value. She is always alive in our thoughts and is permanently engraved in our hearts. Although many of us have been away from her for many years - she is dear to all of us.

Let the book awaken the memory and let it tell our children the story of their parents in the Diaspora. Let it persevere for eternity so that those who come after us will know how their forefathers lived. Silently, with bowed heads we stand at the scattered graves of our dearly departed. We shall never forget them.

The Editor and The Editorial Boar

From right to left: 1. Shlomo Kravi 2. Yosef Segal 3. Haim Shteinman 4. Aharon Lifshitz 5. The Editor, Eliezer Leoni 6. Bat Sheva Fichman (Shohet) 7. Aryeh Geipman

The creation of this book was not easily achieved. The mission was too heavy and too full of responsibility. The members of the Editorial Board dedicated much of their time and spent over three years in backbreaking work. They added brick to brick and helped the Editor in the verification of facts, editing material and in the final preparation for publication. Thus was produced the manuscript of the essence of the lives of the community of Rokitno and its vicinity. The years in which the book was created were years of suspense and great activity of all the members of the Editorial Board. This dedicated work exacted many sacrifices - both physical and emotional. It was done with inspiration and unconditional dedication in order to perpetuate a whole community- a task that only our generation knew. It was teamwork in which much thought and contemplation were invested. We did whatever it was possible for us to do so that the image of our dearly beloved would not, G-d forbid, be diminished and that their memory would not lessen among us.

It is our pleasant duty to heartily thank in the name of the Editorial Board and in the name of all those from our town and its vicinity, our Editor. The author Eliezer Leoni, a native of Kovel, who invested a great deal of energy, diligence, dedication and talent in gathering the literary material, editing it, proof-reading and preparing it for printing. He did not skimp on any effort. He visited many of us who came from Rokitno and its vicinity, encouraged the people and wrote down their recollections. Thanks to his adherence to this lofty task Rokitno has been commemorated in a way that allows us to see all that is good and sacred to us all. Let this monument serve as a recompense for his hard work.

[Page 8]

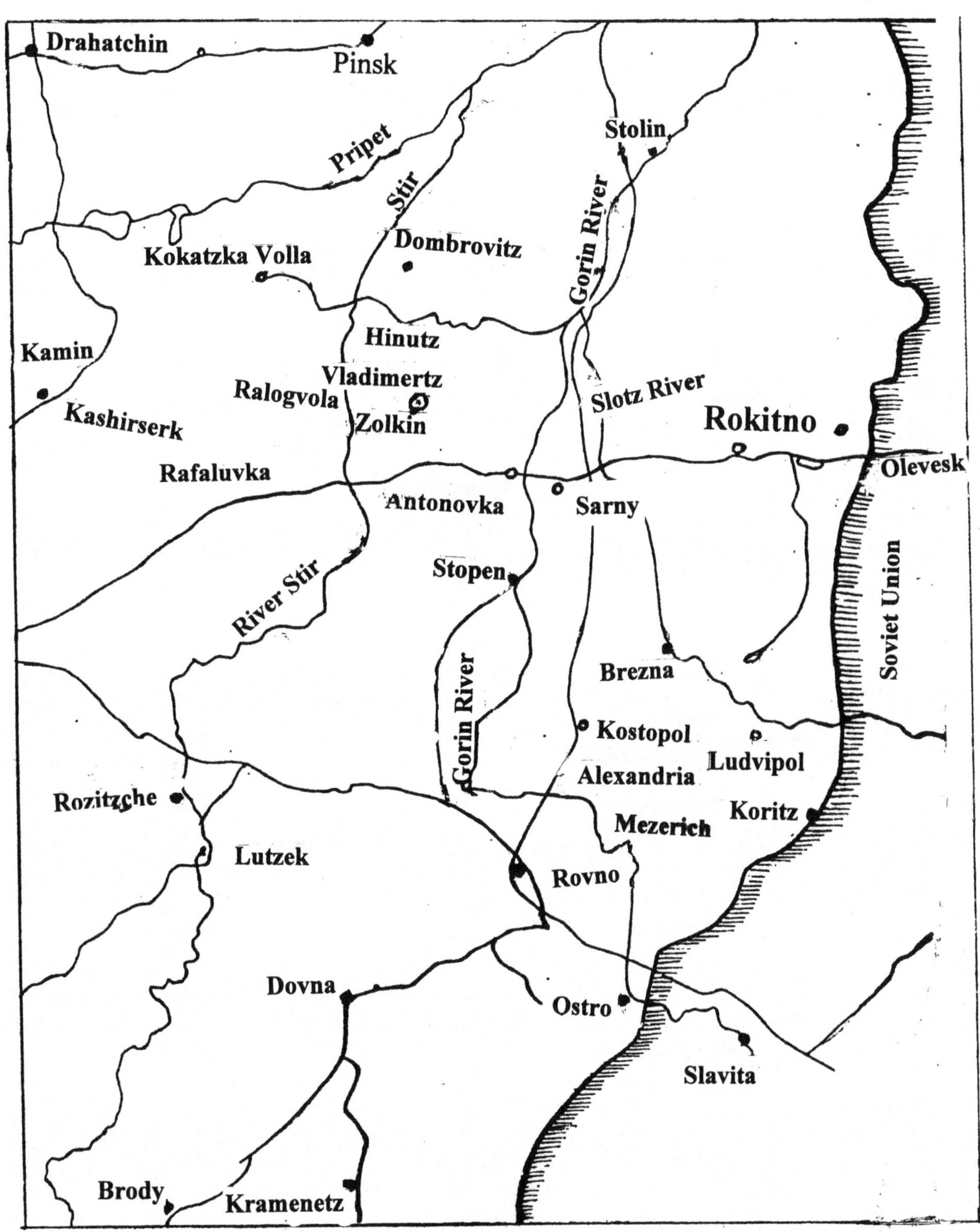

Regional Map

[Page 9]

Rokitno Shall Survive

Eliezer Leoni

Translated by Ala Gamulka

The Jews of Volyn Province were as one family. This Jewish Community did not have borders since “we came from the same well”. Thus, with a slight change of the ancient proverb I will state, “I am a man from Volyn and anything that touches Volyn and its Jewry is close to my heart”. Therefore, I will lament and eulogize the children of Rokitno who were struck down since I think of them as my siblings.

The memory of Rokitno is dear to us since this is where the foundation of our youth was laid. The atmosphere of our parents' homes and that of Rokitno shaped our being. They became absorbed in our being as a cherished heritage. Therefore, the sharp memory of the misfortune lives inside us. Now, sadly all is ravaged. The candle is snuffed. The children of Rokitno were killed mercilessly in a way that cannot be imagined. They will not return to their homes. This is the terror which screams out, but no one can change it.

Man is endowed with the ability that is his alone - to be able to resurrect the dead in a spiritual way. This is possible in print only as S.Y. Agnon says in his book *"A Guest Goes To Sleep"* (p. 332): “Paper is superior even to a gravestone since if a gravestone is large and attractive, the goyim steal it and put it in their buildings. If it is small, it sinks into the ground. Paper is different. When a book is printed, it is sent throughout the land and it lasts for generations”.

Man's life moves in two circles which after some time blend one into the other. One is a narrow circle, the circle of physical existence, which is restricted to a specific beginning, a middle and an end. All human beings are subject to the law since “the road begins in the six days of creation”.

However, man does not live only a physical existence. His life also moves in another circle, the circle of spiritual life, which has no end and which is not as light as the body, but becomes a spiritual essence, an eternal existence.

When it comes to the narrow circle, the Jews of Rokitno have reached a definite end. Death swallowed them for eternity and their light will not shine again. However, when it comes to the endless circle they still exist. In spirit our dear ones are here and they are immortal. This book was meant to give an eternal resting place to their souls.

In addition to perpetuating the soul of the Jews of Rokitno and its vicinity, there is a tragic moral lesson hidden in the book. For us it is like the phrase: "Teach them thoroughly to your children and speak of them while you sit in your home, while you walk on the way, when you retire and when you rise".

We were slaughtered and burned, not because we are one of the rotten nations, but because we are a nation lacking in protection, without a country and bereft of any basic human rights. Our miserable situation in the world- a situation of a defenseless nation - is what encouraged the perpetrators to do their evil deeds.

Rokitno had its own setting. It was a town of youth, of young people, vibrant and active. Thus, the book is mostly dedicated to these wonderful young people with their cravings, their hopes and their dreams of redemption - their own redemption and that of the Jewish Nation. In these young people were found strengths and special talents which unfortunately stayed hidden and were never discovered. They were very young people when they went on their last voyage. The youths were nurtured deeply by a love of Jewish tradition. This is why they did neither kneel nor bow down to the *goyim* and they bore their tradition and their Jewishness with pride. How wonderful was their life and how rich was their experience and how deep and sacred was their inner world. A thrill of sacredness waves over me when I remember them. I am unable to peek behind the screen of its existence. These youths were taken from us by wicked and violent persons while they were still developing, at the height of their aspirations and desires. How can we forget those who are part of our own experience?

Rokitno was a young town when it was cut down. Its foundations were only begun at the turn of the twentieth century. However, in this short period of time vast spiritual and human values were shaped. With recognition and in fear that we may not be able to commemorate these values- they may be forgotten and they may sink into oblivion- we drew out the sweetness of our dear ones. We collected their stories, their jokes, their experiences. We amassed a spiritual wealth which is important not only for us, but also for generations to come. This book is not an impassive gravestone which we honor but keep away from. This is a source of life which flows on the eternal horizon and serves us as an emotional support. Therefore, we see it as our life's path.

We constructed a repository for the soul of the communities of Rokitno and its vicinity. This is a work of rededication. We collected and gleaned the spiritual bones of our dear ones in this modest temple. They will be anchored on the infinite shores of the human experience and their time will never end.

In spite of the large scope of the book, it is only a prologue. We did not include everything in our structure. It is impossible to describe the treasure of Rokitno souls. Many chapters remained behind the scenes because we could not express all that was there. If, G-d forbid, we made any errors, we ask forgiveness from our martyrs. All was done to honor them, not for us, so that their memory would be eternal.

Now, when we look at the world of Rokitno, as it is again being revealed by word and picture, the pain is rekindled and it will not be relieved. I take upon myself the role of community representative and I state that even if we ascend to heaven our grief will not end. A lamentation pours out of the heart. Alas, what happened to Rokitno! Would that G-d had breathed life in our dearly departed who were tortured and slaughtered. Would that He would have rejoined all the bones! How rich our life would have been! How happy we would have been! We cannot really absorb the misfortune without realizing their yearning for Jerusalem and their desire to see the eternal glow of Israel.

The book is the sole and most important sacred remnant of Rokitno. We have nothing else. Without it we would be full of endless misery. This is our "Western Wall". We can let our tears flow in front of it and we can unburden ourselves to ease our pain. Near it we are joined with our martyrs. As long as we are connected to them and we are involved in their lives - we lengthen their lives and the community of Rokitno will persevere and will achieve immortality of its soul.

[Page 12]

"That the generation to come might know them,

even the children which should be born;

who should arise and declare them

to their children"

Psalms 78:6

[Page 14]

HISTORY OF ROKITNO

[Page 15]

On the History of the Jews in Rokitno

Eliezer Leoni (Tel Aviv)

Translated by Ala Gamulka

When one traces the sources for the founding of the village and the town of Rokitno, an interesting phenomenon occurs. A phenomenon that historians of Jewish communities in Poland sweep aside intentionally or unintentionally.

The accepted version is that the life of the Jews in the Diaspora was based on one dimension - the spiritual one. Therefore, the scholars and the thinkers were the ones usually featured. The workers, simple country folk who did not follow the blessing which Isaac gave to Jacob - "Other nations will serve you"- earned their daily bread by working hard. These simple and honest people were almost forgotten by us.

We feel a fresh country wind when we learn the history of the first Jews in Rokitno. We hear about a Jewish tribe that does hard physical labor, suffers from loneliness, has few connections to the outside world and is detached from cultural centers.

The most important source we have about the early days of the village of Rokitno is an excellent essay by Jadwiga Bergerowna titled "*Rokitno Life*". The author taught at the Teachers' College in Lvov and was commissioned to research the early days of the village. For that purpose she traveled to Rokitno in 1932 and she read all the documents. The first authentic historical document that she discovered was from 3/2/1862 which attests that there were 118 houses in the village (there are no population statistics). From this we learn that the village was founded in an earlier period, but we do not know exactly when.

A legend made the rounds among the Jews of Rokitno, one handed down from generation to generation, that the village is a remnant of a big city that spread to the villages of Sohov and Osnitzek and that it was destroyed by earlier government decrees. As proof of this there are ancient graves in the cemetery in Osnitzek where the dead of Rokitno were buried. We learn from the inscriptions that this cemetery is very old. This story has not been verified historically, but we should not discard it completely.

The lands of the village originally belonged to the Princess Anila Rzyszczewska. We do not know if there were any Jews there, but it can be surmised that the

Jews settled in the village in the 1880's. The basis for this belief is that the decree, published by the tsarist government in the second half of the 19th century, ordered the expulsion of the Jews from the area and their resettlement in rural areas. As a result, the migration of Russian Jews from urban to rural areas began. In the 1880's there were 58,427 Jews in the Province of Volyn. They represented 3.9% of the total rural population. Even the *Hasidic* movement was involved in this migration. It is known that Rabbi Menachem Mendel Schneierson, The Lubavicher Rebbe, was instrumental in spreading the idea of working the land among the Jews and he inspired the Jews of Volyn to change their way of life.

The following population statistics of Rokitno date from early in the twentieth century:

Russians	3858
Jews	105
Poles	74
Others	18
Total	**4055**

The Jews mainly earned their living from producing pottery and bartering it in surrounding villages for wheat and potatoes. The Jews also made shoes out of reeds and out of felt and sold them. Other Jews were able to lease facilities. The most famous among them was Yehudah Leib Gendelman, a resident of the village who leased, from Polish aristocrats, factories that produced tar and windmills. The Russians governed Volyn from 1795, the year Poland was divided into three parts. Their policy was to exile the Polish aristocracy from their land holdings and to divide these possessions among the Russian residents. Accordingly, the Russians exiled many aristocrats at the end of the nineteenth century from the Rokitno area and divided the land among the villages. Thus, Yehudah Leib Gendelman's livelihood was cut down.

At the beginning of the twentieth century two important events took place, which changed the lives of the Jews in the village. These changes were both demographic and economic and caused a social migration. As a result, a modern town was built on the other side of the village. These events were: the erection of the glass factory and the building of the railroad from Kiev to Kovel.

Rokitno and its vicinity have an abundance of red and white sand and various silicates needed for the manufacturing of glass. These geological occurrences laid the foundation for the manufacturing of glass in Volyn. At the end of the nineteenth century there were 20 glass factories in Volyn - 16 of them owned by

Jews. 143 Jews worked there. One of these plants was built in Rokitno at the beginning of the twentieth century.

The reason for the founding of these factories is not only because of the availability of raw materials. There was also a political reason. In January 1897, the tsarist government issued an edict that forbade the sale of brandy in glasses or barrels. It had to be placed in glass bottles. This edict increased the demand for bottles throughout Russia.

The glass industry owners reacted to the edict by scouting for locations where the raw materials were available. This is how, at the beginning of the twentieth century, representatives of a well-known Belgian glass manufacturer arrived in Rokitno and decided to build a plant. Heading the plant was a Jew from Petersburg called Eliahu Michaelovitch Rosenberg.

Rosenberg had an important part in the economic history of Rokitno. Therefore, he deserves a few lines of discussion. He was an assimilated Jew from Uman, but he still kept in close touch with his fellow Jews. His second wife was a niece of the Russian Minister of the Treasury. This connection opened many doors for him. Rosenberg had his own office in the Trade Ministry in Petersburg where many Russian industry giants would visit. Rosenberg made many physical improvements in Rokitno. He built a magnificent park filled with blooming oaks and fruit trees and colorful lawns. The park covered several square kilometers. The winter palace of Mr. Rosenberg was built inside the park. It was a fancy three-storied palace, where he resided with his wife during the winter months. In the summer he went to Kiev and Petersburg.

The construction of the *Huta* (glass factory) took two years. Residences for the laborers were built nearby. Each laborer was given his own apartment. This was co-operative housing and it served as a basis for an urban settlement. Most of the houses were built by Germans. From a historical point of view, the basis for the town of Rokitno is the construction of the glass factory and the housing for the hundreds of laborers. Most of the laborers were Polish.

The factory operated around the clock and its products were sent to various parts of Russia. The office clerks were Jews- among them Isaac Eidelman who worked in the factory as a manager in charge of quality control. After his death, Yakov Grinshpan took his place. The accountant and confidant of Rosenberg was a Jew called Hochfeld from Homel.

The Chief Engineer was Rosenberg's son-in-law, a German, and an expert in the manufacturing of glass. When World War I broke out in 1914, he was deported by the Russians to Siberia because he was still a German citizen.

The great distance from the railroad was a deterrent to the development of the factory. The bottles were shipped by ox cart to Sarny- a distance of 40 kilometers. This primitive method of transport was too expensive and the factory was almost shut down. The owners of the factory asked Rosenberg to intercede on their behalf with the powers that be (since he had the connections). Rosenberg was successful and the Petersburg government ordered the construction of the railroad from Kiev to Kovel, through Rokitno. Prior to that, it was necessary to go from Rokitno to Brezno, from there to Rovno and then to Kiev. This trip took two days. The construction of the railroad was begun in 1900 and completed in 1902.

The construction of the railroad broadened the scope of the glass production and the factory was highly successful. When World War I broke out the factory was closed. Rosenberg left Rokitno and died in poverty in Petersburg during the war. After the war, his son Vladimir sold the factory to the Zunder brothers- Aharon and David. The younger Rosenberg felt the Revolution coming and managed to sell his possessions.

Aharon Zunder was the owner of several bakeries in Rovno. In 1915, as the Germans were approaching Volyn, he moved to Kiev. There he became wealthy in the lumber industry. In Kiev he met Rosenberg's son and purchased the *Huta*. The civil war was raging in Russia. Zunder was beaten by Danikin followers and he almost died. His friends begged him to stay in Kiev to recuperate, but he missed his wife and children who had remained in Rokitno and he started for home. The Kiev-Kovel railroad was not functioning properly at the time because of the war and it took him a long time to return to Rokitno. He fell ill with the flu and died soon afterward.

After his death, his brother David tried to revive the *Huta*. He was not successful because of the civil war. After the Bolshevik Revolution in 1917, many Russian leaders escaped to Ukraine where they formed a treaty with the Germans and invited them to attack the Bolsheviks and take over Ukraine. The Germans formed a Ukrainian government led by Skoropedsky. Rokitno was taken over by the German army. After the Ukrainians, led by Petlura, conquered Kiev and evicted the Germans, they arrived in Rokitno and they executed David Zunder.

After David Zunder's tragic death, his father Israel Hirsch Zunder and his younger brother Moshe came to Rokitno. They operated the flour mill attached to the Huta. According to the treaty signed in Riga between the Bolsheviks and the Poles, Rokitno now belonged to Poland. After some dealings, the *Huta* was sold to a group from Warsaw called *Lazaro* (acronym - Lashinsky, Zabedsky, Rosenzweig). They operated the *Huta* for a short time and sold it to Vitrom - a company from Warsaw which owned glass factories, headed by Flanzreich Vranglavsky. Under their management the factory was quite successful.

The building of the railroad helped in the development of the lumber industry completely run by Jews.

Between the glass factory and the railway station sprawled the estate of a Polish princess who owned the large forest in Rokitno. This forest was bought out by the brothers David and Yechezkel Lerner from Kliban.

Researching the history of Rokitno forces us to answer the question: why did the lumber industry flourish at the end of the nineteenth century and the beginning of the twentieth? The reason is that there was a revolution in transportation methods. The extension of the railroad brought a great demand for telegraph poles and extensive construction. The villages near the railroad began to develop and grow and building materials were required. The tree roots were used as raw material for the production of tar and turpentine. In the village of Toupik a factory producing tar was built before the one in Rokitno. Later, the factories were owned by David Shachnovski, Aharon Lifshitz, Avraham Asher Gitelman (from Stariky) and others.

The forests of Rokitno and the villages near it did not only serve as a source of lumber. They were also the hunting grounds of the Tsar's companions. Among them was Senator Ochotnikov, the Tsar's confidant. On one of his visits, Ochotnikov met the Rokitno princess and he bought the forest from her. It included open areas that the Lerner brothers had not bought because they were not interested in developing farming.

Ochotnikov called the railway station Ochotnikov Station. The name remained until the Poles took over the town and renamed it Rokitno Station.

The quick capitalization of Rokitno, thanks to its topographic and geological assets, brought many changes in the economic lives of the Jews of Rokitno and the surrounding villages. The Jewish population shifted from the villages to Rokitno and became a part of its economy. In a short time Rokitno became a town and the surrounding villages were part of its greater area, as far as the economy and organized Jewish communal life were concerned.

Rokitno Train Station

The names of the villages that belonged to Rokitno are:

1. **Ostoki**
2. **Osnitzek**
3. **Okopi**
4. **Boid**
5. **Budki Borovski**
6. **Budki Snovidovich**
7. **Borovey**
8. **Bilovizh**
9. **Brazov**
10. **Glinana**
11. **Dert**
12. **Vitkovich**
13. **Voltche-Gorko**
14. **Zolovey**
15. **Toupik**
16. **Masevich**
17. **Natrava**
18. **Stariky**
19. **Snovidovich**
20. **Kisorich**
21. **Krapilovka**

At the beginning of the twentieth century there were 400 Jews in Rokitno. There was no synagogue yet and services were held at the home of the father of Herzel Lerner who had received a Torah scroll as a gift from the Stolin *Hasidim*. There were also services at the home of Yeshayahu Gendelman. On Shabbat and High Holidays, services were held in the synagogue in the village of Rokitno. Soon, a beautiful synagogue was built in the town of Rokitno. This is the story of its construction: A man called Gelfand, from Odessa, bought large estates in Kisorich and Voltche-Gorko. The Jews of Rokitno asked him to build them a synagogue. Gelfand, a warm hearted Jew, agreed and built a well-appointed synagogue.

The dedication of the synagogue was a magnificent ceremony. Gelfand came with his wife, his daughter and son-in-law. He invited two bands from neighboring towns and the celebration was grand. During the festivities an interesting event occurred. Mrs. Gelfand announced on stage that she wished that half of the *Mitzvah* (merit) should be hers. However, Mr. Gelfand replied in Russian: "I will not allow it! The *mitzvah* is all mine. We are wealthy enough and you can commemorate your own name". It was then suggested that Mrs. Gelfand would commission the inscribing of a Torah scroll in her name. And so it happened - a year later a Torah scroll was brought to the synagogue and again a wonderful celebration was held.

The Jews of Rokitno came from many parts of Russia and Ukraine. These were progressive Jews who came into contact with western culture. It was a monolithic population. In those early days they were not involved in the battles between the *Hasidic* movement and the *Mitnagdim* or the Enlightenment. They were outside these arguments.

The founders were Zionists and educated their children accordingly. In 1913 Sheftel Levin, the son of Feivish the *shohet* (ritual slaughterer) was chosen to go to Eretz Israel to buy land on behalf of the Jews of Rokitno who planned to move there. The money was collected and Sheftel was on his way. When he reached Odessa, he discovered that it was impossible to continue since it was the eve of World War I and the roads were not safe. He reluctantly returned to Rokitno and the plan was shelved.

In the beginning, there was no cemetery in Rokitno because the inhabitants were mostly young people who did not think of death. When necessary, the dead were buried in Osnitzek. The first Jew to die in Rokitno was Shmerl the *shohet* who died more than 60 years ago (at the turn of the twentieth century).

Sources:

Jadwiga Bergerowna: Rokitno 1925. Rokitno, wies (received from the Jewish General Historical Archives HM 7106) (in Polish)

Collection of materials about the economic situation of Jews in Russia, St. Petersburg, 1904. Publication by Jewish Colonial Society (in Russian)

Jewish Industrial Activities In Poland- Eliezer Heller 1923

Personal Recollections by townspeople: Herzl Lerner, Ita Eidelman, Israel Greenberg, Aharon Lifshitz

[Page 21]

The Beginnings of Rokitno

Pinchas Kliger *z"l* (of blessed memory)

Translated by Ala & Larry Gamulka

The first settlers of Rokitno were the Jews from the village of Rokitno. Their names were: my father Avraham Shmuel Kliger (the *Shohet*), Moshe Lifshitz, Sheftel Levin, Alter Vorona, Moshe Leib Zaks, Meir Weiner, Haim David Weiner, Avraham Golod, Moshe Freierman, Yakov Polishuk, Aharon Rotman, Moshe Haim Shapira, Benyamin Meirson, Yeshayahu Gendelman, Betzalel Kokel, Shimon Zaltzbuch, Ben Zion Geipman, Isaac Griever, Shimon Shapira, Gimpel Greenberg, Moshe Gurman and Moshe Hirsch Linn.

Alter Vaisblat, also one of the early settlers, owned a store near the glass factory (*Huta*) and lived in a house which belonged to the *Huta*. In the houses owned by the *Huta* there was a pharmacy run by a Jew called Barzam. He later sold the pharmacy to Noah Soltzman and moved to Sarny where he opened another pharmacy.

The village began to grow with vigor and many Jews and non-Jews from the vicinity came to settle there. A "practical doctor" (*feldsher*) called Zarin came, as well as a government-appointed doctor.

The first thing the Jews did was to build a synagogue with a ritual bath and nearby a house for the sexton - Nahum Eisenman. Gelfand, a rich man from Odessa, had bought a large tract of wooded land in Kisorich. He brought down his son-in-law, Polaver, who built himself a large house in the new town. The lumber business went well and with the help of Gelfand's trusted employee, Moshe Wolf Horman, a new large synagogue was built in the yard. The original small synagogue was moved to a different location.

Rabbi Aharon Yosef Shames came from Brezne, opened a dry goods store and also became the Rabbi of the village.

The pharmacy building also contained the post office. The first mailman, Anthony, and his assistant traveled to the station by horse and buggy to pick up the mail. Those people who wanted to receive their mail faster went on their own to the station.

A tragedy occurred in those early years. A murderer came to the village brandishing a revolver. At night he came to the house of Benyamin Meirson and he shot through the window. The Meirson family began shouting and they sent for help. Their neighbor, Ben Zion Geipman, ran towards their house. The murderer encountered him and killed him on the spot. Benyamin Meirson and his wife, Golde, were injured. The murderer was caught and brought to the station. He was sentenced and the residents calmed down.

This is how Rokitno was in those years.

[Page 23]

THE OLD CEMETERY

Yosef Segal (Neve Oz)

Translated by Ala Gamulka

Since Rokitno was only founded at the beginning of the twentieth century, there were no historical sites as there would have been in other Jewish settlements in Volyn. The only historical site in our area to be described is the Old Cemetery.

The Old Cemetery was located about six kilometers from Rokitno, northwest of the Klesov-Sarny road on a hill near Osnitzek on the river Lvo. It was surrounded by large oak trees and the graves were so old that they were almost indistinguishable. The land was quite rocky and it was fairly common to need a horse to remove a rock.

A popular legend is told about the earlier existence of a large Jewish community, which sprawled over the area between Sohov and Rokitno - a distance of 10 kilometers. All the Jews had been slaughtered in 1648 by the Cossack of Chmelnitzky and the community was totally destroyed. Even the cemetery was obliterated. Many years later when the Jews returned, the cemetery was discovered by a *Tzadik*, a follower of the Baal Shem Tov, who came there by accident. Just before *Mincha* prayers he ordered the caravan to stop, he washed his hands in the river, prayed in the cemetery and informed his followers that these were graves of martyrs, virtuous people and great Torah scholars.

Accordingly, this site was intended as a resting place for area Jews. However, the farmer who owned the land refused to sell it to the Jews. Once he was plowing his field, the earth opened up and swallowed the farmer and his oxen. Actually, at the entrance to the cemetery there was a depression, almost a hole. The elders would point to it and would tell, with trepidation, about the event.

The farmer's heirs eventually sold the land to the Jews and the cemetery served them until the 1920's. There were buried the martyrs slaughtered by Petlura and other murderers. From the 1920's the cemetery was no longer in use since the town grew and a cemetery was opened in Rokitno. The Jews still came every *Elul* to visit family graves in the Old Cemetery in Osnitzek. When the Jews were eliminated during the Holocaust, so was eliminated the Old Cemetery.

Gravestone in the Osnitek Cemetery

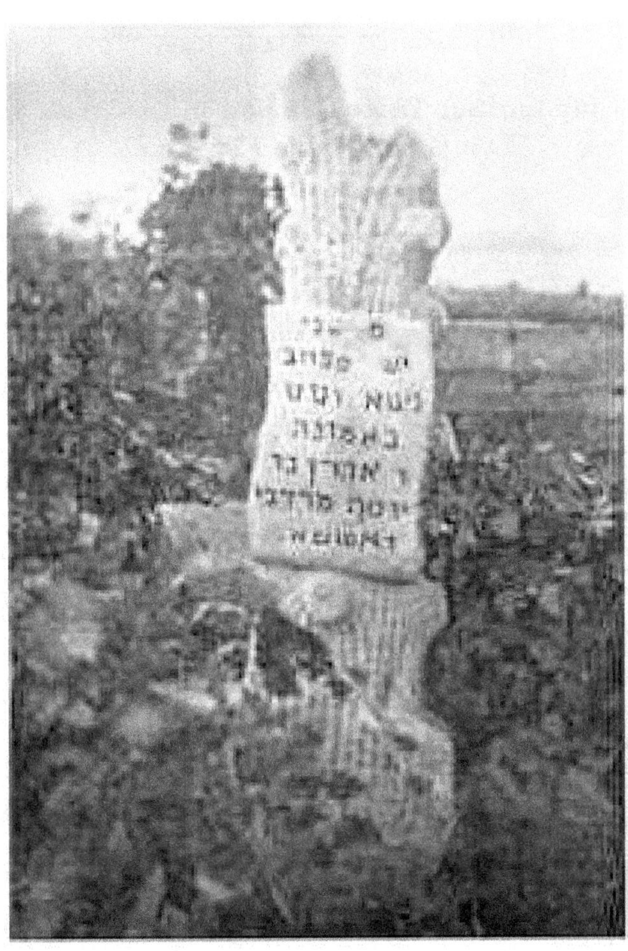

[Page 25]

THE VILLAGE OF ROKITNO (Memories and Experiences)

Dov Ben Yehoshua (Vorona) (Tel Aviv)

Translated by Ala Gamulka

In memory of my mother Tzirel, buried in Osnitzek and my father Yehoshua, buried in Israel.

Its Charm

The village of Rokitno was large and its streets and lanes were numerous. Uvel, a narrow river, divides the village in two. It begins southeast of Rokitno and it becomes a small lake as it reaches the village. From there it flows northwest to the village of Osnitzek. On the edge of the lake stood a flour mill where the residents would grind their wheat. The flour was used in the baking of a wonderful, tasty and aromatic bread.

On one side of the river lived mainly non-Jews. There were very few Jews - only 3 families. This was the center of the Christian community. The church stood out with its colorful steeple. Nearby were the Christian cemetery and the priest's house. Across from it, there was a public school with 6 classes. During the times of the tsar, Russian was the language of instruction. However after the Revolution, when various governments ruled, the teaching was done in Polish and/or Ukrainian. There were Jewish children in the school. Their parents wanted them to be taught secular subjects, in addition to their Jewish studies in the cheder. They felt that these secular studies would prove useful to them in later life.

On the other side of the river, the population was mixed. The Jews were devout and loyal. They educated their children in the Jewish spirit and celebrated all the holidays. The Jewish homes were more attractive than those of the others. A synagogue and a *mikveh* were built. After WWI, the Joint financed the construction of a magnificent bathhouse and *mikveh*. They were also used by Jews from the surrounding areas.

The majority of the Jews made their living by working as tradesmen, as storekeepers, or by using a horse and cart. Several families owned small stores in the surrounding villages. They were not wealthy, but they made a decent living.

Our Teachers

Education was most important for all parents. Torah teachers were brought in from great distances. The first one was Berl Gluzman from Sloveshnia, near Kiev. He would become easily enraged and did not spare the rod. Our parents permitted this corporal punishment as if beatings were a necessary part of our education.

Eventually, he was replaced by a new teacher, also from Sloveshnia, but completely different from the first one. His name was Leibl Shleifman. He was modern, nice, easy-going and good to the children. He never lifted a finger towards us and treated us with respect. He was a slender young man with the spirituality of a poet. He was a wonderful violinist and when he poured out his heart while playing it was as if the Holy Spirit rested on his shoulders. Before lunch he would stop our class and would play a "concert" to please his students. He was also a nature lover. At around 4:00 P.M., he would take his students for a walk along the river bank. He knew the names of all the flowers. The Jews thought this was a waste of time, but we, the children, enjoyed these walks tremendously.

World War I Threatens

The skies of the world and of Rokitno darkened. In the summer of 1914, WWI broke out. The teacher, Leibl Shleifman, announced: "Conscription, children! The war has broken out. I am going home". He left the village immediately. The violin was silenced and we had no school. We were happy, relieved of our studies. Little did we know that this day, the day our teacher left, was not a day of rejoicing but a day of deep sorrow. We would be subject to hunger, pogroms and other misfortunes resulting from war.

Youths were conscripted into the army and their parents ran around trying to get them out of it. One became deformed, another was bought out and a third ran away from the front and went into hiding. The police were paid off.

We, the children, roamed in the village. We were full of mischief even though these were difficult times. We were starving and our existence was in danger. We expected to be attacked by our neighbors and only by a miracle were we spared.

The November Revolution In Rokitno

One afternoon in 1917, when I was a young boy, as I stood near the railway station the train from Olevsk arrived. The locomotive was decorated with red flags and fir trees. When the train stopped, young revolutionaries jumped off dressed in leather jackets and began to remove any signs of the tsar's regime. There was not much to remove since there were only a few policemen, some clerks and the manager of the post office. These people were dressed in uniforms and were decorated with various insignia. The revolutionaries tore the insignia from the uniforms of the tsar's representatives and yelled out loud: “Long live freedom!”

I also recall from my childhood the first day of the November Revolution in Rokitno. I remember the beginning of that period which we hoped would bring us great freedom and equality. However, after the “honeymoon” of the Revolution our eyes were opened and we saw that we were only daydreaming.

In the streets of Rokitno there was an atmosphere of fear and helplessness. The civil war broke out and Petlura's rioters appeared. They were battling the Bolsheviks, but they always began by slaughtering the Jews. David Zunder, the owner of the glass factory, was the first victim. He was killed because it was rumored, incorrectly, that as an employer he exploited the workers. He paid for this lie with his life.

The Synagogue And Its Leaders

A magnificent synagogue stood in a corner of the village. It was one of the tallest and most elegant buildings in the village. There was space for 100-120 worshippers. There were many Torah scrolls in the Ark. Among the worshippers stood out Rabbi Shraga Feivish Levin, the *Shohet*. He was a learned Jew who was also well versed in the every day world. He was involved with the lives of many people. He would visit our home often and would spend time talking to my father about world events. On the High Holidays he led the services. When his booming voice was heard, the worshippers were moved. The rural Jews who were honest and simple and worked hard with the sweat of their palms during the rest of the year would be lifted from their simple existence. They were thrilled to listen to such expert chanting.

Next to Rabbi Feivish the *Shohet*, always stood Hershel (the yellow one) ready to announce the order of the *shofar* blowing. He too was a scholar. He led the morning services on a regular basis and read the weekly portion. He was a kind-hearted Jew who dealt in honey and wax. However, during the war years, when business was slow, he would gather the children who were out of school and he taught them Bible and *Rashi*. The older children were also taught *Gmara*. He did not even charge a fee, for it was important to him that Jewish children should not forget their Bible studies.

On *Yom Kippur*, these two men were joined by David Grinshpan who led the *Kol Nidrei* service. He was a tall man with a long beard. He was handsome and possessed a beautiful melodious voice. Before *Kol Nidrei*, he would stand clad in his *Kittel*, the synagogue packed with young and old. The candles were lit and shone like a forest on fire. Then David would lift his head and look out the window on the western wall, towards Osnitzek. When he saw that the sun was in on the tops of the trees - that was his signal to begin the *Kol Nidrei* prayer. His soft and melodious voice would be heard: “Happy are the just...”

The Opening Of The Cemetery

The village of Rokitno did not have its own cemetery. For many years the Jews of the village were used to the idea that Rokitno was meant for live Jews only and that the dead ones had no place in it. Those who died were buried in Osnitzek or in Olevsk, in spite of the difficulties entailed.

Towards the end of World War I, the Jews of Rokitno were dying of hunger or of disease or they were being slaughtered. Only then did the Jews understand that the dead had to be cared for and that a cemetery was needed in Rokitno.

One day we, the children, found out that a plot of land was being designated as a cemetery. The children did not know what a cemetery looked like because they had never seen one. Unfortunately, I knew about it since my mother was buried in Osnitzek and on the eve of the High Holidays, I used to go to her grave with my older brothers, Noah and Ephraim, to say *Kaddish*.

All the village children gathered and waited impatiently for the big event. An area on the way to Snovidovich was fenced off, not far from the Christian cemetery. The day of dedication was declared a fast day. All the Jews of the village and the town met in the field and circled it many times while reciting the appropriate Psalms. A long time was spent there and at the end they all wished each other not to need the place too soon.

When the first grave in the cemetery was dug, a major problem arose. It is unlawful to leave a lone grave without a guard and it is necessary to watch it until a second grave is dug. However, time quickly resolved the problem.

As I previously recounted, we lived through bad times and Jewish blood was spilled. A Jew was killed in Olevsk. The community helped us by burying him in the Rokitno cemetery. This death saved the situation.

The settlement was destroyed and not all its Jews were even buried according to Jewish law. For this reason our hearts are heavy.

[Page 29]

Rokitno during World War I

Yosef Segal (Neve Oz) and Aryeh Geipman (Ramat Gan)

Translated by Ala Gamulka

The declaration of war in August 1914 came as a shock to the Jews of Russia, among them the Jews of Rokitno. Since many of the farmers and other residents of the town and its surroundings were conscripted, the economic situation of the Jews worsened. The work in the forests stopped almost completely and it was limited to chopping wood for heating purposes or for the war effort.

The recession was already felt at the beginning of the war and became worse as the war continued. The movement of the passenger and freight trains stopped since the trains were needed to transport soldiers and military equipment to the fronts. The Rokitno train station stood on the important Kiev-Kovel-Warsaw line. This was an essential route that led to the battlegrounds. Packed trains went through the station to the front while the wounded and the prisoners (mainly Austrians) were transported in the opposite direction.

The lack of supplies caused a rise in their price and the area farmers often accused the Jews of speculating and of hiding the supplies.

When the war broke out, the authorities began to persecute the Jews. As a result, several families of commercial representatives were hurt because the representatives were accused of being in contact with the Germans. The representatives had to be in correspondence with the Germans regarding the export of lumber products. Avraham Golod was exiled to Siberia. The families of

Aharon Litvak, Avraham Shapira and Zeev Zelikovsky, who were to be exiled, quietly left Rokitno and settled in Tzaritzin (Stalingrad, now Volgograd).

After the conquest of Poland by the German army in 1915, a flow of Jewish refugees began to arrive. These were refugees who had been expelled by the retreating Russian army. Many of these refugees settled in Rokitno. The local Jews gave a helping hand to their poor brethren.

At the beginning of 1916 the front moved closer to the Stir River and the Stohod River - about 100 kilometers from Rokitno. Again, refugees arrived in Rokitno from the villages closest to the front. As the front came closer, several military plants were transferred to Rokitno. These plants were used to repair weapons and for garage space. As well, a military hospital was installed in the Rosenberg Palace (opposite the railway station). These plants slightly improved the economic situation of the Jews of Rokitno.

In March 1917 the Tsar was defeated and Russia became a republic. This happy news reached Rokitno and caused much excitement. It warmed the relationship between Jews and Christians. Local government institutions were established headed by the "Committee of Workers, Farmers and Soldiers". A local militia was also founded and it replaced the tsarist police. It was headed by David Shachnovski, a resident of Rokitno. A special department for the supply and apportionment of food was managed by Moshe Freierman and Betzalel Kokel. The main clerks were Yakov Wolfin and a farmer by the name of Prohor from the village of Rokitno. When the revolution broke out, many young people from Rokitno went to study in the high schools in Kiev, Katerinsolav and Odessa.

In the summer of 1917, elections to the All Russia meeting were held and the local Jews participated. At that time, branches of all of the Jewish organizations, headquartered in Kiev, were founded: *Tseirei Zion, Poalei Zion, Bund, Ahdut, Mizrahi,* General Zionists. In November 1917 we were happy to hear about the Balfour Declaration. It encouraged the Zionist movement and raised our spirits. When the Bolsheviks took control of the central government, a civil war broke out. By the end of 1917, Rokitno had changed hands several times. At the end of 1917, the Ukrainians announced the formation of an independent republic. It was led by Vinichenko (Prime Minister) and Petlura (Minister of Defense). In the beginning, the authorities were friendly to the Jews. As proof of this Moshe Zilberfarb, the representative of the Territorial Zionists, served as Minister for Jewish Affairs.

This government lasted only until April 1918. After the signing of a separate peace treaty between Soviet Russia and Germany in March 1918 in Brest-Litovsk, the Red Army attacked the independent Ukraine. The Ukrainian government asked the German army for help. The German army conquered the whole Ukraine (up to the Black Sea) in April 1918 and a new government was formed, headed by Pavel Skoropedsky. The Minister of Industry and Commerce was Mr. Gutnik, the son-in-law of Mr. Gelfand.

The Germans also occupied Rokitno. Although their headquarters were in the Rosenberg Palace, they did not interfere in local government. All was calm, but not for long. In November 1918, a revolution broke out in Germany and two days later the war ended. The German army in Ukraine prepared to return home. At the same time, the Ukrainian army organized itself under the leadership of Petlura. He quickly took over the whole of the Ukraine and deposed Skoropedsky. Petlura soldiers reached Rokitno - the descendants of the Haidamaks. When they arrived they shot to death David Zunder, the owner of the glass factory. His workers had libeled him. There were other Jewish victims whose names we do not remember. The Petlurists ransacked Jewish homes and punished the Jewish population with harsh taxes. The Jews met in the synagogue and collected the necessary funds, which were given to the rioters.

Fear and depression fell on the Jewish population. There was no traveling to and from the city and there was a great shortage of food. In January 1919, the German army left the Ukraine and the Red Army quickly moved in. Petlura's army was soon defeated and the Bolsheviks came in April 1919. The Red Army advanced to the Bog River. During that time, the Polish army was reorganizing in a rejuvenated Poland. While they were advancing east they defeated the Russian army and reached Olevsk.

That year, a Polish unit from General Haler also arrived. These soldiers immediately began to ruthlessly attack the Jews - to cut the beards of the elderly and to force Jews to do hard labor. They were told to dismantle military equipment that arrived by train and to repair railroad tracks and bridges that had been destroyed by the retreating Red Army. The railroad to the village of Kisorich was built by the Jews at that time.

In the summer of 1919 Yosef Lerner was killed by the Poles. He was the oldest son of Herzel Lerner, who was then on his way to Rokitno.

The Polish - Red Army front moved near the Oobort River (in Olevsk). In spring 1920, the Poles attacked the Red Army all along the front and they quickly conquered Kiev. The Red Army recovered and attacked. Led by Budionov, it defeated the Polish army and quickly reached Warsaw.

Rokitno again became part of the Soviet Regime, but this lasted only three months since in September 1920 the Poles returned to Rokitno and again reached Olevsk. During the transition of governments the Jews of Rokitno organized themselves in civil defense, especially night watch. The Jews and the local Poles cooperated in this endeavor.

In October 1920 a cease-fire was announced by both sides and peace talks were begun in Riga. According to the agreement the Polish army retreated to Tomshgarod. The area between Tomshgarod and Ostoki was declared no man's land. A small Soviet occupation force arrived in Rokitno since the area was divided among the different armies.

The Soviet occupation lasted until the end of March 1921. On 21.3.1921 a peace treaty was signed in Riga. As a result, the border between Poland and Russia was placed near Ostoki and Rokitno became part of Poland.

During the changes of government there was a great lack of food. The Jews of the town - at great personal danger - went to surrounding areas to look for food. Not once were they robbed on the road, but nothing stopped them.

When the Polish rule was established in the town and its vicinity, life slowly returned to normal and the economic situation improved. Again, the lumber industry was thriving and the glass factory was reopened after a long stoppage. The old sawmill was again in operation.

The Zionist and cultural activities were revived. The Tarbut School was founded and the pioneers began to go to Eretz Israel.

[Page 32]

העץ הגדוע..

The fallen tree...

[Page 33]

ECONOMY AND INSTITUTIONS

[Page 35]

The Community

Shlomo Zandweis (Tel Aviv)

Translated by Ala Gamulka

Rokitno was not a community by itself. It originally belonged to the Sarny Community, which included several villages and towns in the area. The Jewish population there numbered 17-18, 000 people, among them 3,500 in Rokitno. In accordance with the electoral laws, which were published in the official gazette of the Polish government (*Dziennik Ustaw*) of 1924, the right to vote was granted to all males over 25 (women were not allowed to vote). When elections were announced a council of 14 was chosen, headed by Moshe Tartakovsky. In addition, there were sub-committees in the communities which were part of Sarny. The first elections were held in the fall of 1927.

The president was Mendel Kercher from Rokitno. He also served for many years as a member of the Administrative Committee of Rokitno. He was a dedicated community worker. He was even active in Slichetz-Lodiopol. He was a bright Jew who defended Jewish interests and knew how to reply to accuser and prosecutor alike. All this was done with wisdom and wit. The alternate head was Noah Perlstein from Sarny. The Chairman of the Council was Moshe Pikman and the Rabbi of the community was Nahum Pechnik from Dombrovitz. The secretary was Moshe Gotlieb from Dombrovitz.

Until 1932 there was almost no activity in the community. The Rabbi opened an office for the registration of marriages, births and deaths. The community, including the Rabbinate, had its headquarters in the home of the widow of the late Rabbi Yosef Pechnik.

As of 1932 the position of secretary was that of yours truly, the author of this article. From that year on, the community council began various activities. The government demanded that the community control all matters of slaughtering, synagogues, ritual baths and other public buildings. After 4 years, the term of office of the first council ended and new elections were announced.

All Zionist organizations participated in the election committee. The Chairman was Shmarayahu Gershonok. Lists of candidates were drawn from all the towns and all levels of society. The public participated eagerly. The following Rokitners were elected to the second council - Mendel Kercher, the teacher Mordecai Gendelman and Yehoshua Gitelman. The chairman of the Executive Committee was Yakov Liberson and his alternate was Shmaryahu Gershonok. The chairman of the council was David Birg and his alternate was Binyamin Kanterowich. According to the regulations of the community, the Rabbi was a member of the administration. The Rabbi was a Zionist and even the extremists among the *Hassidim* never objected to any proposals regarding any funds, *aliyah* or any other Zionist purposes.

A budget of about 30,000 *zloty* was approved (in 1938-39 the budget reached 80,000 *zloty*). The funds and the supervision of expenses and income were in trustworthy hands. The treasurer was Avraham Binder, an honest man and devoted community worker. He watched over every penny of public money and presented the ledgers in an orderly manner. The collector and supervisor was Motl Levin who fulfilled his task loyally. The teacher Mordecai Gendelman, a cultured man, conducted all public business with honesty and integrity.

In matters that required the seal of approval of the majority of the citizens, e.g. - community taxes, charitable distributions to the needy, etc. - the representatives of the council invited the important property owners and community workers of Rokitno. Among them were Rabbi Damata, Moshe Lifshitz, Shimon Zaltzbuch, Moshe Freierman, Avraham Golod, Avraham Levin, Hershel Shteinman, Moshe-Zelig Shulman, the pharmacist brothers Noah and Yakov Soltzman, Betzalel Kokel, Shimon Gendelman, Leibel Gitelman, Leivik Rotman, Yosef-Haim Baum (representative of the tradesmen union) and others.

The income was produced, mainly, from ritual slaughtering. The community received 20% and the *Shohet* the remaining 80%. In Rokitno, the ritual slaughterers were Yoel Shwartzberg and Issachar Trigun. There were other non-official slaughterers, who were not recognized by the Rabbinate for good reasons.

Even in Rokitno the slaughterers had a competitor - an illegal one. He was Rabbi Asher Eisenberg, from Blezhov. He claimed that most of the Jews from Blezhov and Brezov had moved to Rokitno and he lost his means of earning a living. The Rabbinate, other slaughterers and the community representatives did not recognize him. There were many heated discussions, but in the long run, nothing was done to him because the other slaughterers did not wish to hurt him. Who among us does not remember Rabbi Issachar Trigun, a bright, intelligent Jew? He had a noble spirit. He was a scholar and an honest man. He was pious and spoke beautifully. It was always a delight to be with him and to listen to his words of wisdom.

The *Shohet and Bodek* Rabbi Yoel Shwartzberg was an honest and wonderful person. There was no one better. He never caused any unhappiness to another human being and, as it is said, would not even hurt a fly. And last, but not least, the late Rabbi Aharon Shames. He was a spiritual leader not only in Rokitno but also in the surrounding area. He was known as a patient and kind man, a lover of and pursuer of peace. Would these kind Jews hurt another Jew? This is why the slaughterer from Blezhov was able to continue his work and the community was not shamed.

Other income came from the registration of marriages, divorces, births and deaths, sales of cemetery plots and gravestones. The expenses for payments for guards were covered by the community.

Another source of income towards the community budget was membership dues - or as it was called *Kehila etat* - dues established by the state, as it were. The income was used, except for administrative expenses, for the following purposes:

All Rabbis (in addition to the community Rabbi, who received a monthly salary) were given an annual assistance of 600 *zloty*. They were also reimbursed for the birth registration books, which they had to hand in. The Rabbis were: Kunda Vahman from Sarny, Nahum Pechnik and Yakov Zalcman from Dombrovitz, Aharon Shames from Rokitno, Moshe Naidich and Bakun from Brezhnitz.

In the winter, all the schools, religious *yeshivas*, Ort and other educational institutions were given food and warm milk in addition to the regular monetary subsidy. Weak and needy children were also given fish oil as prescribed by the doctor.

All charitable organizations, as for example, “Bread for the Poor”, “Orphans Home”, etc. were given funds.

Jewish National Fund and *Keren Hayesod* were allotted annual amounts.

A specific sum was set aside for the pioneers who were to make *aliyah* and who needed assistance to cover their expenses. Officially the funds were designated as help for immigrants.

Twice a year, on specific holidays, the community opened soup kitchens for the Jewish soldiers in the local army units. When it came to religious matters, the community was in contact with the Chief Army Rabbi of the Lublin district - Captain Raab. He visited Sarny once or twice a year and conducted a service for the soldiers in the Great Synagogue. He also sent copies of all regulations regarding religion, Shabbat and other holidays.

The community had a special fund for needy families who did not want to contact “Bread for the Poor”, sick people who had to be transported to Warsaw. Those who had tuberculosis were taken to Otvortzek or to sanatoriums in other locations. All the expenses were carefully supervised by a committee. All the members of the council and the administration were well-known community workers who volunteered their service.

Usually, all matters were handled in an orderly, responsible, and cooperative manner. At times, difficulties would arise which would cause discussions and lively meetings. In Dombrovitza, for instance, there was a debate about a resident who was an illegal slaughterer. On the other hand, Rokitno did not cause any difficulties and everything ran smoothly. The reason for this was that the economic situation of the majority of the Jews of Rokitno was satisfactory. There were no really wealthy people, but everyone made a living because there were good opportunities locally.

So continued the life of the Rokitno community in peace and quiet and with great respect, love of Israel and a love of fellow human beings, until the beasts who pretended to be humans came - the German Nazis, may they be obliterated. They desecrated our Temple and trampled on the honor of human beings. They looted our homes and on that terrible day, 14 *Elul* 1942, men, women and children were massacred and buried in place. May G-d avenge their deaths and may they be remembered forever.

[Page 38]

The Economy of Rokitno

Natan Gendelman (Tel Aviv)

Translated by Ala Gamulka

Rokitno was a city well situated. There were no millionaires, but everyone made a living. The main reason for this was the fact that there were many villages in the area and they had economic ties with Rokitno. Many villagers came to market in Rokitno and also bought their necessities there. This afforded an income to many Jewish families.

As in many other towns and villages, commerce in Rokitno was extremely important. Storeowners left an indelible stamp on the economy of the town. There were many different stores and they supplied all needs.

Among the stores and businesses that I remember are: the dry goods store of Leibel Gitelman and Avraham Grinshpan in partnership with Haikel Kleinman, grocery stores of Moshe Lifshitz, Motel Kremer, Levi Grinshpan and others.

Building supplies stores belonged to Shimon Gendelman and Avraham Sliep and the glass store was owned by Betzalel Kokel. The stationery stores were run by Avraham Schwartz and Lipa Shpilman. Bakeries were those of Leivik Rotman, Eidelman and Garber.

Storekeeping was only one branch of the economy of Rokitno. The geological make-up of the soil of Rokitno and the surrounding area allowed for the development of several manufacturing plants. The soil in Ostoki was rich in clay - good for the production of building bricks. The Jews took advantage of these natural resources and built plants for the production of bricks. This raw material was mixed with other ingredients. The work was primitive and the machines were powered by horses. The largest brick factory in Ostoki was owned by Klein. The general manager was Haim Torok. There were 200 workers, mostly Poles. The second largest brick factory was owned by Shimon Gendelman and Shpilman.

These factories helped many Jews in Ostoki and Rokitno to earn a living. Payment was made with coupons, which were traded for needed items at the stores. There were always outsiders working there as laborers, clerks, traders and wagon drivers and this created the hotel and restaurant industry in Ostoki and Rokitno.

Our area was rich in stone quarries. The best-known quarry was in Mochilenka, owned by Taras Borovitz. During the German occupation, he led in the destruction of the Jews in Rokitno and the surrounding area. However, during the times before the slaughterers came on the scene, he was quite friendly with the Jews and dealt with them in business. He bought drills, bits for the drills, and blasting materials from the Jewish stores in Rokitno.

The quarry owners in the area were mostly Jews from Warsaw. One was owned by Frantz, a Jew from Rokitno. The foreman was Berkman. They looked after transport, ordered railway cars for the stones and supervised the loading.

This was an important source of livelihood for many Jews. However, there were no quarry laborers among the Jews.

The transport of the goods from the trains to the stores was, in general, in the hands of *Volksdeutsch* (German Poles), but there was among them one Jewish wagon driver, called Moshe Shaintuh. He worked hard for his wages.

The sawmills contributed greatly to the economy of the Jews of Rokitno. There was a large sawmill near the railway. Its managers were Jews, among them the three Golubovitz brothers. Many Jews worked there in all stages of production. Among them were experts in lumber. There was another sawmill in Rokitno owned by Persitz. In Ostoki, there was also a large sawmill owned by Berezovsky and many Jews worked there. When the *preparatory kibbutz* was founded in Rokitno, many of its pioneers worked in those sawmills.

Market Day (Back left - part of Kostushko Street; Center- New Synagogue)

There was also a large agricultural settlement in Rokitno, owned by Shulman. The work was primitive. The wheat was thrashed with sticks, as in biblical times of Gideon. Eventually, machinery replaced the sticks as industrialization reached Rokitno.

There were two factories for soda and lemonade. One was owned by Strelovsky. Rokitno was, to an extent, an "international" town, as businessmen from many European countries came there for lumber. Also, many firms had agencies in town. The hotel industry developed. There were two large hotels in Rokitno. One belonged to Aharon Litvak and the other to Moshe Katz on Kostushko Street. The first inn was owned by Sheftel Levin. These hotels served as a meeting place for lumber traders and some important business deals took place there. This helped in the economic development of the town.

Even the two cinemas in town were owned by Jews. At first, there was a cinema in the area near the glass factory. Later, a new cinema named "Apollo" was built. The concessionaire was a *goy* and he sold it to Moshe Freierman.

There was a Jewish partnership in the large flourmill, which also included a textile mill that produced coarse cloth for the villagers. An important source of income was market day, which occurred twice a month- on the 5th and on the 18th.

There were Jews whose sole source of income came from market day. They bargained over their goods, which contained farm tools, clothes and building supplies.

On market days many villagers would gather to spend their considerable income. The farmer who had money in his pocket on that day would "invest" in liquor, which he would down in large quantities. He would also buy clothes and shoes for himself and his family. However, the market day also served as a day of hatred and fear - a day when the Jews were attacked. Near the market square there was a restaurant for the Polish porters, who were infamous hooligans. When they drank, their hidden hatred of Jews would be revealed and they would attack.

In the last years before the Holocaust the economic situation of the Jews in Rokitno worsened. Poles opened stores and anti-Semitic propaganda, rampant among the non-Jews, was successful in stopping them from trading with Jews. This boycott caused the Jews to lose their means of earning a living.

[Page 41]

The Lumber Trade and the Lumber Yard

Zvi Persitz (Tel Aviv)

Translated by Ala Gamulka

In 1924, my father, Yakov Mordehai Persitz, left Harkov and moved with his family to Vilna. He was a well-to-do lumber merchant, highly experienced in the field. I worked for Mr. Beikovich who was an agent for a paper manufacturing plant called "Papirovka". Its head office was in Koenigsberg. I traveled to Lubinitz on business and an event occurred there which helped considerably in the economic development of Rokitno. By pure chance I met, in the railroad station cafeteria, Mr. Siniavsky, born in Harkov and one of its wealthier citizens. At the time he was residing in Warsaw and he was dealing with a railway company whose head office was in Vilna.

Mr. Siniavsky told me that he was looking for my father. He was ready to conclude a large business deal - buying the forest land of Rokitno and its surrounding area. He himself was not knowledgeable in these matters and that is why he wanted to include my father in this deal. I gave him our address and a few days later he came to Vilna to meet with my father.

This is what it was all about, Siniavsky's offer to my father: there was a large ancient forest area near Rokitno. No human foot had ever stepped in it. Its length was 25 kilometers and it reached the villages of Ostoki, Karpilovka, Borovey and Blezhov. These lands bordered on Soviet territory and served as hiding places for infiltrators and elements unwanted by the Polish government. Therefore, the Polish Defense Ministry decided to cut down a large part of these forests in order to create open spaces and to get rid of the danger from infiltrators or, at least to lessen the danger. The job was given to a non-Jewish firm and it proved unsuccessful. The authorities turned to Siniavsky for help.

My father was interested in the proposition but, before agreeing to it, he wanted to visit Rokitno in order to investigate for himself. In 1925, my father came to Rokitno with my uncle Yehoshua Betzalel Persitz who was also a lumber expert. They slept over in the home of Aharon Litvak and then proceeded to tour the area in a horse and buggy. They visited Ostoki, Karpilovka, Borovey and Blezhov. My father returned to Warsaw greatly encouraged by his visit and told Siniavsky that he would accept the government contract because he felt it was a gold mine and that a great deal of money could be made. My father found in these forests high quality trees for which there was great demand in the world. Among them were beech, oak, pine and other fine trees.

According to my father's recommendation, a partnership was formed. Its members were: the engineer Frumkin from Warsaw, Siniavsky, my father and my uncle. (A year later, my uncle left the partnership and opened a large business in the Grodno forests).

The new plant invigorated Rokitno. In those years it was a large village and there was much poverty. There was economic growth and the population increased quickly. Many Jewish businessmen from the area and from places far away came to settle in Rokitno. They saw great opportunities for good business and for making money. In those days, we referred to our village as “Little America”.

The forest-clearing project (a length of 25 km) became a great source of employment for Jews and non-Jews alike. In order to understand the scope of this era, it is sufficient to say that 3,000 non-Jews were employed with their wagons. It was necessary to mobilize villagers from the area. There was a whole fleet of horse and buggies. They were housed in canvas tents, in the forests. Dozens of Jewish families earned their living by providing food, clothing and felt boots for the forest workers.

A large office was opened in Rokitno. It had 120 clerks - most of them Jews. Some were Jews from other villages. The workers were paid weekly. The payments began on Saturday at noon and ended early Sunday morning. There were three locations: Karpilovka, Borovey and Ostoki.

The New Sawmill

The lumber of Rokitno was well known in all of Europe because of its high quality. Important firms in England, France, Belgium and Germany sent their representatives to Rokitno to buy the outstanding lumber. Because of all the languages spoken in the streets of Rokitno, it looked like an international village. The English firm "Neam and Booth", one of the large lumber export firms, had permanent representatives in Rokitno who stamped the trees with the firm's logo and looked after their transport. The top directors in London even came at times to Rokitno, toured the forests, and selected the best lumber. Even the firm "Parmentier and Partners", one of the large firms representing sawmills in France and Belgium, bought a great deal of lumber. Maurice Parmentier lived in Rokitno for two years and dealt in the transport of oak trees to France and Belgium.

Loading Of Logs On Freight Cars

Standing, third from right below:	**Mordecai Hamer**
Last one on the left:	**Avraham Golod**
Standing on freight car on the right:	**Haim Berezovsky**

However, the partnership did not only send lumber, but it also gave advice on lumber products. For that purpose, my father built a large sawmill in Rokitno which worked non-stop day and night. Aside from the *Huta*, it was the only place that was lit by electricity. The sawmill produced railroad ties, boards, building planks and beams. The products were destined for export and for the local market in many parts of Poland. Rokitno flooded the markets in Poland and other European countries. There was so much lumber that the wagon drivers could not keep up and it was necessary to build a narrow gauge railroad, 12 km in length, to the forests in Borovey and Karpilovka in order to bring the lumber on the freight cars. For the sake of accuracy, I must note that the need to build this railway arose from the fact that in the summer and in autumn the movement of wagons was almost stopped because the roads were full of puddles. The lumber was mostly transported in the winter and not enough time was thus available to transport this bounty.

The sawmill fulfilled an important economic role in Rokitno. Many Jewish families earned their living from it. Some of the young men from the *Hechalutz Preparatory Kibbutz* worked there. My father was a Zionist and he admired the physical labor of the enthusiastic and loyal Zionist youth. He also donated lumber for the construction of the Tarbut School in Rokitno.

In 1927 the sawmill burned down and not a trace was left. My father decided not to rebuild because, in the mean time, the price of the lumber went down and there was not a good opportunity for a new sawmill. The demand for unprocessed lumber at better prices grew. Lurie's factory in Pinsk ordered lumber for their production of matches and an important match factory owner in Vienna also became a customer. The lumber business also brought about the beautification of Rokitno. Beautiful large homes were built and the streets were full of life. Many Jews began to trade in lumber and became wealthy. Energetic young people bought remnants and firewood and resold them.

At the end of 1929, the government contract ended and the partnership was dissolved. The firm fulfilled the conditions to the satisfaction of the authorities.

[Page 45]

CHARITABLE INSTITUTIONS IN ROKITNO

Haim Shteinman (Tel Aviv)

Translated by Ala Gamulka

The tradition of mutual assistance between people existed for many years. Merciful men and pious women dedicated their time to charitable deeds.

One of the institutions was *Gmilut Hasadim* (Free Loan). Its leaders were Mendel Kercher, Shimon Gendelman, Betzalel Kokel and others. The treasurers would change every year, on *Simchat Torah.* The funds were donated by the residents. The Free Loan was an important support vehicle for small merchants, poor craftsmen and other needy individuals. A merchant whose affairs were near bankruptcy would receive a loan at convenient terms. A wagon driver whose horse collapsed suddenly and thus he would have no means of making a living, was helped back on his feet. Also, the Free Loan helped a craftsman who wished to open a workshop.

In time, the dimensions of the Free Loan were enlarged and the Popular Bank (Bank Ludovy) was founded. Its director was Asher Zelig Baratz. The bank was mainly helpful to small merchants by granting loans at low interest. The middle class, which included most of the Jews of Rokitno, was rejuvenated with the founding of the bank.

The Torah commandment: “And your brother shall live among you”, became a prime concept for the Rokitno Jews. Therefore, in addition to these financial institutions which were intended for constructive purposes, there was also an unofficial institution of “Secret Giving”. Its activities were purely assistance to the needy. There were some families in Rokitno who were too embarrassed to beg. In order to save them, many of the residents of Rokitno canvassed the population to collect the means to help them anonymously. It was not necessary to press too hard for people to give. All those canvassed gave willingly. They showed their love for their fellow Jews and their wish to help each other. Our parents felt the pain of their brethren who were impoverished and hungry. Among those who were active in the “Secret Giving” we remember fondly Yoel the Shohet, Zeidel Binder, Shimon Gendelman, Hershel Shteinman, Itzhak Shuber, Betzalel Kokel, Mendel Kercher, Berl Shwartzblat and others.

Among the many important charitable activities, I wish to note one example. It was done by my father and left an indelible impression in my memory. A maid from a village near Rokitno worked in our home. She came from a poor family and her father found her a suitable spouse who was also poor. My father acted as the father of the bride and paid for a beautiful wedding party with Klezmer musicians in the Old Shul. All the town residents participated in the festivities and brought gifts for the couple. The young man was nicknamed “Hershel's son-in-law” in Rokitno.

Another type of institution which existed in Rokitno was *Linat Tzedek* -Righteous Lodging. This institution was active in medical assistance. Its purpose was to provide the poor with inexpensive medications, at times for free. It also covered doctors' fees. The “Righteous Lodging” especially took care of those miserable souls who were chronically ill. In these cases, in addition to providing medications and medical help, nightly vigils over sick beds were made available. In this manner, other members of the household could get a night's sleep.

I recalled here only a few of the charitable and righteous deeds which were performed by the Jews of Rokitno. These are mere examples, which point out the kindness of all Jews and their readiness to help others among them.

The Founders of "Righteous Lodging"**, established 1930**

Standing: Right to left: 1. Yosef Haim Baum 2. Zeidel Binder 3. Baruch Flehendler 4. Levi Grinshpan 5. Daniel Bender

Seated: 1. Aharon Levin 2. Betzalel Kokel 3. Noah Soltzman 4. Asher Zelig Baratz 5. Shlomo Bender

[Page 47]

THE ZIONIST MOVEMENT

[Page 49]

The Origins of the Zionist Movement in Rokitno

Avraham Ben Dor [Binder] (Ramat Gan)

Translated by Ala Gamulka

The population of Rokitno was mainly young. It consisted of people who came from neighboring villages and from distant settlements in Russia. Here, their families grew. Among these people there were three opposing movements: *Hasidism, Bund* and early Zionism. Why early Zionism? In order to answer this question, we must know the public and political image of the population of Rokitno during World War I.

The *Hasidic* movement, which left a deep imprint on the Jews of Rokitno, did not understand Zionism and opposed it. It saw in Zionism an attempt to postpone the end and to bring the Messiah before its time. The second element that dominated the public was the *Bund*. Its influence on the youth was great. Even in 1905, a strong group of *Bund* members settled in Rokitno. Among them were: Moshe and Nissan Polishuk, the dentist Moshe Kutzin and his sister Idel. They were better educated than the rest of the local population. Thus, their influence on the youths was great from an ideological point of view. These youths had not yet defined their view of the world. They were, in general, susceptible to influences and no wonder that the *Bundists*, who were highly educated, were able to direct them to their way of thinking and their worldview. They sowed hatred towards Eretz Yisrael as it was, according to Ansky's declaration, "a land of holy graves" and that it would not solve the problems of the Jews. In their opinion, the change in the Russian governing body would solve the Jewish problem automatically. In these beliefs, there was a great misconception. The youths did not possess analytic skills and could not distinguish truth from nonsense. This nonsense would solve nothing and would only serve as a basis for a losing ideology. These youths, in their innocence, believed that the *Bundists'* beliefs would be redemption for the Jewish people.

In order to deepen their influence among the youths, the *Bundists* established a library, which served as a center for the dissemination of their ideology. Meetings of youths and adults were held there. It was the only cultural center in town.

However, the *Bund* ideology hit a brick wall, which it could not break down. As a result, the movement shattered into tiny pieces. What was this brick wall? It was the stories of the destruction of the Temple in *Eyn Yaakov*, which Jewish children read and studied in the *cheders*. These stories had a tremendous influence. This is where the children received their knowledge of the land of their forefathers and the prophets. In this struggle, ultimately, *Eyn Yaakov* was the winner over the maligning ideology of the *Bund*. The buds of Zionism and the Hebrew language began to develop among the Rokitno youths.

The actual push for the formation of the Zionist movement in Rokitno came from nearby Sarny. The Association of Lovers of Hebrew was founded in 1911 in Sarny. Its goal was to teach and to speak Hebrew, to open Hebrew libraries and, as much as possible, to establish a Hebrew school. The Association influenced and directed the formation of a large branch in Rokitno. It became the basis for the Zionist movement in Rokitno. Since they were young, their power was limited. Still, they were able to overcome the influence of the *Bund*, to stop it in its tracks and to cancel its influence on the streets of Rokitno. The members of the Association kept in touch with the committee of the *Hapoel Hatzioni* (the Zionist worker) in Berlin. They obtained materials from Petrograd. In the circulars that were sent to them, the youths were asked to establish a Hebrew library, evening classes and to open a Hebrew school.

According to the instructions from the central office, the young members of the Association of Lovers of Hebrew intended to open a Hebrew library in Rokitno. Since the population at that time was small, there really was no need for two libraries. As a result, there was a movement to remake the existing library into a Zionist one. All members of the Association took out library cards and in this way they were able to join its administration in a democratic way. After a long struggle, the young Zionists succeeded and became the directors of the library. The leaders were: Gedalya Lifshitz, Pinie Kliger, Haya-Sara Lifshitz, Polia Rotman (Lifshitz), Leibel Geipman, Yeshayahu Meiri (Meirson), Rachel Meirson (Margalit), Haim Zandweis and others. The library became a center for serious Zionists.

While the Zionist movement was organizing itself, the October Revolution began. Tremendous revolutionary forces were in evidence. The fermenting forces in Russia touched the Jewish population in Rokitno. All colors of the rainbow were represented by the many political groups, such as the *Bund*, "Social Revolutionaries", Young Zionists, and *Achdut* (Unity). These groups struggled for the souls of the Jewish population, in general and the young, in particular.

The ideological struggle was won by the Zionist movement. The youths of Rokitno were not blinded by the promises of the emissaries of the revolution who predicted wonderful things for the Jews. In this time of turmoil, the Zionist dream took shape and became a way of life – a way of life which had no alternative. The anti-Zionist parties were beaten and their influence was minimal. Rokitno became a well-known Zionist town.

Receipt from the Odessa Committee

11/XI 1916

Комитетъ Общества Вспомоществованія Евреямъ Земледѣльцамъ и Ремесленникамъ въ Сиріи и Палестинѣ Одесса

№ 4585

ועד החברה לתמיכת בני ישראל עובדי אדמה ובעלי מלאכה בסוריא ובארץ ישראל אודיסה.

Господину Г. М. Лившицу, Охотниково, Вол. г.

Присланные Вами Руб. 14 к. 29 (четырнадцать р. 29 к.)

мы получили и записали по н/ книгамъ согласно Вашему указанію

Съ совершеннымъ почтеніемъ

Бухгалтеръ

Председатель

Receipt from the Odessa Committee

for Funds donated through Gedalya Lifshitz dated 11.11.1916.

To Mr. G. Lifshitz, Ochotnikov, Volyn

Received total of 14.29 rubles sent by you.
Entered in the accounting books according to your instructions:
Donations collected on eve of Yom Kippur.
We give you our thanks. Regulations are herewith attached.

Respectfully yours,
Menahem Ussishkin
Chairman

The Association of Lovers of Hebrew prepared the foundation for a political Zionist movement, which left its mark on the life of the community. The young Zionists took part in every public performance and in elections of various secular and Jewish institutions.

It must be noted that many of the old timers, graduates of the cheder, secretly admired the new movement. However, during elections, they voted for *Achdut* – a religious movement. *Mizrachi* was not acceptable to the *Hasidim*. They rejected it because it was a Zionist movement and they saw its adherents as heretics. However, the Rabbis felt that it was necessary to become involved in political movements and not to stay on the sidelines. For that purpose, the religious political movement, *Achdut* was organized. The Zionists fought it. However, when the choice was between the *Bund* and the Zionists, the *Achdut* people supported the Zionists and the Tarbut School.

When the Revolution broke out, the Association of Lovers of Hebrew declared themselves as the Zionist Party of Rokitno. At that time, there were no sub groups and parties yet. The movement began a difficult struggle to broaden its horizons and to increase its membership. After two years of hard work, the Zionist movement reached its peak. The dream of the Zionists of Rokitno came true in 1912 - the Tarbut School was founded.

The main Zionist activities were centered in three areas: study of the Hebrew language, collection of money and work for the Jewish National Fund. At every event- weddings, Bar Mitzvahs and other happy occasions – pairs of people would appear representing the Zionist movement and would obtain donations for the Jewish National Fund. This was especially true on the eve of *Yom Kippur*. Those active in this area were: Avraham Golod and Moshe Gurman. There were many meetings to collect funds for Jewish National Fund. Its organizers were: Avraham Shapira (from Kisorich), Haim David Weiner and others.

The funds were sent to the Palestine committee in Odessa headed by Ussishkin. Every year a book was published listing the names of donors and the total amount of money collected. This is how the Zionist movement developed in Rokitno, up to the Balfour Declaration.

[Page 52]

Zionist Activity during the Balfour Declaration

Yakov Lifshitz (Givat Hashlosha)
Aharon Heruti [Freierman] (Tel Aviv)
Translated by Ala Gamulka

The trademark of Rokitno was the Zionist spirit and the loyalty to Hebrew culture that permeated the town. All attempts by those opposed to Zionism collapsed against the reality of a Zionist town. The Hebrew language was something indisputable – an axiom. No one even suggested that Yiddish be taught. There was no need for it. Later on, there was a handful of Communists who operated secretly in town. This was a small weak group and it was not able to influence Jewish life.

An obvious indication of the Zionist make-up of Jewish life is the fact that, among all the collection plates placed in the synagogue on the eve of *Yom Kippur*, the one belonging to the Jewish National Fund was the most noticeable one. The largest amount was to be found in this collection plate because there was almost no Jew who would not donate towards the redemption of the land of Israel. The Zionist youths, although they were mainly secular, streamed to the synagogues on the eve of *Yom Kippur* – mainly to make sure that the Jewish National Fund collection plate would be filled and to encourage the congregants to donate.

There were many Jews in town who had donated to the Jewish National Fund before the Balfour Declaration and were in close contact with the Odessa Committee. There were some among them who were involved with the coining of the shekel at the First Zionist Congress and they kept it as an honor certificate.

This Zionist spirit of the parents was also handed down to their children. Their education, mainly in Hebrew, was imbued with a nationalistic-Zionist spirit. The *cheder* in Rokitno was not of the old type common in other parts of Poland. This *cheder* was progressive and liberated. This was the embryo of the modern Hebrew school. At first, secular subjects were taught in Russian, but eventually they were done in Hebrew.

The Russian language teaching material- *Leyaldenu* (for our children), used by the *cheder* teachers, had been specially written for Jewish children. Its content was Zionist. There were selections from Hebrew and Yiddish literature, the poetry of Bialik and stories by Peretz and Frug. The children subscribed to a Hebrew language children's newspaper edited by Aharon Livoshitzky.

The Balfour Declaration brought the Zionist movement in Rokitno to life. A strong light was kindled. Even though we did not know what exactly was coming, we waited for redemption. The historic connection with Eretz Yisrael was renewed and the gates of *Aliyah* were opened.

The Balfour Declaration and the October Revolution were bound together in Rokitno, but the Zionist youths did not follow blindly the alien crowd and did not pin all their hopes on the Revolution as a source of good things for the Jews. They lifted their heads towards Zion. The change in government, the troubles the Jews were suffering and their fears only served to deepen their yearning for Eretz Yisrael. We, the young children, composed a sad song in Yiddish. Its refrain was: "O, that I were far away from here". It meant that we wanted to leave this misery and go to Eretz Yisrael.

The Jewish streets of Rokitno were full of demonstrations in favor of the Balfour Declaration. There were many mass meetings. In those days, the synagogue served as an assembly place for Zionist meetings. At one of the large gatherings in honor of the Balfour Declaration, an announcer from Kiev recited the Yiddish poem by Bialik, "The Last Word". It begins: "I have been sent to you by G-d. " The Hebrew translation by Aharon Zeitlin reads:

A prophetic G-d created me

He saw you in difficulties

He saw you withering and decaying

From day to day you are more bereaved."

The children and the older teens were enthusiastic about revival. From early childhood, we belonged to Zionist youth movements named "Association of Children of Zion" and "Association of Flowers of Zion". The establishment, in 1922, of Polish rule, allowed regular Zionist activities and a fresh wind energized the sails of the Zionist youth movement.

The youth groups presented several plays with all proceeds dedicated to the redemption of land. In a storehouse in the courtyard of Hershel Greenberg, a play was put on. The income of one-and-a-half rubles was used to plant trees in a Jewish National Fund forest. All the plays and parties planned by these groups had a distinct Zionist flavor. We wrote songs which reflected the moods of the time. One song was dramatized by a group of young women on stage wearing straw hats and carrying pitchforks. The floor was covered with sheaves of straw representing the harvest. One girl sang: "Are there any foxes there, my friend?"

The boy who is inviting her to go to Eretz Yisrael replied: “Come here my child, my lovely dove.”

One of the main activities of the Zionist youth groups was the founding of a Hebrew library, which also contained books in Russian and in Yiddish. In those days, Shtibel Publishers was very active and we were among its first subscribers. We thought this was not sufficient and we worked hard at introducing Hebrew books into Jewish homes in Rokitno. Shtibel Publishers sent one of its representatives to Rokitno and we went with him to various homes where we generated orders for Tolstoy's “War and Peace” translated by Trivush and Knute Hansen's “Blessing of the Earth”. Many also ordered volumes of “The Period”. The library was initially located in the home of Yitzhak Pik and later in the home of Haim Yehuda Shohet. This was the only Hebrew library in town and the adults also enjoyed it.

The Zionist hopes came to fruition. The first to make *aliyah*, during the Polish regime, was Gedalya Lifshitz. He joined a group of pioneers from Sarny and came to Eretz Yisrael in 1922. The excitement grew and *Hechalutz*, *Hechalutz Hatzair*, *Hashomer Hatzair* and later *Betar* were founded. They pulled in most of the young people.

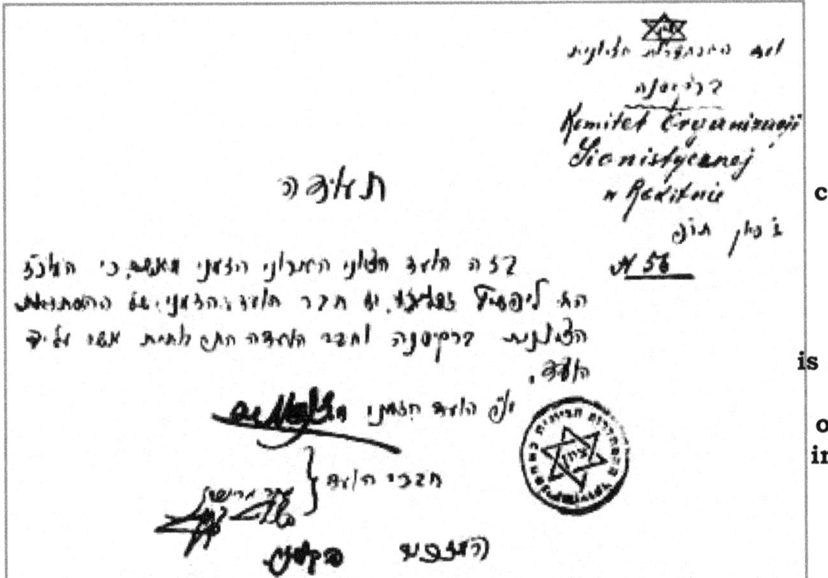

תעודה

N 56

Certificate

The temporary Zionist Municipal committee hereby certifies that

Gedalya Lifshitz

is a member of the temporary committee of the Zionist Organization in Rokitno and is a member of the Cultural Sub-committee.

Signed

The lives of the young people were turned upside down with many of them leaving home to go to *Hachshara* (pre-*aliyah* preparatory settlements) in Klosov and other places. The first to go from Rokitno to Klosov were Sender Lerner, Eli Greenberg, Liova Litvak and Avraham Geipman. Lerner and Geipman made *aliyah*.

[Page 55]

National Funds in Rokitno

Haim Shteinman (Tel Aviv)

Translated by Ala Gamulka

Keren Hayesod

The activities of *Keren Hayesod* in our town were run by a few people only because the residents were canvassed once a year. The amount required was considerable and only the most influential people were involved. They formed the committee and pre-assigned sums to be pledged. It is important to note that the majority accepted the burden cheerfully. Those who argued about the required sums were blacklisted on the bulletin board in the synagogue. This did the job and those listed changed their minds and paid up. Every subscriber paid by bank check.

Jewish National Fund

Unlike *Keren Hayesod*, Jewish National Fund was a more popular fund, which conducted its business throughout the year and involved all residents – young and old. Everyone happily did his or her part as needed.

The local committee consisted of representatives of the Zionist movements in town. Mr. Haim David Weiner devotedly served as deputy for many years. He was followed by the teacher Mordechai Gendelman. The secretary was Avraham Binder and the treasurer- Aharon Lifshitz. Most of the responsibility was carried by the Zionist youth movements. They competed constantly for the title of the largest sums collected. *Hashomer Hatzair* usually led. The methods of collection were varied. First and foremost – the Blue Box which was exhibited in every home as a sacred icon. Mothers would drop coins every Friday night prior to candle lighting. The boxes were emptied monthly. They were always full to the top.

Other activities took place around the holidays. On the eve of *Yom Kippur*, there was a special table in the synagogue which contained various bowls for charity. The Jewish National Fund bowl dwarfed the others. We, the youngsters, watched carefully and encouraged the worshippers to give as much as possible. The results proved us right. At every *Yizkor* service we worked hard: we distributed printed sheets to the worshippers, which they would fold indicating the amount pledged. A few days later, we went to their houses to collect the money. There was a special event at *Simchat Torah* when a special Zionist *minyan* was held. The service leader was always the teacher Mordechai Gendelman. This *minyan* attracted many worshippers, especially the young yeshiva students. All proceeds from those called to the Torah were dedicated to the Jewish National Fund. We even went to other synagogues to collect our share.

The dedication of the Zionist youth to the Jewish National Fund knew no boundaries. We tried different methods to increase the income – be it *Purim* parties, bazaars, raffles or theater productions. We did not refuse any activity that could bring in money. Before *Shavuot*, we went knee-deep in mud to collect greenery in the forest. We braided the branches into wreaths containing the Jewish National Fund insignia.

We came to every wedding (uninvited) with the Blue Box and we did not leave until we filled it up. We did the same at funerals.

The jewel in the crown of our activity for the Jewish National Fund was the 20th day of *Tammuz* when a mass memorial rally was organized in memory of Dr. Herzl, the founder of Zionism. On that day, we used all our artistic ability and we presented a play to the large crowd. Almost all the Jews of Rokitno and its surrounding area attended. The harvest was bountiful. The Jews gave generously to the Jewish National Fund. With great satisfaction we would run to the deputy house, teeming with happy young people, to bring the money. We waited impatiently for the counting to end in order to find out who won first place. It happened that some individuals would leave upset and unhappy because they did not collect as much as the others. At that point, they made a vow to outdo their friends the next time. This was the dedication of the youth of Rokitno to the Jewish National Fund and to their homeland. It was the result of an excellent Hebrew and Zionist education in which they were steeped from childhood.

Women of all ages played a considerable role in the work for the Jewish National Fund. They organized special parties, raffles, prepared the food and decorated the halls elegantly. The atmosphere was that of pioneering in Eretz Yisrael. This was always done with dedication in order to achieve success and to collect money.

This is how the Rokitno residents showed their loyalty to Eretz Yisrael and to its national funds.

Award Certificate

Awarded as a mark of distinction
for dedicated work
for Jewish National Fund
for self-fulfillment
in the year 1931.

To

Haim Shteinman

Rokitno

JNF

the National Agency in Poland

Signed

[Page 58]

The Origins of *Hechalutz* in Rokitno

Dov Ben Yehoshua [Vorona] (Tel Aviv)

Translated by Ala Gamulka

General Background to the Founding of *Hechalutz*

After years of riots, suffering and torture during World War I, peace finally came between Poland- who gained independence, and the Bolsheviks- who annihilated the Kingdom of Tzar Nikolai.

Rokitno became a border village. The Jews awoke to a new energetic life and they resurrected their economic and cultural lives. The lumber trade began to flourish. The sawmills and the glass factory worked at full steam. Brick plants were built and new ways of earning a living were discovered. Everything was blooming and the standard of living improved. Every storage space became a shop and every vegetable garden became a building lot.

The general growth drew many Jews from nearby villages to Rokitno – from Stariky, Osnitzek, Dert, Krapilovka and from nearby towns – Stolin, Dombrovitza, Sarny, Visotzk, etc.

However, the economic growth, which knew no precedent before the war, did not blind anyone. The Zionist movement in Rokitno began to ferment during this time. The youth, in spite of the economic freedom enjoyed in their homes, did not pine for a golden calf, but they were excited by the national Zionist dream. Zionism meant pioneering-Zionism.

This excitement was expressed by a song that was popular in the Zionist movement:

"Bless our G-d who created us as pioneers

He separated us from the General Zionists

He gave us the knowledge of fulfillment

He sowed in us love of group life."

This was not a meaningless excitement. It was translated into practical terms. In 1925, the residents of Rokitno began to make *aliyah* – the Gurman family, Zeidel Binder, Sade Lavan and my brother Nachman.

The Founding of a *Hachshara* (Preparatory) Unit in Rokitno

After my brother's *aliyah*, when I was 15 or 16 years old, I saw my future in Eretz Yisrael and I began to prepare myself. In those days, there was selective *aliyah* and only those who could be productive were chosen. I dedicated myself to learning carpentry with my brother-in-law, Betzalel Eisenberg.

One day I was working with Betzalel Eisenberg in the construction of the new synagogue in the "new town". Usually near a synagogue, one can always see Jews. I entered into a conversation with Vitia Hefetz, Liova Litvak, Avraham Geipman and others. They asked me why I was learning to be a carpenter. My reply was: "In order to prepare myself for *aliyah*. My older brother, Nachman, has made *aliyah* and I do not intend to remain in Rokitno."

Geipman told me that there was no need to learn a trade as there was a better, more useful way. He secretly told me about *Hechalutz* which was functioning in many towns near Rokitno. The Rokitno youth would also found a branch of *Hechalutz* where they would prepare themselves for *aliyah*.

His words fell on willing ears and an eager heart. We immediately became practical. Aryeh (Leibl) Geipman went to Warsaw often and he was entrusted with finding out what were the possibilities of founding a branch of *Hechalutz* in Rokitno and how to go about it. As a result of the information he obtained, we began to work. My task was to organize a meeting between the youth in the village of Rokitno and those in town.

At the end of 1924, the Rokitno branch of *Hechalutz* was founded. Leibl Geipman registered it at the head office. After a few months, we performed a daring deed: we formed a preparatory group in Rokitno. At first, we feared we would not have enough candidates who would give up the comforts of home and who would willingly begin a life of hard labor in a collective. They would have to give up their regular life because of ideology. However, we were wrong. The youth of Rokitno were prepared emotionally for these difficult physical sacrifices. The following song (in Yiddish) sums it up:

"Tell us pioneers,

What is bread?

Rich people think it is

White bread.

For us, the pioneers,

The poor ones,

It is just a piece of crust."

I was one of the first who came forward without hesitating. I left my brother-in-law and my home and I joined the collective. The other members were: Naftali Gilman, Avraham Geipman, Reuven Frital and Itzhak Pik (Itzhak was permitted to sleep at home since he had to help his elderly mother). Others from the village were: Shlomke and Shimon Gendelman. There were also two women: Anka (Hanna) Shlafer and Hava Barman.

We rented an apartment in a Polish house in the new town. We organized the household and prepared sleeping quarters. Each one of us took his belongings from home and came to live in the shared apartment, which we named *Kibbutz.*

The *Hechalutz* center sent to us members from Kremenetz, Shumsk and other villages. When the new members arrived, the Jews of Rokitno looked at us in a more positive light. They began to respect us because they felt that the *kibbutz* would bring an improvement in the lot of the Diaspora Jews.

Our numbers grew and we did not have enough room in our apartment. After much searching, we found a more convenient place. Shlomo the tailor had tried to build a bathhouse on Messiviche Street and did not finish it. He only erected a skeleton. We renovated the unfinished house and adapted it to our needs.

The *kibbutz* rejuvenated the town. It became a meeting place for the youth. They benefited intellectually. The place was full of people in the evenings, especially on Friday nights. They came to listen to lectures and to dance pioneer dances with Hasidic enthusiasm.

The exotic atmosphere of the *kibbutz* caused curiosity. Young people, who were used to drinking tea from delicate cups, felt a special flavor in drinking tea in aluminum and clay cups. There was competition among them to see who would be first to use these cups.

Our visitors especially relished our hit song, which became an anthem of *Hechalutz*. It was the *Ani Maamin* (I believe) of the movement:

"Pioneer, pioneer, am I

Without clothes and shoes

Without any herring

I did not know from where I came

And I did not ask for much

There is work, there is no work

I did not give up

I already forgot my family

Moshe, Hanna, Devora –

These are my brother and sisters

All the Hora dancers

A one and a two

Day and night

Boy will dance with girl."

The Depression Years in *Hechalutz*

In 1926 after several years of existence of the Kibbutz, some members, I among them, were approved for *aliyah*. They did go, but I was forced to postpone my trip because my documents were not in order. The authorities did not allow me to leave Poland. Weeks and months passed until one fine day the British Mandate government did not allow anyone to come. “Stop immigration!”

The news we received from Eretz Israel was not encouraging. Many of the people who came with the Gravsky group for economic reasons, now left due to the poor economy in the country. Even Rokitno had its own returnees. They were Zeidel Binder and his son Moshe. All this contributed to a lowering in the image of the Zionist movement in 1927-28 and one heard voices of despair and helplessness.

I waited for the gates to reopen. In time, there was a change in the *Hachshara* group. It amalgamated with *Kibbutz Klesov* and was now called the “Rokitno Division”. The mood was dark and sad. However, we had been educated in Brenner's motto- “in spite of everything” and we had a strong belief that one day things would improve. We managed to overcome the difficulties and we continued with our Zionist mission.

At the beginning of 1928, I went to Klesov with Shimon Gendelman. Benny Marshak, one of the organizers, commissioned me to direct the new members in their work and in kibbutz ideology. Our motto was: “Work is our life. It will save us from all trouble”.

In due time, the chances for *aliyah* improved. Pressured by the Zionist organization and the Zionist Congress, the British government was forced to reopen the gates. This news blew like a fresh wind and caused a great reawakening in the Zionist movement. The preparatory *kibbutzim* grew and hundreds of members joined. The emissaries from Eretz Israel came to visit and formed strong ties with them. They came to guide, to encourage and to prepare. The visitors were Ben Ari and Tzizling from Eyn Harod and Eliahu Dubkin, Berginsky and Pinchas Kozlovsky from *Hechalutz* headquarters (now Pinchas Sapir, Minister of Finance).

I recall an interesting episode with Tzizling. He came off the train in Sarny, a large man dressed like Tolstoy in white pants and a peasant shirt. He looked suspicious to the police, ever wary for security reasons. He was asked to come for questioning, but the British passport calmed them down immediately. They had no common language because Tzizling announced that he only spoke Hebrew (he did, of course, speak other languages). The police had no choice but to find someone, in the middle of the night, who could speak Hebrew. Naturally, in

Sarny, it was not difficult to find such a Jew to act as translator. After a short while, Tzizling was released and arrived in Klesov.

At the end of Tzizling's visit there was in Klesov, a large *kibbutz* of hundreds waiting for *aliyah*. As the members were approved, the *kibbutz* was almost completely emptied of veterans and in their place arrived new members who were not as knowledgeable in the *Hechalutz* beliefs or the labor movement. The *kibbutz* was forced to organize a core of veterans whose mission was to prepare Zionist youth groups for *aliyah*. I was fortunate to be one of these veterans, but not for long. In May 1929, I was called up to the Polish army and was due to go on active duty in two months. This was a good reason for me to be approved for *aliyah*.

[Page 62]

The *Hechalutz* Branch and its Activities prior to the Holocaust

Haim Shteinman (Tel Aviv)

Translated by Ala Gamulka

When the first members of the Rokitno branch of *Hechalutz* made *aliyah*, in 1928, its activities were curtailed. However, our youth- mostly Zionist- knew how to overcome the decrease in numbers. Soon, enthusiasm was rampant, especially among the older youth who were searching for a social framework, which they had not found in other movements in Rokitno. They looked for ways of achieving the goals of *Hechalutz*. This meant preparation for and subsequent *aliyah*.

The members: Yakov Lifshitz, Haya Berezovsky, Genia Tuchman, Reuven Frital and Haya Lifshitz got busy. They formed the lively nucleus which dedicated itself to revive the branch and to reorganize it in a Zionist bent. They were successful and attracted 60 new members. They were prepared to absorb even more members.

They rented a hall for everyday work. Other active members who were in the Klesov and Tomshograd *kibbutzim* near Rokitno assisted those responsible.

During that time, the branch stopped being a dream and became a reality. There were two reasons for this: spiritual and material. In the few years since the founding of *Hechalutz* in our town, there was an important ideological change.

Hechalutz became a part of life. Slowly, the older youths and their parents began to understand that *Hechalutz* was not only a question of existence for them but for the whole nation. The serious economic breakdown in the 30's, especially at the end of the decade, which caused a lowering in the standard of life of the Jewish merchants, also served as an impetus for the youth groups to join *Hechalutz.*

Thus we find the *Hechalutz* branch in our town in the 30's as an absorption center for young people from the surrounding areas. They all desire to absorb the pioneer ideology, to prepare themselves for *Aliyah.*

As the branch grew, there were many people who put its activities at the top of the agenda. Among them were: Israel Lifshitz, Shoshana Finkelstein, Zissel Meirson, Esther Shuster, Breindel Tendler and others. On a cultural level Itzhak Waldman, Zvi Eisenstein, David Eidelman and Ronka Greber were also active. They were all members of *Hashomer Hatzair* who joined the *Hechalutz* activities according to directives from their headquarters.

The branch was active at all levels of Zionist work in town – the distribution of *shekalim,* and collection of money for workers of Eretz Yisrael, the League for the Workers of Eretz Yisrael and all the national funds.

As part of the branch activities, there were Friday night events with questions and answers, guest lectures on events in Eretz Yisrael and in the Zionist movement. The branch utilized the services of the Klosov *kibbutz* members who often were invited to come. Emissaries from headquarters also visited when they were in the area. These visits encouraged the members because they would receive first-hand information. Among these visitors were Itzhak Tabankin, Feivish Bendersky (Ben Dor), Bankover, Berginsky, and Benny Marshak, a most popular figure.

The branch encouraged the members to learn a trade, to study Hebrew and to read the movement newspapers- *Haatid, Davar, Hapoel Hatzair.* In the center was the need for self-fulfillment within the framework of the kibbutz. The majority of the members did make *aliyah.* Many are scattered today in various kibbutzim in our country.

The branch also absorbed, due to their small numbers, the members of *Haoved.* These were older people with families. They had different trades and wished to continue with them in Eretz Yisrael. They integrated well into the branch activities. A few of them came to Eretz Yisrael and live among us.

Hechalutz Branch in Rokitno in 1932

Standing, top row [from right to left]: 1. Shimon Gendelman 2. D. Baum 3. Avraham Tendler 4. Barman 5. --- 6. ... 7. Dodia Greber 8. Eli Wasserman 9. Yentel Ivry 10. ... 11. Liova Golod 12. Leibl Wolfin 13. Asher Golovey 14. Mordechai Friedman 15. Fuchsman 16. Miriam Linn 17. Hinia Tuchman 18. Hanna Friedman 19. Haya Pinchuk 20. Berezovsky

Second row: 1. Eisenberg 2. ...3. Sarah Wasserman 4. Shmuel Fuchsman 5. Haim Shteinman 6. Rivka Kutz 7. Urman

Third Row: 1. Zipa Wax 2. ...3. Kalman Kleinman 4. Itzhak Waldman 5. Asher Eidelman 6. ... 7. Doba Zaks

Fourth Row: 1. Zvi Eisenstein 2. Esther Shuster 3.Kleinman 4. ...

[Page 65]

Hashomer Hatzair

This article was written by the graduates of *Hashomer Hatzair* in Rokitno:

Ruth Baum [Reis]	**Asher Binder**	**Hanna Gelfand**
Ruchama Gelfand [Oliker]	**Ronka Rosenstein [Greber]**	**Shulamit Grinshpan [Honig]**
Hanan Hatzuvi [Trigun]	**Aharon Heruti [Freierman]**	**Itzhak Waldman *z"l***
Yitzhak Litvak	**Penina Fuchsman [Ortreger]**	**Shmaryahu Kravi [Korobochka]**

Translated by Ala Gamulka

The teacher, David Shtern

The early Days of the Rokitno Branch

The creator and founder of the *Hashomer Hatzair* branch in our town was David Shtern, a young and dynamic teacher from Koritz. He taught music and physical education in the Tarbut School in Rokitno.

In 1926, even when the school was still in the women's section of the synagogue in the old town, he organized a student choir. He began to teach a new Torah, the way of scouting and physical education among the book stands, *Mishna* tomes and ancient scrolls. He believed in the motto: "A healthy soul in a healthy body".

Hashomer Hatzair in Rokitno was built on pure nationalism and Zionism. The teacher Shtern told us that throughout Poland a scout movement existed called *Hashomer Hatzair.* Its main tenet was a return to Zion and it prepares its members for *aliyah.*

The teacher Shtern formed the first scout group called *Gur Aryeh Yehudah.* It consisted of two groups: *Brener* for boys and *Dror* for girls. It was the organized pioneering Zionist youth movement in our town. The first to respond to Shtern and to found the *Hashomer Hatzair* branch in Rokitno were:

1) The brothers David and Shlomo Eidelman

2) Misha Berezovsky (he died while trying to reach Palestine during the Holocaust)

3) Hershel Gutnik (killed during World War II in France)

4) Liova Golod

5) Ronka Greber

6) Batya Grinshpan, z"l,

7) Aryeh Wolfin

8) Syoma Weiner

9) the Hammer sisters

10) Hanan Trigun

11) Hanna Lifshitz

12) Israel Lifshitz (transferred to *Hechalutz*)

13) Zissel Meirson, z"l (transferred to *Hechalutz*)

14) Israel Kek (transferred to *Betar*)

15) Yechiel Shohet (transferred to *Hechalutz*)

16) Haim Shteinman

17) Aharon Burd, z"l.

The main educational activity was learning scouting. Shtern spoke of Baden-Powell (founder of the scout movement) and read to us chapters from his book "Scouting". We learned all the details of camping.

Since there was no hall, we met in the women's section in the synagogue in the "old town". In summer, we went to the forest on the railroad in the direction of Ostoki where a hill served as a central location for the youth. Nature walks were a permanent part of our education. On *Tisha B'Av,* we went on an overnight trip to the village of Osnitzek. We set up a camp between the river and the cemetery.

At night we built a fire and we sat around it. The feeling of camaraderie was forged on these trips. The atmosphere was festive and we sang songs of our land. We felt that we were members of one nation and that we had a common language. We were all involved in one idea: redemption of our land. When we saw the growing fields and the carpets of flowers, we wished each other to live to see the same sights in Eretz Yisrael.

The founding of the branch did not run into any opposition from the parents. The fact that the movement focused on the redemption of the land and involved the youth in powerful desires for the homeland did not worry the parents. On the contrary, they liked these ideas and they were certain that our paths would cross and that we followed in their footsteps. Our dream coincided with their Zionist thoughts.

The fact that our meetings were held in the women's section served as a defense mechanism since no one would suspect that these boys and girls would do any wrong. Our parents saw us as children playing games who would change their minds when they grew up.

However, they did not realize that in these childish games were hidden ideological explosives that would burst and bring changes in the ordinary old lives. This new generation had as its motto the words of the poet David Shimonovitz:

“Do not listen, my son, to your father

Nor lend an ear to your mother.”

***Gur Aryeh Yehudah* Group in 1926**

<u>Standing top row</u> [from right to left]: 1. Israel Kek 2. Syoma Eidelman 3. Aharon Burd 4. Aryeh Wolfin 5. David Eidelman 6. Misha Berezovsky

<u>Second row</u>: 1. Israel Lifshitz 2. Haim Shteinman 3. Liova Golod 4. Meir Rivkin 5. Hershel Gutnik

<u>Third row</u>: 1. Zissel Meirson 2. Hanan Trigun

The excellent conditions that prevailed from the early days served as a "hot house" for the growth and development of our branch. In addition, it must be mentioned that in those days, the Yiddishists, Bundists or Communists in our town did not compete with the Zionist movement. In other places this rivalry caused many difficulties and cultural wars. We did not have to struggle to overcome problems because they did not exist.

An Activity of the Senior Group in Rokitno Forest, 1928

Under these favorable conditions, the elite of the youth of our town joined us. They wished for refinement, simplicity and modesty. We did not create anything from nothing. The first members had been prepared for new ideas by their wonderful teachers in the Tarbut School. They had instilled in them a love for Hebrew, the nation and the land. Reading Bialik's poems like "The Town of Killing" sowed in them seeds of rebellion. The school was the receptacle from which the *Hashomer Hatzair* in Rokitno was watered. This was a pure well from which arose the wonderful human element that became our movement.

The members wore a uniform: gray shirt, khaki pants, gray hat with a blue and white stripe and an orange brim. The scouts and the cubs wore on their shoulders insignias representing their group. The cubs had a green necktie and the scouts- a blue one. The seniors wore a black necktie. When they moved from group to group and from level to level, they changed their neckties at a festive commemoration. This usually took place on *Lag B'omer*, which was officially *Hashomer Hatzair* day. All formal activities happened on that day.

The Crystallization of the Branch and its Contribution to Zionist Life in Town

When Shtern left Rokitno, two members of *Hashomer Hatzair* settled in our town in 1928-29. One, from Alexandria, was called Zvi Finkelstein and the other, Binyamin Zaltzbuch, from Rovno, who was an official in Volyn headquarters (they are both in Israel now). Zaltzbuch was very active in the movement and participated in several executive meetings in Malkin.

These two members integrated well into our work and contributed greatly to the development of the branch.

Every member had to follow the "Ten Commandments" which were the mainstay of the movement.

"*Hatikvah*" and "*Techezakna*" were the main anthems, but each level had its own hymn.

The cubs' hymn was:
One, two
Three, four
Brothers, we swear...

The scouts' hymn was:

Be prepared, Shomer,
For honest activities
You have a difficult
Route to follow
Courage will lead to happiness
Be prepared and remember your documents

The hymn of the senior group was Yaakov Cohen's song:

"**We arise and sing...**"

Although the branch grew continuously, it still did not have its own hall and it wandered from home to home – those of Avraham Golod, Berezovsky, David Kleiman, Moshe Wolf Horman, Shuster and others. We saluted each other in the street, one member to another or the counselors. The salute was accompanied by the motto: "Be strong!" The reply was always: Be strong and become stronger!" While saluting three fingers would be thrust forward, representing the three main principles of our education: one people, one homeland, one language.

During that time, our branch was evident in the Zionist and cultural lives in town. We always had a representative in every institution involved in propagating the Hebrew language and in any activity for the land. We were very active in the Zionist funds so that most of the activity for these funds was done by our members. We helped in collecting funds for the school and for the League of Workers in Eretz Yisrael.

Hashomer Hatzair In Rokitno In 1928

The members of our branch were nurtured on activities for the Jewish National Fund. They excelled in the collection of donations and in the emptying of the boxes. We instituted the Blue Box in every home. Every month, the members of the branch would be sent to empty the boxes. This was a permanent activity. We had a trusted friend in every synagogue. Whenever someone was called up to the Torah, he would donate to the Jewish National Fund. Our trusted friend would send us the name of the pledge maker and we would send our members to collect the promised sum.

Even on the eve of *Yom Kippur*, after *Mincha* and before the evening meal, our representatives would sit in the synagogue and collect pledges and donations for the Jewish National Fund. At every Jewish National Fund bazaar, our members worked hard. On *Purim*, our members would dress up and with boxes in their hands, they would collect for the Jewish National fund.

The Transition from Scouting to Ideological-Political Purpose

In 1928 we ceased being just a scout group and we became more politically oriented. We began to think of the labor movement and socialism. We received two movement newspapers called *Hashomer Hatzair*. One was published by headquarters in Poland and the other was published by the kibbutz movement in Eretz Yisrael. Thus we obtained information on the labor movement. These newspapers formed our worldview. The movement also published books and pamphlets on educational activities with lesson plans for the counselors at all levels of a branch. The material was prepared with specific instructions.

We began to study the history of the labor and socialist movements. We struggled to understand the "Political Economy" of Bogdanov. Not everything written in the "Communist Manifesto" was clear to us. We believed in the statement: "Workers of the world unite!" This was our main belief since socialism meant internationalism – the unity of all workers. It was the only way to achieve socialism.

In spite of this, our connection to our ancient culture deepened. We were eager to acquire the Hebrew language and speak it. The *Hashomer Hatzair* branch was the only youth movement that held all its activities in Hebrew. The members conversed in Hebrew. They were all nurtured on the Bible and Hebrew literature.

Public Appearances and the Struggles of the Branch

From 1930 on, Aharon (Iliosha) Freierman was chairman of the branch. He fulfilled this position for 4 years. We remember this period as a very active time. Iliosha's personality influenced our education. As his disciples, we knew how to appreciate the fact that Iliosha, a graduate of the movement (there were almost no other members his age in the branch), knew how to keep the interest of the youngsters. He persevered and was totally dedicated to representing the branch in the broader Jewish and Zionist community in town. He was our spokesperson whenever necessary.

Our activities grew and we were successful – the best of the town youth.

Our work was well organized. On weekdays, there were group discussions. On Shabbat, without fail, all members showed up. The Shabbat activity was the crowning glory of the everyday activities and it galvanized all the members. The seniors served as counselors at the very young levels. There were regular meetings of the counselors where the planning was done. The counselors had to prepare precise plans. Each activity began with a roll call and the singing of *Techezakna*. The relations between counselors and members were friendly, like those between siblings.

The branch welcomed a new generation, a generation that had decided not to suffer quietly as saints but to change Jewish history. The performances of the members at *Lag B'omer* parades were impressive and heart rendering. We appeared in white shirts and it was an imposing participation.

On Polish Independence Day, May 3rd, we were forced to participate in a parade in order to show loyalty to the government. We did not have warm relations with the local Polish police since it was quite sensitive to any hint of communism. Our town was close to the Soviet border and the least suspicion led to suppression. It was hinted to the police that *Hashomer Hatzair* was left-leaning and that its ideology was close to that of the Soviets. The detectives kept an eye on us and often we would find their representatives standing near our windows and listening.

20th of *Tammuz* Assembly in 1929

Standing in first row from top [from right to left]: 1. Liova Golod 2. Hanan Trigun 3. Syoma Weiner 4. Haim Shteinman

Second row: 1. Ruth Baum 2. Shifra Levin 3. Manya Gendelman 4. Hinia Gorenstein 5. Zelda Gorenstein 6. Batya Levin

Third Row: 1. Israel Lifshitz 2. *Stage director* Avigdor Murik from Sarny 3. Yitzhak Golod 4. Teibl Shapira 5. Ronka Greber 6. Hanna Lifshitz 7. Sheintza Kokel

Fourth Row: 1. Yakov Turovetz 2. Hana Friedman 3. Hinia Gorenstein 4. ...5. Manya Shapira 6.....7. Izia Tzipiniuk

The official organization in Warsaw was legal, but it did not have a permit to open branches in other towns. For that reason, we used a different name for our group. Our permit was given to "The Culture and Sport Club of the Zionist Movement in Rokitno – *Hashomer Hatzair*".

Our activities grew before the elections to the Zionist Congress. We tried to distribute the largest number of *shekels* and to bring electors to the polls on Election Day. The elections presented a difficult task. It was after Arlozorov's murder and his tragic death cast a shadow on the election campaigns of the different movements. There were collisions with the local *Brit Hehayal* and *Betar* and there was great tension.

The ideological chasm served to deepen our pioneering and socialist spirit. Our road became clearer. We increased our activities in the League of Workers in Eretz Yisrael and *Hechalutz*. Our branch greatly enhanced the influence of *Hechalutz*.in Rokitno, especially in educational and cultural spheres.

Berel Frimer Visits as Representative of Headquarters in 1928

Standing in first row from top [right to left]: 1. Avraham Shulman 2. Aharon Burd 3. Liova Golod 4. Syoma Eidelman 5. Yechiel Shohet 6. Rachel Hamer
Second row: 1. Misha Berezovsky 2. Israel Kek 3. Teibl Shapira 4. Sussel Eisenman 5. ... 6. Etia Klorfein
Third row: 1. Hinia Korobochka 2. ... 3. Berel Frimer 4. Aharon Freierman 5. Ronka Greber 6. Hannah Lifshitz
Seated in front: 1. Israel Lifshitz 2. Syoma Weiner

The graduates of *Hashomer Hatzair* were obligated to become members of *Hechalutz*. The local branch served as a meeting place for these graduates as well as graduates of *Hechalutz* and unaffiliated members.

The thirties – prior to the Holocaust – were uninterrupted growth years for *Hechalutz* branches in all towns and villages and *Hachsharot* (preparatory kibbutzim) appeared everywhere. Even the local *Hechalutz* branch was filled with youth, mostly older ones. These were people who saw no future for themselves in town and their only solution was Aliyah.

The graduates of *Hashomer Hatzair* were the main organizers of the movement and concentrated on teaching Hebrew in *Hechalutz.*

There was great debate about "mixed preparation". *Hashomer Hatzair* opposed it because they believed in homogeneous groups made up of people from the same level in the movement. They foresaw a start in the *Hachshara* and a continuation in an independent kibbutz in Eretz Yisrael.

In the Circle of Preparation and Fulfillment

The movement obligated all its members to join a *Hachshara* and to make *aliyah.* This was the guiding tenet of our Zionist ideology. Anyone who wished to postpone *Hachshara* for academic reasons was not permitted to do so. Anyone who tried to avoid going on *Hachshara* had to leave the movement. The only exception was Misha Berezovsky who was the sole support of his frail parents. He became the chairman after Aharon Freierman's *aliyah* and he remained in that position until the Soviets came to Rokitno.

Misha did not live to accomplish his great dream of *aliyah* and of building a kibbutz in the homeland. We are certain that up to his last moments he never stopped believing that a miracle would occur and that he would join his comrades and do the daily work with them. This was the work for which they prepared in *Hashomer Hatzair* and *Hechalutz.* Misha had great capacity for work and he was a wonderful planner. He was a staunch believer in the movement. He had exceptional energy and devotion. When all his comrades went on *aliyah,* he was left alone until the last minute of his life. During the war, he attempted to make *aliyah* and he died in Vilna. We will always cherish his memory as that of a dear colleague and an educator.

Many of the graduates of *Hashomer Hatzair* went to various preparatory places in Poland. Most of them made *aliyah* and to this day many of them are members of *Hashomer Hatzair* kibbutzim.

The Branch in the Last Years of its Existence

In 1935-39, the leadership consisted of Yitzhak Litvak, Betzalel Kek, Aharon Kleiman and Misha Berezovsky who was the chairman. Our activities continued as planned but, unfortunately, difficulties arose. Many members left us – some to *Betar.* We struggled to stop them, but we were not always successful.

The group of graduates was named after Yosef Trumpeldor who became a symbol of courage and hard work in our eyes. His declaration: "It is good to die for our country!" was one that heightened the enthusiasm and longing for our land. The song about Tel Hai and about Trumpeldor's death conquered our hearts and strengthened our spirit. We remember well the song and its melancholy tune.

During those years, a weeklong camp (*Moshava*) was organized in the village of Rokitno in the home of Yona Katz. We worked hard to convince our parents to allow us to be away from home for a whole week. Most of the members participated in this *Moshava.* There were scouting activities and many hikes. We went on an overnight trip to the village of Osnitzek and we pitched tents near the cemetery. We were a little fearful of being in the vicinity of the cemetery, but the fact strengthened us to be prepared for any event. The trip had an educational purpose – to teach us communal living by sharing food brought by all of us.

Some members participated in administrative meetings. One of these, a month long, took place in Dorohosek with the participation of Meir Yeari and Yehudah Guthalf. Our representatives were Yitzhak Litvak, Betzalel Kek and Shifra Finkelstein. In 1937, a winter camp was held in Kremenitz and our Penina Fuchsman attended.

Scout Trip to Osnitzek in 1931

In the last years before the Holocaust, many difficulties arose in our activities. The public identified us with the left. We had to be very careful. Also, by then we were no longer the only youth movement in Rokitno. There was an active and strong branch of *Betar* as well as *Hapoel Hatzair.* We struggled on several fronts. Our battle with *Betar* was in the open – a struggle between two opposing camps. Each one had its own beliefs, which it defended with vehemence.

The school, the main source for our membership, began to close its doors to us. The teacher Gendelman, who had tremendous influence on the students, became involved in founding *Hanoar Hatzioni.* We were pressed to give up our permit since it was in the name of the Zionist movement. Since it was difficult to obtain another permit, we opposed it with all our might. Time was on our side, since *Hanoar Hatzioni* was not established. It was an unsuccessful attempt.

The Dying Branch

When World War II broke out, some of our members were in *Hachshara* in Radom, Chenstohov, Baranovich or Bialystok. They rushed home and tried to find a way to make *aliyah.*

When the Soviets came, we burned all the documents we possessed. We only left the library. The Soviets announced that all Jewish youths must become members of the *Komsomol.* The response was weak since we all hoped to see Zion.

Vilna was still free and it served as an entry gate for *aliyah. Hashomer Hatzair* kibbutzim were concentrated there. Yeshayahu Weiner and Adam Rand (from headquarters) asked us to send our members to Vilna. We tried to encourage our members to go there quickly, before it would be too late, but we encountered indecision and parental opposition.

Soon the following members left Rokitno and went to Vilna: Shoshana and Shmaryahu Korobochka, Yehoshua and Dov Eisenstein, Yosef Ivry, Dvora Golovey, Eliezer Shapira, Misha Berezovsky, Bunia and Beba Kutz and Asher Eidelman. Some of them succeeded in reaching Eretz Yisrael and escaping the bitter end which awaited the Jews of Rokitno.

Those members who remained in Rokitno did not pretend that no harm would come to them. They left the killing fields in various ways. Some managed to save themselves and to remain alive after years of wandering in the forests and fighting the enemy as partisans. Many of them fell in this battle with the enemy and their graves are scattered in forests, pits and barren fields.

[Page 77]

The Jabotinsky Movement in Rokitno

Itzhak [Isia] Golod (Haifa)

Translated by Ala Gamulka

The *Betar* Branch and *Brit Hachayal*

The public atmosphere in Rokitno was Zionist. I came to Zionism not only through Bible studies and parental upbringing - my father was one of the first Zionists in our town - but also by looking at our economic and political situation in Poland. I saw that we had no place on Polish soil. Bloody attacks by our Ukrainian and Polish neighbors spotlighted our miserable situation in exile. From early on I talked to my friends about making our home in our ancient land.

Influenced by the articles of Zeev Jabotinsky, where he described his point of view about a Jewish state and the road to it, I decided that *Betar* was the only way for me. I decided to organize a *Betar* branch in Rokitno, along the lines of the Latvian Betar.

It happened in 1928. We met in Rokitno during vacation from Hebrew High School in Vilna. Leibl Lifshitz, I, Busia Levin, Moshe Binder and Yehudah Kaplan decided, after a lengthy discussion, to explain to the youth of Rokitno the world view of Jabotinsky. He believed that the redemption of Israel would not come through pacifism and socialism, but by armed conflict.

We were successful in organizing a group of 15 boys and girls. The branch was founded on my parents' balcony. There was much enthusiasm because what we told the young people was new and imaginative. We got in touch with *Betar* headquarters in Warsaw and our branch was attached to the other branches of *Betar* in Poland.

Our main activity was in cultural fields and we strongly emphasized sports in many forms. We became part of the cultural and public activities of the Zionist movement in Rokitno. We took part actively in the drama presentations whose income was dedicated to the Zionist movement. Every year we helped in organizing the *Hanukah* bazaar. Income from the bazaar was dedicated to social assistance, such as *Linat Hatzedek, Gmilut Hasadim,* help to orphans and for Zionist funds. Preparations for the bazaar began right after *Rosh Hashana.* First, the musicians established an orchestra. These *Klezmers* were Abrasha Klorfein, Yosef Kitziv, the drummer Syoma Klorfein and I. In addition, we participated also in organizing *Purim* balls where a *Purim* queen was chosen. Among the queens were Etia Klorfein, Manya Gendelman, Polia the milliner, Anya Shlafer and others.

A *Hachshara* unit of *Betar* was founded in Rokitno. Young men and women from different places in Poland arrived and brought a fresh wind to town. Among them were educated people who helped with cultural activities of the branch. The *Hachshara* group was billeted in one of the houses near Motel the Shoemaker, across from the "Palace".

I was the first commander of the Rokitno *Betar* branch. My second-in-command was Busia Levin. In addition to the founding of *Betar*, the Zionist Revisionist movement was also established in Rokitno. Its chairman was Leibl Lifshitz. It operated as a political party, like all parties and movements in Poland.

***Hachshara* Unit of *Betar* in Rokitno**

Third Row from top:
Fourth from right: **Busia Levin**; fifth: **Isia Golod**

In 1933 *Brit Hahayal* was established. Its organizers were: Baruch Felhandler and his father, Moshe Bukstein and Isia Grempler. The bloody events in Eretz Yisrael awakened in us the urgent need to give military training to *Betar* members. Several of the *Brit Hahayal* members were on friendly terms with Polish officers. Their influence enabled us to receive a permit for training with live ammunition.

Brit Hahayal in Rokitno

Standing in first row from top [from right to left]: 1. Isia Grempler 2. Moshe Schwartz

Second row: 1. Alter Pik 2. Herschel Gorenstein 3. ...4. Avraham Shapiro 5. Levi Fishman 6. Aharon Galperin 7. ...8. Herschel Heitchkis

Third row: 1. Aharon Perlov 2. Bukstein

Fourth row: 1. Isia Golod 2. Representative from Rovno 3. Haim Felhandler 4. Rosen, commander of "Brit Hahayal" in Rovno 5. Representative from Sarny

In 1932 the members of *Betar* began to go to Hachshara in Klesov, Orhov, and Rozhishetz. Upon their return to Rokitno they continued their activities in the branch, since the number of *aliyah* certificates assigned to *Betar* was very small. In spite of this, several *Betar* members made *aliyah*. Among them were Busia Levin, his sister Shifra Levin, Israel Kek and Shmuel Shuber. When the illegal immigration began in 1936, several *Betar* members were active and some of them made *aliyah* in this way.

[Page 80]

From *Hashomer Hatzair* to *Betar*

Israel Michaeli [Kek] (Haifa)

Translated by Ala Gamulka

I came to *Betar* from the Hashomer Hatzair branch in Rokitno. It happened in 1929, the year of bloody events in Eretz Yisrael. The Jews of Poland were incensed and were attuned to events in our homeland. At that time, the commander of the Hachshara unit of *Betar* in Klosov, Avraham (Avremke) Axelrod came to Rokitno. (Today he is the vice-mayor of Jerusalem). He was young, 16 or 17, but a talented orator. He spoke in the old synagogue and many of the town Jews came to hear him. His speech was convincing and impressive.

What happened to me is what happened to Bilam in the Bible. I came to disrupt the meeting and to interrupt the speaker. Indeed, the meeting was nearly canceled and the stormy discussions continued past midnight. In the end, my *Hashomer Hatzair* ideology was shaken by this magical speech. When Axelrod came back to Rokitno a year later to give another speech, I was already a member of the command committee of the *Betar* branch in Rokitno.

With Axelrod's influence, *Betar* gained in strength. We went from 15 to 30 members. We were housed in Baruch Felhandler's home. We were very active and our movement went from strength to strength. We had great success in the elections to the 18th congress.

We earned the love of the Jews of Rokitno. Time was on our side. We came out to the Jewish youths with a slogan: The Jews must leave Poland because here only destruction awaited them. Very few heeded our warning.

In 1932, I went to *Hachshara* in Lutsk. After one month, I was appointed by headquarters as commander of the *Hachshara* unit in Volyn. It had 14 sections. After six months, there were 8 section commanders from the Rokitno *Betar* branch. Isia Golod served as secretary. In 1933, I was elected representative of *Betar* at a conference in Katowicz. It ended in a parting of the ways. Some went with Meir Grossman. I remained true to the Jabotinsky movement. In 1934, I returned to Rokitno and I undertook the command of the branch. The years I spent in *Hachshara* made me dislike life in exile, although I lived a life of active Zionism. In 1936, I was fortunate to achieve my dream and I made *aliyah*.

The Hachshara Unit "Edmondia" in Rokitno in 1935

[Page 81]

The Second Generation of *Betar*

Shimon [Syoma] Klorfein (Tel Aviv)

Translated by Ala Gamulka

Yoseph Trumpeldor and his heroic death caused an upheaval in my Zionist beliefs. At one of the sessions of my *Hashomer Hatzair* group, we read about Trumpeldor's death. I was so influenced by these words that I suggested to change the group's name to *Tel Hai*. My suggestion was adopted unanimously.

Therefore, it was not surprising that when Isia Golod approached me I was very enthusiastic. He told me that a youth movement was founded in Rokitno, one named after Trumpeldor and whose purpose was to give the Jewish youth military training, so that they would know how to use arms when they will fight to free the homeland in the spirit of Trumpeldor. I joined *Betar*. In addition, I became a propagandist for *Betar* among my friends in the Tarbut school and in my neighborhood.

My classmate was Yehudah (Nonia) Freierman (now in Argentina). I told him, using my imagination, about the guns we would receive and that we would create a new generation. These would be young people never seen before in exile – a generation of Jewish soldiers, marching together, who would restore our national pride which had been demoted and trampled upon. He did not take me seriously and since he could draw well, he sketched a caricature. In it, I held a gun and I was aiming it at a mouse. In the end, he also joined *Betar*.

In 1934, Yehudah Kaplan returned from the Halpering training course for counselors in Warsaw. He decided to organize a program for members of our unit. Most of the participants were members of the *preparatory kibbutz* in Rokitno. Those who took part were: Hinia Gorenstein, Aharon Shachnovski and I. The discipline and order in this program were of a high caliber. The participants received an excellent military preparation.

1935 was not a successful year in our unit. Most of the leaders made *aliyah* and others were scattered among different preparatory groups in Volyn. At that time, a visitor from *Betar* headquarters arrived in Rokitno. Since I wore the *Betar* uniform, he asked me to call all the members of *Betar* in Rokitno to meet with him. I was able to bring six members to a room in the Zandweis Hotel. In total, there were only 12 members since the unit was not really operating.

At this meeting, I was chosen as leader of *Betar* in Rokitno. Yosef Golubowitz and Haim Weiner helped in this task because I was not able to lead others at my age. The unit was revived and many new members joined us – 10-12 year olds. After a month of searching, we rented a room in Chechik's house in the Halles of the old town. It was a small room, but it suited our purposes. Since the unit grew from day to day, we ran out of space and we rented the gymnasium in Shlomke the butcher's house. A year later, when the representative from headquarters again visited Rokitno, he was pleasantly surprised to see a unit of 60 young and vibrant people.

In 1938 we received circulars from headquarters about *Aliyah Bet* (*Aliyah* In Spite of Everything). When it was rumored that it was possible to make *aliyah* through *Betar* and not in a dangerous adventurous way, many members joined us. Toward the end of the year, several of our members, as well as members of *Hashomer Hatzair* made *aliyah.* The newspaper *Unzer Velt* (Our World) organized a "visit" to the exhibition that was taking place then in our land. The condition was that every "visitor" would remain in Eretz Yisrael. Many joined this "visit". The Rokitno youths did not need this condition because they were dedicated heart and soul to Aliyah.

In 1939, members of our *Betar* unit began to go on *aliyah.* The first was Isia Golod. He went on the boat "Farita". In July, a second group left. It included Moshe Kutz, Israel Greenberg, Baruch Shuber and myself. We reached Shiatin, but the Rumanian border police would not allow us to continue. A tiny group somehow managed to get through. We refused to return to Rokitno and we waited for the right moment to cross the border. We were organized into groups. A group of 25, which included those from Rokitno, settled in Kolomay. We sat there and waited for a proper opportunity to cross the border.

However, World War II broke out and we reluctantly returned to Rokitno. When the Soviets occupied Rokitno we knew our dream of *aliyah* had died. Still, a small group of members continued its activities underground until it was denounced by local Communists. Noah Soltzman, the teacher Mordechai Gendelman, Avraham Schwartz and I were jailed in Rokitno. This is how the Zionist movement in Rokitno, including *Betar*, was extinguished.

[Page 83]

The Activities of WIZO in Rokitno

Fania Freiman (Ramat Gan)

Translated by Ala Gamulka

Rokitno was a vibrant Zionist town, full of lively interest in everything that was happening in Eretz Yisrael. I will describe our activities in the WIZO (Women's International Zionist Organization) branch in Rokitno. I lived 13 happy years in our town and I dedicated my time to the local WIZO branch. We did not look for personal honor. The work itself gave us satisfaction and happiness.

The members of the executive were: Mrs. Baratz, chairman, Clara and Luba Soltzman, Rivka Shapiro, Mrs. Katzenelson, Mrs. Shulman, Mrs. Turok, Clara Zumerman (still with us) and the author of this article. Our relations with WIZO headquarters were strong. Our most important activities were the annual balls we organized. We did not depend on others to do the worrying and preparing, but we did it all ourselves. We worked night and day. When it came to a *Purim* ball, we sewed paper hats and paper flowers in order to increase the merriment.

Some time before the ball, we began the canvassing. We were quite demanding, but we were the first to donate. After we fulfilled our duties we went from house to house to obtain donations. When we knew people had the means, we were more forceful. We walked with baskets. Some people gave money and others bought raffle tickets.

The balls were held on Saturday nights in the school auditorium. It was a day full of planning and activity. We brought carpets, tablecloths, cutlery and towels from home. We decorated the auditorium and we set the tables. The ball would end late at night. We did not feel like going home because we were so elated. We put our poor husbands to work in the coat checkroom, at the cash register and in similar jobs. The women served as waitresses. Our hearts were full and our feet wanted to dance. Even though we were young and we wanted to dance, we did not allow ourselves more than one dance because we were all involved in working for our goal – to increase the income.

When the partygoers left the auditorium, the executive stayed behind to count the money. It turned out that our work was worthwhile because we were pleased with the results.

WIZO Leaders in Rokitno, 1938

Standing [right to left]: 1. Baila Zandweis 2. Berezovsky 3. Tzessia Golod 4. ...

Sitting [right to left]: 1. Batya Grinshpan 2. Trigun 3. Rachel Gutman 4. Persitz 5. Necha Shulman 6. Henya Turok 7. Clara Zumerman

We also worked on JNF donations. The Blue Box was very dear to us. The work for this fund was so sacred in my eyes that even in the last months of my pregnancy, I went out on a winter morning with the Blue Box and I waded through the snow. I would return exhausted, but happy. The satisfaction that I was taking part in a special activity always encouraged me and gave me strength.

[Page 85]

Culture and Education

[Page 87]

History of the Tarbut School in Rokitno[1]

Eliezer Leoni (Tel Aviv)

Translated by Ala Gamulka

The School during its Growth and its Destruction

School memories are the dearest and the most pleasant in the life of man, since this is where the roots of our spiritual being are planted. All of our subsequent experiences stem from them.

This is what shaped our experience. It is said: "When the morning stars sang together and all the sons of G-d shouted for joy" (Job 38:7). Our world was happy and full of hope and beautiful dreams. These were days of glee and devil-may-care days, which will never be forgotten.

I approach these memories of the Tarbut School in Rokitno with trepidation and love. Although I was not among its students, I was educated at the Tarbut School in the town of my birth. I remember my school days as a priceless heritage.

Everything I learned in those days is still with me to this day. I still drink from its fountain of knowledge.

This is not merely a chapter of history, but a memorial to wonderful souls. We were tied to them from early childhood. These young children provided the reason for the wonderful world of Rokitno. They were its beauty and decoration. They gave the strength to the Jews of Rokitno to bear the burden of exile. We see this wonderful group in front of our eyes. We will always cherish their souls. We will bequeath the story of their lives to the coming generations.

[1]. I wrote the history of the school based on notes provided by **Mr. Avraham Grinshpan** (one of the founders of the school).

Teachers: Yosef Bar Niv (Budnayev); Shlomo Bar Shira (Baikelsky); Israel Einav (Weintraub)

Students: Pnina Orteger (Fuchsman); Haya Katz (Gotlieb); Zehava Nevo (Perl); Hadassah Kedem (Freiman); Tzilla Kilim (Kaminsky); Ronka Rosenstein (Greber); Yakov Schwartz; Haim Shteinman

Preparatory Classes *(Propaedeutika*[2]) For the Tarbut School**

Tarbut School in Rokitno held an important place in the network of Tarbut Schools in Poland. The background responsible for its growth and its thriving is inherent in the local population which had an understanding of Hebrew and a nationalistic education. The school did not spring out of anywhere since a great deal of preparation was done. There were preparatory classes, which served as the seeds for the growth of the school.

This preparatory nursery was founded in 1919 by the elderly teacher, Tozman. He rented two rooms in the home of a Polish resident called Dolgert on Soviesky Street and he taught Hebrew to the children of Rokitno. He was followed by his brother. The younger Tozman was a talented teacher, well versed in Hebrew, who produced hand-written grammar manuals.

He was followed by a modern teacher who had a European education – Yosef Melamed from Pinsk. He opened a "modern *cheder*" in the women's section of the old synagogue. There were two groups- 11 seniors and 20 juniors. There were two sessions – in the morning and in the afternoon. The students learned many skills in mathematics, geography, Hebrew grammar and literature from this teacher.

Sounds of Hebrew conversation – with an Ashkenazi pronunciation – were heard throughout the school and even in the streets. Mr. Melamed translated Varshatzgin's mathematics textbook from Russian to Hebrew and the students learned to solve mathematical problems.

When Mr. Melamed left Rokitno, the parents of children in these classes invited the teachers Volmark and Shmuel Volkon to come. The children continued their studies in the house of Leibl Lifshitz and in the old Halles.

In 1920 Israel Feldman founded a kindergarten in the women's section of the old synagogue. It served as a basis for the Tarbut School in Rokitno and Shmuel Volkon became principal.

The Founding of the School, its Teachers and its Curriculum

The founding of the Tarbut School in Rokitno, in addition to the existence of the preparatory classes, was possible thanks to the broad activity of the local Tarbut branch. Rokitno, a Hebrew town, had many cultural activities in the propagation of Hebrew culture, the sale of *"Selah"* and the organization of cultural performances.

At the beginning of the 1920's, there was a gathering of Tarbut activists in Rokitno. Among them were: Avraham Binder, Avraham Grinshpan, Shlomo Grinshpan and Aharon Slotzky. They decided to found the Tarbut School where the curriculum would follow that of the Tarbut organization in Poland. The number of students grew and the school moved from the women's section of the

[2] Preparatory classes from the Greek word "paedeutik".

old synagogue to Shlomke Shapira's house, near the Noyedval Hotel. Soon, this too became too small for all the students and space was rented on the next street – two rooms in the Halles and two in Mr. Shafir's house (the Radomer tailor). From there, the school moved to the house of the *shohet* from Blezhov, across from the post office. This house had large and spacious rooms and was well suited for the purpose.

Foundation classes of Tarbut School in Rokitno with the teacher Yosef Melamed in 1925

Standing Top Row [right to left]: 1. Haya Lifshitz 2. Baruch Schwartzblat 3. Yakov Freitel 4. Yakov Lifshitz 5. Buzia Levin 6. Grisha Litvak 7. Aryeh Chechik 8. Avraham Binder 9. Mendel Schwartzblat

Second Row: 1. Hannah Lifshitz 2. Hannah Murik 3. Yehudah Kaplan 4. Moshe Binder 5. Leibl Lifshitz 6. Motel Shteinman

Third Row: 1. Haya Sarah Grinshpan 2. Tzessia Golod 3. Bat Sheva Shohet 4. Gitel Burko

Fourth Row: 1. Syoma Weiner 2. Teacher Yosef Melamed 3. Polya Kokel

Fifth Row: 1. Aharon Freierman 2. Reuven Freitel

Shmuel Volkon taught Hebrew grammar and literature in the senior classes and eventually was appointed principal. Israel Feldman taught religious subjects and Mordechai Gendelman – history, Hebrew, Bible, Gmara and music. Hillel Volmark – mathematics. Podlis – Polish. Later Mrs. Erlich taught Polish. David Shafran taught art, music and physical education. Other teachers were Shlomo Farber, Yakov Shlita, Chuprik, Atlas, Shpirt, Fishman, Dichter, Bella Muravchik, Hillel Kovner, David Shtern, Sarah Bronstein, Volodavsky, Kulik, Weintraub, Rosenfeld and Budnayev. [3]

[3] Unfortunately, we do not recall the names of all the teachers.

Certificate

"תרבות"
הסתדרות עברית לחינוך ולתרבות בפולניה
הועד המרכזי, ורשה פז'יזד 11.
ס. ק. א. 4191.
סניף רוקיטנה
No 4
כרטיס·חבר
השם והמשפחה שטיינמן חיים
נתן ביום

"Tarbut"

Hebrew Organization for
Education and Culture in Poland
Central Committee, 11 Pzhized, Warsaw
P. O. B. 4191

Rokitno Branch

No. 4

Membership Card

Name: Shteinman Haim

Given on: ...

[Stamp]

The parents committee was highly involved in the hiring of teachers from a pedagogic as well as a social point of view. This is why there were many outstanding teachers during the golden years.

When the student population grew to 200, the *shohet's* house was too small. The leaders in cultural and educational circles decided to build a permanent building for the school. A building committee was elected. It included Aharon Slutzky, Moshe Freierman, Sender Perl and Avraham Grinshpan. They went on a financial campaign. The amount collected was insufficient and they had to buy a lot behind the bathhouse. The parents opposed it saying it was not a proper location for a school.

A Russian by the name of Yozpin owned an appropriate lot in Rokitno. The lots were exchanged and he was paid the difference. This exchange drained the financial resources of the building committee. The committee, connected to the Tarbut organization in Rokitno, had no money left for construction. They turned to Yakov Persitz, manager of the sawmill in Rokitno and he donated lumber for the building. Foundation stones were brought from the nearby Klesov quarry.

Other expenses were covered by donations and pledges from the Jews of Rokitno. Residents were assessed and they gave generously. They understood that as the influence of the synagogue study program waned, the school would serve as a source of learning of Jewish values and culture. Balls and plays were also organized as fundraisers for the school. Slowly the necessary funds were collected.

The construction of the school was begun in 1928 and it was completed in 1931. It was large and beautiful and equipped with furniture and learning tools. It contained seven classrooms, an office and a staff room. The classrooms were in the outer rim and the large auditorium was in the center. It was used as a gym and for assemblies and activities for the town Jews. On the High Holy Days, it was used for services.

The white eagle, the symbol of Poland, hung in the hall surrounded by large pictures of Herzl, Weizmann, Bialik and Ussishkin. Under Herzl's picture sparkled the slogan: “If you will it, it is no dream”.

Next to the building there was a large yard with sports equipment, modern trapezes for all ages, nets and marked spaces for games. A botanical garden surrounded the school and it was used to cultivate plants for study and research, as part of the natural science program. The physiology of plants was learned in a practical laboratory in addition to theoretical studies. The care of these plants served not only for enrichment of the curriculum, but also as preparation for agricultural life in Eretz Israel. The teachers made certain that their students had some knowledge of working the land, as this would be useful in agricultural life in the homeland.

The guard and janitor of the school was Mr. Avraham Lifshitz (now living in Israel). He was highly devoted to the school and involved his sons in his work. They were students in the school. By trade he was a bookbinder and in addition to his official title he bound books for the school. He rang a large bell when he supervised recess. He watched over the order and cleanliness and took care of the furnace. He also collected tuition and he sometimes had to perform an unpleasant task - he would send a student home when his parents were delinquent in payment of the school fees.

The first secretary of the school was Mr. Yakov Frietel. He was an educated young man who was dedicated to the upkeep of the institution. After him, the position was filled by Mr. Yehoshua Gaier. The last secretary was Mr. Weinbrand.

Tarbut School Building

When construction was completed, most of the Jewish students transferred from public schools to the Hebrew school. More than 90% of the children of the town and its surroundings were educated in the Tarbut School. It is important to point out the great dedication of the parents who willingly gave up the free public school whose building was spacious and well equipped. This was not true of the Tarbut School where the parents had to look after its upkeep and had to pay salaries to the teachers and other staff.

The school provided an education in all subjects. In addition to the curriculum of the government schools, Hebrew subjects were taught according to the Tarbut program and under its supervision. The inspector, Mr. Shmuel Rosenhek from Rovno, visited from time to time. There were also government inspectors who visited.

Except for geography, Polish history and language – compulsory subjects taught in Polish, the language of instruction was Hebrew. Until 1932, Hebrew was taught in Ashkenazi pronunciation and from then on the Sephardic version was used. The change to the new pronunciation was difficult, but the teachers became used to it and their Hebrew was precise and clear. The educational level was very high. Textbooks issued by "*Amanut*" in Eretz Israel were used. Basic texts were: *Divrei Yemei Ameinu* (History of Our Times) by Zuta and Spivak, *Lashon Vasefer* (Language and Story) by Yakov Fichman and S. L. Gordon's geography book.

Students of Tarbut School, 1926/7

Standing First Row from top [right to left]: 1.Z. Meirson 2.S. Eisenman 3.Ronka Greber 4.Nissan Kek 5.Taibl Shapiro 6.Misha Berezovsky 7.Yechiel Shohet 8.Israel Kek 9.Israel Lifshitz 10.Syoma Eidelman 11.David Eidelman 12.Gershon Kruchman

Second Row 1. Dina Roitblat 2.Haim Shteinman 3. ---- 4.Meir Rivkind

Third Row:.1. ----- 2.Esther Gertzolin 3.Esther Lerner 4.Batya Grinshpan 5.Izia Tzipiniuk 6.Yakov Olisker 7.Yoel Grinshpan 8.Teodor Linn 9.Mordechai Freedman 10.---- 11.Sonya Naiberg 12.Batya Levin 13.Sheintza Koke 14.Shifra Levin

Fourth Row: 1.Meir Burd 2.Asher Eidelman 3.Katz 4.Vova Kutz 5.Berel Baum 6.Vera Tzipiniuk 7.Manya Gendelman 8. Shulamit Shachnovski

Fifth Row: 1. Yitzhak Waldman 2. Perlstein 3. Roitblat 4. Kalman Kleinman 5. Krupnik 6. ... 7. Syoma Klorfein 8. Shmuel Shuber 9. Esther Shuster 10. Tzipora Wax 11. Rivka Wolfin 12. ... 13. Max Becherman 14. Nachman Vorona

Sixth Row: 1. Israel Trigun 2. Kaminsky 3. Hassia Binder 4. Feigl Kutz 5. Manya Shapiro 6. Hinia Tuchman 7. Teacher Mordechai Gendelman 8. Teacher Shmuel Volkon 9. Teacher Israel Feldman 10. Moshe Feldman(on his father's lap) 11. Teacher Volmark 12. Zaks 13. Sheintza Grinshpan 14. Ruth Baum 15. Grinberg 16. ...

Seventh Row: 1. Michael Shapiro 2. Yonah Rotblat 3. ... 4. Moshe ... 5. Hunia Eidelman 6. Yona Freedman 7. Raizel Shteinman 8. Kopel Zaks 9. ... 10. Moshe Kutz 11. Zinia Berezovsky 12. Sonia Berezovsky

Last Row: 1. Rachel Freedman 2. Haike Shohet 3. ... 4. ... 5. ... 6. Liova Golod 7. Aharon Burd 8. ... 9. Milia Tarilsky 10. Zaks 11. ... 12. Becherman 13. Gendelman

Within the curriculum, handwork held an important position. The handwork teacher was Mr. Gurevitz who also taught physical education and art (replacing Mr. Shtern). The students learned to bind books and they did bookbinding for the school. They also sawed large wooden pieces and fashioned different things out of them. The girls learned embroidery

Special attention was paid to developing the aesthetic side of the students. Singing and music were held in high regard. The singing teacher, Mr. Gendelman, put his heart into it. He organized an excellent student choir, which used to perform at many celebrations and memorial assemblies. The songs were learned from music sheets. In 1938-9 Shlomo Bar Shira (Baikovsky) joined the staff. He taught Polish language, Polish history and music. (He is now the principal of the Amal school in Haifa). He organized a children's choir, which sang every Friday at the school assembly. The students would donate to Jewish National Fund as they listened to the choir. He also organized a mandolin orchestra. This teacher did a great deal to inculcate modern Hebrew singing in the school. This singing created a Zionist pioneering atmosphere in town. Mr. Bar Shira also performed at violin recitals, accompanied on the piano by Mrs. Soltzman.

Woodworking Class in the School

Physical development was of great importance. On rainy days and in winter, the auditorium was used. Students wore running shoes, gym shorts and white shirts. The volleyball and ski teams competed successfully against the teams from the Polish school.

The girls wore uniforms. At first, they wore a black apron with a large pocket and tied in the back with two loops. Later they wore black tunics made of shiny satin with a white collar, white buttons and two large pockets. They also wore berets with blue and white stripes. The school insignia depicted roots of a date palm on a blue background and initials in gold letters. The boys wore hats with the school insignia.

The school made all efforts to complete the curriculum. If a teacher did not finish any material, he would gather the students on Saturdays or after hours in order to give extra classes. Mr. Gendelman had a beautiful custom which did not necessarily depend on the curriculum. On Shabbat morning, after services, he would read to the students stories from *Moladetenu* Publishers (Our Homeland) in Eretz Israel. His students well remember the stories about life in our land: "A Story About An Arab Shepherd", "The Young Heroes of Kfar Tavor", and "Yossi in Eretz Israel". During these story readings he deepened the understanding and breadth of knowledge of his students. He instilled in them an unquenchable thirst for learning. Even in early childhood they knew that there is no end to knowledge. There is always more to learn.

Education for Jewish National Fund in the School

Education about JNF was the mainstay of the school. The students elected a JNF committee, a treasurer and a secretary. It was headed by a teacher- at times Gendelman and at other times Kovner. The committee dealt in the collection of donations from students' parents, as well as those at *Purim* and *Hanukah* celebrations and family get-togethers. Fridays were full of content from Eretz Israel. There was *Kabbalat Shabbat* in every classroom and the blue box was passed around. Every month the boxes were emptied. The students held the box in awe as they had been taught by the song written in its honor: "You are a box, our box which redeems our land. You add fields to the countryside, trees in the valley and on the mountains". In every class there was a corner dedicated to JNF and a central one was in the auditorium.

The students collected JNF stamps which were tied to the map of Eretz Israel, its landscape or to important Zionist personalities.

Every student had a collection of albums. The top class was awarded a prize – a flag or a special certificate. In 1937 the students received a certificate of distinction from the center in Warsaw. On *Hanukah* there was a JNF bazaar in the school auditorium with the participation of all sections of the Zionist movement in town.

The Celebrations In School

There were no better days in school than celebration days. The students were blissful. *Hanukah, Purim* and *Lag B'omer* parties were happy events not only for students but also for their parents. Every celebration was opened by the choir, directed by Mr. Gendelman, singing:

> "The day will come
>
> A day full of light and goodness
>
> In which our nation will live
>
> And will call for freedom.
>
> Then all those exiled will gather
>
> From West and East
>
> From North and South
>
> From the Jordan and the Sea. "

A very interesting experience was the *Hanukah* celebration in the school. There were many intricate preparations. Since there was great interest in the celebration, there was not enough space in the school for the large audience. A big hall was rented, some distance from the school, in an anti-Semitic area near the *Huta.* Usually it was the Apollo. Walking to the hall entailed some risk of physical harm from the locals.

At the celebration there was a two-character play. Its content was mainly longing for redemption depicted by signals and dramatic symbols. On stage snaked the Jordan River made shiny blue and well lit. The front of the stage was dark – a symbol for the exile.

In this darkness, full of yearning and sorrow, was a girl dressed as an old woman gazing sadly at the lit Jordan where her son stood near a tent holding a spotlighted hoe.

Between them a dialogue developed. The mother was emotional and full of longing and heartache. She sang: “What will I see, my son, in Eretz Israel?” The son, the pioneer answered: “Pioneers working on the road with a pick and a hammer. In the winter the trees bloom and in December we bathe in the sea. All over there is an endless sea of blue. “Come, my mother, come.”

First Graduating Class in 1928

Standing [right to left]: 1.Sheintza Kokel 2.Sonia Naiberg 3.Ronka Greber 4.Esther Lerner 5.Freedman 6.Henia Korobochka 7.Asher Gendelman 8.Yehudah Linn 9.Moshe Brach 10.Teacher Kovalsky

Second Row: 1.Teacher Shpirt 2.Teacher Shmuel Volkon 3.Teacher Mordechai Gendelman 4.Teacher Podlis 5.Teacher Yitzhak Dichter 6.Teacher Israel Feldman 7.Israel Lifshitz

Third Row: 1.Gitel Modrik 2.Batya Grinshpan 3.Manya Gendelman 4.Batya Levin 5.Isia Tzipiniuk 6.Yoel Grinshpan 7.Meir Burd 8.Haim Shteinman

The audience was excited and moved by the performance. In this vision materialized all the longings, desires and hopes for redemption. We especially remember the assembly commemorating the 25th anniversary of the death of Dr. Herzl in 1929. The students presented a play on themes from Eretz Israel.

The celebrations at *Shavuot* were quite thrilling. Once, in addition to bringing the first fruits, a dove lost its way and flew into the building. One of the girls caught it and brought it to her teacher, Mr. Kovner and he placed it in a cage. At the end of the celebration he freed the dove and excitedly announced: "As the dove is free, so will the people of Israel merit its freedom in its homeland". As he spoke, his eyes welled with tears. He expressed his dreams and those of all the students. All the celebrations were accompanied by violin playing. The violinist was Mr. Moshe Kaminsky who taught music. On *Tu B'Shevat* the students ate fruit from the land – figs and carobs and they sang: "In the land of Israel the sun shines and the vine blooms and my beautiful sister went to Eretz Israel". On *Lag B'omer* the students went on a nature hike for the day. They went as far as Osnitzek or another village where they pitched tents and sang: "There we will build, we will erect kibbutzim and villages and lead a communal life". On Saturdays they went under the bridge to the lake. In the quiet of the forest one could hear young voices hoping for a better future.

The Hebrew-Speaking Association

A big and rare event in the life of the school was the formation in 1934 of the Hebrew-speaking association named after Eliezer BenYehudah. Mr. Gendelman (the teacher) was the moving spirit behind this event. It was a source for the group whose members promised to speak only Hebrew. It was a renewal of a vow made by Y.L. Gordon: " I am a slave to the Hebrew language to the end of times. I am committed to it for eternity". This association followed the Association for the Revival of Israel founded by Ben Yehudah in Eretz Israel. Its purpose was the slogan: "To speak to each other in Hebrew in company, in council, in the market and on the street. They will not be shy."

The founder of the association was Mr. Avraham Olshansky, principal of Tarbut in David-Horodok. Its purpose was to popularize the use of the Hebrew language and to make it into an everyday language. When a language is alive so is its nation.

The anthem of this association was:

We are the followers of Ben Yehudah
We are the fulfillers of his mission
We did not abandon our language
We will continue his teaching
In every corner of our place
In every forgotten corner
We will enforce our language
Within all our brothers and sisters.

The members of the association kept their vow and spoke Hebrew at home and outside, in spite of the Poles. When they entered a Polish store they used sign language or winking and pointing to show the storekeeper what they wanted. There were some humorous incidents, but they persevered. Anyone who lapsed and used Yiddish or Polish paid a fine.

The members of the association held their meetings in the school. They read Hebrew newspapers, mainly the children's newspaper *Itonenu* (our newspaper) and they enjoyed the stories of Tarzan, which were published in installments. They also published a wall bulletin of high quality.

This association helped a great deal in the acquisition of language, enriched the vocabulary of the students and allowed them to speak naturally. The members of the association wore a pin. The pin was engraved with the initials D.I. (*Daber Ivrit* – Speak Hebrew).

The Teaching Staff

Blessed be the memory of the teachers of the school who always worked in a difficult, yet respected, field – educating children. They enriched their students' knowledge of their Judaism and reared a generation of young people longing for their homeland. In spite of the fact that larger communities competed for their services they left other places in order to inspire the students of the Rokitno Tarbut School. As much as we praise them it will not be possible to fully describe their excellence. We will not finish lauding them: "...beyond all blessings and hymns, praises and consolations..."

All these teachers are unforgettable. They are outside the realm of ordinary memory. The students absorbed from them values and concepts. The teachers awakened in them desires and longings for new ideas and for renewal.

There was no distance between them and their students. They were like older brothers to them. They were not afraid to do anything as long as it was for the good of their students. We know that souls do not rise again. That is why the students kept in their hearts all their wonderful experiences. Their memory remained forever inside their students. Fortunate is the student who was affected by the fire they lit.

Lack of space forces us to draw simple sketches only, even though they deserve an in-depth description of their spirit and inner being. Our sages said: "Every scholar who utters sayings in this world continues to speak in the grave." These lines will revive them and we will erect gravestones of respect to them forever.

Teacher And Principal - Shmuel Volkon

He served as principal of the school and as teacher of science, geography and literature. He was very learned. From childhood he attended famous *yeshivot* in Novogorod-Volinsk (Zvihil) and in Brisk. He studied in Odessa in a rabbinical seminary founded by Rabbi Haim Chernovitz (the young Rabbi). He was a student of Prof. Yosef Klauzner in History; of Bialik in *Agada* (fable) and language; of Prof. Simcha Assaf- in *Talmud.* He studied literature with the poet Yakov Fichman.

Well prepared by these studies he was invited by representatives of the Rokitno community to serve as principal of the Tarbut School. During science classes he used various kinds of equipment to teach Physics and Chemistry. He went on many outdoor trips with his students to help them identify flora and fauna. When the students studied the anatomy of a lizard, they first caught some lizards, performed an autopsy and learned about the secrets of its insides. It was the same with frogs. They placed toads in an aquarium to watch the development of the embryo.

There was a science corner in the school which had skeletons of birds, fish, eagle, reptile and a snake preserved in alcohol. In the forest the students looked inside the tree to guess its age. The students learned from their principal that the age of a tree is discovered by counting the rings around its trunk. His aim was to make the students like nature. He also knew all the scientific terms in Hebrew. He taught general geography by following the books of S.L. Gordon and he always used maps in Hebrew published by Levin-Epstein. All the students respected and admired him.

In the mid thirties he left and settled in Volkorisk where he successfully directed the Tarbut School. It eventually became a Hebrew high school. Mr. Volkon perished in Treblinka.

Israel Feldman

He started his teaching career in Rokitno as a teacher of the kindergarten class which opened in 1920. Due to lack of proper space he gathered his pupils in the synagogue and became a kindergarten teacher. He was able to enter the inner world of his children. He would dance, sing and play with them. When Tarbut School was founded, he served as a Torah and Talmud teacher and he taught "Hebrew in Hebrew". To make it easier for the students to understand the material he used visual aids. When he taught *Parashat Terumah,* where the *mishkan* (ark) is described, he took a cardboard box and drew on it the golden *menorah* in detail.

He was a fanatic about the Hebrew language. He inherited this trait from his teacher, Achad Haam who taught him during his wanderings in Russia. His accomplishments in research in Hebrew language were outstanding. In the evenings, he would discuss language and *halakha* with the Rabbi and the *shohet*.

Mr. Feldman endeavored to make his students like Hebrew books. In his house he had a treasure- a set of old textbooks – some volumes of *Kol Agadot Israel* (All the Fables of Israel) by Lebner and the children's newspaper *Olamenu Hakatan* (Our Small World). He willingly lent them to the students for them to acquire more knowledge. In 1935 he left Rokitno and settled in Kamin-Koshirsk where he perished in the Holocaust.

Yavne School with Teacher Molchodsky

Talmud-Torah School in 1926

In the photo the following teachers appear: Israel Feldman, Kipnis, Tamara Litvak (Lifshitz) and Betzalel Kokel, from the founders of the Bet-Ulpana

Mordechai Gendelman

He was a veteran resident of Rokitno. He was one of the leaders in Hebrew culture circles, an agent of Jewish National Fund. He prepared students for their Bar Mitzvah. On the High Holy Days, he would lead the services in the school auditorium organized by the Zionists. He was well received by the congregants. He organized the choir and was its director and conductor.

He awakened in his students the yearning and longing for Zion with a stanza from a famous poem by Mordechai Zvi Ma'ane:

Where are you, Where are you

Our Holy land

My spirit searches for you

The air of the land is in my soul

It even heals the dead.

He taught Jewish subjects – Hebrew language, Bible, history, grammar and Haftara reading. He was the lively spirit of the school. He implemented the Bar Mitzvah gift of registering in the Children's Book of the JNF in Jerusalem. The Bar Mitzvah boy would receive a large certificate from Jerusalem bearing his picture. It was quite expensive then – 2 pounds sterling.

He also inaugurated the writing of essays about books that interested the student and forced him to go deeply into the book. The student had to explain the theme of the book. He made sure that students would read Hebrew books that would enrich their thoughts and forbade any shallow content. He gave guidelines and only allowed reading choice material. In this way he developed in the students the making of choices, internal selection and proper and deep understanding.

In history classes he added a list of novels that highlighted the period being studied. When they studied about the Maranos he assigned the reading of *The Maranos* by Kantrovitz and *Memories of the House of David* by Friedberg. When they dealt with the false Messiahs, the students read *David Hareuveni* by Max Brodt.

Mr. Gendelman made his students enjoy Bible studies because he saw in it an expression of the original creative forces inherent in our nation. He instituted the "Bible note book" in which the students would make notes in every class according to the following headings: name of class, Hebrew date, chapter number, verse number, vocabulary words and their explanation, special verses as well as summaries and verses to be memorized. Every page had colored margins drawn by the students. These notebooks made the students love Bible studies.

He knew how to teach poetry verses with a special melody and he insisted on proper pronunciation. He read with enthusiasm and intonations. When the students learned *El Hatizipor* (To the Bird) (Bialik) they went through a special experience. He would accompany the poetry by singing since he had a good voice.

With the Soviet occupation, he was jailed because he was the official JNF agent. Others arrested with him were Avraham Schwartz, Shimon Klorfein and Noah Soltzman. He was brought to Sarny for questioning. There he was forced to sign a document which denounced publicly Zionism, his educational work during the Polish regime and his world view.

Certificate-Jewish National Fund

Children's Book of JNF

Yakov Schwartz
Rokitno, Poland
Born: B Shevat 1927
Inscribed by Tarbut School and his Parents

Central Agency of JNF in Jerusalem

"And they shall bring thy sons in their arms, and thy daughters shall be carried upon their shoulders" Isaiah 49:22

We must not speak badly of him and denounce him. Whatever he did, he was forced to do. He accepted his bitter existence which confined him against his spirit. He was completely broken. In those times it is useful to read the words of a great Jewish prophet: "Do not laugh at man's actions. Do not rue them. Do not repel them, but try to understand them." Therefore, it is essential to understand what he did considering the background of these wretched times. If he had a choice, he would have refused to contribute to this destructive deed. He was subjected to ideology that was totally against his spirit and he was caught between the sacred beliefs to which he remained true in his heart and the desecration which he pretended to follow. He walked around disjointed as an abstract being, as if his artistic world and his ideas were blocked off. However, since he saw that the devil was at him at the time, he bowed and scraped and pretended to follow an alien culture. He was afraid to show his true colors to the authorities since he knew what awaited him.

Although he turned in the wrong direction, we must not misjudge him. It was said about Elisha Ben Aboya in the *Zohar* that he was not given the opportunity to come back and that when he died a voice was heard proclaiming all roads above and below would be blocked for that person, that he would not be able to enter the next world. We must not pass judgment and we should not close the roads to the next world for the martyred Gendelman. His promises were not promises and his oaths were not oaths. He was forced to do what he did.

Polia Erlich Volkon

She was the wife of the principal, a native of Zmoshetz. She graduated from the state teachers' college and received a teaching diploma. She taught the Polish language and did her work faithfully. She tried to teach her students proper Polish language and she insisted on a correct and clear Polish accent. She founded a Polish library full of easy and entertaining children's books. Slowly, she acquired more serious books. Polish was not taught every day. She used the newest textbooks. The government inspector would visit her classes every so often and he was pleased with her teaching methods.

Rivka Volodavsky

She came from Yanov-Polsky. Her father was a teacher and her mother a kindergarten teacher. She was a graduate of the teachers' college in Grodno. She was young, pretty and energetic. She was endowed with special pedagogic talents. She was on friendly terms with her students, without any boundaries.

She was an excellent athlete. In her spare time in the winter she went ice-skating with her students. In the summer she took them bicycle riding. She enlivened her students and they truly appreciated her. She did not only teach, but she spent a great deal of time as a counselor in *Hashomer Hatzair.* She taught in the lower grades from 1936 until the Soviet occupation. After much wandering, she managed to return to her hometown and there she perished.

Hillel Kovner

He was born in Vilna and graduated from the teachers' seminary there. He arrived in Rokitno in 1933 as a young man and immediately became a favorite of the students. He was a nice man with impeccable manners. He was an intelligent young man with a fountain of knowledge.

He loved people and he dedicated himself to helping them. He was chosen as the JNF agent, organized beautiful *Shavuot* celebrations, gathered the parents on Shabbat for orientation sessions and dedicated himself to informing the general public about Eretz Israel and Jewish values.

He taught geography of Eretz Israel and general geography. In grade 7 he taught demography, a new subject in those days and he brought the students to Jewish awareness.

His classes were well prepared and were popular among the students. He awoke in them the will to learn, not through rules and punishment, but by his personality. He was a friend to the students and he wished all of them well. They became very close and were part of a mutual admiration society. His home was open to his students and they often came to chat with him. Children who needed special attention received extra help after hours. This was not in order to receive a reward, but to help them to keep up.

He was highly involved in all the cares and worries of the students. He knew how to lower himself to enable a student to rise above. He was quite successful with this approach. There was an atmosphere of trust and friendship and Kovner was thus able to reach deeply and to find talent and capability inside a child without needing tests.

Many schools competed for his services and in the end he moved to Sarny in 1938. He came to Rokitno with love and left it that way.

The Last Days of the School

When the Soviets entered Rokitno in 1939, they found the school at the height of its development from the point of view of the quality of its staff as well as the caliber of its students.

The principal, Mr. Shmuel Kulik came from Sokolka with his wife, also a teacher. He was an ardent Zionist, a big man in all ways. He was an experienced teacher and a dedicated educator. He was well known among the staff and in Jewish circles in Poland for many years as a man of inner peace. His extensive experience in education and his good relations with the staff, parents and students helped to raise the status of the school.

On the staff was: Mr. Israel Einav (Weintraub) who taught general history. During the Soviet occupation, he was appointed educational director and also taught Stalinist constitution in the senior grades. In 1940 he organized a choir, which sang in Yiddish and in Russian. The choir was of a high quality. At a choir convention in Rovno, the school choir won first prize and Mr. Einav, as conductor, received an award of distinction.

Mr. Yosef Bar Niv (Budnayev) taught natural science and chemistry. He replaced Gurvitz who married a woman from Sarny and went to teach there. During the Soviet occupation Mr. Bar Niv was appointed inspector of schools in the area and chairman of the teachers association of the area.

Mr. Gendelman taught Yiddish. Mr. Itamar Zomberg (now a lawyer in Israel) taught mathematics and physics. The teacher of Russian in the senior grades was Mr. Shmuel Weinbrand. He had earlier been the school secretary. Mr. Bronstein, who taught Polish before the Soviet occupation, began to teach mathematics and geography. Mr. Dichter (now a teacher in Kiryat Haim) taught Grade 8 algebra, geometry and physics.

Feigl Rosenfeld (now a teacher in Kibbutz Hama'apil) served as a teacher in the junior grades. She especially shone as a ballet teacher. She organized a ballet group in the school which was highly regarded. Malka Rotenberg, a student, was the ballerina and every performance of hers was amazing. Other teachers in the junior grades were Mrs. Hanna Dichter (now a teacher in Kiryat Haim), Sara Isserlis (she also taught German) and Mrs. Kulik, the principal's wife. Mr. Forman was the school secretary.

The Soviet occupation caused an assault on all aspects of Jewish life, especially in education, culture and Jewish identity. The authorities had as their main purpose depriving the Jews of their national characteristics, their love of past history and Jewish sources. This regime can be defined in one encompassing statement: "Burn the soul and the body!"

The Jews of Rokitno, who were loyal to Zionism and the Hebrew language, began to live forced lives. They were compelled to perform many tasks. These forced lives touched children most seriously. The school children had difficulties in understanding the events that were taking place.

The most tragic and painful surprise for the students was caused by the following declaration, in Yiddish, by the beloved teacher and educator, Mordechai Gendelman: "Go away despicable Hebrew language! Go away the language of the counter-revolutionaries and opposers of progress! Our language is Yiddish only!"

The students could not believe their ears since they did not know that he had been forced to make this declaration by the powers that be. The students did not understand the forces of assimilation that were unleashed or the cruel reality. They announced that they would fight back. They stubbornly refused to get used to the destructive change. This struggle of the students of the school in Rokitno to preserve their Judaism, nationality and Jewish identity, is one of the most wondrous and admirable events. It was a result of an excellent Hebrew education which could not easily be cast aside. The struggle began on *Yom Kippur*. The Soviets had just entered Rokitno. The teachers announced, on the eve of *Yom Kippur*, to their students that they had to attend classes on the next day since it was no longer a holiday, but an ordinary school day. They were ordered to bring books and food. The students of Grade 7 initially decided not to listen to the orders and to stay home on this Holy Day. However, they feared that the authorities would retaliate by arresting their parents and their teachers. They went against their conscience and appeared in school.

The School during the Soviet Occupation

They were in shock when they saw Mr. Gendelman eating a sandwich on Yom Kippur. Gendelman, a *yeshiva* graduate, an exceptionally traditional man who led services on the High Holy Days – eating on *Yom Kippur*! The students could not imagine a worse calamity. Out of deep ties to the people came their decision to fast. They came to school without books and without food and went on strike.

This was the final curtain for the Hebrew school. It was forbidden to study Jewish history. Any mention of Judaism was erased from the textbooks. It was meant to enable the students to become part of the Communist world.

Yiddish became the official language of teaching in the school. Woe to the Yiddish and woe to the printing. The books came from Moscow written in the *Yevseki* font. It was difficult for the students to pronounce *Shabbes* instead of *Shabbat* and *baalmeluche* instead of baal mlacha (tradesman). They were depressed and sad.

The school continued to exist as an elementary school with 7 grades. A high school was opened in a new building originally prepared by the Poles for their school. The official language in this school was Ukrainian. The graduates of the Yiddish school were forced to continue their studies in this high school. Soon the students went on strike. They wrote to the Education Department in Rokitno and asked for continuation classes to be opened in the Jewish school. They were even prepared to study in Russian instead of Ukrainian if Yiddish was not feasible.

At first there was strong opposition as the inspector felt there were not enough teachers who could teach in Russian. In spite of this, a Grade 8 was opened in the Yiddish school and it was taught in Russian.

The strength and courage of the students of the school reached a pinnacle in another instance. The students successfully prepared a Yiddish play. It was presented in the cinema theater to an overflow audience. At the same time, a festival of school drama groups was being planned and it was recommended that this play be presented since there was also an individual Russian recitation in it.

Two weeks before the festival began, its program was received by the school administration. The Jewish school play had been deleted with the excuse that it was too long and in a language not understood by all. This caused great bitterness among the students. They boycotted the festival and decided that even the individual reciters would not perform. All the participants hid in their homes.

They were liable to expulsion from the school for this deed, or perhaps even worse. Their pain was too intense and the insult to their national pride too painful and they were prepared for anything. In their hearts the teachers commiserated with their students and they felt pity for them. The only punishment was rebuke.

The condition of the teachers was not better that that of the students. They walked around looking sad and depressed, full of bitterness and disappointment. The secret police were watching. Under these conditions their sharp teaching skills were dulled. Their resources dried up and they were forced to teach heretical material. Their fields were barren. The teacher became a tool for the authorities. The ideals of the teachers and the students were smashed to pieces. Their work was done under duress and with fear. They became passive and stopped being pro-active. Their faces were somber, but they still hoped that this will pass, that this was a temporary situation.

The teachers were only active in school since they could no longer do any social activity. They lost their contact with the parents and they became a world onto themselves.

This is how the Hebrew school in Rokitno was terminated, together with the Jewish population. The destruction began with the burning of the body and soul and ended with extinction.

The Influence of the School on the Spiritual Balance of the Rokitno Youth

The school spurred the students to continue their studies. Many of its graduates continued their studies in the high school of Rovno, Sarny and Vilna. The students of Rokitno stood out in these institutions with their talent and knowledge.

The school shone its spirit on the local Jewish public. It represented the spiritual world of the Rokitno youth. It was a place where the soul of the youth was created. The students left the school equipped with spiritual and emotional values, which influenced them all their lives. This spiritual crown was ingrained in them and it formed the image of this youth. There were none like them in other towns. The youth were emotionally healthy, built out of strong bricks. They were not torn by doubt. They had the gift of sharpness, strength of spirit, ideas and character. They never succumbed to beliefs other than Zionism and Hebrew. They continued on a straight road, which led them to the Hebrew country and settling on the land. They always looked up towards Jerusalem.

A Group of Young People who left to study in Vilna

From right to left:
1. Grisha Litvak; 2. Leibl Lifshitz; 3. Yakov Lifshitz (standing); 4. Aharon Freierman (Heruti)

The adhesion of these young people to the Hebrew language is amazing and fills us with awe and wonder. There was hardly a Jewish child in Rokitno who did not know Hebrew. This was not just any Hebrew, but one with depth and instilled with holy spirit. Parents denied themselves food to give their children a Jewish education, so they would grow up knowledgeable and comfortable with their background. It is thanks to the understanding and devotion of the parents that the children were educated with Jewish values and Hebrew language. When they made *aliyah*, they seemed and felt like native-born.

*

My story is ended but is incomplete. The memorial that I have created of this wonderful institution is inadequate. Even if my words were poetry as full as the ocean, my language like waves of music and my lips as full of praise as the skies are wide, I still would not complete the praise of these children. "There was nothing lacking in them". They were the offspring of Volyn, our Volyn whose name still makes us tremble. Their names will never be forgotten and we will always remember them in our speeches. We will mourn them for eternity.

[Page 111]

A Teacher of the Tarbut School in Rokitno Remembers

Itzhak Dichter (Kiryat Haim)
Translated by Ala Gamulka

Unfortunately, I will not be able to describe in full, in this article, the tremendous educational experience of the Tarbut Hebrew school in Rokitno. I spent only one year teaching in the school in 1927-8. I have forgotten many details in the interval. Hopefully, there will be others who will fill in the missing parts. The school was located in a rented apartment too small to accommodate all the children of the town. Even in 1928, we spoke of the need to build a proper building for the school. This was not an easy task. Where would we get the money? Wonders will never cease, for when I visited the school several years later, I saw a beautiful new building. I can only imagine the hard work and effort that the people of Rokitno put in until they were able to erect this building. There were about 300 children in the Hebrew school in Rokitno in 1927-8, i.e., almost all the children in town. It seems to me that no Jewish children attended the Polish school, or at least very few did so.

The residents of the town, mostly of meager means, made every effort to send their children to a Hebrew school. Many ate less in order to pay tuition. They knew that only through Hebrew school would their children learn about their heritage. They looked up to this sacred place and they sent their children. They never even noticed that there was a large and spacious free public school right across the street. This was a progressive town. The youth were dear and likable, happy and progressive.

They were interested in everything and they were sports-minded. This was a novelty. Not only the youth – the adults were also more liberal, progressive and enlightened than those of other towns. What a liberal atmosphere reigned in town! I did not meet in Rokitno any people who were stubborn and conservative. I saw neither *shtreimels* (fur hats) nor side curls. Certainly there were observant people in town, but they were not fanatics. They understood the spirit of the times and allowed their children to move with the times.

It was not an easy task for the parents committee to maintain the school, to pay rent and teachers salaries, as well as for the cleaning, heating and repairs. To this day I do not know how they managed it. At the beginning of every school year the committee decided on the tuition that all had to pay – according to their means. There were, of course, some complaints and discussions, but it never happened that a child would leave the school because of the cost.

The educational level of the school was high. The language of instruction was, of course, Hebrew, except for Polish language and Polish history. It is easy for us now to say Hebrew language of instruction. It is hard to imagine the effort, dedication and good will that the teachers invested in teaching in Hebrew. There were no Hebrew textbooks in science, geography or mathematics. The teachers translated from other languages. Can you imagine the effort put into a lesson plan for the study of science? Appropriate material had to be found in Polish, Russian or another language. Then came the translation into Hebrew before the students could be given this material. This went on daily. The teachers spent days and nights in preparation of these materials. There were no manuals or teacher guidebooks. The teachers had to create everything from scratch. Not everyone is capable of doing so.

The Student Library

There was a student library near the school. It was not an easy task for the principal and the teachers to obtain books since they had little money. Every year, books were added to the library. One of the teachers ran the library as a volunteer. There was such dedication to the library. Every book was lovingly handled. Books were exchanged twice a week. Twice a week the school was buzzing after hours. It was a pleasure to see the students hurrying to the school library and exchanging views on the books they read. They recommended books to one another. They had a great thirst for knowledge inside them. I loved to visit the school at that time, to listen to their conversations and to enjoy their evaluations. Who could forget it? Who could forget these sacred moments?

The Wall Newspaper

From time to time a wall newspaper was published in the school. It had two purposes: educational and instructional. The first purpose was to educate the child to read and to know what was happening in his immediate vicinity, in his school, his town, in the world and especially in Eretz Israel. The instructional aim was to develop writing skills.

The richest section was the one with news of Eretz Israel. This was our purpose in life. There were always enthusiastic students standing near that section. You could see in their eyes their happiness in reading about any accomplishments in the land – a new settlement or a new purchase. You could also see the deep sorrow when there were failures or tragedies.

The Work of the Jewish National Fund in the School

The JNF served as a cornerstone for the nationalistic education – the value of the land to the people. The notion: "The land will not be sold for eternity" was well received by the students. Every new purchase of land was received enthusiastically and donations were increased. There was a JNF corner in every classroom and the blue box was the center of the corner and of the life of the class. Every happy event was celebrated with a donation. A good mark or the completion of a book brought a donation. Every event in the life of a child such as a birthday, a Bar Mitzvah, a birth of a sibling also produced a donation. The atmosphere in the school was one of pioneering Zionism. An atmosphere of complete identification with Eretz Israel and all that happened in it. We rejoiced with them and suffered with them. Every happening, of course, was immediately reacted to in the school, in classrooms, in the newspaper, etc.

We celebrated *Rosh Hodesh* (first of the month) in the school. On that day, we emptied the JNF boxes and the agents reported on the activities of JNF and its income. We heard news from Eretz Israel, sang songs from there, recited and danced. These celebrations transformed the children to an atmosphere of Eretz Israel and they imagined that they were also there building and creating and living a free life. How sad is it they did not live to see the freedom towards which they strove and for which they worked so hard.

Holidays and Celebrations in the School

The celebrations held an important place in the work of the school. We tried to discover artistic talents in song, dance and the stage. The teacher spent many hours with the children in school after hours. She selected, taught and guided and she always succeeded in finding a talent – often in unexpected places. The school celebrations were famous in town. The parents and other residents in town crowded the auditorium at every event. The performance was a topic of conversation for a long time on the streets, in the stores and among friends. The teacher encouraged the children. She gave them aspirations and wings to soar on. Not just the teacher, but the whole staff and the parents helped to make it a success. The preparations were extensive in school and at home. They prepared backdrops and sewed costumes.

Students' Committee for the JNF at the Tarbut School in Rokitno, 1937

<u>From top to bottom</u>
<u>First row</u> [from right to left]:
1. …
2. A. Lifshitz
3. Nonia Turovitz
4. …
5. …

<u>Second Row</u>:
1. …
2. Gluzman
3. Ita Volodavsky

<u>Third Row</u>:
1. Dina Nagel
2. Mordechai Gendelman
3. Teacher Rivka Volodavsky
4. Dvora Golovey

Purim Celebration at the Tarbut School Rokitno, 1937

As in all our work, we tried to emphasize themes from Eretz Israel e.g., drying the swamps, harvesting on the *kibbutz*. On Polish national holidays, our school performed together with the Polish school and we always outdid them. We were once asked by the principal of the Polish school how we managed to always do so well and why they could not compete with us. If that principal knew how much work, love and good will the teacher put into every performance, he would have understood how we did it.

Influence of the School on the Spiritual Life of the Town

The school was a beacon of light in the life of the town and its influence was great in all areas – cultural life, Zionist movement, helping the youth groups and general atmosphere.

We often gathered the parents and lectured to them on different topics: education, literature, history, and Eretz Israel. We held these gatherings on Friday nights and the school auditorium was always full. The audience, tired after working all week, came to hear about the revival of the nation and redemption. They hoped for a miracle to happen.

Tarbut School in Rokitno, Grade VI 1937

Second Row bottom to top are seated the teachers [right to left]:
1. Bronstein; 2. Feigl Rosenfeld; 3. Principal Shmuel Kulik;
4. Sarah Bronstein; 5. Mordechai Gendelman; 6. Shmuel Baykelsky;
in the middle: teacher Yosef Budnayev

The school even helped the Zionist movement and national funds. Mr. Gendelman served for many years as the JNF agent and he made certain that every Jewish home had the blue box and he looked after emptying it. One of the teachers was the agent for Keren Hayesod and helped with its collections. Much of our time was spent with the Zionist youth movements. We helped them with advice, guidance and especially in teaching the Hebrew language. It was not done in order to be rewarded. It is difficult to list all the activities of the school in town.

Parents Committee

I would like to recall the names of the members of the education committee and the parents committee (as much as I remember) who worked tirelessly for many years. I mention their names with respect and admiration: chairman of the Tarbut committee Yosef Baratz, Noah Soltzman, Kitziu (Katz), Moshe Ber Gutman, Moshe Roitblat and others (still among us).

These dear people dedicated a large part of their time and energy to building an educational institution in town. They often would not rest in order to do work for the school. I recall their names with trepidation and admiration. I am deeply sorry that these dear souls did not live to see the founding of the State of Israel – their lifelong wish. I bow my head in memory of these people and I pray for their souls. May their souls be bound with all holy souls who toiled for the revival of the Jewish people.

The Teachers of the School who perished in the Holocaust

With sadness and sorrow, with respect and admiration, I mention here my colleagues, the teachers of the school in Rokitno who perished with the rest of the Jews during the holocaust that befell our people: Shmuel Kulik, Shmuel Volkon, Itzhak Shpirt, Mordechai Gendelman, Israel Feldman, Podlis and Bronstein.

Dear teachers of Jewish children, I am heartsick that I must mention your names in a memorial book. We were partners in educating a generation. How much strength, thought and good will you invested in your work. You dedicated many hours to teaching the language in the youth movements. This was not done for any rewards.

You lectured to adults on the history of our nation, Bible and Hebrew literature. You lit the fire of Israel in the hearts of many. You were like a pillar of fire which lit the way for the people in exile. You educated generations of seekers of freedom and people who aspire and wish to achieve.

My dear friends, you must know that you did not labor in vain. Your sacrifice was not unworthy. The dream became a reality. Our country is free from rule by strangers. Our people returned from exile to their homeland. Our children are free of fear of the enemy. It is unfortunate that you did not live to see it. It is most unfortunate that those who worked so hard for redemption did not live to see it. I mention your dear names with those of the residents of Rokitno. You were loyal partners to them in life and now your names will be remembered even after your deaths. The guardian of Israel will bind your souls, for eternity, together with those of other educators who dedicated their lives to the education of others.

The Children of the School who perished in the Holocaust

Dear children of Israel; you wonderful beings, I cry for you and I mourn you.

Dear people of Rokitno. It is acceptable that there are bereaved mothers and fathers. However, no one imagined that the most bereaved would be the few Hebrew teachers who survived. We raised, cultivated and taught generations to perform good work and creativity, to love mankind, to be charitable. We hoped for good results, but evil befell us.

Since the Holocaust, joy has left me. My world is full of sorrow and darkness. What is the meaning of our lives, the lives of Hebrew teachers if our children are no longer with us? I recall those days, when the school was filled with children's voices. I remember this sacred corner that we created inside an alien and hateful world. This was a corner where our children absorbed Jewish tradition, love of mankind, equality of rich and poor, values of charity and truth. I recall the atmosphere of Eretz Israel which permeated the school and the emotional preparation of the children for *aliyah* and for building a new society based on principles of truth and justice. I remember the *Rosh Hodesh* celebrations after the JNF boxes were emptied, the shining eyes of the winners of the JNF flag. When I recall all that, I appreciate only now the tremendous creativity of the teachers, students and parents. Even now it is difficult to get used to the fact that it was all cruelly uprooted. One million children. One million Jewish children were slaughtered in the Holocaust. The world shudders from the extent of the Holocaust. The numbers are shocking. For others, it is only a huge and shocking number. For me, it is not a number. For me these are live children, happy and excited, learning and misbehaving. They are still alive for me. Here are the children of Kokel, Gutman, Gendelman, Turok, Baum, Grinshpan, Korobochka, Binder, Tzipiniuk and Gitelman and many more. Where are you my children! Who cut you down so cruelly when you were so young! How many talents were lost!

Beginning Classes in the School

Standing Top to Bottom [right to left]: 1.Moshe Gitelman 2.Kaminsky 3.Sonia Gendelman 4.Baila Grinshpan 5.Yona Grinberg 6.Itka Gorenstein 7.Matityahu Nafhan 8.Tuvia Turovitz 9. ...

Second Row: 1.Moshe Gendelman 2.Moshe Portnoy 3. ...4. ... 5.Teacher Gitel Atlas 6.Hannah Honigman 7.Eliahu Greber 8.Aharon Gilstron

Third Row: 1.Mozik Katzenelson 2.Natan Levin 3.Shlomo Volman 4. ... 5.Yitzhak Kuziel 6.Etzia Lifshitz 7.Leibl Slep 8.Huna Naiberg

There were so many talented children in the school in Rokitno. To this day I remember that we wrote across one report card in large letters one mark: Very Good. Unfortunately, I do not remember his name. Perhaps it was Freger.

How can the sun shine again if this happened to us? Such children fell victim to cruel hands and were obliterated. They live on in the hearts of their teacher. When I came to Eretz Israel you were still in front of my eyes. I remember you on every occasion and to my dying day I will carry your memory in my heart. I will mourn you forever.

[Page 119]

The Tarbut Library

Yakov Schwartz (Rehovot)

Translated by Ala Gamulka

The Tarbut library was attached to the school, but it was not always housed in its building. It moved, sometimes too often, from building to building. The reason for this was rooted in budgetary restrictions.

There were three sections in the library: Hebrew, Polish and Yiddish literature. Most of the books were in Hebrew, among them the latest editions from Shtibl and Amanut publishers. There was a good selection of children's books as well as adult books. The library served not only the students of Tarbut School, but the general population as well.

I remember that on book exchange days the line ups were long - consisting mainly of young people. During the 30's the number of Hebrew readers decreased and the number of Polish readers increased. The reason for this was that new and interesting books would appear in Polish, but not in Hebrew. The readers demanded the new best sellers.

The catalogues were well organized. The choice was great and the condition of the books was satisfactory. Rebinding was constant. The readers respected the books and never soiled or defaced them. No one wrote his name in the book. There was especially much movement of books during the summer vacation. The youths that studied out of town returned to Rokitno and were interested in reading new books. The cost was minimal and the deposit was usually another book. Although the library was situated far away, it did not stop the thirsty readers and they always eagerly waited for the opening of the library.

The teachers prepared compulsory reading lists and those books were placed in the library. I remember that the most popular and beloved books were those of Yehudah Burla, Knute Hansen, Walter Scott, Emle Zola, Yakov Dingzon (mainly in Yiddish) and, of course, the Hebrew classics. There was a great need for a library since, unlike now, there did not exist secular books in the homes. There were books in almost every home, but they were only sacred texts. For that reason the library was the only location where secular books were available.

In order to widen its activities and to enable the general public to read newspapers and to find out about events in the world and in Eretz Israel, the library established an excellent reading room. However, it did not last. I do not know the reason. The room was quite attractive and served its purpose. It contained newspapers in Hebrew, Yiddish and Polish. Newspapers from Eretz Israel and the Diaspora were delivered. The reading room was located in the home of Avraham Binder on Poniatovsky Street. In spite of its success it was closed, probably due to budgetary constraints.

The last home for the library was on Messiviche Street (Soviesky Street). From there it went to the furnaces of the Red Army. I recall the dismantling of the library. When the Red Army entered Rokitno, the order came to bring all the books to the former officers club of the Polish army. Nahum Turovitz, who served as the librarian, packed the books. He hired a wagon and transported the books to the required location. We hoped that they would save, at least, the Yiddish and Polish books and allow them to be circulated after inspection and censure. Our pain was great when we were told by those who resided nearby that the Soviet soldiers were using the books as furnace material. In the officers club there were also books from Polish libraries. The magnificent bindings from the library of a Polish aristocrat from one of the villages stood out.

Among the refugees that arrived in Rokitno during the Soviet occupation, there was a Jew from Warsaw who owned a large library. He was surprised to find out that a small town like Rokitno had such a rich library.

The Soviets erected a new library on the ruins of our library. It was opened in February 1940 and it contained books published in the Soviet Union – some even in Yiddish.

[Page 120]

The Drama Club in Rokitno

Izia Golod (Haifa)

Translated by Ala Gamulka

It is not known when, exactly, the Drama club in Rokitno was founded. It is not essential to determine this. However, there were real sparks of theater during the national reawakening after the Balfour Declaration. The club fulfilled the tasks of Zionism, propaganda, education and explanation. All that was advocated by the Zionist speakers and orators on synagogue stages was also done by the club through song and dance.

I remember a Zionist presentation in 1920. It was performed in the women's section of the old synagogue. It had the participation of Noach Soltzman, Leitze Kliger (the *shohet's* daughter), Liova Soltzman, Sheintze Lifshitz, Haya Sara Lifshitz and Liova Geipman. The theme was harvest time in Eretz Israel. There were sheaves of wheat on stage. The song: "Are there foxes there, my dear young man?" was accompanied by hand and shoulder movements.

A short time after this performance, a group of young men and women was established. They called themselves the Drama Club. The number of participants grew since the following joined: Fanya Klorfein, Liova Litvak, Moshe Shechtman, Nahum Katzenelson, Avraham Schwartz and Yentl Weiner. Some of the plays I remember are: "God, Man and the Devil", "Mirele Efros" by Gordon, "Motke the Thief" by Shalom Asch. When I think of "Mirele Efros", I must discuss the *prima donna* who appeared in this role and who was a central figure in the club – Fanya Klorfein, the wife of the photographer Pinchas Klorfein. She always found time to actively participate in the club, even though she had three children and a home to run. She often invited the cast to her home for rehearsals. She usually played tragic figures like Mirele Efros and the mother of Motke in "Motke the Thief". Her acting brought the audience to tears. Yonas Turkov said that her acting reminded him of Esther-Rachel Kaminska and invited her to join a professional group. The income from the performances was dedicated to Zionist and civil institutions.

Over the years, a new generation of young people joined the club. They studied in Rovno and in Vilna where they had seen performances by the Vilna Troupe. There they learned to appreciate theater. The leaders of the new addition were the brothers Reuven and Yakov Freitel. The members were: Bat Sheva Shohet, Haya Berezovsky, Breindl Tendler, Esther (Etia) Klorfein, Izia Golod, Baruch Levin, Moshe Binder, Taibl Shapira, Grisha Litvak, Leibl Lifshitz and Rachel Trigun.

This group also functioned for the good of the public. We did not only perform for Rokitno audiences, but we also presented plays in Klesov and Dombrovitza. The big attraction was when Lionka Kublchuk (non-Jew) joined our group. We needed a tsarist-type guard and Lionka filled the role tastefully and pleasantly.

In general, we performed comedies or melodramas. It was the era after World War I and there was much sorrow in town. With our plays we hoped to reawaken the spirit of our Jews. We performed "The Witch", "Tevye the Milkman", "*Dos Pintele Yid* (A spark of Jewishness), and "The Big Lottery". We were inspired by the Ararat Revue Theater of Djigan and Shumacher who sometimes performed in Vilna. We were able to see these comedians and to enjoy their performances.

We also performed revues by combining songs and local current events. We were not satisfied with only local directors and from time to time we invited directors from other towns. They volunteered to work with us for a long time, not for any rewards. We received a great deal of help from Mr. Fridzon from Warsaw who was a talented dramatist. He came to Rokitno for his lumber business and he directed "The Witch". There are many songs as well as musical accompaniment in this play.

Drama Club Performing "Tevye the Milkman"

1.Aharon Freierman 2.Reuven Freitel 3.Buzia Levin 4.Haya Berezovsky 5. ... 6.Tzesia Golod 7.Breindel Tendler 8.Haya Lifshitz 9. ... 10. ... 11. ... 12.Yehudah Kaplan 13.Shimon Shapiro 14.Leibl Lifshitz 15.Pola Kokel 16.Bat Sheva Shohet 17.Vera Tzipiniuk 18.Israel Lifshitz 19. ... 20.Motel Mankovsky 21. ...22.Moshe Binder 23.Yakov Freitel 24. ... 25. ...

I always had a funny part – Hotzmach in "The Witch" or as an experienced matchmaker. There were many such parts since it is almost impossible not to have one in a Jewish play. I tried to look stereotyped: yellow beard, dirty cloth hat, red kerchief and a broken umbrella in my hand. I did not always follow the script and I often improvised and ad-libbed. I added local content and folklore. The audience was always amused.

In addition to the drama club, there was an orchestra conducted by the experienced musician Moshe Kaminsky. At first, the plays were presented in storage places and eventually we were able to use the stage and auditorium of the army barracks. It was the only chance for citizens to visit the barracks.

As to costumes – we adhered to realism. A matchmaker would lend clothes to the actor playing one. We also borrowed clothes from the rabbi, *shohet*, dry goods store merchant and the rabbi's wife. They gave us clothes willingly. When we needed a bridal gown from bygone days, we borrowed from older women who had kept theirs. In this way, we broke the barrier between imagination and reality, between the world of the theater and the real world. The audience was quite influenced by these plays. They laughed and cried at appropriate moments. As proof of this, that the plays touched the spectators, is the fact that discussions and arguments went on after every performance. They analyzed the text, the acting and the staging. There was no giving in during these debates. They discussed everything and they were not afraid to pan the play if it did not reach an acceptable level or if it did not satisfy their artistic expectations. As stated earlier, many of our young people studied in big cities and they were immersed in a high cultural environment in general and in good theater in particular. They knew what to accept and what to reject. This criticism was, after all, for the good of the club since it allowed for growth and prevented deterioration.

The part of the prompters is very important in the theater. The prompter sits in a crate hidden from view. Our veteran, professional prompter was Iliusha Freierman. In addition to his task, he was also asked to report at meetings of the club about the movements and acting of the performers, whether they followed theatrical protocol and if they did their best to portray the roles in an artistic manner. These meetings were very useful since they helped the actors to perfect their art.

Every play was given a permit by an office in Sarny. For that reason we needed to translate every play into Polish. We were obliged to omit the word *goy* from "Tevye the Milkman" since it was insulting and we had to replace it appropriately. Certain Yiddish expressions seemed immoral to the Poles and we had to soften them and to find the proper terms in Polish. This permit was not easily given and we had to travel to Sarny several times in order to obtain it. At times, things dragged on and we needed to ask local Polish dignitaries for help.

In 1936-7 new members joined. A group of young people was organized. They followed in the footsteps of the veterans. The amateur director of this new group was Syoma Klorfein. Its members were: Moshe Kutz, Yakov Levin, Haim Lichtman, Pearl Perl, Zlatke Perl, Toddy Linn, Yosef Golubowitz and others. These years did not produce successful progress in the theatrical life of our town. There were no real plays presented, only revues.

When the Soviets came, I am told it was possible to develop the activities of the club – in Yiddish, of course. However, there were some serious limitations since the Soviets did not permit any plays from our national repertoire. The club participated in regional drama contests. The Soviets called the contest an Olympiad. The club presented two short plays by Shalom Aleichem – "The Doctor" and "The Agents". The performances took place in the cinema near the glass factory.

Although the audience was not entirely Jewish, the performance was well received. If we had not been Jewish, we would have won first prize. The government representative invited the club to another contest, but in the meantime the war and ensuing Holocaust broke out.

[Page 124]

Who will give me the strength, the strength of patriarchs, to rise in the night

And to sit on the ground and express myself and to let tears fall

on the ruins of Israel, on the the hundreds of thousands of youth

and old people, children and women,who were tortured terribly

and slaughtered in such cruel ways of killing that there is not in the strength

of human understanding to portray.

(Dr Yaakov Klatzkin. Writings, diary entries, pages 352-353 - Am Oved Publishers, 1953]

[Page 125]

VILLAGES IN THE VICINITY

[Page 127]

The Village of Ostoki (Childhood memories)

Hinda Bleishtein [Wolfin] (Holon)

Translated by Ala Gamulka

The village is located about half an hour's train ride from Rokitno. We seldom went by train because it was pleasant to go on foot. While walking we passed by factories producing fire-resistant building blocks. The Ostoki station was one of the last ones before the Soviet border. It was always humming with hordes of workers piling lumber on flat cars that were sent far away.

My parents, Yaakov and Dvoshe Wolfin, came to live there, as I recall, in 1920-21. It was the first and only Jewish family in the village. Later, the Berezovsky family joined them. They built a large sawmill in the village, but the family did not live there permanently. In the last years before World War II, two more families settled in the village: the Turoks and Nimoys.

The lumber industry grew and blossomed in the village. It was felt everywhere. The most important lumber merchants, Jews and non-Jews, used to come on business. My father and other Jews from the area also were part of the industry.

Although we were, at first, the only Jewish family among many non-Jews, we still kept our traditions and we received a Hebrew-Zionist education. We started in a *cheder* in the village of Snovidovich that had a sizable Jewish population. When we got older, we studied in Hebrew schools in Rokitno, Sarny and Pinsk. I recall that when I returned home for the summer holidays I refused to speak Yiddish or Polish. It was only Hebrew. My parents also spoke to me in Hebrew. My father taught in the *cheder* and my mother also knew Hebrew. A Hebrew island was created in a sea of strangers and exile.

I remember well the Jewish holidays and festivals that we celebrated with emotion and happiness. We, the children, went with our parents to Snovidovich where there was a *minyan*. We walked a distance of 4 kilometers there and back, but we did not feel tired because we were infused with the happiness of celebration.

Our house served as an inn. The Jewish merchants who came from many parts of the country refused to sleep in non-Jewish homes. Here they felt comfortable in our family atmosphere. This is how we acquired many friends and acquaintances among the Jewish merchants.

In 1939, when the Soviets occupied the village, we moved to Rokitno. The clock did not stop ticking and events developed at a dizzying pace. The year 1941 came, when the war broke out between the Germans and the Russians. The Soviets retreated from Rokitno and the Germans came in their place. My parents, brothers and sisters remained in Rokitno. I escaped to Russia. Already in 1944, I knew no one was left of my family. The world of my youth disappeared, but the memories live on. They reappear every day and thus my heart aches.

[Page 128]

The Village of Osnitzek

David Shuster (Ramat Gan)

Translated by Ala Gamulka

The village lies at a distance of about 5 kilometers from Rokitno on the river Lwa that flows into the Slutz River. There were about 120 Ukrainian families and very few Jews. There were only four families: Shuster, Greber, Trechter and Sheinman. They included several tens of people.

The village of Osnitzek was unique. There is an aura of history in it since an ancient Jewish cemetery is located there. Everyone wondered and asked why there was such a large and ancient cemetery there. It was said that the Jews from all the villages in the area did not bury their dead in their own villages, but brought them to the nearest town. However, how can the existence of the cemetery in this village be explained?

My grandfather knew of a tradition, handed down from generation to generation, that Osnitzek was a remnant of a large town. This town had been destroyed during Chmelnitzky's time. Many Jews were slaughtered, many escaped to other locations and very few remained. Many bodies of the slaughtered were buried there and that is how the size and age of the cemetery were explained.

It was a district cemetery. The departed of Rokitno, Sahov, Tomoshgorod, Klesov and Stariky were buried there- nearly all the villages up to Sarny. It is located in a beautiful area near the river and is overlooked by a hill. Even the trees growing there were as ancient as the gravestones – hundreds of years old. Many gravestones sank in the soil due to age and the graves disappeared. Often, when a hole was dug, human bones were found and the hole would be immediately closed.

Since the cemetery served many settlements, there were many funerals. There were especially many more during Petliura's time. I remember, in particular, the funeral of David Zunder who was killed by the Petliurans and also his brother Aharon's funeral.

The economic situation of some of the Jews was good. The Shuster family leased the water mill and many fields from two noblemen, the Sichovsky brothers. They lived in nearby Tomoshgorod. The income was substantial. My family was able to do this leasing thanks to my grandfather, Mordechai Shuster, who was the administrator of these brothers. When they were young children he used to transport them by wagon from Tomoshgorod to school in Rovno. When they grew up, the relations between them and my grandfather were even stronger. They liked him and they put him in charge of their house and everything they owned. They did not dare make a move without him. They would only sell or buy after consulting with him.

The Greber and Sheinman families were poor and indigent and made their living in small trade. They had a tiny store where they sold *kvass* (fermented juice made out of bread), bagels, tobacco and all kinds of notions.

There were no great scholars among the village Jews. Their knowledge was limited to what a Jew needed to ply his trade. Since my grandfather was wealthy, he had a better understanding of the world. He brought brides for his sons from distinguished families in Olevsk. These brides brought a new atmosphere in the education of the village children. They did not like the low level of education of the village Jews and they wanted to give their children a modern education on two levels – religious and secular. They brought to the village urban innovations, which were full of western culture. They hired excellent teachers to teach their children. These were highly knowledgeable and experienced teachers such as Motel Shapira from Sloveshnia, Papish from David-Horodok and Kashtan from Bereznitz. The children learned Hebrew, Bible with *Rashi* interpretation and some *Gmara.*

However, this was not sufficient for the parents. When the children turned fourteen, they sent them to a Russian high school in Rovno where they learned the Russian language and absorbed western culture. This is how a large gap was created between fathers and sons. However, it did not cause a battle. The parents got used to the new trends and did not stand in their children's way.

The children were very happy. They did not feel the weight of living in exile. They enjoyed sunshine and nature. Their favorite place to play was the river where they spent after school hours during the summer. They practiced swimming and did very well in this field. They had contests in crossing the river. Each one of them was certain he would win.

Once an event occurred which could have turned into tragedy. I raced with Aharon Trechter (now in the United States) to cross the river. I arrived first and stood on the bank. I saw Aharon tangled up in the river current that was 4-5 meters deep. He was going to drown. I called for help and he was pulled out of the water still alive.

Another amusement and play place was the forest. It was a magnificent forest and it attracted all the children in the area. The students of Tarbut School in Rokitno and members of *Hashomer Hatzair* also used to come there.

There was no synagogue in the village, only a Shabbat *minyan* at the house of Nachman Shuster. For the High Holidays, a prayer leader would come from Bereznitz. I vividly recall the name of Kashtan, father of the teacher, who was a good prayer leader. He had a beautiful voice and I can still remember his melodies. I do not know if all the Jews in the village were *Hasidim*. I do know that my father was a Stolin follower. Whenever the Rabbi from Stolin went to Rokitno he would visit us.

I remember a childhood event that is both happy and sad. In 1913 Israel Shuster's daughter was married to a young man from Brezhne. It was a fancy wedding. The in-laws arrived in the village in a large convoy of wagons dancing and playing drums. However, the celebration stopped when it was discovered the bride's jewelry was stolen by one of the wagon drivers. She fainted in sorrow and there was a great commotion. The policeman came and he beat the Ukrainian who was accused of the theft. He confessed and returned the stolen goods.

The end of World War I marked the end of the "seven good years" of the Jews of the village and the lean years began. Their economic situation collapsed and they were at the edge of an abyss. The gangs of Petliura roamed the area and were killing people. They also came to Osnitzek. There were many fans of Petliura in the village. One day a group of murderers came to Nachman Shuster's house. They placed a bomb on the table and threatened to blast the house if all the money, gold and jewelry would not be given to them. Everything was handed to them in order to save souls. Many Rokitno Jews were hiding then in the village. They believed life was safer here, but evil followed them to their hiding place. These difficulties caused the Jews to leave the village. Their eyes were suddenly opened and they saw that they were sitting on a volcano surrounded by a wall of hatred. They deduced quickly that they should leave the village. The Sheinman and Trechter families immigrated to the United States and some members of the other families settled in Rokitno. Only the Greber family and Yeshayahu Shuster stayed in the village. They were killed during the Holocaust. Even my two sisters, Chaya and Genia, who escaped from the Rokitno ghetto to Osnitzek thinking the "good neighbors" would save them, died in the village.

[Page 130]

The Village of Borovey

Zillah Razgovitch [Gampel] (Petach Tikvah)

Translated by Ala Gamulka

The village lies about 20 kilometers from Rokitno. There was a considerable Jewish population who lived together like one family. They were close and attached to one another and helped each other when in need. The happiness of one was the happiness of all, but when tragedy struck a family it touched the hearts of everyone. They all walked around sad and in mourning. These close personal connections were forged on the background of them being strangers among a village population of many non-Jews who outwardly were friendly, but in their hearts lurked a deep hatred of Jews. They waited for the moment where there was neither law nor judge to do with the Jews whatever they wanted.

However, until the terrible events began, the village Jews lived a quiet and peaceful life. They did not aspire to greatness. Their livelihood was comfortable and sufficient. All trade was in the hands of the Jews. There were five groceries and some notions stores. There were two blacksmith shops, one belonging to Meir Zilberberg and the other to Aharon Gendelman (Aharon the yellow one). Shmuel Shapira was a carpenter and the Polish public school was located in his house.

There were fifty Jewish children in the village. Obviously, these numbers could not sustain a Jewish day school and the children attended the Polish public school together with other village children. The parents sent their children to this school with a heavy heart since there, head covering was not permitted.

The parents were not satisfied with the fact that their children should study secular subjects only and they made certain that they also studied holy subjects, so they would not assimilate and would maintain their nationalistic spirit. For that purpose, they invited a Hebrew teacher - Mr. Aharon Eizenstein from Karpilovka - to open a *cheder* in the home of Meir Zilberberg. The children studied secular subjects in the mornings and in the afternoons they studied four hours of Hebrew, Bible and Yiddish daily. The children were involved in learning for many hours a day.

When they finished their studies, the children did not waste their time. While they were still young, they were involved in the Jewish Scouts and spent their evenings in its activities. The organizer of the scout group in the village was Sonia Shapira, a member of *Hashomer Hatzair.* She was a graduate of the Tarbut School in Rokitno and she was also certified as a teacher in Ludvipol. She taught

Hebrew to the younger students in the *cheder* and in the evenings she gathered her pupils in the basement, fearful of the locals, who equated the Zionist youth movement with Communism. They were forced to have their educational activities in secret, by the light of a gas lantern. Sonia used to read to her pupils letters from Zionist leaders and held many discussions about Eretz Israel. The devotion of the children to the homeland was finalized by putting five Polish *grushim* into the JNF box, which was hidden in a corner of the basement. The children were immersed in an Israeli atmosphere every evening.

It is difficult to evaluate in a few words the deep educational activity of Sonia, her devotion to her pupils and her great love for the homeland. Her hope was strong that she would be worthy of making *aliyah* with the children under her care. However, the skies of the world were darkened and all her hopes were dashed.

When the Soviets entered Borovey, Sonia left the village and went to her sister in Ludvipol, where she resided until the German-Soviet war broke out. When the Soviet army retreated, she escaped with Yakov Perlstein who had managed the *Hashomer Hatzair* branch in Borovey with her. No one knows what happened to her.

The village Jews did not oppose Zionism, but they saw in it something for the distant future; when that would be, no one knew. Their attitude to the new Eretz Israel can be summarized with a verse from Psalms: "If God will not build the house, it is in vain that the builders will toil". They believed that they would go with the Messiah to Eretz Israel. They were all followers of Rabbi Israel Perlov who visited his adherents once a year and stayed in our house. The Rabbi once saw a miracle. My father's legs were paralyzed and the doctors could not cure him. My grandmother, Rivka Perlstein, talked my father into going to Brezhne, to the Rabbi. He stayed with the Rabbi for three weeks, received a "*cameo*" (a special note to produce healing) and felt an improvement. On the eve of *Yom Kippur*, he felt well enough to go to services, leaning on his family members for support. After prayers ended, he stayed overnight in the synagogue. On the next day, he continued his prayers, in spite of the pain he suffered. When he returned home, after the fast, a great miracle happened - the pains were gone and he became himself again.

We did not have a *shohet* (ritual slaughterer) in the village and every Thursday and before holidays, Reb David, the *shohet* from Karpilovka, would come. After ritual slaughter was forbidden by the representative of the Polish parliament Mrs. Pristor, known for her anti-Semitism, the situation worsened and the *shohet* had to endanger his life and to slaughter a cow or a calf in secret. A dark shed was attached to our house and that is where the *shohet* did the slaughtering. We were once denounced and before the police arrived, a hole was dug in the barn, the meat was placed in sacks and covered with garbage. The blood was cleaned from the ground and covered with white sand to remove any trace. The police searched and poked and even went up to the attic. There they discovered hog's hair, which was used to manufacture brushes. There was then an inquiry, since the Jews were not allowed to deal in this hair. It was only through the intervention of the governor, who was a friend of the Jews, that a tragedy was averted.

In spite of the suffering, the fear and the oppression, the Jews of the village did not learn their lesson and looked at all these events as a necessary evil because we were in exile and we would have no respite until the coming of the Messiah. They followed the paved road of fearing G-d and adhering to righteous people and never thought about the changes in their lives or about their harrowing existence.

However, a very different change was approaching in giant steps and it came upon us as the Soviet Army occupied our village, after the Ribentrop-Molotov pact. The Soviets entered the village on a Sunday afternoon before *Rosh Hashana* in 1939. Planes appeared in the skies of the village and dropped leaflets that told us to identify with the authorities. We brought such a leaflet to the priest to read for us. He, a sworn enemy of Communism, angrily shouted: "These are the killers, the Communists, the enforcers. They say that they will free us from capitalism". All the boys and girls gathered on the porch of the school to welcome the Soviet soldiers. Two horsemen appeared, greeted us and continued on their way.

Suddenly, the earth shook. The children, who did not know what this strange roaring was about, said that "devils" were approaching and were terrified. In truth, a "devil" in the shape of a big tank approached and scared us. We thought the house would disintegrate. Soviet soldiers were sitting on the tank and they treated us kindly throwing ribbons, beads and other gifts. Following the tank was a column of tanks that were going towards the army barracks in the village. Immediately, an announcement was made on a loudspeaker informing all the citizens to attend a meeting in the barracks. Everyone came; no one was absent. At the meeting the residents were ordered to elect a local committee, which would manage all civil matters. The legion left the village with its armaments and only a few soldiers remained.

However, the Soviet occupation did not last long. When war broke out with the Germans, the Jews felt the earth burning and escaped to Olevsk in order to then escape into Russia. They suffered there for three months and could not go forward because the area was already surrounded by the Nazis. Having no alternative, the Jews returned to Borovey since they saw what the *Bulbovtzis* were planning for the Jews of Olevsk. However, even in Borovey the *Bulbovtzis* did not leave us alone and abused us by forcing us to do hard and menial labor. On Shabbat all the Jews were forced to take brooms and to sweep the church.

On the eve of *Yom Kippur* 1941, we were ordered to wear the yellow star. A ghetto was delineated, free movement was curtailed and no one was permitted outside after 8:00 P.M. In those days, the first victim in the village fell. One Sunday morning Aharon Gendelman wanted to take his cow to graze. A policeman warned him to return home. He refused to follow the order because he saw that my cousins, Batya and Shoshana, were brought from Olevsk to be interrogated about their contacts with the partisans. He lingered outside to see what their fate would be. His wife begged him to come in and he agreed to do so. As he turned away from the policeman, the latter aimed his gun, shot and killed him on the spot. The story of the killing reached Rokitno and filled the Jews with great fear. My father, as chairman of the village committee, traveled to Rokitno and reported details to the *Judenrat*. His words created worry and great sorrow.

Aharon was buried by the locals in a disgraceful grave in an abandoned field where horse were slaughtered and skinned. When the Jews were ordered to leave the village and move to the ghetto in Rokitno, we asked to be allowed to take his body with us and to give it a proper Jewish burial. The *Judenrat* in Rokitno intervened and permission was given. Together with these holy bones we left- men, women and children- knowing for certain that our fate was sealed.

This is how we permanently left the village where many Jewish families had lived for generations in an orderly manner. It is not only my home that was destroyed, but our common home, too, was ruined. Let them be etched in our memories forever and let their images always be in front of us.

[Page 134]

The Village of Bilovizh

Shmaryahu Kravi [Korobochka] (Herzliah)

Translated by Ala Gamulka

The village of Bilovizh is situated about 25 *viorsts* from Rokitno on the border of the Soviet Union. It is surrounded by ancient forests full of pine, birch and oak trees. The name means white hill.

There were several Jewish families living in the village. They earned their living from the Ukrainian peasants who were in the majority in the village. Before World War I, when Poland was divided and conquered by foreign powers, Yoel Grinshpan and his family lived there. He owned the large inn in the center across from the Orthodox Church.

Grinshpan's inn was the center of village life. The peasants met there to exchange news, to do some business, to arrange marriages and even to elect the mayor. The inn was open to all travelers. The few Jews who came through the village on their way to town found there a resting place and even a meal to satisfy their hunger. The owner of the inn was an observant Jew who studied Torah constantly. His family was related to many other families. Some left the village and settled in Rokitno, Stolin, Visotzk, Dubno, etc. Others stayed in the village in spite of the threat of World War I, the Petliura and Bulbovtzis gangs and the destruction of the inn. Thus, three families remained, among them my father, Moshe Korobochka whose wife was a Grinshpan.

My father was an observant Jew, a follower of the commandments. He worked and studied Torah. He was a well-built Jew, clean cut and presentable. He served in the Tsar's army in the Russo-Japanese War and he was injured in Port Arthur and taken prisoner. He often told the story of his conscription and of the attempts of others his age to avoid the service by maiming themselves. He refused to maim himself and preferred to serve. He came out healthy having maintained his Jewishness.

He was handy in many fields and was an all-around man. Although he made his living from a general store, he also managed a farm. Not many of the Jewish farms in the surrounding villages could compare themselves to father's farm. The peasants in the area valued him for his diligence in plowing, sowing and harvesting. They also liked him for his goodness and hard work.

Traveling from the village to Rokitno was done by horse and buggy or by a small train through Ostoki. From there the train service was regular on a direct line from Ostoki to Kovel through Sarny. In the area there were other villages where many Jews resided. They kept in touch and met on holidays and celebrations. The village of Blizhov was located 12 km from Bilovizh. There were many Jewish families there. It was an established Jewish settlement with an active Jewish life. They even had a ritual slaughterer who served the Jews of the surrounding area: the village of Zolovey with two Jewish families, the village of Snovidovich on the crossroads to Rokitno with a sizable Jewish population, and the village of Toupik, about 6 km from Bilovizh which had a Jewish agricultural settlement headed by Yakov Freger.

My father's house was open to all comers. He performed the *mitzvah* of welcoming guests with all his heart and soul. He could not be happier than when a guest stayed overnight or for Shabbat. In 1928-1930 many refugees came through the village from the Soviet Union. There were Jews among them and they always found a meal in our house.

Since the village was close to the border, the Polish Army had guard stations there in addition to a unit that stayed there permanently. It was a unit of border patrol (K.A.P), which was not innocent of anti-Semitism. It followed the general enmity towards Jews that pervaded the Polish security departments. The Jewish soldiers in the unit soon became familiar and welcome figures in the Jewish homes in the village.

The residents of the village had agricultural farms. In the winter they worked in the forests in the area because there was always plenty of work. The lumber industry was highly developed and many large businesses were interested in it.

The residents of the village were calm people. They did not hate Jews. They saw the Jews as equals and treated them with friendship. They even protected them in bad times.

I can never forget Shabbat and holidays as they were celebrated in our home. The village Jews walked to nearby Toupik for services. There a *minyan* was held in the home of Yaakov Freger because there was a Torah scroll. On the eves of holidays and Shabbat (except for the High Holidays when all the families would move to Toupik), my father always took care of the *Eruv* (border). He would send one of his sons, on horseback, to place the marker mid-way on a tree, as is written in the *Shulhan Aruch.*

On the High Holidays my father led the services and the prayers. He was famous in the area. His clear voice and pleasing tunes were beloved. His praying came deep from within and his pleas to G-d made everyone shiver. I was a young child then and even when I grew up I could never forget these haunting prayers of the High Holidays.

I still see my father covered in his white and shiny robe during *Hineni.* When he reached *neilah* (closing prayer), in spite of the difficult and tiring fasting, his voice did not give up and it spread everywhere as he chanted "Open thou the gates of heaven" and "Help us thou, our saving G-d". One would be completely shaken and fearful of the angels who were descending to take back with them the prayers of the leader.

The trip to Toupik was an outstanding experience for us, the children. The road led between tall trees whose green tops almost obscured the sunlight. There were many wild birds among their branches and the squirrels jumped over our heads from tree to tree. Even the fields on both sides of the path presented a holiday atmosphere with their golden sheaves moving as if honoring the Jewish holidays. Serenity was felt everywhere. It was sometimes interrupted by birds chirping. They, too, were enjoying the beauty of nature and the vast spaces.

The adults walked slowly and talked about holy matters. Their main topic of debate was the weekly portion and its various interpretations. We, the young ones, were fascinated by stories of miracles of our great saintly people. We ran ahead along the railroad tracks.

My father was a follower of the Stolin rebbe, Rabbi Moshele, of the Karlin dynasty. He went to his house during the festivals and accompanied him on his visits to Rokitno and the surrounding villages. The Rabbi's teachings were sacred to him and he trusted him implicitly. I remember well the visit of the Stolin rebbe who stayed in our new house in Rokitno. During the week of the rebbe's visit the town was enveloped in an atmosphere absent of worry, full of happiness and joy. The feasting went on every night past midnight. The followers stood out everywhere with their black robes and raised hats.

My father lived a simple life. He raised his children to follow tradition, work hard and to love mankind. The verses such as "Next year in Jerusalem", "Our eyes will see your return", "I will not be silent when it comes to Zion", were meaningful and real in our home. All his children found their way to Zionist organizations because their love of Zion began with these prayers and wonderful stories which our father used to tell us on winter nights as we sat with a cup of tea and we absorbed every word he uttered. The redemption of the Jewish nation and its revival in its homeland by the Zionist movement did not seem to him to contradict his belief in the coming of the Messiah.

There was a special atmosphere in our home from the moment Shabbat came until it ended. All meals were accompanied by singing. There was a special aura in the house that even created respect in the hearts of the peasants. When Shabbat ended there was always a long line of people waiting for the store to be reopened. While they waited they enjoyed the singing that emanated from the house during the Third Meal.

Years passed and times changed. Polish nationalism reared its ugly head. All the minorities in Poland shared in suppression and discrimination. Anti-Semitism grew and engulfed all the towns and villages of the country. It even reached us. Those same serene and good-hearted peasants, so to speak, who lived in harmony with the Jews and respected them, suddenly discovered that the few Jews that lived in the village were the cause of all their problems. The propaganda by the Jew haters told them the Jews sucked their blood and lived off them.

This propaganda of venom did not miss our house and my father fell victim to it. The plotting began on economic grounds. A Polish anti-Semite settled in the village. At first he served in the police and with his wife, a convert, plotted against my father's standing. These were times ripe for all plots and slander. One day, my father was accused of circulating a story that Jesus was illegitimate. This slander was spread throughout our district. My father was arrested and imprisoned in Rovno. He was freed only after a costly bond was posted. His trial took a few years and he was sentenced to a year in jail. After an appeal, he was exonerated by the Supreme Court in Warsaw with the help of a famous brilliant Jewish lawyer called Rotfeld. He admitted that my father did tell the story, but it was done quietly, in his own home and not in public.

Another tale of slander against my father was that, supposedly, he was seen, on May 1, on the Soviet side of the border playing cards and drinking vodka with the Bolsheviks. This was obviously an invented tale. The investigating authorities terminated the case before it became a legal accusation.

The atmosphere of those days suited the Jew haters. This was during Hitler's rise to power. The poison of hatred overflowed the borders of Germany and the Jew haters knew they were operating on fertile soil. An administrative order was issued against my father forcing him to leave Volyn. He was not even permitted in any settlement close to the Soviet border. The order was given just as the war broke out. My father was forced, in spite of his advanced age, to abandon his family and his home. He took a stick in his hand and began to wander in exile, all alone.

His exile did no last long because when Poland collapsed, my father returned. He did not return to the village because we had sold everything and moved to Rokitno.

A day after *Rosh Hashanah*, a few days after the war broke out, the Red Army entered the village. It was quite a paradox. My father, an observant Jew, who knew well about the stance of the Soviets against the Jewish religion, gladly welcomed the soldiers of the Red Army who entered singing and dancing.

However, my father, as all the Jews of Rokitno, did not know that the sound of celebrations was misleading and that the Holocaust was waiting for us. My father escaped from the market square together with his daughter Freidel. He sought refuge with the peasants of Bilovizh, but the Lithuanian murderers found him there. He was killed standing at morning prayers covered in his prayer shawl and wearing his tefillin. His only daughter stood next to him. They were both killed in the village where my father had lived most of his life. He was buried by one of his friends somewhere in this village in eastern Ukraine. The grave is abandoned and covered in weeds and we could never find it.

[Page 138]

The Village of Blizhov

Aharon Blizhovsky (Ramat Gan)

Translated by Ala Gamulka

The village of Blizhov is situated in the forests of Polesia on the banks of one of the streams of the Prift-Stviga. During the Tsarist regime the village was part of the Muzir district, Province of Pinsk. On the other side of the Stviga was another province – the province of Volyn. Across the Stviga there was a wooden bridge built by the Russian engineering corps. The land in the area belonged to the Radziwil family of noblemen. One of its palaces, Josephine, was located there.

At the beginning of the 19th century, it seems Nachman, son of Yehudah Blizhovsky, came from David-Horodok or thereabouts. He leased the village and its income from the nobleman. The peasants tell that it was Yehudah, Nachman's father, who had begun relations with the villagers and he was known as a holy man. It was said that anywhere he stepped, a good crop would soon grow. The family lore says that Nachman could not pay the nobleman. He crossed the river and built a wooden shack on government land near the forests. At night he and his wife locked themselves up in the shack and listened fearfully to the howling of the hungry wolves in the nearby forest.

The descendants of Nachman, who was called Blizhovsky after the village, lived for over 100 years in Blizhov and its vicinity. Akiva, Nachman's eldest son settled in Glinna and his second son, Yosef, (he took the name Perlovich to avoid army service), studied Torah and his wealthy brother Shalom supported him.

At the beginning of their residing in Blizhov, the family earned their living by selling sacramental wine, buying dried mushrooms, pig's hair, pelts, etc from the peasants and selling them in the markets of nearby villages Olevsk and Turov. At the end of the 19th century Shalom Blizhovsky began to deal in lumber. He bought entire forests from landowners in the area. In winter the peasants cut down the trees in the forest and brought them to the riverbank. Shalom used to travel to Kiev and other cities where he met important lumber merchants and sold them his lumber. He returned to the village for Shabbat and holidays. It was said that he did not know the names of his many grandchildren and would ask: "Whose child are you?"

In the 1897 Russian census there were 62 Jews in Blizhov against 565 Russian Orthodox citizens. Relations between the Jews and the others were good. The poor farmers had respect for the lumber merchants since they earned their living in their forests.

The Jews of Blizhov were extremely hospitable. A story is told about Hodel, Yosef Perlovich's wife. She used to go out to the crossroads to invite people to her house so that she could properly fulfill the *mitzvah*. Tradesmen and wandering peddlers and simple poor people used to spend several weeks in the village enjoying the hospitality of the Blizhovskys.

The members of the Blizhovsky family lived in a circle in the center of the village. Their houses stood out in their size and beautiful shape as compared to the shacks of the peasants. The synagogue stood among the houses. It was a nice wooden building. There was a *mikveh* that served all the Jewish families in the surrounding villages. Special questions were posed to the Olevsk Rabbi and the dead were buried in the cemetery in Glinna.

The Blizhov Jews were followers of the rebbe from Stolin. Once a year he visited his followers in Blizhov. The Jews of Blizhov and vicinity prepared for several weeks for the visit. When he came, everything else was forgotten; all would crowd into Shalom or Yosef's house to hear words of Torah from the rebbe, sing with him and eat leftovers from his meal.

The rebbe influenced the Blizhov Jews to hire the best teachers for their children. The second generation sent them, especially the girls, to the Russian elementary school in the village. There was also a Russian library in Yitzhak Blizhovsky's house. The young people used to borrow books there.

Shalom Blizhovsky was well known for his severity. It is told that a new official came who "did not know Joseph". He came to Shalom's house and was not respectful to him. Shalom immediately slapped his face and with his sons threw him out of the house. After the matter was settled with gifts and negotiations, the official was appeased. Shalom was more careful afterwards and he used to say: "I thought a 'little Jew', but it turned out he wanted to 'Jew' me". In 1916 Shalom Blizhovsky was killed in a road accident in Kiev. A car hit him as he was coming out of the hotel where he was staying. He was buried in Kiev. He was 73 when he died. Rabbi Israelke was then in Kiev and he took part in his funeral. According to family tradition, he threw the first spade of earth into the open grave and called out: "Shalom of Blizhov did not die. He is still alive and will live forever".

Afte Shalom's death, his five sons Nachman, Yehoshua, Avraham, Israel and Itzhak and Yosef's two sons - Asher and Aharon – continued the family partnership in the lumber business. However, the good years had ended. First came the civil war, which did not touch Blizhov directly. In 1920 the border between Russia and independent Poland was established and Blizhov was located a few miles from the border. The main artery of the lumber industry was cut. From then on, the business continued on other smaller roads. The most important of these was the train station in Rokitno. Lumber was transported to Danzig from there.

In 1924 Batya Benderski organized a *preparatory kibbutz* in Blizhov. It had twenty youths from Blizhov and surroundings. It lasted for about a year and the peasants were surprised to see the children of the Jewish merchants cutting trees in the forest. The young people did not find appropriate employment in Blizhov and they went to study in other towns, even as far as Vilna. Some joined *Hechalutz* and went to *preparatory kibbutzim*.

[Page 140]

The Village of Berezov

Ruhama Oliker [Gelfand] (Ramat Gan)

Translated by Ala Gamulka

The village lies about 45 km from Rokitno. It was a district center serving other villages nearby. The district headquarters were there and residents from the area came on business. There were 15-16 Jewish families in the village. Most of them were wretchedly poor. Some had small grocery or notions stores and others were tradesmen. Each family had a tiny farm near the house. Some Jews were peddlers and they went to villages and hamlets with a backpack full of notions. They traded their merchandize for skins, mushrooms and wheat. These Jews got up early for work and took with them their *talit* and *tefillin.* They prayed in the forest because there was always an icon hanging on the walls of the homes. It was common to see a Jew praying alone in the forest wearing his *talit* and *tefillin.*

The peasants respected the Jewish religion and did not try to trick the Jews into eating non-kosher food. They boiled milk in brand new pots or roasted eggs or potatoes on embers. All this to make sure a Jew did not eat any forbidden food.

Life in the village was very active. The newspapers "Today" and "Moment" arrived regularly from Warsaw. Several families shared one subscription. The Sunday paper arrived on Tuesday. My grandfather, Israel Berezovsky, had a large house that was also used as a synagogue. Grandfather always led the services. In the last years of his life, when he was weaker, a prayer leader was brought from Blizhov for the High Holidays.

The Jews of the village were followers of the Stolin rebbe. Once a year, in winter, the rebbe toured the area villages. Then, he came to visit us also and he slept in my grandfather's house.

They were all Zionists and encouraged their children to go on *aliyah*. Their main hope was that because of a son or daughter who made *aliyah*, they too would do so. In the years before the war the wish to go on *aliyah* was even stronger. Those were the times when ominous clouds gathered in Polish skies.

In normal times the Jews did not suffer from their neighbors. They kept to themselves and did not mix with the others. They did not have any social contact with their neighbors. The peasants respected the Jews because they believed they were better educated.

Hospitality was quite evident in the village. Whenever a Jew came from elsewhere he would be fed and housed. This was not done for any reward, but out of love of Zion. My grandfather's house was large and became a hotel for guests. It was said of my grandmother that she never took the cloth off the table because there were always guests sitting around it. Any Jew who came to the village was immediately asked: "Where are you from, dear Jew?" A kind invitation followed to eat as much as he wanted. I recall distinctly a poor young man who went around the villages guided by a peasant. Once a year, he appeared in our village and, naturally, he never left empty-handed.

Before the Hebrew school was established in Rokitno, the youths studied in the local Polish school. However, the parents arranged for Hebrew studies by hiring a teacher. When the Tarbut School was founded in Rokitno, the local children went there. The trip to Rokitno was quite difficult. We traveled at night in a wagon pulled by horses or oxen. In summer, it was a very pleasant trip. Due to the heat we left before nightfall and arrived in Rokitno in the morning. The road went through forests. It was a slow ride. The forest was dead still. We, the children, feared wild animals because we knew there were wolves around. Indeed, we often saw the eyes of the wolves, which shone like lanterns. I loved the dawn when everything woke up. The stars would dim, a cool and refreshing morning breeze would blow and the birds chirped and sang. The driver who felt sorry for the tired animal stopped in the forest, collected twigs and lit a fire. We would get off the wagon, stretch on the ground, listen to the peasant's stories.

In winter, because of the cold, the trip went faster. It was pleasing to feast our eyes on the beautiful carpet of snow and on the branches that had buds and flowers. The frost made the sleigh screech. We turned over at times, but we loved and hailed it.

This is how the village children went to study in Rokitno. They wanted to receive a Hebrew education and to remain Jews close to their people. This closeness was planted in us from early childhood. The older ones among us organized a branch of *Hechalutz* that remained in contact with branches in neighboring villages. They would meet in Berezov for talks about Eretz Israel and read together the material sent in from headquarters in Warsaw. The younger ones, who started a *Hashomer Hatzair* group, believed in Eretz Israel, joined a *preparatory kibbutz* and made *aliyah.*

Suddenly everything changed. World War II broke out. The Soviets entered our village and dashed all our plans and our hopes. All the Hebrew books and all Zionist material were hidden in attics and cellars. Life had no meaning. These were purposeless days. We took the books secretly and looked at them, our hearts beating, afraid to be caught in our "sin".

We went through difficult times until we got used to the idea that we had no choice, that the authorities were in charge. It was hard to get used to youth meetings with non-Jews. The collectivity pulled the economic rug out from under the Jews. They were never farmers and they were no longer allowed to trade and mediate. They were in dire straits. The village was slowly emptied of its Jews. They moved to Rokitno with the hope of earning a living there.

This situation continued until the Russia-Germany war broke out. Jewish refugees who escaped from parts of Poland conquered by the Germans told us stories of the horrors the Germans had committed on the Jews. Rumors of a slaughter of the Jews in David-Horodok came, but we did not want to believe it. Two Ukrainians arrived in the village to plunder the Jewish homes and to arouse the local residents to slaughter us. However, decent Ukrainians kicked them out. After a while a Ukrainian police force was organized in the village. They abused the Jews and did whatever they wanted to them. This police of troublemakers established a ghetto in Berezov where Jews of nearby villages were locked up. The crowding was awful.

The Jews worked in the sawmill near Berezov and in other jobs of hard labor. The news about the slaughter in Rokitno came from my uncle Aharon Berezovsky and other Jews who managed to escape.

The appearance of a unit of security police in the Berezov ghetto made us fear that the fate of the Jews of Rokitno awaited us. The unit stayed for ten days and then departed leaving only a few Germans in place. They wore the skull insignia and this worried us. We asked the village mayor what it meant. In his innocence, he told us that some Germans were stranded in the village because their car broke down. This answer did not calm us and we feared what was to come. No one slept a wink. On the next day we discovered the truth. These murderers stayed in the village to organize the slaughter. Our fate was decided when ditches were dug at night outside the village.

Common Grave In Berezov
(250 Martyrs from Villages in the Area are Buried Here)

It was a misty morning. We heard noises from the Germans. A Jew was lying near the window in our house. He peered out and began to shout: "They are coming!" Indeed, the Germans immediately appeared. They blocked all entrances to the house and began to shout: "Get out!" We were expelled from the house. I was the last one to leave. I tried to escape from the trap, but I bumped into a policeman who hit me with a gun handle. I decided that, no matter what, I would not be brought to the ditch. I was ready to die right there. I broke through the row of Germans and I began to run. I was followed by my oldest sister Sonia. My father, my mother, my little sister and my little brother stood embracing. My father was crying and said: "Children, stay near me!" He shouted: "*Shema Israel*".

My sister and I escaped to the fields and we reached the forest under a barrage of bullets. I discovered later that my family escaped to the forest where they remained for ten days until they were denounced to the Germans. Many other Jews from the ghetto managed to escape to the forests, but they were caught and killed. This was the end of the Jews of our village.

[Page 143]

The Village of Glinna

Pinchuk Family (Israel)

Translated by Ala Gamulka

The village of Glinna stood out, in particular, among the ancient villages around Rokitno. It was named after its clay soil (Glina). The village is situated on the bank of the Stviga River. There is a legend that says that Glinna was once a big city that was destroyed in the 17th century. As proof of this legend, there are two actual events. The village was surrounded by fortifications 2 km away, on the road to Yozfin - Prince Radziwil's estate. Also, the flowers growing in the area were beautiful and rare. It was said that they grew from seeds found in the hay fed by the Tatars to their horses.

There was an ancient cemetery in the village, the only one in the area. In 1937, when a new section was added to the cemetery, a skull was found during the digging for a grave. The conclusion was that even this new section was part of an ancient cemetery. The grave was closed and the section was no longer used for burials.

Yosef Shuster, one of the veteran residents of the village recalled that some ancient graves, hundreds of years old, were found in the hills of Glinna. There were also remnants of an ancient factory.

The beauty of the village was an old synagogue, built 500 years ago. It is mentioned in *Pinkas Vilna*. Rabbis came from Vilna to Glinna and confirmed that the synagogue was an ancient one. It was built out of unplaned beams and planks. At the entrance there were three steps to go down, to fulfill the verse: "I called G-d from the depth". Inside were woodcarvings. Akiva Blizhovsky (130 years earlier), the right-hand of the great Rabbi Aharon from Karlin, renovated the synagogue. Prince Radziwil had donated the lumber for that purpose. The renovation was done very carefully so as not to ruin the works of art that had adorned the synagogue for many years. For that reason they left the old carved lintels and also built a women's section.

The ten Jewish families that resided in the village were either in business or they were tradesmen. Every family had a small yard in which they kept cows and chickens. In Yozfin, 4 km outside Glinna, there were sawmills and a tar factory. The village Jews also made their living there. Even the nobles who hunted in the thick Yozfin forests provided an important source of income.

The houses and businesses were inherited by the sons. Every son had first entitlement to his father's business. The Jews of the village were traditional and devout and there were no arguments about faith or difference of opinion. The children were brought up steeped in tradition. However, in time, they also established an advanced *cheder* where secular subjects were taught. The wealthier residents sent their children to Hebrew schools in the area.

The big event in the life of the village Jews was the visit of Rabbi Israelke from Stolin. It usually happened in the winter. The followers from nearby villages came to Stolin on sleighs to bring the rebbe. The trip included the string of nearby villages and lasted about a week. These were days of spiritual awakening and there were many celebrations with Hasidic dancing. In Glinna the rabbi slept in our house. The Jews came to greet him with horse drawn sleighs. The bells on the horses' necks were wonderfully sweet. The sound of the bells harmonized with the Hasidic songs and the roads were sanctified in honor of the Rabbi.

The entire Jewish village population - about 60-70 people -gathered in our house. They danced on benches and tables until after midnight. After a light sleep of two hours, the Jews came back to the Rabbi to present requests, to ask for advice and to give him donations.

Modern times did not miss Glinna. The *Hechalutz* movement came to the village and the youths began to think of new values and of preparing themselves for physical labor in Eretz Israel. The village young people gathered, here and there, and discussed different issues that troubled the Jewish world and the workers' world. The majority went to *preparatory kibbutzim* and some made *aliyah*. Glinna also served as a preparatory place for pioneering youths from area villages.

Although there were usually good relations with the neighbors, in times of upheaval, between governments, the locals would turn against the Jews ready to plunder and to kill. 1920 was a very bad year. The *Bolhovtzis* gangs ran wild in the forests of Polesia. Jewish victims were brought to burial in the Glinna cemetery, from the village of Bukcha. The Jews gathered in the synagogue to fast and to pray. At the last minute, a miracle happened. A Polish army brigade came and saved the Jews from certain death.

However, during the Holocaust, there were no saviors and the village Jews were killed. On the days before the slaughter, my father was deep in study of the unknown and the mysterious. He saw signs of the Messiah in his suffering. The fact that the Holocaust took place in the year 700 (*taf shin*) strengthened his belief in this. In an ancient book he found written that the number 700 (*taf shin*) announced a great disaster and that the strength of the world with the Jews in it, would end (*tash*). Perhaps after this Holocaust the Jewish nation would be revived. He lived and died with this belief.

[Page 145]

The Village of Drozdin

Ruhama Chechko [Polsky] (Givat Hashlosha)

Translated by Ala Gamulka

It was a small village between Rokitno and Stolin. It had five Jewish families. Its wooden buildings were low with straw roofs. The windows were dark. A low light was seen here and there and beautiful singing was heard in the evenings. Jews had lived in the village for many generations. They made a living and educated their children. They hired an excellent teacher even though it was a financial burden. Some of the children studied in the Tarbut School in Rokitno.

The Jews of the village were hard-working. They made a living from physical labor, using spades and rakes, axes and saws. Their main source of food was potatoes and animals and fowl from their tiny yards. We grew up in green fields. There were beautiful gardens around our house. They enriched our soul and our imagination. In the yard we had fruit trees planted by our grandfather and intended for the enjoyment of future generations. We had vegetables and corn, a cowshed, a stable and a barn.

In addition to work in the field, the Jews also traded with poor peasants. The Jewish population was related and there were many children. Their social conditions were equal and they did not need much. However, in spite of the poverty, the children were happy and full of delight.

Hasidism contributed to the spiritual uplifting in the life of the Jews of the village. The Jews of Drozdin were followers of Rabbi Moshele Perlov, may he rest in peace, from Stolin. They fully believed the Rabbi could perform miracles. In times of difficulty and sorrow they went to pour their hearts to him.

The Rabbi from Stolin used to visit his followers in the area every year and he included Drozdin on his tour. Who among us does not recall the tremendous impression the appearance of the Rabbi and his entourage made in our village? We remember the Jews that followed him from village to village and who celebrated till midnight. The circle of dancers even pulled the children into it. Father accompanied the Rabbi and his music to the next village, Berezov, 10 km away. There were wonderful sparks from the aura of *Hasidism* spread among the Jews.

The pioneering Zionist spirit also came to our village and the longing for Eretz Israel enveloped us. My brother Nahum decided to break with tradition and went to a *preparatory kibbutz* to fulfill his dreams. One fall day he left the house secretly and disappeared. There was a pall of mourning in our house. Our mother read her prayer book in a sad voice. Loud crying was heard from the whole family, as if he were, G-d forbid, dead. However, soon, many other young people followed in his footsteps. The parents accepted the fact, were positively influenced and finally helped their children gladly to make *aliyah.* Today there are five sons and daughters from the house of Yaakov of Drozdin here. There are also many cousins who established families in Israel.

[Page 146]

The Village of Vitkovich

Reuven Ory (Jerusalem)

Translated by Ala Gamulka

The village of Vitkovich was situated, from the First World War until the beginning of the Second World War, between the borders of Poland and Russia. Today it is within Russia.

There were 15 Jewish families in the village. Most of them dealt in business. The relations between the Jews and the peasants were mostly normal.

Some of the Jewish youths managed to reach Eretz Israel, through *Hechalutz.* When World War II broke out the Jews of the village were killed, in a most cruel manner, by a group of peasants incited by the Nazis. Not one Jew managed to escape.

[Page 147]

The Village of Zolovey

Sarah Fuchsman (Ramat Gan)

Translated by Ala Gamulka

The village lies 50 km from Rokitno. When I came there in 1924 there were about 200 families of which only 2 were Jewish: the Fuchsmans and the Rosensteins.

My mother-in-law was a hard-working woman (a woman of valor). She earned a good living from a fabric store she owned in the village. The customers were all locals who were on good terms with the Jews.

Our children, Yaakov and Godel, were educated at the Tarbut School in Rokitno. It can really be said of them that they went to a place of Torah since our village did not have the facilities for a modern school and the materials available to the local teachers were not sufficient for us. The children lived in Rokitno during the week. On Fridays we leased a wagon harnessed to two horses and brought them back home. The children were very lonesome for their parents. Every day, when the school day was over, they wandered the streets of Rokitno searching for anyone from Zolovey who brought them greetings from their parents.

The other family in Zolovey was, as I said, the Rosensteins. It included the father, Aharon-Ber Rosenstein, his wife Chava, his two sons Asher (in the United States) and Yaakov (in Canada) and his daughters – Baila and Haika (both killed in the Holocaust).

Aharon-Ber was a businessman. He traveled to the surrounding villages in his wagon. He bought pelts, pig bristles and grain and brought back to the peasants whatever they needed. The mother farmed the land. They had vegetable gardens. Some of the produce was sold and the rest was for the use of the family. The son, Asher, was a blacksmith. His shop was the only one in the village and it provided him with a good income. It was a hard working family.

Transportation to Rokitno was erratic most of the year. When the snow melted, after *Purim*, the area between Zolovey and Rokitno became a marshland. The trip was complicated and dangerous. Often, when *matzos* were brought for *Passover* from Rokitno, the horses would sink in mud and they could not move. Most of these accidents took place during dark nights when no one else was around. The people felt abandoned. They then had no choice but to sleep overnight in the forest or in an open field. They lit a bonfire and waited for daybreak when someone would come by and extricate them from the mud.

The Jewish homes in the village served as guesthouses for visitors from nearby villages on their way to and from Rokitno. In winter they arrived frozen from the cold and whipped by the winds. Hospitality was well developed and all guests were warmly received. When a Jew arrived shivering with cold, a hot drink, a sumptuous meal and a warm bed were immediately offered.

A special type of visitor who came to Zolovey was one who used the *mikveh*. The villages did not have a *mikveh*. The women fulfilled their obligation by immersing themselves in a large copper container. However, the G-d fearing men could not do without a *mikveh.* Therefore, they put their life in danger and walked tens of kilometers in winter storms to reach the *mikveh* in Rokitno. These Jews came out of the *mikveh* clean and pure and prepared for Shabbat. They made their way back on foot. On the way they nearly froze from the cold winds and the snow and barely made their way to us. After a good meal they continued on the way home to their families.

The road from Vitkovich to Rokitno went through Zolovey. Berl Turovitz from Vitkovich always went on foot from Rokitno to his village. When he came to us he was completely frozen. I immediately would say to him: "Reb Berl, wash your hands, eat to your heart's content!"

The tasty meal would revive him and his strength would return. Berl would tell me that this *mitzvah* was as important as that of observing *Yom Kippur.* The many forest inspectors (*brackers*) whose work kept them in the forest and who were quite lonely away from their families also found a warm place in our home.

The two Jewish families in the village kept their Jewish identity and were careful to follow all the rules. Our forefather, Yaakov, said: "I lived with Laban and I kept all 613 *mitzvot*". In addition to making sure the children had a good Jewish and secular education, the families also kept their ties to the community. On the yearly memorial days they walked to Blizhov to say *kaddish* with a *minyan.* As the High Holidays approached, they removed themselves from everyday affairs and left all business to the other villagers. They felt the coming of judgment day. They put their families on wagons, packed food and went to Blizhov for the High Holidays. The trip took a whole night. The wagons traveled slowly since the driver would fall asleep and drop the reins. The horses made their own way since they knew the road. We would arrive in Blizhov at daybreak, tired and broken from a long sleepless night. The trip through fragrant fields and endless forests soothed us and gave wonderful memories.

When the terrible day came, the locals turned from friends to enemies. We left the village and went to the ghetto in Rokitno. We took apart the stable to use the wood for heating. Hershel and my two children returned to Zolovey hoping to find shelter with the villagers. However, they were cruelly slaughtered and buried in a communal grave.

When I was in the forests, the peasants told me that wolves found the pit and gnawed on the bones of my children. A partisan accompanied me to the grave. On the edge, I found parts of my children's clothes torn by the wolves. A local volunteered, in exchange for salt, to help cover the pit. This was the end of the two Jewish families in Zolovey.

[Page 149]

The Jewish Settlement of Toupik

Yitzhak Meir Chechik (Herzliah)

Translated by Ala Gamulka

This tiny settlement has its own history, just like all the Jewish settlements that were destroyed and that had their own past. However, this story is unique since it was founded by Jews exclusively. Its eradication from the world during the Holocaust was therefore, quite final.

Early in the twentieth century the railroad from Olevsk to the middle of the forests of Polesia-Volyn was built. It was meant to transport trees cut down in multitude by Jewish lumber merchants. The single house that was built as an office near the Toupik track was occupied by a Jew called Yaakov Freger. He was nicknamed Yaakov of Toupik. He settled there with his entire family – three sons and two daughters. Eventually, they too built homes there for their own families. The Jewish settlement grew.

At first, the occupation of the area served as a place to earn a living only. Eventually, it became a special place – a Jewish agricultural settlement.

Up to World War I, Yaakov and his family performed different jobs, such as the "trusted employees" of the Jewish lumber merchants and the provision of food to the forest workers and their animals. Yaakov's house always hummed with many workers, clerks and merchants from Russia and elsewhere who were involved in the lumber industry. The house was also used for prayer services by the Jews since it held a Torah scroll.

When World War I broke out all work in the forest and on the railroad stopped. Everyone returned to their homes and only Yaakov's family remained. The war left its mark. Most of the Jews in the area, whether in town or in villages, suffered from hunger and were pursued by criminal gangs.

Since the sources of income were no longer available, Yaakov and his family decided to work the land and live off it. They uprooted trees, prepared the fields and pasture areas, ploughed and sowed, cultivated sheep and cows and lived well. They were highly respected by the local residents and were not bothered by the gangs – in contrast to the suffering of other Jews. Many Jews escaping from the gangs found a haven in the settlement. They were thus saved from starvation.

In this way the residents of Toupik tilled the land during World War I. When the war ended and new borders between Poland and Russia were drawn up, Toupik remained part of Poland. The railroad was moved. Just as once Toupik served as a shelter for those escaping from the Tsar, so now, it sheltered those escaping Communism – Jews and non-Jews alike.

The Jewish lumber merchants continued their business. A small railroad track was built from the nearest train station, Ostoki. A sawmill and a flourmill were also built. The village of Toupik began to bloom again. Many Jews made a living from the stores and many workers were employed in the sawmill and the railroad. However, Yaakov and his family continued to be loyal to the land.

The Jewish merchants in Toupik employed a group of pioneers from the Klesov *kibbutz*. Here many young people were prepared for future pioneering work.

In the thirties the Jews continued to build the railroad from Toupik to Vitkovich. A tar and turpentine factory was built in Toupik. The people of Toupik were pressured by the Polish estate owner to buy the land. Even though the payments were annual, it was a great burden. They worked hard and paid for their land.

In 1933 life stopped in Toupik. The sawmill burned down and all work stopped. Most of the temporary residents moved to other locations. Only the original residents remained and Toupik again became an agricultural settlement.

The residents of Toupik followed tradition. On Fridays and on the eves of holidays the *shohet* came from Blizhov to slaughter animals. On the High Holidays the residents of Blizhov, a nearby village, came to pray together. On *Succot*, Yaakov Freger's *lulav* and *etrog* were brought to all Jewish homes. The younger generation was taught Hebrew by excellent teachers. Many of them studied in Hebrew schools in Stolin and Rokitno. The rabbis of Stolin, Karlin and Brezhne came on annual visits on their way to see their followers in the area.

[Page 151]

The Village of Snovidovich

Avraham Shafir [Shvindelman] (Naharya)

In memory of my father Yaakov Shmuel and my mother Rivka

Translated by Ala Gamulka

The village of Snovidovich was situated 13 km east of Rokitno. It was on the border of Poland and Russia. Foreigners were permitted to enter only by special permit from the Security Office. The crossroads in the center of the village led east to Bilovizh, north to Zolovey, and south to Dert and west to Rokitno. As you stood at the crossroads it seemed that here were the roads that connected the whole area and that its center was Snovidovich.

Some of the natives of the village settled in Rokitno and were active in the life of the town – in business, cultural and social affairs. Any Snovidovich natives who went out into the world adapted to any society because they had a good foundation and they were broad-minded.

There were twenty Jewish families in the village. They were ambitious and energetic and held important positions in business, trades and agriculture. Every family had a house with some land. The Jews worked hard all week and rested properly on Shabbat. The sanctity of Shabbat was felt fully in Jewish homes. All the stores were closed on Shabbat. Everyone rested and the locals knew not to disturb the Jewish day of rest. Shabbat was Shabbat. On Shabbat it was easy to find a place to pray since there were several *minyanim* in the synagogue. There was no need for a cantor from the outside because Shmuel-Yitzhak Spivak with his magnificent white beard, led the services all year and on the High Holidays. Baruch Gluzman, an educated Jew, read the weekly portion on Shabbat. He was the lively one in the village. He was always full of jokes and anecdotes. He never stopped telling stories and he never repeated an anecdote or a joke. Before the war, a new Torah scroll was brought by the residents.

It was a great pleasure to carry pails of "our water" from the river for *matzo* baking. The young people considered this to be one of the most important events in their lives.

The parents looked after the education of their children and brought into the village highly qualified teachers. Among them were Dr. Shvetz and Chuprik. My father, Yaakov Shmuel, was in charge of hiring teachers since he had eight children and they would constitute the majority of the class. For that reason he worked hard to find exceptional teachers. Some of the teachers in Snovidovich were university students who came there to save money. The salary was decent. Every family had to host the teacher in their home for a certain length of time. The school moved from house to house. In addition to Bible and *Rashi,* Hebrew language and literature were also taught. The lessons were conducted in Hebrew. The parents were always concerned with giving their children a proper basic education. They helped those who could not afford to pay school fees. Some of the children studied in the Tarbut School in Rokitno and some went to *yeshiva* in Rovno or Stolin.

The youngsters were educated in the spirit of Zionism. I cannot remember any house that did not have the blue JNF box. It was emptied regularly. The *Betar* branch in the village conducted Zionist, cultural and social activities. There were meetings almost every evening. The Zionist movement captivated most of our young people. They prepared themselves for making *aliyah* in Voltche-Gorko, 3km from our village.

Hebrew School In Snovidovich, 1928

Standing in first row from top to bottom from right to left:
1. Teacher David Schwartz, 2. Avraham Shvindelman, 3. Pessia Shapiro

Second row:
1. Liova Shapiro, 2. Freidl Gluzman, 3. Hassia Shapiro, 4. Haim Shvindelman, 5. Freidl Shapiro, 6. Shlomo Lederer, 7. Ida Lederer

Third Row:
1. Sheindl Gluzman, 2. Moshe Barman, 3. Miriam Gluzman, 4. Sheindl Barman, 5. Mushka Shapiro

Fourth row:
1. Sheindl Barman (daughter of Yitzhak), 2. Henia Shapiro, 3. Moshe Gluzman, 4. Moshe Barman, 5. Haim Barman, 6. Isser Shapiro

A *preparatory kibbutz* of *Hechalutz* was established and the members worked in the sawmill. The *Betar* youths went to the Ostoki *kibbutz* where they worked in the brick factory and the sawmill. In the Rokitno *kibbutzim*, they worked in the glass factory. Even in the *Betar kibbutz* in Klesov there were members from Snovidovich.

Wherever the young people of Snovidovich went they worked hard and were among the leaders. The secretary of Kibbutz Grochov in Warsaw was born in our village – Moshe Gluzman. (He returned home from Warsaw after it was conquered by the Nazis. He was in Russia and then volunteered to the Polish Army. He became a captain and was killed together with Moshe Barman in battle in Warsaw). In 1933-34 Israel Kek worked in the Palestine Office in Warsaw as a representative. He made *aliyah* before the war.

The youths of Snovidovich were healthy and courageous. There were no shy and fearful Jews in the village. When necessary, the Jews knew how to retaliate. However, as a rule, there was no need for it since the relations between the Jews and their neighbors were good. They found a common language and were helpful to each other.

The soldiers of the Nazi machine came and completely destroyed this Jewish settlement – except for those who were in the Soviet Army or who fought, with the partisans, to save themselves and to annihilate the enemy.

I cannot give specific details about the extermination of the Jews of Snovidovich since I was drafted into the Soviet Army before the war and I participated in battles against the Nazis. When I returned from Russia via Poland, I could not go to the village to obtain details about the killing of the Jews who had been there for many generations.

[Page 154]

The Village of Kisorich

Liza Polishuk (Shapira) (Kfar Bilu)

Translated by Ala Gamulka

The village lies about 10 kilometers from Rokitno. There were about 100 peasant families and a few Jewish families who resided in eight houses. My grandfather, Ruven Shapira, nicknamed "Ruven from Kisorich", was one of the veteran settlers in the village. The other families were the family of Yakov "the mailman" who brought the mail to and from Rokitno in his cart; the blacksmith Shimon Gendelman; the Broder family and two other families who owned department stores. In 1910 the Polishuk family arrived from Olevsk. Yakov Polishuk built a sawmill and lived for several years in the village with his family. When World War I broke out in 1914, this family left and settled in Rokitno.

Grandfather dealt in lumber and became wealthy. He used to travel in a fancy wagon pulled by two horses and was like a Jewish "landowner". He was known in the area as a clever and wise man.

Although our home was traditional, we were exposed to western culture. My grandfather, who dealt with the governor, spoke Russian. The sons and daughters received a secular education. Grandfather felt it was important to teach his daughters language and he explained it by quoting one of our sages who said: "It is permissible for a man to teach his daughter Greek since it decorates her". So, in addition to Russian, our mother tongue, we also knew German - we read German books. The children had music lessons and played violin, guitar and mandolin. Higher education was pursued in Zhitomir. His grandson, Kutzin, had a university education. He studied dentistry in Zhitomir. When he graduated, he settled in Kovel where he had a dental practice.

My niece, Hinda, had obvious literary talents. She was born in Kisorich and by herself, self-taught, reached a high level of proficiency in Russian literature. She had a brilliant literary style. She was inspired at a young age and began writing novels in Chekhov's style. She sent her creations to Leonid Andreyev. The famous Russian writer was impressed by Hinda's talent and wrote her letters full of praise. He told her that he was very jealous of her because she knows how to value and to describe the essence of loneliness.

Our house was large. Five families lived in it. One stove did not suffice for cooking and baking. We built a kitchen with two huge Russian stoves. Each stove occupied half the room. They were built with fireproof bricks. Between the stove and the ceiling was a space that was constantly pleasantly warm. Guests, whose feet were frozen and who came to spend the night, would climb up and spread themselves there. There was no lack of guests. Our house was always open and available to passers-by. Everyone came and ate and drank. Grandfather used to say: "They are not eating my food. They are eating food sent by G-d".

Since there were so many people in our house, we had, on a permanent basis, a shoemaker and a tailor who made shoes and sewed clothes for the family. They were always busy with work. These tradesmen had vacations during *Passover*.

There was also a synagogue in grandfather's house. For the High Holidays, Jews from Karpilovka, Dert and Borovey would come. Although we were not many, during the High Holidays there was a spirit of sanctity in the village and even the peasants were afraid of Judgment Day. During the closing prayer (*neilah*), the peasants were afraid to go outside and stayed inside their homes.

Kaparot time was an exciting moment with a mixture of happiness and sadness. At midnight, the children were awakened for the twirling of chickens (*kaparot*) and the *shohet* from Rokitno stood with a sharp knife held in his teeth, ready to perform the deed of sacrifice. It was always a sleepless night. All the children were busy plucking feathers from the chickens and preparing them for cooking. Large vats stood on the fire and the melting chicken fat spread a wonderful, enticing aroma.

Youth Group In Kisorich

Standing Right to Left:

1. Haya Shapiro, 2. Dvora Shapiro, 3. Nissan Polishuk, 4. Eidl Kutzin, 5. Rivka Schwartz (Polishuk), 6. Boria Polishuk.

Second row:

1. Golda Shapiro, 2. Moshe Kutzin, 3. Feiga Gutman, 4. Esther Shapiro.

Third row:

1. Moshe Polishuk, 2. Liza Polishuk (Shapiro).

Mother's blessing of the candles before *Kol Nidrei* was very moving. Her crying created fear and trepidation. What didn't mother ask with her heart-rending prayer? That her sons would remain good Jews, would study Torah and would perform good deeds all their lives, that their homes should be blessed and that they should have a substantial income so they would not need any charity. There was a special sanctity in our home on *Yom Kippur* and even the younger children shed their everyday existence and prepared themselves for the great Day of Judgment.

The baking of *matzos* in our house was a joyful event. The preparation of "special water" was unique. At midnight, my uncle, Moshe Shapira, would wake me up by saying: "Get up, my child. Let us go to the well and pump still water". My uncle meant that at night, when water is not being pumped, it is still. That is why it was called "still water". My eyes were still nearly closed. How I wanted to stay asleep, but I overcame my desire and I went with my uncle. It was deathly quiet outside. The village was asleep. The night was full of magic and my uncle and I were doing sacred work. We went back and forth with pails of water in order to fill a small barrel.

The boys had a traditional education. A teacher was hired and he lived in our house. In the yard there was a tiny house and this is where he taught his pupils. The teacher was mean and he beat his pupils without pity. The children decided to get even with him. How? They went out on a snowy evening and built a snowman near the teacher's window. At midnight the teacher woke up and saw a man covered in shrouds peeking into his room. He almost died of fright. After that day he stopped beating the children.

In the 20's the number of Jews in the village diminished. The elderly died and the young went away.

The fate of the Kisorich Jews was told to us by one witness who remained alive. There was once a family by the name of Knishkov in the village. They eventually moved to Rokitno. When the Germans entered Rokitno, the father escaped to Russia. The mother, with two small children, returned to Kisorich hoping to find refuge with one of the peasants. There was an infamous peasant in the village that dealt in business with Knishkov. When the Germans came to Kisorich, they ordered all of the village Jews to gather in the forest. Even the boy, Yakov Knishkov, was taken to be slaughtered. As they came to the forest, they were surrounded by the peasants who were armed with axes and spades. The killers cut off the heads of the Jews and buried them using their spades. The boy, Yakov, managed to save himself and returned to Kisorich. He went to the house of the infamous peasant. The latter had pity on him and hid him in the yard under a stack of hay. He warned his family not to harm the child. At night he would bring him food and water. The neighbors sensed that something was going on in the yard and they discovered that the peasant was hiding and feeding a Jewish child. This man had many enemies in the village. Now they were ready to take revenge on him and they informed on him to the Germans.

The peasant knew that the boy was in grave danger and he immediately harnessed his wagon. He put Yakov into the wagon, added a sack of bread and pork and took him into the forest. There he told him: "Run straight ahead and you will reach the partisans". Indeed, he reached the camp of the partisans, among them Jews from Rokitno, and he was saved. When the man returned home, a German unit was waiting for him. They ordered him to gather his family inside the house and with them locked inside; the Germans burned them all alive.

Yakov Knishkov remained alive and came to Israel. He worked on the ship "Henrietta Szold" which traveled between Germany and Israel. The father, Moshe Knishkov, who had escaped to Russia, was saved and came to Israel. While he was still in Germany, he found out that his son had been saved and wanted to see him. The father spent some time in Israel and eventually returned to his friends in Germany. One day, he was found dead. He was killed in a mysterious way and to this day, in spite of the son's efforts, the killers have not been caught.

[Page 158]

"I am quite sure that when my own time comes, and the gates of this world open for my exit - at that last hour all the scenes of my childhood will peek forth once again from behind the curtain and raise themselves before me in one array.

Every single one of them will come in all its sweetness and grace and in all its pristine splendor, just as I was shown them in the morning of my life.

They will stand before me bright and clear and watch me silently.

Suddenly, the light of the seven days of creation will shine upon them and fade forever with the light of my soul..."

Haim Nachman Bialik. *Safiah (*"Aftergrowth" or "Random Harvest"*).* Chapter One. Page 14. *Kol Kitvey H.N. Bialik.* Dvir Publishers 1947.

English translation: Patterson, David and Spicehandler, Ezra, trans., Page 27. *Random Harvest: The Novellas of Bialik.* Boulder: Westview Press, 1999.

[Page 159]

ROKITNO AS SHE LIVES IN OUR MEMORIES

[Page 161]

There was a "River" in Rokitno

Yakov Schwartz (Rehovot)
Translated by Ala Gamulka

The river was one of the most beloved and fun places in Rokitno. It was loved by all residents in general and by young people in particular. A river? It is difficult to give that name to the modest stream, which flowed at the outskirts of town. One cannot find it on a regular map, perhaps only on a topographic map. This stream caused us an inferiority complex in discussions with residents of other towns, since it did not even have a name. It is rumored that it was nicknamed *Rokitnenka* (Little Rokitno). This was never proven to be true.

In spite of all that, there are some pleasant and not so pleasant memories connected to this stream. Already at the beginning of spring, in late April and early May, groups of children and youths could be seen on their way to the river. There are many memories - walking, standing near the gated rail crossing, watching the train maneuvers, marching on the winding path for several hundred meters inside the rich vegetation just awakening after a long winter. Of course, it was necessary to be vigilant of the groups of young locals who used any opportunity to beat Jewish children, or at least to scare them. Indeed, once I was badly beaten by a group of infamous *Goncherokes*, when I wanted to walk alone towards the river. It was less dangerous to go in groups and we tried to go together and with the protection of those older than us.

It was not possible to go swimming in the spring. The water was still cold and the fears of the result of swimming in it were quite great. In spite of that, we used to take off our shoes and, at least, dip our feet in the cool water. We also splashed the women washing clothes nearby and disappeared followed by their angry shouts and curses. We walked barefoot to town relishing the feeling of the warm earth and fresh grass, just beginning to sprout, under our feet.

Once I "enjoyed" a spring dip, in my clothes, caused by Kostek "the pig" who approached me. I was standing at the edge of the river deep in thought and he picked me up and threw me into the river while his friends laughed in derision. I crossed the river swimming (luckily I knew how to swim) and I distanced myself from him dripping wet and extremely angry and ashamed.

We learned to swim not in school, not in sports clubs- which did not exist in our town- not through expert teachers and counselors. Each one taught his friends and the fact that the river was shallow was to our advantage. A turning point was the "flood" in Rokitno in the early 30's. The town itself was not really touched by the river, which overflowed and flooded many other areas. The current was too strong and we, the children, abandoned ourselves to its mercy and we were thus transported a great distance. When the water receded and the river shriveled, we discovered that we suddenly could swim. Soon we were able to swim with the older kids near the bridge. This was, practically, the only place where the water was deep - the equivalent of the height of a person.

The River In Rokitno

In truth, it must be added that there were other swimming areas. They were smaller and further away and very few Jews would go there, e.g., behind the glass factory and in the village of Rokitno and behind Messiyeviche Street.

The area around the river also served as a place for nature hikes to study flora and fauna. Often natural science classes, led by our teacher Shmuel Volkon, would be held there. Another "bridge" with a pool of water underneath it was found in Osnitzek, a village some 5 kilometers away from our town. People from Rokitno, mostly youths, would go to this farther place in large, organized groups. On the way we tasted, actually ate, the black and red berries, which grew in plenty along the railroad tracks. This would make our long walk more pleasant.

Although it was small, the river, or stream, provided many unforgettable experiences to the younger generation of our town. It refreshed perspiring bodies on hot summer days. The river also served as a refrigerator. Huge ice blocks were cut out during the winter and kept under a blanket of sawdust for the hot summer days. The manufacturer of soda water provided ice with every container. On the High Holidays, it served for religious purposes. The Jews of the old town performed *tashlich* on its banks. The Jews of the new town used an abandoned quarry filled with water for that purpose.

Because of the distance we did not reach the river in the winter. We used ditches alongside the roads as skating rinks. The stream was small, but it gave us many pleasures. We will always remember it with fondness.

[Page 163]

The Jews of Rokitno

Haim Shteinman (Tel-Aviv)

Translated by Ala Gamulka

"For these things I weep;
mine eye runneth down with water,
because the comforter is far from me".

Lamentations 1:16

The Jews of Rokitno were a mixture of the serious nature of the first settlers and the light-heartedness of the later ones. It can be said that they were Jews celebrating a minor holiday since the sacred and the secular were intermingled in them. They were like birch trees, which surrounded tens of villages in a green belt. The strength that enriches and keeps alive the roots underneath and the treetop above was well hidden. It was just like the white, soft petals of a flower, which have to be removed in order to reach the center.

The style of houses in town was not any different from the other towns. They were not built by great architects or artists with special plans, but by ordinary tradesmen who did everything by themselves. The town structure in Rokitno consisted of Pilsudsky Street (old town) with wooden stairs on its flanks. It continued to the *Huta* (glass factory). There were other wide, long streets (in the new town), but Pilsudsky Street was the main commercial area.

Typically, the town had water wells on every street. In winter they were covered with a thick layer of ice blocks. In summer, they were almost emptied. It then became necessary to haul pails of water from far away.

On the other side of the railroad tracks, among several buildings, the Polish Catholic church stood out. (The statue of Pilsudsky stood across from it.) The church bells cast fear with their loud peals, especially on Easter and Christmas Eves. Another building that stood out for its architecture was the railroad station. There were also two synagogues. The central one - the old synagogue - had people praying and learning Torah day and night and the new synagogue, which was only full on Shabbat and on holidays.

This, more or less, was the daily routine of any Rokitno Jew: at dawn, they took out the cows to join the communal herd. This task was the responsibility of the men and was done, usually, with the *talit* and *tefillin* under the arm. Immediately afterwards, they went to the synagogue and quickly did the morning prayers. They bowed, rocked on their feet for "*Kadosh*" and, suddenly, here is "*Aleinu*". "*Shema Koleinu*", during *Shmone Esre* is an important prayer. One can always add personal requests for G-d's help in improving one's livelihood and having enough food for the children.

Pilsudsky Street

In the meantime, the doors of the stores clattered as the iron bars were removed and the herring barrels were brought to the door. The merchandise was mainly intended for the peasants. Gas lanterns with glass containers hung on hooks and ropes, as well as shovels, rakes and pitchforks. Here is a sack of barley; there is a bunch of mushrooms pungent with the smell of the forest moisture. On the shelves there were bolts of cloth, toys, soap, penknives, wallets, colorful kerchiefs for the women, boot polish, sugar, salt, matches and colored thread. This was a store with everything in it.

There were very few stores with cloth for Jews. Special clothes made of *Samut,* velvet and *Atlas* for sacred objects and for wedding gowns were ordered separately. New clothes were bought every year before *Rosh Hashana* and *Passover.* The clothes were used as initials. Atlas stood for *Ach Tov Leisrael Sela* (It is good for Israel) and Samut stood for *Sur Mera Veaseh Tov* (Get away from evil deeds and do good ones).

In Rokitno there were Jewish tradesmen of all kinds. They liked to sing as they worked. One could hear wonderful melodies from the windows of their workrooms. They sang sacred songs, pioneering songs and even a revolutionary one.

The storekeepers followed an unwritten, but obligatory, code of ethics. The area had many villages with their own Jewish stores. They sold on credit and every store had a thick, oily ledger where entries were written, such as: "I gave Ivan on this day..." "I received from Ivan today...". The peasants were habitual customers and the storekeepers would not accept a new customer unless they investigated why he had left a previous store.

The storekeepers were on friendly neighborly terms. In summer, they sat on tree stumps near the store and, when there was no action, they would chat and discuss world events and local problems: lawlessness, political conditions and taxes.

Sometimes they would discuss the cantor who visited recently, various funds and Eretz Israel. In winter, they would sit caged inside the store. The men wore wrinkled fur coats and the women warmed themselves near a potful of glowing embers, their hands covered in fingerless woolen gloves.

The noon meal was eaten quickly with a short catnap while still seated. Towards evening, there were more customers and the wife came to help her husband. The sunset reminded the shopkeeper of his obligations and he would take a short break from business to pray afternoon and evening prayers in the synagogue.

They came home late at night, frozen in winter and sweaty in summer. They looked in their credit ledgers and the tiny letters would put them to sleep after a hard day's work.

There were some Jews who made their living in the forests. They were inspectors of the cutting and subsequent transport of the lumber. They earned a good income, but no one envied them since they were away from family and community all week.

Aside from the fair in the village, eagerly awaited, there were also merchants who traveled to the fair in nearby Klesov. They suffered all night as they went in a horse-driven wagon and early in the morning they stopped at a self-made stall, emptied the wagon and wondered if they would be successful. They did not expect much and were satisfied with little.

Their life was hard and their income sparse, but they subsidized the household, celebrated Shabbat and holidays with food and drink, donated towards the Rabbi's upkeep and, most important, saved enough to pay the teachers' salaries.

Learning followed a well-known pattern. At first, there was a teacher of basics who taught understanding of the Bible and then another teacher for *Rashi* and *Gmara*. The next step was a more advanced teacher to teach *Tosafot* (annotations to the *Talmud*). After the Tarbut school was founded in Rokitno, most parents enrolled their children there. Some continued in high school and yeshivas in the big cities while others continued in the *Talmud Torah* school.

Poniatovsky Street

The worldview of these honest Jews was simplicity and innocence. During the week they were involved in everyday responsibilities while Shabbat and holidays were special times for the Jews. This is when they were able to devote themselves to G-d as if to make up for the weekday existence.

When the month of *Elul* arrived, the face of the town changed. The shadow of the approaching Days of Awe loomed over everyone. These were days of sanctity and cleansing. During the ten days of repentance, there were some people who would read the whole Book of Psalms daily. They began the reading in the morning in the synagogue and continued in the store between customers. On the eve of *Yom Kippur* they were more pious. Some would stand all day during prayer and there were others who slept in the synagogue after *Kol Nidrei.* When they felt that they had succeeded in being written in the good book, they returned as if reborn. Then everything would begin again.

They were conscientious about receiving guests properly. No guest was left, G-d forbid, standing near the furnace in the synagogue after prayers ended. Honored guests, special emissaries, ordinary people and passers-by were invited as

Shabbat guests into homes. This custom was steeped in a love for Israel and its people.

Those who were learned knew that it was written in the *Zohar* that the poor are the broken tools of G-d. On Shabbat and holidays, G-d comes to visit his broken tools and when he sees that no one is hosting them and that they are hungry and thirsty, he cries for them.

Although the Jews of Rokitno had dealings with non-Jews, they did not follow their customs. There was a division between them when it came to matters of faith and opinion. The locals fed calves for alien work and bowed to emptiness while we thanked and blessed our G-d for his creation. Faith sustained us and provided the source for educating the children for the continuity of the generations and for preventing the links from disintegrating. As Zionists, they encouraged the children when the children decided to go to a *preparatory kibbutz* and to make *aliyah*, since they hoped to follow them.

The Jews of Rokitno loved and sanctified life simply and innocently. The women, the mothers used the supplications of Sarah Bat Tovim and "The G-d of Abraham", composed for Rabbi Shmuel from Kaminka, Ukraine.

This is how generations lived and died, until the brigades of destruction came and with fury uprooted the tree with its seedlings and roots.

Everything disappeared and was eradicated. Now, only unknown graves remain. The remnants of Rokitno and surroundings gather under different skies and sanctify the name and memory of all those who had died in the name of G-d.

[Page 168]

Memories, Impressions and Happenings

Yeshayahu Meiri (Meirson) (Ramat Gan)

Translated by Ala Gamulka

Rokitno At The Crossroads

At the beginning of the 20th century, when it was decided to build the railroad from Kovel to Kiev, Rokitno, a small forlorn village, stood at the crossroads. There had been some Jews there before. With the building of the railroad, a new modern town was built, called Ochotnikov. It was named after Ochotnikov, a senator and a confidante of the Tzar. (The name was changed to Rokitno after World War I when Poland became independent.)

The main source of income of the Jews of Ochotnikov was the railway station. Agents, middlemen, hotel owners, storekeepers and grain merchants appeared. There were forests around our town and they served as a basis for the lumber and sawmill industries. The tar factories also served as an important source of income. One of them was owned by my uncle, Rav Avraham Zelig Guchberg. My father, living in Bersetchka, was asked to come and manage the tar factory. He opened a large warehouse for grain and flour. When this trade was well established, our entire family moved from Bersetchka to Ochotnikov. This was in 1906. The village was just beginning to develop and there were less than 10 houses there. The *Huta* (glass factory) was producing well and promised the village a brilliant economic future. Thus, Ochotnikov began to grow and to develop at a dizzying pace.

Study of Torah

When we arrived in Ochotnikov, there was neither day school nor *Talmud Torah* (supplementary school). There were no teachers. Some residents decided to invite a teacher to teach Torah in our village. The first teacher was Rav Yossel from Sloveshna who was excellent. After him came Leibl from Velednik. This teacher forced us to study in a loud voice and by the third day we were all hoarse. It is difficult to say that we really learned from this Rabbi but, to his credit, it must be said that he imbued in us the desire to learn Torah.

The next teacher was Rabbi Avraham, a knowledgeable man, well versed in worldly affairs. This Rabbi was the one who instilled in us the study of *Torah* and a deep understanding of *Gmara* and interpretations. He used the *yeshiva* method of study, mostly self-study. He gave us a class only once a week and on other days he assigned us a page of *Gmara*, which we had to learn by ourselves. He then tested us to see if we knew what we had learned. (In *cheder* language we called it "a *leinen*" - self study). We made progress in our studies and I was able to read a page of *Gmara* and to understand without difficulty. At my brother Zosia's *bris*, I read aloud the annotations "*Ein Mesichim Beseudah*" – (Do not talk during a meal) and Rabbi Shames gave a loving pinch.

The period of religious study only ended with Rabbi Avraham. Modern teachers came to Rokitno. Among them was Israel Tozman, who introduced the system of *Hebrew in Hebrew*. He also taught us secular subjects. This teacher was one of those who paved the way for the Hebrew school in Rokitno.

The Shocking Murder in Ochotnikov

When we moved to the new town, we opened a grocery store and grain storage in our house. On one of the market days, the proceeds were great and there were a few hundred rubles in the cash box. Most of it would be handed to one of the suppliers leaving on the evening train for Ovrotesh. We heard banging on the door accompanied by terrible threatening words: "Give us the money or I will kill you." My parents, unclear about self-defense, moved from the bedroom to the larger room, where my brother Yona and my sister Batya slept, to wake them up. They were concerned with the danger awaiting them and wanted to seek advice on how to defend themselves.

When my father opened the door to the larger room, the killer shot and hit the gas lantern that my father was holding in his hand. The bullet hit my father and he fell covered in blood. My mother began to cry and to scream for help. My sister Batya went out through the back door to call the neighbors. The killer, noticing that someone came out the back door, burst into the house and found Yona and my mother standing over the bed of my injured father. He shot my mother, the bullet hit her and he demanded from my brother all the money or else he would kill everyone. My brother asked my father to give the killer all he had. My injured father could not speak since he had lost consciousness due to the loss of blood.

Not waiting for an answer, the killer went over to my father, lifted his head and banged it on the wall. He took the purse from under the pillow and began to count the money in it. In the meantime, my sister returned with one of our neighbors, Ben Zion Geipman, a railway agent, a healthy and courageous man. Geipman entered the house in the dark and did not see that the killer was armed. He began to struggle with him, caught him by the throat and tried to throw him down. However, the killer did not lose his cool, shot Geipman twice and killed him.

The neighbors heard the shots and the screams and they immediately came to help. The killer became scared, shot a few times and fled from the house. Several months later, some of the money was found and the killer was arrested. He was sentenced to many years in prison. However, dear Mr. Geipman was no longer with us. I was only a child then, but I vividly remember the mourning that the small group of Jews in Ochotnikov felt when they heard that Ben Zion Geipman had been killed.

Everyone accompanied his body to the cemetery crying as if it had been their brother or son that had died. Geipman was loved by all those who knew him. All tore their clothing and mourned him.

A Heart-Wrenching Episode from World War I

One Friday in 1914, the beginning of World War I was announced in our town. The fear that gripped all the residents cannot be described. Immediately, it was announced that all young men were to be drafted. Rabbi Yossel Shames was still young and he, too, was to be drafted. He had served in the Russian army. He went to Kisorich, which served as a central place for all the draftees from the region. The Rabbi was then in mourning for his wife who had died less than 30 days earlier.

The Rabbi returned from Kisorich at sundown. He changed his clothes and rushed to the synagogue for Friday night services. He looked angry and somber. He began to pray *mincha*. When he reached the verse in "*Ashrei*", "G-d is close to all those who call in Him earnestly", he burst out crying and could not continue praying. All the congregants cried with him for a long time. The mourning was heavy.

However, the Rabbi's crying was heard in the heavens above and he was excused from the draft. He stayed with his congregation throughout the war and afterwards.

Father's House

My father's family was nurtured by the Trisker Court where Torah and commerce were intertwined. However, preference was given to Torah.

My father's attitude to Torah learning can be seen by the following event: When I was 11, I was studying with three other boys, under a Rabbi who was brought for a six-month period. He was paid a respectable amount and was also fed, clothed and shod.

One evening around *Hanukkah*, instead of studying the tractate of *Pessachim*, in addition to our weekly lesson in tractate of Shabbat, we played cards. My father came in and saw my transgression. He said nothing, but asked me to go over the *Gmara* lesson. I was well versed in *Gmara* and interpretations and I was able to repeat the lesson easily. When I finished, to my great surprise, my father slapped me twice. I asked: “Father, why are you doing this to me?” He replied: “The conclusion is that when you play cards, you are so knowledgeable in *Gmara*. If you did not play, you would know even more.”

My father's death was a shock to me. On the 23rd day of Adar 1933, he came home in the evening after helping my sister all day in her store. There was nothing wrong. He sat down with some neighbors and chatted with them. When they left he began reading *The Kuzari*, a book that he enjoyed. While he was reading he felt weak and went to bed where he died during the night. We found *The Kuzari* closed with his glasses inside as a bookmark.

My mother, may she rest in peace, left *The Kuzari* to me in her will and it is still in my library to this day.

The Library and The Struggle With The Bundists

There was a well-known family in Rokitno, the Polishuk family. Two of its sons were *Bund* leaders in Volyn. Their membership in the *Bund* was not merely ideological. They also fought hard against Zionism, Hebrew language, Hebrew school and any nationalistic spark.

In 1916-17, a movement opposing *Bund* arose in Rokitno. It was a strong group of *Tseirei Zion* who were educated in modern Hebrew literature and they were especially imbued with Mapu's love of Zion. They looked up to Zion and they began to prepare the younger generation for aliyah. They organized Hebrew classes, the Association of Speakers of Hebrew, information evenings and meetings with Zionist content. The town pharmacist, Noah Soltzman, belonged to *Tseirei Zion*.

The members of *Tseirei Zion* saw in the founding of a library, a means of increasing Zionist education. In those days, as it did in every village, the library served as a cultural center and as a hot house for the growth and nurturing of the Zionist dream. When the Zionist-nationalist direction of the library was decided, a hard struggle ensued with the Bundists. This was not only a struggle between two ideologies, but also between young and older. The Polishuks were, by then, over thirty years old, while the members of *Tseirei Zion* were younger.

Youthful ardor was the determining factor. The library was taken away from under the influence of the *Bund* and was now run by the Zionist youth. They showed great enthusiasm and endless devotion to the collection of books. To obtain a realistic description of the scope of the library, I must point out that all the books were contained in a small kitchen cupboard. It had been donated to us by one of the housewives. We kept a vigil on this cupboard 24 hours a day. The Zionist youths were afraid that the Bundists would attack it and remove the books.

The Zionist-inspired library was a drawing card for other cultural institutions in town. We, the Zionists, had our own corner for meetings and discussions of our plans as well as for attracting new members and the dissemination of the Hebrew language among the youngsters.

The number of volumes in the library was small. Every book acquired was known immediately by everyone. There was a long waiting list for each book. The thirst for Hebrew books was very deep and they were perceived as holy matter. Besides the books, we had subscriptions to *Hazman, Hatzfira* and *Haolam* (Hebrew newspapers). They contributed greatly to the development of Hebrew-Zionist awareness among the youngsters of Rokitno.

The First Refugees in Rokitno In 1914

When World War I broke out, the stream of refugees from Poland, which had been conquered by the Germans, grew. A group was organized in Rokitno to look after these refugees. When they passed through our town on the train, they were offered financial assistance and food.

One day a few refugee families arrived in Rokitno to stay. Among them was a Jewish family, nicknamed “The Poles”. After we found them lodging in Betzalel Kokel's house, we looked after their absorption. It was a family with many children, dressed in the traditional clothes of Polish Jews and following its customs.

All the young people in Rokitno saw it as their sacred duty to help in the absorption of this family and in accustoming them to everyday life. Actually, after some time, the head of the family opened a grocery store. We helped him by translating for the locals who did not understand his Polish. We looked after the education of the children. We did not stop our work until we saw that his economic situation was settled.

[Page 172]

The Rabbi from Stolin and His Followers in Rokitno

Shlomo Zandweis (Tel Aviv)

Translated by Ala Gamulka

Unfortunately, I can only write about the Karlin-Stolin *Hasidim* and their court. It is not possible for me to write about other *Hasidic* dynasties in Rokitno. These would be the *Hasidim* of the Brezne dynasty, from the court of our master and teacher, Rabbi Shmuelke and his son, our master and teacher, Rabbi Itzikel Pechnik, *z"zl*, our masters and teachers from the court of Rabbi Haimke Toibman from Brezne and his sons, our masters and teachers, Rabbi Aharale and Rabbi Gedalche, *z"zl*. I know they used to come to Rokitno to visit their flock. I also know that there were followers of the Trisker master and teacher in Rokitno. It is not only because I am a follower of Stolin that I want to speak only of them. G-d forbid! They were all holy and righteous (may their merits protect them). However, it is not possible for me to write about them because I do not know enough about them and their flock. I was not fortunate enough to be inspired by them, as I did not spend any time with them. I was educated in the house of my father and teacher, Rabbi Zadok. He was one of the pillars of the Stolin-Karlin *Hasidim*. He was a follower of our master and teacher, Rabbi Israel Perlov and was nicknamed the "nurturer" (*Hayanuka*) from Stolin by his followers and in the *Hasidic* movement. **[1]**

Although there were many followers in Rokitno, I do not recall that the Rabbi from Stolin came for visits for Shabbat or even during the week. Rabbi Israelke had many places to visit: Kiev, Zhitomir, Avrotch, Lutsk, Warsaw, etc. He could not have had time to visit small villages.

Since the Rabbi would visit the nearby villages of Olevsk and Sarny, the *Hasidim* from Rokitno and its surroundings went there to bask in his glory, to celebrate with our friends and to listen to the singing and praying. It was a great *mitzvah* for the *Hasidim* from Rokitno to go on this visit. The sayings of Rabbi Shlomo from Karlin, a pupil of Rabbi Aharon the Great, were etched in their hearts. He said: "The forests and fields which are traveled on the way to visiting the pious help in balancing the scale."

I recall that Rabbi Israelke sometimes stopped for a day or two in nearby villages and would be housed with his famous followers. In Blezhov, he stayed with R' Shalom Blizhovsky and his sons R' Itzie and R' Asher. In Brezov, he stayed with

[1] My father was so described by the *Hasidim* of Stolin-Karlin and his portrait appears in the collection "*Or Zarua*". These are articles and writings about the masters and teacher of the *Hasidic* movement of Karlin-Stolin.

R' Herschel Berezovsky, in Sahov with David Zunder and his son-in-law, R' Menachem-Zalman Briskman, *z"zl.*

R' Israelke died on the second day of *Rosh Hashana* in 1922 and was buried in Frankfurt-am-Mein. His son, R' Moshele, was crowned our master and teacher in Stolin. Most of the *Hasidim* of Rokitno remained loyal to R' Moshele, but some followed his brother, R' Melachlke, who was crowned master and teacher in Karlin.

Thus, only R' Moshele visited Rokitno and he stayed for seven days. These were days of holidays and celebration and uplifting of the spirits. The celebrations attracted not only the Stolin Hasidim, but also almost all the Jews from town and its surroundings. They came from near and far to listen to the Rabbi's wisdom, to receive his blessing, to consult with him on matters of income and matchmaking. They also presented him with "redemption" money, as was the custom in the courts of the masters and teachers.

The hosts, *Hasidim* of Rokitno, were very busy. Among them were R' Mendl Kercher, R' Aharon Levin, R' Herschel Shteinman, the brothers Yehoshua and Leibl Gitelman, may they be spared for life, and others. They served the visiting *Hasidim* who came from the surrounding areas, provided the food, drinks and lodgings. Particularly, they kept a vigilant eye on the Rabbi and did not budge from him. They encircled him, so it was difficult to approach him. After the Rabbi left the synagogue, or when he went back to his room in the inn, the *Hasidim* began to sing and dance with enthusiasm. They often danced on chairs and on tables.

The Rabbi would take part in their dancing only rarely and only on Saturday night during the *Melave Malka.* On weekdays, he danced on Tuesday evenings, a day or two before he left Rokitno. The *Hasidim* would then have a good-bye party. They sang and danced, nearly till dawn. The enthusiastic prayers and the dances warmed all hearts. They even danced in the streets, especially on Shabbat after services. After the big *kiddush* in the synagogue, the *Hasidim* went for *kiddush* in the homes of residents and friends. They started at the home of R' Aharon Levin and the *shohet and bodek* R' Yoel Schwartzberg, who both lived near the synagogue. They went to the town Rabbi, Rabbi Aharon Shames and from there to R' Leivik Rutman and the *shohet and bodek* R' Issachar Trigun. Then they went to the brothers Leibl and Yehoshua Gitelman and R' Mendl Kercher and ended up at the home of Baruch-Yoel Felhandler. They went from house to house, like on *Simchat Torah.* It was not only the *Hasidim* who felt the Rabbi's presence in Rokitno, but also the whole population, young and old. Even the non-Jews said to one another: "The Rabbi from Stolin came."

The preparations in Rokitno for the visit of the Rabbi and his followers began several weeks earlier, as soon as the Shabbat date was determined by the Rabbi. The followers from the area would come for the length of the visit. Extensive plans were made. Where should the Rabbi stay? (Usually he stayed at R' Moshe-Hirsch Linn's) Whom will the Rabbi visit? Who will lead the services, read the Torah, serve, sing, etc. Money was also collected for expenses.

Invitations were sent to followers in Sarny, Dombrovitz, Sahov, Tomoshgorod, Klesov, etc. The invitations were signed, in the name of all Rokitno Jews, by R' Hever Boktzer. R' Hever, the *shohet,* was close to 80, but he was full of energy and humor. He wrote the invitations in verse and metaphor. He had a saying and a metaphor for everything and everyone loved and admired him.

R' Hever nicknamed R' Moshe Hirsch Linn as "Rabbi Bar Tanura" **(2)**, (*tanur* = stove) since he was, by trade, a plasterer and a builder of stoves. When he saw a *Hasid* called R' Yehoshua in the synagogue wearing a new hat, he paraphrased a verse from *Anim Zemirot.* "Yehoshua, instead of *Yeshua* (redemption) wore a hat..."

The *Hasid,* R' Israel Fishbein from Sloveshnia, was once arrested by the authorities. He was accused of maintaining a relationship with his relatives in Poland and was imprisoned in Rovno. All of his friends worried about his fate and when the news came of his release, they ran to R' Hever to tell him. R' Hever was sick in bed, covered in his *talit,* wearing his *tefillin* and praying *shaharit.* He mumbled his prayers quietly, but when he reached "*Shmone Esre,*" he said out loud: "Blessed are you, G-d, the Redeemer of Israel."

R' Hever served as a *shohet* in his previous town of residence. However, when he aged, he settled in Rokitno. He stopped working and lived with his children. He was the prayer leader in Rokitno in the old synagogue and assisted at weddings. He was the master of ceremonies at circumcisions. When the Rabbi, R' Moshele, visited Rokitno, he sang his songs: on Friday night -- "Peace and Happiness" and at Shabbat lunch – "Blessed is G-d in Heaven."

Of the old *Hasidim* in Rokitno, I recall vividly one named R' Yehoshua Wolfin. He was nicknamed Yehoshua from Hrapuna by other *Hasidim.* This Jew was full of stories about our master and teacher Rabbi Israelke, *z"zl.*

R' Yehoshua earned his living by owning a millstone and a store. However, his wife and children were the workers while he served the Rabbi in his court. He would go to Stolin and often spent Shabbat and holidays there. When the Rabbi went to visit villages and towns scattered throughout the marshland of Pinsk, R' Yehoshua would accompany him. He sat next to the Rabbi in a cart or in a sled and served him, even though the Rabbi had a sexton and a *gabbai* with him. For him, it was a great *mitzvah* to serve a scholar. He listened to every word uttered by the Rabbi and remembered everything verbatim, even though he did not write it down.

Everything was stored in his memory bank and he talked of everything he saw and heard with trepidation. All the *Hasidim* surrounded him and listened, cupping their ears with their hands to hear better. They would shake their heads

[2] This is a pun. Rabbi Ovadia, son of Avraham Yera from Bartenura, was a Rabbi and an interpreter of Mishna who lived in the 15th century in Italy and died in Jerusalem in approximately 1500.

and, with a sigh of wonder, said: "His merit will defend us and the rest of our people."

R' Yehoshua traveled with Rabbi Israelke for about 40 years, summer and winter. When he became older, he sat in Rokitno with his grandchildren, great-grandchildren and all the *Hasidim* and told them about the wonderful miracles that happened on the way. He was certain that it was due to his following the Rabbi that he was never sick and that he lived to a ripe old age.

The *shohet and bodek*, R' Issachar Trigun, was different from the jolly and sharp R' Hever. He was always serious and his face was somber. It was obvious that he was a deep thinker and that he weighed every word before he uttered it. He often sang the song of R' Aharon from Karlin – "How I desire the beauty of Shabbat" [3]. Even when he stood far and the words were not heard, one could tell, by looking at his face, which stanza he was singing.

He sang the first stanza:

"How I desire the beauty of Shabbat,

The Shabbat which is special because of you,

Spread the beauty of your being on your people who follow you

Sanctify them with the Shabbat of your Torah

Open your gates to them."

He clapped his hands while he was singing happily. However, when he reached the third stanza, he would sigh and raise his eyes skyward:

"Have mercy on your holy people

Quench the thirst of your followers with a river from Eden

Crown your people with glory.

Your people who exalt you with Shabbat

For six days they inherit the legacy of Jacob."

In a mournful voice he would beseech G-d and he would repeat again: "Dear G-d, Have mercy on your holy people." It was as if he felt, in his gentle soul, that terrible events would be happening to the holy people

3] The Great R' Aharon composed "Song for Shabbat." In this song, he sings from his heart of the sanctity of Shabbat. The song is divided into 4 parts and the acronyms of the first three words of all 4 parts hint of Existence, Aharon, Soul. The *Hasidim* of Karlin sang it every Shabbat with a special tune.

The same happened after Friday night dinner, when they returned from synagogue to the Rabbi's lodgings. There the Rabbi would rest a little and read sacred texts.

When the Rabbi went to his *Hasidim*, R' Issachar would sing mournfully the song: "Protect the Fathers with your words." Full of yearning, he would repeat: "Oy, Protector of the Fathers with his words. Rejuvenator of the dead with his speech...We pass in front of him with fear and we thank him." He was full of love of Shabbat. The spirit of R' Issachar would rise upwards sweetly. "Shabbat is pleasant to the soul. The seventh day pleases the spirit."

The *Hasidim* of Rokitno were joyful and full of life. The Great R' Aharon said: "Sadness is not a sin, but the hardness of the heart caused by it is a greater sin."

The Hasidim were famous for their pleasant tunes. The Rabbi, R' Israelke, had musical talent. When the Rokitno *Hasidim* traveled to Olevsk and Sarny to listen to his tunes, they immersed themselves in a world of song and happiness, Torah and wisdom. They would divest themselves of everyday problems and became aristocrats. The *Hasidim* tell us that R' Israelke and his sons washed their hands in ritual before they performed on Shabbat evening. This meant they prepared themselves to do the holy work of the Levites in the Temple.

The *Hasidim* of Rokitno believed in Zionism. Love of Zion and Zionism were instilled in them by Rabbi Moshele who had visited Eretz Israel twice. (The first time was in the fall of 1933, when he returned from a visit to his father's grave in Frankfurt. The second time was in 1938.) He had strong impressions of the country. He searched and found the positive in the rebuilding of the country and he was happy with every innovation, creation and addition.

It is difficult to describe and to believe that all that is gone. The Jewish population of Rokitno was so full of life and energy. Those dear good Jews, charitable and hospitable were all slaughtered. The Rabbi? The shepherd followed his loyal herd. "The beloved in lifetime are not separated in death." May their memory be cherished.

[Page 177]

The Rabbi Comes to Town

Bat Sheva Fishman (Shohet) (Tel Aviv)

Translated by Ala Gamulka

The visit of the Rabbi in our town was an unforgettable experience. The ordinary face of the town was transformed. What uplifting of the spirits! An atmosphere of sanctity prevailed everywhere. I particularly remember the days the Rabbi spent in our house because he usually stayed in the home of R' Yeshayahu Gendelman.

The Rabbi, Rav Gedaltche from Brezne, was a relative of ours on my father's side. (My father, Haim-Yudel, came from Brezne from a family of rabbis, shohets and arbitrators.) Many weeks before the Rabbi's arrival, the *Hasidim* gathered in the evenings in our home. They discussed and debated how to receive the Rabbi and worked out every detail of his weeklong visit to our town. Sarah, my mother, worked hard to prepare for the event. The preparations were similar to those for Passover. The house was cleaned and shined and made fit to receive the Rabbi and his entourage.

The long-awaited Thursday came. It was the day the Rabbi was expected. All the Hasidim, headed by R' Aharon Shames, went to the railway station to receive him. Lucky was he who was greeted by the Rabbi as soon as he arrived. They all made their way to the house led by the Rabbi and those close to him, and followed by the *Hasidim*.

Friday night and Shabbat were spent in the old synagogue since it was the only appropriate location large enough to accommodate all the *Hasidim*. All heads of households left their homes for this Shabbat to sit at the "Rabbi's table."

On the next day, our house was full of visitors from dawn till late at night. The Rabbi sat in his room and received visitors with "notes." Each visitor would open his heart and tell all to the Rabbi as a blessing or intervention was requested.

Everyone who came out of the Rabbi's room felt as if a heavy load had been lifted from his heart. He encouraged everyone since it was obvious that the Rabbi's prayer would be received above.

We, the children, ignored school and homework and reading of books. These matters were forgotten during the Rabbi's visit. An unforgettable experience seized us – the sanctity of the Rabbi. Although we were warned, we still crept into the house through the back door. We stood on the kitchen threshold or in a hidden corner and followed, open-mouthed, all that was happening. We absorbed everything our young minds were capable of absorbing.

At lunchtime, the Rabbi sat at the head of the table and gave a sermon to the *Hasidim* seated around him. They were all listening intently and drinking in every word that came out of his mouth. The Rabbi seemed to be eating. He touched and tasted a morsel and passed it to others who attacked it and fought for it. Anyone lucky enough to taste something is the happiest person around.

Slowly, the *Hasidim* shed their stiffness and got up from the table. Arm on shoulder, their eyes closed, their faces inspired, they form a circle and with amazing enthusiasm, they begin to dance a long *Hasidic* dance. Everything is then forgotten. They leave the physical world and are transported higher up beyond the everyday gray existence. Who knows, maybe this is where the secret of our forefathers is hidden – how they managed to overcome their difficulties.

[Page 178]

The Choosing of a Rabbi in Rokitno

Aharon Lifshitz (Ramat Gan)

Translated by Ala Gamulka

R' Shraga Feivish Levin served as a Rabbi and *shohet* in the village of Rokitno. When the town began to develop and the number of Jews increased, a second Rabbi was needed and was sought.

In our town, there was a merchant named Aharon Yosef Shames. Although he was a businessman, he was a learned Jew and was certified to teach in the *yeshiva* of Rabbi Yoel Shurin (the "*Gaon* from Poltava") in Zvhil. The *Gaon* ("Genius") thought highly of his student. He, therefore, came to Rokitno, gathered the Jews and suggested that Rabbi Shames would be the most appropriate person to serve as Rabbi.

However, the wishes of the *Gaon* were not enough. The choosing of a Rabbi necessitated the stamp of approval of important citizens. Their opinion counted. They asked my father to be the first to sign. However, since he was a follower of R. Shraga Feivish, he refused to sign.

The *Gaon* spent several days in town and did almost nothing. A small percentage of the population did sign. When he saw that nothing was happening, he gathered some Jews, friends of my father's, in our home. They tried to persuade him to sign. However, my father did not budge because he highly respected the *Gaon* Shraga Feivish.

The *Gaon* lost his patience, arose from his chair, banged on the table and told my father: "I order you, in the name of our holy Torah, to sign!" My father respected learned men, especially this *Gaon* who had great authority in the Torah world. He changed his mind and signed. The others followed quickly. Rabbi Aharon Yosef Shames began to serve as a Rabbi in our town.

[Page 179]

The Old Shul

Yechiel Shohet (Ramat Gan)

Translated by Ala Gamulka

The Magen Avraham synagogue was the center of life for the Jews of Rokitno. The synagogue was busy and noisy every day of the year. At daybreak, the doors were opened to the worshippers in the first minyan and subsequent minyans. In the afternoons, they would gather for mincha and maariv. Those who wished to learn sat late at night and studied *Mishnah* and *Gmara* with annotations.

The synagogue was also used for discussions and decisions in matters of *kashrut* and non-*kashrut*, debates about inheritance and finances, and relations between people. All aspects of the life of the Jews in Rokitno were decided inside the walls of this old and sacred synagogue. The Rabbi officiated at marriages and bar mitzvahs in the synagogue. The members were always served liquor and the famous honey cake prepared by the celebrating family.

The synagogue had a festive aura on Shabbat and holidays, depending on the particular holiday. In the month of *Elul*, the spiritual preparation for the High Holy Days began. This month announced the beginning of autumn and was the month of *shofar* blowing. At the end of prayers, the *shofar* was blown every day. These *shofar* blowings attracted us, the children. We found many ways of practicing the blowing of the *shofar*. At night, in the cool nights of *Elul*, before daybreak, Yankel the sexton passed from house to house, knocked on the windows and called in a hoarse voice: "Jews, get up for *selichot*!" Mother and father arose from bed, careful not to wake up the children, dressed quietly and rushed to the synagogue for *selichot* prayers. This was repeated every *Elul*.

On *Rosh Hashana* the atmosphere of the approaching Day of Judgment enveloped everyone. Even Jews who all year did not come to pray, suddenly awoke to tradition and came to the synagogue. During the ten days of repentance, days of prayer and apology, the tension increased as *Yom Kippur* came closer.

Early in the morning on the eve of *Yom Kippur*, after a quick *shaharit* prayer, came the custom of releasing promises between man and G-d and the forgiving of wrongs between people. Jews made peace on this day, to be clean and worthy of a positive judgment.

An unforgettable event etched in my memory was the ceremony of the punishment by lashing -- forty less one. This was an ancient custom for those who repent. I watched with great interest as my father took off his shoes, lay down on a straw mattress and received his lashes willingly and with love.

On the eve of *Yom Kippur*, representatives of different organizations and institutions, JNF and *Keren Hayesod*, Burial Society, *Bikur Holim*, etc. appeared in the synagogue. They sat at tables, each one with his cause, to encourage the large audience to donate. At that time people were most generous.

It was time to eat the meal before the fast. Everyone hurried home. A few people remained to prepare the sand boxes for the memorial candles. These were large wax candles that every family prepared and lit in memory of their dear departed ones. At nightfall, the houses emptied and all the Jews streamed to the synagogue for *Kol Nidrei*.

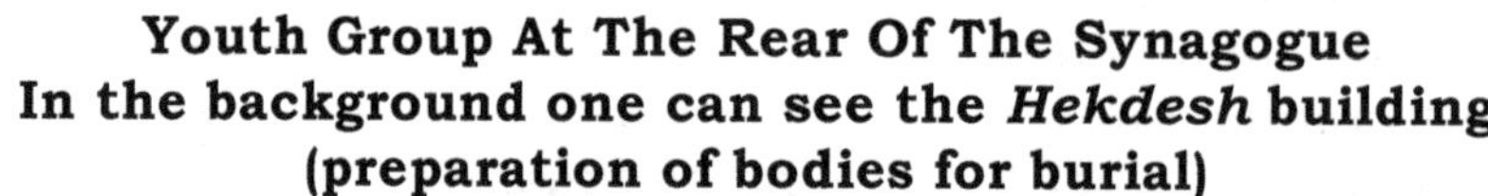

Youth Group At The Rear Of The Synagogue
In the background one can see the *Hekdesh* building
(preparation of bodies for burial)

The synagogue even looked different. An air of mystery hovered everywhere. All the worshippers were filled with awe and fear. The countless memorial candles added to the aura of trepidation.

The spiritual leader of Rokitno, Rabbi Aharon Shames, an aristocratic-looking man, touched our hearts with his *Kol Nidrei*. His praying was pure and entered our hearts. The synagogue was packed and filled with devotion, sanctity and an outpouring of souls. Everyone identified with the merciful G-d. The town was very quiet, as if the world was frozen.

On *Yom Kippur*, the town was empty. There was no sign of life on the streets. Everyone was in the synagogue. It was a long and great day of fasting and prayer. It began with the praying of *shaharit* by R. Betzalel Kokel and continued with the musaf of Rabbi Aharon. He was outstanding in his praying and he touched the hearts of the worshippers. The crowd reached a pinnacle of emotion during "*Unetane Tokef*" composed with blood and suffering by the saintly and tortured R. Amnon of Magentza. *Mincha* was led by R. Moshe Lifshitz. Many of the worshippers suffered a weakening of the senses. *Neila* was led by the Rabbi. The prayers ended with the blowing of the *shofar*. All wished each other a *Gmar Hatima Tova* (a good final judgment), went home and blessed the new moon.

The synagogue fulfilled an important place in the history of Jewish education in Rokitno. The first classes of the Tarbut school were founded there. Sounds of the Hebrew language emanated from there throughout Rokitno.

Several small buildings stood in the courtyard of the synagogue. On the right was the sexton's house, the middle building was used for preparing bodies for burial and the bathhouse was on the left.

[Page 181]

Rokitno at the End of the 1920s

Rachel Konopiata (Tel Aviv)

Translated by Ala Gamulka

In 1928 I was sent by the kindergarten teachers center in Warsaw to serve as a kindergarten teacher in Rokitno. The road to my job is etched in my memory. As the train approached Rokitno, the cars emptied and I found myself alone in the car. I felt uneasy. An uncomfortable feeling overcame me and I was transported to an ominous and secretive atmosphere.

Close to Rokitno, the door opened and a Polish gentleman entered the car. I later discovered he was the head of the secret service. Apparently, there was a network of Jewish and Ukrainian Communist youths in the outlying villages. The secret service kept a close eye on these villages.

He began to speak to me and asked me the purpose of my trip. While I was answering, a Jew entered and sat down at the other end of the car. I breathed a sigh of relief since I no longer felt alone. However, my relief was short-lived since immediately a band of Ukrainians burst into the car and began to mock the bearded Jew. To my surprise, the head of the secret service helped the Jew. He arose from his seat, pointed to his insignia and, miraculously, stopped the band of outlaws.

I did not stay long in Rokitno. I taught there for one year only, but it is well etched in my memory as a cultured and lovable place. The Jewish population kept its national outlook. Its ties with Eretz Israel were close. I don't think the Jewish youth was infected by Communism.

The youth of those days could be categorized in two groups. The majority were Zionist and longed to fulfill the dream. As proof of this was the *preparatory kibbutz* there. Many of the young people were preparing to make *aliyah* and were not afraid of the difficulties involved. The second group were "golden youth" in the positive sense of the term. They were not empty-headed, G-d forbid. They were cultured, healthy in mind and body, loved books and read Russian literature. They did not aspire to make changes in their lives and did not look up to Zion. They only wished to remain in town and continue to do business.

The Jewish population of Rokitno was not dogmatic. The pious Jew was not radical and was quite tolerant of others. For example, when the Rabbi from Stolin came, they all went to greet him. Even the non-believers donated to his cause. It looked odd to me, but to them it seemed natural and acceptable. They saw nothing wrong in their behavior. When I think back about this event, I am convinced that the Jews of Rokitno were, inadvertently, the pioneers of the Reform movement. They did not look askance at anyone who ate on *Yom Kippur* or smoked on Shabbat. I was involved with the community and I write these observations based on my visits to many Jewish homes in Rokitno. The community was progressive, from this point of view, and the youth were imbued with western culture. The secular and the religious were an integral part of their being and the result was a proud Jew who knew how to preserve his national character.

One of the highly respected homes in Rokitno was that of the Geipman family. It was a big and spacious house in the center of town. The rooms were large, as were the hearts of the owners. There was a mother, two sons and a daughter. It was a cultured and hospitable family. The house was always open to visitors.

One of the important locations in those days was the one housing the *preparatory kibbutz*. The Zionist youth met there for discussions, amusement, ideological debates and other occasions. The young people of Rokitno left home and lived on the *kibbutz* because it was theirs. They were always interested in all that was happening there. Occasionally, they went together to regional conferences in one of the other *preparatory kibbutzim*. It was an interesting and important event in the lives of the Zionist youths in Rokitno.

Rokitno was a small town, but it produced good and loyal offspring. They were loyal to their people and to their homeland. My heart aches that so few of them survived.

[Page 183]

A Pioneer Makes Aliyah

Dov Ben Yehoshua (Vorona) (Tel Aviv)

Translated by Ala Gamulka

In 1929, the *Hechalutz* headquarters organized a group of movement members who wished to make *aliyah*. They did not have exit visas from the Polish authorities. This was either because of the draft or for other reasons. This *aliyah* proceeded in two directions: one group went through Berlin and the other through Vienna. At the border, professional smugglers waited together with members of the movement. They helped our members to cross the border without difficulties.

The *aliyah* committee of my *kibbutz* decided that I would leave for Warsaw from the Sarny train station on a Sunday. On Friday, I returned to Rokitno to prepare for my trip. Few knew about it. On Shabbat we received the terrible news about the massacres in Eretz Israel, known as the massacres of 1929. I feared that my trip would be stopped, but the *Hechalutz* headquarters announced that no changes would take place and that we were still going.

I was afraid that my departure from Rokitno would be revealed and I left home in secret. My father said: "Go son. We will meet at the train station." I walked the streets of Rokitno with a sad heart. I was homesick. I grew up here and my roots were here. I knew the war years, but I also had happy times in this generous village. The last stand came. It was the end. I would never again see these fields, streets and lanes.

On the way I met Bender, the husband of my niece Rosa. I weighed telling him about my trip. Without thinking, I blurted: "I am going to the train station. I am leaving Rokitno forever". He blessed me and promised to come to the station.

It was a quick parting. My father shook my hand, kissed me and told me to take care of myself because things were bad in Eretz Israel at this time. He was followed by Bender. He, too, quickly bade me good-bye and left the car. I sat alone and I remembered the poet's words: "No people, no country, no G-d and no person." My heart rejoiced that I had reached the big moment in my life and I was on my way to my desired homeland. Our people will be rejuvenated. G-d and country will be with me and I will be a free man. However, I was also fearful, not knowing if I will be successful in crossing the border. I had no official documents allowing me to leave the country.

The whistle of the locomotive interrupted my sad thoughts. I calmed down. I reached Warsaw and found there friends from Klesov who were also on their way to Eretz Israel. The plan was for us to go the Czech border where we would join a group of hikers. They had permission to cross the river within a radius of 20 kilometers without being stopped. This was according to a cultural agreement between Poland and Czechoslovakia. It was decided that as soon as we would cross the border we would distance ourselves from the group of hikers. We would then reach the train station and go to the Czech -Austrian border. We would cross it illegally and continue on to Vienna.

In order to ensure success, we broke up into small groups. I left Warsaw with my friend, Alenboim, from Klesov. We were dressed as boy scouts. We purchased the outfits in the flea market in Warsaw. Dressed in these uniforms, we sat on the train, which made its way to Zakopny, a famous resort town.

We spent two weeks in Zakopny. We intermingled with the hikers who were most enthusiastic about nature. Our hearts were not capable of rejoicing with every tree and every clearing. We were worried about how and where we would leave these hikers to reach our destiny.

When we reached the train station, we carefully moved away from the hikers and we remained alone. Only my friend and I were there. We removed from our clothes all signs of the country we had just left and we waited for the Czech train going to Brin. We would be met there by members of Bloy Weiss. Late in the evening, we reached Brin. Our friends were waiting as planned and the next morning we continued to Marish-Austro. When we arrived there, we were disappointed. No one was waiting for us. We decided to go to a local member's house to find out what happened. It turned out that the person who was to meet us fell ill and no one could replace him. After some discussion with our sick friend, we decided to continue on our way. According to his instructions, we were to take a bus to the border. When we got off the bus, we were to enter the forest and after walking for an hour we would reach a shallow river. The river was the border between Czechoslovakia and Austria. After we crossed it, we would be in Austria.

We rode to the Austrian border and we hoped to cross it without any difficulties. The Jews of Marish-Austro accompanied us with love and worry.

We reached the place and entered the forest. We walked an unmarked path. We thought we were lost and that we would never reach our destination. Suddenly, the beautiful river was there. Crystal clear water was quietly flowing, surrounded by greenery and mountains. There was no time to enjoy the scenery. We quickly undressed, put the pile of clothes on our heads and we successfully crossed the river. We got dressed and we found ourselves in Austria.

The plan was for us to reach Graz and to board the Vienna train at 6:00 P.M. We reached Vienna by 10:00 P.M. on a Friday night. We had the address of the *Palestine Amt* Office, 2 Kertner Street. We rang the bell, but no one answered. We began to worry. Where would we sleep? Who do we go to? What should we do? We had no documents of any kind.

We had no choice but to ask one of the passers-by how to enter the office. In our incoherent German, we made quite an impression. To our surprise, we received a reply, in simple Yiddish, that the office was closed on Shabbat. We need not worry. Help was coming. It turned out that the man was a Zionist and knew about illegal immigration. He brought us to a hotel and arranged a place to sleep.

According to Austrian law, we should have gone to the police station to report that we had smuggled ourselves across the border. We would have been fined and that would have been the end of it. However, our situation was unusual. We had no documents since our friends in Brin took them away from us. They thought that if we would be caught it would be better not to have any documents whatsoever. They promised to send us the documents care of the *Palestina Amt* [Palestine Office] in Vienna. We waited over a week. We telephoned and were told they had been mailed. We figured that the documents were lost and we decided to report to the police without them. We hoped things would work out.

We came and told them that we had crossed the border and that we had no documents. We were put in central prison for 12 days. A lawyer called Finkelstein was asked to defend us. He succeeded in freeing us. We were given one week to leave Austria.

We managed to organize all the formalities and we obtained a visa. We left Vienna and arrived in Trieste. We boarded a ship on the eve of *Rosh Hashana* 1929. We had neither cabin nor food. We slept on deck and we ate whatever we had brought with us. The days and nights were warm and we did not suffer from the cold. On Friday, the eve of *Shabbat Shuvah* - the Shabbat between *Rosh Hashana* and *Yom Kippur* - we landed in the port of Jaffa. We were accompanied by a police guard since the country was not calm yet after the massacres of 1929. This is how I immigrated to Eretz Israel.

[Page 185]

The Rioters of Petlura in Our Town

Aharon Lifshitz (Ramat Gan)

Translated by Ala Gamulka

One week before *Hanukah* in 1918, I accompanied my father to the train. He was going to Zhitomir. When we reached the station, during twilight hours, the stationmaster advised us to return home. He told us to hide there all night since a train full of Petlura's rioters had reached Olevsk. The rioters attacked Jews.

At 10:00P.M. we heard the wheels of the train approaching the station. A few minutes later we were overcome by screams and shouts of the wild mob. My father's sister, Mushka Grinshpan and her husband, Levi, lived across from us. They owned a grocery store. Loud bangs on the door of the Grinshpan's house frightened us. These were Petlura's rioters who came to rob the store. They stole cigarettes and candies and disappeared, shouting wildly and cursing.

The next morning, before dawn, a shot was heard. Carefully and fearfully, we opened the shutter to see what was happening in town. A neighbor came in and told us the terrible news. David Zunder, the owner of the glass factory, had just been dragged out of his house, taken to the train station and killed. We then understood the meaning of the shot we heard. It was the first Jewish casualty. There was great panic in town and all were petrified and terrified.

In spite of the danger, many Jews gathered to pay their last respects to the deceased. When they reached the lodgings of the glass factory workers, armed soldiers appeared and ordered them to disperse. All escaped and abandoned the cart with the body on the street. A little later, a few Jews, among them my father, Moshe Lifshitz and Alter Weisblat, dared approach the cart. They traveled to Osnitzek and buried the deceased properly. The widow, Batya, and her daughter, Rivka, lived in our house until they made aliyah in 1925.

One winter night we heard banging on the door. We were afraid to open, fearing the rioters. However, we heard Yiddish speech, saying: “Moshe, Moshe, open the door!” It was Binyamin Meirson. He entered, accompanied by a commander of Petlura's soldiers and another soldier. They sat at the table and the commander said that he was stationed, with his unit, at the Tomoshgorod train station. The soldiers were hungry and thirsty, but he would not let them abuse the public. However, he could not hold them back much longer. To save the Jews, he asked to be supplied with sugar, flour and other provisions. To prepare these provisions, it was necessary to call a meeting. In those days, there was a temporary police unit. Two policemen were sent to call the Jews to our house.

There was a Polish worker called Bolik Piskovsky who worked in the glass factory. He was infamous as a thief and a criminal. When he saw the door to our house open, he entered, kissed the commander and asked him: “Why are you asking charity from the Jews? I have resources at my disposal which will scare the Jews into giving you everything they have.” As he spoke, he placed a live grenade, a revolver and a big knife on the table.

He immediately pulled the safety latch and he was ready to detonate. At the last minute, the commander grabbed the drunken Bolik's hand and shouted: “The matter is finished. Get help!” Those remaining in the room were Zvi Gilman and my sister Haya-Sarah. Gilman grabbed the killer, put him on the couch and tied his hands and feet with a towel. The commander was ready to kill him on the spot, but my mother and sister begged him not to do it in the house because it would cause retaliation from the friends of Piskovsky. He was taken away from the house and brought to the commander's car. After that, all the provisions were collected and the town was saved from the rioters.

The terrible ordeal convinced everyone that it was necessary to organize to save lives and belongings. A town committee was elected, headed by a Pole named Gortziongal. He fulfilled his task with loyalty and devotion. When the ruling powers changed, he went to the train station, met with the commander and asked him to direct any requests to the population through him. He never forgot to add: "If you intend to kill a Jew, kill me first."

[Page 187]

The Hill Behind the Bridge

Shmaryahu Kravi (Korobochka) (Herzliah)

Translated by Ala Gamulka

It is spring. The sun is just emerging from the misty skies and sending its rays to the green fields lying all around. Here and there, puddles glisten as if they were forgotten after the last rain. They reflect the sunrays. The colorful flowers add a special beauty to the greenery. One can see young children collecting flowers to bring home.

In those days, the river overflowed. It meanders and crosses the grass covering the hills and under a strong steel bridge. The partitions on both sides direct the speeding train going from Sarny to Ostoki. The area shepherds direct the cows of the town residents. Their loud whistles interrupt the quiet of the morning and their shouts wake up the dogs. Their barking is swallowed in the rest of the sounds and completes the excitement of the morning.

Young men and women, dressed in their uniforms of gray shirts and colored ties, begin to appear next to the train tracks. They are organized according to movement unit and level. The big hill on the other side of the bridge was part of the still of the night only a few minutes earlier. Suddenly, it is full of life and youthful happiness. It is Saturday. *Hashomer Hatzair* of Rokitno has chosen this day to hold its general roundup in the heart of nature. There is no better place than these wide areas among the green trees on the hill.

One by one they arrive. They come in groups, knapsacks on the back and regimental flags in the hand. Their singing and youthful laughter are heard far away. The units stand in pre-arranged groups. The leaders are presented to the commander, Michael Berezovsky, nicknamed Misha. The song "*Anu Olim*" bursts and fills the air. It can be heard beyond the hill. The festive occasion and the feeling of sanctity fill the entire camp with trepidation.

The presentation has ended. The boys and girls disperse in groups. Each one is in his own special area and every group decides its agenda. It was prepared ahead of time. "The Sparrows," one of the groups, organized games. The children skip and jump around their counselor. The cubs and scouts organize scouting activities. The senior group meets away from the others to discuss important matters.

Even the sun does not stay in place. It rises and reaches the center of the sky. Many Polish youngsters, on school vacation, also gather and follow our activities with curiosity. The presentation itself brings a feeling of respect. The title "Jewish Scouts" stops the Polish youngsters from provoking us. They do not dare interrupt the presentation and to fling their usual insults at groups or individuals. They know that this Jewish group will give back more than they got.

Many of the town youngsters were excited about life. They enjoyed the holidays completely. All of them, without exception, found great relief in nature far away from town. Early on, these youngsters had strong ties to nature and to everything in it.

When the official part ends, the youngsters go into separate groups. Some pick flowers to bring home to their parents, to appease them. Some go for a dip in the cool waters of the river. Others go to be alone with their boy or girl friends. They are then called back to join the circle dances in the clearing.

Today, I think back and remember the not so distant past. These were days spent in the movement, learning, playing sports, loving Zion and wishing to become pioneers. I see continuity between these days and the darkest days in our history, when the image of man was kept still alive. The Rokitno youngsters became counselors and leaders in the exile in the Soviet Union. Even there they were not swept up by the filthy stream. They did not forget what they learned in their childhood and they never looked for the easy way out. They always chose to do whatever helped the collective war effort against the Nazi beast.

They were among the first to find a secret way to their homeland. They endangered their lives by crossing borders and bypassing guards, in forests, behind enemy lines, with the partisans. They showed unbelievable courage by taking an active part in defeating the enemy. These youngsters also were involved, day and night, in smuggling the survivors of the Holocaust.

It is not by accident that hundreds of our town folk streamed to the homeland and they were not, as were others, drawn to other developed countries. In the modern "departure from Egypt" there were many young men and women who were nurtured in the Tarbut school and the youth movements. They revived the survivors from Rokitno and brought them to safety.

Railroad Track Over The Bridge

***Hashomer Hatzair* Branch In 1935 at One of its Activities on the Hill Behind the Bridge**

[Page 190]

Eight Oaks Grew in Our Yard

Hagai Baum (Natanya)

In memory of the house of David Baum

Translated by Ala Gamulka

The trees grew before I was born and before Rokitno became a town. They were not single trees then. The area was full of forests. Rokitno slowly became a town, when it was subdivided and fenced in. Houses were built and the forest was cut down. Trees were left here and there, among them the eight trees in our yard.

There were Jews in Rokitno and the children had to be educated. The parents arranged for a *cheder* and a *Talmud Torah.* As Rokitno developed quickly, the Jews thought that this was not enough and decided to found a progressive secular school. This is how the Tarbut school came into being. It did not yet have its own building. The school was housed in several rented locations and the classes were scattered. Several active people dedicated themselves to the collecting of funds needed to construct the school building. The Jews of Rokitno responded positively and with dedication. This was an important project and each one gave according to his ability. The committee assessed those who were wealthier.

Although my father was busy managing his shop, he was a lover of nature. In summer, he worked lovingly in our vegetable garden. There were also eight trees that were cherished by him, for it was a beautiful place and all the children in the area enjoyed it too. The bravest among them climbed on the trees and performed acrobatics. The less adventurous stood beneath and admired their friends. They caught the acorns thrown to them. Somehow, they felt togetherness with their antics.

The collection for the school building was announced. One evening, the committee members came to my father for his contribution. He donated four trees for the construction. The trees were transported for storage. I cried bitter tears when they were cut down. I mourned them as one mourns a living person. All the neighborhood children, who spent many hours playing near them, joined me.

We were happy that the trees were not used for heating purposes, but were taken for a noble purpose. There was an announcement in school that one morning all the pupils were to help heap sand before the floors were finished. All the pupils came to help. I remember, when I was still small, that I made plans with my friend Baruch Shuber, to walk together on that day. We arose early and we went to the building to pile sand. We had no tools. We used broken pieces of wood to move the sand. At 8:00 A.M. most of the other pupils arrived with their teachers and began to work with youthful enthusiasm.

The remaining four trees in our yard served as the foundation for the new Polish elementary school building. Some of the Jewish children in Rokitno attended the school.

[Page 191]

Memories of a Rokitno Communist

Yosef Gendelman (Givatayim)

Translated by Ala Gamulka

The Communist party in Rokitno was founded around 1925. It was not a very large party, but it made its presence felt. The main reason for founding the party in our town was the miserable status of the laborers and tradesmen. They worked 10 - 12 hours a day for little pay and no one took up their cause.

We began to organize these workers. We explained to them that their situation was not carved in stone. It could be changed if they would realize it and stand up for their rights. Workers' strikes broke out after these organizing activities. They demanded better pay. The employers did not, of course, remain silent after these activities. Police involvement followed. They tried to suppress the activities of our party.

In 1930, the Polish police in Rokitno executed numerous arrests of members of the Communist party and its followers. I, too, was arrested. We were held for two months by the police in its cellars until the end of the investigation. We were then transferred to a prison in Rovno. We waited for two years until the trial. Seventy people from the area were placed on trial. Very few were released. The judgment was quite severe. We were sentenced to 6 to 12 years.

After the court decision, we were transferred to Shedlitz. We sat in jail for 6 months and then we were moved to Drohovitz. We stayed there in jail for a year. In that jail we "dared" ask for human rights and political privileges. For this "daring" we were exiled to the fortress of *Swiety Krzyz* (Holy Cross) near Kelc. It was one of the worst prisons in Poland. It was carved into a mountainside more than 600 years ago. It was first used as a holy mosque. It was then turned into a secular prison for political prisoners. The walls were built with gable stones, over 3 meters thick.

Conditions were very poor. We slept on a stone floor and the cold penetrated every part of the body. At night we were ordered to undress down to our shirts. It was a surefire way to impede our escape. Every night, at 7:00 P.M., there was roll call. The windows were open and we stood barefoot on the cold floor for one whole hour.

I sat in jail for 5 years, from 1934 to 1939. Two other Jewish Communists from Rokitno were with me. In 1939, we were moved eastward out of the prison. We were bound in chains, hungry, sick and weak. It was a convoy of 1500 prisoners. Anyone who complained that walking was difficult was shot on the spot. We walked for ten consecutive days. On the 17th of September 1939, we reached

Kovel. The Soviet army had, by then, crossed the border and arrived in Kovel. As it entered the town, the prison doors of Kovel were opened and we were liberated.

I immediately returned to Rokitno. It was already in the hands of the Soviet army. On the strength of my rights as a veteran Communist and a loyalist to Communism, I became a member of the town council. From an economic point of view, as well as a municipal one, we did our best to prevent any wrong to be done to the Jews of Rokitno.

[Page 192]

The Torture Cellar in the Palace

Yosef Segal (Neve Oz)

Translated by Ala Gamulka

Since it was a border town, the Polish authorities built army barracks in Rokitno. It was in open area, at the end of Poniatovsky Street. The border patrol, consisting of foot soldiers and cavalry, was housed there.

The authorities also founded the infamous *Defansiva* (secret service). It was a branch of the counter espionage of general headquarters in Warsaw. The *Defansiva* spied on the Soviets, fought smugglers and Soviet espionage. It was headed by officers from the permanent army units and some White Russian officers who had remained in town after World War I. In the *Defansiva* were all kinds of questionable types of stoolies who sold themselves for the generous funds paid.

The *Defansiva* was housed in the palace, in the Rosenberg's park, in the shadow of the thick trees across from the train station. The broken-down palace was renovated and refurbished. The offices and interrogation rooms were on the top floor and the cellars were fitted with prisoner cells. They were turned into torture chambers.

All kinds of suspects were brought to the palace. They were interrogated and indictment papers were drawn up. They were then brought to trial in the regional courthouse in Rovno.

The palace was closely guarded inside and outside by soldiers. There was no entry allowed. During interrogations, usually held at night, the prisoners were cruelly tortured to force confessions, even from the innocent. Many paid with their lives as a result of these tortures. The bodies were taken out secretly and thrown into one of the lakes near Rokitno. At night, the screams of those interrogated frightened the town residents.

In the thirties, anti-Semitism was surging in Poland and the Polish government was competing with Nazi Germany. The *Defansiva* in Rokitno decided to show the height of hatred and to "prove" the disloyalty of the Jews to Poland.

One summer night in 1936, before dawn, four Jews from Rokitno were taken out of their beds and thrown into the torture cellars of the *Defansiva*. Their homes were searched. The four were: Aharon Burd, Moshe Schwartz (Sliep), Moshe Yankel Grinshtat and Betzalel (Zalek) Kaplan. They were all well-known Zionists and honest men.

Rokitno was in turmoil. All worried about their fate and sympathized with their families. The sorrow and grief of the parents and relatives of the prisoners were boundless. The parents stood for days at the fence of the *Defansiva* to find out the fate of the detainees. They were not successful in finding out any details.

Some time later, the parents received the bloodied underclothing of the detainees. It was proof of their being tortured.

While the detainees were in the cellar, the members of the *Defansiva* made surprise nightly raids on their homes. They even emptied the water from the ritual bath in Moshe Yankel Grinshtat's yard and searched for evidence in its bottom. The four detainees were thus tortured for six months. They were finally released and exonerated by the prosecution in Rovno. There had been no proof whatsoever.

When the news of their release was heard, the Jews of Rokitno were deliriously happy. All greeted each other with "*Mazal Tov*". Finally, the false charges were discovered. They were accused of crossing the border to the Soviet Union, to Olevsk and of participating in a Soviet parade there. At the same time, they had pictures taken with Soviet officers and received orders to bomb the barracks in Rokitno. As proof, the *Defansiva* showed a "photograph" taken in Olevsk.

All the detainees withstood the torture, except for Moshe Yankel Grinshtat. He returned from prison broken in mind and body. The detainees kept silent and did not speak of the tortures they had suffered.

The sudden appearance of the Soviet army on 17.9.1939 was a surprise to the members of the *Defansiva*. They did not have time to destroy their files. They feared capture by the Soviets and they left Rokitno in haste, fleeing westward. All the files and materials were transferred to the Soviet authorities.

The building then served the Soviets and the Germans when they were in our town - for the same purpose as it served the Poles.

[Page 195]

I Made *Aliyah* on the Eve of the Holocaust

Sarah Yasmin (Schwartzblat) (Haifa)

Translated by Ala Gamulka

I was a young girl when I saw that the Polish friends, who only yesterday ate and drank at our table and toasted our health, suddenly changed. They showed their anti-Semitism. It was the first warning that difficult days lay ahead.

I always dreamed of making *aliyah* and the change of atmosphere hastened my decision to do so. These were days when *aliyah* was limited by the White Paper. I decided, therefore, to join the *aliyah* group organized in Warsaw by the Revisionists.

I was on my way on February 21, 1939. I went with Syoma Eidelman and Modrik. We left town secretly. Although all was done in secret, many people came to the train station to say good-bye. I was very excited and afraid that I was seeing my dear ones for the last time.

I went to Warsaw. As I was walking through the city, I saw many anti-Semitic attacks and I thought the ground was going to swallow me. From Warsaw we went to Sniatin. We traveled silently all night in a darkened train car. No one spoke. Our only baggage was backpacks, a Hebrew-Polish dictionary and some addresses of our former town people in Eretz Israel. Our passports included visas for San Domingo. We reached Constanza and we boarded a rickety freight ship meant to carry cattle. We hid under the decks so the British would not see that human beings were on board. As luck would have it, the ship had already been in Eretz Israel and had been photographed by the British. The captain refused to set sail. Four days later, another ship, called *Kafu* arrived. It took our 700 people and set sail on the open seas.

When we were in mid-sea, we were permitted to go on deck to get fresh air. The sanitary conditions were very poor. Two weeks later, there was little food and water. Every morning we had to line up to receive our food and water rations. A few days later, there was no fresh water left and we drank seawater.

It took us three weeks. Once we woke up at night, petrified, because we had been flooded. We were ordered to go on deck and to get into the lifeboats. The ship hit a sandbank near Crete and was beginning to sink. We were forced to leave our meager belongings and we went on the island with nothing. The rescue activities continued feverishly. There were doctors among us and they took care of those who fainted from weakness and terror.

We remained on the cold cement of the lighthouse on Crete watching the ship sink in front of our eyes. The immigrants looked awful. Women and children were crying bitterly. Everyone asked: "What is waiting for us?" We stayed two days on the island and the local residents brought us food and water. We waited in fear for what was coming. We signaled SOS for help. Two days later, an immigrant ship called *Katina* approached the shore. It had been on the seas for 7 weeks and had close to 1000 immigrants from Germany, Austria, the Balkan countries and Poland. It took us in.

The conditions on *Kafu* had been primitive, but enough to bring us to safety. This new ship had unbearable conditions. We slept under the docks, squashed like sardines. We could move neither arm nor foot. Our daily rations consisted of lice, filth, lack of food and water, futile fights.

Our chances to reach Eretz Israel were dim. Several times we neared the shore, but we were forced to retreat. The British airplanes photographed the ship and followed it. One dark night, we were told to be prepared to disembark. We approached the port of Natanya one cold night in March. The ship docked about 20 meters from shore. Women and children were the first to disembark. Young men from *Haganah* swam over and put a woman or a child on their backs. We swam in stormy waters. When we reached land, we walked cautiously into a packing house in an orange grove. We waited there till morning, wet and very hungry.

As soon as the women and children managed to reach the shore, a British airplane appeared in the sky. It noticed the ship and forced it, with the men still aboard, to sail back into the sea. The women and children remained on shore while the husbands and fathers sailed to unknown places.

In the morning, representatives of the Jewish Agency came to the orange grove. They distributed buttered rolls and oranges. We were worn out, dirty and hungry and we did not know our fate. Still, we breathed a sigh of relief because we were in our homeland.

What happened to the ship and the men? The ship came close to land several times. It was finally caught by the British and towed to the port of Haifa. All aboard were arrested and placed in Atlit prison. A mass demonstration was organized in Haifa to insist on their release. I, too, joined the demonstration. It was not successful and the Jewish Agency had to use up official certificates of entry for all the immigrants. These certificates were subtracted from the original schedule. All the prisoners were released.

The story of the ship even reached Rokitno. It was reported on the radio that the ship had sunk with all its passengers. Our home was in mourning. However, when they discovered that I was saved, there was much jubilation in our house.

Although the suffering was great and the trip was fraught with danger, I was very sorry that only a few were, in this way, saved from the Holocaust.

[Page 197]

PERSONALITIES

[Page 199]

Rabbi Aharon Joseph Shames

Rabbi Yakov Pinchas Shir (Tel-Khanan)

Translated by Thia Persoff

The Rabbi's house on Main Street, at the center of town, stands out among its neighbors – the stores at its sides and across the street – in its uniqueness, exuding peace and splendor.

During the day and late into the night, the melody of the *Gmara* wafts from the house, the Rabbi's Torah chanting which imbues an atmosphere of purity and holiness.

Rabbi Aharon Joseph Shames

At a young age, in the year 1935, I left home and emigrated to Israel. I did not have much chance to breathe this atmosphere, but the short time that I was there left its mark on me, and its impression was indelible. I will try to describe those impressions in a few lines.

Our sages of blessed memory defined the Holy Temple and called it *Telpiyot*- a hill (*tel*) that all the mouths (*piyot*) are looking towards. Such was the house of Grandfather, holy *tzadik* of blessed memory, (*z"l = zichron tzadik livracha*) in town - everyone's house, open to all - whether for consultations, questions of law, arbitration, or for matters of charity. Between these walls, couples suffering from family problems found remedy, and persons in dispute or quarrel made peace. Even the *goyim* in town and the surrounding area would go to him when in dispute - trusting him to judge and decide. The house was open to any embittered soul, widows and the poor, every person in distress went in with a heavy heart and exited much relieved.

When an emissary (*ShD"R. = Shliakh de Rabbanan*) from a Jewish institution, or a *tzadik* came to town, this was his home. He was given the best room and never refused hospitality. There were dangerous cases - when a refugee from over the border came, when fugitives from the sword were hunted. All were welcomed, clothed, sheltered, and before leaving, supplied with provisions. All this was done just a few meters from the local police station, while scared but not showing it, so that the guest will not feel bad, G-d forbid! [*Chet"Vav* = chalilah ve'chas]

I remember the days approaching *Pesach*: it was a very busy time in the house, with extensive preparation to supply the needy with *matzot*, potatoes, *borsht* and wine for the holidays. All this was done in the evenings, secretly, so as not to embarrass the needy. The preparation and distribution of the *charoset* was also done. How fairly Grandmother, of peaceful memory (*a"h = aleha ha'shalom*), had divided the *charoset*. She gave generously and with good will.

The days of the *Sukkot* holiday, the blessing of the etrog- when Grandfather, *a"h*, would stand waiting for the sunrise on the first day of the holiday to do the *mitzvah* of blessing the etrog at the proper time. The other householders were already waiting to join the Rabbi in the blessing.

The jewel in the crown was *Simhat Torah*, the *Kiddush* at the holiday eve, and the joyful festivity that enveloped all the town's residents the next day, when all of them would come to Grandfather's house, *a"h*, to enjoy the handiworks of Grandmother, may her soul rest in paradise (*n"e = nishmata b'eden*), and felt at home there.

Grandfather, *a"h*, was tall of stature, great in the Torah; he was a student of the *Gaon*, our teacher and Rabbi (*mvhr'r = morenu ve'rabenu ha'rav*) Rabbi Yitzhak Elkana from Kovna, *z"l*. He was sharp of mind and his wisdom was well known in the whole area. He was very intelligent. He was good hearted and generous with a helping hand to all. He was modest in his ways; he liked his congregants and was liked by them. He used to sign his name Aharon Yosef Shames in acronym,

A.Y.Sh. (in Hebrew it is *ish*, meaning man)- and truly, he was a man of all the best qualities.

He went to the killing-grounds with his congregants, but managed to escape from there at the start of the slaughter, until the evil ones, may their names be erased (*YM"Sh = yimakh shmam*), killed him on the 13th of the month of *Elul*, in the year *TSh"B* (5702). G-d will avenge his blood (*HY"D = Hashem yikom damon*).

Grandmother Lea Rickl, *z"l*, his helpmate, was the daughter of a scholar and a scholar herself, quoting the sayings of our scholars and wise men and from the bible. A homemaker who did her work faithfully and with devotion. She spoke wisely and compassionately – always taking part in doing charity, and adding from her own. She used to say, "It is to be my privilege".

She was with Grandfather for most of his life and at the killing grounds too. She escaped also, but was caught and killed by the hands of the accursed evildoers, on the 14th of the month of *Elul*, in the year 5702, *HY"D*.

The evil reaper came; the town was destroyed and the house was silent. But it lives in the hearts of all those that knew it.

The branches sent out by the house will carry on its traditions wherever they are, and will keep its memory forever.

[Page 201]

Rabbi and *Shohet*: Rabbi Feivish Halevi Levin

Haim Shteinman (Tel-Aviv)

Translated by Thia Persoff

Rabbi Feivish Halevi Levin

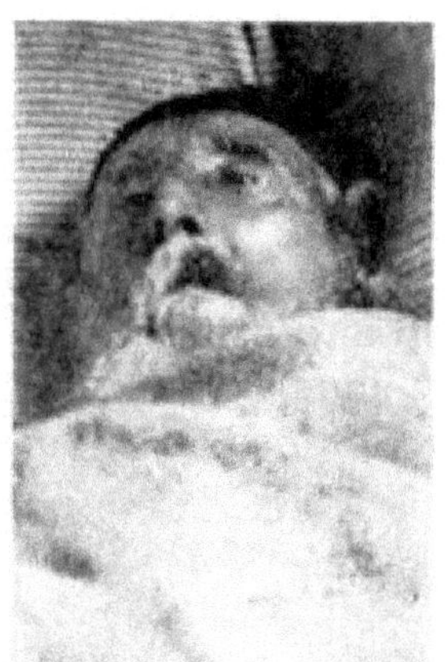

R' Shrahga Feivish was a Rabbi and Shohet in Rokitno village, and continued to do so when moving to the town of Rokitno after it was built.

He was well known for being an eminent scholar, erudite, and of a sharp mind; his greatness radiated over the residents. Even those in the surrounding villages respected and honored him. His actions were guided towards the betterment of the people, whose needs were many, and his heart was open to all the needy. He counseled and consoled, mollified, and gave aid to the best of his ability, and then some. He did not worry about his own needs, was content with little, lived frugally and modestly.

R' Shrahga Feivish was a wise man, knowledgeable in the traditional laws (*halakha*). He interpreted and made decisions according to them in disputes, and made peace among rivals. He was compassionate, though strict, in his judgments; both sides always accepted his decision with honor.

R' Shrahga Feivish excelled also as a reader of the Torah and for his expertise in blowing the *shofar*. He had an established claim to read to the congregation during the High Holy Days. A thrill would pass through the hearts of the congregants, when his voice thundered in "Rise G-d in sounds triumphal, Lord, in the *shofar* call". Sometimes he would entertain his listeners with amusing stories and jokes. His sayings, told also in the local language, were famous.

I remember that when I was a child, at one of the lessons in the weekly portion of the Torah, I asked him a naive question: "Grandfather, please tell me, is there a G-d in the heaven?" Astonished, he thought for a moment and answered me metaphorically. "Show me, my son, an object that does not exist, and is talked about. For example: there is a table, a book, a tree, etc. We talk of them because they are real things. If, G-d forbid, there was no G-d in the world, people would not be talking about him." So, in a simple, understandable way, he would explain away all sorts of problems, and in this was the strength of his great influence.

When he reached a ripe old age and the town developed and grew, a young Rabbi was chosen to take his place- Rabbi Aharon Joseph Shames; but Rabbi Shrahga Feivish, in spite of his old age, continued to do the holy work, the slaughtering (*shekhita*). One winter day, during a riotous snowstorm, he was called to slaughter a calf in Rokitno village. To reach the village in such weather it was difficult even for a young person. He caught a cold, was sick and bed-ridden for a long time. He never recovered. In the year 1924, he passed away at a very old age, and was buried in the Rokitno cemetery. Above his grave a tent-like structure was erected, with an opening, as is the custom for sages (*tzadikim*).

His son Sheftl Levin was buried next to him. On their joint grave was engraved the words: "A tree and its fruit".

Many of Rokitno's Jews would come to the grave at times of distress and sorrow.

[Page 202]

My Father, the *Shohet* Issachar Trigun

Hanan Hatzuvi (Tel-Aviv)

Translated by Thia Persoff

Issachar Trigun

My father settled in Rokitno in the early twenties. He came from the town of Visotzky and was educated and knowledgeable in the Torah, which he studied for many years in the *Yeshivot* of Volyn and Polesie. He was hired as a second *shohet u'bodek* (slaughterer and examiner); the first was Reb Yoel Shwartzberg. As soon as my father came to Rokitno, he became deeply involved in the public life of the community. Being a Karlinny *Hasid,* he hoped to turn Rokitno to a center for the Karlin *Hasidic* movement. My father was a religious man and did not see secular education as the answer to the Jewish-religious awareness. He felt that the Hebrew school education was important as a shield against the Polish schools, where the children were completely estranged from Judaism.

My father followed the rule set by the wisest of men: "It is good to do this, but do not neglect to do that too". Though sympathetic to the secular Hebrew school, he opened a *cheder* in his house, where a group of children studied the Bible and the *Gmara.* In this *cheder,* more than for economic need, my father intended to create a scholarly nucleus, where Rokitno's children would be instructed in Jewish studies. And true to his hopes, some of his pupils went on to study in Koritz *Yeshiva* in the town of Rovno.

This was just one of my father's public activities, which he took upon himself from the day he arrived in Rokitno.

His main activity was in spreading *Hasidism.* For him the Rabbi was an institution, a higher authority of unshakeable laws and axioms. My father tried to impart this to the Jewish community in Rokitno in a religious- *Hasidic* form.

Our house was open for the community's assorted activity groups. My father developed a tradition that was an enticement and attraction for many people: during the holiday of *Chanukah,* he gave a *levivot* (*latkes*) party, in which a large number of guests attended. The great blessing, "*Kidusha Rabba*" and celebration of *Simhat Torah* at his house were famous all around.

My father was a pursuer of peace, and hated discord; he always looked for friendliness among the people. With the Rabbi he worked to block the gaps and repair the breaches in peaceful, friendly relations. As clear proof to his peace loving, we see that in spite of being a Karlin *Hasid*, while most of Rokitno's *Hasidim* were Stolin *Hasidim*, he refrained from having his Rabbi come to Rokitno to avoid discord.

Father searched the way to the Zionist movement. He was impressed by the youngsters in the Zionist youth movements and idealized them as the saviors of Israel – as possibly being this generation's *Lamed Vavniks* (the 36 secret righteous men of lore) who will overcome the wicked Armilos and will bring the redemption. As for himself, he longed for a religious Zionism, one of maintaining the Holy Commandments. His request, before I emigrated to Israel, still echoes in my ears: "Remember, my son, the Sabbath and the laying of the *tefillin*. These are our ammunition for overcoming the wrong temptations (*sitra akhra* = in Aramaic- *sitra* is side, *akhra* is other, used in the *Kabbalah* to mean the other side, or Satan's camp); with their strength we will defeat our enemies and shine above our adversaries".

After I emigrated to Israel we kept a constant correspondence. In those eventful days of 1936, the Arabs rioted and ambushed our people; Jewish blood saturated the land. Concerned and anxious, from the distant land he followed the events in Israel. His letters were full of belief and trust in the future of our undertaking, because our Heavenly Father will see our plight, will pity Zion and will return us to her. By then he was already a devoted and loyal Zionist.

Father was deeply involved with the artisans groups, and sympathetic to all sufferers. He succeeded in establishing close relations with them. He showed interest in their life and knew who was in need of help- who needs shoes for his children, who has no money to marry his daughter. Then Father would walk from house to house, collecting donations for the poor and the needy. He did all his charity work without revealing for whom it was intended, so as not to cause embarrassment to the receivers.

All the week's days, Father was deeply involved in community work. But with the coming of the Sabbath he divested himself from the profane and made his Sabbath in a special style, the Karlin version. There was much beauty in those Sabbaths, and their flavor nourishes me still.

Father did not have much pleasure in his life. He had many dark days; one daughter died at birth, the other got very sick and died during the *Shoah* years. Father sighed and cried in private, but he forbeared, restrained himself and conquered his sorrow. His trust in our Heavenly Father unshakeable, he continued in his way of life, the *Hasidic* way, which was a source of life for him. With this devotion and trust, he went to the killing grounds and gave himself to death.

[Page 204]

The *Shohet* Reb Yoel Shwartzberg

Dov Harari (Neve Oz)

Translated by Thia Persoff

Reb Yoel Shwartzberg, an expert Slaughterer and Examiner *(shohet u'bodek)* from Trisk, came to Rokitno to take the place of the *shohet u'bodek*, Reb Avraham Shmue Kliger after his death. He married Chavah, the older daughter of Reb Avraham Shmuel. R' Yoel was wise and a great scholar. His words, thoughtful, were always measured by logic, and pointed to the one and only truth – the truth of the Torah.

R' Yoel was active in soliciting aid from able householders for the individual's and community's needs- charity for the poor, and support for charitable institutions. He also contributed his own money to the needy.

Yoel Shwartzberg

He was a most generous host. It is told, as an example of his devotion to the *mitzvah* of gracious hospitality, that one winter night a person knocked on his door requesting a place to sleep. Though the house was very small with no room to spare, R' Yoel did not let him leave. Instead he offered his own bed, saying that he has to leave on an important errand and will not be sleeping at home that night. When the guest got up in the morning, he saw that R' Yoel was sleeping on the table...

R' Yoel had a pleasing voice. He would go in front of the ark and sing. Being a Trisker *Hasid*, he knew ear-pleasing *Hasidic* melodies. He was a just man, distancing himself from evil. He would not even touch a fly on the wall. Though he had little, he was content in his lot. After the decree against Jewish ritual slaughtering, his situation was worsened and, like his colleagues, he was forced to do it in secret.

Before the Nazi invasion he went to Trisk, to visit his ailing father. On his way back, he was murdered.

[Page 205]

Asher Zelig Baratz

Aharon Heruti (Freierman) (Tel-Aviv)

Translated by Thia Persoff

Asher Zelig Baratz

Asher Zelig Baratz, one of the outstanding persons in our town, arrived in Rokitno in 1923, from a town in France where he served as a *Rabiner*. Here he was employed as a head bookkeeper in the glass factory of the Vitrom Co.

Since arriving in Rokitno, he involved himself in Zionist activities and devoted much of his time to Zionist institutions and Hebrew culture. He headed the *Keren-Ha'yesod* (Jewish Foundation Fund), and was a big help to its emissaries, accompanying them to the homes of the town's notables and helping to persuade them to donate or to increase their donations to the fund. He also headed the Tarbut organization in town, and initiated forming the committee to build the Tarbut School.

Though he disagreed with the political ideas of the *Hashomer-Hatzair* organization, he nonetheless helped their cell. Calling them a "Scouts/cultural" group of the Zionist organization named *Hashomer-Hatzair,* he agreed to be their guarantor in front of the authorities.

In the year 1928, he left his post at the glass factory to be the manager of the newly formed national bank in Rokitno. Here too, his unstinting help demonstrated his talent and generosity. He was elected to the town's council, then to the post of vice- mayor. The Polish authorities valued and honored him, and cooperated with him in spite of his being a Jew and a proud Zionist, who stood firm on the rights of the Jewish citizens.

Mr. Baratz corresponded with Yossef Baratz from Kibbutz Deganya, and discovered a family link with him. A few times, he showed me Yossef Baratz's replies to his suggestion about the possibility of building a glass factory in Israel, and to find out if the raw material could be found locally. When Yossef Baratz visited Rokitno as an emissary from Israel, he stayed with Zelig Baratz.

Asher Zelig Baratz, 75 years old, died from a heart attack in 1937. He left his daughter, Sarah (a dentist in Rokitno) and son, Yones (a well known violinist) who were killed in the *Shoah,* and a son who was a victim of the first Russian purge.

[Page 206]

Remembering Moshe Lifshitz

Aryeh Geipman (Givatayim)

Translated by Thia Persoff

Moshe Lifshitz

The image of *Reb* Moshe Lifshitz was deeply imbedded in my mind since early childhood- a sharp mind, eyes that seemed to look through you, reflecting a hint of irony. He was determined and reacted sharply to anything that he thought was wrong.

In spite of the fact that in our town his name was synonymous with wealth, I doubt that he was a wealthy man. When someone wanted to tell his children that he cannot afford to fulfill their requests, he would say: "I am not Moshe Lifshitz, and I cannot afford it".

Reb Moshe's house was always open – to storekeepers or persons seeking help in civil arbitration, Jewish law, etc. He was a learned man, and in his free time he studied the Torah.

He was not a public functionary in the regular sense. He was not an official functionary, but he was asked for advice on everything that had to do with the interest of the community. During the period of Petlura with his band of murderers, every time a troop of soldiers would arrive in Rokitno, they demanded contributions – money, foodstuff, or clothing. The leaders of the community would hold council in *Reb* Moshe's house to find ways of raising the needed monies to save the town's Jewish citizens from an imminent pogrom.

Being a prominent wholesaler of flour and other food products, it was only natural that all the grocery-store owners in town and the area received credit from him. Not once did he think to sue for unpaid debts. Moreover, anyone that was in need of charity would receive his help- in secret and in private.

Though he belonged to the older generation and he and his children had different ideas and opinions, he did not force his on them. He saw the importance of going along with the changes in time, and provided his children with higher education in the cities of Vilna and Kiev.

His house was a center for all Zionist and community functions. During the First World War, with the increased flow of Jewish refugees from Poland on their way to Russia through Rokitno, his house was used constantly – for days and weeks – as a food-collecting and packing center for the refugees.

The house was filled with the sound of local youth of all ages – the friends of Chaya Sarah, Gedalyahu, Yehudit, Shunamit, Leibel, and Aharon. As long as the older children were at home, the house was the "heart" of the town when it came to community and social functions.

Although *Reb* Moshe did not favor his children's activities, he treated it with tolerance. When Gedalyahu emigrated to Israel in 1922, a change in his attitude took place and his interest in the youth activities increased.

Reb Moshe made his last way in the company of the rest of our town's people – to the common grave in Sarny.

[Page 207]

Moshe Hirsch Linn

Linn family (Israel)

Translated by Thia Persoff

Moshe Hirsch Linn

To *R'* Moshe Hirsch is reserved a special honor in his profession as a builder; he was one of the first to build in the new Rokitno. In 1920 he built the synagogue in the new town, donating his skill to the holy task, and collected donations for the building fund. When the building was completed, he felt that his foremost responsibility was to install a Torah scroll in it. He went to Hassel Shapira, the father of Avraham the butcher, and received from him a donation of calves' hides. Those he had tanned into parchment. He then gave the parchment to Hershel from Slutzk, the scribe of Holy Scriptures (*S"TM = Sefarim, Tefillin, Mezuzot*), to write the Torah scroll.

In the midst of writing, Hassel Shapira died and left two grown daughters. Moshe Hirsch saw it as his duty to find them suitable worthy husbands. As it was the custom of the Rabbi from Stolin to be our guest on Shabbat-Shira, Moshe Hirsch talked with him about it. The Rabbi sent a young man from Stolin and the match was successful. The marriage took place on the day that the new Torah was installed. Moshe Hirsch provided for and gave the wedding party at his home. In spite of his hard labor, he gave much of his time to help the needy. Following the Commandment to help dower a poor bride was sublime and holy in his eyes.

Moshe Hirsch was a combination of learning and work. During the day he stood on the scaffold, and in the evening he would go to Rabbi Shames to study the daily "page". He was a simple man, and in his simplicity- was his uniqueness. He had in him the folksiness of the Vilna Jew. He was filled with love for the people and for the land of Israel. Without knowing about Herzl and Ehad-Ha'am, he longed to emigrate to Israel. He came to the love and longing from the book of *Eyn-Ya'akov*, which he studied by himself and with others. May his generosity and love for his fellow man be an example to us and our children.

[Page 208]

My Brother, Noah Soltzman

Yakov Soltzman (Tel-Aviv)

Translated by Thia Persoff

Noah Soltzman

In 1914 Noah, a pharmacist, came to Rokitno. He bought Yossi Barzam's pharmacy in the old town (*altshtot*), which was developed and expanded as the population increased.

Being a Zionist, Noah loathed speaking in the local tongue. It surprised his customers that he spoke Yiddish with them, as the previous pharmacist spoke only Russian. He blended fast into Ochotnikov's Jewish community, and was liked by the townspeople.

With his move to the town started his activities – participating in assistance to the needy and in Hebrew education. With the eruption of war in 1914, a large number of Jewish refugees started to flow into Ochotnikov. Noah- along with Moshe Freierman, one of his first friends in town- made all possible efforts to ease their hardships. They collected donations from the townspeople for the "help and assistance fund". But this was only a slight relief.

In addition to the aid for physical needs, Noah was concerned about the Jewish youth that were neglected and uneducated. As a patriotic Jew, he emphasized Hebrew education, and to that purpose he invested a great deal of effort in establishing a Hebrew school, part of the *Tarbut* (culture) association. The beginning was very modest; the budget was very small. Saddened, Noah searched for other sources of financial help to cover the school's deficit. One of them was organizing plays, in which he took part, as did his wife Clara, my wife Luba, Avraham Shvartz, and others. The proceeds helped somehow in balancing the budget, and a certain percentage was allocated for KKL (*Keren Kayemet Le'Yisrael*, Jewish National Fund).

At the end of the summer of 1919 when Poland conquered a large part of Volyn province (including Ochotnikov), Noah, with help from a few of the house-holders, purchased a lot for building a school and registered it to his name.

In a meeting of the Zionist board, it was decided that Noah would be in charge of all the school's affairs. A building permit was acquired, a plan drawn for a school with seven classes and all the necessary supplies. Noah started on this labor of love with devotion. His life's dream was of a Hebrew school for the children, to take them out of the Polish school – where they were educated in a foreign, alien atmosphere – and give them a Hebrew education. The school and its upkeep brought many worries to Noah. He struggled hard to see that the building debts be paid. Its upkeep too was a serious problem as many of the pupils were from poor families that could not pay tuition.

Noah demanded a budget from the town's council to help the struggling school but the Polish councilman Gertzvingel spoke against it saying: "It is not reasonable to support a school that teaches its pupils to leave the country and emigrate to Eretz-Israel. When you send the young people away at the age to join the army, it weakens the ability of the country to defend itself. Do you think that you should be rewarded for that? Is it not our national duty to budget monies to the Polish schools, where the children are brought up to be loyal to their country?"

Those inciting words angered Noah, and he replied: "As long as we live in Poland and pay the country's and the town's taxes; as long as we, the Jews of Rokitno, are loyal to the government not less than the Polish individuals; as long as our sons serve in the army as the rest of the citizens – it is our right to demand and receive a budget for our educational institution, where Jewish children are brought up to love our ancient homeland and to be loyal to Poland, their birth country." His argument won and the town council granted his demand.

A fateful, tragic step in Noah's life was his joining and being active in the Block #16 that Yitzhak Grinboym organized. It included the local minorities – Jews, Ukrainians, Russians, and Germans. Noah was one of the first to join and conducted extensive propaganda for it. The Polish authorities considered this a subversive activity and, as Noah was a Russian citizen, they decided to revoke his pharmacy permit in retaliation. Thanks to interference by his friend General Zabedsky (one of the *Huta* partners), the decision was canceled.

His life proceeded peacefully until the outbreak of the Second World War.

When the Red Army entered Rokitno, Noah- accused of being a Polish patriot, an enemy of communism, a counter-revolutionary, a Fascist, etc.- was arrested and incarcerated in a dark, damp cellar in the Sarny jail. There for two weeks, he was interrogated and tortured. All efforts to force him to admit perpetrating those "crimes", yielded no "confession" or "admission" by this proud Jew to his uncommitted crimes. After two months, he was released. Abused and exhausted, the signs of torture on him, Noah continued to work in the pharmacy in spite of being shaken from his distressful experiences. He overcame the torments of his soul and encouraged himself and his family to hope for better days that are bound to come; the clouds will disperse and the sun will rise again on Rokitno's Jews. In reality there was no chance for this hope, the time was of disorder and chaos. The Russian army retreated from the Germans and its soldiers looted and plundered. They attacked the pharmacy and stole everything they could reach. Noah and I stood by, looking and seeing all our labor and efforts go down the drain- without uttering a sound.

At one time, the Train-Police showed up in the pharmacy accusing him of destroying Russian property. One of the policemen pulled a gun and aimed it at Noah's temple. His wife, Clara and I started crying and begged for our life. Lucky for us, at that very crucial moment a troupe of Soviet soldiers burst in and continued looting. The policemen realized who caused the destruction to the Soviet property and let go of Noah. That is how he was saved from certain death. But for a short time only – the total annihilation was at the horizon already.

Noah's care and responsibility towards Rokitno's Jews were most pronounced during the *Shoah* period. One day the head of the *Judenrat*, Aharon Slutzki, came to him and said that though the Germans demand that the apartment of the German commander be elegantly furnished, it is not being done. Noah understood well the consequence, and asked Slutzki to send some people over to take the furniture from his house, and save Rokitno's Jews from calamity.

I am unable to describe the agonies that my brother suffered in Rokitno ghetto until he was killed. He was taken with his wife, Clara and his daughters, Lucia and Shoshana, to Sarny. Together they left and together they went to the pit. Standing on the edge of it, he turned his head towards his family and the other unfortunate wretched ones, slapped his chest, raised his eyes to the heavens and started justifying the judgment: "Our Father who art in Heaven – We are guilty, We have sinned, We have betrayed, We have transgressed". These were his last words as he died in *Kiddush-Hashem.*

[Page 211]

My Father, Betzalel Kokel

Nehama Kokel (Tel-Aviv)

Translated by Thia Persoff

Betzalel Kokel

It is difficult for a person to write about his father. You can write about anyone when not emotionally attached – but not your father, that you are part of and he of you, so that you cannot see him as a separate image from yourself. It is harder; manifold, to write about a father that you loved very much. How can you dissect a beloved one's image into parts of character, of behavior, and tell about him section by section, when you always see it as a whole, a unit complete and perfect. A wave of warmth floods your heart – the pen shakes, the writing is impossible, the eyes dominate us. There is no stopping them.

The life history of a proud Jew, who existed hardly for himself, but for his household needs and his family's affections, for charity and good deeds, for working on the needs of the community with devotion. Devotion – unbounded. In the belief that with each person he helps, he helps the entire world. And more so, maybe with the feeling that all he does for the good in this world is basically for humanity's soul, and that in this is the greatness of service to the community. To see in the work for supporting an orphanage not only a community project, but first as for an individual orphan, the forsaken human, that you can delve the depth of his emotional distress. Just separate him from the crowd and you can see in him the true embodiment of the human tragedy.

That's the way he was walking around town – and taking in what he saw. Walking fast, in a bit of haste, in a rush to make time. Hardly seen, but always seeing. Returning home saturated with what he noticed and observed. Before even telling and explaining to the family of the worries and problems and failures of earning a living, he would describe what he saw in the streets: children dressed in rags, young ones playing in the street instead of going to school, townspeople that you can see on them how distressed their situation is at home, sometimes to the point of hunger. Those observations weighed heavily on him and caused worries that would not let up. As a result, ideas and plans had formed: to start a *Talmud-Torah* school, to organize a group of teachers, to collect all the children off the streets – into the school, to form a fund for charity to help those that have limited means, to always carry a small bundle for helping privately – to be returned or not, and more – gently in humility and in secrecy, without acknowledgement. Gentility – that was the road that my father followed until his last day. And a parallel road of love – for all men, all creatures.

Beloved father – one of the pearls in the crown of a Jewish town that was felled and is no more, but one more stone among the gravestones on the grave of the slaughtered of the Jewish nation. And our home with it.

[Page 212]

Haim David Weiner

Yakov Soltzman (Tel-Aviv)

Translated by Thia Persoff

Haim David Weiner

Haim David Weiner was one of Rokitno's founders. He was active in community and Zionist work, and the endowing of the Hebrew language to the local children.

After the First World War, when Zionist activities were permitted, he worked devotedly for the Jewish National Fund and the Jewish Foundation Fund in town, and was the J.N.F.'s representative in Rokitno. When someone asked, "How many Jewish families lived in Rokitno?" – the reply was, "Go to Haim David Weiner, the J.N.F. representative, and you will get your answer." The number of J.N.F. donation boxes equaled the number of the Jewish families in Rokitno. He made sure that not one Jewish household in our town will be without a J.N.F. box.

He was a man of few words. Not among the wealthy, he was content with little (he earned his living from a small store and rent from an apartment). During changes in regimes and the scare from attacks by local gangs, Haim David Weiner was one of the organizers of the "Self Protectors" and would go to guard in the nights. He loved work and had a deep feeling for agriculture; the land around his house was always tilled and sown, and the vegetables from his garden were always on his table.

His life was devoted to the national funds. And as such – he was an example to the Zionist youth in Rokitno, who continued with his good work.

[Page 213]

My Father, Aharon Levin

Yaakov Levin (Haifa)

Translated by Ala Gamulka

Aharon Levin

He was a personality that stood out among all other important people in Rokitno. He was well received by everyone as an advisor on many matters and as a great host. His home was open to the Jews of the town. They willingly came to listen to him and to discuss Torah with him. He was an expert chess player and he played many opponents. His main strength was the study of Torah. He had a deep understanding and knowledge of Jewish topics. He was known as an undisputed authority.

As proof, I relate the following story: One night during the month of *Shevat*, the elderly *shohet* Habert came to tell my father that his interpretation had been correct. When the children wondered about this nocturnal visit, my father replied: "Yesterday we were discussing *Mishna sugiat" Tagri Lod"* and there were several interpretations: I accepted Habert's version because of my respect for him. However, R' Habert thought it over and came to the conclusion that I had been right. That is why he bothered to come on this cold night, to confess that I had the correct version."

My father was one of the founders of *Mizrachi* in our town and he was also one of the main supporters of *Linat Hatzedek*. All his life he was devoted to the progressive Zionist movement. He educated his sons and daughters as Zionists and was fortunate that they all made *aliyah*.

When World War II broke out, he called me and begged me to go to Russia. He hoped it would save my life and that I, too, would join my brothers and sisters in Eretz Yisrael. I begged my father to join me in going to our relatives in Kharkov. Father refused, saying: "Mother and I are like an ancient tree. If it is uprooted and replanted in strange soil, it would need too much care. If the tree would go on the road, it would not survive the journey and it might die."

He remained in Rokitno and relied on providence. However, this tree with many roots was uprooted. He and my mother Pearl died as martyrs.

[Page 214]

Yakov Persitz

Aryeh Geipman (Givatayim)

Translated by Ala Gamulka

Yakov Persitz

Yakov Persitz was not one of the veterans of the town nor was he one of its founders. However, his arrival in Rokitno in 1925 was a turning point and the beginning of a new era in the economic development of the town and its vicinity.

Many of the residents of Rokitno, especially those who were involved in the lumber business, wondered about this man who stood as head of a large lumber producing plant. They were all certain that the director would stay in his office in the town and would run the business from there. What a surprise when it became known that Yakov Persitz moved to the village of Borovey to personally supervise the work.

The man regularly arose at 4 a.m. and by 5 he would meet with the many office clerks to instruct them on the daily agenda.

He visited daily all the remote corners in the forests. These forests covered large areas. He checked the progress of each clerk in his place of work and that is how he became so knowledgeable.

Yakov Persitz was well versed in Jewish and in general literature. He had an excellent memory. He spoke few words and listened intently and with infinite patience. His replies were appropriate and short. Even his casual conversation with friends and acquaintances was pleasant. His eyes shone with intelligence. His workers could not understand how he knew their good and bad points in such a short time. An additional virtue attributed to Yakov Persitz was his generosity. He gave with an open hand and without much publicity.

When he completed his tour of duty in the lumberyard, Yakov Persitz settled in Rokitno. He was much attached to the town and he went into his own business. His family spread throughout the world and he was not fortunate enough to see his sons and daughters in his later years.

[Page 215]

My Father, Avraham Golod

Isie Golod (Haifa)

Translated by Ala Gamulka

Avraham Golod

My father Avraham, son of Nissan Golod, was one of the first settlers in Ochotnikov (the former name of Rokitno). He dealt in transport for the lumber dealers to Russia and other European countries. He was referred to as an expediter. He arrived while still a bachelor and when his economical situation was settled, he married Chaya, from the family of Baruch Kleifeld from Koritz, and he started a family.

Due to his business dealings, his house was always full with merchants who worked in his field. He was a popular man who got along with people. He was proud of his Jewish heritage and was always ready to help the needy. He was active in almost all the charitable organizations in town. He was a dedicated Zionist and collected money for Eretz Yisrael from the beginning of the Zionist movement. He was very proud of the pile of letters (which he guarded), handwritten by

Ussishkin regarding the purchase of lands in Eretz Yisrael even before the founding of the Jewish National Fund. My father was extremely active in the election of Zeev Jabotinsky to the Russian *Duma* (parliament).

Since he was in contact with different merchants, including Germans, at the start of World War I, my father was accused by the Russian government of spying for Germany. He spent a year in prison in Zhitomir without being tried. He was then exiled to Siberia where he suffered till the end of the war. He wrote letters to the Zionists in Rokitno from his place of exile. In these letters he encouraged them to continue with their activities.

When he returned to Rokitno, the entire population of Rokitno – including the Christians – led by Rabbi Damata, came out to greet him.

Father stood out in his devotion and his love for his family and made a great effort to educate his children in a Hebrew and Zionist spirit. His hopes were that his children would make *aliyah* and that he and mother would follow them. Sadly, he did not achieve his goal.

Father loved working the soil and much of his time was spent in his garden. He grew fruit and vegetables and he greatly enjoyed the produce. His leisure time was spent in the study of Torah. He was a modern man and he understood the times. He followed the progress in all fields.

Since he was a public personality, he was a member of the executive board of the Tarbut School building committee as well as the *Gmilut Hassadim* (Charity). He felt that assistance was very important and he made speeches in the synagogue on Saturdays- after Torah reading- about mutual help.

At one time he managed the popular bank in Rokitno and he helped many public institutions.

During World War II, he was one of the organizers of self-defense in Rokitno. He fell while on duty. One night, he was hit by a stone thrown by a Christian hooligan as he was running to defend a Jewish family. He died a day later. My father was the first victim of the Holocaust in Rokitno, even before the Nazis arrived.

[Page 216]

Herschel Shteinman

Aharon Lifshitz (Givatayim)

Translated by Ala Gamulka

Herschel Shteinman

R' Herschel was a progressive Jew, but he was quite traditional, from the point of view of "Be a Jew at home and a human being outside." He attended synagogue regularly, but he did not have a special seat, except during the High Holidays, when he sat in a place of honor with other important people. He did not have an official position on the executive of the community, but he was highly involved, especially in matters pertaining to the synagogue. These were the Burial Society and *Kiddush* committee. They organized a *Kiddush* every Saturday after services in different homes. R' Herschel also donated *Havdalah* candles to the synagogue.

Even though he was a *Hasid*, he did not belong to a specific sect. He received all the Rabbis who visited our town. He took part in all festivities and dinners held in their honor and gave them donations.

He had a business – a small department store. The Jews of the area would buy goods in his store and they also ordered merchandise that had to be brought in from big cities. In addition, R' Herschel also had a good heart: if any sick person needed medicine that was unavailable in the local pharmacy, he would make certain that it was brought in as quickly as possible. He was highly regarded by other merchants and they always approached him with arbitration matters. He was successful in this position by mediating without looking for rewards.

Even though he was involved in earning a living, he was always ready to listen to others. Many would come to him with their problems. He would circulate among those who had means in order to collect for the needy. The Jews knew that if R' Herschel came it meant that the need was urgent and they gave readily.

On *Purim* and on the eve of *Yom Kippur* he increased his efforts. He went from house to house with a handkerchief in his hand. When he finished collecting the money he hurried to the homes of the needy and distributed the money. On this occasion he would perform another *Mitzvah.* He wished everyone "*Hag Sameach*" on *Purim* and "*Gmar Hatima Tova*" on the eve of *Yom Kippur.*

R' Hershel was an enthusiastic Zionist although he did not identify himself with any Zionist party. He donated generously to Zionist funds. His end was bitter. His wife was killed with other Rokitno citizens on the day of slaughter. He managed to escape and hid with a Christian acquaintance. However, after a few days he was betrayed for a kilo of salt. His dream was to make *aliyah*, but he did not succeed.

[Page 217]

My Father, Berel Shwartzblat

Baruch Shehori (Shwartzblat) (Haifa)

Translated by Ala Gamulka

Berel Shwartzblat

Although he was born in Rafalovka and came with his wife (my mother) Dvora to Rokitno in 1910, he was considered as one of the early settlers. In his youth he studied at a *yeshiva.* His studies greatly influenced his life. He had a good sense of humor and liked to tell jokes.

He was blessed with a deep intellect and a quick mind. The fact that he was involved in community affairs and yet he was one of the ordinary people made him quite popular in Rokitno. He earned his living from his store, which stood in the center of town. It was one of the first stores in Rokitno. Since most of his time was spent in working for the common good, it was my mother's responsibility to run the store, even though she had many young children.

Our family suffered greatly during World War I. Father and his neighbor Hertzel Binder did not wish to join the Russian army and were obliged to spend a few years "underground". Even under these conditions, my father did not stop his communal activities and he continued to help Jewish refugees who streamed into our town from western districts as the Russians were retreating.

As an observant Jew, he was always among the first to attend synagogue services. He took part in the study of *Eyn Yaakov* or a page of *Gmara*, between

Mincha and *Maariv*. He was involved in major communal decisions. He was a frequent visitor in the home of Rabbi Aharon Yosef Shames, *z"l*, and he was highly respected by him. Often he was invited to be an arbitrator in a *Din Torah* dispute between two opponents who came to the Rabbi.

Father was not a follower of *Hasidism*, but he still participated in receptions for all visiting Rabbis. He also studied with the Rabbi and celebrated with other *Hasidim* till the early morning hours.

Since he was a Zionist, he belonged to *Mizrachi*, but he supported financially all Zionist parties. He educated his children in a traditional and Zionist spirit.

He was involved in all types of charitable activities. He gave all his energy to these activities, not expecting any rewards. He was one of the founders of the Burial Society in Rokitno. Any dying person was "adopted" by my father. He organized bedside vigils to alleviate the burden on the family. When the person died, my father would conduct the funeral in a traditional and *halachic* manner. There were no funerals without his active participation.

During the Polish rule, my father served as a representative of the merchants and tradesmen to the committee organized by the income tax department in Sarny. He was well versed in tax regulations. His expertise proved useful in showing government clerks that they were exaggerating in their evaluations.

On the 13th of *Elul* 1942 he managed to escape from the slaughter grounds, but he was caught by farmers from Kisorich and he was murdered by the German killers in Rokitno.

[Page 218]

A Monument to the Soul of Gedalya Lifshitz

Yeshayahu Meiri (Meirson) (Tel Aviv)

Translated by Ala Gamulka

Gedalya Lifshitz

Gedalya was fascinated by Zionism from childhood. His studies in the cheder did not satisfy him. He belonged to a special group in Rokitno who studied with an important Rabbi from out of town. However, in any spare moment, Gedalya searched for books about *Hibat Zion* and Zionism. Even though he was quite young, he stood out as an instructor of the Zionist youths in Rokitno.

In 1917, when the Balfour Declaration was made,

most of the young students were away from Rokitno, studying in Kiev and other Russian cities. Instead of studying, we listened to lectures about Zionism and we attended many conferences and meetings. All this was not enough. We wanted to do more for our country. When we returned to Rokitno for *Succoth*, we decided to have a mass rally in the synagogue in honor of the Balfour Declaration. Great Britain recognized the historical link between the Jewish people and the land. Gedalya Lifshitz was one of the main speakers at this rally. He stood out as a brave fighter for Zionism in times that were not so receptive to Zionism. In those days there were young people in Rokitno who were blinded by the October revolution and were known to oppose Zionism.

Gedalya Lifshitz electrified the audience with his great Zionist speech, which was full of love for and a strong belief in the Zionist dream. He saw that the Balfour Declaration was a great light that influenced the Jews in the Diaspora. He ended his speech by reading a telegram that he proposed to send to the headquarters of the Zionist movement in Russia. It read: “The youths of Rokitno enthusiastically embrace the Balfour Declaration which announces the founding of a national home in Eretz Yisrael and they are ready to serve, unconditionally, the Zionist cause. They are prepared to make *aliyah* in order to work the land themselves because no mandate in the world could build our national home for us.”

The contents of the telegram excited the participants and Gedalya was warmly applauded. Rabbi Yosef Shames shook his hand and said to him: “May you be blessed!”

Gedalya was not only a talker, but also a doer. He obeyed the spirit of the telegram and in 1922, he made *aliyah*. There he did hard physical labor. He lived frugally and suffered greatly, but his love for Eretz Yisrael fortified him. He continued his work with enthusiasm and participated with other pioneers in the building of our homeland.

Sadly, Gedalya did not live to see his dream come true. He died on *Pessach* 1936, a young man of 37, at the prime of his life.

Great sadness fills me when I remember Gedalya. To this day I cannot get used to saying the Late Gedalya Lifshitz. My ears cannot absorb it. I cannot accept it because he was my friend from childhood. Many wonderful memories are tied to him. These are memories of a new Zionist spirit in Rokitno. We were as close as brothers during our best years. Our work together in the Zionist movement in Rokitno created a very close relationship.

[Page 220]

Baruch (Buzia) Levin

Haim Shteinman(Tel Aviv)

Translated by Ala Gamulka

Baruch Levin

Buzia Levin stood out among the youths of Rokitno as an educated person and as a public servant. He came from a respected family. In his childhood he studied at the Tarbut School in Rokitno and he continued his studies at the Hebrew High School (*Gymnasia*) in Vilna. When he completed his studies, he entered the teaching profession and taught in several villages in the Rokitno area. He was imbued with the Zionist spirit and he spread the Zionist dream among his students. He continued his life's work in Eretz Yisrael.

Buzia believed in Zeev Jabotinsky's Zionism and he took upon himself the mission of disseminating it. In those days there was an ideological battle within the Zionist movement. Buzia knew how to explain and how to influence. He was one of the founders of *Betar* and *Brit Hahayal* in Rokitno and he was intimately involved in all aspects.

Buzia was active with his *Betar* youths in several national funds until the founding of the "New Zionist Movement". However, from an ideological point of view, he strongly believed in a national home following Jabotinsky's ideas.

The movement assigned him many responsibilities. He visited many towns in Volyn in order to found new *Betar* chapters. He was an outstanding speaker with an excellent sense of humor. He was comfortable in any society and was always able to clearly express his ideas. He was well received by his listeners.

Buzia was also a writer. He was a correspondent for the weekly "Life in Volyn" which was published in Rovno. His articles about events in Rokitno or literary selections appeared in every edition.

He was also a talented actor and he performed in many plays presented by the amateur theater group in Rokitno and its vicinity. All income was donated for national and charitable purposes. He had a beautiful voice and liked to sing cantorial selections. He often joined choirs of visiting cantors, among them Moshe Kussovitzky. Buzia utilized his many talents in all aspects of life in Rokitno. He made *aliyah* with his wife.

After some early absorption difficulties, Buzia again was drawn to public life. He settled in Jerusalem and was appointed manager of a local *Kupat Holim* (Medical Clinic). He continued his work on behalf of the national movement. At the beginning of 1939, he was sent to the United States as an emissary. On the way, he visited Rokitno, but he managed to return to Eretz Yisrael as World War II broke out. He now felt a change in the Zionist movement. After much soul-searching he left the Jabotinsky movement, as did many others, and he joined the General Zionists. Here again he held a key position and admirably performed his duties.

Although he was deeply involved in public life, he did not forget Rokitno. When the Association of Rokitno Members was founded in Israel, Buzia was very active and served as a member of the executive to his dying days. We well remember his electrifying appearances at the annual memorial assemblies. He would remember with trepidation and reverence our dearly departed who perished in the Holocaust. He regularly attended meetings of the executive and when it was decided to publish this Yizkor book, he was quite enthusiastic. Unfortunately, he did not live to see the dream come true.

He became deathly ill and could not overcome the disease. I visited him often in the hospital in Jerusalem and, in spite of his agonizing pains, he always asked about the affairs of the Association. Our friend, relative and comrade left us before his time.

[Page 221]

The Teacher Rev. Efraim and the Teacher Israel Tozman

Aharon Lifshitz (Givatayim) & Yosef Segal (Neve Oz)

Translated by Ala Gamulka

Unlike other neighboring towns, there was no traditional *cheder* in Rokitno, maybe because it was a younger town. Until 1916 we had traditional religious schooling by Rev. Efraim from Avrotch, a Torah-teaching center. The teacher was paid on a semester basis (from after *Pesach* to *Rosh Hashana* and from *Succoth* until *Pesach*). He also alternated staying in the homes of his pupils. Our teacher, Rev. Efraim was an old Jew, handsome. G-d fearing, a scholar and well-versed in *Gmara* and biblical interpretations. The *cheder* was located in the house of Old Nahum and later in the old synagogue.

As a pedagogue, he excelled in his explanations. He was able to interpret the most difficult sections. Every pupil understood what he taught. He was easy-going and kind. The course of study was mainly *Gmara* with interpretations, *Tanach*, weekly portion, bible with *Rashi* and prayers for *Rosh Hashana* and *Yom Kippur*. There were no secular subjects. The school day went from morning till after *Mincha*, actually till evening. On Saturday afternoons, we studied *Pirkei Avot*. In winter we also studied at night and we returned home singing and holding lanterns. Since our days were filled with schoolwork, we had no time to play. We did not play any sports.

The pupils of Rev. Efraim were divided into two classes. In the higher class were Gedalya Lifshitz and Pinhas Kliger, *z"l*, and Yeshayahu Meiri (Meirson). In the other class were Yosef Segal, Aharon Lifshitz and Eliyahu Greenberg, *z"l*, who was killed in the Holocaust.

In 1916, the education system changed completely. A Hebrew teacher named Israel Tozman arrived in Rokitno. He was trained in modern methods. He was an experienced teacher who immediately began to teach Hebrew with a Sephardi pronunciation. Our parents were against these methods. They claimed that we would soon forget the Ashkenazi Hebrew and prayers we had learned from Rev. Efraim. However, they could not stop progress. Tozman's classes were mixed-boys and girls together. We studied literature, Jewish history, grammar, *Tanach* and Hebrew songs. As part of our studies, he imbued us with a love for Israel and a belief in Zionism.

After the Balfour Declaration, when the Zionist movement was organized in Rokitno, a new group was founded. *Agudat Yaldei Zion* (Union of Children of Zion) was intended to disseminate the Zionist dream among the youths. We collected money for Jewish National Fund. We even had a rubber stamp with a Star of David surrounded by the name of the Union.

At our Saturday meetings we read newspapers about events in the Zionist movement and in Eretz Yisrael. We donated a portion of our *Hanukah gelt* for the planting of three trees in Herzl Forest in the name of the Union. Among the founders of the Union were: Aharon Lifshitz, Yosef Segal, Malka Weiner, Avigdor Hefetz (he died while serving in the Red Army), Sender Lerner, Avraham Geipman *z"l*, (one of the first pioneers to make Aliyah) and Shunamit Lifshitz (died during the Holocaust).

The founding of this Union was a direct result of the Hebrew education we received from our teacher, Mr. Tozman. He guided us in this direction.

[Page 223]

Interesting Jewish Personalities in the Town of Rokitno

Efraim Vorona (Tel-Aviv)

Translated from Yiddish by Ala & Larry Gamulka

I wish to immortalize several Jewish personalities in the village of Rokitno who are especially etched in my memory. I remember "Herschel the Yellow One", a Jew who never allowed a *Gmara* book to leave his hand. He dealt in honey, wax and sour berries. At Pesach time, one could obtain a special mead. During *Hol Hamoed of Pesach*, we, the older boys, would go to Reb Herschel to drink mead and eat nuts.

His son, "Yosel the Yellow One" lived not far away. He was childless and loved to lead the prayers. When "the boys" saw Yosel leading the prayers they would twist some towels together and let him have it when he overdid the singing.

Yosel then would turn his head, mumble "Oh, ai, you non-believers!" and would continue to pray. Very often, on weekdays, "the boys" would prompt him into a holiday tune. Even the older Jews enjoyed these pranks.

Not far from him resided Berel, son of Yitzhak. Surnames were not too important in Rokitno. It was enough to tell a child "Go to Berel, son of Yitzhak" and the child would know exactly where to go.

Berel, son of Yitzhak, owned a nice home, a small grocery store and two cows. He made a decent living. His son, Shimon, lived in Warsaw. It was understood that he was studying there. Others said that he was an employee in a business. No one really knew the truth. Thanks to these men, Rokitno was privileged to hear good cantors – even on weekdays.

When Shimon came to visit he brought a gramophone with a big speaker, which resembled a giant s*hofar*. Thus the Jews would gather to hear the latest cantorial records. They were all in awe of this box and could never understand how such beautiful voices would emanate from it. Until then, the locals had never seen or heard a gramophone.

Berel the Mechanic

Berel the Mechanic! The younger generation and the newcomers have no idea who was Berel the Mechanic. The older generation probably still remembers the wonderful Jew. He was thought to be one of the "36 just men". This is why more space is used to describe the Mechanic.

He was a tall, skinny Jew whose face emitted goodness. He had a long Orthodox beard, which he would comb through with his fingers.

It is told that he decided to build a house without the services of an engineer or an architect. He worked at it for a long time until he realized that the building was uninhabitable. He gave it to the community to be used as a bathhouse. Since then he was known as "Berel the Mechanic".

He made a living from a small grocery store, which consisted of a cupboard containing sugar, raisins and other incidentals. A barrel of herring, kerosene, a few sacks of flour and a scale stood in an alcove. Since he spent most of his time praying and learning, his profits were barely enough to cover his living expenses.

He had a sick wife who was very swollen. She was very fat and found it difficult to move. Every Thursday, when all the women wanted to be served first, Berel would call on his swollen wife for help. It was understood that even with her best intentions she could not possibly help him. He would then approach her and tell her: "Even at the beginning it was not a good match between us". He continued to say this to her when the total of their ages was 150 years!

Who does not remember *Simchat Torah* with Berel the Mechanic! Children would prepare themselves for weeks for this happy holiday. Berel would think holy thoughts. When other Jews would drink liquor in honor of *Simchat Torah,* Berel would form a circle with the older Jews and would weave the children through them. With a Torah scroll in his arms he would abandon himself in sacred dancing and sing: "*Yavo Adir Bimhera Beyamenu*" and "When will he come?" Everyone would answer: "When the Messiah will come." Berel would continue: "A day of rejoicing, a day of singing." He danced until the middle of the night.

In the morning, after prayers and *Hakafot,* the children would congregate around him. He would line them up and lead them, holding the hand of a child. This is how he marched in the street, singing "*Yavo Adir*" and "When will he come?" "When the Messiah arrives".

Gentiles and policemen would respectfully get out of his way when he marched with the children. This is how he would visit every Jewish home. He and the children would sing "A Good *Yom Tov*" to the residents of each house. The children would be served refreshments. This would go on till evening.

In the evening, he returned home, but not before he brought each child to his or her home.

I remember how we used to discuss politics with the Jews in the synagogue. "The cursed one must fall (referring to Tsar Nicolai), if not, the Jews would suffer a lot more. The Jew-haters will abolish ritual slaughter and G-d knows what else. Bad times are coming to the Jews. G-d in Heaven should take pity on us."

Just before World War I, Berel left for Eretz Yisrael. With his departure, the Jews of Rokitno felt abandoned. This was a big shock, particularly to the children who always waited impatiently for the big holiday of *Simchat Torah*. Each one wanted to join Berel the Mechanic's group, but the waiting was for nothing. Unfortunately, there was no longer anyone who could inject joy among the children and the adults as much as he did.

The streets of Rokitno were empty of that joy which this wonderful Jew managed to awaken in everyone. He was always referred to as one of the "36 just men".

Deep in their hearts many people were envious of Reb Berel, that he was fortunate enough to go to Eretz Yisrael. G-d himself determined this – so the rumors went – and that is why a Jew like Reb Berel spent his last years in the Holy Land.

For some time, the Jews of Rokitno did not hear news of Reb Berel. Later, it was reported that in 1914, because of the war, he was delayed in Turkey and died there. A second version made it clear that he did reach Eretz Yisrael and was buried in Jerusalem.

To this day, it is not known where this great Jew was buried, the one who was known as Berel the Mechanic.

David Grinshpan

He was called "David the Estate Owner". The young and the old knew him and loved him. He was a tall Jew, with a beautiful, long, white beard, round cheeks and dreamy eyes.

I do not know from where came his nickname – the Estate Owner. It is possible that it was because he owned a big, beautiful house with a big backyard. In addition, he was blessed with a voice like an angel. The tunes that came out of his mouth were sweet and heartfelt. When Reb David sang *Kol Nidrei*, you could hear a pin drop in the synagogue. His lyrical voice couched in Jewish suffering would break the hearts of the Jews of Rokitno. The praying people would be enveloped in holiness through his beautiful voice. When the majority of the rural residents moved into town, Reb David also did so since his children were living there.

In his later years he became paralyzed and was bed-ridden. He was alone at home when he overturned a burning lamp and he was burned lying in his bed.

[Page 227]

Personalities of Rokitno

Yosef Segal (Givatayim)

Translated by Ala Gamulka

A. Avraham Gelfand

Reb Avraham Gelfand, son of Zalman, was an extremely wealthy man. He had two country estates: one in Voltche Gorko- east of Rokitno, near the village of Snovidovitch- and the second- south of Rokitno, in the village called Kisorich. On both estates, Gelfand had sawmills and the lumber industry there was highly developed. His business was managed by his clerks, who were all Jews. Gelfand's son-in-law was Minister of Finance in the Ukrainian government, headed by Hetman Skoropedsky.

As was well known in Tzarist Russia, not every Jew was able to legally own property, land and forests. Therefore, all of Gelfand's properties were registered under a Russian called Banov. For this privilege, Gelfand paid him large sums of money. Banov lived a life of drinking and partying in Moscow and Petersburg. In fact, all of the estates and the business were managed by Gelfand, who resided in Odessa.

When Rokitno was settled early in the twentieth century and Jews from surrounding areas moved there, Gelfand built a beautiful synagogue as a gift to the Jews of Rokitno. He furnished it and purchased Torah scrolls and tomes of *Mishna*. Gelfand came all the way from Odessa for the dedication of the synagogue and he participated in the celebration. He was very well received by the community.

The synagogue, in addition to being a house of prayer, also served as a place for national celebrations. I recall that during the Balfour Declaration there was a spontaneous rally in the synagogue. Collections were made for several funds. When bad times came to the Jews, be it Petlura's gangs or the Holocaust, meetings were held there to find solutions, to try to alleviate the difficulties.

Gelfand died of starvation in Odessa during the revolution. The synagogue he built for the Jews of Rokitno was destroyed during the Holocaust, as were the Jews of Rokitno.

B. Moshe Wolf Horman

I

In our town lived a Jew called Reb Moshe Wolf Horman, an older man. He was a craftsman who cut lumber for construction purposes. No one knew him by the name of Horman; however, if you asked for "Moshe Wolf the carpenter" – you would immediately have a response.

He came to our town from Dombrovitz with the first settlers and participated in its founding. As were most of the tradesmen in our area, Reb Moshe Wolf was an honest man who supported his family by hard work and who was content with his lot. Although he was slightly liberal in his beliefs, he went to synagogue daily to attend afternoon and evening services. When those present studied *Eyn Ya'akov* or discussed a section of *Gmara*, he would sigh and sadly say that instead of arguing about an egg which either hatched or not on a holy day, our sages should have thought about producing arms. Then, the Jews would not suffer so bitterly in exile.

Reb Moshe Wolf worked on the construction of the synagogue in Rokitno. Avraham Gelfand liked him and appointed him manager of the farm in Voltche Gorko. Reb Moshe Wolf fulfilled his function loyally and at Gelfand's invitation, he traveled often to visit him in Odessa in order to report to him personally about his holdings and to seek his advice.

So lived Reb Moshe Wolf with his family in Voltche Gorko until the Poles arrived in our area. He was killed during the Holocaust and did not live to see how Jews manufacture arms in their own land at the same time as they argue Talmudic and scientific points.

C. Feivel The Porter

Feivel the Porter was one of the tradesmen and laborers in our town and earned his living by physical labor. We did not know his surname and it was difficult to guess his age. He was a bachelor around thirty years of age and he never seemed to age. He was short and squat with a muscular build.

Feivel came to Rokitno with his parents from Brezne at the beginning of its development. They were quite elderly. Reb Nahum, with his flowing white beard, was his stepfather. Feivel was not too developed intellectually. In addition, he had speech difficulties. He pronounced "k" as a "t" and that created some humorous situations.

As his name indicates, he earned his living as a porter. He would get up early, say his prayers and go to the train situation in the middle of town. The train travelers who arrived in our town would put their luggage on his back. Feivel would put as much as he could on his back, tying it around him with a rope. Slowly he would move and panting, he would reach either the inns of Reb Sheftel Levin and Haim David Weiner or, in the new town, the inns of Buzi Litvak, Hesia Geipman and Sheindel Kagan. Those who used his services were mostly lumber merchants who wandered on business from station to station. Rokitno was their center. They were always in touch with Feivel and paid him well for his work. When a customer tried to underpay him, Feivel would insist on receiving what was due to him and would not give up. He would stammer and redden with anger.

When Feivel was overloaded one could not see whether it was a human being or a walking cargo. Work exhilarated him and you could hear from a distance: "A parcel, a parcel".

In the mornings when Feivel passed the stores, he would receive orders for delivery from the owners. He used the intervals between trains to fill these orders. He would put on his back sacks of flour, sugar or millet weighing 80 – 100 kilograms and he delivered them to the stores. It is no wonder that Feivel was busy from dawn to late at night. He would come home for a short break only to eat a meal.

When he returned home at night he would distribute his earnings. He gave a part to his mother for living expenses and a part he would store away in a locked crate. He kept the key tied to his pocket. Because of his work, he was always dirty and he wore shabby clothes and heavy boots.

This was his daily routine. However, on Friday afternoons, when Feivel came home clean from the bathhouse, he turned into a “prince”. When he came to the synagogue in the evening, he wore a beautiful clean suit, polished shoes and a shirt and tie.

In the synagogue he prayed devoutly, but you could not tell which prayer he was reciting. His lips moved silently. Sometimes he was moved to play a prank. When he saw a praying man who fell asleep during the services, he would quietly approach him, slap him on his ear or his nose and quickly move away from the scene of the crime. When he returned to his seat, he would giggle.

At the end of Shabbat on his way to the train and before he went to work, he cleaned his Shabbat clothes well and put them in his crate until the following Shabbat. He took good care of his clothes. I cannot recall if he ever had new clothes.

Feivel died in the 1920's.

D. Yankel the Shamess

Who did not know Yankel the *Shamess*? He inherited the position at a young age after the death of his father, Reb Eisenman, who served in this position for many years in the synagogue in the old town. Everyone knew him as Yankel, son of Nahum the Shamess. His mother died when he was small and he was brought up by a stepmother. He was feeble in body and mind. He did not learn a trade and did not know how to do any work. However, he was an honest and straight man, full of goodness.

He could not pronounce the letter ”m”. When he addressed his wife (whose name was Malka) the word came out as Nalka. There were many other funny utterances. He also could not pronounce the letter “p”. When the hooligans – who lived near the *Huta* – attacked him, he yelled Tolice instead of Police.

Yankel filled many positions in town such as keeping and delivering the wedding canopy, inviting litigants to the Rabbi, delivering invitations to a circumcision and waking up Jews for *Selichot.* He did not only participate in happy events. He also took part in funerals holding a *tzedakah* box in his hand.

On *Succot,* he would run around from early morning to honor all the Jews with the *etrog* and *lulav* blessing. Not once would one of the pious women complain to him that he was late in bringing the *etrog* and *lulav* and she had to fast as a result. He would excuse himself as much as possible.

However, his main function was guarding and maintaining the synagogue. There were always some people among the worshippers who complained to him: the synagogue is not clean enough, the clock stopped, there is not enough heat in the winter, etc. If it happened, G-d forbid, that the *Shabbes Goy-* who stoked the furnaces of the Jews- did not appear, they would all direct their anger at Yankel. He was one of those people who are insulted but do not insult back. He would listen and sob quietly.

He did not earn a regular salary. With all his many functions, he barely eked out a living. At times he had to ask for charity in order to prepare for Shabbat and to support his wife and only daughter.

Yankel, his wife and daughter were able to escape Rokitno before the Nazis came. They reached the Soviet Union, but no one knows what happened to them.

E. Mindel (Cossack) Eisenberg

Mindel Eisenberg, known as the Cossack, was born into the large and highly respected family of Reb Yehoshua Vorona in the village of Rokitno. She was married, at the age of 16, to Salek Eisenberg from Vistozk. He was conscripted into the Russian army right after the wedding and he was sent to Warsaw. Mindel followed him. She yelled and screamed and succeeded in liberating him from the army. That is why she was nicknamed "The Cossack".

She was energetic, courageous and kind. She feared nothing. She would slap many Christians who threatened her. At the start of World War I, her brother Nachman, together with Salek Kaplan, were arrested by the tzarist police for not joining the army. The prisoners were brought to the jail in Olevsk. All efforts to free them were in vain. Mindel did not give up and was able to return them to their families.

Even the Poles respected Mindel. Due to her recommendations, many sick Jews were able to be seen by the Polish military doctor who was not known to be a lover of Zion.

Secret help to the needy and the unfortunate was to her sacred work. She would run back and forth among the Jews of Rokitno to collect funds for this purpose. No one ever refused her since they trusted her. She performed all these deeds with modesty and without publicity. In general, even the needy did not know who helped them.

Mindel had five sons and three daughters. In 1920 she gave birth to triplets – three sons all at once. Mindel became a sensation. The triplets were named after our patriarchs: Avraham, Yitzhak and Yaakov. Only Avraham remained alive. He was a brave partisan who fought the Nazis in the forests and lives with us in Israel.

She educated her children in the spirit of tradition and Zionism. They all attended the Tarbut School in Rokitno.

On the 13th of *Elul* 1942 when the Jews of Rokitno were executed, Mindel presented herself in the market square. She stood with her grandchildren in her arms and was the first to sense the killers approaching. She screamed out: "Jews, save yourselves! The murderers are coming to kill us!" Many of the remnants of the town were saved by this scream. She herself was not so fortunate. She was taken with her husband and grandchildren to Sarny. Her end was like the end of all the Jews. She was 48 years old when she was murdered.

[Page 232]

Candles of Remembrance

The Editorial Board

Translated by Ala Gamulka

Reb Hebert the *Shohet*

We remember him as an elderly man. His hands trembled and he stopped working as a slaughterer. He would chant his own tunes in the synagogue. He was a scholar and spoke well. He took part in all celebrations in town. One day he was invited to four happy events. The old man sighed and said: "Today I am going to all four" (walking on four legs...).

Shaya Gendelman (Shaya the Blacksmith)

Reb Shaya Gendelman, nicknamed Shaya the Blacksmith, was an honest man who always supported himself by his work. He prayed daily in the synagogue where he sat at the eastern wall. He prayed devoutly. On Shabbat he would not speak Yiddish, only Holy Tongue.

In the synagogue he made certain that no one spoke during services and he would loudly scold those who talked. The young people sometimes used their time in the synagogue for idle talk and they disturbed those praying. Reb Shaya would walk over to them, scatter them and tell them: "Each person to his own station" or he would point at what was written on the eastern wall: "This is a House of G-d" in order to teach them to respect this holy place

Yosef Haim Baum

Reb Yosef Haim Baum was a tailor. However, in our humble opinion, he was rarely seen plying his trade. He was fortunate to have employees to do the work. He neglected his trade in order to do community work such as the Association of Tradesmen. He was their representative in City Hall and fought for their rights, for the lowering of taxes imposed on them. He helped them get their permits since many of them did not have the necessary funds. He spoke for them in the community and in various Jewish organizations. He gave generously of his time and his effort.

He was often seen on a rainy day making his way to one meeting or another. He bore his role as a representative of the Proletariat with pride and devotion.

Shlomo Bender

He was tall, broad-shouldered, round-faced with a perpetual smile. His bearing spoke of strength. He owned a restaurant and most of his customers were Poles who were not necessarily lovers of the Jews. As a result, he had dealings with the ruling class in the town and in the county.

He had a warm Jewish heart and was always prepared to do a good deed. He was one of the founders of *Linat Hatzedek* and helped in many charitable institutions.

He served as a shield and a defender of the Jews of Rokitno. His name alone frightened many of the criminals and hooligans. He came to Rokitno from Warsaw as a sergeant in the Polish Mounted Army Regiment. He married a woman from Rokitno from the Vorona family. He was killed in a bombing raid in 1941 as he was fleeing to the Soviet Union.

Mendel Kercher

He came to Rokitno as an adult from Slichets in the twenties. He integrated into the community and dedicated himself to Jewish communal affairs. When Rokitno was annexed to Sarny, he was elected chairman of the Joint Community. He served in that capacity for many years. He was also a member of city council and the permanent treasurer in the new synagogue that was built at his urging. He was a strong man and he fought courageously for the rights of the Jews in municipal and government institutions. He was respected by the Jews of Rokitno as well as by other non-Jewish citizens.

He died at a ripe old age in 1940 as the Soviets were entering town.

Moshe Zelig Shulman

He was a wealthy and successful lumber merchant. He bought Anikin's ranch near Rokitno in the 30's and managed it successfully. He came with his wife Necha to our town as a young man from the village of Vitkovich.

Reb Moshe Zelig was not selfish since he did not feel that money meant everything. He did communal work, mainly in Zionist circles. He was well known as a charitable man and he donated substantially to the various national and charitable funds in Rokitno. He helped with money and materials in the construction of the Tarbut School in Rokitno and he served on the Parents Committee of the school. As a dedicated Zionist, he visited Eretz Yisrael and decided to settle there. He was on the verge of liquidating his business, but the war changed his plans and he was forced to give up his dream of *aliyah.*

When the Soviets entered Rokitno he had to leave town and he hid in Zdolovonov. He was killed there during the Nazi occupation.

Zeidel (Herzel) Binder

He was one of the first leather goods merchants. He was also one of the founders of the *Hevra Kadisha* (Burial Society) and the *Linat Hatzedek*, and he remained active in these institutions all his life. During World War I, many Jewish refugees- escapees from the army- came to Rokitno. Zeidel collected money and paid off Oradnik and Pristov so they would not be caught.

In 1925, Zeidel was sent by a group of residents to Eretz Yisrael in order to buy them land. Due to the Depression there at the time, he did not succeed in his mission. He returned to Rokitno and continued with his business. Being a Zionist, he educated his children in the Zionist spirit. His home was a center for Zionist activities. All Jewish National Fund activities emanated from his house. He was killed in the Holocaust.

Esther Hassel Rootman

She was considered in our town as a clever woman, full of energy and resourcefulness. She was good-natured and was always ready to help others. Her home was open to the needy. Many unfortunate people, Jewish and non-Jewish, found refuge from the winter cold in her bakery.

She especially stood out as a hostess. On Friday nights and on Shabbat, there were always poor souls who would come from great distances to dine at her table. This wonderful custom became a family tradition. Her home was imbued with an aura of Zionism and a love of Israel. Her children grew up in this atmosphere.

Esther Hassel was fortunate to leave our town before the Holocaust and made *aliyah* in 1935. She died in Jerusalem on the eleventh day of *Nissan*, 1955 at the age of 83.

[Page 235]

DURING THE SOVIET OCCUPATION

[Page 237]

The Soviets Occupy Our Town

Baruch Shehori (Schwartzblat) (Haifa)

Translated by Ala Gamulka

A

When war broke out between Germany and Poland, no one imagined that it would mean World War II. This was what would bring ruin and destruction to many nations.

Poland was completely unprepared for this horrible war. Its military structure fell apart in the first few days. Transportation was paralyzed and its productive administrative life ceased. The deterioration was plainly visible. After only a few days, refugees from the West arrived. Among them was a complete office staff from the ministry in Warsaw. Our town was on the fringe and no one thought yet about the Red Army's approach from the east.

Poland was always afraid of its eastern neighbor and prepared lines of fortification. Part of it was an underground defense along the eastern border. It was well equipped with up-to-date innovations. The fences were electrified along several hundred kilometers and a large area could be flooded in an emergency.

This defense line was never used. It was rumored that when the German attacks began, the chief engineer ran away. He took all the plans and keys with him. Later, the Russians destroyed all the underground fortifications. They took, beforehand, all the food, clothing and other equipment intended for hundreds of thousands of soldiers for many years.

On the second day of the war, two trains, filled with reservists, went westward. Among them were several of our Jews who never returned to their families. Their fate was the fate of tens of thousands of Jews who fell on the front, were taken prisoners or were killed in concentration camps.

The danger of a long war was seen in the frantic preparations of food for a long time. After a few days, the stores were emptied. The train movement was unreliable and additional food supplies no longer arrived.

The movement of the Red Army westward and its intention to penetrate Eastern Poland was only whispered about in secret. There was no reliable source for news. On 17 September 1939, several police and army officers left town. They were joined by tens of Polish families who were quite involved in public life. It was clear that changes were coming. Soon the news came that the Soviet army crossed the border and invaded Poland. A civilian police force was immediately organized. Since the Poles were depressed because of the quick defeat, most of its members were Jews. At 11:00 A.M., the first Soviet tanks entered town. The reception was enthusiastic. We received them with red flags and they greeted us with songs and blessings.

In the first days, many trucks filled with soldiers passed through town. The soldiers stopped on the streets, gave speeches, sang and talked to everyone around them. They promised we would lack nothing.

Several young men had been imprisoned by the Polish authorities for their Communist activities. They suddenly rose to big positions. There were also Communist sympathizers or *Bund* members. They organized the municipal life and became Commissars. Their activities were not helpful to the Jewish population in town. Most of it consisted of storeowners and members of the middle class.

These businessmen were fearful. They were afraid that they would be the first to be sacrificed to the new regime. Soon, an order was given to open the stores and to sell, freely, all the products in them. The stores reopened and soon the soldiers of the Red Army swarmed them and bought everything available. Soon, the supply ran out and the stores were shut again.

Work was done feverishly to repair the railroad tracks. They had been separated from Russia for many years. After 10 days heavy Russian locomotives began to arrive with convoys of freight cars, full of soldiers and war equipment.

The Russians were sympathetic to the population. They took part in our sorrow since we had been slaves to capitalism for a long time. They promised that from now on we would live beautiful productive lives, happy and creative. Soon the Soviet regime was well established. Rokitno officially became the district capital. All the district offices of the present commissariats were quickly established. Many administrators arrived. They needed houses and we were cramped for space.

The Soviet civil servants attracted all the activist residents and they were assisted by suspicious looking and unwanted elements. Even in the first days, several Polish social activists and some Jews were arrested and exiled. The first Jews to be arrested were the pharmacist Noah Soltzman and the teacher Mordechai Gendelman. They stayed in prison in Sarny for several months and were released after undergoing special treatment. The prisoners returned to town mute and it was impossible to get a word out of them.

Mr. Gendelman, the teacher, was active for many years for JNF and he was a distinguished Bible teacher at the Tarbut school. He turned completely and suddenly became a sworn Communist. He announced publicly in school that he felt contempt towards all Jewish cultural values. He had previously taught these values to his pupils. He said they were only reactionary values.

The children had been educated to love Zionist and cultural values and the history of the Jewish people. Their world collapsed when they heard that their beloved teacher was trampling any Jewish sparks. They received his words with aching hearts and could not accept this change to the end. Tarbut school became a government school and Yiddish was taught instead of Hebrew.

Public life was organized. The Jewish population adapted to the new regime. The workers organized cooperatives hoping that their economic situation would improve. Many were disappointed after a short period of cooperative effort. The shopkeepers began to seek jobs. Some found positions in cooperative groceries and others as office clerks. The different plants in town and around it were nationalized. The owners and the managers left because they feared exile to Siberia.

All the residents were issued identity papers. Those who had been well to-do in the past had notes in their documents signifying that they were second-class citizens. They expected to be sent to distant Russia any day.

All connections between our town Jews and their relatives in other countries, including Eretz Israel, were broken. They were afraid that they would be accused of Zionist or espionage activities. This fear robbed most people of energy and initiative. They isolated themselves, spoke little and suspected everyone.

The Soviets were quite successful in one field -- education. They built a wide educational system. They even founded high schools in the large villages. Next to the veteran teachers, they placed young teachers. They were high school graduates and had taken special training. Teachers were given good working conditions. The schools were well equipped with books and maps and even laboratories.

I served as principal of the Ukrainian high school. My main function was to gather all the school children and all the young people in a special evening course. In addition, I had to teach the population the principles of the Soviet constitution, to call frequent meetings and to do propaganda for Communism. It was a great responsibility.

We did not encounter any limits when it came to keeping religious values. The two synagogues were not closed. Services continued without any interruption.

However, the number of worshippers decreased. First, most of the Jews worked on Shabbat and could not come to pray. Second, clerks and laborers who did not want any suspicion cast on them stopped attending.

There was no point in having a gathering of Jews only since there were no longer any parties, debates on Zionism or Hebrew culture as before. The Jews deteriorated from the point of view of their national character. Still, there was no ban on baking *matzos*, on public worshipping or on performing religious rites.

The hardened, dictatorial regime believed in the motto: "He who is not with us, is against us!" The entire population was afraid. This was a population who had known freedom of movement, freedom of speech and freedom of activity. The youth no longer had hopes of fulfilling the promise of *aliyah.* A few individuals managed, secretly, to leave town for Vilna. There, members of *Hashomer Hatzair* and *Hechalutz* were actively smuggling young people to Eretz Israel. The rest pretended to break off any connections to the past and to join the new regime. In their hearts, the yearning and hope never disappeared. This was really the beginning of the destruction of the Rokitno Jewish community.

In spite of the severe prohibition, we received news of events in Eretz Israel. In the evenings, we listened to the radio for world news. The Russian broadcasts contained only propaganda. There were few newspapers -- *Pravda* and *Izvestia* only. Trips out of town were forbidden without a specific permit. There were no mass meetings. Everyone was too busy. Besides daily work, there were study days filled with propaganda speeches and meetings. It was not a good idea to be absent from these study days.

During the Soviet occupation, there were also purges. Many refugees, who had escaped from Germany, were transferred to work in the coal mines (*donbas*). Among them were some of the administrators of the town. A few returned six months later. However, the war between Russia and Germany broke out and they moved East with the army.

B

The war between Russia and Germany went on for several weeks and spread deep into Greater Russia. The Germans conducted a lightning campaign. There was great fear and confusion. There were sad reports that entire units threw down their arms and fled. Others let themselves be captured. In leaflets thrown from airplanes, Hitler called on the Soviet soldiers to abandon their arms and to join the Germans. The Germans would liberate them and set up the Ukraine and Byelorussia as independent states free of Communists and blood-sucking Jews. "It is very bad," the Jews said to one another. "The end of the Jewish people is here if the motto of Germany is the eradication of the Jewish race in the whole world."

"We must pack some belongings, escape deep into Russia and save ourselves," said a Polish refugee in 1939.

Another Jew said: "It is not as terrible as he describes it." He, too, is a refugee. "There are still many Jews in Poland and they are all alive. I just received a letter from my wife and children and they are alive. Many Jews were killed in our village, but they cannot kill everyone. The first wave will pass and the others will remain alive. I am not going to Russia to die of hunger or in forced labor in Siberia."

These arguments were heard everywhere. Only an hour earlier, a train full of refugees passed through. They looked tired and filthy. They asked for bread, water and cigarettes. Our heartache grew daily. A horde of refugees came through. They were on freight trains, wagons, bicycles and even on foot. They carried some belongings. They did not stop. They only asked for a piece of bread and water and continued on their way.

It was difficult for me leave my family alone. My father was sick and could not travel. My mother, too, was ailing. On the evening of July 4, 1941, I packed two backpacks - one for me and one for my sister. The next day, early in the morning, we planned to go to the train station in the hopes of getting on a train going east.

Mother and father wept with us. My father, in spite of the great sorrow he felt, encouraged me to save myself. They would remain under the watch of G-d.

Suddenly, my sister freed herself from my sobbing mother and said: "I am not going. I cannot leave my sick parents. You can go in peace with our blessings, but I am staying."

I was helpless. Finally I overcame my fears, wiped my tears, put on my backpack, quietly took a final look at the rooms, the darkened walls, kissed the *mezuzah* and I left. My sister, broken-hearted, accompanied me part of the way. At 5:00 A.M. I sat on a stone in the station and I waited. There were other Jews alone or with families.

By 4:00 P.M. we still had not succeeded in boarding a train. All the trains were full of soldiers and equipment. The soldiers aimed their rifles at anyone who approached the train. In the meantime, the platform was filled with refugees, soldiers and government employees.

I became despondent from all the waiting. I wanted to return home and to try again at night. Suddenly, we heard a siren. Everyone ran away from the platform and hid in various places. A few seconds later, a loud sound was heard: a bomb had detonated near the station building. It destroyed all the buildings nearby. The street near the station was in ruins and 14 bodies were found there. These were those who had tried to hide behind the stone wall. No one could identify the dead. They were refugees who had died in our town.

Finally, I managed to board a train and I sat quietly. An Uzbek officer appeared and insisted we disembark. Our pleas were to no avail. He aimed his rifle at us and threatened to shoot anyone who did not get off. We waited again.

I then decided to go back home to my family and to be with them through the terrifying times. I would die with them if it were so ordained.

C

Everything is over. On the morning of 10.7.41, the last train going east passed through town. The remnants of the Soviet occupation were on it. Soon an armed train came, bombing behind it all the tracks, bridges and the station. The sounds of the explosions permeated the air. It informed us that the water tower at the station was gone and would no longer supply water for the steam engines. Fifteen minutes later, there was another big explosion and the iron bridge broke in half and fell into the bottom of the stream. The last of the Soviet army burned the sawmill and the glass factory. Flames erupted in the buildings used as government offices. They spread and incinerated the shreds and documents in those offices. It was done to prevent their falling into enemy hands.

They passed through the streets noiselessly and without looting. Some called from the trucks "Wait for us. We will return soon. This is only a strategic withdrawal. We will return in the name of Communism and Stalin."

The quiet remained for a short time. All the Jews locked themselves in their houses sadly and fearfully. A few hours later, the street filled with Poles and peasants from nearby villages. They broke into storage places and government stores and looted. We saw them through the slits in the shutters. They were sweaty, dragging sacks, furniture and dishes. There was great disorder.

Towards evening, several young people came to my brother's house to discuss the situation and the future. We decided to contact some Poles and to organize ourselves. A guard roster would stop the looting and restore peace. A group of 20 young Poles, hooligans and anti-Semites, was formed. They promised to keep order.

We did not trust them and we agreed that men would go out in the evenings to do guard duty. We went in groups holding sticks. The young Poles tried to talk us into going to sleep and leaving them in charge. We did not believe them and we continued our guarding. At midnight, when most of the older men had gone home, we heard shouting: “Help me!” The shouting came from far away, from the new town.

“Do not hesitate. Let's go immediately," yelled Avraham Golod. He led the group. We hurried towards the train tracks and the new town. He ran ahead and we followed. Suddenly, a group of young Poles burst out of one of the houses near the train station. They were shouting, “Attack the Jew!” They threw stones at us in the darkness. We bent down to search for stones, to retaliate. We suddenly heard shouting and we ran ahead.

The attackers disappeared in the darkness of night. Unfortunately, we saw a victim lying on the road. We approached to identify him. It was Avraham Golod, lying lifeless with blood streaming down his face. He was hit with three stones -- two in the head and one in the nose. We carried him back to his house, washed off the blood and called for the doctor. He did not regain consciousness. The doctor thought that he had a brain hemorrhage caused by the stone that hit his nose. He died early the next morning. The whole town attended the funeral. Some people said he was fortunate to have so many people honor his death and accompany him. Who will do it for us?

This is the story of Avraham Golod. He was the symbol of daring and courage. He was a man of action -- the first martyr in our town.

[Page 243]

The Beginnings of the Soviet Occupation of Rokitno

Yakov Schwartz (Rehovot)

Translated by Ala Gamulka

The first two weeks of the German-Polish war passed fairly quietly in Rokitno. Enemy planes that destroyed other Polish towns, missed our town. This was the reason many refugees came to us. They were Jews and families of Polish officers who were crammed in the houses and streets since they were unable to go east.

We waited anxiously for what was to come. The news from the front was bad. The Polish army was retreating constantly. One need not be a prophet to predict the coming battles. A Polish army unit, organized in Rokitno, went to the front. It was stuck near Sarny and some of its members returned. The Jews tried not to think about the future. They occupied themselves with looking after their fellow Jews, refugees from western and central Poland. Among them were refugees from Czechoslovakia and Vienna. We became very close.

The 17th of September 1939 arrived. We awoke to the growing noise of airplane engines. Everything we expected was happening. We dressed quickly, grabbed the baggage we had prepared and we began to run towards the forest. We had not gone very far when the mayor, Bratzky, stopped us and told us that the Red Army had entered Poland. He calmed us, telling us that these were Soviet airplanes. He asked us to keep order and quiet. He was ready to hand over the town without any bloodshed.

We returned and sat on the balcony, in spite of the warnings of our parents. They feared riots during the changeover of regimes. In truth, there was much movement on the streets. The Polish chauvinists from the O.Z.N. Party, among them many laborers from the glass factory, ran to the barracks to obtain arms. Families of Polish officers hurried towards the train station hoping to escape westward, away from the Red Army. This was their despised enemy and they feared them more than they feared the Germans.

The last train left the station. The remnants of the Polish army went to Strashov where they hoped to stop the Red Army. It was tense and quiet in town.

Towards noon, rumors spread that, on the school road, the first tanks appeared. Curiosity overcame fear. We ran to the first Soviet soldiers who were at the town entrance. There we found a crowd of curious onlookers. They stared at the new army and tried to find out something. The soldiers behaved cordially. They distributed cigarettes and candies and tried to endear themselves to the population. They lifted the small children on the trucks and tanks and drove them to town, to city hall. The mayor and his clerks stood waiting for the Soviet commander to hand over the town. The Soviet authorities appreciated the help of the mayor in preventing riots. They kept him as a clerk on the municipal committee.

An endless stream of tanks and cars began to go through. They passed through Rokitno on the way west. We were not accustomed to such sights. The Polish army that had camped in town did not possess any vehicles. Every soldier and officer of the Red Army who stopped in town was surrounded by a crowd of questioners. Our Jewish brothers asked many questions about prices of provisions, clothes, shoes; work and study opportunities; explanations of various terms unknown in Poland. Every fighter in the Red Army saw himself as a propagandist and always had answers prepared in advance.

The Soviet soldiers laughed, told jokes and made propaganda speeches about communal settlements, Dnieprostroy, Stachanov's system, Moscow subway, factories and happy people who lived under the "sun of the people".

The soldiers were thrilled to see awe and wonder on the faces of the listeners. An order to reopen the stores came and a buying spree followed. Even the soldiers and commanders of the Red Army were involved in buying.

We were especially excited to hear the beautiful songs sung during parades. "Brother Vintovka," "*Yesli Zavotra Vaina*" - we did not actually understand the words. However, the music was enthralling. The soldiers were also capable dancers. They played harmonicas or balalaikas and danced.

Within a few days the whole eastern part of Poland -- or the western part of the Ukraine (so called by the Soviets) was conquered. The government began to establish itself. Veteran Communists, among them Jews from Rokitno who had been in Polish prisons for many years, were appointed to important municipal positions. The fancy clubhouse of the Polish officers was now available for the youth of Rokitno as a place to have fun.

They were drawn to it mainly out of curiosity. They were mostly Jewish youngsters. Some non-Jews came, but they did not really fit in and felt uncomfortable. The libraries from the town and from nearby villages were centered there. Among them was the rich Tarbut library. Books could not be circulated until censoring was completed. There was no hurry to do it. We found out later that many books were used as heating fuel in the homes of the soldiers.

The Zionist parties and the youth movements self-destructed. Here and there, secret meetings still took place. There were some young people who endangered their lives and tried to reach Vilna on their way to Eretz Israel. A few succeeded while others were caught and sent to concentration camps in the far North.

A local militia was formed to replace the Polish police. There were many Jews in it. In general, the Jews were prominent in all new government institutions. When the High Holidays came, the synagogues were full (among them the synagogue in the Tarbut school). Everyone prayed as always. The Jews prayed devoutly and thanked G-d for saving them in an unexpected way. Still, the tension was felt. The Jews knew that more was to come.

On the first day of *Succoth*, early in the morning, a soldier came to our house and asked my father to present himself to the military commander in town. Several hours later, when my father had not returned, we went to investigate what was happening. We saw four of our citizens: Shimon Klorfein, Mordechai Gendelman the teacher, Noah Soltzman and my father sitting on a truck. They were surrounded by armed soldiers. Another truck packed with soldiers, their guns cocked, followed them. It was a shocking sight.

We found out that after an inquest they were taken to Sarny. There they were held and interrogated for a month. A former P.K.P. man, a refugee thrown out of Eretz Israel, had accused them of Zionist and anti-Soviet activities. He decided to take revenge on the Zionists and found a convenient location when the Soviets entered Rokitno.

After the arrests and anticipating searches, we decided to get rid of any suspicious materials. We mainly threw out Hebrew books and newspapers.

Our furnace burned day and night. Black ashes covered the area. The search did not happen. After a month of investigations and interrogations, the detainees were released. It is important to emphasize the honesty of the Communists from Rokitno. When questioned by the investigators from the NKVD, they said that the detainees together with other residents had helped them and their families during the Polish regime. They provided them with lawyers and other assistance.

The first to be released was Mordechai Gendelman. It was at great personal cost and most humiliating. He was forced to sign a document promising to publicly announce that his work up to now was meant to delude innocent people and to show them the wrong way. The three others signed a promise to stop all Zionist activities and to be loyal to the Soviet regime.

These arrests and the first public trial of a Jew- a restaurant owner accused of "speculation"-- showed us the other side of the coin.

Autumn ended. The difficult winter of 1939 began to show its signs. Rokitno was designated by the Soviets as the district capital. All the institutions attached to this role were set up. Their titles were composed of initials and abbreviations. The Jews began to be accustomed, more or less, to the new reality. Schools were opened. Tarbut school became a Yiddish school. Transportation to other towns improved. The line-ups at the cooperative stores grew. In short, the Soviet regime became a fact.

[Page 246]

Rokitno in the Years 1939-1941

Bat Sheva Fishman (Shohet) (Tel Aviv)

Translated by Ala Gamulka

On September 1, 1939, Germany attacked Poland. My family and I were in Lahova in western Byelorussia. According to the agreement signed by Molotov and Ribentrop, it was annexed by Byelorussia.

The change was felt as soon as the Soviets came to town. The authorities began to swallow our merchandise. Our situation was very bad and we were subject to Paragraph 11. It meant exile to distant Russia. However, thanks to Jewish soldiers in the Soviet army who helped us, we were able to escape without being noticed. Somehow we reached Rokitno.

We immediately noticed the big changes in town. There was a pall of mourning everywhere. The streets where Jews used to thrive were now silent. The stores, almost the only source of income for the Jews, were bolted shut. Commerce was no longer permitted. The Jewish tradesmen, who used to hum Jewish melodies at work, were silent. They joined the *artels*, i.e., cooperatives. The atmosphere was now different.

The Hebrew language was banned and the children were educated in a foreign language. Jewish children had been educated with the cultural values of our people, the Bible, the commentaries and the greats of modern Hebrew literature. It was difficult for them to become accustomed to the foreign atmosphere. Their souls were injured and they were very confused. The spiritual life of the Jews had nearly stopped. Public life was silenced. Public gatherings, especially in synagogues, decreased. They were not officially prohibited. However, instinctively, the Jews felt it was better not to appear in public and to stay home on Shabbat for now. Devout Jews continued to pray in secret, although the authorities could not legally touch matters of faith.

Trains crammed with refugees passed daily. They were Poles from areas conquered by Germany. They were not able to stay since the Soviets exiled them to distant Russia. The Jews, especially the wealthier ones, were depressed and worried. The constant fear gnawed at them. However, there is no calamity that human beings cannot overcome. Somehow, they become used to their new life. Almost all of them found jobs and were productive.

They tried to uphold their Jewishness. They mourned the loss of the Jewish life. However, they did not imagine that this was the end, that in a short time, they would perish. On June 22, 1941, Hitler canceled the non-aggression pact and declared war on Russia. On July 5, the train station in Rokitno was bombed and the German army was approaching. Again we continued our wandering and went to Russia.

[Page 247]

Missed Opportunities for Rescue

Avraham Kek (Sh'fiah)

Translated by Ala Gamulka

I was drafted into the Red Army when war broke out between the Germans and the Soviets. We were told that we were being sent to the front, to block the rapid progress of the Germans. A Jewish officer in the Soviet army told me that we were leaving for Rovno that night. We would then go to the front.

My brother Michael came to take leave from me at the soldier's club near the glass factory. He hugged me and with tears in his eyes said: "May G-d help you. What can man do at this difficult time? Who knows what happened to my son, Betzalel. He has been in the Soviet army for the past year and we have not heard from him." He embraced me again and walked away sobbing.

An hour later, we heard a siren. German airplanes appeared and bombed the train station. Soldiers were standing there in long lines. Many died and many were injured. The bombing went on for about 25 minutes. It caused death and destruction.

A terrible panic erupted. The Soviet government clerks packed their belongings and fled. Some Jews followed them. Unfortunately, many refused to run away since they thought their life would be better under the Germans than under the Soviets. I remember one event that proved to me the seriousness of the situation. I was standing near the house of the tailor Yosef-Haim Baum. There I met a refugee from Rozishetz. He told us to run away immediately. The Germans spent only fifteen minutes in Rozishetz and managed to kill many Jews. The Jews heard the warning, but they did not understand its depth. They comforted themselves by saying: "This terrible event will not reach us."

At 2:00 P.M., all those drafted, Jews and non- Jews, were ready to go to the train station to join the Soviet soldiers going to the front. Suddenly, the Jewish officer appeared in the club and told us that he was ordered to release us. He told us to return the guns and go home. The Ukrainians were thrilled to hear the news. We, the Jews, understood only too well the meaning of this "release." We asked the officer to try to let us go to the front. It would be better than to stay under the terror of the Germans. He informed us that he could not change the orders, but that we could take our families to Russia. The Soviet government was allowing the Jews to join the soldiers' train. We had to hurry and leave before it was too late.

I returned to Snovidovich, my birthplace, to see my family. I invited my brother, Haim, to hear this news. He wished to leave, but his wife Sonia refused. She claimed that she could not leave her home to become a refugee. Her neighbors were not leaving. They had good reasons to do so.

As we were speaking, the manager of the government bank in Rokitno came and spoke to my niece, Rivochka (Rivka). She was a bookkeeper at the bank. He invited her to join his family who was leaving for Russia. She would save herself by going. She did not listen to him since her mother refused to leave.

I begged my sister-in-law to reconsider and I returned to Rokitno. I waited two days for them, but I had no reply. Two days later, the German army entered deep into Russia. The roads were closed and there was no way out. My brother's reply came too late and we remained under the Germans.

[Page 248]

Aliyah to Eretz Israel During the Soviet Occupation

Dvorah Ferkel (Golovey) (Beit Zerah)

Translated by Ala Gamulka

The Soviets entered Rokitno on September 17, 1939. The Zionist youth movements were banned and youth clubs were opened in their place. The Zionist youth did not accept this cruel decree. They tried, with all their might, to organize secret activities. They did not succeed. The town was small and everyone knew each other. Any suspicious activity would be discovered immediately.

It was difficult to organize any activities, even in secret. We did everything to preserve cultural values and spirit. The Soviets housed the *Hashomer Hatzair* and Tarbut School libraries in a warehouse. At night, we put our lives in danger to save some books. Unfortunately, we could only save a small portion. These books were our only cultural nourishment since there were no other libraries in town. We were used to reading Hebrew literature and we could not be without it.

I hid the unit flag and several socialist books in our yard. These books did not follow the Soviet worldview. The books remained in a deep pit and eventually disappeared.

We were certain that we would not be physically harmed under the Soviets. However, we knew this regime would force a total separation from Eretz Israel and our hopes of reaching its shores. This realization spurred the pioneering youth. They searched for ways to reach Eretz Israel. We heard that there was a large pioneering youth center in Vilna (it was still free at this time). The center concentrated on finding routes to Eretz Israel.

We followed the example of this center. Several *Hashomer Hatzair* members- Shoshana and Shmaryahu Korobochka, Sonia and Misha Berezovsky, Beibe Kutz, the Eizenstein brothers and I- succeeded in reaching Vilna. There were about 1000 *Hashomer Hatzair* members there.

Our departure was kept secret. No one wanted the authorities or the general public to find out anything. There were some denouncers who were ready to stop us. I told my parents of my plans. They were happy that I was on my way to Eretz Israel. However, they also feared that I would not be able to overcome the difficulties entailed in this daring deed. They also feared that if the authorities found out the reason for my departure, they themselves would suffer the consequences. Still, they showed great courage and wisdom because they were certain that this was the only way. They gave me their blessings and hoped that I would soon see my brother and sister in Eretz Israel.

We boarded the Lida train in the middle of the night. Its first stop was Sarny. This was during *Hanukah* and school was on vacation. Our departure did not make anyone suspicious. I met one of my school teachers in Sarny. He urged me to return home.

When we reached Lida, we found an underground office dealing in transportation of people to Vilna. We were separated into small groups with a guide to help us cross the border. It was extremely cold and the snow was knee-deep. We arrived in Ishishock, a village in Lithuania. We crossed the border on New Year's Eve 1940. From Ishishock we went to Vilna. There was a large camp of *Hashomer Hatzair* on Tartaky Street. We managed to find a place to sleep and to rest up from our difficult voyage. Conditions in the camp were very harsh. We spent a full winter working hard in the daytime and studying at night. In the meantime, the Soviets conquered Vilna. They announced that those who had travel certificates would be permitted to go. I obtained a certificate through *youth aliyah* and I reached Eretz Israel in March 1941.

[Page 249]

A Frightening Episode From the Soviet Occupation

Eliahu Freger (Kiryat Frustig)

Translated by Ala Gamulka

The Soviets did not harm the Jews of Tupik. They saw us as honest, innocent and hard-working people. They allowed us to continue to farm. However, they took away from us the flourmill and appointed Aharon Chechik as its manager.

They were very angry with my brother, Shlomo. They suspected him of collaborating with the Poles. He was sentenced to 8 years in prison and he was taken to Stolin. From there, he was exiled to Siberia. Eight months after he was sent to prison in the distant North, his wife and 3 children were exiled to Kazakhstan. His children were Hannah, Taibele and Shmulik. Shlomo did not know that his family was exiled. Two months before the Germans came, he wrote a letter to his wife. He was certain that she was still in Tupik. He asked for tobacco and sugar in his letter. We sent him her address and they continued to correspond.

When the war between the Soviets and the Germans broke out, the Soviets released Polish citizens. Among them was my brother. He immediately went to search for his wife and children. He traveled for three months and he finally reached a place 50 kilometers from Kazakhstan.

Shlomo did not know that his wife was there. The Soviets brought her there to work in a maternity hospital. As he was walking near the shacks in the refugee camp, he heard a child sobbing. The child told his mother in Ukrainian, "My father will come soon. I will tell him you spanked me". He thought he recognized the voice, but continued on his way.

At the crossroads stood the school. He recognized his daughter Taibele playing in the yard. His heart almost stopped. He quickly recovered and with a voice full of happiness and sobbing, called out, "Taibele, Taibele, my daughter!" The girl approached him, but she did not recognize him. His beard was fully-grown and he looked different. The girl was in shock. She asked, "What do you want, stranger?" His voice choked as he replied, "Taibele, I am your father!" The girl laughed and said, "I have many fathers like you in the village. Go away!" She pushed him away. Taibele was only 3 years old when her father was exiled. Three years had passed and she did not know that the man standing in front of her, dressed in a uniform, was her father.

The strange encounter with the "stranger" caused her to think. With a beating heart she ran into class and told Hannah, her older sister, "Hannah, a soldier called me Taibele and said he was my father! Go and see who is this man."

Hannah immediately recognized her father. Shlomo took his daughters in his arms and sobbed with happiness. He stayed there and worked in the communal settlement. His wife continued her work.

When I was in Rokitno in 1945, I received a letter from him from Zhitomir. He was in a hospital. When I came there to see him, a soldier said simply, "Your brother died yesterday." I did not believe this terrible rumor and I went to the command center. The secretary told me my brother was alive and had been transferred elsewhere. In spite of my pleading, I was not allowed to see him and I returned to Rokitno.

Eight days later, I received a letter from him. He told me that he had recuperated and was returning to Rokitno. Time had ravaged Shlomo's body. I placed him in the hospital and when he felt better, we left Rokitno. We went to Germany where we parted company. I went to Italy on my way to Eretz Israel and he reached Graz. There he became ill again and was in the hospital. Before he died, at the last moments of his life, he told his wife, "I am going and I will not return. You are alive. You suffered so much from the Gentiles. Do not go anywhere else. Go to Eretz Israel. Go to Eliahu". She did not fulfill his wishes. She moved to Canada where she quickly died.

[Page 251]

Leaving Rokitno in 1941

Yakov Schwartz (Rehovot)

Translated by Ala Gamulka

Who can ever forget, even for a short time, that fateful day, when we took our belongings and left our town? We left everything good and dear to us and we went to Russia- the big country.

The war had already lasted for over a week. Bad news kept coming. The Red Army- "unbeaten and fighting on the enemy's land"- was retreating. Everything we did not want to believe was actually happening. Rokitno was full of refugees and many of the residents were themselves preparing to become refugees. Many rumors circulated: the roads in Russia were full of bodies of dead soldiers; there was no food; the former border was closed, etc... Many who had planned to escape decided to stay home, come what may. No one believed that this decision to stay could bring death. We expected to do forced labor, to be enclosed in ghettos, to suffer difficulties. We did not expect physical destruction. The general belief was that men and young people were in danger. Plans were made to leave temporarily because of the bombing, changes of regime and rioting.

One day there was a rumor that the NKVD in Rokitno was distributing permits to enter Soviet Russia. At dawn, there was a long line of interested parties. They were mainly Jews who waited anxiously for the piece of paper that would save them. Indeed, it was true. Permits were distributed and the Jews began to search for a method of transportation- horses and wagons. Train travel was only a dream.

The central committee of the Communist Party was successful in obtaining a train car for the members of the town's *komsomol*. On the day of departure, everyone felt that fate was not kind to Rokitno. This time, the horrors of war would not bypass us. On Friday afternoon, the city felt, for the first time, the brunt of the fascist bombings. A military train, standing in the station, was bombed. The results were frightening. The number of injured and dead was high. Many cars and the station itself became ruins. The streets were full of broken glass from the blown windows. The residents were deeply affected. Depression and fear of the bleak future filled our hearts. The noise abated and everyone was deep in thought. Those who planned to leave Rokitno and had postponed their departure decided now was the time to go. Preparations continued all night. Food for the travelers and the horses was packed. Suitcases and backpacks were filled. They contained all the essentials for the road. On Saturday morning, July 5, 1941 after an emotional parting, we went on the road towards the unknown.

Four young men joined us. In all, we were seven people on a packed wagon. Of course, this was not an actual trip. We were happy that the horses freed us from the burden of carrying our packages. The convoy of wagons stretched along the old town to the village of Rokitno. The looks of neighbors, friends and acquaintances followed us. We left town quietly, sadly, accompanied by secret jealousy mixed with pity. The quick glances expressed the emotions. No one thought of the terrible holocaust coming to our town. This was the fate of those who remained. We were certain that the German army would be stopped near the fortified border between Poland and Russia. We hoped we would find shelter in one of the nearby Ukrainian villages. We would wait there until the Red Army, we were sure, would regroup and defeat the Germans. We would then return home to our dear ones.

Thinking sad thoughts and trying to figure out our chances, we passed Ostoki and Snovidovich. We reached the old Polish-Russian border gate. The few soldiers who manned the gate could not control the crowd that wished to cross. Our documents were inspected and we were allowed to continue to Olevsk. How surprised we were to discover that most of its inhabitants had run away and abandoned their houses.

The picture was repeated in many other towns and villages. Only then did we understand the size of the tragedy. All the hopes we had nursed in our hearts in the last few days turned to disappointment. Our hearts were heavy. We thought of returning and taking all those left behind in Rokitno, to save them. However, the road was blocked. We could only move forward. Even this was difficult because there were retreating units of the Red Army on the road.

Olevsk was behind us. Towards evening, we reached a communal settlement to spend the night. We unharnessed and fed the horses. We also ate. The people from the settlement looked after us with great devotion. They brought us bread and milk and offered us straw pallets in one of the public buildings. We were very tired and, in spite of our worries, we fell into deep sleep.

The next few days passed like a kaleidoscope. We traveled hundreds of kilometers in the next week until we reached Nizhin, across the Dnepr. There, we finally boarded a freight train. Many times we found ourselves in difficult situations. Enemy planes hovered over us, threw bombs and shot at us. At times we had to disembark and lie cramped together for hours waiting for the bombing to end. We tried to use nighttime to move ahead. We had enough food with us. The local authorities and citizens helped us everywhere we went. We made 40-50 kilometers a day, sometimes even more. We were driven by our wish to live. We felt as if all of Russia was traveling with us. We met many people and heard many stories. The picture was very gloomy.

There was no purpose in continuing to Kiev. It was being bombed and was itself preparing for evacuation. Our aim was to cross the Dnepr as soon as possible and to continue by train because the horses were losing their strength.

We managed to cross the Dnepr at night in a convoy of thousands of wagons. We were unfortunate enough to be greeted on the other side by a German airplane that caused havoc. We reached Nizhin. It was a big station at the crossroads. Tens of trains and hundreds of cars were concentrated there. They were filled with soldiers, arms and military equipment. The soldiers were singing, commands were given, political speeches were heard calling for a battle "for country and for Stalin".

We handed the horses to the firefighters and we settled ourselves in a freight car on a train going east. It was going away from the front, away from the German bombs and parachutists. It was also far away from home, from family, friends and from Jewish life in our town.

Our peaceful life was over, more or less. Our never-ending wanderings began. They continued for many years, until many of us made *aliyah*.

[Page 253]

Mushka Shuster – The Committee Representative

Yosef Segal (Givatayim)

Translated by Ala Gamulka

One of the tradesmen in Rokitno was Yehoshua Shuster (Yehoshua the painter). He lived with his wife, Mushka, and his young son and daughter in a small rented house. It was situated in the yard of the Trossman family on Soviesky Street (Messeyevitch Street). Yehoshua was a good and diligent tradesman. He was always occupied with his work. He earned a good living for his family and was always satisfied with his lot. In the winter, when there was no work painting, he tried to do other work. He was never unemployed. His home was a traditional Jewish home, like all other Jewish homes.

Mushka was a good housekeeper and looked after the education and well being of their two children. They received a Zionist education in the Tarbut school. It was an ordinary, simple family that led a quiet life.

In 1939, after the 17 th of September, the Soviet occupation was established in the Ukraine and western Byelorussia (previously belonging to Poland). The authorities announced the formation of two committees: one, in Lvov, the capital of western Ukraine, and the other in Baranovich, the capital of western Byelorussia. Their purpose was to approve, by the representatives of the people of the area, their annexation as republics of the Soviet Union. The representative of the Rokitno district to the Lvov committee, chosen by the Party, was Mushka Shuster. Great publicity was involved in her election. There were articles in the local newspaper about the biography of Mushka Shuster. She was described as a loyal daughter of the working people and the Ukrainian nation. She was deemed worthy of this great honor, to be a delegate to the committee and to represent the Ukrainian people. Her picture was displayed in store windows. She herself was not thrilled with the election. She was forced to represent the district. It was not done out of her free will. Why was Mushka chosen? Perhaps it was due to her simplicity or her innocence? It remains a mystery.

Mushka took part in the historic committee in Lvov. It was chaired by Marshal Timoshenko and included many important personalities from the central Communist Party and Ukrainian leaders. The 600 delegates voted to annex western Ukraine to the Soviet Union. Mushka was soon forgotten. She continued to live with her family in the small house in the yard of Yechiel Trossman. Their condition did not improve.

When the German Nazis occupied Rokitno in 1941, Mushka remained with her family. In the confusion of war, no one even tried to save Mushka, the representative of the Ukrainian people. She was executed by the Gestapo in Rovno when the Germans entered Rokitno. Yehoshua and their son were killed in the Rokitno holocaust. Their daughter was saved and now lives in the United States.

[Page 254]

The *Bulbovtzes*

Yakov Soltzman (Tel Aviv)

Translated by Ala Gamulka

Who were the *Bulbovtzes* who murdered us in the years 1941-1944? In the 30's a Ukrainian called Taras Borovitz came to Rokitno from Dubno. He was an expert in quarries and owned one in Karpilovka.

I knew him well since he used to come to my pharmacy to buy first-aid products for his laborers. He was known as a radical nationalist and always made intense propaganda among those who knew him. Once, one of his laborers became intoxicated and began to riot at the outskirts of Rokitno. When the police came to arrest him, he struggled with the officers and told them, "Why did you, the *liachs* (slur word against Poles), come to rule over our land? One day we will murder all of you." He was sentenced to three years in prison for this mutiny against the authorities.

Once, in the summer of 1938, I was sitting with Borovitz in the pharmacy and we spoke about politics. I asked him, "Mr. Borovitz, where is it stated that Ukraine was ever, in history, an independent state?" He replied with cunning, "History is like a violin. He who knows how to play will play as he wishes and as he sees fit. The Soviets wanted to hold on to the wheat fields of Ukraine. They proved that Ukraine and Russia are one indivisible entity. Now the *liachs* are saying the same thing."

In June 1939, Germany attacked Poland to defend itself on the Ukrainian side. (It was well known by the Polish government that Bandera murdered Minister Piritzky. He then made a pact with the Germans and promised them the assistance of the Ukrainians.) The Polish authorities arrested the national Ukrainian leaders, Taras Borovitz among them. They exiled them to a concentration camp in Kortoz-Bereze. When the Soviets conquered Kortoz-Bereze, they released all the prisoners including Taras Borovitz. He returned to Rokitno and the Soviets appointed him manager of the quarry in Rokitno. He was considered an honored citizen and they did not harm him.

Taras Borovitz served in this position for two years. Eventually he realized that the hopes he had placed in the Soviets, that they would award independence to the Ukraine, were in vain.

According to the secret pact between Stalin and Hitler, the Ukrainian section of Poland, with its capital Lvov, would be annexed by Russia. The national Ukrainian leaders, who had been released by the Russians, began underground activities against their Soviet liberators.

The Ukrainian leaders in Volyn, led by Taras Borovitz, were convinced that with the German's defeat of the Russian army they would be able to have an independent state. Its capital would be Kiev. Even their cohorts, the Banderovtzis in Galicia, believed that Hitler would keep his promise.

When the Germans attacked Russia, there were riots in our area. We were close to the front and the Germans bombed Rokitno on the third day of the war.

In these dark days, Taras Borovitz held a meeting in the village of Borovey in the house of the priest, Alexander Simonovich. Those who attended were the priest's brother, Boris (he helped the Germans to murder the Jews of Olevsk), his wife (a teacher), medically trained Kramer from Karpilovka, a teacher from Korostin, Sharat from the village of Netreba, Afansiuk (veterinarian technician from Rokitno), and others. It was decided to elect a committee of Ukrainian nationalists headed by the *Bulbovtzes*.

The Soviet army was in disarray and the *Bulbovtzes* used the fact to take arms and to cross to the German side. The removal of arms was done with great craftiness. A huge funeral was organized. Arms and ammunition were put in caskets instead of bodies. This booty was buried in the cemetery.

When the Germans reached the Sluch River, 45 kilometers west of Rokitno, Taras Borovitz (calling himself Bulboy), gathered his laborers, deserters and hoodlums from Karpilovka, Borovey, Mocholnoka, Kisorich and other villages. He armed them and informed the residents of Rokitno that he would soon come with his army.

When the Soviets left Rokitno, a drunken shoemaker, boorish and illiterate, appeared in town. His name was Ratzlav. He organized a police force from among the laborers in the glass factory. Its task was to rob the Jews of Rokitno and vicinity. When Taras announced the date of his arrival in Rokitno, Ratzlav ordered all the residents, except for the Jews, to greet the "liberating redeemer" with flowers.

All the residents of Rokitno, Body, Messevich and the outlying farms in the area drowned the Bulbovtzes in a sea of flowers. They shouted, "*Slawa*! (freedom)" as they entered the park. There they gathered near the broken statue of Pilsudsky. The priest, Alexander Simonovich from Borovey, conducted a prayer service and thanked G-d for saving the residents from the cruel Soviet government. A local government was chosen (*Rada*). Dr. Anishtchuk was very active in it.

Taras Borovitz stayed in Rokitno with his group for two weeks. He drafted young people into his army. Except for a few robberies, the *Bulbovtzes* conducted themselves in Rokitno in an orderly manner. They did not murder anyone because Taras was very popular in Rokitno and he had many Jewish friends. Avraham Golod and I came to him and we asked him to look after the Jewish population. He promised us that nothing would happen in Rokitno. He kept his word.

When Taras Borovitz expanded his group, he went to Olevsk with fresh recruits. There he staged many pogroms and killed 10 Jews out of the 550 Jews who lived there. In Olevsk he established his command and published a newspaper in Ukrainian, edited by Bozhovsky the teacher and with the participation of Vasilenko, son-in-law of the priest from Rokitno. Boris Simonovich, the brother of the priest from Borovey, became head of Olevsk. Constant propaganda for an independent Ukraine began in earnest.

When the Germans entered Olevsk, Boris handed them a list of all the Jews in town. The Bulbovtzes helped to take out all the Jews to the village of Ivankovo (5 kilometers from Olevsk). They were all exterminated.

Soon the Germans no longer cared for *Bulbovtzes*. The Germans realized that the Bulbovtzes were only interested in an independent Ukraine and not in helping them. After allowing them to plunder the belongings of the slain Olevsk Jews, they disarmed them and sent them home. However, Taras Borovitz and some of his relatives managed to escape into the forest and from there to Karpilovka. There, he gathered some tens of robbers to help him achieve his goal.

Taras managed to organize an army group. His people wandered in the area forests and continued to function for an independent Ukraine. They killed and destroyed. Even when Rokitno was liberated by the Soviet army, the *Bulbovtzes* continued to riot and killed Motel Shapira from Zolovey and Yechiel Trossman.

[Page 257]

THE HOLOCAUST

[Page 259]

I Call Upon Mourning

Rabbi Yehudah ben Kolonimus

Translated by Rabbi Avrohom Marmorstein

I call upon mourning and elegy,
May my eyes pour forth tears,
And let them roll down night and day without being silenced.
I will surely cry with ashes I will adorn,
I will join with for my dirge seeking out every man whose soul is bitter,
Do not grant silence or relief (from these tears).
Let your eyes fill with tears and wail,
And let our hands lose their grip as tragedy has gripped us,
Clap your hands in aggravation,
Wail from heartache as old and full-of-days speak,
Make many cries and groans, with screams of pain,
Make your outcry more and stronger,
And dress in sackcloth over this tragedy.

[Page 260]

The Destruction Of Rokitno

Baruch Shehori (Schwartzblat) (Haifa)

Translated by Ala Gamulka

A.
The Beginning of the Suffering

When the Soviets left Rokitno, our suffering increased. Our daily fare consisted of beatings, robberies and lootings. Everyone closed themselves in their houses under lock and key. They peeked through the shutters in fear of seeing what was going on outside. The Biblical curse was upon us: "In the morning you will wish for night and at night you will wish for morning."

Some of the town leaders met to seek counsel. Should they ask the Germans in Sarny to come and establish order so they would not fall into the hands of thieves and criminals?

A despicable non-Jew, a half-German called Ratzlav, came to us. He earned his living from shoemaking and from fishing. He was always drunk on the streets. He offered to go to Sarny to invite the Germans to come. We had to provide food, money, clothing and a wagon for a few travelers.

Our people went out to prepare what he demanded. A few hours later the wagon was packed and ready. Ratzlav was well-dressed and had two Poles with him. The wagon was filled with food. Ratzlav took out a bottle, half-emptied it and shouted: "I will return from Sarny a big man. You will see! *Deutschland uber alles*!" (Germany above all others!) He climbed on the wagon and was on his way.

The group of Jews that remained on the street watched the departing wagon with sinking hearts. "God help us if this fellow will be pleading our cause". A discussion ensued. Some maintained that we should crawl on our stomachs, if necessary, and escape this hell. Others thought that we should wait patiently for redemption. They soon dispersed because it was dangerous to be seen in groups.

Three days later, Ratzlav arrogantly returned. He wore a khaki hat with a large iron cross. He brought back a sack full of posters and announcements, 6 guns and grenades. An hour later, we saw the posters. The first was decorated with an eagle and an iron cross. Written in large letters in Ukrainian and German was: "At the will of the *Fuhrer*, Eric Koch has become governor of western Ukraine. His office is in Rovno and he is in charge of all matters." Next to the poster there was a manifesto written in Ukrainian by Eric Koch thanking the Ukrainian population for helping to free the country from the Jewish Communists and from the corrupt Jewish government headed by their "*Shabbes goy*" – Stalin. The Jews are well-known to him and are advised to obey all orders. Next to the manifesto a large drawing was hung showing three NKVD men disguised as Jews running away from the approaching Germans. Below was the heading: "Run away, the murderers will not return".

Two hours later two young armed Ukrainians appeared on the street. They were hanging posters which said: "I, Ratzlav, have been appointed chief of the police of Rokitno. The population is ordered to hand in all ammunition in its possession. I expect 3 Jews to appear in my office at 5:00 A.M. *Heil Hitler*!" It was signed – Ratzlav. His signature was illegible as he could neither read nor write.

Several of the town leaders met in the Rabbi's home to make decisions. No one wished to go to Ratzlav as all were afraid. After a short discussion, 3 Jews were chosen: pharmacist Noach Soltzman, Aharon Slutzki and Mendel Schwartzblat.

Ratzlav was situated in a large house, but the delegation was ordered to wait outside. There, 20 police officers were busy moving furniture. Ratzlav sat comfortably on a couch, red-faced from liquor and he began to speak in a mixture of Polish and German interspersed with Russian swearwords.

"You Jews know well that I have been appointed as chief of police, not only of Rokitno, but also of the entire area. When we conquer Kiev I will be promoted. Who knows how high I can reach? Since I am in charge of you, you must obey me like loyal dogs. First you must furnish 4 rooms with the best furniture as well as provide linens and dishes. Daily, you must provide food and drink for 10 people. Of course, Vodka must also be brought. Since you burned the town, you must remove all the ruins. Therefore, all able-bodied Jews must present themselves tomorrow at the police to be placed. They will not be paid for their work, since Jewish labor has no value. Tomorrow morning you must send 4 women to clean this house. This will be done on a daily basis. I now require a pack of excellent cigarettes and a gold wristwatch.

As to the Germans, I have arranged for 200 of them to come here in two days. We will have a fancy party for them in the palace. Tomorrow, the big rooms must be cleaned and 200 plates, other utensils and a lot of food must be provided."

One of the delegates took out of his briefcase a pack of excellent cigarettes and a bottle of Vodka and placed them on the table. Ratzlav's eyes lit up. He opened a drawer to look for a glass. When he could not find one, he uncorked the bottle and began to drink. When he had finished about half of the bottle he raised his hand and screamed: "Why are you silent? You dogs! You must reply *Heil Hitler*! When you see me on the street, you and all the other *kikes*, you must remove your hats and greet me." When he finished screaming a bout of giggling overtook him and his head fell on the table. The Jews stood up embarrassed and heartsick.

"Yes. I have something here – a paper for the *kikes*!" he said when he had stopped laughing. "Here, look among these papers because I am a little drunk and I can't read." The paper was immediately found. It was a letter from a lieutenant informing the Jews that they must form a *Judenrat* consisting of 5 representatives. They would have the responsibility in all Jewish matters in town and in the area around it. The *Judenrat* is to appear in Sarny in front of the commander to receive further orders.

The delegation left the room. Only Soltzman stayed and told Ratzlav that if he would be kind to the Jews he would want for nothing. "Well done!"- was the reply.

When the delegation left, the Jews were told to meet in the synagogue. Several tens of Jews met and were given a report on the situation. The rabbi and the *shohet* spoke. They emphasized that unity would save us and bring us redemption.

B.

The Germans Enter Town

We began to work. Every morning we went out in groups to jobs. The main location was the demolished glass factory. We quickly removed the piles of heavy stones left after the bombing of the factory. Some Poles served as foremen and treated the workers cruelly.

I belonged to a group of 14 people that worked on repairing the railroad tracks. We had to take apart the bombed tracks and to replace them with new ones. We also had to make them narrower to adapt to the German trains. We worked on a section between Osnitzek and the bridge outside town. The work was back-breaking. We did everything with our hands since there were no tools. We piled the old tracks on a platform and pushed it several hundred meters along the tracks to the repair shop. Our supervisor was an angry and mean Pole. He used 6 workers, instead of 10, to raise large pieces of track. It was very difficult, but we got used to it. Our bodies strained, but we hoped that all our problems would only amount to hard labor. There was a benefit to working since those who worked hard received half a loaf of black bread each day. This was a great thing at the time. Nothing was available in the stores and we were not rationed any food.

On our return from work we would run into the large poster board, which contained new orders every day. The Jews were not permitted to leave town. Anyone who tried would be shot. Jews were not allowed to do any business with non-Jews. We could not buy any food and we were sentenced to starvation.

The first Germans arrived. There were only 10 and not 200 as Ratzlav had announced. The Jews stayed indoors and peeked out. There was a parade to welcome the Germans. The Ukrainian police officers, dressed in clothes supplied by the *Judenrat*, were followed by the Germans arranged in pairs. They wore summer clothes- shirts with sleeves rolled up, short pants and a belt filled with guns and grenades. Flashlights hung from a button and compasses were on their wrists. They wore steel helmets and had backpacks.

They marched proudly in goose steps, their heads raised and their faces fierce. Onlookers were filled with fear. They were followed by a crowd of young Poles and Ukrainians. They passed through the main street and went towards the palace. They were well received there. The sounds of the glass factory workers' band were heard till late at night as well as screams and shouts of the drunken Germans and their friends.

"Let us hope all will be well", whispered the Jews in their homes. However, their hopes were quickly shattered. At night, when the party was over, the Germans, accompanied by some Poles, went on a rampage. They divided themselves into two groups. The Poles led them to two Jewish homes where they raped the women at gunpoint.

On the following day, Shabbat, no Jews dared leave their homes. They were afraid. At 9:00 A.M. we saw two police officers escorting Alter Pik to the police station now located in Levik Grinshpan's house. With our hearts beating we waited for what would follow. Twenty minutes later we heard three shots, one after the other. It was clear to us that Alter Pik was gone. He was killed without a trial.

The Germans left town a few days later and returned to Sarny. Ratzlav continued his cruel deeds.

C.
The *Judenrat* and Its Mandate

The *Judenrat* was organized by the town residents in order to look after urgent matters and to avoid rampages. It actually began its work with the first arrangement to send the thief Ratzlav to Sarny to plead on our behalf. Later, it took care of the needs of the police.

The *Judenrat* was an administrative unit that centralized all Jewish matters. To outsiders it functioned as an official institution with influence on the Germans. There was the possibility of obtaining some easing of restrictions – perhaps even to save a Jewish life. It became a "valley of tears" where many hungry, depressed, suffering Jews would shed their tears. It was also a meeting place for Jews who came to hear news. There were those who invented happy items. However, after they read the only newspaper, "The Voice of Sarny", they found out the opposite.

The German army was advancing and taking revenge on the Jews. The Poles, who tended to wander in the fall to other locations to buy food, spread rumors. They said that there were massacres in Koritz, Ludvopol and Kostopol and that anyone still alive was imprisoned. The *Judenrat* tried to cast doubt on those rumors since the Poles wanted to befriend us and get clothes and food from us at a cheaper price. Unfortunately, the rumors proved to be true eventually. Refugees from David-Horodok came to Sarny and reported that the local police gathered all the Jews on the bridge and threw the children into the river. Refugees from other villages, where local farmers had gone berserk, arrived in Stolin.

The German Police soon arrived. It was headed by officer Sokolovsky who spoke Polish and was probably a *Folksdeutch* (German-Pole). They looked more or less human. No one seemed cruel. Sokolovsky was short and skinny and his first name was Henkel, but he was nicknamed Tiny.

As soon as he arrived, Sokolovsky invited the *Judenrat* to a meeting. He informed the Jews that if they obeyed all instructions no ill would come to them. His only request was the Jews must prepare a location where they would come to him daily to receive orders and requests which must be fulfilled. He also asked that three young women would come to clean and work in the kitchen and two young men would shine boots, groom the horses, clean their stalls and do other chores. He then presented a list of household and kitchen needs and linens to be supplied within a few days.

The staff of five was at the disposal of the five police officers who represented the German government in town and in its surrounding area. The police officers were satisfied with the efforts of the *Judenrat* and they did not exhibit any special signs of animosity. The Jewish population was calmed by this. It also increased their trust in the *Judenrat*. The fact that the Ukrainian police was no longer in charge also helped. The Germans disarmed the Ukrainians and gave them sticks instead of guns. When a Jew was caught doing business with the Poles or the farmers, they did not have the authority to punish him. They had to bring him to the German police. The *Judenrat* was then able to free him with bribery.

However, the imagined peace and quiet that we enjoyed did not last long. In mid September 1941, three new evil orders were given to the community:

1. Every Jewish home was to be marked with a Jewish blue star. It was an omen for what was to come. There was fear of riots and the Jewish homes were marked so the non-Jewish ones would not be attacked.

2. The *Judenrat* was ordered to provide to the Ukrainian police 50 pairs of boots and 50 black suits. The materials had to be provided and the craftsmen were gathered to make the boots and suits. All was ready in two weeks.

3. The Regional Office of Agriculture was to be given 12 cows. No one wanted to give up his cow since it was needed to feed the household. It was decided to collect 12,000 rubles. Anyone who gave up his cow was compensated 1,000 rubles. This is how the order was filled.

During the High Holidays we received bad news. In Rovno, 18,000 Jews were exterminated in one day. Hearts were heavy with worry and people seemed like dark shadows who were even afraid to talk about the news.

On the eve of *Yom Kippur* another order was given. All the Jews had to wear a yellow star- a round piece of yellow cloth, 5cm in diameter- one over the heart and one on the shoulder. I silently cut the circles for the family and my mother sewed them on the clothes, her tears streaming.

At *Kol Nidrei* everyone came to the synagogue wearing the yellow star. The atmosphere was tense. The synagogue was lit with small candles. The praying tore our hearts. Everyone prayed in a loud voice full of pleas and sighs. The prayers expressed deep sorrow and fear for the lives of our families. Never before had we prayed like this. During *Shema Koleinu*, heart-rending sounds came out of the synagogue.

Yom Kippur was spent in prayer. After the reading of the Torah the Rabbi gave a speech. The *shohet* Rev Issachar Trigun connected our difficult times to other periods when our leaders were killed in the name of G-d. Their belief in G-d remained strong. He called on the worshippers to have faith so that we would all be redeemed. Loud sobbing came from the women's section and from the entire synagogue during *Unetaneh Tokef.* They did not know it would be their last prayer.

Horrible Meetings during *Shemini Atzeret* and *Simchat Torah*

After services on *Shemini Atzeret* the chairman of the *Judenrat* came to the podium and announced that a new order was given and he hoped we would overcome it. He demanded that all men would gather at 3:00 P.M. in the synagogue for consultation. Our minds were full of doubt. Everyone tried to guess what was coming. At the appointed hour the synagogue was full. The chairman announced that the community was being assessed, one time only, 30 rubles per person. Pure gold was to constitute 10% of the total. If we could not collect the amount we would be in danger of being killed. Since among us there were refugees who had no means and there were Jews who had been robbed and had nothing left, it was up to those of means to look after the others. On a preliminary basis there were two suggestions: to prepare an accurate list of the Jewish population to help with the assessment and to choose a committee who would send emissaries to the surrounding villages to collect money. For this purpose wagons were prepared. They would be accompanied by the Ukrainian police who would look after their safety.

The Rabbi came to the podium. He showed that in the times of Moses, a similar procedure took place. The people of Israel were assessed one *shekel* per person. Unity is essential for the continuity of the Jewish people. "Jews are responsible for one another." Truthfully, our town is poor and low in assets, but if we do not succeed, our existence will be in great danger. Therefore, he calls on the Jews of the community to think carefully and to fulfill the requirements so that we all will be redeemed.

A member of the *Judenrat*, Avraham Binder, followed him. He was an intelligent and thinking man. This is what he said: "Jews! Your chairman, Mr. Slutzki, has already told you some details about this task and what we must do now. Time is short and the coming moments are full of danger. We must begin immediately. The latest events that occurred in our area proved that wealth has no value. The greatest wealth is life itself. I propose to choose a committee of 3 people and to hand them money and valuable objects immediately."

The proposal was accepted. To accomplish it the following were chosen: the Rabbi, *shohet* Trigun, and the pharmacist Noach Soltzman. In addition, a committee of five was chosen to do a proper census of the population. The committee quickly began its work in the streets. They soon returned to the *Judenrat* with an exact list of all the Jews. The *Judenrat*, located in the home of Betzalel Kokel, received the cash. Gold and other valuable objects were brought to the Rabbi's house. The women arrived with small packages wrapped in kerchiefs. They brought gold rings, necklaces, bracelets, watches, brooches- all pure gold. They were all placed in a large box.

As I stood near the Rabbi's house I was flooded with thoughts and memories. When I was still a child there was another collection of gold. However, that project had to do with a happy occasion for the Jews. There was a parade in town and, young and old, we marched in the street with a blue and white flag towards the synagogue. It was filled with people. On the Eastern wall a banner announced – in large letters- “A new light will illuminate Zion and we will all bask in its beams”. It was a party inaugurating the Hebrew University in Jerusalem. Emotional speeches were made. Everyone was dressed in holiday clothes. When the event was finished, we greeted each other with “Happy holiday”. A few hours later the collection of gold began. Couple after couple went to the Rabbi's house to donate items of gold for the university. They were happy to donate for such a great cause.

Now everyone was still marching, but the picture was different: sad-faced, bent people came and went. The groups were not dense. They were reluctant to visit the Rabbi. On the next morning it was discovered that the wealthier Jews did not even appear. They waited for the end, to see how much they needed to add.

All the Jews were called for morning services at the synagogue. Nahum Katzenelson, a member of the *Judenrat*, went up to the podium. He reported bitterly that a large portion of the population did not heed the call and did not participate. It was as if their hearts were made of stone and they did not feel part of the terrible fate that awaited us. He demanded that the Rabbi excommunicate those who refused. Rabbi Shames went next to the podium and, in a hoarse and shaky voice, said: “Jews, our brothers. It is not so easy to excommunicate Jews. The law allows us to do it only in exceptional cases. How can I excommunicate people who have already been punished by G-d? These are people full of suffering and problems.” He then quoted verses from the *Midrash* and the Torah which described the suffering the people of Israel had gone through for many generations. The crowd stood still. Sobs were heard from the women's section.

Still, the Rabbi ordered that the “bed” covered in black be brought in and placed on the podium. Candles were put into candlesticks and placed near the “bed”. The candles were lit and the Rabbi announced: “I decree that everyone in the audience vow by a handshake that they have given everything. If not, I will be forced to use the “bed” and the black candles to cast a curse from G-d on those who refuse.”

The synagogue was quiet. All turned their heads towards the Rabbi, to see what was happening. A man came up to the podium and said that the committee will call on those who had not yet appeared and that we should continue with morning prayers.

“It is *Simchat Torah* today! Woe to us and to these holidays! We allow the Rabbi, the *shohet*, the pharmacist and all those who still must appear to perform their tasks and to miss prayers. Let us hope that we can overcome the excommunication and to come out of this whole."

The shohet, Rev. Issachar Trigun, came up to the podium and said: "Dear brothers, woe to us that we have reached the moment where our holiday becomes a time for mourning. Instead of rejoicing with our Torah we cry for our martyrs and for ourselves. Who will cry for us? At this moment, when life and death are in our hands, we do not want to "choose life". We close our fists and we do not see the sword over our heads. Our town is in flames. Save it! Has G-d turned his back on us? No! He is testing us to see if we can withstand the situation. G-d tested Abraham our father and ordered him to kill his beloved son. At the last minute the angel appeared and stopped him from slaughtering his son.

My dear brothers! We are facing black candles and we ask G-d for mercy. We ask him to forgive us our sins. We must know what to ask so that we do not fail by saying the wrong words. We are sinners and we are obstinate. I warn you. When you come to give a handshake in front of the "bed" and the candles, you must not use the wrong words. Do a proper soul searching and be truthful. I am confident that we will defeat Satan. We will manage to forget all our problems and we will be redeemed. Amen! May it be so!"

The committee left the synagogue. The noise grew louder. Screams were heard. The women cried. Some women broke through to the podium shouting: "Jews, save our children! Don't let them kill us!"

Two hours later the committee returned. It was very quiet. Soltzman came up to the podium and announced: "We failed! We did not succeed in fulfilling our task. The worst will now come. Let the audience be excommunicated. Jews, this is the Day of Atonement!" He pointed eastward and the *shofar* was blown near the ark. A shudder went through those present.

"Jews, you can still change your minds at the last minute. It is not too late!" shouted Avraham Binder. "Open your hearts and your wallets and let us not allow the curse to come upon us. Our community has never before been tested in this way. Give us whatever you have and we will be redeemed."

The community was split in two. Some were for and others were against the excommunication. Those against yelled: "Stop! Do not excommunicate. You will be punished by G-d!" The synagogue was in turmoil. Finally, the money was collected in full.

All heaved a sigh of relief. The ark was opened and the Torah scrolls were taken out for *Hakafot*. The next day, the *Judenrat* took the money to Sarny, to the governor.

D.
The Atrocities in Vitkovich and the Cruelty of Ditch

In October 1941 the railroad was repaired. It was very difficult work. We had to remove the broken tracks and to bring in tracks from far away. All this was done without proper tools. The Polish overseer kept at us constantly with curses and screams. We worked hard. At night we received our "pay" – half a loaf of black bread. This was a dire necessity in those days.

When we repaired the tracks connecting the bridge in town to the bridge in the village of Osnitzek, our work was finished. We them began to work in the yard of the glass factory. There we removed the ruins and we rebuilt the factory. We worked with the Poles and it was a nightmare. We were constantly badgered and denounced, but we had to keep silent.

One day, a horrible rumor was heard. A ghetto was to be formed where all the Jews would be enclosed. It was clear that the Germans were planning in this way to steal, with ease, the belongings of the Jews. It was not permitted to transfer belongings to the planned ghetto. Necessary items were packed and we waited for what was to come next. Finally, the order was given. The Jews had to give an inventory of all farm animals, wagons, harnesses and farming tools. It was a rainy Friday. Everyone brought their cows or horses to the collecting station in the yard of the abattoir. I stood in line for many hours until my turn came. I registered and brought my cow in to the yard. I removed the rope from its horns and I left. She smelled the wet earth, turned her head to me and mooed as if to say good-bye. I was saddened to see the poor creature that was now to be locked up.

In those days terrible events occurred in Vitkovich. About 40- 50 Jews had lived there for many years. They were well established in the village. They owned stores and large farms. However, evil reached even this village. The farmers, their good neighbors, who used to spend time in the Jewish homes, began to ravage and steal. It happened that Soviet partisans infiltrated the village and killed some of its residents because they were Nazi sympathizers. They only stayed for a short time and quickly returned to the forests. A rumor spread that the local Jews had organized the attack. Some even testified that local Jews were among the partisans. The Jews immediately understood that they had to leave. They rented wagons and left for Rokitno during the night. Several hours later, when the convoy came out of the forest and into the plain, they were attacked by their murderous neighbors with axes and other utensils. They were cold-blooded and did not listen to the pleading of the women and children. It was a terrible massacre. The bodies were thrown into a ditch. Only two families managed to escape and safely reached town.

This event cast fear in the hearts of all the Jews in the villages. They ran away and came to Rokitno.

In November 1941, the news came that a whole S.S. division was on its way. The residents immediately began to prepare food, bed linens and other items the murderers would require. Luckily, only 30 killers arrived. They came to assist the *Kreislandwirt* (District farmers) in the collection of taxes from the non-Jews. They were headed by a short Kreislandwirt, Captain Ditch. He was dressed in a khaki uniform. He was the cruelest German we had ever met. The first time he passed Jews on the street, he hit them for walking on the sidewalk instead of in the middle of the road, as required.

When he came to the *Judenrat*, everyone stood up. He cast an angry look at those present and immediately went to the office of the chairman, Mr. Slutzki. We soon heard shouts and screams coming from the room. He demanded that all his office equipment, which included more than 100 items, be prepared within 4 hours. Four hours later exactly, Ditch reappeared. He entered the chairman's office screaming: "*Alle heraus*!" (Everyone out). He then evicted all the members of the *Judenrat* and remained alone with Slutzki. We heard his terrifying screams and then a countdown: One! Two! Three! – to 25. Fragmented sighs emanated from the room. Suddenly, the door flew open and Ditch, sweaty and wild-eyed quickly exited the room and slammed the door. We rushed inside and found Slutzki on the couch, half-naked, his back covered in bleeding welts. His jacket was on the floor and he looked lifeless. We threw water on him and he recovered slightly. In a weak voice he told us how Ditch attacked him, tore off his jacket and slammed him on the couch. He then lifted his shirt, took off his wide belt. Pistol in hand he whipped him with the belt. Slutzki lost consciousness on the 11th hit and could not remember anything else. After some medical attention, Slutzki was taken home. He recuperated a few weeks later.

The month of November was full of fear and trepidation. The 30 SS men in town were destructive. We had to supply them with 30 pairs of boots, clothes and top-notch tobacco daily. The committee did not have these items. Therefore, a delegation went to Sarny and from there to Dombrovitza to buy leather and tobacco. A new order was given forbidding the Jews from any gatherings, including prayer services. The two synagogues in town were closed. A week before the order was given, when the Jews were praying in the synagogue, Ditch suddenly broke in screaming. He took out his pistol and shot in the air. Panic ensued and people jumped out of windows. Ditch, pleased with the results, left. Public praying stopped.

Soon an order was issued to provide craftsmen only with licenses, to close individual workshops and to organize workers in craft guilds. A great rush on licenses followed since everyone believed this would save lives. Indeed, after the slaughter in Rovno, many Jewish craftsmen were spared. The craft guild was located in the old synagogue. It consisted mainly of tailors and shoemakers. There was more work every day since all orders were filled according to instructions of the Germans and the Ukrainian police. They were paid a symbolic salary of 60 *kopeks* per hour. The work day was 10 hours long. Each craftsman earned 6 *rubles* per day- a measly sum. However, they lived in the hope that work would spare them from death.

E.
The Atrocities of the 15 and the Hardships in the Ghetto

In the winter of 1942 heavy fines were imposed on the town Jews. However, the most frightening decree was the mobilization of 15 expert craftsmen who were to be sent to an unknown location. Our experience was that when someone was sent away, it meant death. However, this decree was puzzling: why were craftsmen chosen? We believed that craftsmen were spared from death because of their licenses. If so, why were they chosen?

The *Judenrat* stayed up late struggling with the list. After much self-torture, 15 people were selected. They were all sick or crippled. It was felt that the Germans would eliminate them since they were helpless. The next day their wives came to the *Judenrat* and begged with tears and screams to release their husbands. The men lifted their shirts to show their scars and wounds and begged for mercy.

The *Judenrat* stood helpless in front of the angry women who attacked them with their nails. One woman told her friends to tear their clothing and to sit *shiva*. They sat on the floor and heart-rending screams could be heard. The crying and screaming attracted the attention of a policeman who came to the street. When he saw the grieving women he asked what was wrong. The women, thinking the policeman would help them, got up. Each woman wanted to present her own case. The noise was deafening and the policeman did not understand anything. "Quiet!" shouted the policeman and pointed his pistol. The women immediately fled and shouted: "Help. They are shooting!" A great panic followed. Everyone ran away from the street and hid at home. The policeman was pleased with himself.

However, the shouting and crying did not help. The men had to present themselves. The parting from wives and children was frightening. There were heart-wrenching scenes which cannot be described. They knew this was the last parting. It was forever. All present cried. Only 3 of them returned. They told about the slaughter in Rovno.

In April, I was busy at work because the Germans decided to enclose the Jews in the ghetto. They demanded that the *Judenrat* prepare 3 maps of the town. They chose me as the cartographer and I had to draw these maps. I spent day and night bent over my papers drawing the maps. I was required to mark the non-Jewish homes in one color and the Jewish ones in a different color. In the second half of April a detailed map of the ghetto streets was read. The *Judenrat* began to assign lodgings. There were some bitter fights. Each person wanted to choose his neighbors. We were assigned 25 square meters per person. In reality, we did not even enjoy this much space and the crowding was terrible.

On May 1, the Jews of Rokitno were enclosed in a narrow and suffocating ghetto. Eight souls shared one small room. The heat was unbearable. To make life even more difficult, we were forbidden from going out for fresh air. We were isolated from the outside world and from supplies. We could not even think of buying food. Hungry people ate grass from the fields bordering the ghetto. They picked leaves from wildflowers and boiled them to quiet their hunger pangs. Those who had some seeds of grain, ground them secretly in a mill that was hidden underground in the ghetto. The entrance was camouflaged with a large crate used as a table. The crate was moved to allow descent into a dark low-ceilinged cellar. A small petrol light was lit and with their last strength people managed to turn the wheel. The flour was thick as groats. Each piece of grain was worth as much as a diamond and all were careful not to drop any on the floor.

Whenever a policeman appeared on the street, everyone shivered. They immediately stomped their feet as a warning. It became deathly quiet in the cellar. We had to spend many hours crowded in the dank airless cellar breathing the vapor from petrol lamp until the all-clear signal was given. We could then continue our grinding. The flour was mixed with millet, spelt, potatoes and *lebede* (grass leaves). It was quite tasty and flavorful. Our only food for many months was a thin soup made with groats and water and a piece of bread. Many people did not even have this much and they were swollen with hunger. The *lebede* was our main food. We made cutlets, biscuits and other dishes from it. We did not have tobacco. Everything was smoked: cherry tree leaves, ground raspberry stones, ivy leaves and nettles. It was rolled in paper and lit.

The situation of the *Judenrat* worsened daily and with it that of the Jews. The Germans became crueler in their demands and they slowly revealed their true purpose – extermination.

Life in the Enclosed Quarter

The enclosed quarter was not a real ghetto because no walls or barbed wire fences were built. It was enough that an order was given forbidding the Jews from leaving the street. It was as if they were locked inside a house. Since the main street of Rokitno was not large enough to contain all the Jews, a small ghetto was organized in the new town. There were about 10 houses around the market square. One of them was used by the Germans from the Economic Department. Behind the ghetto, near the railroad tracks, was a camp of a German army with reserves mainly from Czechoslovakia and Hungary. They were rebuilding bombed bridges.

There were about 50 houses on the main street. Some were occupied by Polish squatters. The Ukrainian militia remained in its building. The windows opened to the street and provided a view of all that was happening there. At the end of the street, the regional police occupied Grinshpan's house.

The ghetto was overcrowded. Each room was occupied by at least one family. It was forbidden to leave the ghetto or to go from the main ghetto to the small ghetto without permission from the *Judenrat*. Two Jewish policemen stood at the beginning of the street and watched the traffic. Every day, those who worked for the Germans lined up at the square near the militia building. They were then sent to the workplaces.

The guild in the synagogue, where the tailors, shoemakers and other craftsmen were concentrated, was supervised by the Department of Labor. They were forbidden from doing any work for Jews. They either served the Germans and the militia or did work ordered by the *Judenrat*. They were not paid for their work. Their only salary was the hope that they would remain alive because of their skills. The *Judenrat* did compensate them for any work done for them.

The Jews were not even permitted to linger on the street and to enter into any discussions among themselves. It was prohibited to bring any food into the quarter. Once a week, the weekly bread was distributed – 40 grams per person per day and groats or millet – 400 grams per person per week. Kenig, the police officer, would sometimes do searches in the streets. He entered houses where smoke was rising from the chimney, to make certain they were not cooking meat or boiling milk. One day, four Jews were caught with bottles of milk given to them by their Polish neighbors. Immediately, a large fine was imposed on the *Judenrat.*

The economic hardship increased. In addition to the constant fear of the future and the difficult work, which was becoming worse every day, hunger depressed everyone. Many people wandered around dizzy and weak, their bodies swollen. In the evenings and at night, people sneaked out of the houses, went to the fences and exchanged clothes for food – bread or flour or some butter and cheese. The food was then well hidden.

There was no contact with the outside world. No newspapers arrived and radio did not exist. We were afraid to speak to the Poles and to discuss politics. Sometimes, the members of the *Judenrat* traveled to Sarny, on orders from the governor, to deal with various decrees. They would then bring back some news. None was good news. It was during the time when the Germans continued to advance in Eastern Europe and were approaching Georgia and Stalingrad. Their aim was to reach and conquer oil supplies and to separate the Russian army from important supply centers.

While we were in the ghetto, some partisan groups began activities in the forests. Their nucleus was Russian soldiers who were either "accidentally" separated from their units or who remained behind to harm the enemy. They were joined by Russian youths who feared that the Germans would massacre them. At first, the situation of the partisans was bad. They needed guns and detonating materials. Their purpose was to attract more fighters to the forest and to dispense information in different ways. Even those few made life difficult for the Germans. It was enough to destroy a small bridge on the railroad or part of a track to frighten the Germans in town. At first, there were only 5 police officers supervising an area 40 kilometers in diameter. After some sabotage activities by the partisans, more German troops came to guard the tracks. They built shacks near every bridge, surrounded the area with a barbed wire fence and even put in land mines. In important locations, like the railroad station, they built watchtowers. Only when I came back from the partisans, did I realize how much the Germans feared them.

The activities of the partisans in the area greatly distressed the Germans. Many more German soldiers arrived in town. They erected cannon positions at the town entrance and at the bridge on the small river.

The fear inside the ghetto also grew. We prayed that the nights would be quiet and that the partisans would not attack. We knew that each one of these attacks would bring retaliations on us. The Germans became more and more nervous and cruel. They began to suspect the Jews of assisting the partisans. Every bit of news about any activity made us shiver. A few days before the last massacre the partisans attacked a train in the Osnitzek station and 20 Germans were killed. Soon strange characteristics were noticed in the local Germans.

The Bitter End of Rokitno

On August 25, 1942, the strict order was given that all Jews, including the sick, were to present themselves on the following day, a Wednesday, in the market square for roll call. We were suspicious because the police officers and the Germans spent the day collecting all the goods in the various workshops. Also, additional police officers from the surrounding areas arrived in town. Some people thought of running away, but the *Judenrat* tried to calm us by saying that the purpose of the roll call was to verify whether Jews had escaped to join the partisans during the previous attack. If one of us were to escape it would be proof that we were guilty. The entire community would be punished because of a few escapees. The next day, August 26, 1942, 13 *Elul* 5742, at 9:00am, the entire Jewish community – 1631 people – stood in the market square and waited for the verdict. The chief of police stood with a bandaged hand. Next to him were several Germans. The roll call was done quickly and, to our surprise, we were not ordered to go home. Instead, we were told to stand in two lines – men in one, women and children in the other. We were 6 people abreast. Our hearts were beating and we were scared.

The head of the *Judenrat* came to me and asked me to go to the chief of police to ask him what was going on. As I moved from my place the women began screaming. Mindel Eisenberg's voice was heard shouting: “Jews! Save yourselves!” I immediately saw a large group of policemen and Germans coming from everywhere, their guns cocked. The chief moved back two steps from me and drew his gun in his left hand and, swearing, shot twice.

Before I was able to lower my head I heard shots from hundreds of automatic guns. People began to run crazed trying to escape the bullets. Terrible screams, groans, “*Shema Israel*” and non-stop shooting were heard. The market square was drenched in Jewish blood. Blood was streaming from all directions. If not for the beating sun, the blood would have become an angry stormy river. The market square was covered with broken bodies of men, women and young children.

Many Jews were caught and put into train cars waiting at the station. The next day, they were slaughtered in Sarny together with other Jews from Sarny and other villages. 10,000 Jews were murdered in 3 hours. 300 Jews were killed in the market square and 700 others managed to escape into the forests.

This is how the Jewish community of Rokitno was terminated.

[Page 275]

Lamentation on The Destruction

Natan Gendelman (Tel Aviv)

Translated by Ala Gamulka

In memory of my dear mother and sister
and all my family who were slaughtered in Sarny
and in memory of my dear father,
killed by soldiers in the village of Berezov.

The twenty-second day of June nineteen forty-one
Will not be erased from my memory.
Early in the morning, it was announced on the radio
That the enemy had suddenly infiltrated.

The residents of Rokitno were in a quandary.
Should they hide? Should they run? That was the question.
Run eastward, my brothers,
Leave your homes, remove yourselves from danger.

It was all in vain - only some took walking stick and backpack
And went east in any way or path.
The rest did not budge. They remained attached to the place, believing
Help would come from above. My heart was full of fear
For those who stayed home.
Their misery and suffering would know no end.

That day I cannot forget how I said good-bye to my parents.
I gave my sister and my dear ones those last kisses.
How they cried bitterly.
Their pain was obvious with every word.

I hear my mother's voice that night and I absorb her words
"My son! Who knows if we will ever meet again?
Go in peace. I will pray for you. Perhaps redemption will come
And you will be saved from this burning inferno."

This is how I left town. This is how the convoy disappeared
My family's moans remain in my heart forever.
Man, how bitter is the destiny of those who remain.

Angels of peace, stay and protect them from harm.
My heart is open and aware of all that happens at home
To all my town folk who are waiting to be caught.

The enemy approached the town and waved its sword
It spread its black wings over its prey.
Dark shadows covered the road
Everything is hidden. There is no one on the street
All passers-by are cowering in darkened entrances.

From time to time you hear dogs barking
Suddenly you hear the sound of boots marching.
"The Germans are in Rokitno" - one Jew tells another
New orders come every minute. Reside in a separate area,
Ghetto, yellow stars, life without hope,
Tasks for the town elders, shots, killings.

***Rosh Hashana*, 1941, do you remember?**
This is the old synagogue - it is surrounded.
The S.S. is all around it, drunk and wild,
Killers holding guns, bayonets,
In harsh voice they shout "*Juden Raus*!"
Doors are rammed and thresholds shake.

Who will dare open the gates? Everyone is praying
They are pouring out their bitter hearts to heaven
They cry over their fate, the difficult times,
Such wickedness was never seen before. These evil men
Intend to exterminate us - "Pour your wrath" on them.

In a secluded corner stands Reb Shimon, covered in a talit, his eyes tearful,
His brow is furrowed, his hair white, his hands raised upwards,
He begs for the safety of his son, who ran away with the Bolsheviks,
To his family, standing near him, - "Give them life, send redemption to your people, the people of Israel".

Then is heard the shaky voice of the prayer leader:
"On *Rosh Hashana* it is written and on the fast day of *Yom Kippur* it is decided,
Who will be killed by earthquake, or by epidemic or by choking or by stoning".

Months of anguish have passed and there is no end to the suffering
It is a life of an abused prisoner, broken in mourning,
As all are immersed in sorrow and suffering, an order thunders
All must present themselves in market square, all to be counted.

This terrible news is immediately spread everywhere
At daybreak the miserable souls leave their homes
Young and old, women with babies in their arms,
Some latecomers arrive from the ghetto streets
Followed by police marching with rubber sticks
Whipping their backs and the rest of the villains
Are rushing to discover those in hiding.
They remember the sick who are in their beds
And they quickly condemn them to death.

This is how the ghetto was emptied of its Jews
They gathered in the square, so miserable.
They never imagined they would be slaughtered.
They ask each other, what did we do,
What are they planning for us?

The S.S. counts, separates and divides
The first shots hit some tens of people.
There are dead bodies lying in piles.
They lie in pools of blood, their souls have not yet left.
How terrible is this place!

In the morning the enemy will shove the unfortunate ones into cattle cars
The train will move. Where to? For what?
The ditches of Sarny are waiting for them, where thousands are shot
Deep ditches, dug by our brothers by force

You scan with your eyes a large field and you see
The first ditch has not been dug and the last one not yet filled.
The barrage is starting
The bullets are fired in rapid succession.

Thousands of bodies fall off the edge
Into the ditch, limbs and bodies covered in blood,

Horrible screams for help and "*Shema Israel*" are
Called by the unfortunate and reach the skies.

Moans of pain are swallowed by the laughter of Satan
He is crazed. There is no law nor judge
Ukrainian soil, in its breadth and length,
Absorbs the blood of martyrs and saints.

The news of the destruction is quickly disseminated
It hits my heart like a dart, I shout and scream
I grind my teeth and seek a path
To the animals' cave - to Berlin - to annihilate it.

Our pure blood is pouring in Europe
And will never be absorbed by the earth.
We will never be quiet and calm
We will seek revenge from door to door.

You may be alive, but you are in a trance.
Will you not awaken and feel the heat?
Are your ears blocked? Do you not hear the bitter crying?
Answer me, will you avenge the martyrs?

My son, only yesterday your father was slaughtered in front of your eyes.
Are you not agitated, do you not roar like a lion?
Will you blow the *shofar* to alert the hearts?
Will you march erect to the land of the beasts?

The liberation army is approaching, its star is beckoning
These are your comrades in misery. Wake up! Volunteer!
We are all remnants ready to join
Together we will put an end to darkness.

I run like a dog from yard to yard
I grab any bone thrown my way, but I am awake
I bark, I bark to penetrate the hearts of the remnants
Our hour of revenge is here, my brothers!

We avenge the tears of fathers,
The cries of children and humble mothers.
My slaughtered brothers, hanging from trees.
We avenged your suffering and endless torment.

Silently, I look into the clear eyes of my friends.
I remember how we sat in school together
We hiked to the bridge together, the river water underneath rippling,
We breathed the odor of the wheat fields, we forged friendships in the woods
Mysteries of the night were sweet, the stars were shining
Suddenly, a storm of destruction came
It uprooted the trees and pulled you all down.

You struggled hard for your lives, you did not offer your necks for slaughter,
You did not go out like sheep to be slaughtered, but defended yourselves properly.
You joined the partisans in the forests and you showed your courage.
As ghetto fighters you defended the honor of man and nation.
In the Red Army you fought for freedom like lions.
You received strength from the defenders of Moscow and the fighters of Stalingrad
Are you really gone, does no one know your names?

How bitter is your legacy. Let us hope your memory
Will be valued by history. You will be memorialized as heroes
Who were born in the twenties and fell in the forties.

Somewhere in the forests of Volyn I quietly look around
I search for you day and night, I find a grave in the grass,
I approach you, you are so many. I look inside.
I see only your tender bones, lifeless,
I stand trembling at the grave of my brothers and I honor them.

I cannot believe that they are silent forever. There are times
When the silence speaks for them at night
Their lips whisper: Remember the day of atrocities
Remember to avenge, to save mankind!
I remember them forever and I will fulfill their last wish
I sit alone on the roadway,
I listen to the distant wind
Which disappears, but leaves an echo of their last request.
This is how I stand on the land of destruction.

Oh Poland, the land of my youth,

You gave us young people full of life
There we studied and played, we swam in your rivers
We enjoyed your gardens and we forged friendships in your forests.
We were raised in your midst and we were creative. We established communities
So many writers and poets emerged from among us.

My good brothers lived there, from them I received
My strength to bear the heavy load on my shoulders
To suffer and to wander, from village to town
Like a ship on the seas thrown by the waves.
A storm came, heavy clouds obscured the light.
A chapter in our life has ended and will never return.

I returned to you and I did not recognize you, the land of destruction.
You must know that I did not come to cry over you.
I am a Jew and I have only one question for you
Where are my dear brothers? I ask you in vain.

Oh, brother! If you wish to know, go to the ditches of destruction
Look in and tremble. You will get the correct reply.
Sound is choking in my throat, my eyes are full of tears,
My fists are banging and demanding
Judgment for the bloodbath, the innocent blood
That was shed everywhere and was absorbed by you. Do you know why?
The witnesses are the mass graves in Majdanek, Treblinka
The big death machine in Auschwitz.
You can see mass graves scattered in thick forests.
They faced the barbaric enemy in terrible times.

Your soil is completely covered in ashes
Of father, mother and the People of the Book
The dust of the martyrs will not cover the sins of the murderers
Look, blood stains are appearing on your soil
They protrude and show evidence of the destruction of millions
Of our brothers performed by the followers of Hitler.
Your trees, fruit trees, were used as gallows
By the executioners who hung bodies on them.

It will still be told of the Jews of Poland, of the large Jewish population,

That their way of life has ended forever.

And you, son of Rokitno,
From the depth of my heart I send this poem to the sound of bitter cries
If no one listens, it will drown in heavy waters
You must promise to remember our dear ones and to never forget the Holocaust
Tell this to your children, from one generation to another, to always remember.

[Page 282]

Tearful Events

Israel Greenberg (Afula)

Translated from Yiddish by Ala Gamulka

On Tuesday, August 25, 1942, we received an order for all the Jews, without exception, to present themselves at 8:00 a.m. on the following day in the market square near the new synagogue. If anyone would be absent, the whole family would be punished. Late at night, Lifsha, my brother Hershel's wife, came to us crying. She told us that a police officer had come to collect his boots from the Zeshlichov shoemaker. The work was incomplete and the policeman whispered a secret: All the Jews will be murdered on the next day.

We yelled at her that she should not panic for anything and she went back home sobbing. We felt uneasy and did not sleep a wink all night. In the morning we went to the market place and stood together as a family. When the militia began to shoot, I escaped with Pessyah Kutz's son and hid in a garden. We could not stay there for very long and we had to continue running. A German caught us and took us to the train cars waiting at the station. Some 400-500 people, crammed into the train, were taken to Sarny. Sender Perl's daughter and Moshe Turok's wife had been badly wounded, but they were still thrown into the cars, as were all the wounded. In Sarny we encountered a train full of Jews from Dombrovitza. We were all taken to a camp on Polske (on the road to Tutovich, past the hospital). We were heavily guarded. We were housed in four or five barracks.

We had nothing to eat or drink for two days. Whenever anyone approached the fence, he or she would be shot. We were not allowed to bury our dead. Sender Perl's daughter died on the third day. Her mother and I carried her out and we placed her body among the dead. At around 12 o'clock, one of the Rokitno *Judenrat* was called to present himself. Noah Soltzman immediately went and returned crying. He gave us the terrible news that we were all to be annihilated. Soltzman and his family, my father Avraham Itzhak and I, my father-in-law Yehoshua Wolfin (from Hrapon) and a few other Jews went together. There were approximately 20 of us. Soltzman beat his chest and said: "We have sinned. We are guilty." My father prayed *Vidui.*

We reached the narrow gauge railway. Nine of us were sent to the side. They were: 1. Israel Greenberg, 2. Motel Levin, 3. Levik Rotman, 4. Moshe Grinshpan (son of Avraham), 5. Hershel Hailcheks, 6. A Jew from Karpilovka, 7. Aharon Levin, 8. Michael Keks' brother-in-law (He owned a flour warehouse), 9. Buzik Portnoy (from Stariky). All the rest were ordered to undress – women and children separated from the men. They were led to the ditches. The miserable souls lay down and were immediately shot.

The slaughter went on till evening. Those who were still alive knew the end was near. They ignited one of the barracks. They were able to run away because they cut the fence as they were protected by the smoke. Unfortunately, not many were able to escape. Blood was streaming like water.

I knew that my situation in the camp was dreadful. I tried to think of a way out. In the meantime a truck was brought to remove the clothing of the dead. I climbed on the truck and began to pack the clothes. I hid under a pile of clothing.

When the truck was filled, it left immediately. On the way I decided to try to jump off. However, the truck was accompanied by another one full of killers. The driver did not know that I was hiding on the truck.

When I was sure that there was no one else around, I revealed myself to the driver. I begged him for my life. After I gave him a generous tip he told me to jump over a fence and to lie down. I crawled on my stomach to an open cattle car and I lay there till nightfall. The train was on the Rovno track.

On the way I saw many men, women and children. I left the train at the Mokvin station by jumping off. It was late at night. I started on the road to Brezhne. A kind local warned me that all the Jews of Brezhne had been killed and that I would be in danger there. I went in the opposite direction and reached the village of Ilova.

There I found my uncle Yakov Greenberg, my aunt Zlate, her son-in-law Shlomo Rekkes with his three children. I asked Shlomo to go with me to look for our wives. His wife and daughter had also escaped from the market square.

We sat together for an hour crying and then we said our good-byes. We went towards Rokitno. On the way, I heard children crying, but I did not see anyone. Near Rokitno, at the graves, I saw something black approaching. It was Avraham Grinshpan. He was injured and was hidden by a local man called Frohor Lukian. At night the man hid him in the barn and in the daytime he was in the forest.

I asked him to tell my wife, if he ran into her, that I was going to the forests of Zolovey. I came to a hamlet near Zolovey. The forest warden who lived there was called Lavoren Tzalkovsky. I went to sleep in the barn. In the morning I went to another local man in the Blizhov hamlets. His name was Miron. There I found Aharon, Nachman and Yosef Blizhovsky, Aharon Perlovich and Noah Rafalovich. The next night Asher, the blacksmith from Zolovey, arrived. He told us that the local residents of Zolovey had captured his father, mother and sister and took them to Rokitno. It was a miracle that he had escaped.

We stayed together. Once Tzalkovsky came with Miron and demanded that we find another hiding place. The locals were talking about him. Asher and I went to a hamlet in Kopele and stayed with another local called Alexander Yanevich. He took us to the loft in his barn and brought us food. He told me that if I found my wife, Yentl, he would hide her, too.

From there we went back to Miron. I asked him if he knew where my wife was. He answered: “If you give me some liquor, I will tell you where she is”. I fulfilled his request and he took me to a place 3 kilometers away. We came to a thicket in the forest. Our dear ones were lying there covered with a tarpaulin. We cried quietly looking at the terrible situation in which people could find themselves. They were sleeping and did not hear our crying. I woke them up. It was an emotional reunion. There lay my wife, Yentl, her sister, Henya Kutz, her daughter Hindl and Ita Trossman (Yechiel's wife) with her 3-year-old daughter Marel. We immediately built a fire and they warmed themselves up a little. My wife asked me if I had a piece of bread for little Marel. I actually had some bread and I gave Marel a piece of it. She tasted it and told her mother: “Hide the rest for tomorrow”. We stayed together for three days. On the fourth day at midnight, I noticed someone approaching us. It was Adam, Lavoren Tzalkovsky's brother. He whispered a secret to me – his brother intended to kill me and my wife. He came to warn us so that we should leave the forest. When we reached his home he gave us a loaf of bread and informed us that he could not hide my wife.

We went to another local resident called Frank Garvovsky, from Berezov. I told him about our terrible situation and asked him for advice. He cried profusely about our calamity. We looked awful – hungry, scared and panicky. He was moved by our appearance. He offered us a place for the night. Asher left and went to Blizhov, to Miron.

Frank hid us in the loft of his barn. It was extremely cold there and we had no food. One day, in daytime, we heard a noise in the yard. Through a slit we saw 10 police officers with guns. Frank had invited the police officers to his house and he was plying them with food and liquor. When it became dark, Frank's son came and told us to run to the forest. He would call us back when the police leave.

Early in the morning we heard shooting. We immediately put out our fire and we hid in a thicket. Only G-d knows how we got in. When it quieted down I told my wife that Vatzlav Raviky lived in a nearby hamlet. I wanted to go to him to find out why there was shooting. On the way, I saw three people hiding under a stump. When I came closer I heard them speaking Yiddish. They were Asher Binder, his cousin Katya Binder and Baruch Schwartzblat. They told me that they had hidden with a group of 23 Jews. They were attacked on the way and those who fell were: 1. Nahum Katzenelson, 2. Misha Berezovsky, 3. Leibl Lifshitz, 4. Yehoshua Itzhak Zilberman and his son Boria, 5. Shalom Zilberman, 6. Mendl Schwartzblat and a few others.

Eventually, I found Yechiel Trossman. I told him that I had seen his wife a few weeks earlier. Trossman reacted to the news with an emotional outpour and went to look for her.

The partisans came closer to our area. Once I met a partisan officer – a Jew from Kiev. He brought us to a site where there were many partisans armed with machine guns. They gave me a pair of boots, a large fur piece and other clothes and I became one of them. The partisans were very tired and they assigned me to do night watch. I was told to wake them up if I heard anything suspicious.

The officer believed it was still too early for us to join the rest of the partisans. He urged me to wait. “However,” he added, “I want you to go back as free people. I will, today, give a speech in the village to all the local residents. I will tell them that if they mistreat any Jews or kill them, we will burn down the entire village”.

We parted from the officer. We hugged and kissed each other and then we left. We went back to Blizhov. My wife and I had received new woven shoes and we began our journey. It was extremely dark. My wife had no strength to continue and we went into a hamlet near Blizhov. There we met Baruch Blizhovsky and Baruch Perlovich. They told us that we did well in coming there. This village belonged to the partisans and it was safe.

It was really true. The Jews were free to roam the village and were employed by the local residents. One of the locals told me that my sister-in-law Henya Kutz was nearby. She was sewing jackets. We spent a whole day with her. At night we went with her to the forest to a lean-to made of branches where Yechiel Trossman and his family and Henya Kutz and her daughter had hidden. They told me that not far from there in another dugout were Avraham Gotlieb and his family, Leah, Haya, Hindl, Vitka, Hiska and his sister's two children, Haya and Haim Wasserman. We stayed with them. We built a proper lean-to for the whole family. Later, Baruch Schwartzblat arrived. The women and the girls knitted sweaters from threads. Avraham Gotlieb and I would exchange the sweaters for eggs at night.

Once, on a Friday, we heard loud shooting. We jumped up, not knowing what was happening. Soon, a local acquaintance came and told us that a large number of partisans had come. They surrounded the village of Yelena and burned it. The loud bangs came from a warehouse where bombs were stored. The partisans killed around 100 people. The rest ran away and were hiding near us. He advised us to run away from our lean-to because our lives were in danger. We followed his advice and we ran wherever we could. In fact, the murderers immediately came and burned down our lean-to. These were murderers who had fought with the partisans. They helped the Germans who had promised them an “independent Ukraine”.

The good man was really a messenger from G-d. His advice saved our lives.

[Page 287]

Pages from the Holocaust

Israel Pinchuk (Haifa)

Translated by Ala Gamulka

In normal times there were cordial relations between the Jews and their Christian neighbors. However, when the Nazis entered, our neighbors became our enemies and washed their hands in our blood. We heard rumors that in David-Horodok the local residents killed all the Jewish men. A short time later, the Jews left the village of Vitkovich. They were pursued by the locals and, 3 kilometers away from the village, they were all brutally murdered.

Three months later the *Judenrat* managed to obtain permission to remove the bodies of the Vitkovich martyrs from the forest. This is where they were killed and their bodies hidden. We wanted to give them a proper burial in Glinna. Words cannot describe the horrors we witnessed. Most of the bodies were cut into small pieces and could not be identified.

After the destruction of the Jews of Vitkovich, we ran away to Rokitno where we performed forced labor. I was attached to a work unit whose task was repairing the railroad tracks and the bridges. We carried on our backs metal tracks, heavy planks and beams. Life was difficult. The food supplies were meager and hunger oppressed us. Rumors of destruction were rampant. We heard that the Jews of Olevsk were annihilated.

On August 26, 1942 the final roll call of the Jews of Rokitno was held. As I stood next to my father, Avraham, I heard shouts: "The German police are surrounding us!" I escaped into the synagogue yard. I hid in a garbage can and I put the lid on. A few minutes later, a German came and threatened to kill me. He removed me from the garbage can and brought me to the train station.

The market place resembled a killing field. The Germans were yelling at those who were trying to escape: "Stop! I will shoot!" I remember that Noah Soltzman's daughter was begging "chief" Sokolovsky: "Please don't shoot!" This plea softened his heart and he ordered the shooting stopped.

At the station there were freight cars used for transporting cattle. They were guarded by men armed with machine guns. We were put into the cars which were tightly packed. Some of us were badly injured.

When we reached Sarny we were taken out like sheep to a slaughter. One of the last to leave was my mother, Hava-Shifra. I caught her in my arms. She had been caught by the Germans when she hid in the stable in Dr. Anishtchuk's yard. From the train station we were brought to a field fenced with barbed wire. It was located on the other side of the tracks (Zapoliska). The heat was unbearable. The SS men, assisted by the Ukrainian militia, surrounded us holding machine guns. Soon we were joined by Jews from Dombrovitza, Bereshenitz, Klesov and

Tomoshgorod. We did not eat all day. We waited with heavy hearts for what was to come.

We exchanged gold and jewelry for some water which the local residents brought us in a shoe or a hat. Everyone wanted a swig of water and we pushed towards the fence. The Germans shot at those crowding together. Some were injured and many were killed. I recall that I succeeded in obtaining a tomato which had been thrown over the fence by a local woman. The *shohet* from Blizhov asked me for a slice of tomato for his granddaughter. I gave it to him and he blessed me with long life. In the meantime, we heard rumors that we would be taken to a central location. There the families would be separated and the young men would be sent to do forced labor. We stood tense and nervous on the field for a day and a night. We did not close our eyes. Crying and sobbing were heard from several directions. The rumor was whispered that the Sarny *Judenrat* was trying to free us. This filled us with hope and encouraged us. Even when the sharp sword was on our necks, we still remained hopeful. Then, the Jews of Sarny were brought in and our hopes were dashed. It was extremely crowded and we knew something terrible was coming.

At 3:00 p.m. the Jews of Rokitno were informed by the Jewish police to prepare to leave. We knew that we were being led to a slaughter because the injured and the dead were with us. The Nazis even took pictures of this death march. I will never forget the shudder that overcame me when I saw, from a distance, the ditches. My mother whispered to me: "My dear son, these are the final minutes of our lives and there will be no one to say *Kaddish* for me". I replied that her son Shalom was in Russia and her son Baruch was in Eretz Israel and they would remember her. (Unfortunately, Shalom fell in the battle of Berlin and Baruch in the War of Independence).

We approached the ditches. The SS and the Ukrainian militia stood around them armed with automatic rifles and machine guns. They were prepared to annihilate us. Fear of death befuddled and numbed us. We stood in groups of four. We did not know what would happen to us. We were ordered to undress completely. The men were separated from the women and children. I parted from my mother and I stood in the fourth row close to the ditches.

That moment I decided to escape, no matter what. I whispered to those standing near me to run away since we had nothing to lose. At least we would be part of the spilling of the blood of those close to us. We jumped shouting "*Shema Israel*" and we began to run with our last strength. We fell down and got up and the killers shot at us from all directions. I reached the forest alone – naked as a baby.

In the forest I met the two sons of Avraham and Haim Blizhovsky from Sarny. One of them gave me a shirt and the other – a pair of pants with a belt. (I still have the belt). A young girl from Nimovitz (near Sarny), the daughter of Hannah, was with them. She was covered in blood from those who were wounded when they were trying to escape.

We crawled for about two kilometers and we pondered our next move. The Blizhovsky boys went to the side and whispered. I understood that they intended to leave me. This is, indeed, what happened. The young girl remained with me. We waited for them all night. There were armed forest wardens all around us looking for escapees so that they could hand them over to the Nazis. By morning, the brothers had not returned.

On Shabbat, the third day of the slaughter, we saw a farmer from a distance. We asked him the way to Nimovitz. He shuddered when he saw us and he continued on his way. Two hours later he returned with food for us. He told us that he was a Baptist and that two young Jews had been caught and killed nearby. We understood that the Blizhovsky brothers were dead.

We stayed there till nightfall and we started towards Nimovitz. The young girl was a native of that village and she knew the residents. When we reached a hamlet near Nimovitz, we saw farmers returning from Sarny. They were laden with goods they had stolen from Jewish homes. We went to the hamlet and the farmer's wife gave us food and allowed us to sleep in the stable. The next day, the farmer brought us potatoes and showed us the way to Nimovitz. He calmed us down by telling us the residents were also Baptists and would not hurt the Jews.

On the way the young girl thought of one of her acquaintances called Hovodor. We decided to go to him. We reached his house in the evening, but we did not go inside. We slept outside. At dawn when the shepherds went out with their herds, they began to shout: "Jews! Jews!" The forest warden arrested us and was taking us to Sarny to hand us over to the Nazis. We passed through a village whose residents were Baptists. They asked the warden to hand us over to the mayor. One of the Baptists noticed that I was murmuring Psalms: "To the victor, a psalm of David. G-d will help you in your difficulties!" He consoled me saying that they would try to save us. The residents distracted the warden and motioned for us to escape. The young girl managed to escape. I was very weak and I could not run. However, the villagers delayed the warden and enabled me to run away.

I ran to Hovodor's house and there I found the young girl. He built me a shelter from branches, about 300 meters from his house. He provided me with food all the time. On the eve of *Succoth*, Hovodor, one of the Righteous Gentiles, came to me and told me that the rainy season was approaching and the shelter would not suffice. Also, there was another great danger since the Germans were hunting for partisans who had been seen in the area.

He suggested that I move to a different location. I walked to the Rokitno forest hoping to find some remnants of my family. Hovodor accompanied me to the railroad tracks and showed me the direction to the forests of Strashov. Before he parted from me, he hugged and kissed me and told me: "Let G-d be on your side and let him keep you from harm. May you reach your destination in peace."

At night I crossed the Slutz River and I waded in ponds and swamps. I walked through the forest for a long time until I reached, at dawn, the village of Osnitzek. My feet were swollen, but I continued on my way until I reached the village of

Glinna. I stayed around there for two weeks until I found some members of my family.

Some time later, a partisan camp was established in the area. I received propaganda materials from them and I distributed them with my brother-in-law, Yechiel Trossman, among the area residents. I urged them to rebel against the Germans. When the camp left the area we joined the Kotovsky division. I fulfilled various tasks there. When the area was liberated by the Soviets in 1944, I joined a special reconnaissance unit which functioned behind enemy lines near Kovel. We had clashes with German reconnaissance units. As the Red Army was advancing, most of the partisans were fighting the Banderovtzis who were anti-Soviet. I stayed in this function until the end of the war.

At the end of 1945 I left and reached Germany. After many trials and tribulations I was on my way to Eretz Israel.

[Page 291]

Self Sacrifice of a Mother

Yosef Segal (Neve Oz)

Translated by Ala Gamulka

My sister Gitel Segal-Wolman, and her 15 year-old son Shloimele, were confined in the Rokitno ghetto, as were all the Jews in town. They felt the holocaust coming and decided that when the worst moment came, they would escape and hide with a peasant they knew. He lived in a village called Netrebe, 20 kilometers from Rokitno. They agreed that if they could not run together, each one of them would try to get there on their own.

The terrible day came – the 13th of *Elul*, 1942. The Germans and their Ukrainian cohorts gathered all the Jews in the market square and began to shoot at them. My sister and her son ran from the killing area in different directions and they lost sight of each other. My sister was the first to reach the peasant. She waited for her son for several days. She assumed that he had been killed in the market square. Out of sorrow and longing she decided to give herself up to the Germans. The peasant tried to talk her out of this dangerous decision. He was prepared to continue to hide her in his place. However, one day, early in the morning, she left the peasant's house, returned to Rokitno and was murdered by the Ukrainians.

Several days later, her son Shloimele reached the peasant's house. He had hidden in the forest. His mother was gone. Some time later, he too was murdered by another peasant.

[Page 291]

The Destruction of Toupik

Eliahu Freger (Kiryat Frustig)

Translated by Ala Gamulka

On the eve of Yom Kippur 1941, the Jews of the village of Vitkovich were slaughtered. Immediately after the massacre, a peasant woman came to our house and advised us to run away to Bilovizh. She heard that the murderers were coming to Toupik on the following day. My father did not want to desecrate the Holy Day and refused to move from his place. On the morning of *Yom Kippur* the same woman returned with terrible news: The murderers had already arrived in Toupik. I went outside to verify the news. I saw our shepherd signaling with his hands. I did not understand the signals. However, another peasant from Vitkovich, called Durko, immediately approached me. His hands and clothes were bloodied. After he excused himself for interrupting me on this day holy to the Jews, he said, "Yesterday we killed all the Jews of Vitkovich. Only Yoel Korobochka, his wife Hinka and their four children escaped the execution and found a haven in our house." He now wanted to get his hands on the family to add them to the pile of dead bodies. Then he would be happy.

I begged him to spare their lives. Since he respected my father, he agreed and cancelled the death sentence he had passed on the Korobochka family. On my way home I saw armed peasants returning to Vitkovich. I found out that these were the killers the peasant woman had warned us about. The peasants from Bilovizh immediately came out and formed a defense wall around our house. They guarded us so that we would not be killed.

They asked us to move to Bilovizh since we would be better protected there. My father refused to go with them because he was afraid that he would be forced to eat non-kosher food. The Bilovizh police posted an officer at his house to guard him. He stayed at home from *Yom Kippur* to May 3.

When the Germans ordered the concentration of all the Jews of the area in Rokitno, my father was uprooted. The peasants harnessed the horses. My father took my mother and the Torah scroll of the village and went to Rokitno.

We suffered terrible hunger in the ghetto. The cold and the hunger distressed my father who was over eighty years old. My mother had great staying power and faced all the difficulties bravely. She collected potato peels that were even rejected by the cows. She salted them and fed them to my father. This abominable food caused my father to swell and he lost consciousness. A week before he was killed he regained consciousness and he spent day and night praying and reciting Psalms.

The Germans came to execute him. All those who were ill were exterminated in their homes. The house was full of people. These were the peasants from Bilovizh who came to say good-bye to my father. When the interpreter asked what they saw in this Jew, the peasants replied that Yakov was a good man. He never hurt anyone. They were begging for him to be spared. The only "special" treatment my father received was that he was not killed at home like all the other ill people. He was killed in Sarny.

Before he was killed, my father covered himself in his prayer shawl and prayed in a voice choked with sobs. While he was praying a bullet hit him. He died together with my mother.

Aharon of Toupik was blind in both eyes. His wife, Haya-Sarah, was crippled in both legs. They could not move from the ghetto. They were killed in the house together with their son, Moshe and their daughter, Nehama. Others who were killed were Naftali and Rachel Dubinski, their son Eliahu and daughters Fruma, Leah and Sarah; Hava Freger, her daughter Haya and son Yoel; 13 year-old Eliahu Chechik; (Mordechai and David, the sons of Aharon Chechik, fell on the front in 1944. David dreamed of reaching Germany and of making *aliyah* from there. He fell in battle on Polish soil.)

I escaped, under a shower of bullets, with my son Shimon, into the forest. There I was shocked by an event that I will never forget. In our household in Toupik we had a dog that had been with us for many years. When we were exiled from the village, the dog could not find a place for himself. He roamed around searching for us. We found him in the forest and he began to lick us with happiness. We had to send him away because his barking would have endangered our lives. My son Shimon began to cry when he saw the dog sadly making his way back to the village. The peasants told us that the dog stopped eating and drinking and lay in his corner making horrifying sounds.

This is how the village of Toupik was annihilated. Its Jews loved the land and always worked hard.

[Page 293]

Blizhov During The Holocaust Years

Aharon Blizhovsky (Ramat Gan)

Translated by Ala Gamulka

By the time the Nazis took over Polesia in the summer of 1941, most of the Jews had left the village and had moved to Rokitno and Sarny. A few old timers stayed in the village. All the young people had left the village. For almost a year the Nazis did not bother the Jews. In the summer of 1942, they took them to the village of Berezov. All the Jews from the area were concentrated there in a few houses. On the eve of *Rosh Hashana* 1942, the Jews were taken a few kilometers away from the village. They were shot. Some managed to escape into the forests.

During the German occupation, I lived in Rokitno. As we all know, those Jews of Rokitno who survived the market square were taken to Sarny. On the day of extermination in Sarny a few Jews managed to break through the barbed wire fence surrounding the killing field. They began to run in all directions. The Nazis and the Ukrainian guards shot at them. I was among the escapees. Out of town I met an unfamiliar peasant. I asked him the way to Tomoshgorod. I hoped to reach Blizhov from there. He not only showed me the way, but he also gave me bread and cucumbers. I turned east and I crossed one of the rivers on foot. On the road I met a refugee from Sarny. We walked together for four days until I reached Blizhov. I went to a farm early in the morning. I was shoeless and my feet were bleeding. The peasant began to cry when he saw me. He gave me a piece of bread and shoes made out of reeds (*halanot*)*. He said to me: "I can't bring you to my house. Go in peace!"

I reached the village and I went to see Vatzek, a Polish forest warden. He fed us and told us that members of my family and other Jews had made it to the forest. Within two weeks we were a group of 50-60 people, scattered in the area. We roamed the forest. The peasants asked the village mayor what to do about the Jews. He replied: "I did not ask you about the Jews. Don't tell me about them." The peasants understood that he meant that the Jews should not be persecuted or handed over to the Germans. In Blizhov there were no Germans. It was only in January 1943 that a unit of soldiers settled in the village of Glinna. These Germans sometimes passed through Blizhov on their way to Rokitno.

Until the difficult winter came, we were scattered in the forest. We moved in groups of 3 or 4 people. At night we went to the village to beg for food. In daytime we hid in the forest. We dug for potatoes in the fields close to the forest. In the winter, as it became colder, we began to ask the peasants to let us stay in their barns, stables and wells.

I must say that these peasants treated us fairly well. In the area of Blizhov there

**Fastalas*

were no attacks or denunciations of Jews. In other villages some peasants killed the Jews that strayed into their area.

Yosef Blizhovsky testified about the good relations between the peasants and the Jewish refugees. He tells of one peasant that worked his family's land and who brought him payment for his share of the potato crop and for the rental of his land. Another peasant took his mother's cow and gave him as much milk as he wanted. He even returned the cow when the Nazis left.

There were especially good relations between the Jews and those peasants who belonged to a religious sect called Shtundists. They saw the hand of G-d in the horrors that befell the Jews. They believed in the prophecy that only a remnant of the Jewish people – "one from a city and two from a family" – would stay alive on judgment day. I visited one of these peasants many times and I read aloud his sacred books.

There are three reasons for their good behavior.

1. For several generations, the peasants knew most of the Jews of the Blizhov forests and they had good neighborly relations with them.
2. The village was situated in a remote corner of Polesia, far from the center of the German authorities.
3. The influence of the religious sects (Shtundists).

In the winter of 1943 small units of Russian partisans arrived in the Blizhov forests. They were mostly Russian prisoners of war who had escaped. Younger refugees joined the partisans. They received arms and took part in various activities such as the bombing of the railroad tracks near Rokitno. There were also reprisals against collaborators with the Germans.

In the village of Glinna a peasant denounced Shimon Gendelman of Rokitno to the police. Shimon had come to beg him for bread. He was killed by the police. A few days later, Asher Binder of Rokitno penetrated the village with a Russian partisan. They removed the peasant from his house. After they made certain that he was the one who had denounced Gendelman to the authorities, they killed him on his doorstep.

Those who did not join the partisans lived in the forest. We learned how to make brandy (*samogon*) and we exchanged it with the partisans for bread, meat, etc.

Sometimes the rumors came that the Germans were coming to search the village. We would immediately leave the village and go into the forest. On such a night, a cold winter night, one Jew froze to death near one of the houses. The peasant lent us a sled and we brought the body to the forest for burial.

At the beginning of 1944 we heard that the Red Army had liberated Rokitno and Sarny. We began to return to the towns after a year and a half of living in the forest.

[Page 295]

A Child's Memories of the Destruction of Rokitno

Haim Bar Or (Svetchnik) (Haifa)

Translated by Ala Gamulka

The 22nd of July 1941 was a beautiful summer day. Since it was summer vacation, we were off from school. I was playing with other children in the Tarbut school yard. I felt strange when I saw the movement of the Soviet soldiers near the school. I felt something out of the ordinary was about to happen. Actually, that morning we were informed that the Germans had bombed Kiev and other cities.

This event was a "red alert" for the Jews of Rokitno. It was a warning of what was coming. However, they did not even think of what could happen. Save for a few, they did not believe that anything bad would reach us.

I remember the day the Soviets retreated. They burned offices, central buildings and bridges. The town was in flames and in the middle of the fire, the Ukrainians came from the villages to rob the well-stocked warehouses.

Tzvi Olshansky, who was serving as a soldier in the Red Army, came to our house and begged us: "Go to Russia! Escape from the hell that is coming upon us!" He said these words during the last days of the retreat of the Soviet army. In reply to his pleading, my mother said she would not leave her property and her belongings. She had worked too many years to acquire them and she did not wish to begin a life of wandering as a deprived refugee.

We stayed. However, not too many days passed and we saw what our imagination could not have conjured up. The Germans entered the synagogue, dragged out a Jew who was praying and slaughtered him near the cemetery. The Jews deluded themselves, thinking that this one Jew was the scapegoat. The murderers would stop with him.

As time went by we heard all kinds of rumors about the formation of ghettos in various towns and about the murders of Jews for no reason. No one imagined that our turn would come. The winter of 1942 passed and summer came. Rumors were spreading that a ghetto was to be established for the Jews of Rokitno and its vicinity. It turned out that these were not merely rumors, but that the plan would soon come to fruition. The *Judenrat* members interpreted the establishment of the ghetto as a good thing, since inside the ghetto; Jews would be better protected from the Ukrainian hooligans.

The ghetto was filled to capacity. Families with many children were crammed into tiny rooms. It was horribly stifling and the hunger was unbearable. I cannot even describe what my eyes saw. I well remember a Jew who came to the ghetto with his family and they were housed in the synagogue. He was a handsome Jew, about 50 years old, full of energy. However, starvation destroyed him. He was constantly depressed. He became bloated from hunger and died.

The Germans and the SS did not sit with folded hands and they came up with actual plans for our destruction. At first, their satanic plots were modest and they were satisfied by counting the Jewish population. This was done with the help of the Jewish police and the *Judenrat.* The Germans were pleased with the counting. No one was missing. After several roundups we reached that bloody Wednesday in August - the last day in the lives of many of the Jews of Rokitno. It was a beautiful hot morning. All the Jews of Rokitno were assembled in the market square for a new roundup. After the names were carefully read and everyone was present, an order was given for new line-ups. The women and girls older than 10 were separated from the men (including all boys older than 10). So we stood for a quarter of an hour.

Suddenly, a loud horrifying scream was heard from the women's side. Our hearts were beating faster and the crowd, which had been standing up to now, began to run every which way. A barrage of shots was fired at the unfortunate souls. Shouting and crying erupted. The screams were deafening. As I was running I fell into a ditch near Gotlieb's house.

When I climbed out of the ditch I saw that the market square was strewn with dead bodies and the soil was red with blood. I heard the cries of the injured and the sobbing of the children. I began to run towards the forest through backyards. On the way, I met petrified Jews who did not know where they would find help.

Everyone was searching for family members. Mothers looked for their children and children wanted their parents. I found my 11 year-old sister and together we searched for my mother. On the way I saw groups of Jews who were desperate and crazed, afraid of what was to come.

Suddenly a group of Jews came towards us and among them was my mother alone. My little brother, older sister and grandmother were not with her. After the war I found out that my sister and grandmother died in Sarny and my brother was killed in the market square.

We broke up into small groups. Our group included my family and the Schwartz family. My mother went to a neighboring village to obtain food for us so that we should not die of starvation. However, since she was late in returning, we went with the Schwartz family to look for her. On the way we met a group of 50 people - children alone, women and elderly people. Among them I found my mother. They were thinking of going back to Rokitno because they believed that no one would bother them now. I was against this and I maintained that a return to Rokitno would bring certain death. Indeed, those who did go back - their bitter end is known to all of us. My family joined the family of Yosef Kaplan who knew the area well and we felt safer and stronger with him.

In Okopi we found Gitel Burko and her son, Rachel Wasserman, her two daughters and her sister. A terrible calamity happened to me at that time. My mother fell ill and died after a few days. We buried her not far from where we were staying. My sister deeply mourned my mother and after two weeks of suffering and longing, she too died. She was only 11 years old. I buried her next to my mother. I was left all alone.

On the way I met Niussa Kokel. She was terribly depressed after everything that had happened to her. She could not accept her lot having lost everyone dear to her. When we passed the graves of my mother and sister, she would burst out in bitter tears and would say: "At least you have a grave. You have a place to shed tears. I don't have it". (After the liberation she died in Lvov).

One day Theodore Linn and Avraham Eisenberg came with rumors about partisans who were nearby and their group wanted to join them. I, Shmuel Levin and his brother Shaike, decided to try our luck with the partisans, but we were not successful.

The winter of 1943 ended. The behavior of the Germans towards the Poles worsened. As a result, the Germans were faced with a belligerent attitude from the Polish population. In this way we, the residents of the forests, became allies of the Poles. After several robbery and murder raids by the Ukrainians, the Poles escaped into the forests. We received them with open arms because when we were with them our economic and safety conditions improved. The word "liberation" was on our minds. Rumors of the advancement of the Red Army encouraged us. In January 1944, the Red Army came to our area. I immediately joined a convoy and returned "home" - to Rokitno. Instead of our house I found a pile of rubble. Our homes had been totally obliterated from the faces of the earth.

[Page 298]

Yarzheit - The Yearly Memorial (Poem)

Haim Shteinman (Tel Aviv)

Translated from Yiddish by Ala and Larry Gamulka

Many memorial candles are lit
They spread sparks and flames
They remind us of many memories-
The love of mother and father.

Their charming eyes shine together
For us through the years
The glances of our parents
Glow in our memory.

The candles are lit
They spread sparks and flames
With memories connected
To our mothers and fathers.

[Page 299]

THE ROAD OF SUFFERING

[Page 301]

Wanderings and Hardships During The Holocaust

Haya Volkon (Pinchuk) (Haifa)

Translated by Ala Gamulka

When the Germans occupied Russia on 22 June 1941, I wrote my parents in Glinna to come to Rokitno so that we could go together to Russia. Since they did not reply, I went with my brother, Yisrael, to Glinna to take our parents with us. They refused to leave saying that the war would not last long and the Germans would not reach us. When we parted, my father shed tears and said that he and my mother will be alone and abandoned in their old age. I could not watch them suffer and I decided to stay in Glinna. My brother was advised to escape since, according to all the rumors, the Germans abused men, especially those who had worked for the Soviets. My brother Yisrael parted from us and went on his way. However, he returned ten days later because all the roads were already blocked by the Germans.

It was quiet during the first three weeks under German occupation. Soon gangs of criminals from nearby villages were formed. They demanded from the Jews their belongings. One day, a *Folksdeutch* (German Pole) called Ratzlav, arrived from Rokitno. He was accompanied by twenty men from the glass factory (Huta). They were going from village to village inciting the Christian population against the Jews and they stole anything that came their way.

The situation worsened from day to day. We were afraid of attacks on our houses and we slept away from home every night. I remember one Shabbat eve when the table was set and the candles were lit. Suddenly we heard that in David-Horodok the peasants had killed Jewish men even before the Germans arrived. They were now going wild in the area and slaughtering Jews. We were shaken by the news and everyone went to the forest. We spent the night there.

Three frightening months passed. One day a peasant told us that all the Jews of Vitkovich were exterminated. At first, it seemed that they would be allowed to leave the village. However, they were soon chased and tortured. Their hands and feet were broken and they expired with terrible suffering. Now the criminals were preparing to come to Glinna to exterminate the Jews.

When our family heard this terrible news, we left for Rokitno. We went to live with Asher Schwartz. This is where we had stayed during the Soviet occupation. When the ghetto was formed and the yellow star had to be worn, we moved to Yudel Kleiman's house in the "new town". The ghetto was divided into two sections and was spread over Pilsudsky Street in the "old town" and a few streets in the "new town". We did very hard work. Some of the young women were employed in a cooperative located in the old synagogue. They knitted sweaters and did sewing for the Germans. We were taken to work from the "new town" to the "old town" in the middle of the road. We were not permitted to walk on the pavement. At times we even went to dig ditches and to bring lumber from the forests.

Life in the ghetto became more difficult and bitterer every day. Hunger plagued us especially those who had not hoarded food and who did not have clothes for bartering. It was possible to get food from the peasants in exchange for clothes. We had no choice but to eat weeds and wild flowers. All kinds of stems were cooked, especially poison ivy nettles. We were tormented by the hunger.

In the first roll call by the Germans we were gathered in the market square across from the new synagogue. We were led to the abattoir. The Poles watched us with a smile of pleasure spread on their faces. After this roll call, as well as the next one, we came back home. We were broken and dejected because we knew it was the end.

On August 26, 1942, the SS gave an order for us to present ourselves for a third roll call in the market square across from the synagogue in the "new town". This time it was a comprehensive roll call. It included children, the elderly and the sick. At first we stood scattered. However, soon the order came to stand six abreast – men and women separated. My sisters and I stood near our mother. The Germans, including Sokolovsky, chief of police, were going back and forth in the square. At times the chief of the Ukrainian militia would appear, speak quietly to Sokolovsky, and then leave.

The members of the *Judenrat* mingled among us and calmed us by telling us we would soon be going home. However, troubling swings told us it was not time for optimism. Sima Zaks, who stood near us, asked for water for her children. It could not be done. We waited for a long time. We found out later that the reason for the delay was that the train taking us to Sarny had not arrived.

My mother, always full of confidence and hope, encouraged us saying that in two weeks we would be praying the *Rosh Hashana* service in the synagogue across the road. We must not lose hope because there is a great G-d up above and he delivers salvation quickly. However, suddenly we heard shots fired by the Ukrainian militia. We saw armed officers approaching us from a street next to the synagogue. When we saw the killers, terrible screams erupted and many of us began to run.

Sokolovsky pointed his pistol and yelled in Polish: "Don't run or I will shoot". My mother held my hand in hers and said: "Come my daughter! Let us run away. The end is near!" That moment we were bombarded by a shower of bullets. I managed to run with my mother to Noah Rafalovich's house. Somehow, I dropped her hand. I threw a coat over my head and I ran without looking back. On the way I saw many wounded, but I did not stop. A powerful force was propelling me forward, through backyards and fields until I reached the forest. The escaping Jews, 600 or so, were running mainly on the street leading to the forest. Most of them were caught by the bloodthirsty police officers. Here and there, young children ran without mother or father, scared and exhausted. They fell on the road. I will never forget the image of a young boy, about four years old, who ran after us yelling: "I am Malka's child. Take me with you!" No one paid any attention to him. We ran like crazed people.

In the forest I met Haike Horman (She died a year later in the Osnitzek forest), Tzipah Wax and her family, Motel Kramer and his two children, and Feiga Brach. We sat down and listened to the screams echoing from town. When my head cleared and I understood what was happening, I could not forgive myself for abandoning my mother to certain death as I was saving myself. To this day, my heart is heavy with guilt.

We walked five kilometers away from Rokitno into the forest. Towards evening Motel Kramer, Tzipah Wax and her family and Feiga Brach decided to return to town. They hoped that those who remained alive would be allowed to live in the ghetto. This had happened in other towns. They did not think they could survive in the forest. Haike Horman and I and two Jews from Karpilovka went in the direction of Karpilovka. On the way I went to a peasant's house to ask for clothes to guard against the cold. At the door I met Hershel Gornstein's wife with her baby girl. She was begging to be allowed inside the house. I did not receive the clothing I was seeking and I continued to walk parallel to the narrow railroad tracks. We were depressed and frozen when we arrived in Karpilovka. We went to a peasant's house where we were given bread and hot potatoes. The peasant's daughter commiserated with us and cried about our bitter predicament. She brought Haike and me to the barn to sleep. At night she came and told us that Jews were hiding in the house. I was amazed to find my two brothers-in-law – Sender Golovey and Yechiel Trossman. With them were Issachar and Moshe who was wounded in the leg (he was wounded in the market square). Haike Horman, too, found her sister Sarah with her husband Pinhas Fuchsman.

We could not all stay there. Therefore, we continued on the road. We met other Jews and we entered the forest. On the first night we discovered how cold it could be and how difficult life was without any possessions. Danger lurked everywhere. We began to search for partisans. When we were still in Rokitno we heard that, near Brezhne, ten days before the extermination, they had attacked partying Germans. They killed 30 of them. My brother-in-law, Yechiel, decided to go with his children, Issachar and Moshe, to look for his wife Ita and his daughter Miriam. Before the extermination they had agreed to meet at a certain peasant's house. He was hoping to find them there. He invited me to join them. I thought I would be a burden to them and I parted from him. I joined a group, which included my brother-in-law Sender. It was difficult to say good-bye. My heart told me we would not meet again.

Yechiel stayed with the children in the forest and I walked away from them. From time to time I turned my head and looked at them. Suddenly, the children shouted: "Wait for us. We don't want to part from you. Let us go together!" We continued in the direction of Brezhne, through the forest, through unmarked ways. Two days later we noticed footprints of spiked boots. We realized that partisans had walked there. We asked the peasants where they were and they said they were in the area. We decided to send a delegation of three men to look for the partisans. We were a group of 19 people waiting for their return. We anxiously waited for two days and feared for their well-being. One night we heard rustling in the forest and we soon saw our delegation of three together with the partisans. They wore Red Army uniforms and had a red star on their caps. We were unbelievably elated. Some of us hugged them. They urged us to start walking since there was a long road ahead of us. We had to reach camp before daybreak.

In the morning we reached the tents and we saw uniformed men and women. There were some Jews among them. Some were officers. I particularly remember an officer, a woman from Odessa called Sima. Most of the partisans had come from the forests of Briensk (the hub of partisan activity). They numbered about 100. We were well received. They gave us hot food and medical attention. Slowly our sense of confidence returned and we felt like human beings again. We were ready to fight the Nazi beast.

After we had a short rest, General Medvedev spoke to us. He promised to help us and to set up a special camp for us so that we could defend ourselves. For a while we were part of the larger camp. The elderly were assigned to do housekeeping chores and the younger ones were given arms. The women cooked. When we arrived we found a few young men from Brezhne that we knew from earlier days. We were 150 Jews including 13 children. One of the women was a kindergarten teacher. Haya Gitelman and her husband sewed children's shirts out of parachutes. We waited for an airplane that would take the children to Moscow. A temporary runway was prepared, but the plane sank in the mud and we could not get it out. The pilots took out the ammunition and the medicines and the plane was set on fire. Of course, it was no longer thinkable to get the children out.

Two weeks after the extermination, Moshe Golovey, Shoshana and Shlomo Grinshpan arrived in our camp. Shlomo told us he had seen my father, Avraham, and Hershel Shteinman in the forest. They were too old to join the partisans. Unfortunately, I was not able to see my father. He and Shteinman were caught near Osnitzek and killed. It was three weeks after the slaughter in Rokitno.

One evening, all the Jews in camp were gathered. General Medvedev appointed three Jewish officers to supervise us. We were given ammunition: 18 guns, two wagons harnessed to horses, and enough food to last for a few days so that we would not have to raid the villages and annoy the peasants.

As soon as we covered a distance of 15 kilometers from camp, the three Jewish officers disappeared. They did not believe that, burdened with the elderly, the young and the sick, we would be able to reach safety. The parachutists who had accompanied us went back to camp to seek advice as to how to proceed. We waited for them in a very dangerous area. We were close to the German stations and we had to be absolutely silent.

In our group we had a doctor from Brezhne with his wife, sister-in-law and his two children. One child cried constantly because of mosquito bites, lack of food and the cold. Some members of the group went over to the doctor and asked him to keep the child quiet because he was putting us all in danger. The doctor replied: "Take the child. I cannot keep him quiet. Do with him as you wish. Let us not all be lost!" The people bowed their heads and returned to their places.

When the advance people returned with the commander we were all assembled. We were warned, in case of capture, not to give any details to the enemy. The commander said they could not help us defend ourselves. We were to do it on our own. We could stay as a unit or we could disperse. Some of our group went off on their own. They were caught by the Germans and killed. About 40 of us remained. We decided to continue as an independent partisan unit. Our leaders were Yitzhak Shapiro, Yechiel Trossman and Yechiel Freger (still with us).

We continued to advance. A few days later, we were joined by three Jews from Koritz – Moshe Gendelman (Uncle Misha), his son Simcha and his nephew. Uncle Misha joined the command. In one of the forests near Rokitno we met Rachel Hammer who was all alone. We invited her to join us. However, she refused saying she was used to being there. We parted from her in great sorrow and we left her alone in the forest.

On the way we had to cross a bridge near Osnitzek. It was well guarded by the Germans. In those days, trains would pass through every twenty minutes. They were used to transport stolen Jewish property. We had to cross the bridge between trains. If we ran into guards, we had to eliminate them. We waited for two days in the forest. Our people surveyed the area to decide on the right moment to cross the bridge. Indeed, we were successful. When we had gone a few kilometers from the tracks we sat down to rest.

Early in the morning we saw a peasant arranging a pile of fodder. Some of us wanted to eliminate him so he would not tell the enemy about us. However, since we were Jews who had pity on him, we only warned him to say nothing. One should not feel pity for cruel people. The peasant informed on us. From a distance of 200 m we suddenly heard shouts: "Stop! Stop!" A shower of bullets fell on us. We began to run. Some of us stayed in place to defend those who were retreating. The Germans and the Ukrainians did not dare come closer. They believed we had a larger force.

We were separated from the unit and we roamed the forest aimlessly. We did not know how to go back. When we retreated we had left our parcels. One contained a picture of the family of Yechiel Trossman. The Germans immediately posted, in Rokitno, a reward for the capture of Yechiel. We walked towards the villages of Blizhov and Glinna. The situation in the new area was even worse than in the partisan camp. We discovered that Uncle Misha had remained independent with 15 men. We were forced to break up into small groups so that the peasants would not be suspicious. Also, if something happened, we would not all be caught.

I will never forget those days. They were extremely difficult – days of rain and cold. The peasants did not allow us to come near their houses and tried to avoid us. When we approached a house to ask for bread, they would meet us with axes and send their dogs after us. One rainy night I went to the house of a peasant I knew, to find out if anyone in my family was still alive. I saw him on his knees praying devoutly. When he got out and saw me he began to shout at me for coming there. He said: "G-d ordained that you die. Go and give yourselves up to the Germans. You will not be able to escape from the verdict of G-d in heaven".

From then on we began to wander aimlessly in the forest. As the cold weather worsened from day to day, we lay under the stars on a bed of wet leaves. One evening we reached a hamlet not far from the village of Toupik. Yechiel and Moshe went to the house to beg for food while I stayed outside with Issachar. Suddenly we heard rustling in the forest. I whispered to Issachar: "We are lost!" When those approaching heard my whisper, they began to run away. I understood they were Jews and I called to them: "Don't run away. We, too, are

Jews!" When they came closer I saw my sister Rivka and Motel Shapiro. We called out each other's name in disbelief. I told her that Sender and Moshe were alive and in the area. Rivka had been told that I was killed in Sarny. I was told, by a peasant, two days earlier, that Rivka had been killed by Lithuanians with a group of Rokitno Jews. Rivka told me that Ita and Miriam were near Blizhov. We went to the place where my sister was staying and there we found Shimon Gendelman, Aharon Perlov and two brothers, Moshe and Mordechai Chechik from Toupik. That night Shimon Gendelman, Perlov and one of the brothers went out to search for food. The peasants caught Shimon Gendelman and the young man from Toupik and gave them over to the police. Perlov fought them off and fled. (The peasant who informed on Gendelman and the young man from Toupik, for 2 kg. of salt, was killed by Asher Binder when he was with the partisans).

The next day we parted again from Rivka. She stayed in place and we left to meet Sender and Moshe who were in the area. We continued to wander towards Blizhov because Yechiel hoped to meet his wife Ita, and his daughter, Miriam. We arrived at a hamlet near Blizhov and we spoke to a peasant. Rivka said that he had information about the Jews located near Glinna. We searched fruitlessly for a few days. We settled in the forest near the road from Glinna to Blizhov. We were successful in finding Ita, Miriam, Henya Kutz and her daughter. We were overjoyed. That night we decided to go back to Blizhov because the peasants were kinder there. Yechiel and I went over to a peasant in the Hamel hamlet to ask him to tell anyone who asked about us that we were in the Blizhov area. When we came in at dawn, the peasant told us that my brother, Yisrael was there. My grief was unspeakable when I saw Yisrael swollen with hunger. We went back to the forest intending to remain together without parting. However, the next day we found out that Yehoshua Olisker and his family from Glinna were caught and killed. For security reasons we had to separate. I remained with my brother Yisrael. Yechiel and his family with Henya Kutz and her daughter returned to the Blizhov area.

One night we crossed the Stviga River near Glinna. Yisrael carried me on his back because my shoes were torn. We sat on the other side of the river across from our house in Glinna, which had been taken over by the Ukrainian police. We were alone, hungry, shoeless, frozen and petrified. We watched our home, occupied by strangers, but we could not reach it.

One night, the woman in whose barn we were hiding came and told us that the Soviets had arrived and had conquered the area. I understood her to mean partisans. Yisrael also confirmed that the partisans took over the area and destroyed the police holdings. They spent three weeks there. However, when the German advance forces came they retreated after a bloody battle in the village of Gloshovitz.

When the German forces appeared in the area, we were obliged to escape into the forest to a place called "Island of Wolves". The Germans went through all the settlements killing and burning. They especially took revenge on all those who supported the partisans. We stayed in the forest. The cold was unbearable. We lay on snow under the stars. This cruel cold caused the death of my brother-in-law Sender. He became weaker and one night died in my sister Rivka's arms.

At that time, Rachel Shuster, who was blind, joined us. Her sister Ethel and three children were saved from the Berezov ghetto. When the Germans entered their home to take them out, Rachel jumped, with two children, out of the window and she escaped into the forest. The peasants saw the hand of G-d in this escape and helped her.

In March 1943, the German forces came again to the area. They stayed for 18 days. We were very careful not to be caught by them. When we were on the Island of Wolves, 3 Shtundist brothers from the Hamel hamlet fed us. They brought us information about the movement of the Germans. They endangered their lives many times to save ours.

A short time later the Germans left the area and were no longer to be seen. However, they still bombed the area. In the spring, life was a little easier and we went to live with one of the peasants from the Hamel hamlet. Partisans came into the area. Kovpek with his large army passed through on the way to the Carpathians. Local detachments were formed. The Kotovsky detachment provided propaganda material. We joined the Kotovsky partisan detachment of Sovorov. One of the outstanding members of this detachment was Zvi Olshansky, chief saboteur and right-hand man of the commander.

From time to time, the Germans bombarded us because the peasants told them where we were located. They were never successful in hitting us. At the end of 1943, the Nazis were losing the war. We felt our redemption was near.

Unfortunately, I had an infection in a wisdom tooth. My mouth was completely shut and I had high fever. There was no one who could pull the tooth. One of the peasants tried to pull it out with pliers, but was unsuccessful. I was near death for three weeks. My condition was very serious. It was suggested to have my throat cut open to install a pipe for breathing. I refused. After lengthy treatments I had surgery under the tooth. The pus was drained and I improved.

When the Soviets liberated the area, the partisans left. Yisrael joined them. We went back to Rokitno. We found an empty, destroyed town. Jewish voices were no longer heard. Every street, every house and every corner reminded us of our dear departed souls. The loneliness was oppressive. Our only hope was to find a way to leave the place. A while later we received a letter from my brother in Russia.

He informed us that he had gone there in 1941 with the Red Army. In February 1945, on his way to the front, he visited us. The day after he left Rokitno, my brother-in-law Yechiel went out to battle the Banderovtzis in the village of Decht. He never returned. Two months later, on April 19, 1945 my brother Shalom died. Our only hope was to make *aliyah* and to join the remainder of the family. We left Rokitno for Poland. After much wandering, we arrived in Israel in 1948. I still managed to see my brother Baruch who was a soldier in the Israel Defense Forces. He died defending his country in 1948, two weeks before the ceasefire.

[Page 308]

The Road of Suffering

Bronia Lifshitz (Kogan) (Givatayim)

Translated by Ala Gamulka

On the eve of that fateful day, we knew that, the next morning, we had to go to the market square. My mother Sheindl had a bad feeling. Her heart told her the end was near. She prepared us for judgment day and told me and my sister Bella to save ourselves. We did not need to worry about her. Our neighbor, Fanya Klorfein, told my mother off for panicking everyone. There was no basis for it. She felt that since the first two roll calls ended well this one would also be like them. My mother was not convinced by these worthless consolations and she could not sleep. We did not sleep a wink all night and we prepared for judgment day. One cannot describe the suffering we went through that night. Jews have always consoled themselves with the saying: “Even when a sharp sword is placed on a person's neck, compassion is still possible”. However, the coming extermination was so certain that we could not console ourselves with this saying.

In the morning we put on our best clothes as if we were going on a festive outing. (It turned out that these clothes saved us because they kept us warm and also served as an exchange for food). I stood near my mother and my sister and near us stood my aunt, Esther Cherpichnik. When the police arrived, my mother began to sob and said: “Children, they are coming to kill us!” She pushed us and said: “Run, my children, run. Save yourselves!” To this day I feel the push on my back. My senses were blurred. I began to run frightened and lost my mother and sister. I later found out that my mother ran to a peasant called Claudia. She had stored some belongings there. I was told that the woman informed on my mother to the police and that they took her back to the market square. My sister with her two-year old son in her arms escaped to a peasant called Stankevich and hid in his garden. She, too, was taken back to the market square.

As I ran between the bullets, I was caught in an iron bar sticking out of the fence. I do not remember who freed me from this trap. I do remember that I continued to run with my last strength. I reached the forest where I met Aharon Lifshitz, the three Golubovitz brothers and a few others. We walked together. A troubling question filled my head: Where is my family? What was their fate? I felt guilty because I had saved myself. I very much wanted to return to Rokitno to die together with my mother and sister. However, the hope that in spite of everything, they had managed to escape from the market square, kept me from performing this desperate act.

We walked a whole day without any food or drink. Towards evening we found a well of dirty water. Felix Golubovitz took off his hat, filled it with water and gave us a drink. We heard that in the village of Budki-Borovski there were good peasants who hid Jews. We went there and we came to Liucik Zalevski. When I arrived I asked the good man to go with me to the village of Borovey. We had hidden goods there at the home of the priest's brother. We left at night. The road was very difficult. He was afraid to be caught by criminals who roamed the area. Zalevski went back and I stayed alone in Borovey. I was separated from my group. When I came to the priest's brother, he and his wife began to threaten me. They told me to leave immediately because they were in contact with Germans who visited them regularly. They were prepared to give back some of our belongings. However, they wanted me to leave immediately. I cried bitter tears and I begged them not to abandon me because I did not know how to reach a place where I could find Jews.

They told me that their farmhand would accompany me. I took two suits and some cloth and we were on our way. We came to his house and I stayed in the attic a whole day and half the night. At midnight the man came and told me the time was right to be on our way. Later on he stole the suits and cloth. I was suspicious from the beginning and when he reached the forest he stopped and said: “You are on your own from here on”. It was pitch black outside. With tears in my eyes I begged him not to leave me. I did not know the way. How could I walk in the dark? Wild beasts could attack me or the killers would find me. He answered stubbornly: “If you are not tired of your life- run now!” I was covered with a blanket to protect me from the cold. He took the blanket from me and in cruel voice repeated: “Run now!” I asked him to give me back the blanket because I could freeze in this extreme cold. When he heard my begging he took out an axe, put it to my forehead and said: “If you wish to stay alive, do not ask me for anything”. I was afraid that he would fulfill his threat and I escaped. I sat down in the thick of the forest and I wept silently. I resolved to wait for morning.

At daybreak I arose and began to walk. I did not know in which direction to go. I saw railroad tracks and I said to myself: If I cross them I may cross the border. I am already lost. I should go wherever my feet carry me. I suddenly discovered houses. I passed a few of them because my heart was beating hard. Eventually, I stopped at a house. An inner voice whispered to me: “Go inside and you will be safe”. I traversed the fence and I saw a huge scary dog. To my great surprise, he opened his eyes, looked at me, but he did not budge from his place and continued to doze. When I knocked on the door a petrified peasant came out. He was totally surprised. How did the dog remain silent and allow me to enter? It was something unusual. I was worthy of coming inside the house for that reason alone.

The peasant offered me a meal. I told him my story and he was in shock. He told me not to be afraid. He was a Shtundist and the Shtundists love Jews. He promised to accompany me at night to my destination. I lay all day hidden in the yard. At noon he came with a bible and read a few chapters to me. He saw me as a mysterious figure. His frightening dog only spared spirits and miracle workers. The fact that the dog did not bare his teeth proved that it was a sign from G-d that I should live.

While I was hiding in the yard the Ukrainian police conducted a thorough search in his house. This too was a sign from above because he originally had intended to hide me in his house. He only changed his mind at the last minute.

At night he went with me to Budki-Borovski and brought me to Yuzik Zalevski's house. He was renowned as a savior of Jews.

Zalevski accepted me willingly and arranged a hiding place for me in a potato cellar. He hid me in a crate that resembled a coffin. I shrunk myself into this living tomb. There was no air and no light and I thought I would faint. I called for help. Zalevski came immediately and found me unconscious. He took me out of the crate, rubbed my temples with snow until I came to. As soon as I felt better, he put me back in the crate because it was dangerous to be seen in daylight. At night I would come out for a breath of fresh air. I lay in this coffin for three months. I was certain that I would come out a cripple.

One day Yuzik came to me and said: “You can come out. The partisans came and they are accepting members into their ranks. Go to them and they will receive you well.” After three months of darkness I thought daylight was a miracle – something from a distant world. I felt as though, for the first time in my life, I was seeing this precious light. It bothered my eyes and I had difficulty adjusting. I was very happy because I was fortunate enough to see the sun again and to breathe fresh air. Great elation overcame me. In my heart there was hope that if I was fortunate enough to come out of this darkness into daylight, I would also be free again.

I joined a group of Jews hiding in the village and we went together to the partisans. However, they only wanted a few men. The women were not wanted. I had no choice but to return to Zalevski. The situation had worsened. Germans and Ukrainian militia had appeared in the village looking for partisans. He asked me to hide in the forest until the storm passed.

In the forest I met Avraham Eizenberg, the Burd brothers and Niuska Kokel. We were dirty and very weak. We could not stand up. We fell after walking a few steps. We wanted the end to come. Death seemed to us the redemption from unspeakable suffering. Avraham Eizenberg brought us potatoes and other food. We broke our fast and we slowly recuperated.

One day the happy news came. The Soviets were coming closer to our area. A few weeks later we were free. The enemy was defeated. Rokitno was liberated and we could return as free people. In January 1945 we returned to Rokitno. I looked at the terrible destruction and I saw what was left of our Rokitno where we had spent our best years.

[Page 311]

My Experiences in the Years 1942-45

Asher Rosenstein (America)

Translated from Yiddish by Ala and Larry Gamulka

The escape from the market square in Rokitno was in such confusion and so sudden that it is impossible to concentrate on details. I remember only that I was holding the hand of Godel, Pinie Fuchsman's younger son and we ran not knowing in which direction to go. Running out of Rokitno, we were three by the time we reached the forest. The older boy, Yakov, was also with us. Suddenly, a peasant came out from behind a tree holding a pitchfork and began to shout: “Jews! Jews!” We began to run again and he followed us yelling: “Where are you running cursed Jews? May the devil catch you!” We ran without stopping until we collapsed exhausted under a tree. Fear and hunger did not permit us to waste time thinking and we continued to run until sunset.

We wandered for two days and two nights until we reached Zolovey, the village from which both the Fuchsman boys and I came. Our hope was that our former neighbors would help us and feed us.

The Fuchsman children, who were very hungry, decided to go to a peasant called Trachim, with whom their parents had left their belongings for safekeeping.

Trachim did hide them, but he immediately went to the police to inform that he had hidden two Jewish children. It did not take long for the murderers to arrive and to shoot them on the spot. They also shot their uncle Modrik (the husband of Hava Modrik who is now in Israel with her children). This was the first chapter in the story of the Zolovey escapees who had hoped to be rescued by their former neighbors whom they had known for many years.

I went to Evelyn, my close Polish friend. We had a child, Kalman, who was born shortly before the war began. Evelyn hid me in a barn filled with hay. Even though it was a safe place, I knew that Evelyn and her family would sacrifice their lives rather than give me away.

While I was hiding in the barn Evelyn brought me terrible news. My parents escaped the slaughter and came to Zolovey. The killers arrested my mother and my sister Haya and were holding them in the police station. They announced that they would wait until my father and I will be caught to decide our fate.

My father did not hesitate for a moment and he gave himself up to the killers. It must be understood that these killers were local boys who used to constantly eat and drink in our house. Their parents were life-long neighbors of our family. My mother and father begged them to allow them to escape into the forest.

What was the answer? The killers led them out of the village in the direction of Rokitno through the forest. All the way my father talked to them and asked them to, at least, spare my sister's life and allow her to live. He told them to shoot in the air, pretending to shoot at us.

The killers of Zolovey, Adam and Trachim Turgansky and Pavel Djukovsky were drunk from killing Jews and took pleasure in killing more. A few kilometers before Rokitno, a horrible tragedy befell my parents and my sister. My sister begged to be shot first so she would not see her dear parents killed. They were killed in a small forest. Their bodies were not buried, but were left for wolves to drag through the forest. (The fate of my parents was told to me by a local peasant who had been given all the details by the killers).

After liberation, I collected their bones and hid them hoping to give them a proper Jewish burial. Unfortunately, it was not possible to do it because I was drafted into the army.

After the slaughter of my family, the killers came to look for me. They knew that Evelyn would be the first to know where to find me. When they arrived, Evelyn went out to meet them. With guns in their hands, they asked her: "Where is your Asher?" Her answer was: "You can search for him". You must understand that if I had been found, Evelyn and her entire family would have been burned to death.

Two of the killers took pitchforks in their hands and began to hack away in the hay to see if I was hiding there. They reached all the way to the wooden boards above me. I was lying there really without breathing. Suddenly, the pitchfork hit my hand. The pain was unbearable, but I managed not to cry out. The killers gave up the search when Evelyn begged them not to mess up the barn since her stepfather would kill her when he would see it. They shook off the hay from their bodies, took their rifles and went into the house. When night fell, I crawled out from under the hay and I hid under a cross in a Christian cemetery. That night I escaped into the forest and eventually I was hidden by a local peasant on an outlying farm.

These were terrible times. The winter was hard and bitter in all respects. It was easier for me because Evelyn brought me food and clothing. I also knew what was happening in the area.

In spring, when the partisans began to show themselves, I joined them and stayed with them until I was drafted into the army. While I was in the forest and later with the partisans, I remained in contact, through Evelyn, with her uncles, especially Lavren. He was a Pole on whom I could depend. He also had some guns. I planned my revenge on the killers of my family and many other Jews from the area with his help.

I was informed that the killer Adam Turgansky would attend a party with some girls in a specific place in the village. Lavren, the other uncle and I planned to visit him at the party. We, the three men, disguised ourselves and with handguns we entered the house where the party was held. The hero, who took part in the Jewish tragedy, the pride of the Third Reich, hid himself under a bed. When the gun was pointed at him, he crawled out, pale with fear, and begged us to spare his life. We took him outside and shot him several times. The locals gave him a fine funeral. They put into his grave everything he had taken from Jewish homes. The other two killers, when they heard of their leader's fate, became very cautious and seldom showed themselves in the village. I tried to catch them in various ways, but I was not successful. On the other hand, they, with the help of the Germans, killed Evelyn's uncles who had helped me to kill Adam Turgansky.

Years later, Pavel Djukovsky was found living a financially secure quiet family life in Poland. He was arrested and sentenced to seven years in prison. The third one, a cold-blooded killer, disappeared off the face of the earth and could not be found. He used to boast that when he shoots a Jew, he jumps for joy.

The years spent with the partisans and in the army were full of bloody battles. I was twice wounded on the Byelorussian front. Our unit was one of the first to march into East Prussia and took part in the toughest and bloodiest campaigns. When I was wounded the second time by shrapnel, I lost consciousness and awoke in a hospital where I recuperated until the end of the war.

After the war, I found my Evelyn and my son and we left Poland for America where we still reside.

[Page 314]

The Struggle with the Horrors of Life*

Ita Trossman (Pinchuk) (Ramat Gan)

Translated by Ala Gamulka

When the Jews of Rokitno were assembled for the third counting, many deluded themselves with the hope that it would be similar to the previous two and that there would be a good ending. There was a refugee tailor in town that arrived from Warsaw during the Soviet occupation. He managed the tailors' *artel*. He came over to my husband Yechiel and whispered to him that the Germans had already packed all the cloths and materials and they were taking them out of town. This is how he surmised that the Germans had decided to liquidate us, since on the previous occasions the goods had been kept in place. I told my parents what the tailor had related. Nahum Katzenelson of the *Judenrat* shouted at me: "Don't create a panic! Nothing will happen and soon you will all return home!"

The Germans lined us up alphabetically. Since my name began with a "T", I stood in the last few rows. A few minutes only after the soothing words of the *Judenrat* member, the Ukrainian killers from the Shutz-Politzei swarmed all over us and began to strafe us with machine guns.

A great panic arose and in this general confusion I took my three-year old daughter, Miriam, in my arms and I fled to the forest. I went into Zavienko's garden and there I found Dina, Nachman Blizhovsky's wife, her mother Sarah and her two daughters. A few steps further, I saw Haike Grinshpan lying dead with her head crushed. I climbed the fence and went into the forest. I was immediately captured by Stefan of the Ukrainian police. He aimed his rifle at me

*Footnote: This testimony was received in cooperation with Henya Kutz - Pesach Kutz's wife

and was ready to shoot. I begged him: "Don't shoot! If you want me to return to town, I am ready to do it immediately." The policeman turned his head and saw escaping Jews. He began to chase them and left us alone. He was certain that we would return to town. I used the situation to my advantage and I ran into the field where I lay down till evening. In the dark I went to see Prochtor, a non-Jew. He took my clothes with the yellow star and exchanged them for an old coat.

When I left him I hid in the bushes not far from the road, to hear what the locals were saying about the fate of the Jews of Rokitno. I heard one telling his friend that 80 Jews were killed in the market place and that the others were taken to Sarny. I understood that it would not make sense to return to Rokitno. In spite of this, Mordechai Kramer and his two sons, and Rachel Barman put on their yellow stars and returned to town. They thought the killings were over and that no more Jews would be killed. However, it was all in vain. The killers found them as they entered town.

Suddenly, I heard dogs barking in the forest. It was 3 a.m. I went in that direction and I met Henya Kutz and her daughter Hindel. Finding them encouraged me and from then on we wandered around together. We were 5 kilometers from Rokitno. We had to move every half-hour because the police were after us. The blueberries staved our hunger and we drank dew in the fields to slake our thirst. As we walked we heard the Rebbetzin Raykale begging: "Take me with you!"

In the morning we met Shimon Gendelman and Yentel Greenberg (Henya Kutz's sister) who joined us. On the way, we met Jews from Rokitno who were petrified. Near the outskirts (Hutor) of Ilova we found, in the bushes, Haim Turok and Shachnovski. We met Rachel Tochman, her husband and two daughters and we continued together.

Not far from the outskirts (*Hutor*) lived a local by the name of Michel Kanonich who was a family friend. When we were in the ghetto, he brought us food in exchange for clothes. He would tell us that in times of danger we should run to him and he would hide us. When I came to Ilova, I met Yakov Greenberg and his wife Zlate, his brother-in-law Shlomo Rekkes and his two daughters, and Yentel Potroch and her child.

I approached the house quietly and I called to him: "Michel". He opened the door and took us in. He gave us a pitcher of milk and some bread. I asked about my husband Yechiel. He told me that the day before he had slept in Karpilovka at his uncle's house, but that now he did not know where he was. Michel hid us in a bush near his house. We hid there for 4 days and the good man gave us hot food daily. One night it was pouring and we had to find a new shelter. Michel took us to the threshing shack. The forest guard had warned Michel's children that if he found Jews there he would burn the whole village. To their credit it must be said that although they knew about us, they did not give us away.

However, we had to find a new hiding place because there was a hunt for Jews in the outskirts (*Hutor*). The forest guard chased us and overtook us. We threatened him that our husbands were partisans and that they would avenge us. He let us continue out of fear for himself.

We had to cross a river. We did it at the risk of our lives. We reached the forest guard in Kovila. He gave us the bad news that on that day the two sons of Pinie Fuchsman had been killed. He took us into the threshing shack and in the morning he told us to follow the canal where we could meet other Jews.

That day there was a downpour and we could not leave the place. We spent two months alone in the forest - two women with two little girls. No one helped us because we were a burden to others. When there was no more food and we were near starvation, we left the girls alone in the forest, we crossed the river and we went to look for food.

The peasants had pity on us and they filled two sacks with bread and cabbage. We returned laden and tired, but we lost our way. We were certain that beasts had attacked our girls. We sat on the wet ground and we cried. We cursed our lot.

Suddenly, an old man appeared, as if from heaven and told us: "Don't cry. Come and I will show you where your girls are." We found them and from then on we carried them on our backs, as if they part of our bodies. Our bodies protected them.

One of the miracles that I cannot explain was the conduct of the girls. Under ordinary circumstances, when a three-year old girl is left alone in the thick, scary forest, she would die of fear. This was not the case with these two girls. They were as mature as any adult and they understood well the dangerous situation in which they found themselves. They never cried. They were neither afraid of the dark nor of the forest animals. They became very close. One took care of the other. They were totally devoted to each other. What courage they displayed! When I discovered that my husband was alive, I went from one place to another to look for him. We were chased by some local peasants who told us to stop. My daughter said: "G-d forbid. If the killers overtake us we will throw ourselves into the river and we will not give ourselves up to them." The girls developed an excellent sense of direction. As soon as they traveled on a road, it became a part of their memory and they always knew how to return. They never lost their way.

In our wanderings we reached a thick forest. The trees were tall and dense and they formed a natural defense wall. Nothing from the outside could penetrate them. Wolves howled and birds of prey flew over our heads. We were scared that we would be attacked by wolves. We did not sleep at night and we made sure the fire did not go out. We piled branches and we lay on top of them. Every rustle frightened us. One night we heard a hissing near our heads and I saw a snake lying near me. We took the girls and fled.

Two months after we had come to this horrible place, Nachman Blizhovsky and Baruch Perlovich arrived to tell us that Shlomo Grinshpan had told them that my husband Yechiel and the children, my sister Chaya and Moshe Golovey were alive. We went to search for them and we found them between Blizhov and Glinna.

Yakov Wolfin, the brother of Henya Kutz, went into the village of Hrapon with his wife Dvoshke and his son Nachum. The peasants in Hrapon did not want to shelter them and told them to go to Berezov. There they were put to death.

Pessi, Henya Kutz's husband, managed to escape from the ghetto, but he was killed in Karpilovka with a group of 30 Jews. Her son, Aharon and her father Shaya, 83 years old, were killed in Sarny.

[Page 317]

Miracles Which Happened and Miracles Which Did Not Happen

Rachel Wasserman (Reznik) (Kiryat Bialik)

Translated by Ala Gamulka

The Germans came to Rokitno to a “well-prepared” location. The Ukrainians and the Poles prepared lists of Jews suspected of being Communists. Alter Pik was also on the list. The Germans took him outside, stood him near a tree and killed him in front of his wife and other bewildered Jews.

It was a punishment meant to set an example. At the beginning the Germans were not yet interested in extermination. They needed the Jews as a work force.

Howver, conditions were so cruel that many were swollen with hunger and were incapable of working. These were the last days before the day of the roll call.

The work was accompanied by abuse. The women were ordered to bring water. They were harnessed like horses to the carts and, with their last strength; they pulled the heavy water barrel. A German sat on the barrel holding a whip, which he flung mercilessly to make the women hurry. Naturally, many women collapsed and could not get up.

At first, my husband, Moshe Wasserman, worked hauling rafters. However, when the Germans discovered that he was a watchmaker by trade, they freed him from this physical labor. He was allowed to work in the ghetto in his trade. One night I heard loud knocks on our door. I looked through the slits and I saw that Germans and Ukrainians were the ones knocking. Since I had no choice, I opened the door, but I sent my husband and my son, Yakov, to the attic. I was certain that they had come to get them.

I opened the door holding my two-year old daughter, Taibele, in my arms. The killers hit me and demanded watches. I gave them all the watches I had. This did not satisfy them. They took my child out of my arms and flung her on the couch with such force that it was a miracle that she remained alive. They aimed their fists at my nose causing it to bleed profusely. I lost consciousness and stayed that way for five days.

In the ghetto I lived in the house of Hannah Hessel Levin, the grandmother of Haim Shteinman. There was another woman there who was critically ill. She was terribly swollen from hunger. She could only relieve herself with the help of a doctor. The killers would not allow her to see the doctor and she would writhe in pain day and night. There are not enough words to describe her suffering. She was "redeemed" on that fateful Wednesday morning when the Jews were gathered for the third roll call. Death came after that roll call. The sick were exterminated in their beds. This is how the poor woman was also exterminated.

Early Wednesday morning, my good friend Manke, who lived in the Baratz house, came to see me. She worked for me as a washerwoman for many years. I tried to help her as much as I could. When I was in the ghetto I never ran into her. She suddenly appeared in the middle of the night. Without any preliminaries she told me the end was near for all the Jews of Rokitno. She hurried to come and tell me so I would seek refuge under the protection of darkness. She left immediately after telling me the news. I reported this to the *Judenrat*, but they did not believe it. They said it was idle talk. They just would not believe that a slaughter was coming.

That night we heard the unusual sounds of wagons moving. There was great movement in town. Trumpets and crowds were heard. We saw the town was being surrounded on all sides. We could not sleep and we went from house to house, trembling with fear. The approaching sound of death was heard throughout the ghetto.

What we feared came indeed. It was not an ordinary third roll call. It was a sendoff to the death ditches of Sarny. The fact that the sick were shot in their beds forecast the terrible end. When we came to the market square shots were heard and many fell immediately. My older daughter cried to me: "Let us run, mother!" We began to run towards the forest with Taibele in my arms. I reached Avraham Gotlieb's house. The ditch near his house was full of bodies. I fell in and bodies fell on top of me. My older daughter stood at the edge and screamed: "Mother, you are alive. Let us run away!" With my last strength I managed to get out from under the pile of bodies. I was unable to pull out Taibele. I held her little hand while her body was squeezed by the dead bodies. My older daughter helped me to take her out. She was unconscious. I shook her and she began to cry. I knew then that she was alive.

I ran with my two girls continuously looking back. I was hoping to see other family members. I suddenly heard a voice calling me. It was my sister Dutzia. I wanted to run with Mrs. Shachnovski to the tar factory. But my sister stopped me saying it was not a hiding place, but a burial place. The forest was full of Jews who had escaped from the killing field. Among them were many who were injured and were writhing in pain. Soon the Ukrainian police came to the forest to bring back the Jews to Rokitno. They were going to put them on the waiting train cars.

The Jews began to run and the Ukrainians chased them. I used the opportunity and I ran into a pigpen with my daughters. Freidl Linn and Hannah Kasher came with me. The pigs were grazing in the field and the house was locked. We found out that the peasant had gone with his wife to Rokitno to steal Jewish belongings. Indeed, soon he returned with his wagon loaded with goods. We heard him tell his wife: "Unload the wagon quickly so we can go back for more."

When he returned the second time it was dusk. We escaped to the forest in the darkness. I found my relative Nachman Levy. I said to him: "Let's run away!" He asked me to wait a few minutes because he had to go into one of the nearby houses. He went in, but he never came out. He died inside. We roamed all day and in the evening we entered a house in the forest. We saw a peasant roasting potatoes. He received us warmly, gave us hot potatoes and told us to go to the attic where we would find other Jews. There we found Ziske Kissel and his family from Karpilovka and Israel Eizenstein (Zvi Barzilay's father).

The next day the peasant informed Ziske that he could no longer hide us. We had to find a new hiding place. I wanted to join him and to go to Karpilovka, but he refused. This refusal saved my life. Ziske advised me to hide in the garden of the forest warden. This was friendly advice, because the warden knew my parents. He gave us food and a place to sleep. In the evening, the warden told us he was going to Karpilovka to see what was going on there. He soon returned, ashen-faced, and told us: "Run away from here. The village is full of Germans. They killed Ziske Kissel and his family and another forty Jews from Rokitno."

The peasant gave us some food for the road and advised us to cross the marshes. Once we reached dry land we found a Jew roasting potatoes. We saw Haim Trossman (Yechiel's father) standing alone in the field roasting potatoes. He told us that he was not afraid because he trusted G-d in heaven. Whatever would happen, he was calm. He was happy to see us. We stayed near his fire all night. The next day we decided to go to the village of Netrebe. Haim knew all the roads, but for safety reasons we went in a roundabout way. We walked a whole day. We reached the village at night. It was pitch black all around us, but there was a light shining in one of the houses. We were frozen, hungry, barefoot and half-naked. Dogs began to bark and would not let us approach the house. The peasant came out and warned us to run away. There were policemen in the adjacent house. We took a chance and went inside to rest. His wife saw our misery and brought us food. The man took us outside and said: "Do you see the fire in the distance? My children are watching my horses graze there. Go and sleep there." We went there. The saying goes: "Like father, like son". The man was kind and his sons were also good-hearted.

When the boys saw us they got up and offered us their mat so we would not lie on the cold ground. We lay down to rest near the fire. Our feet were swollen from the cold and we needed to rest them.

The next day we looked around and saw no one. Trossman was afraid that in this empty area we could be killed and no one would know. He asked the peasant for his opinion. The peasant advised us to go to the village of Okopi. Its residents did not hurt Jews. When I mention this village, I must praise it highly. Just as we must condemn our killers and slaughterers, we must also commemorate our saviors. This village was merciful to all the Jews. The village priest said in his sermons that his followers must help the poor refugees (he did not specifically say Jews), treat them kindly, not hurt them, give them food and drink, and offer them a place to sleep.

We reached Okopi and we stopped at the crossroads. A peasant called Cesar Zalevski came out and said to us: "Hear me, my brothers. I know about your terrible situation. Do not despair. Your redemption will come in this village. The residents swore in the name of the redeemer that their village will not spill Jewish blood. The war will not go on forever. It will end and you will remain alive. Come with me." He took us deep into the forest and brought us to a pit. He told us to go inside. He camouflaged us with branches and told us to stay here until daybreak. At sunrise he brought us a pot of milk and some bread.

(I now must tell about the bitter end of Haim Trossman. At that time a group of approximately twenty people was formed. They lived together in the forest for two months. They were denounced by the Ukrainians and the Germans attacked them. The younger people managed to escape, but Haim was old. He was caught and brought back to Rokitno. He was killed in exchange for two kilos of salt.)

A few days later some partisans came. My sister Dutzia decided to join them. She thought she would help me, too, in this way. They did not want to take me because of the children. This decision brought about Dutzia's death. These were Soviet parachutists from Moscow who did not know the roads well. They were ambushed by the Germans and killed. Dutzia was killed in the exchange of fire.

We could not stay long under Cesar Zalevski's protection. The *Bulbovtzis* in the area knew well that the residents of Okopi welcomed the Jews. They waited for the opportunity to attack them. After the defeat of the soviet parachutists they burst into the village and set it on fire. Cesar harnessed his wagon and placed his family and me with my two daughters on it. He tried to find a way to escape the revenging *Bulbovtzis*. We were surrounded by the fire. The *Bulbovtzis* came to the wagon and killed his wife and family. He managed to escape. By a miracle, I got out of the wagon. The killers saw other villagers and left me alone. They chased the others and killed about 80 of them.

I ran with my daughters and I reached a small bridge over a ditch. It was winter. Barefoot and half-naked we went into ice-cold water. We were covered up to our necks. I held Taibele in my arms because otherwise the water would have covered her completely. At night, it was even colder. The water froze and a layer of ice surrounded us.

We were saved by a miracle. What was that miracle? In the village of Netrebe, Avraham Grinshpan and his family and Yosef Kaplan and his family were hiding in a lean-to. When they heard that 80 people were killed in Okopi, they were certain that my daughters and I were among the dead. Grinshpan said to Kaplan: "Let us bring Rachel and her daughters to a proper Jewish burial." They took shovels and were on their way. When they saw three heads peeking out of the ice they were sure we had frozen to death. I began to shout: "Come here! I am alive!" They broke the ice with their shovels and pulled us out of the water. They carried the girls on their shoulders because they were frozen. Grinshpan brought us to his lean-to which had a stove. The ice melted off my daughters and they began to show signs of life. Grinshpan obtained various creams from the peasants, which he rubbed on our wounds. Slowly our limbs revived.

This was the end of our suffering. The war was coming to its end. The area was conquered by the Soviet army and we returned to Rokitno. To my great surprise, I found there my father, Aharon Reznik. What miracle allowed him to be saved? It was beyond understanding. He could not fathom how he had escaped with my brother from the market square and which angels had guarded him in the forests. However, sadly, he told me of my brother Yeshayahu's death.

My brother was forced to do hard labor in the ghetto and he fell seriously ill. As long as we were in the ghetto we did everything to look after him. His condition improved. However, the conditions in the Blizhov forest were too difficult and he fell ill again. His condition worsened. One cold winter day he expired. Father buried him with his own hands and said *kaddish.* Inside my brother's hat he found a crumpled piece of paper. My father took a small branch, put into the fire and used the ashes to write my brother's name and the date of his death. He took a flask, broke its opening and put the note inside. He placed the flask on the grave as if it were a gravestone. It was to be a marker so that on the day of liberation his grave would be found and he would be given a proper Jewish burial. However, snow and storms erased everything. In spite of the hard work my father put in, he could not find the grave again.

[Page 321]

The Great Rescue

Baruch Goldman (Attorney) (Ramat Gan)

Translated by Ala Gamulka

The Germans were so devious that we did not have an inkling that they were planning to annihilate us. Truthfully, there was no indication that the end was near.

Firstly, we did not know what was happening in other places because we were isolated from the outside world. Secondly, no cruel deeds had been perpetrated on the Jews of Rokitno. We had no indication that the end was coming. Therefore, when the order was given to gather in the market square for the third roll call, there was no panic. It was felt that if the two previous roll calls had ended with people returning home, then this one, too, would end well. There was a rumor that the purpose of the roll call was to determine that all were still in town and that no one had escaped to join the partisans.

This time the Germans and their Ukrainian helpers had decided to annihilate the Rokitno community. The shots in the air and at the people were proof enough. It is impossible to describe the bedlam that followed. Everyone went in his own direction. Mothers abandoned their children. Even if they escaped together, they became separated while running. I stood near my father (I was 13 years old then) and I held his hand. We began to run towards the saw-mill. We were constantly chased and shot at. I suddenly could not see my father and I did not know what had happened to him. I ran alone and met other youngsters my age that had also become separated from their families. They were looking for shelter in the forest. On the way we met Jews returning to town. They were saying that they wished to die with their families since there was no purpose to their lives once their dear ones were torn away from them.

We were a group of 4 or 5 children. After we rested in the forest we decided to return to town to see if any Jews remained. We met some peasants and they told us that the Jews were being taken to Sarny by train. Anyone who returned was shot in the synagogue. On the way we saw the earth soaked in blood and we found pictures and papers belonging to Jews. We understood that the end had come to the Jews of our town. In order for our fate to be different from theirs we decided to search for shelter in one of the villages nearby. I remained with one young lad. The others left us. In a village near Rokitno, there was a peasant called Feodor Tzaruk who was friendly with my father. I decided to go to him hoping to meet my father. Indeed, when I came there, he told me my father was hiding there.

My father told me that he hid in the military cemetery. There was a thick tree with all its leaves intact. He climbed it and hid in it from morning till nine in the evening.

Since his hiding place was close to town, he saw how the Jews were taken to slaughter in the synagogue. Some terrible sights were etched in his mind. There was a Jew in our town called Michael Shuster. He worked in the saw-mill that the Germans built near the train station. He was an expert in the field. He had good relations with his superior. Shuster escaped with all the others, but his superior chased him and found him hiding in a potato field.

"Get out, dirty Jew!" shouted the superior and aimed his gun. Shuster fell on his knees and begged the superior: "Let me live and I will serve you to the end of my days". "Forward!" yelled the killer. Shuster, pale, got up. He was taken to the synagogue and shot there.

A young woman hid about 100 meters from my father. A German chased her and yelled at her to stop. She ran like a mad woman. She fell, got up again and continued to run. The German shot her in the arm. When she saw the blood streaming from her body she was alarmed and stopped running. This is how the poor woman was taken to slaughter in the synagogue.

After we met at Tzaruk's, my father and I walked together. We learned that it was safer to stay in small groups and not to remain permanently in one place. We had to be on the move. During our wandering we met Aharon Lifshitz and the hat maker Yakov Landau (son-in-law of the hat maker Michael Steinberg). With them were Batya Grinshpan and Rachel Hammer who did sewing and embroidery for one of the peasants.

Aharon and my father Yakov are credited with a big rescue effort. We were in the marshland between the villages of Chabel and Lenchin when two Baptists, acquaintances of my father, passed by. One of them, Afanas, told us he was returning from a large gathering of Banderovtzis in the village of Tinna. It had been decided there that night they would go to Berdocha, an agricultural farm near Tinna, to kill 21 Polish families. The following night they would go to kill the Jews hiding in the forests in the area. The Banderovtzis even knew the names of those Jews.

When my father and Aharon Lifshitz heard about the fate awaiting these Jews, they decided not to waste a minute and to save them immediately. They hurried to the site and told them they must escape or else they would not remain alive. At first, they refused to leave. Firstly, they did not believe the situation was so drastic and secondly, they did not want to abandon their belongings. However, the pleas of Lifshitz and my father finally opened their eyes and they joined us. We went together to the village of Bober where Medvedev's regiment was camped.

On the way my father and Lifshitz wanted to save two young women hidden by a peasant, but they were too late. The Banderovtzis had, in the meantime, killed Batya Grinshpan. Rachel Hammer managed to run out of the house. She hid in a barrel in the yard and was spared.

Our acquaintances, peasants from the vicinity, reported that the Banderovtzis did come at night to kill all the Jews. When they did not find them, they became angry and burned all the shelters where they had hidden.

Most of those saved made *aliyah* and reside among us to this day.

[Page 323]

I Was a Mother to Unfortunate Children

Esther Naiberg - (Bnei Brak)

Translated by Ala Gamulka

The story of the children who were separated from their parents during the panic and the shooting in the market square is a horrifying tale. They ran petrified crying for their mothers. As they ran they held on to any adult and begged to be taken along. When I ran from the market square I saw a group of small children who were sobbing. I gathered them as any mother would and we ran together to the forest. (My younger son Baruch ran alone and we met later). I sat down with them on the ground, gathered blackberries and fed them. The children clung to me and begged not to be abandoned.

I stayed with them for four days and them I gave them over to Jews who were roaming the forest. With me remained Sima Katz, the daughter of Moshe-Leib, and her two daughters. I put one on my shoulders and we wandered together. The child was almost out of strength. On the way we met Yitzhak Forman with his young son, Yehudah Schiff and his son Yeshayahu and Avraham Wax from Sahov.

I had to part from them because I went to search for my children Baruch and Sonia and her two daughters Raya and Shoshana. I reached the village of Borovey. On the way I met a peasant who told me that Jews were hiding in the forest. Two children came towards me. One was Yitzhak Gendelman's son. They told me they saw my son-in-law Binyamin Shtedler (He later died fighting with the partisans) and my son Baruch. I found them and we stayed in Borovey for 14 days.

We had to run away because the peasants plotted to kill us. We reached the village of Berezov where we had a flourmill. It was the night of "*Remember the Covenant*". We wandered for 3 days in the forest and we reached Berezov on the eve of Yom Kippur. One peasant hid us until after Yom Kippur. He was afraid and urged us to continue on our way. We went into the forest where we saw a large fire. Two young boys were nearby. One was Monik (Michulchik's son) and the other was Syoma (the son of Avraham the Bookbinder). They told me that they had been in a group of 20 Jews, but they had all left them. The children were afraid that I, too, would leave them. I told them not to fear, that I would look after them as if I was their mother. I was a devoted mother to them during our hard times until we were liberated.

In the forest, my son and I became ill with typhus. I was so concerned about my child that I ignored the fact that I, too, was sick and that I felt dizzy. I took my son in my arms and ran to a peasant called Michael Kohonivich in the Blizhov hamlet. I went to him and asked him to give my child shelter because he was very sick. The peasant said: "You are very sick also". He laid us on the ground and we stayed there burning with fever for 14 days without food or water. The fever broke by itself. When we opened our eyes the peasant fed us honey from his own beehive. We recuperated. As a result of the illness and the lack of food we lost our hair, but it grew back later.

My son Baruch worked as a shepherd for one of the peasants. He excelled in his duties. I stayed with him until liberation. My eleven-year old son Sossik, my daughter and her two daughters Raya and Shoshana were killed escaping from the market square.

[Page 325]

Preserving the Jewish Image in the Ghetto and In the Forest

Issachar Trossman (Ramat Gan)

Translated by Ala Gamulka

When the Jews were enclosed in the ghetto we made a trade - we exchanged our houses - the large and the small - for a small, two-family house. It stood at the edge of the ghetto and belonged to a *Folksdeutch* (ethnic German). He was a veteran resident of Rokitno. Greber lived in that house.We came to live there with grandfather Haim and grandmother Tema.

At first the Germans did not make children aged 13 work. As a result, we were idle. Some parents, who were afraid that their children would forget the Scriptures, secretly organized a Hebrew school. The secretary of the Tarbut School, Mr. Weinblatt, was the teacher. We studied all subjects usually taught in senior elementary school.

However, we did not spend a long time on our studies. The ghetto was made smaller and our parents, fearing the authorities, interrupted the studies. The Germans began to force even children my age to do hard labor. I worked in the peat fields and I had to dig for 400 peat bricks. The person in charge was a mean Pole who in peacetime was a telephone repairman. We worked from 7 in the morning to 4 in the afternoon in miserable conditions, oppressed and mistreated.

As luck would have it, I managed to escape into the forest with my family. (My grandfather was murdered in the village of Decht) In the forest, we met my aunt Rivka Golovey (my mother's sister) and her son Moshe. From her we learned that her husband Sender died in the forest. We also met Ethel from Glinna with her three children and "Rachel the Blind One". They joined us and we hid together in a *kurin* (underground dugout). One time, the Germans were hunting for Jews in the forest and we had to run away into marshland. Above it, for a distance of several hundred meters, there was a very narrow crossing. It was an acrobatic feat to cross this span and to not fall off. Many of us fell and got thoroughly wet. It was a miracle that "Rachel the Blind One" went through without falling. It was said that an angel was protecting her from above. Believers saw it as a sign that we remained alive because of her.

The partisan movement spread in our area and we joined a unit called Plasnosov. Its base was in the houses outside the village of Vizhitz. Among these partisans was the famous hero, Zvi Olshansky from Staro-Cielo. He had escaped from a German prison and he organized the unit. He was a proud Jew and because of him we were able to keep our Jewish image, even in caveman conditions.

On the Holy Days, we were freed from everyday work in order to be close to our creator and to remember our dead. Tens and hundreds of Jewish partisans from the area came to Blizhov and spent *Rosh Hashana* and *Yom Kippur* in fasting and in prayer. A great sorrow engulfed everyone. We also thought about our broken and ruined world.

In order not to assimilate and to keep our Jewish spirit, we did not eat *chametz* on *Pesach*. We prepared ourselves spiritually. We even baked *matzo* cakes from dark flour. Although they were hard as stone and became gravel in our mouths, they instilled a holiday feeling in us. It was as if we were sitting at a *seder* as in previous years. We even read from the *Haggadah*. Each one of us read from memory. These miserable, dried flat breads with shriveled potatoes became, in our eyes, a symbol for our belief in the Jewish nation. They also told us that we will be free again in the near future.

However, we were not always in an uplifted mood. We had days of sorrow and of crying. Every time we heard that a Jew from Rokitno fell in battle or was caught by the Germans was like a sword thrust at us. With great sadness we heard the news that Yosef Olshansky and Moshe Barman had fallen. They died during an attack on a German arms train. Immediately after that we also heard that the partisan, Shepsel Shteindel had died. He was a young man in the Kovpek unit. He had gone through hell, had come back from the Carpathian Mountains and had arrived in the village of Vitkovich. He entered one of the houses in the village and took a spool of thread. The locals libeled him saying he was going into homes and threatening the residents with a gun. He was killed because of this lie in front of the camp of partisans.

This is how Haim Turok died as well. Even Yakov Gitelman was put to death by the partisans for a lie. He was accused of forcing the villagers, with a gun, to give him clothes and food.

Our hearts were gladdened when we heard of heroic deeds performed by the youth of Rokitno. We heard a tale of Asher Binder's heroism. In the vicinity of Blizhov there was a group of partisans, the most famous among them were Asher Binder, Nachman Blizhovsky and Baruch Perlovich. The housekeeper of the staff of the partisans, Rivka Golovey, was well known for her wonderful deeds.

Every piece of information about a Jewish partisan from Rokitno filled our hearts with pride. We did not sit empty-handed and we contributed to the struggle. My father was very active in the procurement of food and clothing for the Jews in the forest. It was not enough for him. He endangered his life and visited nearby villages in order to get news about the locals who directly or indirectly participated in the killing of Jews. He was killed on one of these visits.

[Page 327]

In The Shadow of the Gallows

Shmuel Levinson (Levin) (Ramat Gan)

Translated by Ala Gamulka

When the Germans conscripted the Jews of Rokitno to do forced labor, I was ordered to work in *Tod-organizatzion*. This was a group of German officers and soldiers whose task was to supervise the construction of bridges and railroad tracks. Three hundred soldiers occupied the Palace and the officers lived in the New Town across from the market. I was a servant to 5 officers and my job was to shine their shoes, to bring firewood and to clean their guns. I was given a pass to come and go. Every morning, before daybreak, I would run to a gentile I knew in the village of Rokitno and I would take from him bread, milk, at times flour, for my starving family.

Once the Polish cook fell ill and I was sent to bring food to the officers from the army kitchen. The cook identified my nationality by my yellow star. Even though he knew very well why and by whom I was sent, he beat me badly and ordered me to chop wood with other Jews. At noon he let go of me and sent me back with food.

One day officer Lemel went out on the porch and ordered me to bring a brush and shoe polish and to polish his boots. While I was doing so he announced with great joy: "If the Jews will be killed, come here. We will not kill you". From his promise I learned that the Germans were actually planning to kill the Jews. I reported this to the *Judenrat*, but they did not take me seriously because they could not imagine that all the Jews would be killed. The bubble in which the members of the *Judenrat* lived was soon burst and the final and third roundup soon came. I asked the officer if I, too, had to present myself and he replied with a sarcastic smile: "Yes!" I obeyed the command and I stood next to my brothers Yeshayahu (Shaike) and Moshe and my parents.

As the commotion started when shots were heard, I remembered the promise made by the officer and I ran to the building where I was working. The door was locked. I tried to enter thorough an open window, but the cook stopped me. I forced the window open and I jumped inside with Shaike, my little brother. I passed through several rooms and did not see a soul. I ran to the hallway and I reached the dining room. A machine gun was standing on the piano in the room and the Germans were shooting at the escaping Jews. With great fear I ran to the cellar and a few minutes later I heard knocking on the door. I was afraid to open it since I did not know who was knocking. To my great horror, I found out later that it was my father. I jumped with my brother over the fence and we ran towards the railroad tracks. We saw our neighbor, a heavy woman, running. She was shot and she fell. The whole road was covered in blood. I heard yelling coming from the railway cars. I saw how poor souls were forced into the cars, but we continued to run under a barrage of bullets, which were aimed at those who were escaping from the town. My brother was hurt by a metal post and asked me to leave him there because he could not walk. I dragged him and we escaped the bullets and entered the forest. In the forest we were joined by Shepsel Shteindel and Meir Krupnik. We were four boys and we did not know which way to go. We decided to go towards a nearby village. There we met Asher Binder, Lipa Shpilman, Lola Shachnovski and others. For safety reasons we had to divide ourselves into small groups. Therefore, we left them and in our wanderings arrived in the village of Glinna. Shteindel and Krupnik remained in the forest and my brother and I went to a farmer to ask him for food. He received us nicely and told his wife to prepare a meal. He then sneaked out of the house. We became suspicious and we ran away.

We lived in misery and we began to think of going back to Rokitno. We were certain that the killing was a one-time event and those returning to the town would not be hurt. Besides, we were hopeful that someone in our family was still alive. We were 4 kilometers from Rokitno. On the way, we met gentiles carrying stolen Jewish property. They warned us not to endanger ourselves by going back because the police was lying in wait for returning Jews.

In the forests we walked for three days and three nights until we reached the cemetery and we hid there. In the dark we saw some silhouettes. These were Jews, but we were afraid of them and they were afraid of us.

On the following day we continued on our way and we met a farmer plowing his fields. He recognized us to be Jews by our clothing and suggested to us to go over to the former Soviet area. There we would have a chance to join the partisans. We took his advice, but he warned us not to go to Karpilovka because its residents hated Jews. We went around the village and arrived in Netrebe. We stayed there 3-4 days and from there we went to Midan. We wandered aimlessly. We returned to Netrebe and from there to Okopi. Early that evening we saw a bonfire and we approached it. There we found Rachel Wasserman, her sister Dutzia and her son, Dvosil the blacksmith's daughter with her son and daughter, Shmuel Bagel, Avraham Eisenberg and Linn. In the evening we heard rustling noises and suddenly three armed men appeared and presented themselves as partisans. They gave us food and left. The next evening they returned and informed us that they could only take a young woman with them. They took Dutzia and left. We discovered later that they were not partisans, but criminals and hooligans. To this day we do not know what happened to Dutzia.

Death took its toll. We held two funerals. We buried Dvosil and her daughter. Dvosil had leaned on me all night long and in the morning when I tried to wake her, she was frozen to death. Her daughter died right after her. At night we wrapped her in a blanket and we buried her next to her mother.

We were worried about getting caught and we went deeper into the forest. There we built a *kurin* in the ground and we camouflaged it. We dug a well and at night we went to look for food. In Okopi there was a teacher who helped us as much as she could. She was killed for her generosity. She traveled to Rokitno to bring us news and on the way she was killed.

Eventually we were not alone in the forest. The *Mazuris*, Ukrainians converted to Catholicism who had also escaped from the *Banderovtzis*, joined us with their wives, children and cows. We felt safer among them. They employed us as sheepherders.

Among the *Mazuris* there were some partisans and we went with them on revenge raids. One day the partisans told us that the Soviet Army had liberated Rokitno and we could go back.

We returned in torn clothing. The first thing I took care of was clothing. I went to one of the collaborators, Yanek Byalouse, and forced him to hand over clothes for my brother and me.

A Jewish major who was with the Soviet Army in Rokitno took my brother with him as a messenger boy and dressed him in army clothes. He sent him to Moscow to the Sovorov Cadet School.

I reached Berlin as a soldier in the Soviet Army. At the end of the war, I was liberated as a Polish citizen and I came to Israel in 1948 as part of *Aliyah Bet.*

[Page 329]

The Struggle for Life

Aharon Lifshitz (Givatayim)

Translated by Ala Gamulka

On the 13th day of *Elul* (26.8.1942), the day of destruction of the Rokitno community, we gathered at the market square by families. We did not know what was waiting for us. Our hearts predicted bad events, but we never imagined the extent of the annihilation. My father consoled me by saying all will be well because it was the 13th of *Elul.* Thirteen is a lucky number. However, as we were encouraging each other, the order was given by the chief of police, Sokolovsky, that all men and boys older than 10 should line up in rows, 5 abreast. Women and girls would line up separately. My eight-year old son, Gershon, stood next to me. My father said to me: "Give me little Gershon and I will pass him on to mother. Maybe we will be taken to a work camp. Why should the child suffer because of us?" As he left the line we heard screams and shots. I threw myself on the ground and I searched for my family. I lost sight of them in the great panic.

I heard a warning: "Don't stand! Run!" I ran bent low and I reached Avraham Gotlieb's house. I saw many people escaping and I joined them. I entered the forest 10 kilometers from Rokitno. There I met the three Golubovitz brothers, Toddy Linn, Bronia Kogan, Batya Grinshpan, a Polish refugee called Farber, and Herschel Gendelman's young son from the village of Rokitno.

In the evening we reached the village of Borovey, but we did not find one living soul there. We discovered that all the villagers had gone to Rokitno to steal Jewish property. We continued on our way looking for the partisans. We heard rumors that they roamed the Soviet side. Petya Golubovitz knew the paths through the forests and he led us to the Russian-Polish border. In the evening we reached the village of Voniatzy on the Soviet side. We were afraid to enter because we were told that there was a German retribution action there only recently. Residents had been punished for allowing the partisans to enter.

We changed direction and waded through marshes and ponds. We climbed trees and with great difficulty we reached the villages of Budki-Borovski. There we met many Jews from Rokitno. One of the *Righteous Gentiles*, Yuzik Zalevski, lived there. His home became a meeting place for many of the Jews from Rokitno. In his yard I met Shimon Gendelman, Herschel Shteinman, Motl Shapiro and the Eisenberg brothers. I found out from them that my brother-in-law Misha and my brother Leibl were in Stariky near my tar factory. They thought that if I survived I would hide in the tar factory. Although I yearned for them, I had to wait because Ukrainian policemen were circulating in the area. They shot anyone they met on the way.

I organized a group, which consisted of Yakov Krantzberg, Batya Grinshpan and the Eisenberg brothers. We decided to return to Stariky. We left on a dark and rainy night and we walked holding hands because there was no visible path. At daybreak we saw that we were near the village of Ilova. We went into the forest and sat down to rest. Suddenly, we heard rustling and a voice said: "Don't be afraid. We are Jews!" Indeed, we saw Shlomo Grinshpan and Yonah Katz. Shlomo told us that he sent a messenger to Dr. Anishtchuk to find out what was going on in Rokitno. Anishtchuk sent back a newspaper in which it was written that the Fuhrer had decreed that all Jews be wiped off the face of the earth.

The Eisenberg brothers went towards Karpilovka. Yakov Krantzberg, Batya Grinshpan, and I walked towards Stariky. I went to see an acquaintance by the name of Yasku. He offered to hide me only in his house. He said that if I was spared from death I would now remain alive. He would help as much as he could. He told me that all the Jews of Stariky were saved and were hiding nearby. He was hiding another Jew, but he would not tell me his name. I went to sleep in a storehouse full of fodder. I was exhausted and I fell asleep immediately. When I opened my eyes I saw in front of me David Shachnovski, my partner in the tar factory. He heard that his son Lulik and his son-in-law Mulik Berkman had escaped and were hiding in the tar factory near Rokitno. I told him that my brother and my brother-in-law were seen in our tar factory and I wanted to go there. He advised me not to budge because there was great danger on the roads.

Shachnovski was hiding in a haystack and had no fresh air. I asked him to come to the forest because the place seemed dangerous and the peasant was not trustworthy. He refused and wanted to convince me not to leave.

I did not listen to him and I was on my way. One of my workers, Marcel, lived in the area and I was certain he would welcome me. I approached his house. When the dog began barking some children came to the window and shouted: "Run away, Jew. The Germans will catch you!" I ran into the forest. There was a great downpour and I stopped to pray *Shmone Esre*. My tears mingled with the raindrops. My chances for remaining alive were minimal. I thought of returning to Rokitno to die there.

In this hopeless despair, I saw Marcel's wife coming out of the yard. I went to her and asked about her husband. She did not recognize me. When she heard who I was, she burst out crying. She told me that there were Jews near a bonfire not far from there. Indeed I met Yakov Landau, Moshe the shoemaker, Dvora Greenberg, Hava Modrik and Batya Grinshpan. They told me they had been there for several days without any food or water. I gave them a few potatoes to satisfy their hunger. A little while later, I heard a voice in Polish saying: "Aharon, come here!" I turned my head and I saw Marcel. He fell on me, burst out crying and kissed me. He told me he was afraid to come closer to the bonfire because it was too close to the road. He brought me half a loaf of bread and a bottle of milk. He advised us to transfer the fire deeper into the forest because we were in mortal danger so close to the road.

On the next day I went to look for my brother Leibl and my brother-in-law Misha. I came to a peasant called Sokol who was hiding some Jews. I did not find them. I found out that my sister Sarah's children were looking for me. A Polish peasant wanted to hide Rivka, my niece, in his house, but she did not want to part from her brother Chen (named after Haim Nachman Bialik). They went together to the village of Osnitzek and were killed there by the Ukrainians.

It was the eve of *Yom Kippur*. Marcel brought us hot food. We told him not to bring us any food on the following day because we fast on Yom Kippur. At the end of the fast he brought us food and told us that, to his great sorrow, he could not feed the whole group, not even potatoes. He could only feed me. I could not accept his offer. I told him the fate of my friends is my fate. He advised us to go to the other side of the river Lave where the peasants were wealthier. The place was suitable for shelter because it was heavily wooded. We crossed the river. Yakov Landau and I went to scout the area. We entered one of the houses. The peasant called Adam Garvovsky treated us well. He stood guard outside so we would not be harmed. The Jews of Stariky used to come to him to bake bread and to cook. The peasant befriended me, but he only allowed me into his house at dusk. At night I had to go back to the forest and I was petrified. Every sound made me think the end had come.

Adam Garvovsky told me there were many women and children in the forest and he advised me to go there to look for my family. Indeed, I found David Schwartz's wife and some other women and young children. They told me that David Schwartz and Shvindelman from Snovidovich had gone to the forest to find moss (to be used instead of matches). I also met Menashe Zandweis who was looking very pale. I went over to greet him, but he did not recognize me. When I told him my name he became very excited and asked me if I heard any news of his daughter Bailtze. I knew she was killed, but I kept it from him. I consoled him by saying she was probably saved. I asked him why he was so pale. He replied that when Esther Cherpichnik was alive she brought him water from time to time to revive him. Since she was killed, he did not even have this much. A few days later, Menashe died. Shmuel Shvindelman left the place and died of cold in the forest.

Shachnovski came to us every morning and in the evening he went back to Yasku. Once he told me Rachel Hammer was also at Yasku's. Her face was singed because she had fallen asleep near a bonfire and fell into it. The next day he brought her to my shelter. It was called Aharon Lifshitz's shelter. When I saw her I almost fainted. We prayed she would not die while with us. She lay for a few weeks and improved from day to day. When her strength returned she would go with Batya Grinshpan to bring us food.

The villagers in the area began to complain that the Jews were a burden and asked us to look for food and shelter elsewhere. From time to time I went to Stariky where they felt sorry for me and gave me food. Once I saw, from a distance, a young man chopping wood in the yard. When he saw me he stopped working and he looked at me. He went back into his house and then came out again. He approached me and asked me who I was. I told him I was one of those who lost the right to live.

He asked me: “If so, what are you doing here? You should be in Rokitno and I will take you there.” I begged him: “Is it worth it to you to have me killed for a kilo of salt? There are people in the forest who will avenge my death.” He relented and said: “Run quickly and don't show your face here again!” I went to another house. The peasant gave me some leftover food and told me to run away immediately because he could pay with his life for the charity he was extending to me. Another peasant gave a pair of woven shoes and some rags and showed me how to swaddle them. Miraculously, I found a bible with *Rashi* interpretation and a prayer book in his house. I was thrilled with both items. My feet would be warm and when food was scarce I could pray. We collected straw that served us as a mattress and we built a bonfire. We went to sleep inside the shelter. The wind drew the fire towards us and everything went up in flames. We managed to escape, but the bible, the prayer book and the shoes were burned.

One day I went out to chop some trees and I heard shots nearby. I went back scared to the shelter and I called all the people. They stood tense and fearful and listened to the sound of the bullets. We scattered in the forest and each one of us went into a pit covered with snow. We camouflaged ourselves with snow and we lay there for about an hour, until the shooting stopped.

Towards evening I went with Yakov Landau to Adam Gravovsky's to find out about the shooting. We discovered the Jews of Stariky were killed in the forest. As we walked out of his house we saw Germans driving by. We fell into the snow. It was a miracle that they did not see us.

We went back to the shelter and at night we decided to leave. To my great sorrow, Dvora Greenberg and Moshe the shoemaker were ill and could not join us. The Germans came and killed them.

We went towards Haim Turok's shelter. It was difficult to walk because there was a great deal of snow on the ground. Shachnovski told me to return to Stariky because the Germans would not come once they had annihilated all the Jews.

We found out that Haim and Yakov Gitelman joined the partisans. They told us to go to the forest warden, Sokolovsky, who knew where to find the partisans. When we reached him, he let us warm up by his stove and his wife gave us some warm milk. She then took us to the attic and covered us with a pile of rags. They told us to go to a village whose name I don not recall. There we would speak to a peasant called Aleksei who would take us to the partisans.

Shachnovski, who up to now was our guide, stepped back. He asked me to go ahead of him because he had difficulty walking. On the way he disappeared and we did not know what motivated him to leave us. We came to Aleksei who received us warmly. He believed it was not the right time to join the partisans. We stayed with him. Yakov Landau sewed hats in his house and I helped him.

The women settled in various peasant homes. A few days later I found out that Shachnovski returned to Stariky. He stayed with Yasku for a few days and then decided to return to us. On the way, he went to see Sokolovsky to find out where we were hiding. While he was sitting in the house, the police came and caught him and a young woman from Klesov who was also hiding at Sokolovsky's. The young woman and Shachnovski were killed there. Sokolovsky was severely tortured and killed. The next day his wife was taken away and the house was burned.

In this village I met Yakov Goldman (Burd) and his son Baruch. They were hiding in a shelter in the forest. One day we heard that the Germans were planning to search the villages in the area. We went to the partisans' command and begged to be accepted. They replied that they were now going to battle with the Germans and they could not accept us. We went back to the forest. For a long time we heard the sounds of incessant shooting and we saw fire lighting up the skies. It was reprisal action by the Germans.

Many of the villagers escaped into the forests for fear of the Germans. We felt safer among them. However, this sense of security did not last. The *Banderovtzis* threatened the villagers that they would kill them if they helped Jews. Landau and I stayed with a kind-hearted peasant. We sewed hats and earned our keep.

At Easter 1943 there was a big conference of *Banderovtzis* in the village of Tinna. Our host also attended the conference even though he was not one of the *Banderovtzis*. Yakov and I went to the village to watch the Easter festivities. We felt that many of the young people were lying in wait for us. We took a roundabout route back to our shelter. Late in the evening our host returned full of fear. He told us that at the conference an officer of the *Banderovtzis* gave a speech warning everyone that anyone who hid Jews would suffer the consequences. He asked us to leave immediately. Since it was raining and it was night, he allowed us to stay till dawn. We did not sleep a wink all night. At dawn a young man came to call on the host. He was known to be one of the *Banderovtzis* and he had a gun. The host told us the young man was a relative and did not harm us for that reason. In light of the situation, the peasant urged us to leave or else the young man would burn our shelter with everyone inside.

We left the place with a heavy heart and with trepidation. A Shtundist called Kirila accompanied us. He loved the bible and sympathized with the fate of the refugees. He parted from us with tears in his eyes. He said that he believed that soon our troubles will be over and we will see happiness again.

We went to the village of Bober where there were partisans. We entered their camp and met a Jew. He asked us why we had come. When he heard that we wanted to join the partisans, he advised us to leave immediately. Two Jews had come only a few hours earlier and were killed. These were Haim Turok and Yakov Gitelman.

We went to the forests of Votche where there were partisans. There we found Aharon Slutzki, his daughter Miriam, Leibl Gitelman and his wife and many other Jews who were reasonably free. Avraham Eisenberg was a partisan there and he helped us to obtain food and clothing.

At the end of 1943 we heard the news that the Germans were defeated near Stalingrad and were retreating from Russian lands. Our will to live was revived. We wanted to see the defeat of our torturers and we hoped to see the remnants of our families. We lived to see the great day, the day of liberation.

[Page 334]

About the Righteous of the World

Yosef Segal (Neve Oz)

Translated by Ala Gamulka

When they conquered the western Ukraine, the Nazis found among the Ukrainians loyal partners and active assistants in their goal of exterminating the Jews and stealing their property.

The Ukrainians had a long tradition of killing members of the Jewish people. It went back to the days of Bogdan Chmelnitzky in the 17th century, Petlura and bands of killers and robbers (May their names be eradicated) of the civil war in 1918-1920. (In those days the Ukrainians spilled the blood of many innocent Jews).

The Ukrainians from Rokitno and vicinity and some of the Poles who worked in the glass factory began to kill and rob the Jews even before the Nazis established themselves in Rokitno. Ukrainians who earlier seemed to be friendly and honest showed their true colors and became killers thirsty for Jewish blood.

Many Jews managed to escape from the market square on the 13th of *Elul* (1942) and roamed the fields and forests. Many were either cruelly murdered by the Ukrainians or caught and handed over to the German murderers in exchange for a kilo of salt per Jewish soul.

However, on the contrary, there were some Ukrainians who had pity on the miserable souls and treated them humanely. At night, they took the escapees into their homes and fed them at great personal risk. Not once did they pay for their generosity with their lives and property.

About 20 kilometers south of Rokitno, in the Polish village of Netrebe, tens of Jews from Rokitno and the area found shelter. They were helped by the villagers who not only did not harm them but also hid them near the village during the day. At night they took them to their homes. Many Jews survived there until the liberation by the Red Army. In the Polish village of Budki some Jews survived, but the Poles who saved them had their property burned by the Nazis.

In the same area, in the Polish village of Okopi, some tens of Jews were saved thanks to two special individuals. They are worthy of being considered part of the *Righteous Gentiles*. They are: the Catholic priest and the village teacher. The priest used to give sermons to his followers telling them not to be involved in the extermination of Jews. He asked them to help the Jews to survive until their redemption. At that time justice will prevail and the evil Nazis and their helpers will be wiped off the face of the earth. The village teacher also had compassion for the unfortunate Jews. Their suffering touched her heart and she helped in any way possible. She was killed by a Ukrainian gang on the way from the village of Rokitno while she was helping a Jewish family.

The priest was burned alive in his church. The memory of these two saintly beings stands as a ray of light in the darkness of the Nazi rule.

Others who must be mentioned are Yuzik Zalevski, Miron and Ivan Borsovich from Blizhov, Horoder from Nimovitz, Michael Kohonivich (from a hamlet near Ilova), Franko Garvovsky (of the village of Berezov), Sokolovsky and bearded Simon who endangered their lives simply to save Jews.

A special honor must be paid to the Shtundist sect who showed special love to the Jews. Thanks to these wonderful people many Jews from Rokitno and area were saved from certain death.

[Page 337]

VENGEANCE AND REPRISAL

[Page 339]

From Sheep to Slaughter – Punishment to Our Killers

Asher Binder (Neve Oz)

Translated by Ala Gamulka

The first blood-shedding occurred in July 1941. The Ukrainians attacked the blacksmith Yechiel Freger. We heard his screams from a distance. We ran to help him and we dispersed the mob. During this attack Avraham Golod was injured by a stone hurled at his head and he died on the next day.

When the Germans entered town they caught Alter Pik and killed him. He was accused of denouncing German parachutists to the Russian authorities when the war broke out. After him, David Baum was killed. He had left town to find partisans. However, when he could not find them, he had no choice but to return to Rokitno. The Germans discovered the fact and had him killed.

At the end of December 1941, the first transport of Jews from the vicinity left for work in Vinitza. Among the 68 Jews in this forced labor group there were 14 Jews from Rokitno. Among them were Meir Eisenberg, Baruch (Borya) Shuber, Yakov Linn, Avraham Zolotov, David Roitman, myself, the tinsmiths Svetchnik and Weisman and another refugee.

David Roitman, Yakov Linn and I managed to escape and we hid in Rovno for a few months. We then returned to Rokitno. During the last roll call I escaped with 13 other Jews and hid in the village of Moshia. At the end of October 1942 a peasant came to us to tell us that the Germans and Lithuanians had arrived in the village. We intended to leave the village immediately, but we decided to wait till daybreak. However, during the night the killers found us and killed Mendl Schwartzblat, Leibl Lifshitz, Misha Berezovsky, Nahum Katzenelson, a refugee doctor called Levin, the two Zilberman brothers, their son and someone else whose name I do not remember.

At the end of November 1942, I was with my cousin Mordechai Binder in the village of Bilovizh. We stood near the bridge called Haim's bridge (after Haim Berezovsky). A peasant saw us and immediately called the Germans. I managed to cross the river, but my cousin was caught and killed. A few days later a peasant called Simon Slavuk caught Shimon Gendelman, Aharon Perlovich and Moshe Chechik. Perlovich managed to escape. The other two were tied with ropes with the help of another peasant. He brought them to the Ukrainian police in Berezov where they were killed.

After my cousin's murder I went to the village of Kopele. I came at night and went to a Pole's house. He pretended to be a friend and offered me supper. After this meal he said to me: "Come, let us go into the fields to search for Jews". I had an axe, which I used to chop wood for fire. I put it aside and lit a fire. I bent my head and warmed myself up. Suddenly, I felt a hard bang on my head. The peasant hit me with the sharp edge of the axe. If I had not worn a soft hat, my head would have been split in two. Streams of blood ran down my face and my clothes. With superhuman strength I began to run, chased by the peasant. He yelled at me: "You will not get away from me!" He held the axe covered with my blood. I reached an open field and I saw a house. There was a wedding party going on. The peasant was afraid of coming too close to the house. Its owner was a Ukrainian with whom he had a dispute. This was my lucky break. The host put slices of bread on my bleeding wounds and used a rough towel to bandage my head. I kept the bandage for about a month until my wound was covered with a scab.

After this terrible event that happened to me I was very angry. Until when will we be sheep to be slaughtered? I renewed my search for the partisans. At the end of December 1942 I met five partisans at a peasant's house in Blizhov. I told them that I wished to join them. They replied: "We derailed a train on the tracks near Tomoshgorod. Go and find out how many cars were derailed and write down the number of the caboose. Then we will accept you." They gave me a pistol without any bullets and a live grenade. The area was infested with Bulbovtzis who terrorized everyone. I walked for 30 kilometers and did not meet anyone. I found the train and wrote down the number of cars, but I could not find the caboose number.

Although I only fulfilled half of the task, I was still accepted at the encampment. It was located in the airport of Markovesk near Leichitz. I stayed for a week and then went on a long trip. I had a chance, for the first time, to retaliate. From there I returned a distance of 70 kilometers and I reached Blizhov. Nachman Blizhovsky, Baruch Perlovich and I joined a regiment of Russian parachutists-partisans. The regiment was named after Kremlink. The commander was Veramchuk. Our task was to derail trains. We were active in the area of Olevsk-Rokitno-Klesov. Later, we went to Kovel and Pinsk. I participated in 12 operations.

When our regiment was near Glinna I looked for Simon Slavuk who had denounced Shimon Gendelman and Freger. I did this on my own. I knew that I might have to pay for it later because partisans cannot perform any operations without the commander's permission. There was a gypsy woman in Glinna who knew where this murderer was located and she took me there. I told him that the commander of the partisans was calling for him. He did not recognize me and took the announcement at face value. On the way he started talking to me. He said: "I obey every authority. When the Germans made me kill Jews, I did it. Now I am called to the partisans and I am going to them!" My blood boiled when I heard these words. I could not control myself and I shot him with my pistol. I used 30 bullets.

I returned to my regiment and told Baruch Perlovich and Nachman Blizhovsky what I had done. Ten minutes later the commander called me and told me that I will be severely punished for the killing of Slavuk. I shivered. The commander immediately added, with a smile: "You should be punished because such a murderer should not be killed in secret. A despicable person like that should be brought alive to the regiment to be killed in front of the partisans".

Since I knew the area well, I dedicated myself to the capture of Ukrainian policemen who had spilled Jewish blood. I listened to the commander and I brought them back alive to the camp. After he questioned them in detail, he gave an order for them to be shot.

In my regiment was also Yehuda Grempler from Rokitno. During our stay at the airport in Markovesk he was wounded accidentally by one of the partisans. He was immediately flown to a hospital in Moscow, and although he received devoted treatment - his ability to participate actively in revenge attacks was marred.

In May 1944 we were liberated in Rovno. I remained there. Part of the regiment was ordered to go to Olevsk to return equipment. Among them was Baruch Perlovich. When they reached Brezhne the *Bulbovtzis* attacked them and killed 8 partisans. The rest escaped to Brezhne. Perlovich saw a peasant being brought to the police. He went over and shot him explaining that this was one of the *Bulbovtzis* who had attacked the regiment.

A few days after Rokitno was liberated I came back to town. I found there three Ukrainian policemen who had served during the German occupation. I transferred them to the NKVD in Rovno, but I do not know what happened to them.

Among the youth of Rokitno who courageously stood up to the enemies, my brother Moshe must be mentioned. On the third night of his wandering in the forest he saw what could happen to an unarmed Jew. He decided to return home to take the pistol he owned. He arrived safely in Rokitno and took his weapon. When he reached the other side of the forest he ran into three armed policemen. My brother did not lose his cool and decided to "die with the Philistines". He shot and killed one of the policemen, wounded another and died a hero.

When I came back to town I was told by an NKVD officer that my brother deserved to be commemorated among the proud Jews who faced a larger group without offering themselves to be slaughtered.

[Page 342]

In The Forests and Reprisal Activities

Avraham Eisenberg (Tel Aviv)

Translated by Ala Gamulka

Judgment Day came to Rokitno, too. The Gestapo henchmen, accompanied by their Ukrainian helpers, began to stream into town. We saw them through the night.

The *Judenrat* members were summoned to the police and were told that all the Jews in town were to assemble in front of the new synagogue near the municipal market square. The news spread very quickly, but no one knew its true meaning. The murderers did not even wait for the Jews to come on their own, but they began to kick them out of their houses using sticks and gun butts.

There was great panic and pandemonium in the square. Parents sought their children and children looked for their parents. The crying and shouting reached the heavens; people fell and their blood covered the area. The wounded and the dying were groaning with pain.

Suddenly, a scream was heard. It was my mother who shouted: "Jews, run away! Death is coming to all of us!"

This scream galvanized the assembled. In a blink of an eye hundreds of people who had been sitting bent and cowering, stood up. They began to run as if carried by a strong gale. They jumped over fences and other stumbling blocks. The bullets were flying over their heads and the groaning of the wounded accompanied them.

I was among those who escaped. I did not believe I would remain alive, but a miracle happened. I reached the forest, far enough to be out of the range of the shooters. Ukrainian shepherds were lying in a circle around a bonfire and were enjoying themselves singing and whistling.

They looked at me as if I were a ghost. They could not imagine how I escaped when death was lurking in every corner. I was hungry and thirsty. I asked them for some bread and water to satisfy my hunger and slake my thirst, but I was denied.

From there I walked to Karpilovka, to Soltis who was a friend of the family. He received me warmly and could not believe his eyes. He was certain I had been killed with my family. He gave me food and I went to the forest. I heard that there were some mysterious people there called partisans. I wanted to join them. I walked in roundabout ways. I fell, got up and fell again. I wished to die so my suffering would end!

Suddenly, I heard rustling in the bushes. I began to shake. I was sure the murderers were lying in wait for me. My end was near. However, I heard Yiddish spoken and I recognized the voice to be that of Malka Kaplan. The heads that popped out of the thick bushes were those of her husband Yosef Kaplan, Shimon Gendelman, Toddy Linn, Dodya Burd, Yitzhak Vorona and his son Dov. To my great surprise I also saw my brothers Hershel and Velvel and my brother-in-law Haim Hanzanchuk. They told me that my sister Ronka, her husband Fishel Shechter and their child in her arms had gone to a peasant's house to beg for food. When they left him, German and Ukrainian policemen appeared and killed them there.

My brother-in-law Haim found a shelter in a peasant's hut. He was a tailor and was given food in exchange for his work. We began to get used to the conditions.

I dug a *korin* (shelter) for my brothers and me. The Weiner family was hiding in a shelter not far from us. However, we could not be calm. Murderous gangs arrived in the forest. My brother-in-law Haim heard that groups of Germans and Lithuanian policemen were hunting for Jews in the forests.

Suddenly, the sounds of gunfire filled the air. The shots became louder and the shouts of the murderers could be heard. Malka Weiner became hysterical. She started to run and I ran with her. In her haste and panic she forgot to wake her little daughter and she only took her son Baruch in her arms. We were exhausted and we fell on the ground. The night cold woke us up. I told Malka that we should return to the shelters to see if anyone was alive. We wandered for many hours in the forest. It was a dark night and we could not see our way.

At daybreak we reached the shelters. It was very quiet everywhere. Malka, scared, entered the shelter and immediately a horrible scream was heard: "My child! They murdered my daughter!" The poor girl was killed in her sleep and her body was lying in the damp and dark hiding place. Her daughter Breindl was dead. In the light of dawn her face looked peaceful, as if with a special smile.

When I saw the dead girl I feared for my brothers' welfare. Who knew what happened to them? I ran crazed to our shelter. I did not see my brothers there, but on one side I found the body of a Jewish refugee who had joined me in my wanderings and on the other side I found the body of my wife Rosia.

I searched in the dark touching every grain of earth with my hands. As I was bending down I found the bodies of my brothers. One was smashed with a rifle butt and the other was shot. About 20 meters away was the body of Berel, the son of Yitzhak Vorona.

Struck with fear, I began to run away from this killing field to search for Jews to tell them about my problems and to try to forget the bigger fear. I found some Jews, among them the wife of Avraham Barman from Snovidovich and others.

She asked me to go with her to the shelter where her husband was hiding at one of the peasants. We walked a whole night in pouring rain. At dawn we reached a bridge. We suddenly heard loud whistles, which then stopped, and all was quiet.

Rustling was heard among the bushes. In this quiet I recognized the voice of Yitzhak Vorona who had been saved by a miracle. When he was escaping from the house of a forest warden the Germans passed by and did not see him.

We walked together. We wanted to cross the bridge before dawn. We climbed on it, our shoes muddy and wet and our clothes filthy and full of lice. We sat down on the bridge to rest a little and we dozed off. Suddenly a suspicious sound woke us up. When I opened my eyes I saw the Germans coming after us. I immediately jumped under the bridge and I covered myself with thick underbrush. The others also jumped after me. The murderers came close to where we were hiding and yelled: "Get out quickly, Jews! We will not harm you!" We held our breath and did not move. I heard orders given in Ukrainian: "Comb the area and catch them alive!" I decided to escape, no matter what. I crawled forward in the bushes. I fell and became tangled in the thick vegetation. A barrage of fire came at me. It was automatic rifles as well as grenades. The shrapnel hit the bushes. Everything was on fire.

I crawled a great distance and I heard, from a distance, sounds of shots and blasting. The danger passed, at least for a while. I sat down in the shade of a bush, tears streaming from my eyes. I was all alone and I was being hunted like an animal. I decided to return to the shelter to bury my brothers and my cousin. I made my way in the dark. I stumbled on a body and I was frightened and jumped back. It was Dvosil Svetchnik*, the wife of Yitzhak the hat maker.

I could not go over to bury them because I was petrified. I looked for other Jews to help me to perform the last rites for my brothers. However, there was no one in sight.

It was a Saturday. Around noon I dug a trench and put in one brother and my cousin Berel. I dug a second trench and put in my older brother. I kissed the cold bodies, covered them with soil and parted from them forever.

I then went to look for my brother-in-law – the only one left alive from our large family. When I reached the village of Netrebe I discovered my brother-in-law was no longer alive. I found out he had gone to collect his belongings from a peasant. The latter wanted to get rid of him and served him some poisoned food for dinner. The last remnant of my family was gone.

One of the villagers told me that his brother-in-law, who lived on the other side of the village, had contact with some Jews, among them Toddy Linn. I went to him, but he told me that "strange" people had taken him with them. He returned a while later and gave me the happy news that Toddy was taken by the partisans. He told me that Russians had come to give him a test. In order to test his courage they tied him to a tree and aimed a rifle at him. When he burst out crying they calmed him down by telling him they were Russian partisans and they only wanted to test him. A few days later the partisans told Toddy that they

*an error in the name since her death and burial are witnessed elsewhere. Also husband's name and occupation do not match.

had to leave the area because there were too many Germans there and they could not take him with them. His begging did not help. Again we remained isolated and subject to attacks.

We approached a barn where we wanted to sleep. Suddenly we heard terrible groans and we discovered Niuska Kokel. We were shocked by her appearance. She looked swollen from hunger. Her body was covered with wounds and she could barely talk. She told us that she was hiding in the barn for a week and she decided to lie down to die. She preferred death to falling into the hands of the Germans. We tried to calm her down and to encourage her. We washed her face and fed her milk. We then took her in our arms and we brought her to a peasant's house. We ordered him to take care of her. He would pay for it if anything happened to her, since we were partisans.

We continued in our efforts to join the partisans. We searched for them everywhere. On the way we saw, from a distance, three men standing in the shadow of a broken wooden fence on which there was a machine gun. When they noticed us, one of them threatened us with a live grenade and ordered us toidentify ourselves. We told him we were Jews and that we wished to join the partisans. He immediately put down the grenade and motioned with his hand to come closer. They began to question us. One of us, a refugee, said he was a printer's apprentice. Dodya Burd said he knew how to tile roofs and I was a carpenter.

Of the three of us only the printer was welcome. We begged to be taken. We explained that the three of had wandered together in the forest and we were united by the suffering. We could not be separated now. Our begging softened the heart of the commander and he agreed to let us join.

In mid January 1943 we were accepted by the partisans. Everyone received a gun, bullets and three grenades. We now felt the time for revenge and punishment of our murderers had come. One day a long column of tens of carts with hundreds of fighters was organized in the thick of the forest. Dodya Burd and I were among them. We began to move when it became dark. This time we did not go into battle, but only went to collect food from villages in the area for the partisans. In Netrebe I went to see how Niuska Kokel was doing. Her wounds healed from the ointment put on by the peasant's wife. Her health had improved considerably. I encouraged by telling her the time of redemption was near and she would soon be free. Indeed, she remained alive and returned to Rokitno. However, there she contracted blood poisoning. She was taken to Lvov, but all efforts to save her failed and she died.

Our first battle with the *Bulbovtzis* took place in the village of Karpilovka. It was a reprisal for the murder of a unit commander. We marched in columns towards the village. We soon reached the first huts. It was the lull before the storm. A shot rang in the air followed by the ringing of bells. All the local churches were summoning the villagers against the approaching partisans.

The noise and shooting increased. Shouts and screams, shots and explosions were heard. I advanced with three men and came upon *Bulbovtzis* firing a cannon. We finished them off with grenades.

An order was given to gather all the men, to burn the houses and the barns, to destroy the wells – to teach the *Bulbovtzis* a lesson. The *Bulbovtzis* were punished. Those with guns were killed. We took revenge on these murderers who had spilled so much Jewish blood.

As long as I was a partisan, I searched for Jews to help them with food. At night I rode on a horse packed with all kinds of food and went from place to place. In a shelter I found Aharon Lifshitz, Mara Slutzki, her father Aharon and two Jews from Ludvopol. In this way I also helped Raphael Burd's daughter from Karpilovka and the daughter of the Rabbi from Brezhne. After Karpilovka was burned, I met Esther Ivry and I gave her a package of food. This saved her from starvation. The most audacious operation I participated in was the battle of Rokitno. One time, the commander called me in and told me that the regiment intended to conquer Rokitno from the Germans. Since I knew the roads he appointed me as scout and guide. I happily undertook this task. The regiment assembled and we were on our way. Near Messiviche, not far from the flourmill, we stopped. At night a small advance group went to Rokitno. The commander told me that as we enter town we must signal with red flares. The group divided itself into smaller groups. Some crossed the bridge and went to the glass factory and the others went towards the Tarbut School.

When we approached the school, the signal was given and the partisans who surrounded Rokitno from all sides opened fire. My group began to fire at the Germans who were in the building and they ran away. In the meantime the rest of the regiment, 1200 people, entered town. When the Germans saw what was coming, most of them escaped to an armored train. A group of 20 of them hid in the glass factory, which had been fortified. We overcame them. We took more than 20 Germans and Polish policemen to the forest and we eliminated them.

We returned to town and we burned the houses of all the collaborators. Many of the Polish and Ukrainian murderers fell into our hands and we administered due justice. We bombed the glass factory, destroyed the railroad tracks, and burned the police station and the houses inhabited by the SS. It took a whole night. When this daring operation was over, although we had no losses, we were told to retreat from Rokitno. The Germans were returning with many troops. We went to Messiviche where we took out all the flour in the mill and burned the building. The whole village was also burned.

After these two operations we went deep into Poland and we reached the Bug River. At night I went with two partisans to bring food for the regiment. Avraham Zolotov was with us. On the way we ran into Germans and a battle ensued. Avraham Zolotov was killed. This was a bloody battle. We killed many Germans, but we suffered many casualties. We continued with these reprisals until the war ended.

[Page 347]

My Participation in the Partisan Activities

David Burd (Ramat Yosef)

Translated by Ala Gamulka

In October 1942 I was sitting in a camouflaged tent near the village of Netrebe with my brother Berl, Avraham Eisenberg, Toddy Linn, the three Golubovitz brothers and some others. At dusk, a cow suddenly emerged from the bushes, followed by a young local lad. He eyed us suspiciously and we realized that we had to escape from there. This is exactly what we did. We went 4 or 5 kilometers further. On the following day, Toddy talked me into returning to the tent. My heart told me that a return to the tent meant an encounter with death. However, he begged me so much that I relented.

We came to the tent and we lit a fire. As soon as we lit it we saw a German soldier coming out of the bushes holding a rifle. He wanted to catch us alive. Toddy was barely able to tell me: “Run quickly!” He ran and I followed. The Germans shot from all directions. When G-d allots years to a person, that person escapes even from such danger. The Germans chased us, but they did not catch us and we were saved.

We wandered in the forest for two weeks and we then went to a house of our acquaintance, Yuzik Zalevski. We found his wife crying. When we asked the reason, she replied that ten armed men had taken her husband and were on their way to his father's house.

We followed the trail and we reached the house. We knocked on the door and Yuzik opened it. We asked him if the men were partisans or *Banderovtzis*. He replied that he could not identify them. However, he remembered one of their slogans: “G-d is up above and Stalin is far away”. As we were speaking, a group of men suddenly appeared shouting: “Jews, stop! You are all *kaput*”. They ordered us to go to a place where they guarded us – two in front, two in the rear and two on the sides.

They searched us and did not find anything. They pretended to be German policemen and threatened to kill us immediately. One of them spoke to us and wanted to know from where we came. We told him we were from Rokitno. “What are you doing here?” We said we were searching for food. “You only want food? That's all? Do you hear, Grishka, they are hungry. Give them food!” Grishka took out from his backpack some pork. He put slabs on large pieces of bread and said: “Eat to your heart's content”. From this action we understood that these men were partisans. After we ate enough they told us to leave. They warned us not to tell anyone about this encounter. After liberation we discovered that they were parachutists from the Medvedev division – the first group to be parachuted on Polish soil.

Finally, the time we had hoped for came. We would now take part in the defeat of the enemy. We heard there was a unit of partisans not far from us. We decided to send my brother to find out if this was true and if they were partisans or *Banderovtzis*. Two or three days passed and my brother did not return. We were certain he had fallen into the hands of the *Banderovtzis*. I went to see a local acquaintance and I burst out crying. I told him that I feared for my brother's life. When he heard this he began to shout: "You should only be so lucky to be where your brother is now". He told me my brother had visited him wearing a red ribbon on his hat. He told him the partisans were not allowing him to leave the area and he asked him to tell us to come to this partisan unit because we would be well received.

We were on our way. When we reached their location, one of the partisans brought us to the commander. He asked us if we had any arms. We replied that we did not have any arms, but we had trades. For example, Avraham Eisenberg was a carpenter. "Good", said the commander. "We need a carpenter to build us tents." They accepted all of us, even those who did not have a trade.

We waited for the day when we could avenge the spilled blood of our families. The hoped for that day came. I was a machine gunner and a sapper. We planted landmines in the fields where the Germans were passing. As they approached the site, we pulled wires to explode the landmines. We also fired a barrage of shots from all sides. It was an operation of "hit and run". We would immediately go into the forest where we were certain the Germans were afraid to enter. One of the operations in which I participated was the blasting of the glass factory.

[Page 348]

A Partisan in The Kovpak Regiment

Todres Linn (Kiryat Motzkin)

Translated by Ala Gamulka

After wandering in the forests I discovered there were Russian partisans in the area. I, along with other remnants of our town, joined them. We went out on all kinds of operations. Life was a little freer, but still dangerous. At that time, the Kovpak division arrived in our area. It took 100 people from the local unit. I, too, joined them. There was a special Jewish unit, famous for its battles with the Nazi invaders.

We advanced to the oil pits in Drohovich. On the way we destroyed all the bridges and the railroad tracks. We conquered towns and villages and we defeated the

Germans thoroughly. When we conquered the town of Skalat in Galicia, we liberated a camp of Jews. We then arrived at the oil pits and we decided to bomb them. The Nazis organized many SS divisions and army units. They surrounded us in the hills and we suffered heavy casualties. In a decisive battle in the town of Dlatin one of the important division commanders fell. We retreated in haste and confusion.

I was once sent to reconnoiter a village with 10 other men. We were surrounded by *Banderovtzis*. During the short battle, many of us were caught. However, I was able to escape with two other Jews. We could not return to our division because there were ambushes everywhere. In the evenings we went on raids to obtain food. In spring 1943 we were closer to the front and we were free from the threat of the enemy.

In the Kovpak division, I met Nechama Gelfand, Borya Nagel, Shteindel and other young people from Rokitno. (Some of them were killed in battles). In March 1944 I returned my ammunition to the Russian authorities and I asked permission to go to Rokitno. I was hoping to find some family members still alive. To my sorrow, I found Christians in my house. The town was burned and there were very few Jews. I will never forget those moments when I went up to the attic and I found clothes belonging to my parents and my sisters. My tears choked me and I cried bitterly. At every step I saw sad ruins. Our dear departed ones were gone forever.

[Page 349]

The Hour of Reprisal Came

Moshe Marshalek (Kibbutz R'shafim)

Translated by Ala Gamulka

When the Germans entered Rokitno I remained in the ghetto with my sister Shoshana (she was later killed in the forest, I was told by the Ukrainians). We were isolated from the family. We lived with my aunt and uncle Hershel and Lifsha Greenberg. We suffered great pains and humiliation in the ghetto. I still remember how a former Polish corporal took my uncle Aharon Pik to the palace forest to kill him there. All the efforts of the Jewish committee and the begging of my grandmother Hannah in front of the commander (*Folksdeutch*) did not help. The town residents were shocked by the first casualty – before the great extermination.

Everyone heard that the Germans intended to exterminate us, but we did not believe it would happen here. The Jews paid the Germans a new head tax every so often. The older generation remembered the Germans from WWI and they were certain they could be bought off. They did not believe that a whole population could be murdered - even though they heard about mass killings of Jews in the area.

The terrible day came. I was able to escape from the killing field with some other Jews. We felt terribly alone. Our family members were gone. What purpose was there to live? Some despaired and returned to town to be killed. I was determined to stay alive. We roamed the forests and we ate mushrooms and blackberries. For safety reasons we broke up into small groups. I stayed with Aharon Reznik and his son and a few other young people – Shepsel, Meir, Syoma Lifshitz and Moshe Greber. We went towards the hamlets of Blizhov. We hid among the thick trees and the marshes became our home. We were afraid to be seen in daylight. At night we went to the villages and the hamlets to beg for food. Many times we were chased by various killers, but they did not succeed. We built fires where we roasted potatoes and we warmed ourselves up. Every sound was suspicious. At times peasants with axes tried to kill us. We were saved by miracles.

I learned the secrets of the forest – the paths, marshes and trees. I remembered every tree in a special way so I would not lose my way. We learned to dress like the peasants. We wove shoes from marsh reeds. In the hard winter we went to the peasants to ask for food and to warm up. Luckily, the hamlet residents were Shtundists and they helped us. In exchange for food I worked for Pavlo Zankov. At that time the partisans began to appear in the area. When we were searching for the partisans we once saw horse riders in the forest. In our naiveté, we thought they were partisans (the farmers only used oxen). We were happy to see them, but we soon saw they were Ukrainian policemen hunting for Jews. We hid in the thick branches and they did not see us.

I helped old man Reznik and his son in the forest. The son died and we buried him there. The father felt it was better to die in the hands of G-d than in the hands of the murderers. Sometimes we went to visit Pavlo in the evenings to read a chapter of the bible. He loved sacred texts and I read them to him willingly. Aharon Reznik interpreted the verses and argued with him. The bible reminded me that somewhere there was Eretz Israel. Would we ever reach it? In those days, in the middle of war, it was only a dream.

One evening the partisans appeared. They were members of the famous Kovpak division. They only accepted Shepsel and Meir. They said I was too young. They consoled me by saying I could be useful to the local partisans as a guide.

The time for revenge on the Germans and their Ukrainian helpers came. The partisans wrote a brilliant chapter in the history of the war against the Germans. Harsh battles took place. Trains were hit by landmines and the enemy was afraid. In the evenings the Germans locked themselves up in fortresses for fear of the partisans. This went on until the Red Army dealt a heavy blow and came closer to us. The town was liberated. We, the few remnants, came back to town. We tried to somehow rebuild our lives, but it was not for long. We could not bear the terrible tragedy that befell the Jews of Rokitno. When the opportunity came, we left. We wandered in various countries trying to reach our homeland. After much wandering and after meeting remnants of other families, I discovered that my two brothers had remained in the Soviet Union. I was fortunate to meet them again in Israel.

[Page 351]

The *Kol Nidrei* Prayer of Haim Kek

Gad Rosenblat

Translated by Ala Gamulka

...In the morning we found ourselves not far from the village of Snovidovich near Rokitno. We decided to stay there for a while. Something special drew us to that area. In the summer, when we had gone through the Rokitno area on the way to the Carpathian Mountains, we heard that many Jews were either hiding in the forest and peasant homes or they joined the Medvedev, Davidov, and Shitov partisan divisions. This time, since we did not wish to go north, we decided to search for other Jews.

We did not have to search for very long. In a Polish village near Snovidovich, we found a few Jewish families working in the houses and fields of the villagers. We stayed with these Jews for several days. They told us about their troubles and the operations of the local partisans as well as those of the *Banderovtzis.*

It was two days before *Yom Kippur* and they did not know if they would find a place to pray. A tall skinny Jew told me about it. It seemed as if all the troubles of exile were on his shoulders. This Jew was Haim Kek from Rokitno. He was brought to slaughter with his family, but he managed to escape into the forest nearby. He lived in villages, forests and ditches. His troubles were many, but he focused all his thoughts on preparations for *Yom Kippur* prayers. A minyan was needed. Kek said: “Two members of my family and I – make three. All of you, that is more than a *minyan.* When we pray each one of us will lead, each will remember some parts and others will continue”.

My heart was moved and I agreed to Kek's request. I went to a peasant's house and I asked him to remove pictures of the Holy mother and her son from the walls because we wanted to conduct prayers for *Yom Kippur* there. The floor was cleaned thoroughly. We placed a small table on the eastern wall and Kek brought four large wax candles and lit them. The sun was setting. Kek walked around, looking at the candles and the clean tablecloth on the table. Many of us had moist eyes.

We took off our guns and placed them in the corner. Four armed partisans guarded the house and its entrances. The time for *Kol Nidrei* came. There was no prayer book. Who could do the whole prayer from memory? Our troubles made us forget how to pray, but, as if by magic, all of us suddenly were able to recite it aloud. The mournful voices filled the house and seemed to escape outdoors, to reach the heavens. “May all the people of Israel be forgiven ...for all the people are at fault.”

Through the open window we heard sounds of suppressed sobbing. It was the women and the girls who came, but remained outside near the window to hear the prayers. Every man took a turn in leading the service, beginning with Haim Kek. Everyone remembered something from their childhood and the others joined in.

We prayed for a long time. We did not want to part one from the other. Something bound us together. In the middle of the service, I was told that a famous local partisan, Zvi Olshansky, had come to pray. He heard about the *minyan* from some Jewish families and he came. He was a big, tall and broad-shouldered man and very handsome. He had the spirit of a Jewish partisan who was ready to avenge the honor of his people. All the peasants in the area mentioned his name with admiration and respect. There were many legends about him and his achievements.

Olshansky put his rifle in the corner and joined the prayers. When we finished praying I spoke with Olshansky for a long time. I heard from him about many Jewish partisans from Rokitno who were in the Shitov, Medvedev, Ploskonosov and other divisions.

(From the book: A Fire Took Hold of the Forest" by Gad Rosenblat, pp 260-263, published by Hakibbutz Hameuchad, 1957)

Lighting of Shabbes Candles

[Page 353]

Our Brothers – We Shall Remember!
(In memory of the martyrs of Rokitno, murdered by the Nazis)

Hannah Segal (Neve Oz)

***Written by the author at the age of thirteen.**

Translated by Ala Gamulka

Our brothers, we shall remember how together
We hid in the forest, back to back,
We will still remember, our brothers,
How the bridge was bombed,
And everything that followed...

Father, how you mourned your son!
And you, unfortunate mother, whose baby
The murderers flung at the wall
We shall remember, our brothers.

You, young orphan boy,
Your courage, dear daughter
How you fought the murderers.

We shall remember you to eternity and we will not forget
Your suffering and affliction, we too, felt.
We will tell the world what
Our enemies did to you.
Forever we will whisper – revenge...

Brothers, we shall avenge your blood
You who jumped to certain death,
So that the others could be saved.

You, whose ears no longer hear
The birds chirping.
You, who will never again lift
Your eyes to the heavens.

We shall remember you forever
You, our heroes
Who suffered and shivered.

You who escaped the death camps
Who entered the forests
To save your brothers.
Those who remained
And never returned.

You who held a rifle
In one hand
And a grenade in the other.
You whose courage
Is an example for us
Forever and ever.

We shall remember you, our brothers
To our last days.
We will hope for revenge on those
Who spilled your blood,
Clean and pure blood.

[Page 354]

Dates of the Holocaust Period in Rokitno

Compiled by Haim Shteinman

(Note that dates are European style Day/month/year)

World War II Breaks Out	17 Elul – 1.9.1939
Rokitno Conquered by Soviets	4 Tishrei – 17.9.1939
Soviet-German War Breaks Out	27 Sivan – 22.6.1941
Soviet Army Retreats from Rokitno	15 Tammuz – 10.7.1941
Rokitno Conquered by Germans	12 Av – 5.8.1941
Ordered to Wear Star of David on Sleeve	17 Av – 10.8.1941
Ordered to Wear Yellow Patch	9 Tishrei – 30.9.1941
Ghetto Founded	28 Nissan – 15.4.1942
Ghetto Annihilated	13 Elul – 26.8.1942
Germans Retreat and Town Liberated by Soviets	8 Tevet - 4.1.1944

[Page 355]

IN THE TOWN OF SLAUGHTER

[Page 357]

My Heart, My Heart Is Yours Rokitno!

Haim Shteinman (Tel-Aviv)

Translated by Ala Gamulka

In memory of my dear parents, Herschel and Malka - May the Lord avenge their blood, who died in the Shoah.

At midnight I trembled with fear to hear your name pronounced specifically by the announcer on Radio Moscow, among the names of other settlements in Western Ukraine.

My dear town! You too were liberated by the Red Army. I shuddered when I thought that the bitter day was approaching when that terrible tragedy with all its frightful events would be revealed in its stark reality. Troubling and frightful thoughts came in to my mind. Was it true? My whole family, all my acquaintances, my friends, my colleagues from charitable and Zionist organizations and all the other dear town folk, young and old, men, women and children! Can it be true they were all slaughtered?

And you, overcrowded houses standing on both sides of the railroad tracks, you stand gloomy and deep in mourning, abandoned, alone, saddened because the inhabitants left and no one returned.

And you, the old synagogue, you stand empty, full of despair. You are in mourning, without congregants to visit you. What is the fate of the Torah scrolls, the Torah crowns, the Trees of Life, the *Talmud* books, the *Mishnah* volumes, *Yore De'ah, Hushan Mishpat*, the *Zohar* and all the other sacred books? And what is the fate of the ark that stood on the eastern wall, overlaid with copper animals and birds? Over the two tablets of the ark an eagle spread its wings (symbolizing: "*as an eagle hovers over its fledglings...*"). And above the column stood two guardian lions with beautiful manes (symbolizing: "*Like a lion's whelp, O' Judah*"). And on both sides of the Holy Ark, two stags with large horns (symbolizing: "*Naphtali is like a fleet hind...*"). And you, the Eternal Light, that in your glow the Jews sat at night all year long swallowing pages of *Gmara* while holding a candle between their fingers to keep their eyes open so they won't doze off. Was this Light extinguished forever?

And the house of study, that always hummed like a beehive between *minha* and *maariv* services. In one corner sat the students of *Gmara* and in another politics were discussed. Here one Jew came in for a charitable donation and there, "*mitzvah* emissaries" came to collect quietly, for someone needy. The sounds of prayers, crying, singing and chanting of students that studied Torah were always supplemented by the voices of the various preachers and Zionist speakers. Even you are standing empty and forlorn and "grass has grown in your pathways"?

And you, lovely Blue and White Boxes, are you still hanging on the walls- embarrassed! Does a spider now settle among you, weaving its web on you without disturbance? For there is no hand depositing a coin or taking one out- as the delicate hands have been severed by the cruel slaughterer... or are you empty, you? Or maybe the looters- the villagers- the sons of the "good neighbors" have benefited unexpectedly when they were searching the houses that had been emptied of Jews. Some of you found a new home in a strange surrounding, underneath the pictures of the "Holy Christ" or the "Holy disciples". Do the old village women now collect in your "saintly coins and expiation offerings" for the village priest before Christmas to pardon the sins of the house dwellers?

Rokitno, my town! You always set an example for others with your Zionist and public works and Hebrew language and cultural activities. Indeed, you sent your best sons and daughters to be pioneers to Eretz Israel. Some of them entered Palestine during the British Mandate in strange ways- some by foot, some by jumping from historic boats into the sea. They are now in the cities, villages, *moshavim* and *kibbutzim*, where they embroider green carpets in the fields of the flourishing farms of their homeland.

Indeed, you wrote a brilliant chapter in the history of our people and our land. You deserve to be memorialized for the future, so you will remain in our hearts and in those of our descendants. Forever after, you must be a memorial to those that didn't succeed in reaching a safe shore.

My heart, my heart is yours, my dear town of birth. Your disaster, our disaster, is as deep and large as the sea.

[Page 358]

After The Destruction

Baruch Shehori (Schwartzblat) (Haifa)

Translated by Ala Gamulka

It happened at the end of 1943! General Sovorov's partisans managed to cut through the German lines. In the Baronovich forests in Byelorussia, they joined with the Russian army, which attacked the Germans from the east. By then real Soviet soldiers came to us in the forest to rest after the attacks on the rear of the enemy. We were instructed by Moscow to conscript the younger people who had not yet served as partisans. They were to be trained for a few weeks and they were to join the Red Army. In only one month, 10,000 soldiers were added to the Red Army.

As the Red Army came closer to the former Polish borders, the partisans were instructed to move west, to clear the area of the enemy and to perform sabotage activities. Our regiment was divided into two parts: one group went to the Kovel-Rovno area while we, the second group, stayed in the Polesia forests. In December of that year we received a telegram telling us to go towards the Red Army. It meant returning to Rokitno. We advanced towards the town and a week later we reached its outskirts. At night some partisans were sent to the village of Rokitno to collect information. The scouts returned the next day with the news that the Germans were running away, the regime was collapsing and the road to town was open.

A group of saboteurs went to the railroad tracks north of town, to plant landmines in order to inhibit the retreat of the Germans. At noon we were ready to enter town. When we reached the entrance two hours later, we heard blasts in the distance. We discovered that the last armored train left for Sarny and on its way it blew up all the bridges behind it. However, near Osnitzek, it was stopped by the landmines placed there by the partisans. An exchange of fire between the partisans and the Germans followed. The Germans were shooting from the train to cover their escape into the forest. When the shooting ended only five dead Germans were found. The others managed to escape into the forest under the cover of darkness.

It was December 31 and a light snow was falling. Here and there lights were burning in the houses. Our convoy, which consisted of 50 sleighs full of armed partisans, passed through Rokitno with cries of happiness. I began to shake and my heart beat loudly when I entered our street and came to my empty house. I did my best not to burst our crying hysterically when I saw the town to which I returned after so much suffering and sorrow. I left Rokitno in fear and with grief and I came back broken-hearted.

On the street leading from the direction of Kisorich, distant lights began to glimmer. These were the tanks of the advance regiments of the Soviets. We drove towards them. We held the red flag in our hands and we sang partisan songs. We stopped. Soldiers peered out of the tanks and greeted us. We hugged and kissed and our happiness was indescribable. Some time later the advance 113th division arrived led by General Poliakov. We introduced ourselves and I, as a resident of Rokitno, took it upon myself to find them lodgings. I took them to the new town, which had not been destroyed. Some of its beautiful houses were occupied by the Germans. The Poles cleared some of their houses for the officers. They received the Soviets with restrained warmth. The partisans found lodging with other Poles on the same street. I was the commander of the group and its commissar and we settled in my aunt's house. A woman was living there with her children. She immediately cleared three rooms for us.

In the evening we went to Commander Poliakov's house. We ate dinner there with the officers and then we received our appointments. My commander became chief of security for the area and all the partisans were under his command. The commissar was temporarily named district secretary of the party and I was the representative of the Soviet government for the Rokitno area.

That evening I met some Polish acquaintances. Some of them wondered how I had remained alive. Others were pleased to see me. The owner of a restaurant on Messiviche Street would not leave me alone. He wanted me to sleep in his house that night. I willingly accepted his invitation. They boiled a lot of water so I could take a bath and change my clothes. The bath was a great undertaking because I had not seen soap for a year and a half. I cleansed myself thoroughly. I changed my underwear and lay down in a bed filled with pillows. I woke up after a deep sleep. I felt all my troubles had disappeared. It seemed to me that it had only been a nightmare. I wondered how I had withstood such inhumane conditions for so long.

On the next day, after I made my first visit to town, I met several residents of Rokitno. As soon as they heard that it was possible to return, they came out of the forests and hiding places. They were quite miserable. They wore rags and shabby shoes tied with ropes. They looked shrunken and their faces were pale as if after a serious illness. We hugged, we kissed and we cried together. Only now could we realize the extent of the tragedy. We could see how alone and miserable we were. And the utter sadness!

The streets were deserted. The old synagogue was no longer standing. Only its foundation stones were visible. The place was empty and even the sexton's house and the building used for the preparation of bodies for burial were destroyed. It turned out that the Germans sold the buildings to farmers who took them apart and built stables and storage sheds from the stones.

In the morning, I was appointed representative of the Soviet government. I had to organize offices to deal with ongoing problems of the civilian population as well as the army passing through town. That same day I issued orders asking the population to cooperate with the authorities and to hand in any arms in their possession. It was important because we did not have enough time to take revenge on the Poles who had collaborated with the Germans. On the first night only, a few Poles were killed by Jewish partisans and that was that. The next mission was to bring the traitors to the Soviet security authorities. Some tens of Poles and Ukrainians were sent to Siberia or to prison. They were never seen again.

In midday I continued to tour the town. The houses on our street, which used to be packed with Jews, were taken over by the Poles. The row of stone houses used to serve as residences and stores. Many were now uninhabitable. The Germans had turned them into storage sheds and horse stables. Even the new town was full of destruction. The new synagogue had been broken into and it was full of filth and dung. All industrial buildings were bombed and destroyed. Before they retreated, the Germans had burned the glass factory, the saw-mill and any other public buildings.

Within a week all the Jews still alive came out of the forests and returned to town. They either entered the empty houses or they forced the squatters to leave. There was no intention to settle down again. Everyone knew it was only temporary. Therefore, three or four families occupied one apartment. Loneliness and sadness were prevalent. Those who remained alive searched for intimacy to ease their despair.

On the fourth day of our stay in Rokitno, the Germans bombed the town from the air. There was a casualty among those who returned from the forests. Haim Kek, a Jew in his fifties, who had suffered in the forests and in hiding with the peasants, was looking for cover between the houses. He was hit by shrapnel and died on the spot. The bombings continued for several months. The Germans intended to blast the railroad tracks, which the Soviets had quickly erected. When they succeeded in repairing the tracks east of town, they built a storage house for bombs and ammunition in the thick of the forest near the tracks. The Germans must have known this and they bombed the location non-stop. The bombing was mostly at night. Planes would first drop flare bombs by parachute and the area was brightly lit. Then the bombers would drop their load. It was impossible to use anti-aircraft artillery since the light was blinding.

The front lines settled for several weeks on the River Slutch near Sarny. Difficult battles took place there. There were bloody battles with the aim of conquering Kovel and its vicinity. The partisans, who performed miracles in the forests behind the lines, were sent to help the advancing army. In these areas the partisans met the enemy head on for the first time. Thousands were killed due to lack of military training in open warfare.

Most of the Jews who came back from the forests quickly found employment. They had managerial positions. They remained in their important positions in offices and were not conscripted into the army. Only one or two Jews were conscripted and their fate was unknown. Soon refugees from the west came as well as residents of nearby villages who were afraid to stay there. There were gangs of Ukrainian nationalists, *Banderovtzis* and others attacking in the area. Several times groups were organized with local citizens to go on raids to eliminate these gangs. In one of these operations, Yechiel Trossman died. His body was brought back from the battle. He was buried in the cemetery in Rokitno.

After the town was liberated and trains began to run again, letters arrived from Rokitno residents who had escaped to Russia. They were anxious for news of their families. One letter arrived from Natan Gendelman who was in Kazakhstan. It was the first address I could use to send a letter to my sister Sarah, in Israel. I wrote her a long letter detailing all the hardships, suffering, killing and extermination of our community. The letter reached Gendelman and he sent it to Teheran to the Jewish Agency. They sent the letter to Israel. It was the first terrible pronouncement about the fate of the Jews of Rokitno and Volyn. The letter appeared in the newspapers *Davar*, *Ha'aretz*, *Hamishmar*, *Hamashkif*, and even in the Argentinean press. I began to receive letters from various people in Israel. I did not even know these people, but they begged me to find out the fate of Jews in other villages. I did not have much to tell them. Unfortunately, I had to tell all of them there was no trace left of their families.

Some of our former residents living in Israel organized themselves as an association (*landsmanshaft*) and began to send us packages. Each package contained a blanket, clothing, soap and other necessities. The authorities did not make it difficult and the packages were directed by the Jewish Agency in Teheran. We organized a secret committee to make sure the items were properly distributed. The committee also took care of other matters. There were some orphans and singles that came out of the forests. We looked after food and shelter for them. There were a few couples that adopted these orphans, looked after them and brought them up.

One spring day we went to Sarny to the cemetery. Residents of Sarny joined us and we went together to the burial place. We saw that on the street near the forest, on the other side of the tracks, where the killing took place, the gravestones were strewn on the path and were used as a sidewalk. No one, especially the authorities, bothered to put them back in place. The large cemetery in Sarny was destroyed and abandoned. Past the cemetery we found the site where 10,000 Jews were killed and buried. There were remnants of whitewash on the sand. It had apparently been poured after the slaughter to stem the flow of blood from the common grave. One only had to scratch the sand to find human skulls with hair still attached. It was a horrendous and terrible sight. Our hearts ached and we said *Kaddish* together. Crying and wailing filled the air. For a long time we continued to cover the protruding bodies with sand. We also marked the graves. We decided to apply to the authorities for permission to fence the area and put up a proper gravestone. The residents of Sarny undertook that task.

There was also a common grave in Rokitno. A pit had been quickly dug on a sand dune, near the tracks on the road to Mochulnaka. Three hundred bodies were placed in it. They were either killed in the market square or were mortally wounded later on. Those killed in the forests who had been brought in by the peasants for a reward, were also buried there.

One summer day the authorities informed us that they wanted to open the grave. We came with spades and we carefully removed the top layer of sand. A horrible sight awaited us. In the pit were bodies of men, women, and children completely deteriorated. There were parts of clothes, flowery dresses and men's overcoats covering the skeletons. When the bodies were exposed the committee began to take pictures. We tried to overturn some bodies, but we could not identify any of them. We asked the authorities for permission to transfer the skeletons to the Jewish cemetery. We were refused. We discovered that the committee only intended to take pictures as proof of the German atrocities. We covered the grave and after some time we received permission to put barbed wire around it.

On my first visit to Rovno on glass factory business (I was its manager for a while), I met a group of partisans. My wife Genia was among them. They lived in one building. The head of the group was Lidovsky. One evening he explained to me what they were doing and he included me in the group. It was a Zionist group that was active in transporting survivors to Israel. One evening, it was all formalized. They swore an oath holding a pistol in one hand and a Bible in the other. The intent was to secretly transport young people to Poland or Rumania. From there, contacts would be made to leave illegally for Eretz Israel. When I returned to Rokitno we held a secret meeting, organized ourselves and began our activities. My mission was to go to Rumania illegally to meet people there who would begin to arrange the travel to Israel. However, my wife was pregnant and I had to give it up. Asher Binder was sent in my place. When he reached his destination he found the organizers of the *Bricha* ("Escape") and joined them. He went to Poland several times on a mission and succeeded in transporting some young people to Italy.

It was an extremely dangerous undertaking. On one hand we were members of the Communist party still, from our days as partisans, but, on the other hand, we were secret Zionists. All the activities were done in secret under the noses of the authorities.

The number of Jews who returned to Rokitno eventually reached two hundred. Several whole families returned from Russia, and also Jews from the east who desired to join us in the hope that there would be border changes. In order to relieve the loneliness, they started to marry. Each wanted to create a framework for a family and to find content in life.

In a certain way, the authorities treated the Jews fairly. They did not give us back our destroyed old synagogue, but they did not oppose the organizing by the elders of Shabbat services in a private dwelling. This synagogue was packed on the High Holidays and other festivals.

Most of Poland was conquered and the Soviets wanted to prove to the world that western Ukraine was an integral part of the Soviet Ukraine. An order was issued by Stalin that all Polish citizens were permitted to go west to their homeland, while Ukrainians living in Lublin – Chelm – Hrobishov, etc. could go to the western Ukraine. We were delighted with the order. The time had come to leave this cursed place that had taken its revenge on us. It had turned on us and ended the lives of our dear ones. We all registered to leave. The authorities were not pleased. The best local elements, which Russia had rescued from death and had revived, wanted to run away? They thought we were ungrateful.

Before we left we held a burial for the remnants of the Torah scrolls, which had been strewn everywhere. They were torn and dirty. We brought them to the cemetery and we buried them among the graves. It was our last visit to the cemetery.

Funeral of the Torah Scroll Remnants

We planned to depart on June 5, 1945. We were afraid. What could happen? Perhaps at the last minute we would not be allowed to leave? We took almost nothing with us on the road. Towards evening we climbed on an open train car and we mingled with the Polish villagers who were headed west. They were bringing cows, horses and sacks of produce. The only closed car was assigned to mothers and young children. The cars were being loaded until midnight. The train left at midnight and I heaved a sigh of relief. Finally, we were on our way. Maybe we will be lucky and we will reach our destination quickly.

I sat between the sacks for many hours and I thought about my town of birth. Everything that happened went through my head. It began with my childhood. I remembered events that I had never thought about. Thirty-two years passed like a movie in my imagination, in a few hours. My heart was aching and the blood rushed to my face. Rest in peace my town, where I spent happy years, but where I also suffered terrible sadness.

This is how all the survivors, two hundred people, left town. Only two families who had returned from Russia remained in the town. The majority of the Rokitno residents went to Israel and they are still among us. A shiver of sanctity went through us as the train whistle was heard. We began our journey west.

[Page 364]

Regards From a Destroyed Home

Henia Gendelman (Warsaw)

Translated from Yiddish by Ala Gamulka

After a long wandering during wartime, I am returning to you, my little town, my little town Rokitno. I hardly recognize you. Your streets are empty, your houses ruined. I don't see any familiar or friendly faces. The houses are burnt and broken. Entire streets are destroyed. Occasionally, one sees a wall with a yellow *mogen david.* It seems to me that the rain and the cold wind tearfully lament the destruction.

It is autumn, 1945. While walking around, my heart lets out a shriek. Why? For what sin? I come to the Tarbut school where our children used to study. It was silent, empty and desolate. Only a hospital is there now. Sick people in gowns are dragging themselves around here and there. Sometimes a nurse in a white uniform runs by.

I am reminded of the happy resounding voices of the children, the ringing laughter and the patter of their feet. Was it a dream or a fantasy? It reminded me of the children's evening program when my oldest son, Ruvinke, graduated from the school in the spring of 1939. The hall was packed with parents, teachers and children. The children were beautiful and all dressed up with their shining faces and sparkling little eyes- black, blue and gray eyes- who don't know about trouble and worries and are full of hope and confidence about the future.

The music is playing and we, the parents, are singing and dancing, "*Shalom Alechem, Shalom Alechem*" (Peace to you). We are singing; the children are clapping their hands. It is festive and cheerful and one's heart grows with pleasure. The teacher comes out with a speech. The parents make their speeches. Although the parents went home late, the children were in the street till dawn, strolling and singing, fantasizing about a rich and beautiful future for all.

How could we possibly imagine what kind of black cloud was moving from the west over our heads? The tragic end that befell us all is well known to us. The children were annihilated. My son fell on the battlefield and only a few others saved themselves. I am sitting on the grass near what used to be the school and I grieve.

> *How can I not cry and grieve?*
> *How should I not sit on the ground?*
> *Since they slaughtered and killed our children*
> *And stuffed them into pits and burnt them.*

Those Were The Days...

[Page 366]

In The Destroyed Town

Issachar Trossman (Ramat Gan)

Translated by Ala Gamulka

At the beginning of 1944, I returned to Rokitno with my family. Prior to our return, my father went to reconnoiter and he announced to us the good news we had hoped for - our town was liberated. The way back was very dangerous. The *Banderovtzis* waited for us at every step. They terrorized the area and we battled with them.

We came back on a Sunday morning. The sun was shining on the carpet of snow. It was a beautiful day. For a moment, I pretended that the years I suffered in the forest were only a nightmare and that surely, my school friends would greet me noisily. Unfortunately, to my great sorrow, they did not come out to greet me. It was the local residents who wore smiles of deceit and hypocrisy. They put on a friendly face, but inside they were sorry that I had remained alive.

It was difficult to recognize the town. The Germans turned the large Polish school into a fortress. They surrounded it with a sand hill 3 meters high and with barbed wire. All the houses that blocked a direct view of the forest had been taken down. This is how many houses disappeared.

The synagogues became horse stables. When you passed by the houses that had been homes to many Jews, it was as if they were quietly sobbing. My heart broke when I saw a local wearing a coat or a suit that had belonged to a Jew. He murdered and inherited. The cemetery was desolate and abandoned. Many gravestones had been pulled down and many were being used for mundane purposes - as millstones for grinding flour.

Soon the remnants of the town had gathered - more than two hundred souls. The horrors of the Holocaust united them into one family. The mourning survivors came out of the forest, from bunkers, hiding places in friendly non-Jewish homes and from daring partisan activities. The center of public life was a synagogue that was located in one of the houses. It served a different, special and sad purpose. It mainly was used as a place to remember those who died, to say *Kaddish* and to pray the *Yizkor* service.

Our first activity was to bury the Jews who had been buried outside the town. We searched for every grave and brought all the bodies to a mass grave which we had dug in the cemetery in Rokitno. We even placed there the torn Torah scrolls, which we found on the streets and in the houses. We gave them a proper burial in our destroyed town.

The *Banderovtzis* lay in ambush for us and planned to finish what they had not accomplished during the Nazi occupation. The authorities instituted severe security regulations including night curfew. In spite of the danger, we searched for collaborators who had spilled Jewish blood. We went to many dangerous locations and when we caught them, we turned them over to the authorities.

In one of the battles with the *Banderovtzis*, my father died near the village of Decht. I went out with a group of soldiers to bring his body back to a proper Jewish burial. His funeral was held under armed guard because the *Banderovtzis* were everywhere. Toddy Linn dug the grave and put up a stone. His work was done under difficult circumstances. *"With one of his hands he did the work, and with the other held the weapon" (Nehemia, 4, 17).*

When I got up from *Shiva* for my father, I decided to avenge him. There was a fellow in Rokitno by the name of Leon Yarchun, a relative of Schwartzblat. He was friendly with the Poles who were also involved with fighting the *Banderovtzis*. Seven of us took two automatic rifles and we set out towards Decht. At the entrance to the village, the locals informed the *Banderovtzis* that Yechiel Trossman's son came to avenge his father's death. We were immediately surrounded by the *Banderovtzis* at a distance of 200-300 metres.

We saw that we were in great trouble and not wanting to fall into their hands, we decided to retreat slowly towards the forest. One of the *Banderovtzi* horsemen chased us. We shot towards him and we injured his horse. He went down and hid among the trees. We used the opportunity to go deeper into the forest.

Meanwhile, a group of Soviet soldiers arrived and extricated our seven Poles who had been taken by the *Banderovtzis*. The latter returned to town and spread the rumor that Yarchun and I had been taken by them. The Jews were worried for us and greeted us with cries, kisses and hugs when we returned.

Each one of the survivors did his own reckoning. We knew that, without a doubt, this was not our place and we went as a group to Poland. From there, we went to Bytom. Toddy Linn was one of the first organizers of *Hashomer Hatzair* there. In the camps in Germany and Poland, we were among the first to organize orphanages, youth camps and assistance to the needy. The survivors of Rokitno, who were loyal to Zionism and to Hebrew - most of them went to Israel.

[Page 368]

The Fortunes of a Jewish Orphan after the Liberation

Yakov Israeli (Rosenstein) (Canada)

Translated by Ala Gamulka

The liberation of Rokitno and its surroundings did not solve the problems of the survivors. The most serious problem was that of the forsaken orphans who were left without parents or any other family. The older remnants, although they were like broken pottery, living skeletons, somehow rehabilitated themselves, married and temporarily rebuilt their lives in Rokitno. This did not happen to the young Jewish orphans. They remained alone and abandoned and had no one to turn to for help. Not much had changed for them since the frightful times when they hid in attics and underground in order to save themselves. They were all alone in the liberated town.

When Rokitno was liberated, I was 15 years old, but I looked like a ten year old. I felt that I was an old man nearing the end of his life. I saw myself as a man of 100 years, where 90 years were a long nightmare full of fear and trepidation. I stood near our house (it had been taken over by Polish refugees and their families). The broken windows, shattered glass and peeling walls made it look like a mourner. It too, seemed like a miserable orphan complaining about the atrocities. I went up to the attic and I spent a long time there. I looked for traces and mementos of my mother and my two dear sisters. The only item I found was a pair of dusty and worn shoes. I held them to my heart and I sobbed. My tears reminded me of my happy childhood, too short, before the Holocaust. We used to play in the yard and the laughter of happy children still echoed in my ears. In that attic my soul was tormented with a terrible question: Why? For what sin? This question still pierces my mind to this day, as it must do to other survivors.

Hunger woke me from my sad thoughts and I slowly made my way down, tired and drained, in order to satisfy my hunger. My body did not participate in the sad thoughts that tortured my soul. Like an alarm clock, it woke me up and brought me back to continue on, in spite of everything.

My only hope was that my father had been drafted by the Red Army and that he would come back to me. I would then have someone to lean on, someone who would let me cry. I would not be so alone. This hope encouraged me and instilled in me belief in the future, in better times to come.

How did the survivors in liberated Rokitno look to me? Life was like a torn cloak, badly mended. It could disintegrate at any moment. The Germans continued to bomb at night. The nights were awful. Death lurked at every turn and every step. The enemy wanted to destroy army buildings and especially the railway, which was used to transport thousands of troops to the front. The small Jewish nucleus lived in fear of the Ukrainian killers who roamed the forests well armed. They slaughtered Poles, Jews and Soviet soldiers whenever they could.

The main park in Rokitno became a cemetery for the soldiers of the Red Army who were killed almost daily by the Ukrainian killers. We had no hope for a normal life in Rokitno. Everyone waited for the war to end so they could run wherever they could.

The thought of escaping this hell occurred to me also. I went to the authorities and I asked to be sent to a children's home where I could live until war's end and where I could pursue my studies. They promised to fulfill my request as soon as possible.

However, the matter dragged on for several weeks. In the meantime, I received letters from my father telling me he had been transferred to Archangelsk to do hard labor and that he was constantly hungry. I could not help him much, but I did sell some belongings and I sent him some money so he could feed himself. His letters were like arrows in my heart because they were very sad and depressing. My father was very ill, yet he still had to do forced labor. My heart was full of sadness. My father, who had suffered so much, was now forced to do this work. There was no one to help him or to save him.

Eventually, I and a few other children were sent to an orphanage in Kiev. I arrived by train and I saw a horrifying town. It was totally destroyed and defeated. We arrived at the home and were received by the lady director.

The place did not appeal to me at all. I saw children torn, dirty and wild like animals. It turned out to be a reform school for young offenders. The children in my group decided to return to Rokitno. One of them still had a mother in Rokitno while others had some distant relatives. For me there was nowhere to return. I began walking the streets of Kiev without knowing where I would find help.

Suddenly, a woman approached me and stared at me. “Aren't you a grandson of Gedalke Feldleit from Dombrovitz?” she asked me. The woman was from

Dombrovitz, my mother's village, and she knew my family. After she heard my pitiful story she took me home, gave me food and encouraged me not to worry.

This wonderful woman quickly introduced me to the writer David Hofstein. He asked me several questions and after he heard my sad tale took me to his home. The Hofsteins were very nice people and I felt very happy with them.

I continued to receive letters from my father. He complained that his illness was worsening. With Hofstein's blessing, I wrote a letter to the President of the Soviet Union, Kalinin, and asked him to liberate my father from army service. What was the purpose of keeping an ill man? I discovered that I was too innocent, since Kalinin's reply read: "We cannot free anyone from serving as long as the war is still on and the fascist criminals have not been defeated". Soon after I received that reply, my father died from his illness and hard work in a Soviet concentration camp. He was only 39 when he died.

The shock that befell me when I heard the bitter news of my father's death created in me a hatred of everything around me. I surrounded myself with a wall of silence. The silence was very painful for Mr. Hofstein. I informed him that I had decided to make *aliyah* and he was very hurt.

I returned to Rokitno and I obtained documents which enabled me to leave Poland.

Before I left, I returned to Kiev to say good-bye to my wonderful friends - the family of the writer Hofstein.

[Page 370]

Over a Glass of Tea with Nikita Khrushchev

Baruch Shehori (Schwartzblat) (Haifa)

Translated by Ala Gamulka

Ten days had passed since we, the partisans, had entered Rokitno. That night we met with the advance forces of the Russian army. That evening, on January 10, 1944, I met with General Poliakov, the commander of the 113th division. He appointed me representative of the Russian government to the Rokitno area, commissar of our partisan unit as local secretary of the party. On the following morning I issued the first order calling on the population to organize, to return any arms in their possession, to stop any plunder and robbery, etc.

I had a lot of work and a great deal of responsibility in the first days after liberation. The first survivors came from the forests and they found shelter either in their own homes or in homes of friends. I took Betzalel Kek to be my assistant and he was in charge of providing food to our soldiers on a regular basis. He also took care of fodder for the cavalry horses. I gathered all the workers of the glass factory, mostly all Poles and I spoke to them about the urgent need to rebuild the burned down factory. They volunteered to clean up the area from all the ruins and to begin by reconstructing the big oven in the factory. In the meantime I discovered that there was one whole generator left in the saw-mill. We energetically began to transfer it to the glass factory to be able to restore the only electrical power station in town.

At noon on that 10th of January, a policeman informed me that a certain general wanted to see me. I was in the factory yard and I did not rush back to my office. It was located in Turok's house on the road to Messiviche. When I entered my office, I was shocked to see Nikita Khrushchev standing in front of me. I recognized him from the pictures that hung in the school when I was still a teacher and a principal.

“Is that really you, you who made me wait so long?” he asked.

I became scared and I asked for his forgiveness, saying that I did not know that such an important guest was with us. I asked him to come inside the room, but he said, with a smile: “I do not have much time now. I am going to the front and I will see you on the way back”. We decided to meet at 9:00 in the evening in my house.

I was prepared to greet my guest at the appointed hour. Policemen stood outside waiting to receive him and to direct him to my house. A festive meal was prepared. The house was lit with several large lanterns. Exactly at nine o'clock, the guests began to appear in a convoy of about ten shiny cars. Nikita Khrushchev led wearing a general's uniform, a long fur coat and a Persian lamb hat. He looked fresh and happy. He came in with his friend Major Kozlov, followed by about 20 high-ranking officers.

I immediately invited him in to the large room and everyone sat around the tables. I addressed him as one would address a general, but he asked me to call him simply Nikita Sergeyevich.

At first he wanted to know the story of my life, as is the norm in Russia. I told him I was a Jew, that I had been a teacher and a principal, how I had spent time in the forest as a partisan, how we had met the Red Army and how we had reached this point in time.

He was quite interested in the economic situation of the area. What there had been and what was left after the destruction and how I intended to continue. He wanted to know what I planned to do in my capacity as governor of the area.

I presented to him all my plans. First, we had to restore the electrical station and the glass factory. This was essential in wartime as well as being a main source of income for the local residents. “What is the status of the restoration now? What do you have and what do you still need?” he asked.

I explained to him that the factory yard was cleared of debris and that we were now dealing with the restoration of the big oven. We hoped that if everything went as planned we would rekindle the oven in a month and two weeks later we could produce glass.

He took out a pocket calendar, looked at it and said: “I want to shake your hand on your promise that on the 20th of February I will receive a telegram from you informing me that the factory had begun production.”

I solemnly promised him that I would try my hardest to fulfill this promise. He shook my hand warmly.

“If you need any help in fulfilling your task come to see me in Kiev. I will help you.” He took out of his pocket a small calling card and gave it to me. I thanked him and invited everyone to dinner. However, when Khrushchev replied that they had just eaten on the road and would only have tea, it was served quickly.

While we were drinking I tried to talk him into sleeping over. The *Bulbovtzis* and *Banderovtzis* were still roaming the forests and there was danger in traveling at night.

He laughed and said: “Have no fear. I have to be at work in my office in the morning.” (He was then secretary of the party in the Ukraine and a member of the Central Committee).

Soon, when the drinking was finished, one of the drivers brought in a large basket full of excellent apples and placed it on the table.

"This is for you, Boris Borisovich!" he said with a smile and rose to say good-bye. We parted amicably and we accompanied them to the cars.

Four days passed. Within two weeks the technical divisions of the railroad accomplished a great deal. They repaired the tracks, all the bridges and we resumed contact with the east.

Four days later the chief engineer and two other engineers from the glass factory management appeared in my office. I treated them to dinner.

The manager told me that Khrushchev had informed him that there was a Jewish partisan in Rokitno, Boris Borisovich, who was restoring the factory there without any facilities. It was essential to help him immediately with guidance and with materials. That was why they came to see me.

They really helped a lot. In the meantime, the party secretary, who was there before the Nazis, resumed his duties. In my innocence I told him about Khrushchev's visit here. He became very excited and started to visit the factory daily, to encourage the workers, to make speeches and to conduct propaganda. He kept it up to the promised deadline. On February 20, 1944 he sent a telegram to Khrushchev saying the factory was in production. He signed: Nebobo, Regional Secretary of the Party.

[Page 372]

With Our Stick and Our Backpack

Yosef Segal (Neve Oz)

Translated by Ala Gamulka

In 1946 there were pogroms in Kielce. Tens of survivors of the Nazi holocaust were cruelly murdered. The pogroms were organized by Polish murderers who could not accept the fact that some Jews had survived. They wanted to finish the extermination project that the Nazis had not completely terminated.

The Jews began to escape westward, in dismay, from the bloody land and in attempt to reach Eretz Israel. Emissaries from Israel were active then in Poland and other European countries where convoys of survivors traveled. They organized the illegal immigration.

Survivors from all of Europe were centered in Germany, Italy and Austria. Many were Polish Jews and among them were residents of our town and its vicinity.

A Reunion of Some of the Survivors from Rokitno in Leipheim (Germany), 1946

I joined the Dror *kibbutz*, which was part of the *Kibbutz Hameuhad* (United Kibbutz) organized in the town of Bistrezhitze in Lower Silesia. The *kibbutz* had more than fifty members who had returned from the Soviet Union after the Holocaust. We were mostly singles of various ages, but some of us were young married couples. Some residents of Rokitno were members of this *kibbutz*, among them the brothers Eliahu and Itzhak Zaks and their families.

We left Poland two weeks before *Rosh Hashana* 1946 and traveled through Czechia, Slovakia and Austria. We traveled a little by train, but mostly we went on foot. We rested for two days at the famous Rothschild Hospital in Vienna. Thousands of Jews passed through there. Austria at the time was divided into three areas conquered by the Allied forces. It was extremely difficult to go from one sector to the other.

From Vienna we reached Camp Bindermichel near Linz in Austria. The camp was built by Dutch Jews who were exiled there by the Nazis. They had done forced labor in constructing fancy houses for the Nazi murderer Goering, *may his name be erased*. When the construction was finished they were all killed and buried near the camp. I met there the family of Leibl Zaks from Rokitno on its way to Israel.

After a short rest we moved to Camp Saalfalden in the Austrian Alps, near the Italian border. Here there was a concentration of convoys, which crossed the border illegally into Italy. There I met another resident of Rokitno – Israel Hirsh Zaks, the carpenter.

A convoy of 800 people was organized in the camp to cross the Alps on foot. Those going had to undergo a serious physical examination to see if they were medically sound to march through the high Alps. They were only permitted to take a small shoulder bag with them.

On a rainy fall night, in absolute quiet, we started on our way through the Alps near us. The members of the *Bricha* urged us to move as fast as possible before daybreak so we would not be seen by the locals.

We ran up the high mountains covered in snow. We went as far as we could and we even threw off the shoulder bags to make the walking easier. Some did not have the energy and stayed back. Before dawn we arrived, tired and worn out, at a fenced building called *Givat Aliyah.* After a march of 16 kilometers and a day's rest we continued at night. This time we traveled with army vehicles to the border. At 1:30 AM, we were smuggled across the Austria-Italy border through the famous Brenner Pass. We spent the rest of the night under the stars in Italy. We traveled a whole day from a small train station. In the evening we reached Milan and we settled on the Via Unioni in the center of town. It was a place that served as a transfer point for many Jewish survivors who arrived illegally from other parts of Europe. The house and the yard teemed with Jews. I met there a resident of our town, the partisan Asher Binder. He was active in smuggling Jews to Italy from other European countries.

After a few days' rest we moved to a suburb of Milan to a former officers' school called Scuola Kadorno. In the meantime we visited the beautiful city of Milan and we marveled at the buildings built in a magnificent architectural style. The Italians were extremely hospitable at all times. We were not used to such niceties and we really appreciated them. Since this was a temporary location only, we left Milan and went to a camp near the village of Rivoli near Turin. This camp had a high concentration of pioneers. There were *kibbutzim* from all political streams. The commander of the camp was an officer from the Jewish Brigade, from Eretz Israel, named Aryeh Avissar. He was a well-educated young man who was esteemed by everyone. Every morning we raised our national flag in the camp. On Friday nights we had Shabbat celebrations at tables set in the dining room. The commander read to us from the weekly *parasha* and sang songs from Eretz Israel, accompanied by his accordion. On the first night of *Hanukah* the whole camp paraded with torches throughout the streets of the village of Rivoli. The Italians received us with applause and shouts. We spent the whole winter of 1946-47 in this camp. We spent most of our time studying. In spring of 1947, on the second night of *Pessach*, early in the morning, in complete silence, we boarded the immigrant ship Moila Bugliska that was anchored in one of the Mediterranean ports.

The ship was built 70 years earlier for the purpose of transporting coal within Europe. It was bought by the *Haganah* and quickly became an immigrant ship used for bringing survivors to their homeland. It was not really intended to transport human beings. The ship set sail under the pretense of a South American flag bringing freight to Turkey. The crowding was unimaginable. There were 600 people without any sanitary facilities. We received a ration of half a liter per person of drinking water. In daytime we stayed on deck and at night we went down into the hull of the boat to sleep. It was very stuffy. The captain, a veteran, highly experienced seaman, was an Italian, as were the rest of the crew.

In the middle of the Aegean Sea, near the Greek Islands, we stopped for one day. At night 200 more people came on board. These were immigrants from another ship that had to return for another purpose. This ship took with it some of the Italian crew members who refused to continue on this voyage. They were replaced by members of the *Haganah* who were the actual commanders.

When the ship approached the shores of Palestine, the *Haganah* members informed us that if the British discovered us we would have to fight back and not give in. The opposition was only symbolic because we knew they would overcome us. British planes discovered us. They were followed by two destroyers. The British wanted at first to board the ship and warned us not to oppose them. We greeted them holding iron springs from our mattresses and cans and we hit them. Finally, the British boarded and a face-to-face battle ensued. At the end of the battle the British took over the ship. Seventeen of our people were injured, I among them. (I had a head injury.) As a result of the battle, the ship was completely destroyed. It was towed listing sideways to Haifa. Even here we refused to get off the ship. However, the British removed us with force after we sang *Hatikvah.* We then found out that the name of our ship was *Sh'ar Yishuv* (Remnant of the Nation).

In the port of Haifa we were taken to the exile ship “Isun Veigur” and we arrived at night at a detention camp in Cyprus. At the end of April 1947 we were taken to a new camp, No. 67. It was fenced with barbed wire and surrounded by watchtowers. British soldiers guarded us day and night.

Here I met a resident of our town, Mrs. Polya Lifshitz-Rotman, who was an emissary of the Jewish Agency in the detention camp in Cyprus. In the camp were also, among others, Raizel Shteinman and her husband Pinhas Binder, Avraham Eisenberg, the brothers Shmuel and Natan Levin and Moishele Trossman, Yechiel Trossman's son. He fooled the British and escaped from the camp with the help of his brother Issachar. The trip in our ship from Italian shores to Eretz Israel took 18 days. I stayed in the camp in Cyprus for 7 months. My wanderings, which began in the summer of 1946, terminated at the end of 1947. All through the traveling I met survivors from Rokitno who, like me, intended to reach the Eretz Israel. In early 1948, I reached Eretz Israel as a free Jew.

[Page 376]

Portions of Letters

Nyusia Kokel, *z"l*

Translated by Ala Gamulka

Rokitno, 31.7.44

My dear sisters and Shaike,

My letter will, most likely, sadden you because I describe in it our bitter and terrible fate. We suffered for many months under the cruel Nazi beasts. In the end we lost all our unforgettable dearly beloved – father, mother and sister. What can we do? Crying will not help us. We are not the only ones! This calamity touched thousands of Jews. We must continue our life of loneliness and mourning and worry about our subsistence. We must avenge the blood of our dear ones, which was spilled like water.

My dears! I cannot describe what happened to me and how I was saved. It was a miracle. We lived in the ghetto. We wore a yellow patch on our back. We worked and we were continuously abused. In the end we were gathered in the market square and shot. I managed to escape from the killing field to the forest. I lived there for 18 months. Life in the forest was a series of fear and atrocity. We walked about hungry, barefoot, naked and chased like animals. We were not allowed to live. We were denounced and we were pursued. Only a few managed to hide and stay alive.

After I returned to Rokitno, the town of my birth, it was often difficult to believe everything was in ruins and would never be revived. Here and there, bare walls stood nearly falling as silent witnesses for life that was snuffed out. Now, there is nothing here for me. I am completely alone, without any friends or relatives. I hope I will meet you again and then, I hope my mood will improve.

I receive letters from Sarah'le in which she writes that she is happy and this encourages me very much. There is no one left alive of the Shachnovski family. They are all dead. Even our dear grandfather and grandmother were exterminated. We, who remained alive, have no choice but to take heart and to stand up, if not for ourselves, for our own happiness, then to avenge the spilling of the blood of our beloved ones.

Rokitno, 7.12.44

Sarah'le went to Lvov. She is trying to continue her studies. We, the orphans, have nothing left but education. It is our lifesaver, the basis of our lives. When Sarah'le returns, we will decide if we will stay in Rokitno or go to Lvov.

I have already written to you about my suffering under the Nazis. However, I cannot even describe what I am going through now. Perhaps when I will be with Sarah'le, life will improve.

Lvov, 16.4.45

After months of wandering I am here with Sarah'le. My happiness is boundless. We live together and we seem to manage. Sarah'le is studying at the medical school. I am working for now because there is no opportunity to study. We live like students, but never mind! As soon as Sarah'le finishes her exams, I will take time off from work and we will go together to visit relatives. We can then rest a little.

Lvov, 10.7.45

The weather is awful. My heart is in pain. There is no hope. I went to look for work, but there is none. The situation is desperate. The room I live in is large and cold. I run the household. I read a little and I study. It is six months since I have met anyone. There is no one to meet. I envy those who are studying. I would like to learn to play the piano, but I have no way of doing it. I must find employment. Life without work is useless.

Sarah'le's birthday is coming up. I have no money to buy her a gift. It hurts me very much. I will prepare supper, read a little and go to sleep. Another boring and sad day has passed.

Everyone has left Rokitno. I have no contact and no news of it. It is not good. G-d has averted his face from us because of our sins and he has abandoned us. There is no purpose to my wandering. My eyes are directed there, to the land of Eternal Spring! As of now I have no hope of reaching you. It is very sad.

[Page 378]

A Letter Sent From Russia to My Uncle Yankel and My Aunt Feigl

Nyuniek Gendelman

Translated from Yiddish by Ala Gamulka

I have not written to you all this time because I have not had any news from home. I waited impatiently for 3 years for a letter from Rokitno. For the last 3 years I did not sleep, spending day and night wondering about my home since I did not know if our dear ones had been evacuated or not. Did they manage to escape in time because the Germans were very close to Rokitno.

Finally, yesterday, the terrible and shocking news came from my brother-in-law's brother, Baruch Schwartzblat. My dear parents, my dear sister Maniale and my dear brother-in-law Mendl Schwartzblat, their daughter Malkale and other relatives, the entire Schwartzblat family and other friends were slaughtered by the murderous Germans.

Bitter tears are flowing as I write this letter. It is a cry of despair to the heavens. It is difficult to believe that my dear father wandered aimlessly in the forest for seven weeks. Can you imagine his suffering? Later he was caught, tortured by the killers and then he was killed in the village of Berezov. At the same time, the others were executed in Sarny, a nearby town, on that mournful Thursday, August 27, 1942. Around 600 Jews from Rokitno were brought there.

In Sarny, 9000 Jews from the area were gathered and within three hours all were shot, thrown into ditches and covered with earth. My dear mother, my dear sister Maniale and her child and the rest of the family as well as hundreds of Jews from Rokitno were brought to Sarny. This happened on the 19th day of *Elul* (1942).

Many Jews were killed in the synagogue. This was the destiny of our family. My brother-in-law managed to live another six weeks in the forest. They lived like animals eating grass and stolen potatoes. One Saturday morning their lean-to was surrounded by well-informed Germans who released a barrage of bullets.

Of the eleven people who were hiding in the lean-to, the only ones to remain alive were my brother-in-law's brother and Betzalel Kek, Michel Kek's son.

There are two graves in the forest. In one lies our dear brother-in-law Mendl and in the other one - a man called Katzenelson from Rokitno and Moshe Lifshitz's son, Leibl.

How did my brother-in-law's brother and the second person remain alive? He himself does not know how. They were left forlorn, shoeless, hungry, dirty and covered in lice in the forest among many menacing peasants.

The peasants caught Jews and took them to Rokitno. For each one they would receive a kilo of salt from the Germans. The peasants would remove clothes and shoes from those caught. The Jews begged them not to kill them with a hatchet. It is only thanks to the partisans with whom the two made contact that they remained alive. It is from my brother-in-law's brother that I now know the fate of our dear ones.

It is difficult to believe that our dear ones have departed forever to their heavenly repose. We are left all alone - orphans. My heart is hardened with sorrow. The wild Germans took their revenge on those dearest in the world to me.

Rokitno is sad and in mourning - writes my brother-in-law's brother. More than half of the town is ruined. A great many of the Jewish homes were destroyed together with their owners. 83 Jews emerged from the forests. No more remained of the 1631 Jews. There are only a handful of helpless, poor, sick and broken souls.

It is difficult to overcome the tragedy. Write to all the relatives about it. Let the world know about the horrors and the cruelty of the killers. Let the world cry out about the millions of innocent victims and let those alive take revenge for the innocent spilled blood and for the murders and robberies. Respond to your one and only relative who remained alive.

My dear ones, we stand with our heads bowed over this sad yet true event. This is what happened. It cannot be denied. You did not live through the horror and you did not see the mass slaughter. Please honor with us the memory of my parents, my sister, my brother-in-law and our beloved child Malkale as well as the rest of our friends.

More than 1200 Jews from Rokitno, 18,000 from Rovno, 71,000 from Lublin, 16,000 from Kovel, and thousands more Jews were killed as martyrs.

My tragedy is already known. I am now an orphan. The deaths of my dear sainted family awaken in me, as they should in you, a desire for revenge on the Germans. My blood is boiling and will not subside until the name of the Germans will be eradicated from this earth. Let our terrible curses fall on them for eternity.

Your only relative,

Nyuniek Gendelman

(Printed in “The Forward”, America, 26 April 1944)

[Page 381]

Two Stones

Hannah Segal (Neve Oz)

Translated by Ala Gamulka

The sea is blue and calm
The waves innocently swerve – wave after wave
On the bottom, on its golden bed under the water
Two stones rest.
One is hard and red as blood
The other is soft and blue.
Blood is red and the grave is hard
Happiness is blue and peace is soft.

The sea is stormy and tossing
The stones are flung from their resting place
They wander far from the sea.
Peace and happiness are carried
They are thrown in a forsaken corner
The second stone falls into an empty space
And blood and death now run the world.

Children sob bitterly
Fathers are taken away from their sons
Mothers are mourning their offspring
Blood rules the world
Screaming is heard on the other side of the water.

Human beings threw
The bloody stone, people to people
The world stormed and tossed
There was a war in the world
There is no pity and no fear of G-d.

The blue stone is far in a corner
Blood is streaming and death is near
Casualties fall...
This is how the world storms and tosses, will it be quiet?

Then the blue stone will fall
To the bloodthirsty world.

The world is quietly standing still
The hard stone
Is forgotten for now...
On the ruins of war
A golden sun is shining
With the sadness a smile is seen
There is a light in the eyes.

By a war-blackened stone
Children play peacefully
The world is quiet and resting
The soft stone is now in charge
Satisfaction and good rule the world.

The sea is calm again
The waves are clean and playful
Mothers are again happily hugging their children
Children are laughing with joy.

[Page 383]

We Will Remember

Haim Shteinman (Tel Aviv)

Translated from Yiddish by Ala Gamulka

Our Jewish Rokitno. You were, for many years, the transit point for Jews longing for their homeland and on their way to Eretz Israel. We will not forget you.

We, who spent our lives in you and were fortunate enough to reach Eretz Israel – we remember you.

We remember your twisted streets and lanes where we stepped barefoot as children on your mud and your cobblestones.

We remember your bare little houses which were very close to one another as if to express the love of Israel, which was rooted inside them.

We remember your Jews adorned with beard and earlocks, so as not to lose even one hair off the appearance of a Jew. They wore their Jewishness like a crown – the crown of the People of Israel.

We remember you dear and wonderful Jews, you who did not separate yourselves from the generations who received the Torah at Sinai. You who even though you were driven from your home, you took with you your heavenly Torah and your culture. You walked with them as if they were your homeland. Each one of you was a soldier of good will to guard and defend, ready to sacrifice yourselves. It is to their merit that we reached this country.

Jews of Rokitno! You are the true believers and you are surrounded with the love of Israel! We will not forget your houses of worship, the old and the new synagogues, where three times a day you declared: "May our eyes behold your return to Zion in compassion". This is where our souls were shaped and the truth of the Torah was planted in us.

We will not forget the beauty of your Shabbat, High Holidays and other festivals where you demonstrated your freedom to live among other people.

You touched our souls to prepare for the Messiah "*even though he is tarrying, we will wait for him daily*".

Jews of Rokitno! We will not forget your sons and daughters. Redemption is approaching for those who had the faith. This is the faith that was planted in their souls by you. This is the faith to believe in the liberation of the Jewish people without having to search for unorthodox beliefs for Jews and others. They wanted redemption for our people, but, unfortunately, they did not attain it.

We remember your efforts and your straining to build cultural institutions to give us a proper upbringing.

We will not forget your pain, your need, your suffering and your horrendous death.

We, the remnants, will tie our lives together with yours in a free homeland.

Whatever we will achieve will be in partnership with you.

You are partners in redemption, in building and working the land, in sowing and in reaping. You are partners in guarding at night and in our fight for peace.

As long as we will breathe, we will remember you, brothers and sisters, relatives and friends. You were so cruelly exterminated in Rokitno and its surroundings by the Nazi and Ukrainian killers.

We will remember you because you gave us hope and love and we will draw on that source.

We, the remnants, will remember because we were their emissaries to liberate the homeland. They fell on the way.

We will breathe with their last breath.

We will remember them forever.

[Page 385]

Remember

Professor Marek Dvorzhetzky

Translated by Ala Gamulka

Remember the destruction of Israel.
Remember the loss and the rebellion
They will be symbols and lessons for generations to come.

Let this memory forever accompany you – when you walk
And when you go to sleep and when you rise.

You will always remember the brothers who are no longer here
The memory will be part of your flesh, your blood and your bones.

Grind your teeth and remember: when you eat – remember
When you drink – remember: when you hear a song – remember
On a holiday and a festive day – remember!

When you build a house, leave an opening to always keep in mind
- The destruction of the House of Israel.

When you plough a field, put up a pile of stones - a memorial to our brothers
Who were not given a proper Jewish burial.

When you bring your children to the wedding canopy, you will, in your happiness
Remember first those children who can no longer be brought to the wedding canopy.

They will be as one – those alive and those dead, the empty and the remnant,
Those who are gone and are no longer here and those who survived.

Listen, you people of Israel, the voice coming from the deep
Go in silence, quietly.

[Page 386]

IN THEIR BLESSED MEMORY

Partisans and fighters from Rokitno and its vicinity who fell during the war with the Nazis

Translated by Ala Gamulka

YOSEF OLSHANSKY

Son of Yaakov Shmuel, he was born in Karasyk near Sarny. He joined Ploskonosov partisan brigade and excelled as a sapper. He was appointed commander of a sappers unit. In 1943, on the way to bombing a German train, he was ambushed by the Germans and was killed.

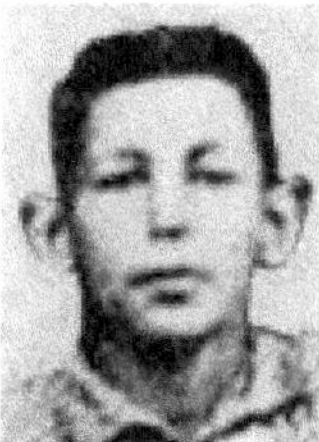

MOSHE BARMAN

Son of Avraham. He fell near Rokitno in 1943, while a member of the Kovpak partisan brigade, in an attack on a German ammunitions train.

MOSHE BARMAN

Son of Yeshayahu, he was born in 1925 in Rokitno. He fell near Olevsk.

AHARON BURD

Son of Michael and Faigel, he was born in 1910. He was conscripted to the Polish Army in 1935. When WWII broke out in 1939, he was again conscripted to the Polish Army and he fought the Nazis. He was captured by the Germans and was imprisoned in Lublin for 3 months. He was transferred from there to a concentration camp where he was exterminated.

MOSHE BURKO

Son of Aharon, he was born in the village of Borovey. He fell while serving in the Polish Army.

YOSEF BINDER

Son of Avraham and Miriam, he was born in 1919. He was conscripted to the Soviet Army in 1940 and was killed near Minsk in 1941.

AVRAHAM (AVREIMELE) BINDER

Son of Zaidel and Shifra, he was born in Rokitno in 1911. He fought with the Polish Army in 1939 and was taken prisoner. He returned from there after the Soviets reached Rokitno. He was conscripted to the Soviet Army in 1941 and was killed in battle near town of Chernigov in August 1941.

YONA GOMULKA

(Husband of Gitel Burko). He served in the Soviet Army. He was taken prisoner by the Germans and was killed.

ZVI HERSHEL GORNSTEIN

Son of Yaakov and Rachel, he was born in 1908. He was conscripted to the Soviet Army in 1941. He was sent to the Ukrainian front where he died in battle.

MOSHE GITELMAN

Son of Yehoshua and Fruma, he was born in Rokitno in 1924. He was conscripted to the Red Army in 1942 and he fell in Bucharest, Rumania, in 1944

YEHUDA GAIYER
He was conscripted by the Soviet Army in 1940 and fell in battle.

MOSHE GLUZMAN
Fell in 1944 while serving in the Polish Army.

YEHUDA GENDELMAN

Son of Michael and Nechama, he was born in the village of Rokitno. He was conscripted to the Soviet Army and he fell in battle.

SHMUEL GENDELMAN

Son of Michael and Nechama, he fell while serving in the Soviet Army.

ZVI GENDELMAN

Son of Yaakov Shimon, he was born in Rokitno in 1912. He fell in battle in the forests of Volyn in 1943.

REUVEN GENDELMAN

Fell in battle while serving in the Soviet Army in 1944.

SHOSHANA GRINSHPAN

Daughter of Levi and Mushka, she was born in Rokitno. She fell near Tomoshgorod while serving as a partisan in the Medvedev brigade.

YISRAEL GREENBERG

Son of Zvi and Lifsha, he was born in Rokitno in 1917. He was conscripted in 1940 and fell while serving in the Soviet Army.

AVRAHAM ZOLOTOV

He was born in Sarny in 1912 and was in the Rokitno ghetto during the Holocaust. He escaped to the forest after the liquidation of the ghetto. After four months of suffering and wandering, he joined the Shitov partisan brigade. He was appointed commander of a patrol unit. He fell in a battle with the Germans on the Bug River.

YONAH ZAKS

Son of Yaakov and Genendel, he was born in the village of Kisorich in 1918. He was conscripted to the Soviet Army in 1940. After serving for several months, he was sent to the front at the Rumanian border. It was reported that he died there at the age of 22.

AVIGDOR HEFETZ

A son of Zvi and Esther (Sterl), he was conscripted to the Soviet Army and fell in battle in Latvia on 3/3/1945.

TUVIA TUROVITZ

The son of Reuven, he was conscripted in May 1941 and fell while serving in the Soviet Army.

YECHIEL TROSSMAN

Son of Haim and Tema, he was born in the village of Dort in 1903. He led a group of Jewish fighters and looked after women and children who had escaped from ghettos in the area. He joined the Ploskonosov partisan brigade. When he returned to Rokitno after liberation he headed a unit of fighters looking to eliminate the *Banderovtzis* gangs. He fell in battle with them near Rokitno in 1944.

PINHAS FUCHSMAN

He was born in 1898 in the village of Zalavie and joined the Medvedev partisan brigade. When the brigade was disbanded he stayed in the forests near Blizhov. He came to Israel after the war and died here in 1959.

YAAKOV PIK

He was conscripted to the Soviet Army in 1941. He fought near Stalingrad where he was injured and remained handicapped. In 1948 he came to Israel and died here in 1967.

SHALOM PINCHUK

Son of Avraham and Chava, he was born in the village of Glinna in 1919. He was conscripted to the Soviet Army in 1940. When the war broke out between Germany and Russia, he was transferred to Kirov. In 1944 he volunteered for the Polish Army in order to take revenge on the Germans. He was sent to an officers' course and upon completion he earned the rank of second lieutenant. Two weeks before the end of the war he fell in the battle of Berlin, on April 19, 1945.

YISRAEL PIK

Son of Yaakov and Mindel, he was born in Rokitno in 1923. He was conscripted to the Soviet Army and he fought in Stalingrad, Crimea, Sevastopol, Lvov and Cracow. He fell in battle on German soil in March 1945.

SHLOMO FRIEDMAN

Son of Natan and Sarah, he was born in the village of Dort. He fell as a soldier in the Soviet Army.

YAAKOV PERLSTEIN

He was born in the village of Borovey in 1914 and he fell while serving in the Soviet Army.

DAVID CHECHIK

Son of Aharon and Chaya-Sara, he served in the Red Army and fell near Warsaw in 1944.

MORDECHAI CHECHIK

Son of Aharon and Chaya-Sara, he fell in the Carpathian Mountains in 1943.

AVRAHAM (ABRASHA) KLORFEIN

Son of Pinchas and Fania, he was born in Rokitno in 1915. He was conscripted to the Soviet Army in 1941 and he served in an engineering division. He was sent to the front and was never seen again.

AHARON KLEIMAN

Son of David and Henya, he was born in Rokitno in 1917. He was conscripted to the Soviet Army in 1940 and served in paratrooper brigade #449. In 1941, he was sent to the Byelorussia front and fell in the battle for Warsaw.

ZVI ROSENSTEIN

He was born in the village of Zalavie and was conscripted to the Soviet Army and fought the Germans. Although he was innocent, he was sentenced by the Soviets to forced labor in Archangelsk. He died there on November 29, 1944 as a result of the hard work, hunger and illness.

YOSEF SHUSTER

Son of David and Batya-Rachel, he was born in the village of Glinna in 1908. (Approximate date). After the Berezov ghetto was liquidated, he escaped to the forests. In winter 1942 he joined the Kovpak partisan brigade and became a fighter. He fell in battle in the Carpathian Mountains.

BENYAMIN SHTEDLER

He was born in Salisetz in 1902 and joined the *Za Rodinu* (For the Motherland) partisan brigade, located near Rovno. He fell in the village of Shatzek in July 1944 when he was ambushed by the Germans as he was returning from patrol.

SHABTAI (SHEPSIL) SHTEINDEL

Son of Meir and Susel, he was born in Rokitno in 1926. He was a member of the Kovpak partisan brigade that fought in the Carpathian Mountains. He fell near the village of Vitkovich.

YITZHAK SHAPIRA
He fell in a partisan activity.

KALMAN SHAPIRA
Son of Moshe-Ber and Raizel, he was born in Snovidovich. He fell while serving in the Soviet Army.

SHLOMO SHAPIRA

The son of Moshe Haim, he was born in Salisetz in 1897. A veteran settler of Rokitno, he was a member of the Fyodorov partisan brigade. He showed great courage. He went out every night to destroy the German infrastructure. He blew up bridges and railroad tracks. After the war he came to Israel where he died in 1957.

(Page 393)

YIZKOR

MAY THE SACRED AND PURE IMAGES OF OUR DEARLY BELOVED BE ETCHED IN OUR HEARTS AND BE ATTACHED TO THE SOULS OF ALL THE MARTYRS OF ISRAEL WHO WERE MURDERED DURING THE HOLOCAUST AND MAY THEIR NAMES ILLUMINATE FOR US THE ROAD TO COMPLETE REDEMPTION.

(Page 395)

Kaddish

May the sacred memory of our mothers and fathers, our brothers and sisters, our sons and daughters, our descendants and relatives, grow exalted and be sanctified. They were murdered and slaughtered, smothered and hung, frozen and starved to death, in the forests, the pits and ditches, but they were not eulogized, their bodies not collected and not given a proper Jewish burial.

May the memory of our children and infants, pure as angels and the heavens, grow exalted and be sanctified. May their cries for help and their groans be in our ears day and night because their blood was spilled while tortured beyond human comprehension. May their name be blessed forever and ever. Our eyes are full of tears because the gates of compassion and acceptance were closed to them when the cruelty surrounded them.

We will cry for their misfortune because it is etched in our hearts. They were our pride and joy. Our tears will accompany their image. Our heart will be in the killing square, in the graves of our brethren, because this is where everything dear to us remained.

In your lifetime and in your days – your life will be attached to the living and you will follow your destiny to the end of days.

He will have mercy and He will give us strength to carry the burden of the Holocaust, our terrible fate, which is incomparable.

(Page 396)

REMEMBER

(Names of Our *Kedoshim* and Their Pictures)

In blessed memory of my beloved Uncle, David Schreiber, a pillar of strength and faith
who was always there when needed, and his son Mark Hal Schreiber, cut down too young.

Haim Sidor

A	B	C	D	E	F	G	H	I	J	K	L	M
N	O	P	Q	R	S	T	U	V	W	X	Y	Z

NOTES:

- CODE: is the page number of the entry and R/L is the side of the page the entry is found on (right or left).
- FAMILY NAME - FIRST NAME - as listed
- MAIDEN NAME - If listed - also sometimes used for a man's nickname
- SPOUSE - as listed
- FAMILY CODE - cc = children, w = wife, daught = daughter, otherwise self explanatory
- FATHER - father's name where given M- mother's name where father's name not given - left blank where no information is given
- ORDER NUMBER - the order that the name appears in the actual list
- **PICTURE - page number of the Original Yizkor Book (note that this is NOT the page number in the upper corners of the pages)** where picture appears. IF blank, there was no picture.

* indicates an entry which does not appear in the original book but which was collected later

** Another addition: Dvosia Schmolko Katz, her sons Aaron, Gedalie and Ben Zion Katz

Code	Family name	First name	Maiden Name	Spouse	Family code	Father	Order #	Picture
396R	Adler	Natan David		Rivka			1	
396R	Adler	Rivka		Natan David			2	
396R	Adler	Rafael		Zlata			3	
396R	Adler	Zlata		Rafael			4	
396R	Adler	Yaakov			son	Rafael	5	
409R	Arender	Moshe		Gisia			720	
409R	Arender	Gisia	Grinshpan	Moshe			721	
396R	Avramel	(Zagotovchik)			w & 4cc		23	

Code	Family name	First name	Maiden Name	Spouse	Family code	Father	Order #	Picture
397R	Babchuk	Chanan		Golda			56	
397R	Babchuk	Golda		Chanan			57	
397R	Babchuk	Leah			daught	Chanan	58	
397R	Babs	Yeshayahu		Esther	& cc		54	
397R	Babs	Esther		Yeshayah u			55	
397L	Baigel	Shmuel		Aidel	& 2cc		92	
397L	Baigel	Aidel	Friedman	Shmuel			93	
397L	Baizman	Haim		Yahah	& cc		94	
397L	Baizman	Yahah		Haim			95	
398R	Balgola	Benzion		Chesia			112	
398R	Balgola	Chesia		Benzion			113	
400R	Baratz	(Dr) Sarah					226	
399L	Barman	Avraham		Maniya			203	
399L	Barman	Maniya	Spivak	Avraham			204	
399L	Barman	Moshe			son	Avraham	205	448
399L	Barman	Aharon			son	Avraham	206	
399L	Barman	Aharon		Pesia			207	
399L	Barman	Pesia		Aharon			208	
399L	Barman	Yeshayahu					209	
399L	Barman	Moshe			son	Yeshaya-hu	210	
399L	Barman	Mordecai		Rachel			211	
399L	Barman	Rachel		Mordecai			212	
399L	Barman	Zalman			son	Mordecai	213	
399L	Barman	Yisrael			son	Mordecai	214	
399L	Barman	Moshe Leib			son	Mordecai	215	
400R	Barman	Sima					216	
400R	Barman	Arie		Chana Rivka			217	
400R	Barman	Chana Rivka		Arie			218	

Code	Family name	First name	Maiden Name	Spouse	Family code	Father	Order #	Picture
400R	Barman	Moshe			son	Arie	219	
400R	Barman	Haim			son	Arie	220	
400R	Barman	Feivish			son	Arie	221	
400R	Barman	Sheindel			daught	Arie	222	
400R	Barman	Meir		Miriam			223	
400R	Barman	Miriam		Meir			224	
400R	Barman	Yosef			& 2cc	Meir	225	
399R	Bastus	Chasel					166	
399R	Bastus	Mendel		Hinda Leah			167	
399R	Bastus	Hinda Leah		Mendel			168	
399R	Batcherman	Wolf		Raizel			169	
399R	Batcherman	Raizel		Wolf			170	
399R	Batcherman	Max			son	Wolf	171	
399R	Batcherman	Hershel			son	Wolf	172	
396L	Baum	David					34	421
396L	Baum	Mordecai Zvi	(Hirsh)	Rivka			35	421
396L	Baum	Rivka	Horman	Mordecai Zvi			36	421
396L	Baum	Moshe			son	Mordecai Zvi	37	421
396L	Baum	Alexander			son	Mordecai Zvi	38	
396L	Baum	Yisrael		Sarah			39	421
396L	Baum	Sarah	Gilstron	Yisrael			40	421
396L	Baum	Hannah			daught	Yisrael	41	421
396L	Baum	Rachel			daught	Yisrael	42	
396L	Baum	Yosef Haim		Devora Rachel			43	
396L	Baum	Devora Rachel		Yosef Haim			44	
396L	Baum	Rasel			daught	Yosef Haim	45	
396L	Baum	Bela			daught	Yosef Haim	46	
396L	Baum	Yehoshua		Chesia			47	

Code	Family name	First name	Maiden Name	Spouse	Family code	Father	Order #	Picture
396L	Baum	Chesia		Yehoshua			48	
396L	Baum	Yisrael			son	Yehoshua	49	
397R	Baum	Bela			daught	Yehoshua	50	
397R	Baum	Ruth			daught	Yehoshua	51	
397R	Baum	David		Rikel			52	
397R	Baum	Rikel	Gendelman	David			53	
399R	Beck	Benyamin		Naomi			173	
399R	Beck	Naomi	Fuchsman	Benyami n			174	
399R	Beck	Leah			daught	Benyam-in	175	423
399R	Beck	Moshe			son	Benyam-in	176	
399R	Bender	Shlomo					162	424
399R	Berezovsky	Michael	(Misha)	Shunam-it			177	424
399R	Berezovsky	Shunamit	Lifshitz	Michael			178	424
399R	Berezovsky	Rivka			daught	Michael	179	424
399R	Berezovsky	Haim		Malka			180	423
399R	Berezovsky	Malka	Guberman	Haim			181	423
399R	Berezovsky	Michael	(Misha)		son	Haim	182	423
399R	Berezovsky	Yisrael					183	
399R	Berezovsky	Yerachmiel			son	Yisrael	184	
399L	Berezovsky	Aharon		Hindel			185	
399L	Berezovsky	Hindel		Aharon			186	
399L	Berezovsky	Raizel			daught	Aharon	187	
399L	Berezovsky	Chaya			daught	Aharon	188	
399L	Berezovsky	Moshe			son	Aharon	189	
399L	Berezovsky	Yosef			son	Aharon	190	
399L	Berezovsky	Michael		Chaya			191	
399L	Berezovsky	Chaya		Michael			192	
399L	Berezovsky	Abba			son	Michael	193	

Code	Family name	First name	Maiden Name	Spouse	Family code	Father	Order #	Picture
399L	Berezovsky	Chava			daught	Michael	194	
400R	Berkman	Feivish		Miriam			227	
400R	Berkman	Miriam		Feivish			228	
400R	Berkman	Shmuel		Shulamit	& cc		229	
400R	Berkman	Shulamit	Shachnovski	Shmuel			230	447
399L	Berlinski	Haim		Chasia			200	
399L	Berlinski	Chasia	Binder	Haim			201	422
399L	Berlinski	Ezriel			son	Haim	202	
398R	Bik	Mirel					109	
398R	Bik	Riva			daught	M- Mirel	110	
398R	Bik	Yitzhak			son	M- Mirel	111	
397L	Binder	Moshe		Tzisia			96	422
397L	Binder	Tzisia	Golod	Moshe			97	422
397L	Binder	Baruch			son	Moshe	98	
397L	Binder	Naftali Herz	(Zaidel)	Shifra			99	422
397L	Binder	Shifra		Naftali Herz			100	422
398R	Binder	Avraham			son	Naftali Herz	101	422
398R	Binder	Yehudit			daught	Naftali Herz	102	422
398R	Binder	Avraham		Esther Chaya			103	
398R	Binder	Esther Chaya		Avraham			104	
398R	Binder	Mordecai			son	Avraham	105	
398R	Binder	Yosef Haim			son	Avraham	106	
398R	Binder	Yitzhak			son	Avraham	107	
398R	Binder	Tzivia			daught	Avraham	108	
399R	Binshchuk	Yitzhak					163	
399R	Binshchuk	Asher			son	Yitzhak	164	
399R	Binshchuk	Yona			son	Yitzhak	165	
398R	Blizhovsky	Aharon					114	

Code	Family name	First name	Maiden Name	Spouse	Family code	Father	Order #	Picture
398R	Blizhovsky	Brunia			daught	Aharon	115	
398R	Blizhovsky	Penina			daught	M- Brunia	116	
398R	Blizhovsky	Avraham		Rivka			117	
398R	Blizhovsky	Rivka		Avraham			118	
398R	Blizhovsky	Asher			son	Avraham	119	
398R	Blizhovsky	Zippora			daught	Avraham	120	
398R	Blizhovsky	Dina	Eizenberg				121	
398R	Blizhovsky	Esther			daught	M- Dina	122	
398R	Blizhovsky	Penina			daught	M- Dina	123	
398R	Blizhovsky	Haim		Zippora			124	423
398R	Blizhovsky	Zippora		Haim			125	
398R	Blizhovsky	Etel			daught	Haim	126	423
398R	Blizhovsky	Rachel			daught	Haim	127	
398R	Blizhovsky	Leah					128	
398R	Blizhovsky	Yaakov			son	M- Leah	129	
398R	Blizhovsky	Shlomo			son	M- Leah	130	
398L	Blizhovsky	Peretz			son	M- Leah	131	
398L	Blizhovsky	Nachman			son	M- Leah	132	422
398L	Blizhovsky	Bunia					133	422
398L	Blizhovsky	Shlomo		Sarah			134	
398L	Blizhovsky	Sarah		Shlomo			135	423
398L	Blizhovsky	Ita			daught	Shlomo	136	
398L	Blizhovsky	Avraham			son	Shlomo	137	
398L	Blizhovsky	Rivka	Shulman				138	423
398L	Blizhovsky	Chaya			daught	M- Rivka	139	
398L	Blizhovsky	Reuven			son	M- Rivka	140	
398L	Blizhovsky	Gershon		Michal			141	
*	Blizhovsky	Michal		Gershon				

Code	Family name	First name	Maiden Name	Spouse	Family code	Father	Order #	Picture
*	Blizhovsky	Hinda			daught	Gershon		
*	Blizhovsky	Tzalel			son	Gershon		
*	Blizhovsky	Hadassah			daught	Gershon		
398L	Blizhovsky	Yitzhak		Chana			142	
398L	Blizhovsky	Chana		Yitzhak			143	
398L	Blizhovsky	Nachman		Chaya			144	422
398L	Blizhovsky	Chaya		Nachman			145	
398L	Blizhovsky	Shalom			son	Nachman	146	
398L	Blizhovsky	Yaakov		Shifra			147	
398L	Blizhovsky	Shifra	Zinger*	Yaakov			148	
398L	Blizhovsky	Shalom			son	Yaakov	149	
398L	Blizhovsky	Faigel	Perlovich				150	423
398L	Blizhovsky	Miriam			daught	M- Faigel	151	
398L	Blizhovsky	Yehoshua		Chesia			152	422
398L	Blizhovsky	Chesia		Yehoshua			153	422
398L	Blizhovsky	Yisrael			son	Yehoshua	154	
398L	Blizhovsky	Shlomo			son	Yehoshua	155	
399R	Blizhovsky	Anshel		Malka			156	
399R	Blizhovsky	Malka		Anshel			157	
399R	Blizhovsky	Hinda			daught	Anshel	158	
399R	Blizhovsky	Bracha			daught	Anshel	159	
399R	Blizhovsky	Braindel			daught	Anshel	160	422
399R	Blizhovsky	Mordecai			son	Anshel	161	
399L	Brach	Moshe		Faiga			195	424
399L	Brach	Faiga		Moshe			196	424
399L	Brach	Simcha			son	Moshe	197	424
399L	Brach	Avraham			son	Moshe	198	424
399L	Brach	Nechama			daught	Moshe	199	424

Code	Family name	First name	Maiden Name	Spouse	Family code	Father	Order #	Picture
397R	Bukov	Dov		Pesia			59	
397R	Bukov	Pesia		Dov			60	
397R	Burd	Michael		Faigel			61	421
397R	Burd	Faigel		Michael			62	421
397R	Burd	Aharon		Genia			63	421
397R	Burd	Genia		Aharon			64	
397R	Burd	Yitzhak					65	
397R	Burd	Haim			son	Rafael	66	
397R	Burd	Moshe		Devora			67	421
397R	Burd	Devora		Moshe			68	
397R	Burd	Eliyahu			son	Moshe	69	
397R	Burd	Sarah	Blizhovsky				70	
397R	Burd	Shifra			daught	M- Sarah	71	
397R	Burd	David		Chava			72	
397R	Burd	Chava		David			73	
397R	Burd	Dov			son	David	74	
397R	Burd	Batia			daught	David	75	
397L	Burd	Mordecai		Hinda			76	
397L	Burd	Hinda		Mordecai			77	
397L	Burd	Rachel			daught	Mordecai	78	
397L	Burd	Leah					79	
397L	Burko	Aharon		Elka			80	
397L	Burko	Elka		Aharon			81	
397L	Burko	Moshe			son	Aharon	82	
397L	Burko	Yitzhak		Liba			83	
397L	Burko	Liba		Yitzhak			84	
397L	Burko	Mordecai Meir		Pesil			85	
397L	Burko	Pesil		Mordecai Meir			86	

Code	Family name	First name	Maiden Name	Spouse	Family code	Father	Order #	Picture
397L	Burko	Avraham			son	Mordecai Meir	87	
397L	Burko	Gedaliyahu		Miriam			88	
397L	Burko	Miriam		Gedaliya hu			89	
397L	Burko	Devorah			daught	Gedaliyahu	90	
397L	Burshtein	Bobel					91	
406L	Chaitchkas	Zvi		Pesia			583	
406L	Chaitchkas	Pesia		Zvi			584	
406L	Chaitchkas	Zev			son	Zvi	585	
406L	Chaitchkas	Henoch			son	Zvi	586	
406L	Chamer	Mordecai		Bracha			587	431
406L	Chamer	Bracha		Mordecai			588	431
406L	Chamer	Maniya			daught	Mordecai	589	431
406L	Chamer	Sonia			daught	Mordecai	590	
413R	Charnota	Michael		Sarah			949	
413R	Charnota	Sarah		Michael			950	
413R	Charnota	Moshe			son	Michael	951	
406L	Chazanchuk	Haim	(Shulman)	Miriam			579	420
406L	Chazanchuk	Miriam	Eizenberg	Haim			580	420
406L	Chazanchuk	David			son	Haim	581	
406L	Chazanchuk	(daughter)			daught	Haim	582	
413L	Chechik	Aharon		Chaya Sara			956	440
413L	Chechik	Chaya Sara	Freger	Aharon			957	440
413L	Chechik	Ruchama			daught	Aharon	958	
413L	Chechik	Mordecai			son	Aharon	959	
413L	Chechik	Moshe Zvi			son	Aharon	960	
413L	Chechik	David			son	Aharon	961	
413L	Chechik	Eliyahu			son	Aharon	962	
413L	Cherpichnik	Yehoshua		Esther			952	

Code	Family name	First name	Maiden Name	Spouse	Family code	Father	Order #	Picture
413L	Cherpichnik	Esther	Greenberg	Yehoshua			953	440
413L	Cherpichnik	Rivka			daught	Yehoshua	954	
413L	Cherpichnik	Dina			daught	Yehoshua	955	
406L	Cuvres	Henia	Korobochka				577	442
406L	Cuvres	Nachman			son	M- Henia	578	442
404R	Dach	Pesia Brunia				(listed twice)	457	429
404R	Dubinski	Naftali		Rachel			450	
404R	Dubinski	Rachel		Naftali			451	
404R	Dubinski	Fruma			daught	Naftali	452	
404R	Dubinski	Leah			daught	Naftali	453	
404R	Dubinski	Sarah			daught	Naftali	454	
404R	Dubinski	Tama			daught	Naftali	455	
404R	Dubinski	Eliyahu			son	Naftali	456	
396R	Eizenberg	Asher		Sarah			9	
396R	Eizenberg	Sarah		Asher			10	
396R	Eizenberg	Bezalel		Mindel			11	420
396R	Eizenberg	Mindel		Bezalel			12	420
396R	Eizenberg	Zvi	(Hershel)		son	Bezalel	13	420
396R	Eizenberg	Meir			son	Bezalel	14	420
396R	Eizenberg	Wolf			son	Bezalel	15	420
396R	Eizenstein	Asher		Chava			16	
396R	Eizenstein	Chava		Asher			17	
396R	Eizenstein	Efraim			son	Asher	18	
396R	Eizenstein	David			son	Asher	19	
396R	Eizenstein	Chaya Rachel					20	
396R	Eizenstein	Yisrael		Tamar			21	
396R	Eizenstein	Tamar		Yisrael			22	
396L	Elshtein	Meir			& w		29	

Code	Family name	First name	Maiden Name	Spouse	Family code	Father	Order #	Picture
396L	Elshtein	Tzirel			daught	Meir	30	
396L	Elshtein	Malka			daught	Meir	31	
396L	Elshtein	(daughter)			daught	Meir	32	
396L	Elshtein	Moshe			son	Meir	33	
411R	Faigelstein	Dov		Miriam			817	
411R	Faigelstein	Miriam		Dov			818	
411R	Faigelstein	Meir			son	Dov	819	
411R	Faigelstein	Hodel					820	
411R	Faigelstein	Sarah Gittel			daught	M- Hodel	821	
411L	Falik	Yosef		Chaya			861	
411L	Falik	Chaya		Yosef			862	
411L	Falik	Zvi			son	Yosef	863	
411L	Falik	(child)				Yosef	864	
411L	Falik	(child)				Yosef	865	
411L	Feldman	Yisrael		Rachel			852	438
411L	Feldman	Rachel		Yisrael			853	438
411L	Feldman	Avraham Kopel			son	Yisrael	854	438
411L	Feldman	Aharon Shmuel			son	Yisrael	855	
411L	Feldman	Chaya Pesil			daught	Yisrael	856	
411L	Feldman	Bracha			daught	Yisrael	857	
411L	Felnzreich	Leon		Rozia			858	
411L	Felnzreich	Rozia		Leon			859	
411L	Felnzreich	Zisel			daught	Leon	860	
411R	Finkelstein	Yehoshua					825	
411R	Finkelstein	Paltiel					826	
411R	Finkelstein	Yisrael					827	
411R	Finkelstein	Liber		Sheindel			828	438
411R	Finkelstein	Sheindel	Weiner	Liber			829	438

Code	Family name	First name	Maiden Name	Spouse	Family code	Father	Order #	Picture
411R	Finkelstein	Moshe			son	Liber	830	438
411R	Finkelstein	Michael			son	Liber	831	438
411R	Finkelstein	Noah	(Nionia)		son	Liber	832	438
411R	Finkelstein	Yosef		Miriam			833	438
411R	Finkelstein	Miriam		Yosef			834	438
411R	Finkelstein	Rachel			daught	Yosef	835	438
411R	Finkelstein	Raizel					836	
411R	Finkelstein	Rachel			daught	M- Raizel	837	
411R	Finkelstein	Rivka			daught	M- Raizel	838	
411L	Fishman	Mina					851	
412R	Freger	Yaakov		Zlata			870	439
412R	Freger	Zlata		Yaakov			871	439
412R	Freger	Chava	Grinshpan				872	439
412R	Freger	Yoel			son	M- Chava	873	439
412R	Freger	Chaya			daught	M- Chava	874	
412R	Freger	Shmaryahu		Freda			875	
412R	Freger	Freda		Shmarya hu			876	
412R	Freger	Rachel			daught	Shmaryahu	877	
412L	Freierman	Moshe					902	439
412L	Freierman	Yaakov	(Yasha)		son	Moshe	903	
412L	Freierman	Zvi	(Grisha)		son	Moshe	904	
412R	Freitel	Yaakov		Toiva			878	
412R	Freitel	Toiva	Shapira	Yaakov			879	
412R	Freitel	Faigel			daught	Yaakov	880	
412R	Freitel	Reuven		Chana			881	
412R	Freitel	Chana		Reuven			882	
412R	Fried	Zvi		Chava			883	
412R	Fried	Chava		Zvi			884	

Code	Family name	First name	Maiden Name	Spouse	Family code	Father	Order #	Picture
412R	Fried	Miriam			daught	Zvi	885	
412R	Fried	Esther			daught	Zvi	886	
412R	Fried	Rachel			daught	Zvi	887	
412R	Fried	Hadassah			daught	Zvi	888	
412R	Friedman	Sheindel					889	
412R	Friedman	Natan		Sarah			890	
412R	Friedman	Sarah		Natan			891	
412R	Friedman	Zvi		Rivka			892	439
412R	Friedman	Rivka		Zvi			893	
412R	Friedman	(son)			son	Zvi	894	
412R	Friedman	Shlomo		Aidel			895	439
412R	Friedman	Aidel		Shlomo			896	
412R	Friedman	Sarah					897	
412R	Friedman	Shlomo			son	M- Sarah	898	
412L	Friedman	Mordecai		Sarah			899	
412L	Friedman	Sarah		Mordecai			900	
412L	Friedman	Rachel			daught	Mordecai	901	
410L	Fuchsman	Asher		Kaila			799	
410L	Fuchsman	Kaila		Asher			800	
410L	Fuchsman	Maniya			daught	Asher	801	436
410L	Fuchsman	Haim Arie		Rassel			802	
410L	Fuchsman	Rassel		Haim Arie			803	
410L	Fuchsman	Yaakov		Godel			804	437
410L	Fuchsman	Godel		Yaakov			805	437
410L	Fuchsman	Zvi		Maniya			806	436
410L	Fuchsman	Maniya		Zvi			807	
410L	Fuchsman	Pesil			daught	Zvi	808	436
411R	Furman	Yitzhak			w & cc		816	

Code	Family name	First name	Maiden Name	Spouse	Family code	Father	Order #	Picture
402L	Gafterman	Michael		Chesia			374	
402L	Gafterman	Chesia	Greber	Michael			375	
402L	Gafterman	Yentel			daught	Michael	376	
401R	Gaiyer	Chava Gittel					288	
401R	Gaiyer	Nachman			son	M- Chava Gittel	289	427
401R	Gaiyer	Yehoshua			son	M- Chava Gittel	290	427
401R	Gaiyer	Yehuda			son	M- Chava Gittel	291	
401L	Galperin	Lipa		Esther			310	
401L	Galperin	Esther		Lipa			311	
401R	Gechman	Zev		Miriam			293	
401R	Gechman	Miriam		Zev			294	
401R	Gechman	Malka			daught	Zev	295	
401R	Gefman	Chesia *					287	427
401L	Gelfand	Zvi		Malka			304	428
401L	Gelfand	Malka		Zvi			305	428
401L	Gelfand	Sarah	(Sonia)		daught	Zvi	306	428
401L	Gelfand	Etel			daught	Zvi	307	428
401L	Gelfand	Michael			son	Zvi	308	428
401L	Gelfand	Haim			son	Zvi	309	428
401L	Gempel	Yehoshua Baruch		Batya			312	
401L	Gempel	Batya		Yehoshua Baruch			313	
401L	Gempel	Noah			son	Yehoshua Ba ruch	314	
401L	Gempel	Shailik			son	Yehoshua Ba ruch	315	
401L	Gempel	Zvi					316	
401L	Gempel	Leib					317	
401L	Gempel	Yaakov					318	
401L	Gempel	Etel					319	
401L	Gempel	Chava					320	

Code	Family name	First name	Maiden Name	Spouse	Family code	Father	Order #	Picture
401L	Gendelman	Asher		Vita	& son		321	
401L	Gendelman	Vita		Asher			322	
401L	Gendelman	Mordecai		Pesia			323	
401L	Gendelman	Pesia		Mordecai			324	
401L	Gendelman	Rivka			daught	Mordecai	325	
401L	Gendelman	Ora			daught	Mordecai	326	
402R	Gendelman	Hersh		Bela			327	
402R	Gendelman	Bela		Hersh			328	
402R	Gendelman	Chava			daught	Hersh	329	
402R	Gendelman	Leah			daught	Hersh	330	
402R	Gendelman	Chaya			daught	Hersh	331	
402R	Gendelman	Asher			son	Hersh	332	
402R	Gendelman	David			son	Hersh	333	
402R	Gendelman	Hodel					334	
402R	Gendelman	Miriam			daught	M- Hodel	335	
402R	Gendelman	Moshe			son	M- Hodel	336	
402R	Gendelman	Yaakov Shimon			& w		337	
402R	Gendelman	Rivka					338	
402R	Gendelman	Shlomo		Leah	& 3 daught s		339	
402R	Gendelman	Leah		Shlomo			340	
402R	Gendelman	Shmuel		Sheindel			341	
402R	Gendelman	Sheindel		Shmuel			342	
402R	Gendelman	Tamar			daught	Shmuel	343	
402R	Gendelman	Noah			son	Shmuel	344	
402R	Gendelman	Simcha					345	
402R	Gendelman	Zippora					346	
402R	Gendelman	Rachel					347	

Code	Family name	First name	Maiden Name	Spouse	Family code	Father	Order #	Picture
402R	Gendelman	Sarah					348	
402R	Gendelman	Moshe					349	
402R	Gendelman	Shimon		Bracha			350	427
402R	Gendelman	Bracha		Shimon			351	427
402R	Gendelman	Shimon		Fruma			352	427
402R	Gendelman	Fruma		Shimon			353	427
402L	Gendelman	Zvi		Hanna			354	427
402L	Gendelman	Hanna	Barman	Zvi			355	427
402L	Gendelman	Leah			daught	Zvi	356	
402L	Gendelman	David			son	Zvi	357	
402L	Gendelman	Reuven					358	
402L	Gendelman	Michael		Nechama			359	
402L	Gendelman	Nechama		Michael			360	
402L	Gendelman	Shmuel			son	Michael	361	
402L	Gendelman	Yehuda			son	Michael	362	
402L	Gendelman	Nechama					363	
402L	Gendelman	Arie			son	M- Nechama	364	
402L	Gendelman	Hinda					365	
402L	Gendelman	Esther			daught	M- Hinda	366	
402L	Gendelman	Arie			son	M- Hinda	367	
402L	Gendelman	Meir					368	
402L	Gendelman	Malka					369	
402L	Genzel	Avraham		Aida			370	
402L	Genzel	Aida		Avraham			371	
402L	Genzel	Gershon			son	Avraham	372	
402L	Genzel	(3 other children)			(children)	Avraham	373	
404R	Gershkovitz	Yoel		Zisel			446	
404R	Gershkovitz	Zisel	Blizhovsky	Yoel			447	

Code	Family name	First name	Maiden Name	Spouse	Family code	Father	Order #	Picture
404R	Gershkovitz	Shifra			daught	Yoel	448	
404R	Gershkovitz	Shulamit			daught	Yoel	449	
403L	Gertzer	Avraham		Devora			441	420
403L	Gertzer	Devora	Linn	Avraham			442	
404R	Gertzer	Theodore			son	Avraham	443	
404R	Gertzer	Simcha			son	Avraham	444	
404R	Gertzer	Pesia			daught	Avraham	445	
401R	Gilstron				& wife		292	
401R	Gitelman	Avraham Asher					275	
401R	Gitelman	Yaakov		Bela			276	
401R	Gitelman	Bela		Yaakov			277	
401R	Gitelman	Yosef			son	Yaakov	278	
401R	Gitelman	Hodel					279	
401R	Gitelman	Moshe			grands on (Hodel)	F-Yehoshua *	280	428
401R	Gitelman	Musiya			grands on	Gr- Hodel	281	
401R	Gitelman	Rivka			Grand daught (Hodel)	F-Leibel *	282	428
401R	Gitelman	Ziskind			grands on (Hodel)	F-Leibel *	283	428
401R	Gitelman	Sonia					284	
401R	Gitelman	Zvi			son	M- Sonia	285	
401R	Gitelman	Bela			daught	M- Sonia	286	
401R	Gluzman	Baruch		Baila			296	
401R	Gluzman	Baila		Baruch			297	
401L	Gluzman	Miriam			daught	Baruch	298	
401L	Gluzman	Ita			daught	Baruch	299	
401L	Gluzman	Aharon			son	Baruch	300	
401L	Gluzman	Moshe			son	Baruch	301	

Code	Family name	First name	Maiden Name	Spouse	Family code	Father	Order #	Picture
400L	Goldfarb	Meir		Rivka			260	
400L	Goldfarb	Rivka		Meir			261	
400L	Goldfarb	Yentel			daught	Meir	262	
400L	Goldfarb	Pesil			daught	Meir	263	
400L	Goldfarb	Sarah			daught	Meir	264	
400L	Goldfarb	Yaakov			son	Meir	265	
400L	Golod	Avraham		Chaya			266	428
400L	Golod	Chaya		Avraham			267	428
401L	Golomb	Rivka	Gitelman				302	
401L	Golomb	Aharon			son	M- Rivka	303	
400L	Golovey	Sender					259	426
400L	Golubovitz	Hertzel		Etel			256	424
400L	Golubovitz	Etel		Hertzel			257	424
400L	Golubovitz	Yisrael			son	Hertzel	258	424
400L	Gomulka	Yona					268	
401R	Gorin	Zev		Chaya Sarah			269	433
401R	Gorin	Chaya Sarah	Lifshitz	Zev			270	433
401R	Gorin	Rivka			daught	Zev	271	433
401R	Gorin	Chen			son	Zev	272	433
401R	Gornstein	Hershel		Chaya			273	427
401R	Gornstein	Chaya	Zaks	Hershel			274	427
400R	Gotleib	Zalman		Sarah			235	
400R	Gotleib	Sarah		Zalman			236	
400R	Gotleib	David			son	Zalman	237	
400R	Gotleib	Eliyahu			son	Zalman	238	
400R	Gotleib	Gershon			son	Zalman	239	
400R	Gotleib	Rachel			daught	Zalman	240	
403L	Grachovsky	Avraham		Chaya			438	

Code	Family name	First name	Maiden Name	Spouse	Family code	Father	Order #	Picture
403L	Grachovsky	Chaya	Eizenberg	Avraham			439	420
403L	Grachovsky	Rivka			daught	Avraham	440	420
402L	Greber	David		Raizel			377	
402L	Greber	Raizel		David			378	
402L	Greber	Freida			daught	David	379	
402L	Greber	Yosef		Malka			380	426
402L	Greber	Malka		Yosef			381	426
402L	Greber	Eliezar			son	Yosef	382	426
403R	Greber	Miriam					383	
403R	Greber	Avraham			son	M- Miriam	384	
403R	Greber	Leah					385	426
403R	Greber	Yaakov			grands on	Gr-Leah	386	426
403R	Greber	Rivka			Grand-daught	Gr-Leah	387	426
403R	Greber	Shmuel		Risel			388	
403R	Greber	Risel		Shmuel			389	
403R	Greber	Moshe			son	Shmuel	390	
403R	Greber	Chaya Rachel			daught	Shmuel	391	
403R	Greber	Zisel			daught	Shmuel	392	
403R	Greenberg	Avraham Yitzhak		Esther Sheindel			397	425
403R	Greenberg	Esther Sheindel		Avraham Yitzhak			398	425
403R	Greenberg	Zvi	(Hershel)	Lifsha			399	425
403R	Greenberg	Lifsha		Zvi			400	425
403R	Greenberg	Yisrael			son	Zvi	401	425
403R	Greenberg	Zev			son	Zvi	402	425
403R	Greenberg	Yaakov		Zlata			403	
403R	Greenberg	Zlata		Yaakov			404	
403R	Greenberg	Devora					405	
403R	Greenberg	Sender			son	M- Devora	406	

Code	Family name	First name	Maiden Name	Spouse	Family code	Father	Order #	Picture
403R	Greenberg	Chana Raizel					407	
403R	Greenberg	Eliyahu			son	M-Chana Raizel	408	428
403R	Greenberg	Nisan		Anya			409	
403R	Greenberg	Anya		Nisan			410	
403R	Greenberg	Giorg			son	Nisan	411	
403L	Greenstat	Miriam					435	
403R	Greiver	Michael		Raizel			393	
403R	Greiver	Raizel		Michael			394	
403R	Greiver	Sarah			daught	Michael	395	
403R	Greiver	Hinda			daught	Michael	396	
403L	Grempler	Luba	Zaks				436	
403L	Grempler	Dvorsia			daught	M- Luba	437	
403L	Grinshpan	Levy		Mushka			412	426
403L	Grinshpan	Mushka		Levy			413	426
403L	Grinshpan	Yoel			son	Levy	414	426
403L	Grinshpan	Shoshana			daught	Levy	415	426
403L	Grinshpan	Aharon		Chava			416	
403L	Grinshpan	Chava		Aharon			417	
403L	Grinshpan	Batia			daught	Aharon	418	426
403L	Grinshpan	Leah			daught	Aharon	419	
403L	Grinshpan	Gisia			daught	Aharon	420	
403L	Grinshpan	Esther			daught	Aharon	421	
403L	Grinshpan	Rivka			daught	Aharon	422	
403L	Grinshpan	Boaz			son	Aharon	423	
403L	Grinshpan	Moshe					424	426
403L	Grinshpan	Bela					425	
403L	Grinshpan	Shlomo		Batia			426	
403L	Grinshpan	Batia	Meirson	Shlomo			427	425

Code	Family name	First name	Maiden Name	Spouse	Family code	Father	Order #	Picture
403L	Grinshpan	Shoshana			daught	Shlomo	428	425
403L	Grinshpan	Zippora			daught	Shlomo	429	425
403L	Grinshpan	Meir		Chaya			430	
403L	Grinshpan	Chaya	Kaplan	Meir			431	
403L	Grinshpan	Baila			daught	Meir	432	426
403L	Grinshpan	Genia			daught	Meir	433	
403L	Grinshpan	Nechama			daught	Meir	434	
400L	Gurberg	David					253	
400L	Gurberg	Baruch			son	David	254	
400L	Gurberg	Miriam			daught	David	255	
400L	Gutman	David		Rechel			241	425
400L	Gutman	Rechel	Meirson	David			242	425
400L	Gutman	Raya			daught	David	243	425
400L	Gutman	Genia					244	
400L	Gutman	Arie			son	M- Genia	245	
400L	Gutman	Pira			daught	M- Genia	246	
400L	Gutnik	Mordecai		Leah			247	
400L	Gutnik	Leah		Mordecai			248	
400L	Gutnik	Aharon		Sheindel			249	
400L	Gutnik	Sheindel		Aharon			250	
400L	Gutnik	Minka			daught	Aharon	251	427
400L	Gutnik	Arie			son	Aharon	252	
400R	Guz	Moshe		Gisia			231	
400R	Guz	Gisia		Moshe			232	
400R	Guz	Yisrael			son	Moshe	233	
400R	Guz	Yocheved			daught	Moshe	234	
404R	Halprin	Hanka	Chechik				463	429
406L	Hefetz	Stara					591	

Code	Family name	First name	Maiden Name	Spouse	Family code	Father	Order #	Picture
406L	Hefetz	Avigdor	(Vitia)	Batia			592	431
406L	Hefetz	Batia	Berezovsky	Avigdor			593	431
406L	Hefetz	Musik			son	Avigdor	594	431
404R	Hendelman	Yosef		Sheindel			464	
404R	Hendelman	Sheindel		Yosef			465	
404R	Hendelman	Rachel			daught	Yosef	466	
404R	Horman	Moshe Wolf		Esther			458	429
404R	Horman	Esther		Moshe Wolf			459	
404R	Horman	Chaya			daught	Moshe Wolf	460	
404R	Horman	Sheindel			daught	Moshe Wolf	461	
404R	Horman	Shlomo					462	
410R	Ivry	Avigdor		Zlata			781	436
410R	Ivry	Zlata		Avigdor			782	436
410R	Ivry	Yosef			son	Avigdor	783	
410R	Ivry	Noah					784	436
410R	Ivry	Moshe		Zlata			785	436
410R	Ivry	Zlata		Moshe			786	
410R	Ivry	Yentel			daught	Moshe	787	436
410R	Ivry	Shifra			daught	Moshe	788	436
410R	Ivry	Dov	(Berl)		son	Moshe	789	436
413L	Kagan	Gershon		Etel			963	
413L	Kagan	Etel		Gershon			964	
413L	Kagan	(children)				Gershon	965	
413L	Kagan	Sheindel					966	441
414R	Kailer	Taivel	Baruch				994	
414R	Kailer	Baruch			son	M- Taivel	995	
414R	Kailer	Chesia			daught	M- Taivel	996	
*	Kalichisky	Haim	Raikel					

Code	Family name	First name	Maiden Name	Spouse	Family code	Father	Order #	Picture
*	Kalichisky	Raikel	Haim					
*	Kalichisky	Zvika			son	F-Haim		
*	Kalichisky	Breindel			daught	F-Haim		
414L	Kaplan	Yosef		Dosel			1023	
414L	Kaplan	Dosel	*Pinchuk	Yosef			1024	
414L	Kaplan	Devora			daught	Yosef	1025	
414L	Kaplan	David			son	Yosef	1026	
414L	Kaplan	Chaya	Schwartz		w/son & daught		1027	
414L	Kaplan	Chana			w/ 3cc		1028	
414L	Kaplan	Braindel					1029	443
414L	Kaplan	Yehuda					1030	443
407L	Kasher	David		Ita			636	
407L	Kasher	Ita		David			637	
407L	Kasher	Chana			daught	David	638	
407L	Kasher	Yitzhak			son	David	639	
407L	Katz	Yisrael		Sima	& cc (twins)		627	
407L	Katz	Sima	Zaks	Yisrael			628	
407L	Katz	Moshe		Rachel			629	
407L	Katz	Rachel	Tuchman	Moshe			630	
407L	Katz	Chaya			daught	Moshe	631	
407L	Katz	Batia			daught	Moshe	632	
407L	Katzenelson	Nachum		Chana Baila			633	
407L	Katzenelson	Chana Baila		Nachum			634	
407L	Katzenelson	Sonia			daught	Nachum	635	
414L	Kek	Yeshayahu Baruch					1031	442
414L	Kek	Chaya					1032	
414L	Kek	Aharon			son	M- Chaya	1033	

Code	Family name	First name	Maiden Name	Spouse	Family code	Father	Order #	Picture
414L	Kek	Shmuel			son	M- Chaya	1034	
415R	Kek	Haim		Sonia			1035	
415R	Kek	Sonia		Haim			1036	
415R	Kek	Rivka			daught	Haim	1037	
415R	Kek	Devora			daught	Haim	1038	
415R	Kek	Avraham			son	Haim	1039	
415R	Kek	Michael		Mindel			1040	
415R	Kek	Mindel		Michael			1041	
415R	Kek	Rasel			daught	Michael	1042	
415L	Kerentzberg	Yaakov					1064	
415L	Kerentzberg	Ita			daught	Yaakov	1065	
414R	Kimmel	Esther Chaya					997	
414R	Kimmel	Batia			daught	M-Esther Chaya	998	
414R	Kimmel	Shmuel		Braindel			999	421
414R	Kimmel	Braindel	Baruch (Burd)	Shmuel			1000	421
414R	Kimmel	Ziskind		Shifra			1001	
414R	Kimmel	Shifra		Ziskind			1002	
414R	Kimmel	Fradel			daught	Ziskind	1003	
414R	Kimmel	Chaya			daught	Ziskind	1004	
414R	Kimmel	Simcha			son	Ziskind	1005	
414L	Kleiman	Aharon					1009	441
414L	Kleiman	Sonia	Shapira				1010	443
414L	Kleiman	Maniya			daught	M- Sonia	1011	443
414L	Kleiman	Yaakov		Chava			1012	
414L	Kleiman	Chava		Yaakov			1013	
414L	Kleiman	Devora			daught	Yaakov	1014	
414L	Kleiman	Chana			daught	Yaakov	1015	
414L	Kleiman	Riva			daught	Yaakov	1016	

Code	Family name	First name	Maiden Name	Spouse	Family code	Father	Order #	Picture
414L	Kleiman	Masha			daught	Yaakov	1017	
414L	Kleiman	Zelig			son	Yaakov	1018	
414L	Kleiman	Avraham Dov			son	Yaakov	1019	
414L	Kleiman	Yehuda		Chana			1020	
414L	Kleiman	Chana		Yehuda			1021	
414R	Klorfein	Pinchas		Fania			1006	441
414R	Klorfein	Fania		Pinchas			1007	441
414R	Klorfein	Avraham			son	Pinchas	1008	441
414L	Knizchnikov	Pesia					1022	
414R	Kokel	Bezalel		Raizel			980	441
414R	Kokel	Raizel		Bezalel			981	441
414R	Kokel	Shaintza			daught	Bezalel	982	441
414R	Kokel	Niosia			daught	Bezalel	983	441
413L	Kokoiv	Zvi		Batia			977	441
413L	Kokoiv	Batia	Geipman	Zvi			978	441
413L	Kokoiv	Benzion			son	Zvi	979	441
414R	Korland	Fradel					993	
414R	Korobochka	Moshe		Miriam			984	442
414R	Korobochka	Miriam		Moshe			985	442
414R	Korobochka	Fradel			daught	Moshe	986	442
414R	Korobochka	Yoel		Henia			987	442
414R	Korobochka	Henia	Gendelman	Yoel			988	442
414R	Korobochka	Benyamin			son	Yoel	989	442
414R	Korobochka	Natan			son	Yoel	990	442
414R	Korobochka	Asher			son	Yoel	991	
414R	Korobochka	(son)			son	Yoel	992	
413L	Koziol	Yosef		Chaya			967	
413L	Koziol	Chaya		Yosef			968	

Code	Family name	First name	Maiden Name	Spouse	Family code	Father	Order #	Picture
413L	Koziol	Haim			son	Yosef	969	
413L	Koziol	Arie			son	Yosef	970	
413L	Koziol	Michala			daught	Yosef	971	
415R	Kracher	Roza					1063	443
415R	Kramer	Mordecai		BatSheva			1055	
415R	Kramer	BatSheva		Mordecai			1056	
415R	Kramer	Haim			son	Mordecai	1057	
415R	Kramer	Kalman			son	Mordecai	1058	
415R	Kramer	Mordecai		Devora			1059	
415R	Kramer	Devora	Eizenstein	Mordecai			1060	
415R	Kramer	Feivish			son	Mordecai	1061	
415R	Kramer	Chaya			daught	Mordecai	1062	
415R	Kravchik	Baruch		Masha			1043	443
415R	Kravchik	Masha		Baruch			1044	
415R	Kravchik	Baila			daught	Baruch	1045	
415R	Krivola	Moshe		Faigel			1049	
415R	Krivola	Faigel	Levin	Moshe			1050	443
415R	Krivola	Yehoshua	(Shepsil)		son	Moshe	1051	443
415R	Krupnik	Yosef Dov		Batia			1046	
415R	Krupnik	Batia		Yosef Dov			1047	
415R	Krupnik	Meir			son	Yosef Dov	1048	
415R	Krychman	Eliezar		Rachel			1052	
415R	Krychman	Rachel		Eliezar			1053	443
415R	Krychman	Chana			daught	Eliezar	1054	443
413L	Kutz	Pesach					972	440
413L	Kutz	Aharon			son	Pesach	973	440
413L	Kutz	Gedalyahu		Sarah			974	
413L	Kutz	Sarah		Gedalya-hu			975	440

Code	Family name	First name	Maiden Name	Spouse	Family code	Father	Order #	Picture
413L	Kutz	Beiba			son	Gedalya-hu	976	440
408L	Landau	Leah	Steinberg				692	431
408L	Landau	Chava			daught	M- Leah	693	
408L	Landau	Veirtzel			daught	M- Leah	694	
408L	Landau	Faigel			daught	M- Leah	695	
408L	Landau	Rachel			daught	M- Leah	696	
408L	Langer	Yitzhak		Chaya			688	434
408L	Langer	Chaya		Yitzhak			689	434
408L	Langer	Batia			daught	Yitzhak	690	434
408L	Langer	Zippora			daught	Yitzhak	691	434
407L	Levi	Nachman		Tzivia			640	423
407L	Levi	Tzivia	Blizhovsky	Nachman			641	423
407L	Levi	Yisrael		Dina			642	
407L	Levi	Dina		Yisrael			643	
407L	Levin	Aharon			son	Yisrael	644	432
407L	Levin	Pearl			daught	Yisrael	645	432
407L	Levin	Mordecai		Mindel			646	432
407L	Levin	Mindel		Mordecai			647	432
407L	Levin	Moshe			son	Mordecai	648	
408R	Lichtenstein	Zvi		Miriam			656	
408R	Lichtenstein	Miriam	Burko	Zvi			657	
408R	Lichtenstein	Shmuel			son	Zvi	658	
408R	Lichtenstein	Masha			daught	Zvi	659	
408R	Lichtman	Mordecai		Esther			652	432
408R	Lichtman	Esther		Mordecai			653	432
408R	Lichtman	Haim			son	Mordecai	654	433
408R	Lichtman	Malka			daught	Mordecai	655	433
408R	Lifeman	Benzion		Braindel			673	

Code	Family name	First name	Maiden Name	Spouse	Family code	Father	Order #	Picture
408R	Lifeman	Braindel		Benzion			674	
408R	Lifeman	Esther			daught	Benzion	675	
408R	Lifeman	Pesach		Miriam			676	
408R	Lifeman	Miriam		Pesach			677	
408R	Lifeman	Esther			daught	Pesach	678	
408R	Lifeman	Hindel			daught	Pesach	679	
408R	Lifshitz	Moshe Simcha					680	433
408R	Lifshitz	Arie	(Leibel)		son	Moshe Simcha	681	433
408L	Lifshitz	Hiyuta	Margalit				682	433
408L	Lifshitz	Gershon David			son	M- Hiyuta	683	433
408L	Lifshitz	Yosef Haim			son	M- Hiyuta	684	
408L	Lifshitz	Golda			daught	M- Hiyuta	685	
408L	Lifshitz	Sarah Chava					686	433
408L	Lifshitz	Zisel			daught	M-Sarah Chava	687	
408R	Linn	Moshe Hersh		Yentel			660	434
408R	Linn	Yentel		Moshe Hersh			661	
408R	Linn	Yaakov		Fraidel			662	
408R	Linn	Fraidel		Yaakov			663	
408R	Linn	Susiya			daught	Yaakov	664	
408R	Linn	Sarah			daught	Yaakov	665	
408R	Linn	Devora			daught	Yaakov	666	
408R	Linn	Pesia					667	434
408R	Linn	Pinchas		Ita			668	
408R	Linn	Ita		Pinchas			669	
408R	Linn	Mordecai			son	Pinchas	670	
408R	Linn	Yitzhak			son	Pinchas	671	
408R	Linn	Michela			daught	Pinchas	672	
407L	Litvak	Buzia					649	432

Code	Family name	First name	Maiden Name	Spouse	Family code	Father	Order #	Picture
407L	Litvak	Arie	(Liva)	Tamara			650	432
407L	Litvak	Tamara	Lifshitz	Arie			651	432
408L	Mahler	Chava	Korobochka				704	442
408L	Mahler	Raya				M- Chava	705	442
409R	Makler	Etel					714	
409R	Makler	Yehuda			son	M- Etel	715	
409R	Margalit	Yosef		Yehudit			716	433
409R	Margalit	Yehudit	Lifshitz	Yosef			717	433
409R	Margalit	Golda			daught	Yosef	718	433
409R	Marshalek	Shoshana					719	
408L	Meirson	Yona		Musia			697	434
408L	Meirson	Musia		Yona			698	434
408L	Meirson	Mary			daught	Yona	699	434
408L	Meirson	Yosef			son	Yona	700	
408L	Meirson	Zissel		Itka			701	434
408L	Meirson	Itka		Zissel			702	
408L	Meirson	Benyamin			son	Zissel	703	
409R	Meizler	(husband)		Mirel			712	
409R	Meizler	Mirel	Vorona				713	
408L	Modrik	Zvi					706	
408L	Muchnik	Aharon		Leah			707	434
408L	Muchnik	Leah	Pinchuk	Aharon			708	434
408L	Muchnik	Moshe Yaakov			son	Aharon	709	
409R	Muchnik	Raizel			daught	Aharon	710	
409R	Muchnik	Vitka			daught	Aharon	711	
409R	Nabozhnik	Faiga					722	
409R	Naiberg	Yisrael Michael					730	434
409R	Naidich	Moshe Aharon		Batia			731	

Code	Family name	First name	Maiden Name	Spouse	Family code	Father	Order #	Picture
409R	Naidich	Batia		Moshe Aharon			732	
409R	Naidich	Anshel		Sarah			733	
409R	Naidich	Sarah		Anshel			734	
409L	Naidich	Shlomo			son	Anshel	735	
409L	Naidich	Zarah			son	Anshel	736	
409L	Naidich	Meir			son	Anshel	737	
409R	Negel	Eliyahu		Zippora			723	
409R	Negel	Zippora	(Faigel)	Eliyahu			724	435
409R	Negel	Buzia			daught	Eliyahu	725	435
409R	Negel	Shlomo		Dvorsia			726	
409R	Negel	Dvorsia	Trossman	Shlomo			727	431
409R	Negel	Zisel			daught	Shlomo	728	
409R	Negel	Nisan			son	Shlomo	729	
396R	Olicker	Yitzhak					6	
396L	Olisker	Libka					24	
396L	Olisker	Chana			daught	M- Libka	25	
396L	Olisker	Genia			daught	M- Libka	26	
396L	Olisker	Yaakov			son	M- Libka	27	
396L	Olisker	Avraham			son	M- Libka	28	
396R	Olshansky	Yitzhak		Ita			7	
396R	Olshansky	Ita		Yitzhak			8	
412L	Perl	Sender		Toiva			905	440
412L	Perl	Toiva		Sender			906	440
412L	Perl	Meir			son	Sender	907	440
413R	Perlman	Shmuel		Zippora			929	
413R	Perlman	Zippora		Shmuel			930	
413R	Perlman	(son)				Shmuel	931	
412L	Perlov	Chaya Sara	Grinshpan				908	426

Code	Family name	First name	Maiden Name	Spouse	Family code	Father	Order #	Picture
412L	Perlov	Miriam			daught	M- Chaya Sara	909	
412L	Perlovich	Chaya	Blizhovsky				910	
412L	Perlovich	Asher			son	M- Chaya	911	
412L	Perlovich	Bela					912	
412L	Perlovich	Nachman		Shosha-na			913	
412L	Perlovich	Shoshana		Nachman			914	
412L	Perlovich	Dina			daught	Nachman	915	
412L	Perlovich	Asher			son	Nachman	916	
412L	Perlovich	Aharon		Perl			917	
412L	Perlovich	Perl		Aharon			918	
412L	Perlovich	Esther			daught	Aharon	919	439
412L	Perlovich	Peretz			son	Aharon	920	439
412L	Perlovich	Yosef			son	Aharon	921	
412L	Perlovich	Nachman		Rachel			922	439
412L	Perlovich	Rachel		Nachman			923	439
412L	Perlovich	Penina			daught	Nachman	924	
412L	Perlovich	Hodel			daught	Nachman	925	
412L	Perlovich	Chava					926	
412L	Perlovich	Esther			daught	M-Chava	927	439
413R	Perlovich	Avraham			w & son		928	
413R	Perlstein	Feivish			w & 2cc		932	
413R	Perlstein	Leah					933	
413R	Perlstein	Chana			daught	M- Leah	934	
413R	Perlstein	Rivka					935	439
413R	Perlstein	Zippora					936	
413R	Perlstein	Batia			daught	M- Zippora	937	
413R	Perlstein	Chana			daught	M- Zippora	938	
413R	Perlstein	Rachel			daught	M- Zippora	939	

Code	Family name	First name	Maiden Name	Spouse	Family code	Father	Order #	Picture
413R	Perlstein	Yaakov			son	M- Zippora	940	
413R	Perlstein	Yaakov		Leah			941	
413R	Perlstein	Leah		Yaakov			942	
413R	Perlstein	Mattiyahu			son	Yaakov	943	
413R	Perlstein	Yehuda			son	Yaakov	944	
413R	Perlstein	Miriam			daught	Yaakov	945	
411L	Pik	Yosef		Chaya Leah			843	
411L	Pik	Chaya Leah	Fuchsman	Yosef			844	436
411L	Pik	Yisrael					845	437
411L	Pik	Alter		Babel			846	
411L	Pik	Babel		Alter			847	
411L	Pik	Chaya			daught	Alter	848	
411L	Pik	Moshe			son	Alter	849	
411L	Pik	Chana Ita					850	437
411R	Pinchuk	Avraham		Chava Shifra			822	437
411R	Pinchuk	Chava Shifra		Avraham			823	437
411R	Pinchuk	Shalom			son	Avraham	824	437
411R	Pischenski	Arie					839	
411R	Pischenski	Sima			daught	Arie	840	
411R	Pischenski	Zippora			daught	Arie	841	
411R	Pischenski	Miriam			daught	Arie	842	
411L	Pkach	Bela					866	
411L	Pkach	Batia					867	
411L	Pkach	Shimon			son	M- Batia	868	
411L	Pkach	Leah			daught	M- Batia	869	
410L	Polishuk	Chaya Faiga					792	
410L	Polishuk	Baila					793	
410L	Polishuk	Devora			daught	M- Baila	794	

Code	Family name	First name	Maiden Name	Spouse	Family code	Father	Order #	Picture
410L	Polishuk	Mindel			daught	M- Baila	795	
410L	Polishuk	Dina					796	
410L	Polishuk	Yaakov			son	M- Dina	797	
410L	Polishuk	Yitzhak			son	M- Dina	798	
*	Polsky	Yaacov		Malka				
*	Polsky	Malka		Yaacov				
*	Polsky	Masha			daught	F-Yaacov		
410L	Portnoy	Dov					809	
410L	Portnoy	Moshe			son	Dov	810	437
410L	Portnoy	Pesil			daught	Dov	811	437
410L	Portnoy	Naftali		Minka			812	
410L	Portnoy	Minka		Naftali			813	
410L	Portnoy	Buzik			son	Naftali	814	
410L	Portnoy	Efraim			son	Naftali	815	
410L	Potroch	Mendel		Yentel			790	
410L	Potroch	Yentel		Mendel			791	
416R	Raidman	Azriel		Raizel			1102	
416R	Raidman	Raizel		Azriel			1103	
416R	Raidman	Avraham			son	Azriel	1104	
416R	Raizelis	Henoch		Kraina			1105	
416R	Raizelis	Kraina		Henoch			1106	
416R	Raizelis	Raizel			wife (daugh t?)	Henoch	1107	
416R	Raizman	Michael		Hasel			1108	
416R	Raizman	Hasel		Michael			1109	
416R	Raizman	Yentel			daught	Michael	1110	
416R	Raizman	(son)			son	Michael	1111	
416R	Raizman	Mottel		Chana			1112	

Code	Family name	First name	Maiden Name	Spouse	Family code	Father	Order #	Picture
416R	Raizman	Chana		Mottel			1113	
416R	Raizman	Michala			daught	Mottel	1114	
416R	Raizman	(son)			son	Mottel	1115	
416R	Reiss	Arie		Rivka			1116	
416R	Reiss	Rivka	Zaltzbuch	Arie			1117	430
416R	Reiss	Moshe			son	Arie	1118	
416R	Reiss	(daughter)			daught	Arie	1119	
416R	Rekkes	Shlomo		Taivel			1120	
416R	Rekkes	Taivel	Greenberg	Shlomo			1121	
416R	Rekkes	Sarah			daught	Shlomo	1122	
416R	Reznik	Liba					1094	
416R	Reznik	Haim			son	M- Liba	1095	
416R	Reznik	Chesia			daught	M- Liba	1096	
416R	Reznik	Dozia			daught	M- Liba	1097	
416R	Reznik	Yeshayahu			son	M- Liba	1098	
416R	Rivkin	Arie		Musia			1099	
416R	Rivkin	Musia		Arie			1100	
416R	Rivkin	Meir			son	Arie	1101	
415L	Roitelman	Rachel					1091	
415L	Roitelman	Rivka			daught	M- Rachel	1092	
415L	Roitelman	Roniya			daught	M- Rachel	1093	
415L	Rosenstein	Aharon Dov		Chaya			1077	443
415L	Rosenstein	Chaya		Aharon Dov			1078	443
415L	Rosenstein	Chava			daught	Aharon Dov	1079	423
415L	Rosenstein	Zvi		Rachel			1080	444
415L	Rosenstein	Rachel		Zvi			1081	444
415L	Rosenstein	Zippora			daught	Zvi	1082	
415L	Rosenstein	(daughter)			daught	Zvi	1083	

Code	Family name	First name	Maiden Name	Spouse	Family code	Father	Order #	Picture
415L	Rosenstein	Baila					1084	
415L	Rosenstein	Avraham			son	M- Baila	1085	
415L	Rosenstein	(daughter)			daught	M- Baila	1086	
415L	Rotman	Levi		Riva			1087	444
415L	Rotman	Riva (Rivka)	Yungstein	Levi			1088	444
415L	Rotman	Aharon			son	Levi	1089	444
415L	Rotman	Genia			daught	Levi	1090	444
415L	Rozenberg	Mordecai		Baila			1069	
415L	Rozenberg	Baila	Schwartz	Mordecai			1070	
415L	Rozenberg	Aharon			son	Mordecai	1071	
415L	Rozenberg	Reuven			son	Mordecai	1072	
415L	Rozenberg	Yisrael			son	Mordecai	1073	
415L	Rozenzweig	Mordecai		Hindel			1074	
415L	Rozenzweig	Hindel	Gendelman	Mordecai			1075	
415L	Rozenzweig	Shmuel			son	Mordecai	1076	
415L	Rubinstein	Chana					1066	
415L	Rubinstein	Sarah			daught	M- Chana	1067	
415L	Rubinstein	Avraham			son	M- Chana	1068	
419L	Schreiber	Meir		Sarah			1297	
419L	Schreiber	Sarah	Yuz	Meir			1298	
419L	Schreiber	Yocheved			daught	Meir	1299	
419L	Schreiber	Shifra			daught	Meir	1300	
419L	Schreiber	Yaakov			son	Meir	1301	
419L	Schreiber	Nissan			son	Meir	1302	
417L	Schwartz	Rivka	Polishuk				1181	444
417L	Schwartz	David		Chana			1182	
417L	Schwartz	Chana		David			1183	
417L	Schwartz	Yisrael			son	David	1184	

Code	Family name	First name	Maiden Name	Spouse	Family code	Father	Order #	Picture
417L	Schwartz	Shammai			son	David	1185	
417L	Schwartz	Rachel					1186	
417L	Schwartz	Asher					1187	
417L	Schwartz	Avraham					1188	
417L	Schwartz	Pesia					1189	
409L	Segal	Shoshana	Hendler				743	
416L	Shabatzki	Chana					1123	
416L	Shabatzki	Moshe			son	M- Chana	1124	
416L	Shabatzki	Golda			daught	M- Chana	1125	
416L	Shabatzki	Esther			daught	M- Chana	1126	
416L	Shabatzki	Miriam			daught	M- Chana	1127	
418R	Shachnovski	David		Mirel			1219	447
418R	Shachnovski	Mirel		David			1220	447
418R	Shachnovski	Aharon	(Lulik)		son	David	1221	447
418R	Shachnovski	Freida			daught	David	1222	447
418R	Shames	Yosef Aharon	(HaRav)	Rikel			1227	445
418R	Shames	Leah-Rikel	(HaRabbanit)	Yosef Aharon			1228	445
418L	Shapir	Yitzhak Meir		Chana			1234	
418L	Shapir	Chana		Yitzhak Meir			1235	
418L	Shapir	Devora			daught	Yitzhak Meir	1236	
418L	Shapir	Bela			daught	Yitzhak Meir	1237	
418L	Shapir	Dova			daught	Yitzhak Meir	1238	
418L	Shapir	Gershon			son	Yitzhak Meir	1239	
418L	Shapira	Avraham		Chaya			1240	
418L	Shapira	Chaya		Avraham			1241	
418L	Shapira	Hesel			son	Avraham	1242	
418L	Shapira	Dova			daught	Avraham	1243	
418L	Shapira	Yisrael			son	Avraham	1244	

Code	Family name	First name	Maiden Name	Spouse	Family code	Father	Order #	Picture
418L	Shapira	Alta					1245	
418L	Shapira	Moshe			son	M- Alta	1246	
418L	Shapira	Batia			daught	M- Alta	1247	
418L	Shapira	Zippora					1248	
418L	Shapira	Dov			son	M- Zippora	1249	
418L	Shapira	Moshe Haim			son	M- Zippora	1250	
418L	Shapira	Mottel		Rivka			1251	
418L	Shapira	Rivka		Mottel			1252	
418L	Shapira	Maniya			daught	Mottel	1253	
418L	Shapira	Chaya					1254	
418L	Shapira	Esther			daught	M- Chaya	1255	
418L	Shapira	Mordecai		Lipsha			1256	
418L	Shapira	Lipsha		Mordecai			1257	
418L	Shapira	David			son	Mordecai	1258	
418L	Shapira	Shlomo			son	Mordecai	1259	
418L	Shapira	Chesia			daught	Mordecai	1260	
418L	Shapira	Sonia			daught	Mordecai	1261	
418L	Shapira	Moshe Ber		Taiva			1262	
418L	Shapira	Taiva		Moshe Ber			1263	448
419R	Shapira	Yocheved			daught	Moshe Ber	1264	448
419R	Shapira	Chesia			daught	Moshe Ber	1265	448
419R	Shapira	Yitzhak		Sarah Leah			1266	
419R	Shapira	Sarah Leah		Yitzhak			1267	
419R	Shapira	Yocheved			daught	Yitzhak	1268	
419R	Shapira	Faiga			daught	Yitzhak	1269	
419R	Shapira	Shmuel			son	Yitzhak	1270	
419R	Shapira	Rasel			daught	Yitzhak	1271	
419R	Shapira	Yitzhak		Rivka			1272	

Code	Family name	First name	Maiden Name	Spouse	Family code	Father	Order #	Picture
419R	Shapira	Rivka		Yitzhak			1273	
419R	Shapira	David			son	Yitzhak	1274	
419R	Shapira	Yaakov			son	Yitzhak	1275	
419R	Shapira	Shmuel		Nechama			1276	
419R	Shapira	Nechama		Shmuel			1277	
419R	Shapira	Mordecai			son	Shmuel	1278	
419R	Shapira	Yaakov		Golda			1279	
419R	Shapira	Golda		Yaakov			1280	
419R	Shapira	Eliezar			son	Yaakov	1281	
419R	Shapira	Yocheved			daught	Yaakov	1282	
419L	Shapira	Shlomo		Rivka			1283	448
419L	Shapira	Rivka		Shlomo			1284	448
419L	Shapira	Benyamin			son	Shlomo	1285	
419L	Shapira	Raizel					1286	
419L	Shapira	Luba			daught	M- Raizel	1287	
419L	Shapira	Rasel			daught	M- Raizel	1288	
419L	Shapira	Mushka			daught	M- Raizel	1289	
419L	Shapira	Fradel			daught	M- Raizel	1290	
419L	Shapira	Pesia			daught	M- Raizel	1291	
419L	Shapira	Kalman			son	M- Raizel	1292	
419L	Shapira	Nachman		Etel			1293	
419L	Shapira	Etel		Nachman			1294	
419L	Shapira	Asher			son	Nachman	1295	
419L	Shapira	Zvi			son	Nachman	1296	
*	Shapira	Dvorah	Horman					
*	Shapira	Ben-Zion			son	M-Dvorak		
418R	Shechter	Fishel		Runiya			1215	
418R	Shechter	Runiya	Eizenberg	Fishel			1216	420

Code	Family name	First name	Maiden Name	Spouse	Family code	Father	Order #	Picture
418R	Shechter	Yehiel			son	Fishel	1217	
418R	Shechter	(son)			son	Fishel	1218	
418R	Shechtman	Dina					1214	
418R	Sheintuch	Moshe		Malka			1206	
418R	Sheintuch	Malka		Moshe			1207	
418R	Sheintuch	Esther			daught	Moshe	1208	
418R	Sheintuch	Yentel			daught	Moshe	1209	
418R	Sheintuch	Zahava			daught	Moshe	1210	
418R	Ship	Faiga					1211	
418R	Ship	Yeshayahu			son	M- Faiga	1212	
418R	Ship	Raitza			daught	M- Faiga	1213	
418R	Shlaifer	Baila					1223	
418R	Shlipak	Shaul		Esther			1224	
418R	Shlipak	Esther	Gitelman	Shaul			1225	
418R	Shlipak	Moshe			son	Shaul	1226	
416L	Shohet	Haim Yehuda		Sarah			1134	444
416L	Shohet	Sarah		Haim Yehuda			1135	
416L	Shohet	Moshe		Rachel			1136	
416L	Shohet	Rachel		Moshe			1137	
416L	Shohet	Shmuel	(Sioma)		son	Moshe	1138	
416L	Shohet	BatSheva			daught	Moshe	1139	
416L	Shohet	Chaya			daught	Moshe	1140	
418R	Shpeilberg	Mina		Baila			1229	447
418R	Shpeilberg	Baila	Kagan	Mina			1230	447
418R	Shpeilberg	Muzik			son	Mina	1231	
418R	Shpilman	Sonia					1232	
418R	Shpilman	Moshe			son	M- Sonia	1233	
417L	Shtedler	Benyamin		Sarah			1196	447

Code	Family name	First name	Maiden Name	Spouse	Family code	Father	Order #	Picture
417L	Shtedler	Sarah	Naiberg	Benyam-in			1197	447
417L	Shtedler	Rasel			daught	Benyam-in	1198	
417L	Shtedler	Shoshana			daught	Benyam-in	1199	447
417L	Shteindel	Meir		Susel			1200	
417L	Shteindel	Susel		Meir			1201	
417L	Shteindel	Shepsil			son	Meir	1202	
417L	Shteindel	(daughter)			daught	Meir	1203	
417L	Shteinman	Hershel		Malka			1204	447
417L	Shteinman	Malka		Hershel			1205	447
417R	Shulman	Moshe Zelig		Necha			1153	445
417R	Shulman	Necha		Moshe Zelig			1154	445
417R	Shulman	Yosef			son	Moshe Zelig	1155	445
417R	Shulman	Rivka			daught	Moshe Zelig	1156	445
417R	Shulman	David					1157	
417R	Shulner	Yitzhak		Chava			1158	
417R	Shulner	Chava		Yitzhak			1159	
417R	Shuster	Chaya					1160	
417R	Shuster	Genia			daught	M- Chaya	1161	
417R	Shuster	Batia					1162	446
417R	Shuster	Yehuda			son	M- Batia	1163	446
417R	Shuster	Necha			daught	M- Batia	1164	446
417R	Shuster	Yeshayahu		Bela			1165	
417R	Shuster	Bela		Yeshaya-hu			1166	
417R	Shuster	Zisel			daught	Yeshaya-hu	1167	
417R	Shuster	Asher		Esther			1168	
417R	Shuster	Esther		Asher			1169	
417R	Shuster	Chana			daught	Asher	1170	
417R	Shuster	Yisrael			son	Asher	1171	

Code	Family name	First name	Maiden Name	Spouse	Family code	Father	Order #	Picture
417R	Shuster	Michael		Devora			1172	
417R	Shuster	Devora		Michael			1173	
417R	Shuster	Eliyahu			son	Michael	1174	
417R	Shuster	David			son	Michael	1175	
417R	Shuster	Yehoshua		Mushka			1176	
417R	Shuster	Mushka		Yehoshua			1177	
417L	Shuster	Chana Hodel			daught	Yehoshua	1178	
417L	Shuster	Yitzhak			son	Yehoshua	1179	
417L	Shuster	Yosef					1180	
*	Shuster	Miriam						
416L	Shuver	Baruch					1128	445
416L	Shuver	Genia					1129	445
416L	Shvindelman	Yaakov Shmuel		Rivka			1141	444
416L	Shvindelman	Rivka		Yaakov Shmuel			1142	444
416L	Shvindelman	Yehoshua		Hinda			1143	437
416L	Shvindelman	Hinda		Yehoshua			1144	
416L	Shvindelman	(son)			son	Yehoshua	1145	
416L	Shvindelman	Paltiel		Bela			1146	437
416L	Shvindelman	Bela		Paltiel			1147	
416L	Shvindelman	Faigel			daught	Paltiel	1148	
416L	Shvindelman	Moshe			son	Paltiel	1149	
417R	Shvindelman	Yisrael		Chaya			1150	437
417R	Shvindelman	Chaya		Yisrael			1151	
417R	Shvindelman	Moshe			son	Yisrael	1152	
416L	Shwartzberg	Yoel	(ShU"B)	Chava			1130	446
416L	Shwartzberg	Chava	Kleiger	Yoel			1131	446
416L	Shwartzberg	Sarah			daught	Yoel	1132	446
416L	Shwartzberg	Yitzhak			son	Yoel	1133	446

Code	Family name	First name	Maiden Name	Spouse	Family code	Father	Order #	Picture
417L	Shwartzblat	Dov	(Berl)	Devora			1190	445
417L	Shwartzblat	Devora		Dov			1191	445
417L	Shwartzblat	Fania			daught	Dov	1192	445
417L	Shwartzblat	Mendel		Maniya			1193	446
417L	Shwartzblat	Maniya (Miriam)	Gendelman	Mendel			1194	446
417L	Shwartzblat	Malka			daught	Mendel	1195	
410R	Sliep	Sarah					774	
410R	Sliep	Arie	(Leibel)		son	M- Sarah	775	435
410R	Slutzki	Aharon		Chaya			771	435
410R	Slutzki	Chaya		Aharon			772	
410R	Slutzki	Isser			son	Aharon	773	
409L	Socher	Leah					754	
409L	Socher	Faigel			daught	M- Leah	755	
409L	Socher	Yaakov			son	M- Leah	756	
409L	Soltzman	Noah		Klara			757	435
409L	Soltzman	Klara		Noah			758	435
409L	Soltzman	Lusia			daught	Noah	759	435
409L	Soltzman	Shoshana			daught	Noah	760	435
409L	Soltzman	Luba	Weiner				761	435
409L	Soltzman	Meir			son	M- Luba	762	435
410R	Soroka	Shlomo	from Borovoiya	Hanna			763	
410R	Soroka	Hanna	Burko	Shlomo			764	
410R	Soroka	Zalman			son	Shlomo	765	
410R	Soroka	Gedalyahu			son	Shlomo	766	
410R	Soroka	Osnat			daught	Shlomo	767	
*	Sorovitz	Moshe						
*	Sorovitz	Gershon			son	Moshe		
410R	Spivak	Shmuel Yitzhak		Leah			776	

Code	Family name	First name	Maiden Name	Spouse	Family code	Father	Order #	Picture
410R	Spivak	Leah		Shmuel Yitzhak			777	
410R	Spivak	Haim					778	
410R	Spivak	(wife)		Haim			779	
410R	Spivak	Hezkel			son	Haim	780	
410R	Strilovski	Zelig		Malka			768	
410R	Strilovski	Malka		Zelig			769	
410R	Strilovski	Sarah			daught	Zelig	770	
409L	Suka	Aharon		Leah			745	435
409L	Suka	Leah		Aharon			746	435
409L	Suka	Rachel					747	
409L	Suka	Pesach			son	M- Rachel	748	
409L	Suka	Shmuel		Sonia			749	
409L	Suka	Sonia	Gendelman	Shmuel			750	
409L	Suka	Zvi			son	Shmuel	751	
409L	Suka	Zalman			son	Shmuel	752	
409L	Suka	Malka			daught	Shmuel	753	
409L	Svetchnik	Feivish		Dvorsia		(also listed on p41 6)	738	444
409L	Svetchnik	Dvorsia	Drach	Feivish		(also listed on p416)	739	444
409L	Svetchnik	Doba			daught	Feivish	740	
409L	Svetchnik	Henia			daught	Feivish	741	
409L	Svetchnik	Yisrael			son	Feivish	742	
409L	Svitcher	Fradel					744	
407R	Tarlo	Chaya	Levin				620	432
407R	Tarlo	Dunya			daught	M- Chaya	621	432
407R	Tarlo	Leah			daught	M- Chaya	622	432
407R	Tendler	Pearl	Perl				613	440
406L	Tomrin	Yaakov					595	

Code	Family name	First name	Maiden Name	Spouse	Family code	Father	Order #	Picture
407R	Trigun	Isachar	(ShU"B)	Pesil			617	431
407R	Trigun	Pesil		Isachar			618	
407R	Trigun	Yisrael			son	Isachar	619	431
407R	Trossman	Haim		Tema			614	431
407R	Trossman	Tema		Haim			615	431
407R	Trossman	Yechiel					616	431
407R	Turkenich	Avraham					612	
406L	Turok	Chaya					600	
406L	Turok	Nisan			son	M- Chaya	601	
407R	Turok	Wolf			son	M- Chaya	602	
407R	Turok	Yenta			daught	M- Chaya	603	
407R	Turok	Haim		Henia			604	
407R	Turok	Henia		Haim			605	
407R	Turok	Gisia			daught	Haim	606	
407R	Turok	Wolf			son	Haim	607	
407R	Turok	Yitzhak		Chana			608	
407R	Turok	Chana		Yitzhak			609	
407R	Turok	Yocheved			daught	Yitzhak	610	
407R	Turok	Luba			daught	Yitzhak	611	
406L	Turovitz	Tuvia					596	
406L	Turovitz	Leah					597	
406L	Turovitz	Gershon			son	M- Leah	598	
406L	Turovitz	Bunia			daught	M- Leah	599	
413R	Tzipiniuk	(family)					948	
405R	Vitas	Moshe		Gittel			497	
405R	Vitas	Gittel		Moshe			498	
405R	Vitas	Bela			daught	Moshe	499	
405R	Vitas	Avraham			son	Moshe	500	

Code	Family name	First name	Maiden Name	Spouse	Family code	Father	Order #	Picture
404L	Vorona	Gunya					478	
404L	Vorona	Yitzhak			son	M- Gunya	479	
404L	Vorona	Miriam			daught	M- Gunya	480	
404L	Vorona	(daughter)			daught	M- Gunya	481	
404L	Vorona	Chana					482	
404L	Vorona	Miriam			daught	M- Chana	483	
404L	Vorona	Yehudit			daught	M- Chana	484	
404L	Vorona	Avraham			son	M- Chana	485	
404L	Vorona	Yitzhak		Feiga			486	
404L	Vorona	Feiga		Yitzhak			487	
404L	Vorona	Miriam			daught	Yitzhak	488	
404L	Vorona	Dov (Berl)			son	Yitzhak	489	
404L	Vorona	Shlomo		Osnat			490	
404L	Vorona	Osnat		Shlomo			491	
404L	Vorona	Miriam			daught	Shlomo	492	
404L	Vorona	Yosef			son	Shlomo	493	
405R	Waldman	Moshe		Esther			515	
405R	Waldman	Esther		Moshe			516	
405R	Walman	Gittel	Segal				517	
405R	Walman	Shlomo			son	M- Gittel	518	429
405R	Wasserman	Batia			& 3cc		519	
405R	Wasserman	Moshe					520	430
405L	Wasserman	Yaakov			son	Moshe	521	
405L	Wasserman	Sarah					522	
405L	Wasserman	Penina			daught	M- Sarah	523	
405L	Wasserman	Nachman			son	M- Sarah	524	
405L	Wasserman	Eliyahu			son	M- Sarah	525	
405L	Wasserman	Avraham Leib		Hannah Sarah			526	

Code	Family name	First name	Maiden Name	Spouse	Family code	Father	Order #	Picture
405L	Wasserman	Hannah Sarah		Avraham Leib			527	
405L	Wasserman	Zvi			son	Avraham Leib	528	
405L	Wax	Zippora					529	
405L	Wax	Raizel					530	
405L	Wax	Chaya	Klapper				531	429
405L	Wax	Devora			daught	M- Chaya	532	429
405L	Wax	Shlomo					533	
405L	Wax	Raizel			daught	Shlomo	534	
405R	Weider	Shabtai		Rivka			494	
405R	Weider	Rivka	Gendelman	Shabtai			495	
405R	Weider	Nechama			daught	Shabtai	496	
405R	Weiner	Aharon		Nechama			501	429
405R	Weiner	Nechama		Aharon			502	429
405R	Weiner	Haim David					503	429
405R	Weiner	Hanya				b-in-law Haim David	504	
405R	Weiner	Kaila				b-in-law Haim David	505	
405R	Weiner	Yosef Leib		Yocheved			506	
405R	Weiner	Yocheved		Yosef Leib			507	
405R	Weiner	Fruma			daught	Yosef Leib	508	
405R	Weiner	Zisel			daught	Yosef Leib	509	
405R	Weinstein	Berl		Yocheved			510	429
405R	Weinstein	Yocheved	Greber	Berl			511	429
405R	Weinstein	Penina			daught	Berl	512	429
405R	Weisman	Shmuel		Sheindel			513	
405R	Weisman	Sheindel		Shmuel			514	
404L	Wolfin	Yehoshua					467	430
404L	Wolfin	Yaakov		Devora			468	
404L	Wolfin	Devora		Yaakov			469	

Code	Family name	First name	Maiden Name	Spouse	Family code	Father	Order #	Picture
404L	Wolfin	Nachum			son	Yaakov	470	
404L	Wolfin	Roza			daught	Yaakov	471	
404L	Wolfin	Yaakov					472	
404L	Wolfin	Nechama					473	
404L	Wolfin	Chava Gittel			daught	M- Nechama	474	
404L	Wolfin	Esther					475	
404L	Wolfin	Minka			daught	M- Esther	476	
404L	Wolfin	Asher			son	M- Esther	477	
407R	Yuz	Leibel		Yentel			623	
407R	Yuz	Yentel	Ivry	Leibel			624	436
407R	Yuz	Avigdor			son	Leibel	625	
407R	Yuz	Tzirel			daught	Leibel	626	
406R	Zaks	Mindel					570	
406R	Zaks	Kopel			son	M- Mindel	571	
406R	Zaks	Brushka			daught	M- Mindel	572	
406R	Zaks	Genendel					573	430
406R	Zaks	Henia			daught	M- Genendel	574	430
406R	Zaks	Chaya			daught	M- Genendel	575	
406R	Zaks	Yona			son	M- Genendel	576	430
406R	Zaltzbuch	Raizel					558	430
406R	Zaltzbuch	Moshe			son	M- Raizel	559	430
406R	Zaltzman	Yaakov Leib		Golda			560	
406R	Zaltzman	Golda		Yaakov Leib			561	
406R	Zaltzman	Moshe			son	Yaakov Leib	562	
406R	Zaltzman	Yisrael			son	Yaakov Leib	563	
406R	Zaltzman	Yehudit			daught	Yaakov Leib	564	
406R	Zaltzman	Matel			daught	Yaakov Leib	565	
406R	Zandweis	Menashe		Fraida			554	

Code	Family name	First name	Maiden Name	Spouse	Family code	Father	Order #	Picture
406R	Zandweis	Fraida		Menashe			555	
406R	Zandweis	Baila			daught	Menashe	556	
406R	Zask	Mindel	Linn				566	430
406R	Zask	Chaya Leah			daught	M- Mindel	567	430
406R	Zask	Yitzhak			son	M- Mindel	568	430
406R	Zask	Mordecai			son	M- Mindel	569	430
406R	Zeligson	Anya	Shlafer		& daught		557	
405L	Zhuk	Tova					539	
405L	Zhuk	Dov			son	M- Tova	540	
405L	Zhuk	Penina			daught	M- Tova	541	
405L	Zilberberg	Meir		Machla			542	
405L	Zilberberg	Machla		Meir			543	
405L	Zilberberg	Berl			son	Meir	544	
405L	Zilberberg	Moshe			son	Meir	545	
405L	Zilberberg	Avraham			son	Meir	546	
405L	Zilberberg	Gittel			daught	Meir	547	
405L	Zilberberg	Shnior		Raizel			548	
405L	Zilberberg	Raizel		Shnior			549	
406R	Zilberman	Yehoshua Yitz hak		Taivel			550	
406R	Zilberman	Taivel	Greenberg	Yehoshua Yitzhak			551	
406R	Zilberman	Baruch			son	Yehoshua Yitzhak	552	
406R	Zilberman	Shalom			w & cc		553	
405L	Zolotov	Avraham		Riva			535	
405L	Zolotov	Riva		Avraham			536	
405L	Zolotov	(son)			son	Avraham	537	
405L	Zolotov	Chava	Blizhovsky				538	
413R	Zveibaum	Chana	Hefitz				946	
413R	Zveibaum	Tamara	Tanya		daught	M- Chana	947	440

[Page 420]

YIZKOR

יזכור

בצלאל איזנברג | מינדל איזנברג | הערשל איזנברג

מאיר איזנברג | וולף איזנברג | רונקה שכטר (איזנברג)

חיים הונצ'יק (שולמן) | מרים הונצ'יק (איזנברג)

אברהם גרציבסקי | חיה גרצובסקי (איזנברג) | רבקה גרצובסקי

420

Photos Page 420

Left to right

Hershel Eizenberg Mindel Eizenberg Bezalel Eizenberg

Ronka Shechter (Eizenberg) Wolf Eizenberg Meir Eizenberg

Miriam Chazanchuk (Eizenberg) Haim Chazanchuk (Shulman)

Rivkah Gertshovsky; Haya Gertshovsky (Eizenberg); Avraham Gertshovsky

[Page 421]

יזכור

דוד באום, בניו: מרדכי־צבי, ישראל, כלותיו: רבקה (הורבן) ושרה (גילמשרון), נכדיו: משה וחנה

אהרן בורד	פייגל בורד	מיכאל בורד
משה בורד	בריינדל קיטפל (בורד)	שמואל קיטפל

421

Photos Page 421

Top photo:

David Baum His sons: Mordechai Zvi, Yisrael

His Daughters-in law: Rivka (Horman) and Sarah (Gilstron)

His grandchildren: Moshe and Hannah

Left to right

Aharon Burd Faigel Burd Michael Burd

Moshe Burd Breindel Keysal (Burd) Shmuel Keysal

[Page 422]

יזכור

נפתלי הרץ (זיידל) בינדר	עפרה בינדר	אברהם בינדר
יהודית בינדר	משה בינדר	צפיה בינדר (גוליד)
חביה ברלינסקי (בינדר)	נחמן בליזובסקי	בריינדל בליזובסקי
יהושע בליזובסקי	חביה בליזובסקי	בוניה בליזובסקי

422

Photos Page 422

Left to right

Avraham Binder Shifra Binder Naftali Herz (Zaidel) Binder

Tzisia Binder (Golod) Moshe Binder Yehudit Binder

Braindel Blizhovsky Nachman Blizhovsky Chesia Berlinsky (Binder)

Bunia Blizhovsky Chesia Blizhovsky Yehoshua Blizhovsky

[Page 423]

יזכור

נחמן וצביה לוי (בריזובסקי)

שרה בריזובסקי

פייגה בריזובסקי (פילוביץ)

חיים ואטל בריזובסקי

חיה רוזנשטיין

לאה באק

רבקה בריזובסקי (קילמן)

מישה ברזובסקי

חיים ומלכה בריזובסקי (גוברסן)

423

Photos Page 423

Left to right

Nachman and Tzvia Levy (Blizhovsky) Sarah Blizhovsky

Faigel Berlinsky (Perlovich) Haim and Etel Blizhovsky

Chaya Rosenstein Leah Beck Rivkah Blizhovsky (Shulman)

Misha Berezovsky Haim and Malka Berezovsky (Guberman)

[Page 424]

יזכור
מיכאל ברזובסקי
שולמית ברזובסקי (ליטביץ)
רבקה ברזובסקי
משה ברך
פייגה ברך
שמחה ברך
אברהם ברך
נחמה ברך
שלמה בנדר
הרצל גולובוביץ
עטל גולובוביץ
ישראל גולובוביץ
424

Photos Page 424

Left to right

Rivka Berezovsky	Shunamit Berezovsky (Lifshitz)	Michael Berezovsky
Simcha Berekh	Fayga Berekh	Moshe Berekh
Shlomo Bender	Nechama Berekh	Avraham Berekh
Yisrael Golubovitz	Etel Golubovitz	Hertzel Golubovitz

[Page 425]

יזכור
אברהם־יצחק גרינברג
אסתר־שיינדל גרינברג
הערשל גרינברג
ליפשה גרינברג
ישראל גרינברג
זאב גרינברג
דוד גוטמן
רעכל גוטמן (מאירזון)
רעיה גוטמן
בתיה גרינשפון (מאירזון)
שושנה גרינשפון
צפורה גרינשפון
425

Photos Page 425

Left to right

Hershel Greenberg; Esther-Sheindel Greenberg; Avraham Yitzhak Greenberg

Zeev Greenberg Yisrael Greenberg Lifsha Greenberg

Raya Gutman Rechel Gutman (Meirson) David Gutman

Zipporah Grinshpan Shoshana Grinshpan Batya Grinshpan (Meirson)

[Page 426]

יזכור

בתיה גרינשפן

בלה גרינשפן

משה גרינשפן

יוסף גרבר

מלכה גרבר

אליעזר גרבר

לאה גרבר ונכדיה: רבקה ויעקב

426

Photos Page 426

Top

Levi Grinshpan, his wife Mushka and their children: Chaya Sara Perlov (Grinshpan), Yoel and Shoshana

Left to right

Moshe Grinshpan Baila Grinshpan Batia Grinshpan

Malka Greber Yosef Greber Sender Golovey

Leah Greber and her grandchildren: Rivka and Yaakov Eliezer Greber

[Page 427]

יזכור

שמשון גנדלמן | ברכה גנדלמן | חיסיה גייסמן

שמעון גנדלמן | פרומה גנדלמן | בינקה גושניק

צבי גנדלמן | חנה גנדלמן (ברמן) | יהושע גייער

נחמן גייער | הרשל גורנשטיין | חיה גורנשטיין (זקס)

427

Photos Page 427

Left to right

Chesiya Geipman	Bracha Gendelman	Shimon Gendelman
Minka Gutnik	Fruma Gendelman	Shimon Gendelman
Yehoshua Gaiyer	Hannah Gendelman (Barman)	Zvi Gendelman
Haya Gornstein (Zaks)	Hershel Gornstein	Nachman Gaiyer

[Page 428]

יזכור

צבי גלפנד, אשתו מלכה וילדיהם: מניה, עטל, מיכאל וחיים

אברהם גילוד   חיה גילוד   אליהו גרינברג

משה גישלמן   רבקה גישלמן   ויסקינר גישלמן

428

Photos Page 428

Top

Zvi Gelfand, his wife Malka and their children: Sonia, Etel, Michael and Haim

Left to right

Eliyahu Greenberg Haya Golod Avraham Golod

Ziskind Gitelman Rivka Gitelman Moshe Gitelman

[Page 429]

יזכור

פסיה־בריינה דראר | משה־וולף הורמן | חינקה הלפרין (צ'צ'יק)

אהרן וינר | נחמה וינר | חיים־דוד ויינר

ברל ווינשטיין | יוכבד ווינשטיין (גרבר) | פנינה ווינשטיין

שלמה וואלמן | חיה וואקס (קלפר) | דבורה וואקס

429

Photos Page 429

Left to right

Hanka Halprin (Chechik)	Moshe Wolf Horman	Pesia-Breina Drach
Haim-David Weiner	Nechama Weiner	Aharon Weiner
Penina Weinstein	Yocheved Weinstein	Berl Weinstein
Devorah Wax	Chaya Wax (Klapper)	Shlomo Walman

[Page 430]

יזכור

יהושע וולפין	משה וסרמן	רייזל זלצבוך
רבקה רייס (זלצבוך)	משה זלצבוך	מינדל זאסק
חיה־לאה זאסק	יצחק זאסק	מרדכי זאסק
נגבדל זאקס	יונה זאקס	חיניה זאקס

430

Photos Page 430

Left to right

Raizel Zaltzbuch	Moshe Wasserman	Yehoshua Wolfin
Mindel Zask	Moshe Zaltzbuch	Rivka Reiss (Zaltzbuch)
Mordecai Zask	Yitzhak Zask	Chaya Leah Zask
Henia Zaks	Yona Zaks	Genedel Zaks

[Page 431]

Photos Page 431

Left to right

1.Maniya Chamer Bracha Chamer Mordecai Chamer

2. (left) Haim Trossman

2. (right) Avigdor Hefetz, his wife Batia (Berezovsky) and their son Musik

3. Dvorsia Negel (Trossman) Yechiel Trossman Tema Trossman

4. (left) Leah Landau (Steinberg) Yisrael Trigun

4. (right) The ritual slaughter and examiner R' Isachar Trigun

[Page 432]

יזכור

חיה סדלו (לוין) | דוניה סדלו | לאה סדלו

בוזיה ליטבק | ליווה ליטבק | תמר ליטבק (ליפשיץ)

אהרן לוין | פרל לוין | מרדכי לוין

מינדל לוין | מרדכי ליכטמן | אסתר ליכטמן

432

Photos Page 432

Left to right

Leah Tarlo	Dunya Tarlo	Chaya Tarlo (Levin)
Tamar Litvak (Lifshitz)	Liva (Arie) Lifshitz	Buzia Litvak
Mordecai Levin	Pearl Levin	Aharon Levin
Esther Lichman	Mordecai Lichtman	Mindel Levin

[Page 433]

יזכור

מלכה ליבמן — חיים ליבמן — שרה־חוה ליפשיץ

משה ליפשיץ — ריזהה ליפשיץ (מרגלית) — גרשון ליפשיץ

יוסף ויהודית מרגלית (ליפשיץ) — גולדה מרגלית

וולף גורין, אשתו חיה־שרה (ליפשיץ) וילדיהם: רבקה וחן — לייבל ליפשיץ

433

Photos Page 433

Left to right

Sarah-Chava Lifshitz	Haim Lichtman	Malka Lichtman
Gershon Lifshitz	Hiyuta Lifshitz (Margalit)	Moshe Lifshitz

Golda Margalit Yosef and Yehudit Margalit (Lifshitz)

Leibel Lifshitz Wolf Gorin, his wife Chaya-Sarah (Lifshitz) and their children: Rivka and Chen

[Page 434]

יזכור

משה'הערש לין

פסיה לין

חיה לנגר

יצחק לנגר

בתיה לנגר

צפורה לנגר

יונה ומוסיה מאירזון ובתם מרי

זיסל מאירזון

אהרן ולאה מוצ'ניק (פינצ'וק)

ישראל מיכאל נייברג

Photos Page 434

Left to right

Chaya Langer	Pesia Linn	Moshe-Hersh Linn
Zipporah Langer	Batia Langer	Yitzhak Langer
Zissel Meirson	Yona and Musia Meirson and their daughter Mary	
Yisrael Michael Naiburg	Aharon and Leah Muchnik (Pinchuk)	

[Page 435]

Photos Page 435

Top:

Faigel (Zipporah) Negel and her daughter Buzia

Noah Soltzman, his wife Klara and their daughters Lusia and Shoshana

Left to right

Aharon Slutzki　　Meir Soltzman　　Luba Soltzman

Leah Suka　　Aharon Suka　　Leibel (Arie) Sliep

[Page 436]

יזכור
אבינדור עברי
משה עברי
יענקל עברי
שפרה עברי
ברל עברי
נח עברי
צבי פוקסמן
מאניה פוקסמן
פעסל פוקסמן
436

Photos Page 436

Left to right

Zlata Ivry	Moshe Ivry	Avigdor Ivry
Berl (Dov) Ivry	Shifra Ivry	Yentel Ivry
Chaya-Leah Pik (Fuchsman)	Yentel Yuz (Ivry)	Noah Ivry
Pesil Fuchsman	Maniya Fuchsman	Zvi Fuchsman

[Page 437]

יזכור

יעקב וגודל פוקסמן

שלום פינצ'וק

אברהם וחיה פינצ'וק

חנה פיק

ישראל פיק

משה פורטנוי

פעסל פורטנוי

יהושע שוינדלמן

פלטיאל שוינדלמן

ישראל שוינדלמן

437

Photos Page 437

Left to right

Shalom Pinchuk	Yaakov and Godel Fuchsman	
Chana Pik	Avraham and Chava Pinchuk	
Pesil Portnoy	Moshe Portnoy	Yisrael Pik
Yisrael Shvindelman	Paltiel Shvindelman	Yehoshua Shvindelman

[Page 438]

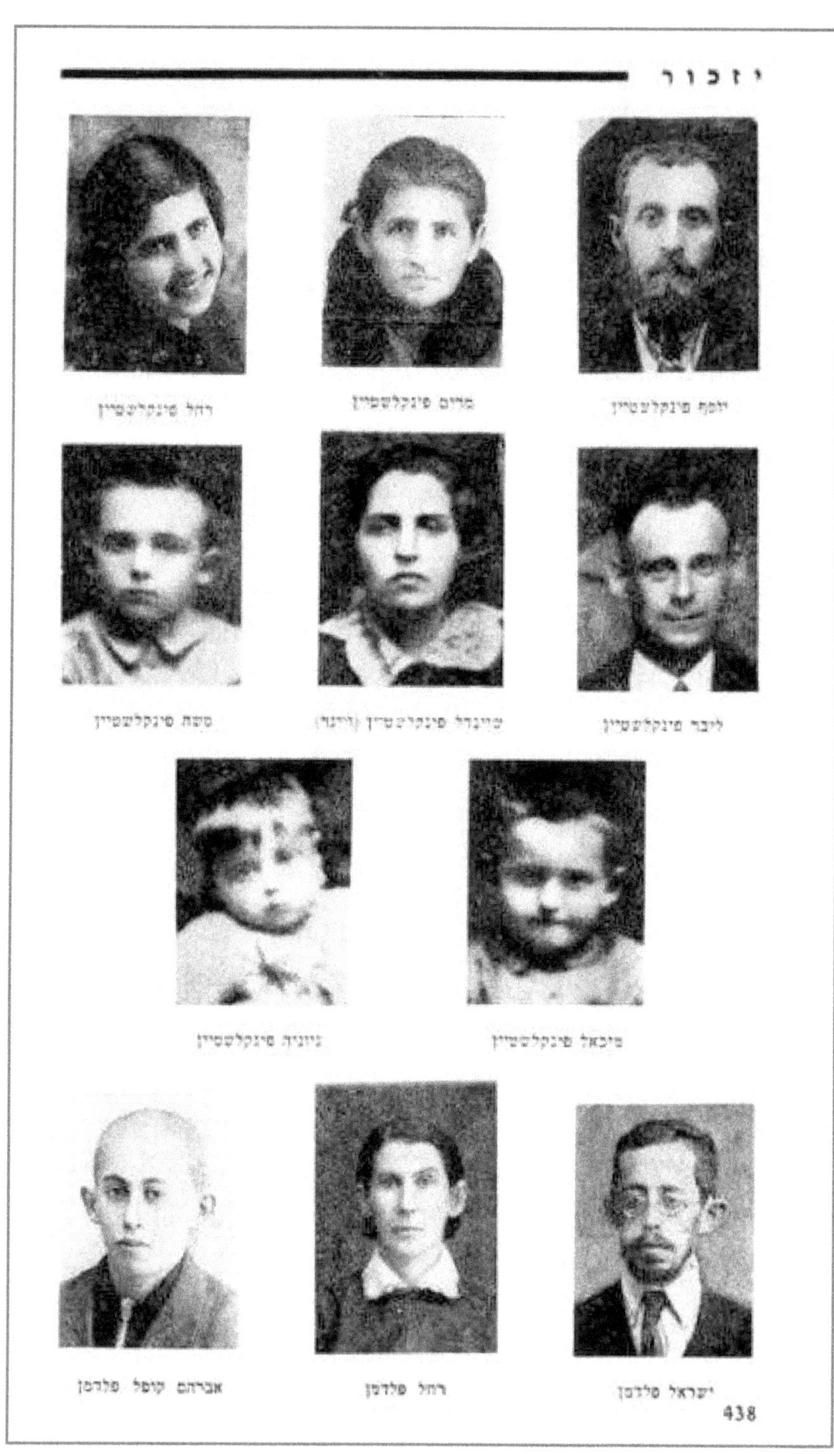

יזכור

יוסף פינקלשטיין
מרים פינקלשטיין
רחל פינקלשטיין

ליבר פינקלשטיין
מינדל פינקלשטיין (ווינער)
משה פינקלשטיין

מיכאל פינקלשטיין
גיוניה פינקלשטיין

ישראל פלדמן
רחל פלדמן
אברהם קופל פלדמן

438

Photos Page 438

Left to right

Rachel Finkelstein Miriam Finkelstein Yosef Finkelstein

Moshe Finkelstein Sheindel Finkelstein (Weiner) Liber Finkelstein

Nionia (Noah) Finkelstein Michael Finkelstein

Avraham Kopel Feldman Rachel Feldman Yisrael Feldman

[Page 439]

יזכור
שלמה והרשל פרידמן
פרץ פרלוביץ
נחמן פרלוביץ
רחל פרלוביץ
אסתר פרלוביץ
יעקב פרנר
שלמה פרנר
חוה פרנר
יואל פרנר
מינה פרידמן
רבקה
439

Photos Page 439

Left to right

Peretz Perlovich Hershel (Zvi) (left) and Shlomo Friedman (right)

Esther Perlovich Rachel Perlovich Nachman Perlovich

Chava Freger (Grinshpan) Zlata Freger Yaakov Freger

Rivka Perlstein Moshe Freierman Yoel Freger

[Page 440]

יזכור
סנדר פרל
טייבה פרל
פערל שנדלר (פרל)
מאיר פרל
אהרן ציציק
חיה שרה ציציק (פרגר)
טניה צווייבאום
אסתר צ'רפיצ'ניק (גרינברג)
שרה קוץ
פסח קוץ
אהרן קוץ
בייבה קוץ
440

Photos Page 440

Left to right

Pearl Tendler (Perl) Toiva Perl Sender Perl

Chaya Sara Chechik (Freger) Aharon Chechik Meir Perl

Sara Kutz Esther Cerpichnik (Greenberg) Tanya (Tamara) Zveibaum

Beiba Kutz Aharon Kutz Pesach Kutz

[Page 441]

יזכור

צבי ובתיה קוקייב (גיטמן)

בן־ציון קוקייב

פנחס קלורפיין

פניה קלורפיין

אברהם קלורפיין

שיינדל קגן

בצלאל קוקל

דייזל קוקל

שיינצה קוקל

ניוסיה קוקל

אהרן קליינמן

441

Photos Page 441

Left to right

Ben-Zion Kokoiv	Zvi and Batia Kokoiv (Geipman)	
Avraham Klorfein	Fania Klorfein	Pinchas Klorfein
Raizel Kokel	Bezalel Kokel	Sheindel Kagan
Aharon Kleiman	Niosia Kokel	Shaintza Kokel

[Page 442]

יזכור
משה קורובוצ'קה
מרים קורובוצ'יקה
פראדל קורובוצ'קה
יואל קורובוצ'קה
היניה קורובוצ'קה (גנדלמן)
בנימין קורובוצקה
נתן קורובוצ'קה
חוה מהלר (קורובוצ'קה)
רעיה מהלר
חיניה הוברס (קורובוצ'קה)
נחמן הוברס
יהושע־ברוך קעק
442

Photos Page 442

Left to right

Fradel Korobochka	Miriam Korobochka	Moshe Korobochka
Benyamin Korobochka	Henia Korobochka(Gendelman)	Yoel Korobochka
Raya Mahler	Chava Mahler (Korobochka)	Natan Korobochka
Yeshayahu-Baruch Kek	Nachman Huvers	Henia Huvers (Korobochka)

[Page 443]

יזכור

טוניה קליינמן (קסירא) | מניה קליינמן | ברוך קרבצ'יק

בריינדל קפלן | יהודה קפלן | רוזה קרצ'ר

פייגל קריבולה (לורן) | יהושע עפשל קריבולה | רחל קריצ'מן

חנה קריצ'מן | אהרן־דב רוזנשטיין | חיה רוזנשטיין

443

Photos Page 443

Left to right

Baruch Kravchik	Maniya Kleiman	Sonia Kleiman (Shapira)
Roza Kracher	Yehuda Kaplan	Braindel Kaplan
Rachel Krychman	Yehoshua Shepsel Krivola	Faigel Krivola (Levin)
Chaya Rosenstein	Aharon-Dov Rosenstein	Chana Krychman

[Page 444]

יזכור

צבי ורחל רוזנשטיין

לזיק רוטמן

רבקה רוטמן (וינגשטיין)

אהרן רוטמן

גניה רוטמן

חיים־יהודה שוחט

פייביש שבצ'ניק

דבוסל שבצ'ניק (דראר)

יעקב־שמואל שוינדלמן

רבקה שוינדלמן

רבקה שורץ (פוליטוק)

444

Photos Page 444

Left to right

Levik Rotman Zvi and Rachel Rosenstein

Genia Rotman Aharon Rotman Rivka Rotman (Yungstein)

Dvorsia Svetchnik (Drach) Feivish Svetchnik Haim-Yehuda Shohet

Rivka Schwartz (Polishuk) Rivka Shvindelman Yaakov-Shmuel Shvindelman

[Page 445]

Photos Page 445

Left to right

Yosef Shulman Necha Shulman Moshe-Zelig Shulman

Genia Shuver Baruch Shuver Rivka Shulman

The Rabbanit Leah-Rikel Shames The Rabbi R' Aharon-Yosef Shames

Fania Shwartzblat Dvorah Shwartzblat Berl (Dov) Shwartzblat

[Page 446]

יזכור
יהודה שוסטר
נחה שוסטר
בתיה שוסטר
חוה שוארצברג (קליגר)
הרב יואל שוארצברג
איציק שוארצברג
שרה שוארצברג
446

Photos Page 446

Left to right

Miriam Shwartzblat (Gendelman) Mendel Shwartzblat

Yehuda Shuster Necah Shuster Batia Shuster

Chava Shwartzberg (Kleiger) Ritual Slaughterer and Examiner Yoel Shwartzberg

Itzik (Yitzhak) Shwartzberg Sarah Shwartzberg

[Page 447]

יזכור

הרשל שטיינמן | מלכה שטיינמן | דוד שכנובסקי

מירל שכנובסקי | אהרן (לוליק) שכנובסקי | פרידה שכנובסקי

שולמית ברקמן (שכנובסקי) | מינה שפילברג | ביילה שפילברג (קגן)

בנימין שטדלר | שרה שטדלר (נייברג) | שושנה שטדלר

447

Photos Page 447

Left to right

David Shachnovski Malka Shteinman Hershel Shteinman

Freida Shachnovski Aharon (Lolik) Shachnovski Mirel Shachnovski

Baila Shpeilberg (Kagan) Mina Shpeilberg; Shlomit Berkman (Shachnovski)

Shoshana Shtedler Sarah Shtedler (Naiberg) Benyamin Shtedler

[Page 448]

יזכור

רבקה ושלמה שפירא

טויבע שפירא

יוכבד שפירא

הביה שפירא

ברמן משה בן אברהם

448

Photos Page 448

Rivka and Shlomo Shapira

Left to right

Chesia Shapira Yocheved Shapira Taiva Shapira

Moshe ben Avraham Barman

[Page 449]

Communal Grave Of Our Martyrs Slaughtered By The Nazis
Cemetery In Rokitno
Gravestone reads in Russian and Hebrew:
"Killed By Hitler's Murderers 1942"

[Page 450]

Translated by Ala Gamulka

My eyes have witnessed the bereavement
And my twisted heart is filled with outcries
My inner compassion has always led me to forgive
Until the times came that would not allow me to forgive
I then made an oath: to remember everything
To remember and never to forget.

Never to forget – up to the tenth generation,
Until my sorrow will subside, until they all will be gone,
Until all chastisement will end.
Mourning is in vain if the angry night passes
Mourning, if in the morning I return to my ways
And I will learn nothing again.

Avraham Shlonsky

[Page 451]

ASSOCIATION OF FORMER RESIDENTS OF ROKITNO AND VICINITY IN ISRAEL

[Page 453]

The Executive Committee

History of the Organization and its Activities

Translated by Ala Gamulka

Until the second half of 1944 we did not know the fate of the Jews or of Rokitno and its surroundings. We did know that the well-known Bundist activist Shmuel Mordechai Zigelboim committed suicide on May 1, 1943, on the threshold of the British Parliament building in London. It was a protest against the disinterest the free world was showing about the murder of a whole nation. However, we did not imagine and we did not want to believe that it was actually extermination.

The person who did tell us this horrifying news, that the Rokitno community no longer existed, was our own Baruch Shehori (Schwartzblat). In 1944, he sent a postcard to his sister Sarah in Palestine. The postcard contained the following:

> "Rokitno is alone and in mourning. More than half of it is in ruins. Many Jewish houses were erased off the face of the earth together with their owners. Eighty-three Jews came out of the forests and have gathered here. This is the remnant of a Jewish population of 1630 who were on the killing-field. There is now a small group of sick, poor, broken and dejected."

This letter erased any false hopes and presented the sad truth to us. We were orphans. The letter was printed then in the local press and even in other countries. It touched many people. We toyed with the hope that "maybe, after all" someone remained alive. Many wrote letters to Shehori to ask about the fate of their relatives. He had no answer for them. His only reply was: "There is no one left of your family. They were all exterminated".

This terrible news roused us to rescue the remnants from hunger and deterioration. This required proper organization. One Shabbat in 1944 the following members gathered in the Kupat Holim building on Ben Ami street in Tel Aviv: Yosef Eisenberg, Meir Burd, Dov Vorona, Hanan Hatzuvi (Trigun), Aharon Heruti (Freierman), Baruch Levin *z"l*, Yeshayahu Meiri (Meirson), Rachel Margalit (Meirson), and Haim Shteinman. It was decided to set up an organization of former residents of our town and its surroundings.

We began by collecting addresses of former residents of our town and its surroundings residing in the country in order to organize them in an institutional framework. This was not enough for us and we immediately began assistance activities. We sent packages of clothes and food to the survivors in Rokitno. The packages arrived and were used to save lives and were also a source of encouragement.

These activities were not continuous. Five years passed, during which we continued to collect addresses and to search for former residents. The first survivors, who came illegally to Eretz Israel, testified about the terrible destruction and this urged us to organize properly.

In 1949 we began in earnest (up to then we met as a small group). On the 13th of *Elul* 5709 (7th September 1949) we held the first gathering and the first memorial service in Tel Aviv. Many former residents of our town and its surroundings came from all parts of the country – from cities, settlements and kibbutzim. At this gathering, survivors spoke about the terrible destruction. It was decided to establish the organization and the first executive committee was elected. It consisted of the following: Dov Vorona, Aharon Heruti (Freierman), Baruch Levin z"l, Aharon Lifshitz, Betzalel Kek, Baruch Shehori (Schwartzblat) and Haim Shteinman. The chairman was Haim Shteinman.

On 8th of *Tevet* 5710 (28th December 1949) the first newsletter was sent to all former residents. The formation of this organization and its purpose were announced. The need to commemorate our martyrs who were exterminated in the Holocaust was emphasized. We attached a questionnaire and sent it to all those whose addresses we had. We asked them to pass the questionnaire on to others whose addresses we did not have.

In order to finance the activities of the organization we asked each member to pay one *lira* per year. We opened an account at the Bank of Savings and Loans in Tel Aviv. The response was good and we began our work. Haim Shteinman, who organized all activities, worked diligently and the organization has functioned smoothly since.

At the first meeting of the executive it was agreed that the first and foremost item was the commemoration of our martyrs. Accordingly, a newsletter was issued on 5th of *Tammuz* 5710 (20th June 1950) in which we explained and emphasized the importance of commemorating our martyrs in a memorial book. We wanted to find appropriate material that pertained to Rokitno and its surroundings.

During all this time we never forgot our martyrs and we met every year to commemorate them. Eight years after the annihilation of Rokitno and its surroundings, a large gathering was held. We had managed to reach many of our former residents. At this gathering our member Aharon Heruti (Freierman) expressed, in a few sentences, our great pain and our terrible loss. Among the rest, he said:

"Today represents eight years since the Jews of our town and its surroundings were murdered. On 13th of *Elul*, eight years ago, our dearly beloved parents, brothers and sisters were called to the market square and they did not return. We meet today, as we have every year, to remember all those who were so dear to us. We are left with wonderful memories. These are memories of Rokitno and its surroundings where we spent our best years, where we dreamed of Zion and our capital Jerusalem. Our beloved memories are full of sorrow because this beautiful world was annihilated and became a pile of bones."

He was followed by Baruch Shehori (Schwartzblat) who spoke about Rokitno during the Soviet occupation at the outbreak of the Holocaust. When he finished, Baruch Levin *z"l*, reminisced about the vibrant life in Rokitno in the past and he eulogized the fallen. Haim Shteinman discussed the administrative activities of the organization. He announced that the assistance to the survivors in Rokitno was over since they had all left Rokitno, either to Israel or overseas.

At this memorial service, the first national executive committee was elected. The following were its members: Ziporah Blizhovsky, Zvi Barzilay (Eizenstein), Yitzhak Golod, Dina Vardy (Roitblat), Dov Vorona, Aharon Heruti (Freierman), Baruch Levin *z"l*, Aharon Lifshitz, Yeshayahu Meiri (Meirson), Yitzhak Freger, Israel Kek, Baruch Shehori (Schwartzblat), Haim Shteinman, Zvi Shapira *z"l*.

The committee slowly broadened its sphere of activities. On the 29th June 1952 we gathered all former residents living in the north in order to tighten our contacts. The meeting took place in the hall of *Mitbah Hapoelim* on Hechalutz Street in Haifa. There was lively participation. At this gathering, Haim Shteinman spoke representing the committee, about its activities, plans for the future and preparations for the tenth anniversary of the extermination of Rokitno and the surrounding communities.

When the survivors arrived in the country, some of them turned to the organization for financial help. We saw the need to have a fund for assistance and *Gmilut Hassadim*. It was begun in 1951. The following members formed the committee: Shlomo Blizhovsky (Chairman), Aharon Heruti (Freierman), Aharon Lifshitz, Haim Shteinman, Zvi Shapira *z"l*. Some former residents who had means contributed large sums of money to this fund. The fund was very helpful to those who were needy. The loans were small, but they saved the recipients. They, in turn, knew how to appreciate the value of the fund. After it was decided to produce a memorial book, the fund was closed and any remaining money was transferred towards this project.

Our first commemorative activity was the planting of a grove of trees (with the help of the Jewish National Fund) in memory of the fallen from Rokitno and surroundings in the Martyrs Forest (Forest of Poland) in the hills of Jerusalem.

This activity necessitated intensive organizational work. On 29th of *Kislev* 5713 (17th December 1952) a special newsletter was issued to all our former residents to announce the project. We attached a questionnaire in which we asked for the number of people that each family wished to commemorate and any other details.

Participants In Planting Ceremony In Martyrs Forest In 1952

First row from top, right to left: 1... 2... 3. Ziporah Fishman 4. Rivka Kutz 5. Nachman Fishman 6. Avraham Tendler 7. Henia Tochman 8. Yosef Vorona 9. Greber 10. Nachman Vorona 11. P. Lichtman 12. Brach 13... 14. Avraham Eisenberg 15. Yosef Eisenberg 16. Nachman Vorona 17. Haim Shteinman
Second row, right to left: 1. Freiman 2. Aharon Freiman 3. Fania Freiman 4. Naiberg 5. Shoshana Shteinman 6. Breindl Tendler 7. Vorona
Third row, right to left: 1. Ephraim Vorona 2. Dov Vorona 3. P. Fuchsman 4. Sara Fuchsman 5.... 6. Ziporah Blizhovsky 7. Natan Levin 8. Grinshpan 9...... 10. .....11. Hagai Baum 12. Turovitz 13. Dov Baum

After we went over the questionnaires we discovered that, for now, there would be 600 trees. We hoped, in the future, to reach the goal of 1000 trees. In cooperation with the Jewish National Fund the first planting was held on *Tu B'Shevat* 5713 (1953). We invited our members to the ceremony. Many arrived from all parts of the country and planted the first seedlings with their own hands in the area assigned to us. A sign was placed reading "Grove of the Martyrs of Rokitno and Surroundings". We stood together to memorialize our martyrs and our members. Yeshayahu Meiri (Meirson) and Haim Shteinman eulogized our dearly beloved with emotional speeches.

The planting of the grove occurred ten years after the extermination of the community of Rokitno and surroundings. That year we held a memorial assembly, with many participants, in the hall of the Educational Center on Raines Street in Tel Aviv. Haim Shteinman presided over the assembly. Baruch Levin z"l, concentrated on discussing the ten years since the extermination. Baruch Shehori (Schwartzblat) reminisced about the Holocaust period and the announcer Shamai Rozenblum (survivor of Lodz ghetto) read chapters on the Holocaust. Haim Shteinman reported on the activities of the executive committee and on plans for the future. Aryeh (Liova) Geipman reported on the *Gmilut Hassadim* fund. At that assembly we distributed certificates provided by the Jewish National Fund to those who had planted trees. At the end a film was shown.

Presiding Committee At The Memorial Assembly In Tel Aviv Commemorating The Tenth Anniversary Of The Destruction Of Rokitno And Area

Right to left: 1. Aryeh (Liova) Geipman 2. Dina Vardy (Roitblat) 3. Baruch Levin *z"l* - speaking 4. Zvi Shapira *z"l* 5. Haim Shteinman. 6.Aharon Lifshitz

On 13th of *Elul* 5717 (9th September 1957), a memorial assembly was held to commemorate the 15th anniversary of the extermination in the new hall of "Our Home" in Haifa. Among other remarks, Haim Shteinman said the following:

"We have gathered here tonight to remember a Jewish town and its surrounding area which have been annihilated forever. Let us together commemorate our dearly beloved. We will view the images of mothers and fathers, brothers and sisters, who were slaughtered by the Nazi beasts and their Ukrainian helpers. In our minds we see the market square, surrounded by killers, where our town members were brought, helpless.

We see the ditches full of bodies, the fields full of the spilled blood of our dearly beloved and their unmarked graves. A cruel fate unites them in their deaths there and their memories are with us here. Let us pray tonight, in their memory, a special prayer."

The Audience At The Memorial Assembly Commemorating The Tenth Anniversary Of The Destruction Of Rokitno And Area

After this opening statement, Haim Shteinman gave over the chairmanship to Yaakov Rotman. The latter said:

"On this day, 15 years ago, we were all orphaned. Today is the *Yarzheit* (Memorial Day) for them. We, the few survivors of the community of Rokitno and surroundings, lit an eternal light near the memorial board commemorating our community on Mount Zion in Jerusalem.

We will also light 15 candles in memory of that day. We will pray the evening prayer and we will recite *Kaddish* together."

One of the survivors from Rokitno who had just come from there, told us about the present look of our town. Then the girls Ronit Shabad and Edna Barman (both from our town) did special readings. This was followed by a report of the activities of the organization.

After the grove was planted we began a second commemorative project – to commemorate the partisans and soldiers from the Rokitno area who served in various armies and who fell in World War II.

At one time, Yad Vashem management approached our executive committee asking for details about our partisans who fell in battle against the Nazis. They planned a general memorial book published by Yad Vashem and dedicated to all the fallen partisans.

For that purpose we issued a special newsletter on 27th of *Tammuz* 5720 (22nd July 1960) to all partisans from our town who were residing in Israel. We invited them to a meeting in the Yad Vashem offices in Tel Aviv with the editorial committee of the memorial book. Many responded and gave details. Their stories appeared in the "Book of Partisans".

As was previously explained, the project of commemorating the martyrs of our town and its surroundings was our prime concern since the association was founded. The above-mentioned participation served as a modest prelude to the bigger commemorative project – publishing the Rokitno and Surroundings Book.

We knew the organization served a purpose – to stoke the dying embers and to not allow the flame of our martyrs to go out.

Presiding Committee At The Memorial Assembly In Haifa Commemorating The Fifteenth Anniversary Of The Destruction Of Rokitno And Area

From right: 1. Aharon Lifshitz 2. Yeshayahu Meiri (Meirson) 3. Dina Vardy (Roitblat) 4. Ziporah Blizhovsky 5. Yitzhak Litvak
From left: 1. Yaakov Rotman 2. Haim Shteinman 3. Issachar Trossman

Audience At The Memorial Assembly In Haifa Commemorating The Fifteenth Anniversary Of The Destruction Of Rokitno And Area

Part of The Audience At The Memorial Assembly In Haifa Commemorating The Fifteenth Anniversary Of The Destruction Of Rokitno And Area

For that reason, our dearly beloved were always in front of our eyes. We continuously discussed their commemoration at every meeting and assembly. There was no doubt that the only method of commemoration of our dearly beloved was a literary one, a memorial book. This book would serve to relive the way of life of our parents, to keep the cultural heritage of the Jews of Rokitno and surroundings. We were convinced that as long as we did not fulfill our debt to the martyrs there was no purpose to our activities.

Our Children Participating In The Memorial Assembly In Haifa Commemorating The Fifteenth Anniversary Of The Destruction Of Rokitno And Area

On left: Edna Barman **On right:** Ronit Shabad

To our great sorrow, not many of us remained alive. We were afraid that we could not fulfill this great mission of publishing a memorial book on our own. A great deal of money would be needed. Thus, we agreed to the request by the Sarny Association to publish a joint volume, which would contain Sarny, Rokitno, Bereznitz and Dombrovitz. The executive committee elected the late Baruch Levin, Yitzhak Litvak, and Haim Shteinman to speak to representatives of the Sarny Association to obtain details.

Later, a joint meeting of the representatives of these associations was held where the form and contents of the book were discussed. It was clear to us that we could not achieve real results because we were afraid, and rightly so, that Rokitno would be swallowed in a common book. We saw that we could only rely on ourselves. This decision entailed new and more strenuous activities. It was most important to dedicate all our energies to publishing the Rokitno and Surroundings book.

In order to collect the necessary funds for publishing the book, the following members worked very hard: Itzhak Golod, Haya Volkon (Pinchuk), Issachar Trossman, Binyamin Modrik, Israel Pinchuk and others. They acted with dedication, understanding and reverence.

However, collecting the literary material was not as easy. We could not do it on our own. For many years we approached our members, in writing and at the annual memorial assemblies, asking them to provide us with material for the book.

Unfortunately, all this work was not successful. The little that did arrive was so thin that we could not think of publishing a book. Thus, it was decided to approach a professional, someone who was experienced in publishing memorial books and to assign him this sacred task.

Members Of The Editorial Board With The Editor

Standing right to left: 1. Shmaryahu Kravi (Korobochka) 2. Aharon Heruti (Freierman) 3. Aryeh (Liova) Geipman 4. Yosef Segal
Seated right to left: 1. Haim Shteinman 2. Bat Sheva Fishman (Shohet) 3. The Editor Eliezer Leoni 4. Aharon Lifshitz

At the executive committee meeting of 31st July1963 it was decided to contact the editor Mr. Eliezer Leoni (born in Kovel) for the task of publishing the book. At the beginning of 1964 we signed a contract with the editor and we began our work. We issued a newsletter announcing the appointment of the editor and we asked the members to quickly produce material for the book. The editorial board also decided that the editor should interview some of our former residents and write down their stories.

The editorial board consisted of the following: Aharon Heruti (Freierman), Hanan Hatzuvi (Trigun), Aharon Lifshitz (treasurer), Shmaryahu Kravi (Korobochka), and Haim Shteinman (secretary and coordinator). As activities were expanded, the following were added: Aryeh (Liova) Geipman, Yosef Segal, and Bat Sheva Fishman (Shohet).

The one who stood out among the members of the editorial board was our dear member Haim Shteinman who guided the organization from its inception and who serves as its secretary and coordinator until today. He undertook many tasks. He envisaged, organized and chaired successfully and ably the annual memorial assemblies and the numerous conferences. He corresponded with our former residents in Israel and overseas. He wrote newsletters and reminders and made sure they were mailed. His address became the address of the organization. His home was open to all those who needed help, advice and guidance. In 1954 he was inscribed in the Golden Book of the Jewish National Fund in appreciation for his productive work for the organization.

Our colleague Haim Shteinman can only be described with the honorary title of a man of "burning dedication". A great sage once said: "If we did not have people with burning dedication, the world would be destroyed". Without his energy, boundless and continuous dedication to activities of the organization, to its various sections, it is doubtful that we would have succeeded in achieving this worthy goal.

We all were fearful when the idea of the book was first brought up. We all knew the value and importance of the project, but we had some doubts about our own abilities in fulfilling this difficult task. Haim Shteinman's steadfastness in wishing to produce the book enthused everyone who came in contact with him. The mountain of hardships, real and imagined, was overcome. Haim Shteinman placed the publication of this book at the top of his agenda. His whole being was involved in it. His private life and personal needs were set aside and he dedicated himself to fulfilling the mission. He was the fresh breeze on the editorial board. He met with many of our members throughout the country and he urged them to prepare material for the book. He sat in their homes and he went through their documents and collected appropriate photographs. He took care of the various proofs and he followed the printing process. He visited the printer regularly. He also cooperated tirelessly with the editor in all matters concerning the publication of the book.

Due to his great dedication, the rest of the editorial board was able to do excellent teamwork. Many hours and a great deal of thinking were put into this. For all of this, for his hard work, may the book repay him for his sleepless nights worrying about the success of this sacred project.

Another hard and consistent worker who must be praised is our dear member Aharon Lifshitz. Since he arrived in the country from the killing fields he served as a member of the executive board and as treasurer of the editorial board. He worked hard at collecting funds. He reacted to every request, urged the others and dedicated himself to any task, big or small.

All members of the editorial board are to be commended for their loyalty and dedication, for giving their time to proof-reading and editing, deciding on titles of chapters, organizing names in the Yizkor section and collecting photographs of those who were killed. The book itself is their reward.

The publication of the book was greatly helped by our dear and loyal former resident of the town, Yakov Israeli (Rosenstein) who resides in Canada. He performed an outstanding deed and sent us a considerable sum to help finance the publication of the book. He has our highest esteem for this help.

Reception In Honor Of Yakov Israeli (Rosenstein) On His Visit To Israel In 1968

Right to left: 1. Aharon Heruti (Freierman) 2. Yosef Segal 3. Aryeh (Liova) Geipman 4. Yakov Israeli (Rosenstein) 5. Haim Shteinman 6. Aharon Lifshitz

From the point of view of available material, we could have drawn a more detailed picture of the life of the Jews of Rokitno and surroundings. However, due to financial constraints we were forced to shorten the tale. We worried that due to cutting down, Rokitno and surroundings would not be properly depicted. We made certain it not be so. The book is true to everything that once was and is no longer. It is a tale of a wondrous world that has disappeared. It only exists now in the pages of the book.

The book appears almost entirely in Hebrew because the people of Rokitno and surroundings learned Hebrew from childhood. Hebrew was their mother tongue.

The organization made certain our dearly beloved were commemorated appropriately. We were among the first communities to put up a marble plaque in memory of our martyrs in the Holocaust Cellar on Mount Zion in Jerusalem. By putting up the marble plaque, the continuity, symmetry and heritage of the Jews of Poland are maintained.

On Tuesday, 13th of *Elul* 5716 (21st August 1956), the commemorative day for our community, the ceremony of uncovering the memorial was performed. There was great participation. The ceremony was opened by Haim Shteinman who explained the meaning of this commemoration.

לזכר נשמות קדושי קהילת
רוקיטנה
והסביבה הי"ד (פולין וואהלין)
שהושמדו נרצחו נשרפו ונקברו חיים
ע"י הרוצחים האוקראינים
והנאצים ימ"ש
ביום י"ד אלול תש"ב
ת׳נ׳צ׳ב׳ה׳
הונצח ע"י ארגון יוצאי רוקיטנה והסביבה,
בישראל ובתפוצות בשנת תשט"ז

Memorial Plaque In The Holocaust Cellar
On Mount Zion In Jerusalem

The plaque reads:

"In Memory Of The Souls Of The Martyrs Of The Community Of ROKITNO And Area (Poland and Volyn) ***G-d will avenge their blood*** **Who Were Exterminated, Slaughtered, Burnt And Buried Alive By The Ukrainian And Nazi Murderers (*May Their Names Be Obliterated*) On The 14th Day Of Elul 5702 -1942**
May Their Souls Be Bound In Eternal Life

Commemorated By The Association Of Survivors Of Rokitno And Area In Israel And In The Diaspora In 1956"

Among the rest, he said:

"Fear and tremor take hold of me when we stand silently in front of the Commemorative Stone. It is a memorial for eternity to our town and its surroundings that were destroyed and are no more. My heart aches and my mouth cannot speak, for my lips cannot express the depth of the pain and sorrow.

With a tremor of sanctity and with tearful eyes I remember our childhood on foreign land. In my imagination I see the town and its Jews who were slaughtered by the Nazis and their Ukrainian helpers.

This memorial is dedicated to our parents, our dear brothers and sisters, who were cruelly tortured and who died pure and holy. This is the eternal light for all our honest, straightforward and fine dearly beloved. They drank the poison and died in the killing field, alone, abandoned and helpless.

The magnificent trees were cut down and were uprooted. How can we be repaid?! We will carry their memory in our broken hearts and we will never forget them. Our soil, do not cover their blood!"

Our member Yaakov Rotman was honored to be the person to uncover the board and to recite *Kaddish.* After the ceremony we gathered in the synagogue on Mount Zion. Our member Yeshayahu Meiri (Meirson) gave the eulogy. After praying *El maley rachamim* and *Kaddish* together the ceremony was over.

As is well known, those who could not escape from the market square were taken by the Nazis by train to Sarny. There they were exterminated together with other Jews from the area. They were buried in a mass grave with Jews from neighboring villages. The associations of Sarny, Rokitno, Bereznitz, Sahov, Tomoshgorod and Dombrovitz decided to commemorate them together by putting a memorial board in the Karlin-Stolin synagogue on Bar Kochba Street in Tel Aviv. Our representatives to the committee, Aharon Lifshitz and Haim Shteinman, participated in preparing the commemoration. In 1966 the ceremony of uncovering the board in the synagogue was held with the participation of many former residents of these villages.

Rabbi Briskman (from Sahov) initiated the studying together of a chapter of *Mishna* in memory of the souls of these martyrs. A special ceremony was held on the *Yarzheit* (Anniversary Day) to celebrate the end of the studies.

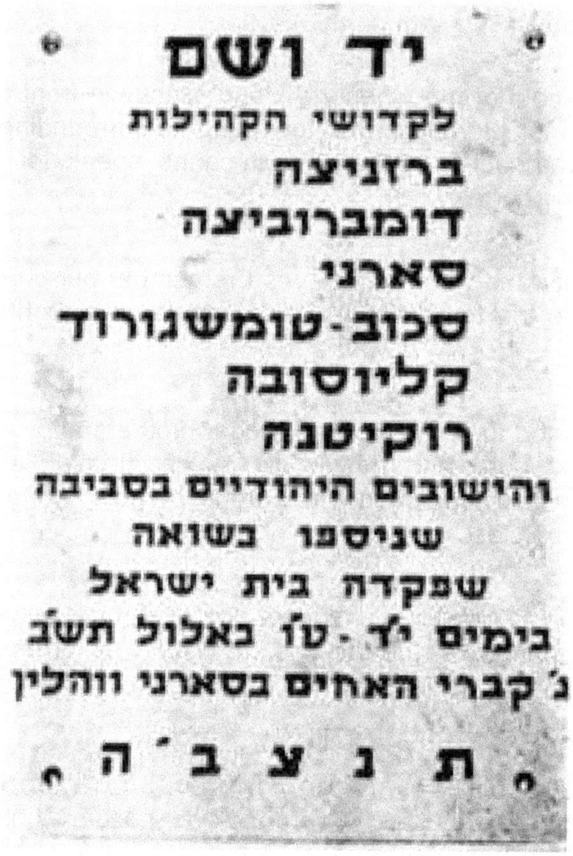

יד ושם
לקדושי הקהילות
ברזניצה
דומברוביצה
סארני
סכוב-טומשגורוד
קליוסובה
רוקיטנה
והישובים היהודיים בסביבה
שניספו בשואה
שפקדה בית ישראל
בימים יד׳-טו׳ באלול תשב׳
נ׳ קברי האחים בסארני ווהלין
ת נ צ ב ׳ה

Communal Memorial Plaque In The Karlin-Stolin Synagogue In Tel Aviv

Plaque reads:

"YAD VASHEM
To The Martyrs Of The Communities Of
Bereznitz
Dombrovitz
Sarny
Snov-Tomoshgorod
Kliesov
Rokitno
And Jewish Settlements In The Area
Who Were Exterminated During The Holocaust
Which Befell The House Of Israel
On 14-15 Elul 5702 -1942
Buried in the Mass Graves In Sarny Volyn
***May Their Souls Be Bound In Eternal Life*"**

Presiding Committee At The Memorial Assembly In Tel Aviv Commemorating The 25th Anniversary Of The Destruction Of Rokitno And Area

Right to left: 1. Yosef Segal 2. Aharon Lifshitz 3. Shmaryahu Kravi (Korobochka) 4. Haim Shteinman - speaking 5. Aharon (Liova) Geipman 6. Bat Sheva Fishman (Shohet)

Although memorial assemblies were held every year, there were two assemblies that were especially etched in the memories of our members. In 1962, 20 years after the annihilation of our community and the surroundings, there was a touching ceremony in Tchernikhovsky School in Tel Aviv. Our children participated in candle lighting and in recitations. The children's performance was organized by our member Syoma Klorfein.

Aharon Lifshitz opened the gathering. Baruch Shehori (Schwartzblat) spoke about "20 years since the annihilation of Rokitno and surroundings". Mr. Eidelman, a representative of Yad Vashem, addressed the gathering.

The second memorial assembly, in 1967, 25 years after the annihilation, was held in Tel Aviv. The hall overflowed. Haim Shteinman addressed the crowd, saying:

"Twenty five years have passed since that bitter and terrible day when our dear families were lost. It seems like a long time, but we, the survivors, feel the terrible tragedy as if it happened only yesterday. Much has happened during these years, like the Six Day War which was forced on us. We withstood a strong enemy who wanted to exterminate us. We held up with courage and strength, unprecedented in history. We did it because we knew we were fighting for our survival and that our martyrs bequeathed us life. How painful it is that **they** who gave their all for the return of the Jewish people to Israel, are not here with us to participate in our struggle here as proud Jews. Thus, we who remained alive and who reached this great event must proudly bear their names to our dying days."

After remembering our martyrs and praying *El maley rachamim* and *Kaddish* together, the memorial assembly ended.

In the second part of the evening Haim Shteinman gave a general report and a special report on the coming publication of the Rokitno Memorial Book. Members Shmaryahu Kravi and Aryeh Geipman gave a financial report and asked those present to pay what they owed so the publication of the book would not be delayed.

Part Of The Audience At The Memorial Assembly In Tel Aviv Commemorating The 25th Anniversary Of The Destruction Of Our Community

Part Of The Audience At The Memorial Assembly In Tel Aviv Commemorating The 25th Anniversary Of The Destruction Of Our Community

In March 1968 our member A. Turok, principal of the A.D. Gordon School in Holon, proposed that his school adopt our community. We replied positively and we held a meeting with him where he explained the purpose of the adoption. He wished to implant the memory of the Rokitno and surroundings community in the hearts of the generation born and raised in Israel. It was decided that after the publication of the book a meeting would be held with the education committee of the school and plans would be drawn up.

On the 25th of March 1968 a conference of partisans from our town and its surroundings was held in Tel Aviv. The secretary of the editorial board, Haim Shteinman, participated. He explained the purpose of the meeting. He asked all participants to write their memories of what happened to them during the struggle with the Nazi enemy. This would serve as educational material for the students of the Gordon School in Holon, which is planning to adopt us. The students will learn from it and will know we did not simply go as sheep to the slaughter, but that there were many incidents of exceptional heroism. These incidents added honor and pride to our nation. This heroism must be told to our children.

Meeting Of Partisans From Our Town And Its Surroundings

Standing right to left: 1. David Burd 2. Bronia Blizhovsky 3. Baruch Negel 4. Haya Volkon (Pinchuk) 5. Asher Binder 6. Issachar Trossman
Seated right to left: 1. Avraham Eisenberg 2. David Turok 3. Nachman Blizhovsky 4. Baruch Shehori 5. Zvi Olshansky

And "the river continues to flow". Rokitno and surroundings is still alive. The fact that the book was written is proof that the cruel enemy did not succeed in annihilating our nation. There is continuity; there is the guarding of the candle, which will not die out. The proof is our attachment to our martyrs and our book. We will keep watch over this treasure – the Rokitno and Surroundings Book. This is all we have left.

During the writing of this article we marked twenty-five years since our town and its surroundings were destroyed and twenty-four years since the organization was founded.

We do not intend to end our work. As long as we are alive - our dearly beloved who were exterminated and erased from the Book of Life, will remain in our hearts. We have a sacred duty to bequeath the story of the Holocaust to the future generations.

Our organization will keep up the fire so it will never go out. Proof of this intention will be seen in our activities in the coming years. Our dearly beloved will not be forgotten.

[Page 472]

THY GLORY, O ISRAEL!

IS SLAIN UPON THY HIGH PLACES;

HOW ARE THE MIGHTY FALLEN!

(Samuel II, 1:19)

[Page 473]

By Right of Their Sacrifice

(Rokitno And Vicinity Members Who Died While Serving In The Israel Defense Forces)

Translated by Ala Gamulka

MOSHE GOLOVEY

Son of Sender and Rivka, he was born in Stolin in 1927. His family settled in Rokitno in 1935 and he graduated from the Tarbut School. He was educated in a Zionist atmosphere and was a member of *Hashomer Hatzair.*

He suffered in the ghetto and in the forests together with his mother. He came to Israel on the immigrant boat "Birya". He served in the War of Independence in the Carmeli Brigade and participated in the battles to liberate the Galilee.

He died from an illness on 3rd November 1949 and was buried in the military cemetery in Haifa.

BEN ZION GEIPMAN

Son of Avraham and Hannah, he was born in Kibbutz Yagur on 4th June 1944 (12th *Sivan* 5704).

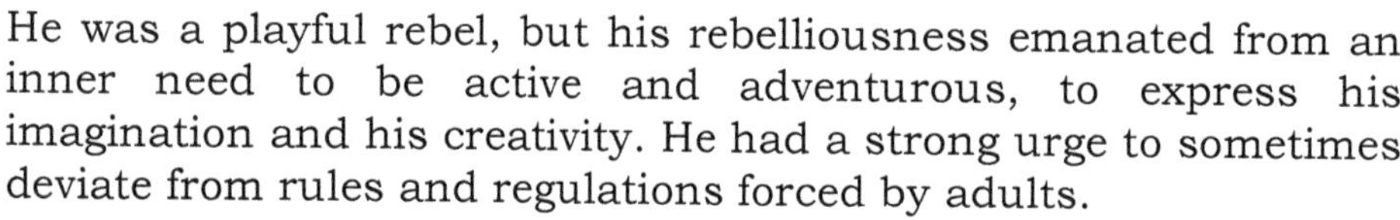

He was a playful rebel, but his rebelliousness emanated from an inner need to be active and adventurous, to express his imagination and his creativity. He had a strong urge to sometimes deviate from rules and regulations forced by adults.

Bentzi had natural technical ability. He showed a strong inclination towards the sciences and he excelled in them. He loved the slopes of Mount Carmel where he hiked. He knew all its paths and its mysteries.

He was enchanted by flying, probably because it presented a personal challenge. Perhaps he searched for an outlet for his boundless energy, his sense of adventure and daring.

The military regime and his strong wish to become a pilot changed him completely. It was as if he had grown up instantly. He would come home and shut himself up in the shed with a pack of books and booklets. He studied willingly and diligently all flying instructions, engines, airplanes, ammunition, etc.

He achieved his dream and became a military pilot. When the course for pilots was finished he was awarded his wings by the Prime Minister as an outstanding student.

During the Six Days War he served as a pilot of a Super-Mystere. He fell on the Golan Heights on 10th June 1967 (2 *Sivan* 5727). He was buried in the cemetery in Yagur. He was awarded the rank of captain posthumously.

EMANUEL MARGALIT

Son of Nehemiah and Rachel (Meirson), he was born on 20th September 1929 in Tel Aviv. An outstanding and conscientious student, he loved learning and was highly respectful to his teachers. He loved music and played the violin. He was also a good athlete. In the summers, he volunteered with his friends in farming communities and devoted himself to his task. He tried to instill the sense of duty, self-discipline and honesty in his friends at work. He had a healthy outlook on the world as a human being and as a Jew and he reacted, in his diary, to political and social events in Israel and in his small personal circle. When the Jewish Brigade went to the front in WWII, he wrote in his diary that he was sorry he was too young and could not join his elders in avenging his nation. He was a member of *Haganah* from the age of 14. He completed a course for counselors and excelled in it. He took part in struggles against the British as part of the *Haganah* youth group. After completing successfully an officers' course he was sent to teach sergeants.

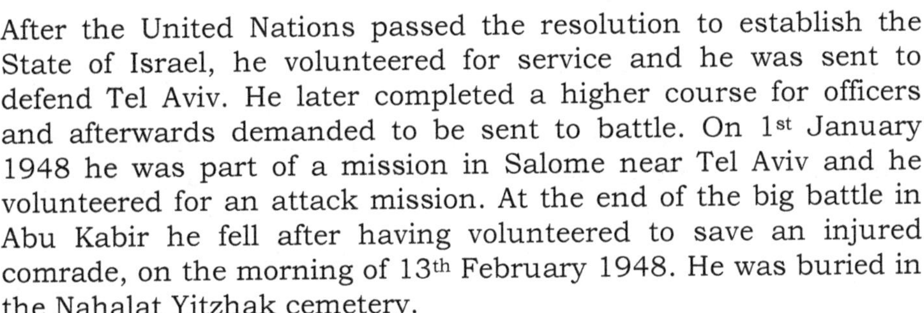

After the United Nations passed the resolution to establish the State of Israel, he volunteered for service and he was sent to defend Tel Aviv. He later completed a higher course for officers and afterwards demanded to be sent to battle. On 1st January 1948 he was part of a mission in Salome near Tel Aviv and he volunteered for an attack mission. At the end of the big battle in Abu Kabir he fell after having volunteered to save an injured comrade, on the morning of 13th February 1948. He was buried in the Nahalat Yitzhak cemetery.

ASHER NEGEL

Son of Moshe and Haya, he was born in the village of Sahov on 15th October 1926 (7 *Heshvan* 5687). He began his education in the *cheder* where he drank in the Bible with *Rashi* interpretation. He was lively and happy from childhood and attracted everyone who met him.

After several years at the *cheder* he transferred to study at the Tarbut School. There he absorbed Hebrew culture and he breathed the atmosphere of Eretz Israel, which was being revived. World War II put an end to his studies. He was only 14.

He managed to escape the Nazis and hid in the forests. There he joined a small nucleus of young Jewish partisans who fought in the forests.

When the war ended he came to Rokitno; he found out that his entire family was exterminated.

He went to Bytom, in Germany, and joined the Dror *kibbutz*. The *kibbutz* moved to France and from there he came here on a small immigrant ship called Tel Hai.

He went with his Dror friends to Kibbutz Beit Ha'aravah, north of the Dead Sea. He became attached to the place, in spite of the difficult climate, and he hiked throughout the area.

Asher was active in the struggle for independence. Among other activities, he participated in the night of the bombing of the bridges.

Upon discharge he moved with his group from Beit Ha'aravah to Kibbutz Alonim – his last home.

He fell during the Six Day War when a Syrian plane was brought down and crashed on an Israeli army camp, on 27 *Iyar* 5727 (6th June 1967). He was buried in the military cemetery in Haifa.

BARUCH PINCHUK

Son of Avraham and Chava, he was born in the village of Glinna in 1911. He was interested in Zionism and in pioneering. He worked in several *preparatory kibbutzim* until he immigrated in 1939 on the ship Tiger Hill. He immediately joined Kibbutz Na'an and spent 7 years there. When the British searched for arms in the kibbutz, he was arrested and brought with other members to Latrun. After some time he left the kibbutz and moved to Herzliah. He worked there in construction and later in agriculture. He was a member of Haganah since he arrived in the country. His warm and calm disposition attracted many friends at work and in the Haganah.

When the War of Independence broke out he volunteered to the IDF and proved himself a good and well-disciplined soldier. He joined a unit of sappers and took part in many battles. He fulfilled his dangerous assignments carefully and responsibly. He died during an operation while placing mines against terrorists near Ramat Hakovesh. He was killed in the explosion on 5th December 1948 and was buried in Netanya. He was awarded the rank of lieutenant posthumously.

MEIR FINKELSTEIN

Son of Yosef and Miriam, he was born on 28th August 1915 in the village of Dort. Even as a youngster he was involved in working in the field and in the stable. When his family moved to Rokitno he studied in the Tarbut School. He loved the Hebrew language and taught it in adulthood to members of *Hechalutz* in town.

When his family's economic situation worsened, he began, at the age of 14, to work in the glass factory in order to help out. He was a member of *Hashomer Hatzair* and went to a *preparatory kibbutz* in Lublin.

He came here in 1939 and belonged to a *kibbutz* in Netanya. From there he went with his friends to establish Kibbutz Yad Mordechai. During the War of Independence he defended the gates of his kibbutz. He was hit by an Egyptian bomb at the entrance to Yad Mordechai and he fell on 19th May 1948. He was buried in the cemetery in Yad Mordechai. He is remembered in the book "Yad Mordechai in Battle".

HAIM FREGER

Son of David, he was born in 1948 in Kibbutz Yagur. He was modest and did not speak much. He was proud of two facts in his short life: he was a member of one of the best units in the IDF and he was a defenseman on the *Hapoel* Soccer Team in Yagur.

When he came home on leave he never missed a game. He played with enthusiasm and great interest.

"He was lovable, modest and quiet", said one of his friends on the kibbutz. He finished his studies on the kibbutz and went with his classmates to establish Kibbutz Yad Hannah Senesh. A year later, he joined the IDF.

On Thursday, 21st March 1968 he went with his unit to chase an *Al Fatah* group. He fell on this mission and was buried in Yagur on 21 *Adar* 5728 (21st March 1968).

[Page 477]

Rokitno and Vicinity Members Who Died In Israel

Translated by Ala Gamulka

SHMUEL OLISKER
Came in...
Died in 1967.
Was... years old when he died.
Buried in Holon.

MICHAEL EIDELMAN
Born here in 1950.
Died in 1963
at the age of 13.
Buried in Kiryat Shaul.

HASSYA BEINSHCHIK
Came in 1947.
Died in 1961
at the age of 61.
Buried in Kiryat Shaul.

HAVA (SEGAL) BARMAN
Came in 1947.
Died in 1949
at the age of 46.
Buried in Jerusalem.

NAPHTALI GOLDFARB-HALEVI
Came in 1937.
Died in 1967
at the age of 59.
Buried in Pardes Hannah.

AVRAHAM GOTLEIB
Came in 1947.
Died in 1954
at the age of 62.
Buried in Kiryat Shaul.

MIRIAM GURMAN
Came in 1924.
Died in 1965
at the age of 76.
Buried in Holon.

YAKOV GORNSTEIN
Came in ...
Died in 1943
at the age of...
Buried in Haifa.

RACHEL GORNSTEIN
Came in ...
Died in 1958
at the age of...
Buried in Haifa.

AHARON GALPERIN
Came in 1948.
Died in 1963
at the age of...
Buried in Haifa.

AVRAHAM GEIPMAN
Came in 1929.
Died in 1965
at the age of 57.
Buried in Kibbutz Yagur.

HAYA-SARAH GALPERIN
Came in 1948.
Died in 1965
at the age of 61.
Buried in Haifa.

HANNAH GENDELMAN
Came in 1945.
Died in 1949
at the age of 55.
Buried in Jerusalem.

YITZHAK (son of Shimon) GENDELMAN
Came in 1936.
Died in 1948
at the age of 70.
Buried in Kfar Saba.

YITZHAK (son of Shlomo) GENDELMAN
Came in 1950.
Died in 1951
at the age of 59.
Buried in Givat Rambam.

AVRAHAM GREBER
Came in 1946.
Died in 1964
at the age of 41.
Buried in Haifa.

SHMUEL GENDELMAN
Came in 1948.
Died in 1952
at the age of 43.
Buried in Rehovot.

MALKA GRINSHPAN
Came in 1948.
Died in 1965
at the age of 71.
Buried in Haifa.

BRACHA HUBERMAN
Came in 1934.
Died in 1952
at the age of 74.
Buried in Holon.

YEHOSHUA VORONA
Came in 1934.
Died in 1950
at the age of 82.
Buried in Kiryat Shaul.

YITZHAK WALDMAN
Came in 1938.
Died in 1965
at the age of 50.
Buried in Kibbutz Yad Mordechai.

TONYA (GEVIRTZ) VARDY
Came in 1933.
Died in 1949
at the age of 49.
Buried in Haifa.

RIVA HAMMER
Came in 1938.
Died in 1945
at the age of 38.
Buried in Nahalat Yitzhak.

MOSHE TUROK
Came in 1949.
Died in 1954
at the age of 56.
Buried in Kiryat Shaul.

REUVEN TUROVITZ
Came in 1949.
Died in 1967
at the age of 86.
Buried in Holon.

BARUCH LEVIN
Came in 1936.
Died in 1957
at the age of 47.
Buried in Jerusalem.

GEDALYAHU LIFSHITZ
Came in 1922.
Died in 1936
at the age of 37.
Buried in Nahalat Yitzhak.

ARYEH (LEIBL) LIFSHITZ
Came in 1935.
Died in 1951
at the age of 70.
Buried in Petach Tikvah.

HAVA LIFSHITZ
Came in 1935.
Died in 1962
at the age of 80.
Buried in Petach Tikvah.

HERZL LERNER
Came in 1934.
Died in 1965
at the age of 90.
Buried in Jerusalem

SENDER LERNER
Came in 1926.
Died in 1956
at the age of 49.
Buried in Jerusalem.

SARAH LERNER
Came in 1934.
Died in 1961
at the age of 91.
Buried in Jerusalem.

YAKOV LANDAU
Came in 1957.
Died in 1966
at the age of 66.
Buried in Dimona.

GOLDA MEIRSON
Came in 1936.
Died in 1953
at the age of 78.
Buried in Kiryat Shaul.

RACHEL (MEIRSON) MARGALIT
Came in 1922.
Died in 1965
at the age of 63.
Buried in Nahalat Yitzhak.

MOSHE MARGEL
Came in 1948.
Died in 1966
at the age of 65.
Buried in Haifa.

SHMUEL NAFCHAN
Came in 1947.
Died in 1967
at the age of 84.
Buried in Holon.

DOV (BORYA) POLISHUK
Came in 1927.
Died in 1944
at the age of 51.
Buried in Jerusalem (Mount of Olives).

PINHAS FUCHSMAN
Came in 1949.
Died in 1959
at the age of 60.
Buried in Kiryat Shaul.

ZVI FINKELSTEIN
Came in 1948.
Died in 1954
at the age of 66.
Buried in Haifa.

YAKOV PIK
Came in 1950.
Died in 1967
at the age of 74.
Buried in Holon.

ITA FREIERMAN
Came in 1947.
Died in 1951
at the age of 83.
Buried in Kiryat Shaul.

IDA FREIERMAN
Came in 1949.
Died in 1967
at the age of 75.
Buried in Nes Ziona.

MORDECHAI PERLSTEIN
Came in 1948.
Died in 1965
at the age of 70.
Buried in Holon.

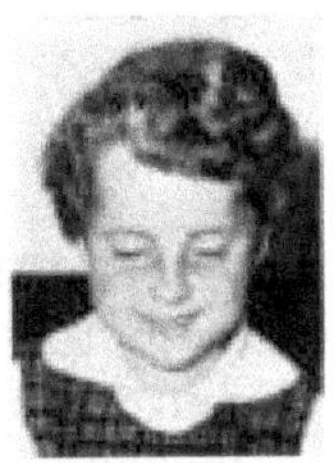

HAYA (DAUGHTER OF YITZHAK) KOZIOL
She was struck by a car on 11th June 67 while she was serving drinks to IDF soldiers returning from the front, during the Six Day War.
She was 9 ½ when she died.
She was buried in Beersheva.

ELIAHU CHECHIK
Came in 1946.
Died in 1965
at the age of 84.
Buried in Jerusalem.

SHEINDEL CHECHIK
Came in 1946.
Died in 1952
at the age of 66.
Buried in Jerusalem.

YEHUDAH-LEIB KRYCHMAN
Came in 1936.
Died in 1947
at the age of 69.
Buried in Haifa.

GERSHON KRYCHMAN
Came in 1934.
Died in 1950
at the age of 37.
Buried in Kiryat Shaul.

RIVKA KRYCHMAN
Came in 1936.
Died in 1958
at the age of 78.
Buried in Haifa.

DAVID KLEIMAN
Came in 1948.
Died in 1963
at the age of 71.
Buried in Haifa.

YAKOV KUTZ
Came in 1948.
Died in 1950
at the age of 31.
Buried in Herzliah.

AHARON KREPEL
Came in 1948.
Died in 1952
at the age of ...
Buried in Kiryat Shaul.

ESTHER-HASSEL ROTMAN
Came in 1935.
Died in 1956
at the age of 83.
Buried in Jerusalem.

ELKA ROITBLAT
Came in 1935.
Died in 1968
at the age of 88.
Buried in Haifa.

HAYA SHUVER
Came in 1948.
Died in 1965
at the age of 72.
Buried in Haifa.

MOSHE SHUVER
Came in 1949.
Died in 1966
at the age of 43.
Buried in Haifa.

HAVA (SHAMES) SHIR
Came in 1935.
Died in 1940
at the age of 69.
Buried in Jerusalem, Mount of Olives.

DAVID SHUSTER
Came in 1948.
Died in 1967
at the age of 62.
Buried in Holon.

DOV SHAPIRA
Came in...
Died in 1963
at the age of 18.
Buried in...

HANNAH (HONIGMAN) LECKER
Came in...
Died in 1966
at the age of...
Buried in Kiryat Bialik.

ZVI SHAPIRA
Came in 1925.
Died in 1961
at the age of 65.
Buried in Rehovot.

SHLOMO SHAPIRA
Came in 1949.
Died in 1957
at the age of 60.
Buried in Haifa.

[Page 490]

From That Fire

From that fire which marked your charred and tortured body
We carried a torch which lights our souls
We lit with it the flame of freedom
We carried it to battles for our land
We took the pain, the unimaginable pain,
And we poured it into stonecutters' tools and sharpened ploughs.
We turned your humiliation into guns.
Your eyes became a beacon directing ships at night.

We took a sooty and broken stone
From the calamity of your destroyed town.
It became a cornerstone and a foundation
For an impenetrable wall.
Your words, smothered in flames,
Are sung by our frontline units.
Honor and courage accompany it.
Also the ancient hope, which will not disappear.

We have avenged your bitter and lonely death
Our fists are heavy and strong.
Here we built a memorial to the burnt-out ghetto.
It is a living eternal memorial.

Haim Guri

Index

This Index Only Covers Material In The Original Book, And Not The Appendices That Follow.

A

B

W

Y

Z

Appendix A: Photo Album of Yosef Golubowitz

Introduction

Below are photos brought from Rokitno by Yosef Golubowitz, as described by his daughters Levava and Ethel. We are very fortunate to have this rare and authentic record of the life and people living in Rokitno and surroundings before the Holocaust, and consider it to be of historical importance. Many people in the photos are not identified because the dedications were scraped off. Nevertheless, we have managed to identify quite a few and hope that at a later date, working with survivors of Rokitno and their families, more will be identified. If anyone reading this book identifies further photos, I would be happy to hear from you. **We will add the new names into the online JewishGen translated Yizkor book file.** Please contact *ybip@jewishgen.org*

I have tried to group the photos in some sort of order, if they are family photos, friends, locations, but because many photos were loose it was not possible to be accurate. We bring short biographies of two of his friends below also.

Yosef's parents were Ethel and Herzel Golubowitz. Herzel had a son Ozer from a previous marriage, who went to Argentina before the war, and a photo from him appears in this collection. There may also have been other sons from the first marriage. Yosef had a younger sister Feigeleh, who went to the United States, and a younger brother Yisrael. Herzel, Ethel and Yisrael were murdered in the Holocaust.

Ann Belinsky (Publication Assistant)

*****

Yosef Golubowitz

My father was born in 1917 in Rokitno. As a youth he worked as an assistant with Pinchas Klurfein who was a photographer in the town and later he became a professional photographer. This enabled him to acquire an impressive amount of pre-war images, especially from the late thirties. Some of the photos document events and views of the town from that time. Others show family and especially friends. Some of the photos were accompanied by dedications on the back, as was the custom in those days.

In 1941 my father moved to the city of Kiev, to try to find work. Among his few belongings, he packed the album of his youth. In Kiev my father met my mother Sonia. In 1942, the German army came to Kiev. The great hunger and poverty forced my father, my mother and her parents to escape to Uzbekistan, where my parents were married. Two years later they returned to Kiev and my father found out that his parents and brother who had remained in Rokitno had perished in the great *Aktion* in the summer of 1942.

After the war, the Soviet government allowed foreign citizens to return to their home countries. My father was a Polish citizen but above all he was an ardent Zionist, the result of moral education received in the Tarbut School and in the Betar Youth Movement. In 1946 he took my mother and my sister Ethel, who was a baby at the time, and together they set off an arduous road. During this period the border crossings in Europe were risky and not simple. At the border between Poland and Germany my parents had to obtain false documents and destroy any document testifying to their original identity. They ripped up and threw into the toilet - birth certificates, identity cards, and certificates of educational institutions, as well as photos of relatives and friends. My father refused to destroy the Rokitno album. This refusal could have cost him his life, but it was important for him to preserve the last remnant of his former life. In order not to reveal the identity of the people in the pictures, my parents took a razor blade and scraped off all the dedications on the back of the images, leaving only the date and year as a historical record.

In 1948 the young family came to Israel. For many years my father refused to dig into the open wounds of the Holocaust and the album that he carried throughout the period of the war and after. Childhood friends and their families replaced the original family members that were lost. After his death, we, as part of the second and third generation, decided to honor the memory my father, his family and friends and publish these photos. The photos in the album are authentic evidence of a world that has disappeared.

Levava Roiz (Golubowitz)
Ethel Regerman (Golubowitz) (sister)

*****

Syoma Klurfein, Yosef Golubowitz's good friend

Syoma Klurfein was the son of Pinchas Klurfein, a photographer in the town of Rokitno. Syoma was the same age as Yosef, and also became a photographer. His photo appears many times in the album. His daughters have also written about Syoma's life during the Holocaust and after, in Appendix B.

*****

Zehava Nevo (born Zlatka Perl)

Zehava was a good friend of Syoma Klurfein and Yosef (Yosseleh) Golubowitz and travelled with them to Kiev when they left Rokitna in 1941. Her photo appears several times in the album. See more information about her in Appendix C.

Fig. 1A

The Golubowitz Family Before the Holocaust

Standing, L-R: Yosef Golubowitz, his brother Yisrael Golubowitz
Sitting, L-R: the parents, Herzel Golubowitz, Ethel Golubowitz

Fig. 2A
Herzel Golubowitz

Fig. 3A
Ethel Golubowitz (née Weiner)

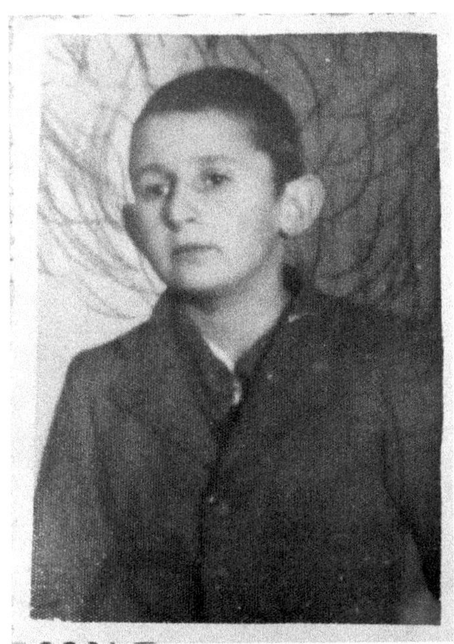

Fig. 4A
Yisrael Golubowitz

Fig. 5A
Yisrael Golubowitz

Fig. 6A
L-R: Yisrael Golubowitz, cousin Shimon Krepel, and Yosef Golubowitz

Fig. 7A
Aharon and Dvorah (née Weiner) Krepel and
their children Dov Berl (left) and Shimon (right)
(Dvorah is Yosef Golubowitz's aunt, sister of Yosef's mother)

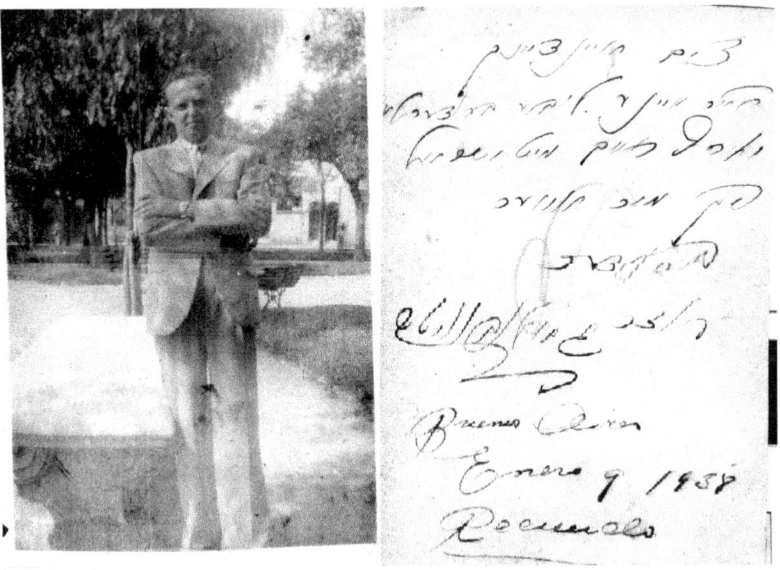

Fig. 8A

Photo Inscription: In remembrance
For my dear brothers Yosef Chaim and Yisrael from me your brother Ozer Golubowitz
Buenos Aires, January 9, 1938. Regards.
(An elder half-brother, Herzel's son)

Fig. 9A
Back, L-R: Yosef Golubowitz, Yisrael Golubowitz, Ethel Golubowitz, Herzel Golubowitz
Others unknown, possibly relatives

Fig. 10A
L-R : ---, Yisrael Golubowitz, ---, Yosef Golubowitz, ---, ---, ---

Fig. 11A

Fig. 12A

Fig. 13A
Behind: Herzel Golubowitz
Looking out of window: Ethel Golubowitz
Front: Feigeleh Golubowitz (assumed), Syoma Klurfein, Chenia Turchin (née Tuchman)

Fig. 14A
Feigeleh Golubowitz (assumed), Yosef Golubowitz, Chenia Turchin (née Tuchman)

Fig. 15A
Yisrael Golubowitz, Feigeleh Golubowitz (assumed), Yosef Golubowitz

Fig. 16A
Yisrael, Ethel, Herzel and Yosef Golubowitz, Feigeleh Golubowitz (assumed)

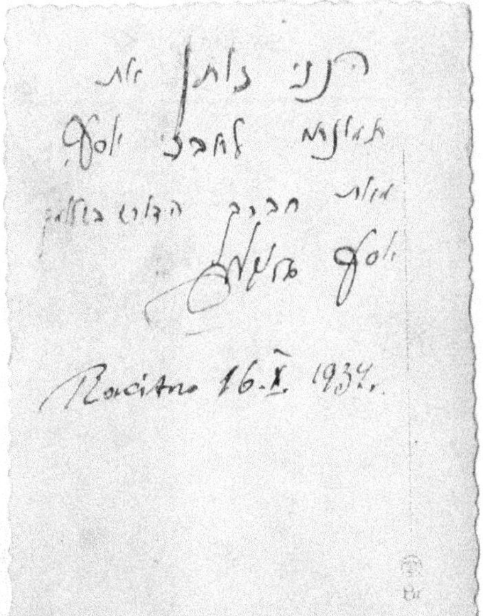

Fig. 17A
Dedication:
I give this photo to my friend Yosef. From your friend who wishes you well,
Yosef Gluzman
Rokitno 16.X. 1934

Fig. 18A
L-R Yosef Golubowitz, Syoma Klurfein

Fig. 19A
Syoma Klurfein

Fig. 20A
Above L-R Syoma Klurfein, Yosef Golubowitz
Below ---, Zehava (Zlatka) Nevo (nee Perl)

Fig. 21A
Zehava Nevo (Zlatka) 1.X.40

Fig. 22A
13th March, 1939 Pearl Tendler (née Perl)
(Zehava Nevo's sister)

Fig. 23A
Zehava (Zlatka) Nevo
1939

Fig. 24A
Syoma Klurfein

Fig. 25A
Syoma Klurfein

Fig. 26A
Etya Klurfein Ravino, sister of Syoma Klurfein. Rokitna 20.XI 38

Fig. 27A
Etya Klurfein
Photo Inscription: To Yosef from Esther
Rokitna 6.12.38

Fig. 28A
L-R: Yosef Golubowitz, -----, Syoma Klurfein

Fig. 29A
Top Left: Syoma Korflein, ---, ---, ---, ---

Fig. 30A
Above: L-R: Syoma Klurfein, Yosef Golubowitz, Chanan (Huna) Edelman
Below: L-R: Saraleh Shwarz, Zehava (Zlatka) Nevo, ?Taibel Greenberg

Fig. 31A
L-R: Haya Greenberg, Mara Slutzky, Yosef Golubowitz, Taibel Greenberg (cousin of Hinda Kotz, according to Tzipporah Miller, née Gruber)

Fig. 32A
Mara Slutzky 26. III. 38

Fig. 33A
Mara (Miriam) Slutzky 17.III 45 (or 49?)

Fig. 34A
Back **R-L**: ---. Soreleh, Chanan (Huna) Edelman, Zehava Nevo, Syoma Klurfein, ---, ---,---
Front right - violin player - Yosef Golubowitz, Saraleh Shwarz, ---. ---, ---

Fig. 35A
Drama Club

Fig. 36A

Photo Inscription:
In everlasting remembrance. To (our) brother Yosef Rotblatt on the occasion of his going to live in the Land of Israel from (his) brothers **(R-L)**: Shmuel Shuber, Haim Barman, Yehuda Friedman.
Rokitna, Dec, 30 1934. "Tel Hai"

Fig. 37A
R-L: Yehuda (Niyoni) Friedman, Haim Barman, Shmuel Shuber

Fig. 38A
---, Yosef Golubowitz

Fig. 39A
Syoma Klurfein, ---

Fig. 40A
Centre row, L-R: ---,Syoma Klurfein, Yosef Golubowitz

Fig. 41A
Bottom to top: Syoma Klurfein, ---, Yosef Golubowitz,---, Yitzhak Litvak, ---

Fig. 42A
Yitzhak Litvak, Yosef Golubowitz, ---, ---

Fig.43A
L-R: ---, ----, Yitzhak (Itzik) Litvak, ---, Yosef Golubowitz,---

Fig. 44A
The frozen river

Fig. 45A
R-L: Mottel Friedman, Yosef Golubowitz,---

Fig. 46A
Top: Yaacov Friedman
Below: **L-R**: Mottel Friedman, Yosef Golubowitz, ---

Fig. 47A
Yosef Golubowitz and friend

Fig. 48A

Fig. 49A
Top: 3rd from left -Aharon (Lolik) Shachanovsky
Front L-R: Yosef Golubowitz, Syoma Klurfein
Photo Inscription: In memory of all my friends For Chanan from Yosef Gluzman

Fig. 50A
Left - Yosef Golubowitz

Fig. 51A
Yosef on the right

Fig. 52A
Friends

Fig. 53A
A Festive gathering

Fig. 54A
L-R: Chanan (Huna) Edelman---. ?Esther Friedman,---, Yosef Golubowitz

Fig. 55A
13th...1939
Esther Friedman (?), Yosef Golubowitz

Fig. 56A
(?) Esther Friedman, Yosef Golubowitz

Fig. 57A
Back: Yosef Golubowitz

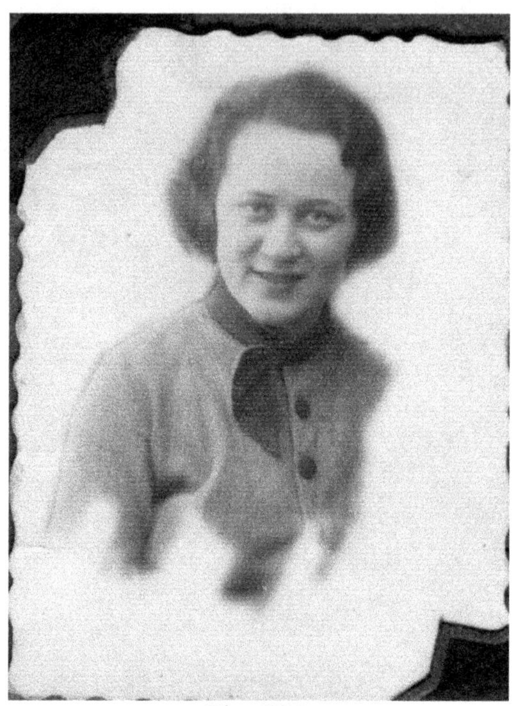

Fig. 58A
Doba Edelman

Fig. 59A
Chanan (Huna) Edelman. 1.X 1940

Fig. 60A
Yosef Golubowitz, Chanan (Huna) Edelman

Fig. 61A
L-R: Yosef Golubowitz, Natan Gendelman, Chanan Edelman

Fig. 62A
L-R: Yosef Golubowitz, Natan Gendelman, ---. Chanan (Huna) Edelman

Fig. 63A
L-R: Yosef Golubowitz, Natan Gendelman, Chanan (Huna) Edelman

Fig. 64A
L-R: Yosef Golubowitz, Natan Gendelman, Chanan (Huna) Edelman

Fig. 65A
?

Fig. 66A
?

Fig. 67A
Rokitno?

Fig. 68A
?

Fig. 69A
?

Fig. 70A
---, Yosef Golubowitz

Fig. 71A
L-R: Shmuel Shuber, ---, ---

Fig. 72A
Back L-R: Taibel Greenberg, Chanan Edelman, ---, Yosef Golubowitz

Fig. 73A
Bottom right: Chanan Edelman
Sitting left: Taibel Greenberg
Top bending over: Yosef Golubowitz

Fig. 74A
---, Yosef Golubowitz

Fig. 75A

Fig. 76A

Fig. 77A
Bottom L-R: Yosef Golubowitz, Chanan Edelman, ---

Fig. 78A

R-L: ---, Yosef Golubowitz, Chanan Edelman, ---, ---, ---

Fig. 79A
Yosef Golubowitz, ----

Fig. 80A
---, Yosef Golubowitz, --- 1939

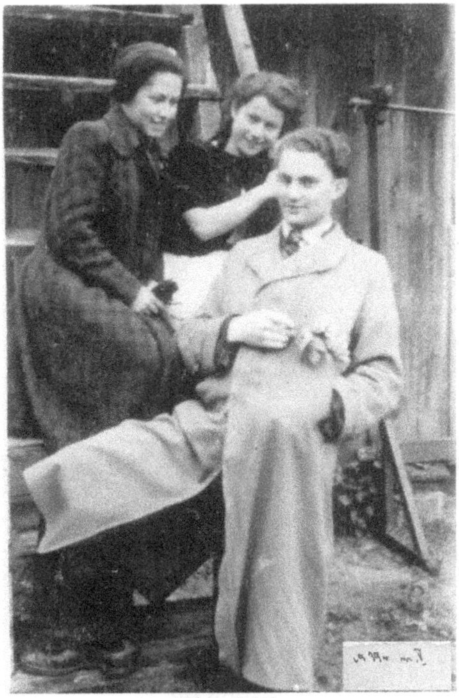

Fig. 81A
---,---, Yosef Golubowitz, 1939

Fig. 82A
---, Yosef Golubowitz, ---

Fig. 83A
---, Yosef Golubowitz, ---, ---, ---

Fig. 84A
---, Syoma Klurfein

Fig. 85A

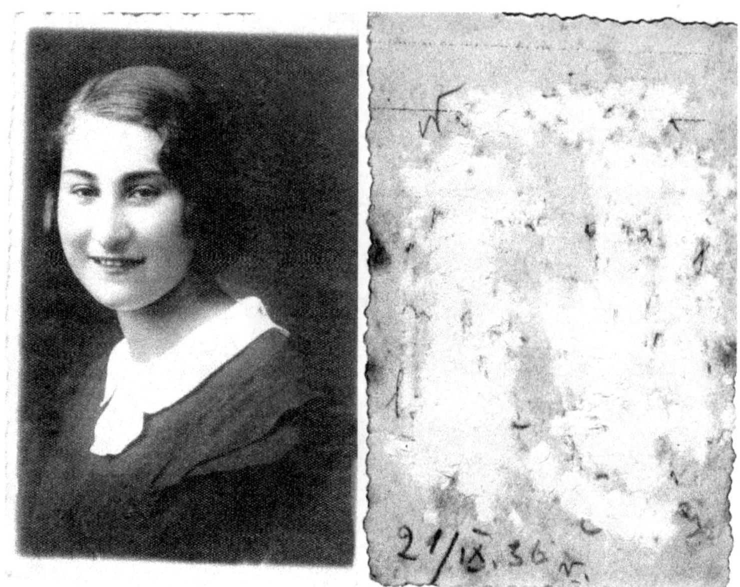

Fig. 86A
21.IX. 36

Fig. 87A

Fig. 88A
Saraleh Shwartz? (Zahava Nevo's identification)

Fig. 89A
Yosef Golubowitz, ---

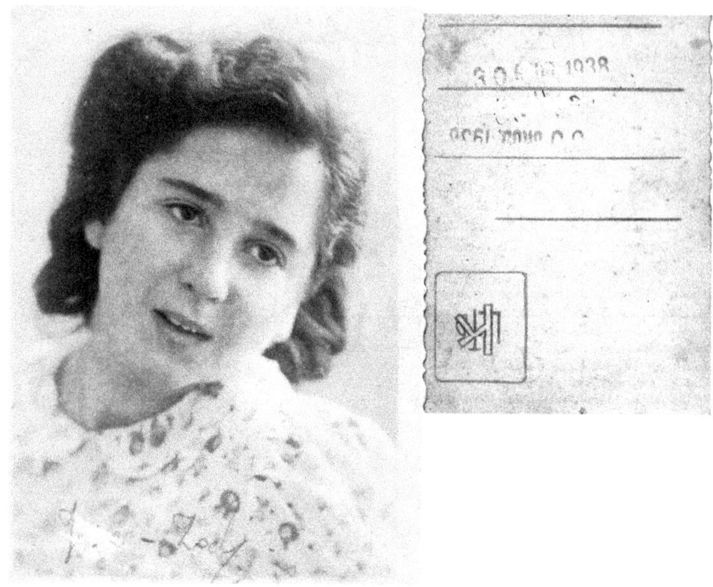

Fig. 90A
30th ---1938

Fig. 91A
1st Right: Taibel Greenberg

Fig. 92A
Girl on Lower right - Naomi Chechik (sister of Tsila Klurfein, Syoma's wife)
Girl 5th from right - Paula Gruber (née Ivry) -aunt to Yaacov Gruber
Teachers at back: 4th from right: Mordechai Gendelman

Fig. 93A
?The Tarbut School

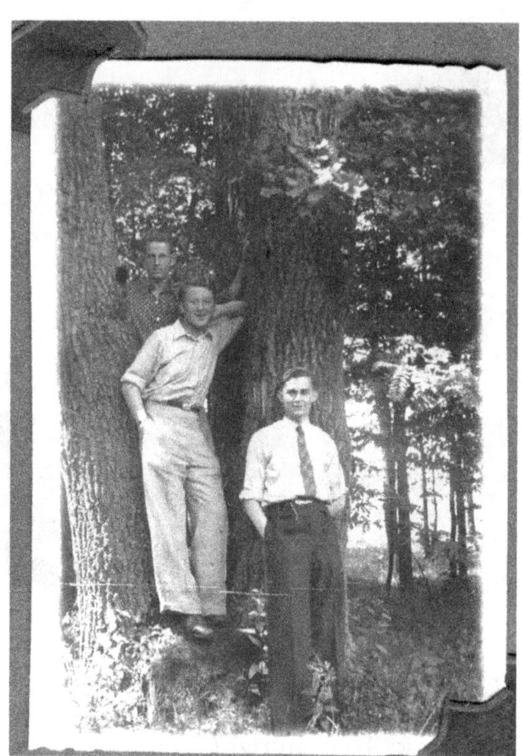

Fig. 94A
L-R: ---, Syoma Klurfein, Yosef Golubowitz

Fig. 95A
L-R: Yehuda (Niyoni) Friedman, Yosef Golubowitz

Fig. 96A
L-R: ---,Yosef Golubowitz, Syoma Klurfein, ---,---

Fig. 97A
L-R: --- Syoma Klurfein, Yosef Golubowitz, ----(??)

Fig. 98A
Yosef Golubowitz, ---, Mottel Friedman

Fig. 99A
Simcha Nagel (Uncle of Eli Sharon)

Fig. 100A

Fig. 101A

Fig. 102A

Fig. 103A

Fig. 104A

Fig. 105A

Fig. 106A
3.1.39

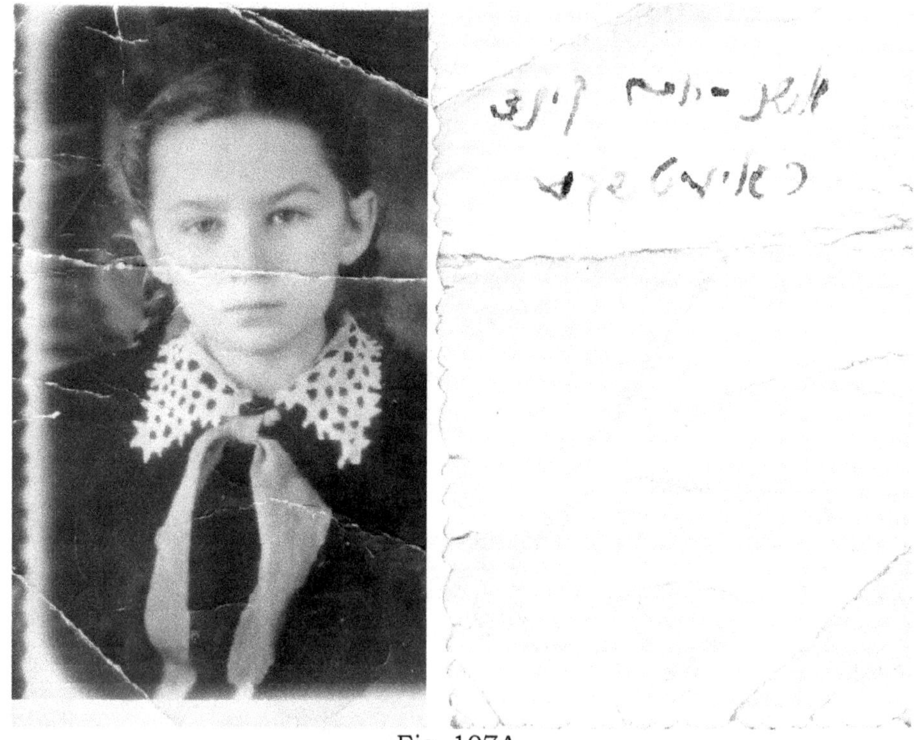

Fig. 107A
Asher-Yoram -his child
Rayatchka

Fig. 108A
2/V/1941

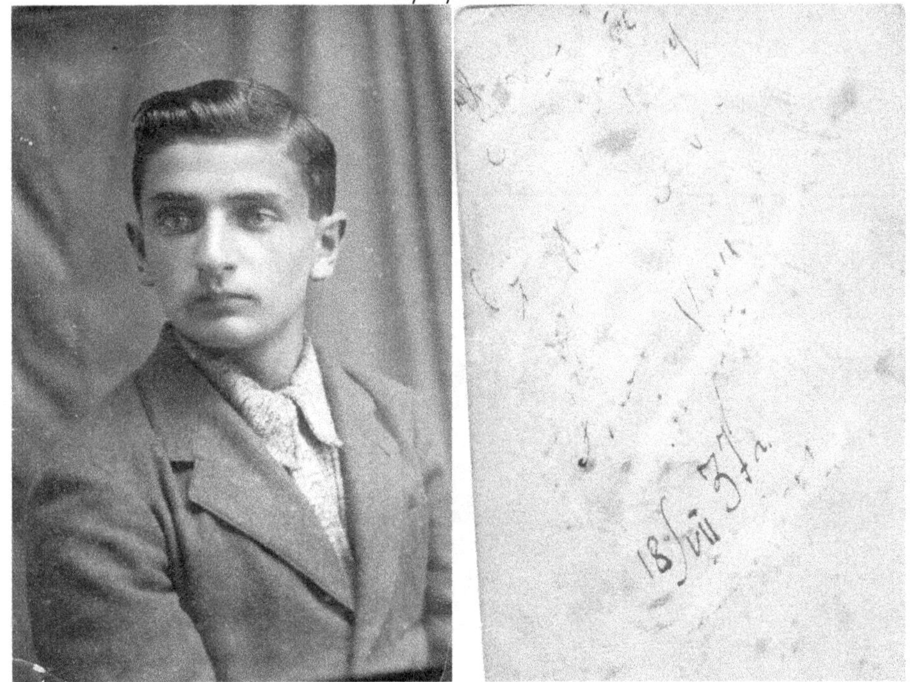

Fig. 109A
18.VII.37

Fig. 110A

Fig. 111A

Fig. 112A

Fig. 113A
Not in Rokitno. Yosef plus friends

Fig. 114A
Not in Rokitno

Fig. 115A
Not in Rokitno (Yosef 2nd from right)

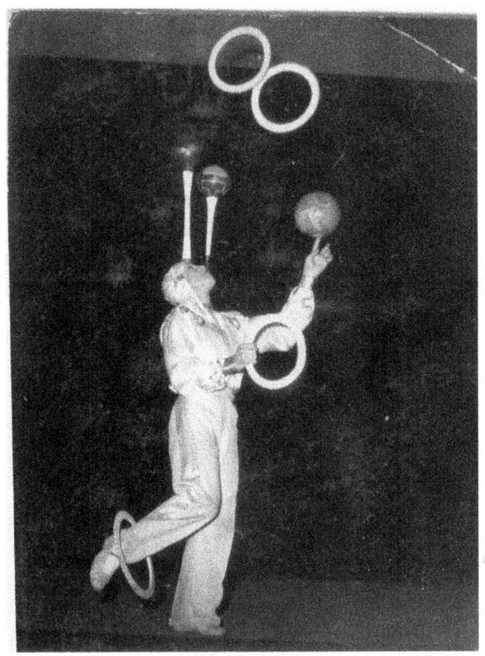

Fig. 116A

Fig. 117A
Not in Rokitno

Fig. 118A
Not in Rokitno
---, ---, ---. ---, Yosef Golubowitz,---, ---, ---

Fig. 119A
Not in Rokitno
L-R: ---, Yosef Golubowitz, ---, Syoma Klurfein

Fig. 120A

Fig. 121A
L-R Syoma Klurfein, ---, Yosef Golubowitz

Fig. 122A
Saraleh Shwartz

Fig. 123A
Yosef Golubowitz, Saraleh Shwartz

Fig. 124A
Yosef Golubowitz, Saraleh Shwartz

Fig. 125A
Saraleh Schwartz

Fig. 126A
L-R: Yehuda Friedman, Yosef Golubowitz

Fig. 127A

Fig. 128A

Fig. 129A

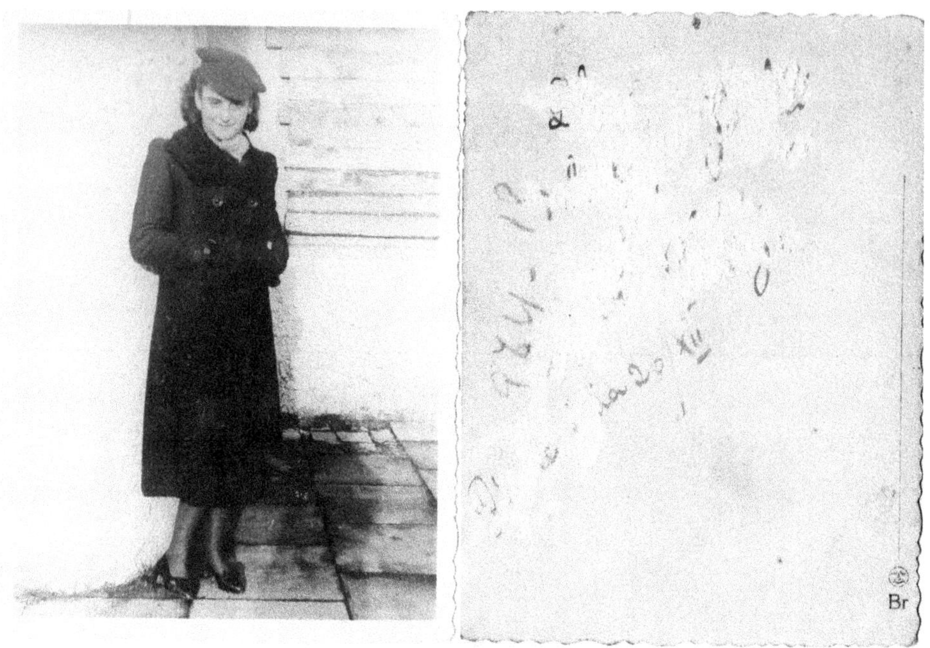

Fig. 130A

Fig. 131A

Fig. 132A
L-R: Syoma Klurfein, Yosef Golubowitz, -----

Fig. 133A
Left: Yosef Golubowitz

Fig. 134A
L-R: Yosef Golubowitz, ---, Syoma Klurfein

Fig. 135A
Left: Yosef Golubowitz

Fig. 136A

Fig. 137A

Fig. 138A
Center -Yosef Golubowitz

Fig. 139A
Right: Yosef Golubowitz

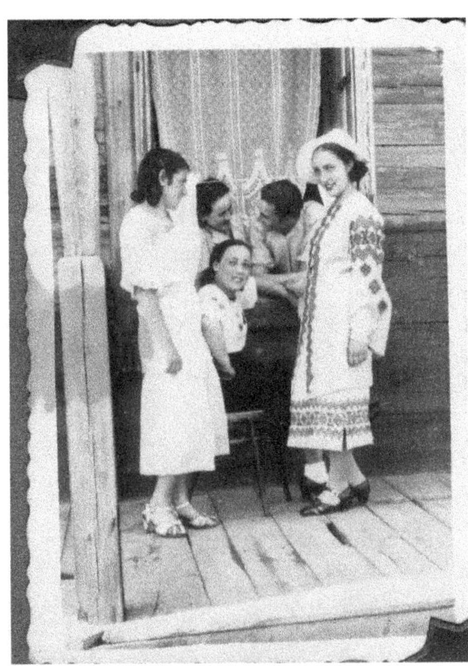

Fig. 140A
Doba Edelman (mother of Batya Weiss) is looking out of the window

Fig. 141A
Left: Yosef Golubowitz

Fig. 142A
Left: Yosef Golubowitz, ---

Fig. 143A
Syoma Klurfein sitting, Yosef Golubowitz behind him

Fig. 144A
KISLOVOSK - Healing "Sour waters" - the Gallery
(A spa in Russia)
Photo Atmanskoy 2715

Fig. 145A

Fig. 146A

Fig. 147A
Possibly Shoshana Greenshpan

Fig. 148A
Left: Yosef Golubowitz

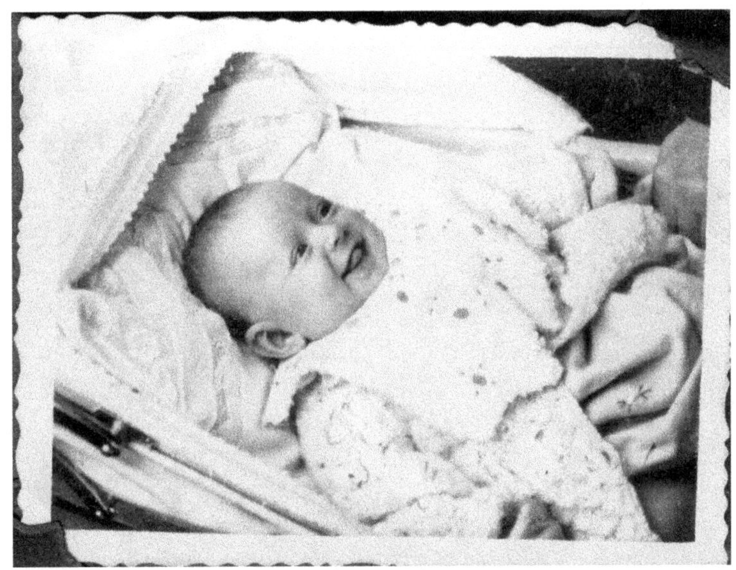

Fig. 149A
Saraleh Amir - (identified by herself)
Photo taken by Grandfather Pinkas Klurfein in Rokitno

Fig. 150A

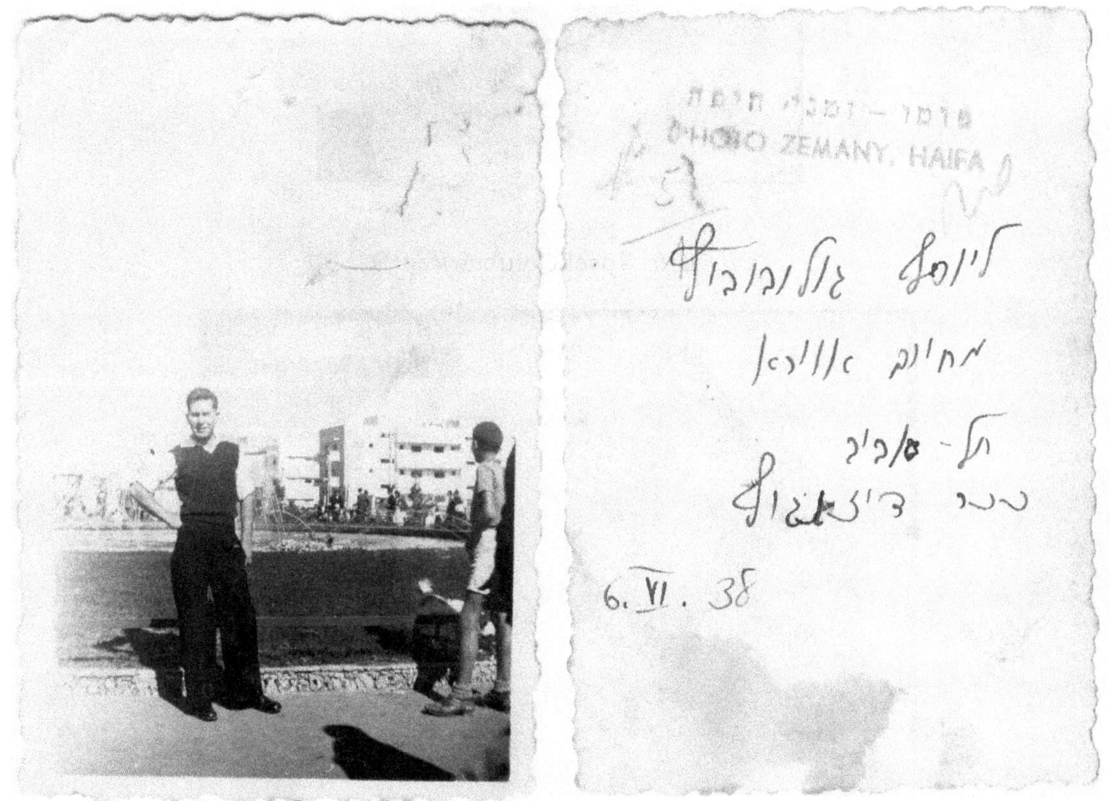

Fig. 151A

To Yosef Golubowitz
From Haim Avira
Tel Aviv Dizengoff Circle
6 VI 38 (6th June 1938)

AFTER THE WAR

Fig. 152A

The residential building in the Leipheim (Germany) Displaced Persons (DP) camp

The memorial plaque behind them, inscribed in Hebrew and English, reads: "Dedicated to the Jewish soldiers and partisans who fell in the fight against fascism 1939-1945. Honor to the fighters of the nation! The Ghetto Fighters" Probably photographed in 1946.

Lower right: Syoma Klurfein; Lower left: ?Shmuel Fuchsman

Fig. 153A

Survivors from Rokitno at the Leipheim (Germany) DP camp

Standing from left: ---, Shmuel Nafchan, Pinkas Fuchsman, ---. ---, ---, ---. Mordechai Perlman,---. Berl Turovitch, ...
Sitting top row: 4th from right - Miriam Ganya Genzel from Olevs'k

(Berl Turovitch and Miriam Ganya Genzel identified by Zack Oryan Oracz)

Fig. 154A

Possibly Displaced Persons in a room or building under the control of the US and/or the US Military (based on the photo of President Truman, the US flag and the soldiers making some type of presentation)
(with thanks to Jo Mintz Seligman for the identification)

Appendix B: Syoma Klurfein and Family

Syoma and Tsila Klurfein and their daughter Fanya, 1948

My Father Syoma Klurfein

Fanya (Tzipi) HaYisraeli (née Klurfein)

Syoma Klurfein was the son of Pinchas Klurfein, a photographer in the town of Rokitno. He was born in 1917. He was a good friend of Yosef Golubowitz and his photo appears many times in the Golubowitz album (Appendix A).

During the war, Syoma fled to Russia where he received a job laying railroad tracks. One day he broke out in a high fever and did not come to work so they decided he was a *provocateur* and put him in prison until the end of the war. Since the conditions there were similar to a concentration camp, he came out weighing 48 kilograms only. He was like a *Muselman*!

From there he made his way back to Rokitno, where apparently he met Yosef Golubowitz. Yosef probably saved Syoma from death when he forbade to him to eat a lot in his condition.

He also met another Rokitno survivor, Tsila Chechik, they fell in love and married. Then they probably continued on to DP camps in Germany. The chronology from here onwards is not so clear. I was born in the DP camp of Pocking in August 1948.

The Story of my Family

Yaffa Bonwitt (née Klurfein)

When the war ended my mother returned with her family, back to their town, which was destroyed and devastated. Almost nothing remained, even the houses were destroyed and burned, and the people who had remained were killed by the Germans.

Appendix B: Syoma Klurfein and Family

My father, who also grew up in the same town, returned to the same chaos, so then they organized youth groups to go to Eretz Israel. They left the town and somewhere on the way they set up a big camp. Youth - boys and girls - came from all over Russia, and regrouped to continue to a port where they could get on a ship and go to Eretz Israel. In that same camp, my father and my mother met again and decided to marry. Later on the way, there was another stop in the city Pocking, Germany, where my older sister Fanya was born.
They came by ship to the port of Haifa. My sister was 4 or 6 months when they arrived in Eretz-Israel. At first they lived in tents in Haifa and later moved to the Tel Aviv area, to Sheikh Munis which became Ramat Aviv. In Sheikh Munis there was a large Arab building, built in the form of square. In the middle was a huge yard and around it were rooms where several families lived. There I was born. When I was five we moved into the apartment buildings which were not far away from the Arab building. I probably loved the house and the big yard, and if I disappeared, they searched and always found me there.

The Story of the journey of Tsila Chechik, my mother

At the beginning of the story we see grandfather Eliyahu and grandmother Sheindel in their very poor home, in a small town named Rokitno, in Ukraine, in Russia. Their home was the edge of town. They were 8 brothers and sisters, studying in the Hebrew Tarbut School in the nearest city, Lvov. Jews from all the surrounding villages and towns learnt there. Social life there was very extensive, including meetings, trips, parties, and singing.

Probably Zionist education was very strong there at the time because most of the older youth made *aliyah* to Eretz Israel. Even Tsila's older brothers - Aryeh, Rachel and perhaps Joseph and Naomi came to Israel in the 30s (maybe related to the "Lovers of Zion" movement). Also Etya, the older sister of Syoma, my father, immigrated to Israel at that time - the Pre-war period!

Tsila, Haya and Meyer, who were young, remained at home and then the war started and rumors reached the town that Germans are invading Russia, entering all the villages and collecting the Jews in the market square.

So Grandfather Eliahu and Grandma Sheindel took the children, Tsila, Haya and Meir (and possibly Naomi) by horse and wagon and drove east, to his uncle who lived in Uzbekistan in a village where they lived on the farm until the war ended. This trip was probably very hasty, with much fear. They lived with the uncle on the farm, as guests, refugees. When they returned to Rokitno and saw that their house was completely destroyed, they decided to immigrate to Eretz Israel. Until they arrived to Eretz Israel it took another two or three years. In the meanwhile Tsila had joined Jewish youth groups, met Syoma, married and immigrated to Israel.

But Tsila for about 10 or 12 years of her life, from the age of about 15 to 27 had not lived in a stable, orderly house. The home she had known had been destroyed and all her pleasant childhood had fallen to pieces. The Youth Brigades lived in camps on the way from Russia to Poland and Germany and then finally they lived in a tent camp in Haifa before going to Tel Aviv. She had no sense of home, but also missed it and wanted a neat and beautiful house. So she wanted to tidy up all the time but did not know how to. She could not organize and pull herself together.

The comforting visits of Aunt Etya (Syoma's sister)

Aunt Etya (see Figs 26A and 27A on page A16) was pleasant, quiet and relaxed. There was something very soothing and comforting in her presence. She had very beautiful facial features, her long hair was always in plaited in two braids that circled her head in a typical Russian style. Legend has it that once there was a kind of beauty contest in Rokitno, and my aunt, who did not want to participate in the competition, won first place, the title of beauty queen!

A True Event in Syoma's childhood

The Big Lie!

Syoma Klurfein

It was the summer of 1928, the summer vacation. Among those who came to Rokitno on vacation was a nice boy of my age named Syoma Polonsky (his first name was like mine). He came to stay with cousins - the Perlmutter family, who lived on our street, Kostioshko Street. In this street lived several friends of my age: Lolik Shachnovsky, Milia Tribelsky, Izia Litvak, Nyonia Roitblat and others. Syoma Polonsky, the guest, was readily accepted to our group, because he was just like us. Every morning we met and would play all kinds of games, or go for a walk along the fields and forests in the area.

That morning was very hot, a real heat wave. I got up quite early, wandered around, looking for something to do. My sister sat in her favorite corner, on the laundry basket and reading a book. My older brother was working on something in the storeroom and when I came to him in hope that he needed some help, I was greeted by "Go, go away you bother me!" I left and went out into the yard, thinking to myself: "The other boys must still be asleep."

I just went outside and who do I see? Of course - "the Group" - Izia Milia, Lolik, and Syoma the guest.

- You know what? - Izia says to me.

Appendix B: Syoma Klurfein and Family

What? I respond immediately.
We're going to the river to swim! - says Milia.
Great I say, let's go! But at that moment, my mother calls: Syoma! Come and eat breakfast before you go to play!
Then everyone remembered that in fact, none had eaten breakfast. We decided that we go to our homes, eat and meet back here in half an hour.

After we met again, we went off to the river. But here the question arose: which part to go to? For you should know that what we called the "River", is nothing but a small stream with no name, which you can cross on foot, or by jumping at almost any part and if there are places where the river is wide, then it is so shallow that if you enter barefoot, it barely wets the ankles.

But there were a few places where the townspeople would come to bathe or sunbathe on the grass, while the children played in the bushes.
In fact there were three such places:
1. Our place, namely for the Jews, was near the big railway bridge which we called *Nabavsky*. It was quite pleasant, the grass was soft and clean, and at 20 meters (65 feet) distance from both banks of the river were shrubs. You could play there, change clothes or do your biological needs ... the water was very clean, the bottom was sandy with fine gravel, but it was very shallow, at the deepest place the water barely reached our knees.
2. The beach behind the *Huta* (the glass factory), was the best in the town, the river was quite wide (about 20 meters) and there were places whose depth reached more than one and half meters (5 feet), you could swim there - those who knew how, and to learn to swim - whoever didn't know and had someone who to teach him. But the "fly in the ointment" was that since it was situated behind the *Huta*, it was the place for the Polish workers. After all, it was the place of the Poles, workers at the *Huta*, and children of the workers, the *shiksim* (gangsters - as we called them) would come there in droves. For us, the Jewish children, it was quite dangerous to go there as single individuals or even in small groups as the *shiksim* would require us to cross ourselves as they did, before entering the water. Obviously we never agreed and then they would beat us, push us into the water with our clothes, steal our clothes after we stripped and throw mud at us after we got out of the water, and caused all kinds of trouble. So if we walked there, it was in large groups accompanied by adults, parents or older siblings.
3. The beach behind the *Mesivichi* area (that was the name of the street that led from it to the village Mesevich -actually it was Dombrowski Street). We often came there, but also the *shiksim* from the village would come and we were treated badly by them - for they too harassed all the Jewish children. In addition, it wasn't very clean, the river bottom was muddy and the beach was pretty high.
4. There was a fourth place to bathe in it. In fact it was the best place, wide and deep enough (up to five feet), had good grass and shrubs close by, in short an ideal place for bathing in the river. But it was not our river. It was in the village

of Oznitzek about 3 or 4 miles (5- 6 km) from us, by the railway bridge there. Although the *shiksim* from the village of Oznitzek came there too, and they did not always have mercy on us and took pleasure of picking on the *ziddim* children, it was there we would go to on special occasions such as: Lag B'Omer, Tisha B'Av or summer trip with the Movement or with the school, which meant it was always in large groups with a guide or teacher.

We walked and discussed amongst ourselves to which of the above places we should go... To Oznitek it was too far and our group was too small. The *Huta* was two kilometers away and dangerous. Therefore we continued, to the bridge (the *Nabavsky*).
And who do we meet on the street? Haya the "blind one" (she had one eye which was a little odd so we called her "blind Haya "), and since she did not have girlfriends because they did not want to play with her, she was always sidling up to the boys.
"Where are you going, kids?" - she asked.
"To bathe in the river" - we answered.
"Take me with you to bathe" - she pleaded.
"What's with you - it's impossible" - I say. "We have no bathing suits! We bathe naked!" "The blind one" laughed and let us go.

We continued to railroad tracks and turned right with the tracks towards the bridge. We had just gone about 200 meters when suddenly we heard a locomotive whistle and saw a train coming towards us. We got off the tracks on the south side and continued. Usually we went to the river on the north side of the bank. When we arrived at the bridge, Polansky - the guest - asked "Is it still far?" "That's it, here we are". "Ha, ha, ha!" He burst out laughing "You bathe in that puddle? And where can you to swim here? I want to swim". We were very embarrassed and then I suggested that we go to the Mesivichi beach. So then Lolik said he was not going to the Mesivichi beach. If we were not staying here, he was going home. We told him to go and he really went and we turned with the river towards the Mesivichi beach. We were not even surprised that Lolik went, because we knew that he was a coward.

Soon we reached our destination and there was no living soul there. Great! We quickly stripped (we really did not have bathing suits) and entered the water. Syoma Klurfein demonstrated his ability to swim. The water was only up to our bellybuttons, but we could swim a little. We wallowed there but soon became muddy and dirty because there was a lot of mud on the bottom. So we got out of the water and lay in the tall grass to dry off.

Then we dressed and headed home, but this time we did not go the same way we came, by the railway tracks, but took a shortcut through the fields and vegetable gardens of the homes on Mesevich Street. We went out into the street and from there passed by the Christian church (not forgetting to spit at it 3 times) and arrived at the sports field with the statue of Jozef Pilsudski. The lot was empty, so we could play there without interruption (which was quite rare). We played "Polenta" (similar to baseball) because Milia Trilavsky had a rag ball in his pocket. After we were really exhausted and dripping with sweat, as if we had just then left the river, we went home, but not before stopping at Kniz'kov's well, because there was a bucket hanging over it. We drew water from the well, drank and washed our faces. At that moment a Jew passed by, looked strangely at us and murmured "There you are!" And when we asked him what he meant, he did not respond and continued on his way. Also we continued on our way home together.

Even before I reached home, I noticed that the street was deserted, not a soul in sight. I thought that because of the heat everyone was at home, but when I got home I was shocked! The house was locked! Also the photography studio (my father was a photographer)! I could somehow enter the house (I had several ways) but why should I enter an empty house?
I ran to the neighbors to ask what had happened. But, alas! All the houses were locked! Even the store of Rosa, Izia's aunt, was locked and bolted! I went onto the street to ask the boys what was going on but I saw them walking and looking very confused. I shouted at them: "My house is locked and I do not know where everyone has gone." "Us too" they chorused. "Even our hotel is closed and no one is there" - Izia says (his parents had a hotel). "What do you mean!?" I say. "It is very strange, what could it be?"
And here we meet that man, who we had seen earlier by the well (I cannot remember who he was)
"Excuse me, sir," we say - "Perhaps you have an idea of what happened here, why all of our homes are locked?"
"Yes!" he said, with a strange smile on his face, "I have an idea."
"???"
"They all went to look for you in the river where you drowned!" He said stoically. "Because I did not believe that you can drown in our stream" he replied and laughed.
We headed back toward the river on the main street, which was now completely deserted. Before we got to the meeting of the tracks, we saw them! A huge crowd, coming towards us. When they saw us, there were shouts of "Here they are, here they are!" Everyone started running towards us and we on the other hand, remained fixed in amazement. Soon Izia, Milia and Syoma Polansky were being embraced and kissed by their families, with shouts of "My dear child! My sweet, here you are, we were so worried ..." and so on. Not so I ... Why? Well this is where my uncle Nota enters the picture - by chance he was staying with us (one of many times). Uncle Nota raised his heavy stick and waved it threateningly, shouting "Where is he, where is he? I'll show him, how you go to drown! I'll show him ....! "
At first I thought that my uncle was joking, so I ignored him and went on my way to my mother to be hugged and kissed. But my uncle grabbed me and started spanking me. Believe it or not, it hurt me, and even a lot. He shouted: "You will drown, huh? You will drown"? I'm floundering in his strong arms of

my uncle, trying to break free, crying and shouting: "What drown, What drown? Who thought of drowning, it never occurred to me to drown!!!" At this moment my sister Etya came to my aid. She caught me, freed me from my uncle and took me aside while hugging and kissing me. The crowd, amazed at first at what had happened, laughed and laughed for a long time... [This sentence: "It never occurred to me drown!" pursued me for quite a long time. Everyone who met me, after saying "Hello, how are you", immediately asked: "So what, you didn't think of drowning? Ha, ha ha!"].

As well as me and my uncle Nota, there were others who did not laugh. These were my parents. They blushed with shame and looked for a crack in the ground that would swallow them up. My mother ran and caught me while mumbling "What an idiot! What an idiot"! I was so scared and said to her "you too?" But she said to me "Not you. It's him, Nota" and she hugged and kissed me.

On the way home I laughed too, when my brother Abrashka, told me how Mr. Katz (owner of the hotel across the street from Litvak) took off his shoes, rolled up his pants down to his knees, went into the water, bent down and shouted: "Izia, where are you? Milia, where are you? .... ". How the passenger train which came from Otseki (final stop before the border with Russia) stopped on the big bridge and Izia's brother Lova and several people got out and joined the "saving" masses. (Apparently they sent him a telegram to Otseki on business matters and he returned with the first train).

As I say, the townspeople laughed for a long time about this. But we still had a puzzle to solve: where did the rumor that we had drowned, start? All our investigations were to no avail. Anyone we asked would say lamely: "I do not know who said .... I heard this and that ..." Even my brother could not find a better answer than that.

Now you surely ask: "What is this to do with "The Big Lie "here?" Well here is the solution to the puzzle.

A few months later, when we returned to school, we received homework from the literature teacher: an essay on the topic "The lie I told, and was believed". Each of us in the class found a small white lie, and wrote about it. But it turns out that the biggest story was by Lolik Shachanovsky. He wrote about how we went to the river, he refused to go to the *Mesivichi* because of the muddy water there and returned home in sorrow. On the south bank, he met Haya "the blind one", who was probably following us. She asked him: "Where are you going and where is the rest of the group"? Without thinking much Lolik said: "The rest have drowned and I'm going to get help!" At this Haya wrung her hands and shouted: "So why are you going so slowly?" She turned back and ran very fast back to the town yelling all the way: "The boys have drowned! Help!"

That's it! And I ask: "Who can compete with the lie like that?!

Appendix B: Syoma Klurfein and Family

Appendix C: Zehava Nevo

Zehava Nevo (born Zlatka Perl)

Zehava (born in Rokitno in 1924) studied at a prestigious Polish-Jewish school in Rovno and learnt Hebrew privately. She was very active in the Hechalutz Youth group and also in choirs in the town. She had planned to go to Eretz Israel and study at the University there, but the Holocaust changed her life. Zehava's sister Pearl (Tendler) urged her to flee when the Germans were advancing. Zehava was a good friend of Syoma Klurfein and Yosef (Yosseleh) Golubowitz and travelled with them to Kiev when they left Rokitno in 1941. From there she travelled to Central Asia to Kulkand (Tajikistan), where she had friends. During the war years she worked in the kitchen at the local Italian hospital. After the war she returned to Rokitno and found out that all her family (parents, sister Pearl and her daughter, and brother Meir), had been murdered. Zehava met and married Sioma Nabozny from Sarny. After the war she was active with the *Dror* Youth Movement in rescuing Jewish children from the monasteries where they had been hidden. This was very dangerous work. They came to Eretz Israel in 1946 via Italy on the boat "Yagur" as illegal immigrants. All those on the boat were arrested by the British authorities outside the Haifa port and sent to a detention camp in Famagusta, Cyprus. Their daughter Tova was born in Nicosia. Then the family received a "certificate" entitling them to come to Eretz Israel and they went to live at Kibbutz Alonim for three years. From there they went to Jaffa, near Tel Aviv where Aryeh Nabozny, Sioma's brother, also a Holocaust survivor, lived.
Zehava now lives in Givatayim, a city near Tel Aviv. She appears in several photos in the Golobowitz album. Her Russian appearance helped save her life.

Fig. 21A (Golubowitz album)
Zehava Nevo (Zlatka) 1.X.40

A Few Words about Chana Kleiman

By her daughter Tzipi Yoel

Chana Kleiman was born in Rokitno in1924 to Henia and David Kleiman. It was a warm family with two more sisters - Dvorah and Ruth, and two brothers - Aaron and Dov.
Chana went to the Tarbut school and after several years moved to the Polish school.

When the war broke out, two Russian officers lived in the house with her mother's family. They warned them that the last train was leaving that day and the family must take it. Thus their lives were saved, they boarded the train and moved around Russia.

Hannah's brother Aaron was recruited to fight in Russia and till this day we do not know of his whereabouts.

After the war, my mother came to the *kibbutz* in Germany where she helped prepare survivors before coming to Israel.

After many hardships in crossing borders and arrival to Eretz Israel by ship, they were sent by the British to Cyprus. There my mother married my father Yitzhak Goldman, and after a year my sister Chava was born.

My mother came to Israel in 1948 to Haifa, where she worked as a social worker and then for many years until retirement as a secretary at the Kupat Holim Clalit (General Medical Care Organization).

My mother volunteered for years in nursing homes with singing and crafts groups and twice received the "Honor of Haifa Award".

She continues to attend meetings of the Rokitna Survivors Association in Israel, and has donated these photos for the book.

*****

Family relationships

Moshe Hirsh and Pessiya LIN had 5 children: Yaacov, Yehuda, Miriam, Mindel and Henia.

Mindel Lin married Yaacov PIK. Their children are Yisrael and Leah. Yisrael was drafted during the war and killed. Mindel, Yaacov and Leah survived the war and came to Eretz Israel. Leah married Yosef Chen.

Yaacov Lin married Friedel Kleiman (sister to David), and they had 4 children: Theodore (Todros, Toddy), Dvorah Beba, Sussia and Sarah.
Theodore survived the war and married Sonia.

Henia Lin married David KLEIMAN. David had 2 brothers: Yosef and Heikel-Heikel's daughter is Ruth. David's sister was Friedel.

Henia and David Kleiman had 5 children: Aharon, Dvorah, Chana, Ruth and Dov.
Aharon was enlisted to the Soviet army in the War and disappeared.
Henia, David, Dvorah, Ruth, Dov and Chana survived and came to Eretz Israel after the war.
Chana married Yitzhak Goldman in Cyprus in 1947, and has 2 children: Chava and Tzipi. Yitzhak died in 2013.

Fig. 1D
Pessia and Moshe Tzvi Lin (Chana's grandparents)

Fig. 2D
Henia (née Lin) and David Kleiman (Chana's parents)

Fig. 3D
Yehuda and Miriam Lin (Henia's brother and sister)

Fig. 4D
Bottom: (L-R) Yaacov Lin, his daughter Sarah
Row 2 (L-R): Yaacov's daughter Sussia and her husband
Above Sussia's husband: his father and mother
Top L-R: Dvorah Beba Lin and her mother Friedel

Fig. 5D
L-R: Dvorah Beba Lin, Malka Lichtman
Dvorah Beba Lin is a daughter of Yaacov Lin
She is a cousin to Chana

Fig. 6D
Theodore (Todros, Toddy) and his wife Sonia Lin
Theodore is the son of Yaacov Lin
Theodore is a cousin of Chana

Fig. 7D
L-R: daughter---, Yaacov Kleiman, son Kalman Kleiman, daughter---
Yaacov Kleiman is Chana's uncle

Fig. 8D

The Nafchan and Pik families

Seated: R-L - Mindel Pik (née Lin); Shmuel Nafkhan; Shmuel's wife?; Yaacov Pik? The little boy on the left in front is Srulik (Yisrael) Pik who got his name from Rabbi Srulik Stolin who used to come to Rokitna. Mindel's children would die young and the Rabbi told her to give the boy the name Srulik after the name of the Rabbi and thus he was saved from death.

The Nafkhan family were neighbors.

Fig. 9D
Joseph and Leah Chen
(Leah née Pik is Mindel's daughter, Chana's cousin)

Fig. 10D
Chana (Kleiman) and Itzik Goldman on their wedding day in Cyprus, 1947

Fig. 11D
---, Aharon Kleiman,---
Aharon is Chana's brother, who was drafted into the Soviet Army in WWII and disappeared

Fig. 12D
Ruth and Heikel Kleiman
Heikel is David Kleiman's brother
Ruth is Heikel's daughter (Chana's cousin)

Fig. 13D
Hinda Kutz
A neighbor of the Kleiman family

Fig. 14D
Sima Sherman
Sima is not our family member, she was one of the students who came from another village to study at the Tarbut school and she was living in Henia's house (Chana's mother) during the week.

Fig. 15D
Sima's brother Shlomo Sherman

Fig. 16D
The Sherman family
Below L-R: Sima's brother Shlomo. Sima's father, Sima
Above ---, --- (siblings, cousins?)

Appendix E: Photograph Album of Meir Burd

Album of Photos - Meir Burd

Meir Burd was born in Rokitno in 1912.
He made *aliyah* to Eretz Israel in 1935, at first living in Kibbutz Ein Hashlosha. Most of his family was killed in the Holocaust, except for two brothers who joined the Soviet Army at that time. One brother, David, made *aliyah* to Israel, the other - Berl -returned to Rokitno and continued to live in the house which the family had occupied before the Holocaust. **Meir's son Itzik Burd has contributed these photos** which Meir brought with him to Eretz Israel.
Many of the captions are translations of dedications written on the backs of the photos. They were written in Hebrew or Yiddish. In some instances, the writing is illegible. Some photos have stamps of official groups on the back.

Fig. 1E
Meir Burd

Fig. 2E
Back of Photo, L-R: In remembrance of our stay in Kolosova; Grisha ---; H. Lerner Klosov 18 VIII 1932

Fig. 3E
Stamp on the back:
Fotographia A.B. FBLD
SARNY Wesola 9

Fig. 4E
As a keepsake
From your friend, Zeivel Friedman
April 8, 1931

Fig. 5E
Stamp on the back:
Fotographia A.B. FBLD
SARNY Wesola 9
(Meir is lying 2nd on the right)

Fig. 6E
Stamp on back: *Histadrut Hechalutz* in Poland. Kibbutz Kolosova

Fig. 7E
I'm sending my photograph for my best friend, Meir Burd.
From me, Ivri Aryeh
June 14, 1932 Kibbutz Klozov

Fig. 8E
The Senior *Hechalutz* group in Kolosova 1933
Back of Photo:
For eternal remembrance to my friend Meir Burd from Hillel Gimshel(?)
Stamp:
SZ BLIZNIUK, M BEREZNICA, POW. SARNY
7.I.33

Fig. 9E
A keepsake to my friend Meir from your friend Chana Friedman

Fig. 10E
As a keepsake,
To Meir from Chantze
Kolosova, 3.IX.33

Fig. 11E
19.XI.33
Dedicated to our friend Meir Burd
From M.S. (or Sh.)
Novo-Stav

Fig. 12E
As a keepsake!
To my friend Meir Burd
Health Resort (*Bet Havra'a*) in Novo-Stav
19 $\frac{26}{XI}$ 33

Fig. 13E
As a keepsake for my friend Meir Burd from Chantze Stern (bottom)
"Health Resort" Novostav 26 IX, 1933

Fig. 14E
10.IX.34
To my dear brother Meir
As a keepsake from your brother Aharon

Fig. 15E
In remembrance forever.
To my important brother Meir
From your brother Aharon
To Zahava Friedman
Rokitna 28.IX 1934
Stamped: Foto-Film APOLLO
Radom - Stowbo

Fig. 16E
To my dear friend Meirka
From ---,
Itzik....

Fig. 17E
---, Meir Burd,---

Fig. 18E
Rokitna, Sept. 8, 1935
I'm sending you my picture. This is my gift. See who your friend is.
Keep this always in memory so that our love may never be lost.
For the best little brother, From your sister Breindel (right)

Fig. 19E
(Top left -Breindel Burd)
For Malka, from Chana
Rokitna. 27. III.38

Fig. 20E
For my faithful niece, Tzvia _______ (last name?)
I'm sending you a picture of the Shapira (Shapiro) family as a souvenir.
Your aunt Tzvia.
(It's interesting that the aunt and niece have the same name, Tzvia)!
Sept. (or March) 24, 1936

Fig. 21E
As a keepsake (to) our dear cousin Meir Burd
From me, your cousin, Tzvia Nov. 3, 1937

Fig. 22E
Rokitna 16.IX.36
To my dear brother and sister
From your sister Breindel

Fig. 23E
Unrhymed translation (from Yiddish) of poem:
The flying machine carries us quickly away/ And it disappears from view
Tell me whether this is from the flying/ or from the happiness of love!

Happy New Year! May you be inscribed for a good year!

Back of photo: Dedicated to Meir and his sisters from---- 19.12.1936

Appendix F: Photograph Album of Haim Bar-Or

Haim Bar-Or was born in Rokitno in1929 as **Chlavna Zechariah Svecznik**. His father Feivish was sent away by the Germans and never returned. On the day of the Great Massacre in the market place, Haim ran into the forest and hid there. His younger brother Shmuel (Srulik) died in the market place and his sister Duba and grandmother Pessiya were killed at Sarny. Haim was later reunited with his younger sister Henileh and mother Dvossel in the forests, but tragically they both died there from illness and he was left alone in the forest to survive together with several others. He was taken in by a family in a small village and spent the rest of the war with them. Haim arrived in Eretz Israel on the boat Tel Hai and decided to change his name with his new life. His extraordinary story of survival is told in the book "*Yaarot Avoodim* (Lost Forests) by Ruth Milrad (in Hebrew). Haim now lives in Haifa.

Fig. 1F

The Svetchnik (SWECZNIK) family in 1936

Top R-L: Father - Feivish Svetchnik, Mother - Dvossel Svetchnik (nee Drach)

Bottom R-L: Children Henia (Henileh), Duba and Haim

After the war, only Haim remained alive

Photo taken in Rokitno

צולם ב: אוליזרקה
בתמונה: סבא יוסף דראך.
צולם בשנת 1937.

Fig. 2F
Haim's grandfather Yosef Drach (photo 1937)
Died before the Holocaust in Olizarka
Photo taken in Olizarka

צולם ב: אוליזרקה
בתמונה: פסיה דראך לבית בראט.
צולם בשנת 1937.

Fig. 3F
Haim's grandmother Pessiya Drach (nee Braat) (photo 1937)
Lived in Olizarka but moved to her daughter's house in Rokitno when Yosef died.
Photo taken in Olizarka

Fig. 4F
Haim's mother and siblings (photo from the 1920's)
R-L: Mother - Dvossel Drach, Michael Drach, Esther Drach
Photo taken in Olizarka

Appendix G: Photographs from Lora Metelits

Lora Metelits, who coordinated the translation project, has contributed 2 photos.

Fig. 1G
Gendelman family in Rokitno - 1930

Avram Gendelman is seated on the far right.
His sister Dora Shapiro is standing behind him with her son Harold.
Next to Avram is his brother Tzvi who is holding his son David.
His wife Hanna is behind them and their daughters Sonia and Leah are on the steps.
Seated in the center are Shimon and Fruma Gendelman.
Behind Shimon is his son Itzak and wife Henia.
Their boys, Borys and Reuven are standing arm in arm in the front.
To the left of Shimon is his daughter Elka holding her daughter Chaya, Elka's husband Aharon Burko and their older daughter Hanna-*Hanka* (who married Shlomo Soroka).
Elka and Aharon's sons, Itzik and Moshe are behind them.
Their other son Mordechai is standing in the front.

Fig. 2G
Barman, Katz and Gendelman Family Reunion in Rokitno - 1937

Seated in the center is Shaya/Seymour Barman, behind is his uncle and above the uncle is his aunt (names unknown). This was a celebration of their visit from the US.
To the left of his uncle is Shaya's father, Haim Barman.
Shaya's grandmother, Pessya is standing fifth from the left.
To the left of Shaya's aunt is Devosia Katz and her husband (both above Haim Barman); their daughter, Elka is seated on the far left step.
Second from right on the porch is Sonia Gendelman, fifth from right is her mother, Hannah Barman Gendelman holding her son, David and then left her husband, Tzvi Gendelman.
Their daughter Leah is seated to the left of Shaya.
Standing second from left is Shmulik Gendelman.

Appendix H: Photographs by Esther Gilbert ©

We would like to acknowledge **Lady Gilbert** for giving us permission to publish several photos she took while on a "Roots" visit with her husband, Sir Martin Gilbert, to the area of Volhyn in 2011.
In addition we are publishing her photos in Israel of the Rokitno and Surroundings Memorial Stone at the Holon Cemetery and the Yad Vashem memorial to Rokitno and other villages/towns.
Other photos taken by her of her trip through many villages in the Rokitno and Volhyn area can be seen at:
picasaweb.google.com/101835228506722847482?authkey=Gv1sRgCNyDt

Fig. 1H
Near the **Rokitno** marketplace - as if time stood still

Fig. 2H
The old Jewish cemetery of **Rokitno**

Fig. 3H
Sarny: The trench where 10,000 Jews were shot. The first mass grave and memorial is in the distant right.

Fig. 4H
Sarny: The memorial on the mass grave.

Fig. 5H

Sarny: The memorial stone erected in 2002 by the Russians.

Hebrew text:

In memory of the Jews of Sarny, Rokitno, Dumbrovitza and the surroundings, who were tortured and murdered by the German Nazis and their collaborators, may their names be obliterated, on 13-14 Elul, 5702 - 26-27.8.1942

May their souls be bound up in the eternal bond of life

Fig. 6H

Memorial stone erected in memory of

Yechiel Trossman

23rd Shvat 5705

6.2.1945

Fell in battle

Fig. 7H
Memorial Stone at **Rokitno** Cemetery:
KOROBOCHKA
Our father and grandfather
Moshe Korobochka, son of Nathan z"l 1883
A worker, Torah scholar and God-fearing man
And his daughter Freidel Korobotchka
Who were murdered by fascist murderers in autumn 1942 in the village of Bilovizh. May their blood be avenged

----

In memory of his wife Miriam from the house of Greenspan
His son Yoel and wife Hinia and their children Benyamin, Nathan, Asher and their baby
His daughter Henia Cuvres and her son Nachman Cuvres
His daughter Chava Mahler and her daughter Raya Mahler
Who were murdered by the fascist murderers in the autumn 1942 in Rokitno and the surroundings
May their blood be avenged

And in memory of his children Shmaryahu Kravi and Shoshana Yoz
Who made aliya to Eretz Israel and died there, leaving children and grandchildren in the State of Israel

(See their photos, page 506)

Fig. 8H
<u>Holon Cemetery, Israel</u>
The memorial stone for the Holy Community of ROKITNO and the surroundings (Volhyn)
May their blood be avenged
In memory of the Days of Slaughter 13-14 Elul, 1942

Fig. 9H
Memorial, <u>Valley of the Lost Communities</u>, **Yad Vashem, Israel**

Appendix I: Photographs from Prof. Arieh Kochavi (Starec)

Prof. Arieh Kochavi's family lived in Rokitno and moved to Russia during WWII. From there, they made aliyah to Eretz Israel.

Fig. 1I
The Rokitno Railway Station before WWII

Fig. 2I
The Dublin family from Rokitno
L-R: Arieh Leib, Judith Ida their daughter (Arieh Kochavi's mother), Sonya
Their daughter Lila is sitting in front

Fig. 3I
The Starec family from Rokitno
L-R: Chava, Moshe, Rachel and David
David is Arik Kochavi's father

Fig. 4I
Josef Starec, Chava's husband, who was a photographer in the Polish army

Appendix J: Our Pilgrimage to Rokitno, 2003

by Ala Gamulka

My husband, **Larry Gamulka**, grew up in Rokitno, a small town in Volyn Province, western Ukraine. However, he was born in Kovel, a larger city in Volyn and the home of his paternal grandparents Manya and Yerucham Gomulka. He spent an idyllic childhood as the only child of loving parents, Gitel Burko and Yonah Gomulka. They lived in a house in "the halles" across from the train station. Their small grocery store was located in the front of the house. It had previously belonged to Leah and Leibl Burko, Gitel's parents (Yonah's aunt and uncle).

Fig. 1J
Gitel Gamulka and her son Larry (Lova) 1946

In 1939, World War II broke out and the Soviets took over the town. Life was difficult, but not dangerous. Since private enterprise was no longer permitted, Yonah worked for the local authorities in the tax department. He was then drafted into the Soviet army. In 1941, the Soviets retreated and the Germans were in charge. The Jews were forced to wear a circular yellow patch and eventually they were all herded into two small crowded ghettos. On August 25, 1942, 1631 Jewish men, women and children were ordered to assemble in the market square for a roll-call on the following day. They stood six abreast, women and children under 13 on one side and men and older boys on the other side. The fear was palpable. Suddenly a woman's voice was heard: "Jews, they are going to shoot us! Save yourselves!" (The woman was very tall and was the first to see the German and Ukrainian police). Sounds of shooting and screaming filled the air. Hundreds of people were killed or wounded. Others, including Gitel and Larry, managed to escape into the forest. All others were put on cattle cars and taken to Sarny, where they were killed together with thousands of Jews from nearby villages.

Larry felt a need to see his childhood hometown and I knew I had to go with him. We were fortunate to join a group of Israelis with roots in Rokitno. They consisted of survivors, their spouses, children and even grandchildren. This has become a yearly pilgrimage organized by the Association of Former Residents (and their descendants) of Rokitno and Its Surroundings.
The simplest way to describe our trip is to do so chronologically. The group included our close friend Haim Bar Or, who had spent 18 months hiding with

Larry in a small dugout in the forest during the war. His wife, three children, son-in-law and oldest grandson were with him. We knew most of the others from other meetings in Israel. Our eldest son Daniel, who lives in Jerusalem, was also in the group. In Rokitno we were welcomed by Nina Ivanovna, former vice-mayor of Rokitno and a dear friend of the Jews and by the hotel manager, Luba Antonovna.

We began walking the streets of Rokitno almost immediately. Haim found the location of his home. Slava looked for her home. We wandered off to the market square, the scene of the bloody happenings. Larry was apprehensive about going back there. However, it looks completely different and there are many permanent stalls now. We walked to the train station, which had been destroyed and rebuilt. Larry's house used to stand diagonally across from the station. All the houses on his block had been burned down by the Soviets as they were retreating.

On Day Two we went to the Rokitno Jewish cemetery. As I walked through the old section, I found the grave of Larry's maternal grandmother, Leah Burko, who died in 1933. Everyone was excited and congregated around us. We lit a memorial candle and Larry recited *El Maleh Rachamim.* We now had a connection to the past. The only Jews still left in Rokitno are the dead ones. We searched for the grave of Larry's grandfather, but were unsuccessful.

There is a mass grave of those who were massacred in the market square. A large gravestone commemorates the fallen. We held a memorial ceremony. Our son, Dani chanted a special recited *El Maleh Rachamim.* It was truly a meaningful moment. The Israeli flag was draped over the gravestones and a special *Kaddish* was recited. Moshe Trossman spoke about his father who was buried there in 1944 and Benny Shapira played a haunting Yiddish song. We all dissolved in tears.

We went to Okopi, a Polish Catholic village which was completely destroyed by the Ukrainians. Only the cemetery remains. This is the area where Larry and Haim had hidden in the nearby forest. Some of the local peasants had fed them. The local priest encouraged his parishioners to give food to Jews. The local teacher, Mrs. F. Massajada, was very good to the Jews. Both were killed for doing so. Towards the end of the war, Haim lived in Okopi with the Romanewicz family and was instrumental in obtaining for Anieleh Romanewicz and her daughter Weronike Kozuiska the title of Righteous Gentiles, awarded by Yad Vashem.

We were joined by Larissa, a teacher from the village of Borovey. She knew a local man who remembers where houses once stood in Okopi. She took us through the village of Netrebe to Okopi. Larry was frozen in time. Netrebe is where he, his mother and six others were denounced and caught by the Ukrainians. They lined up parent and child in order to save bullets. The others were shot and it was Gitel and Larry's turn. Gitel reached into her clothing and threw several strands of pearls at the militiaman. He was distracted and they managed to escape into the forest. Once more Gitel saved her child's life.

We were invited by Larissa to her home for lunch. A wonderful spread was on the table- *varenikes* filled with blueberries! What memories for those who grew up there. On the way back to the hotel we stopped at Moshe Trossman's childhood home.

On Day Three we rode to Sarny. This is where eighteen thousand Jews from surrounding towns and villages were murdered. It is located 40 km from Rokitno and is a larger town. We got off the bus near a football stadium which was built over the Jewish cemetery. We crossed the train tracks and we followed the road our people had walked to their mass grave. They were made to undress there. We heard the story of two people who managed to escape either by hiding in the piles of clothing or by just running. There are three memorials. At the largest one, which the Association had recently refurbished, we held a memorial ceremony. Once again, our Dani chanted the recited *El Maleh Rachamim* and *Kaddish*. The original mass grave was just a pile of bones covered in earth. Haim read the names of his relatives who were killed there. I added the names of Pessach and Sarah Burko, Gitel's uncle and aunt and the names of Larry's aunts, uncles and cousins. They are the children and grandchildren of Leah Burko, whose grave we found the day before. Benny read a famous poem by Bialik. We visited the other memorials which are all next to a heavily-guarded military camp.

On the way back to Rokitno we stopped at the ancient Jewish cemetery of Osnitzk. There are many old, broken-down gravestones. The cemetery has not been used since 1920, but shows signs of a Jewish presence in the area several hundred years ago.
We returned to Rokitno and walked to the old Tarbut School which is now a geriatric hospital. The Tarbut School was a wonderful day school with outstanding and dedicated teachers. All subjects were taught in Hebrew. Larry's mother was one of the first graduates of the school and spoke Hebrew well. Haim, Moshe and Slava had attended the school.
We celebrated a *Kabbalat Shabbat* in our dining room. The women lit the candles, Dani recited *Kiddush* and we all sang and told stories. It was amazing and yet sad.

Day Four is Shabbat. Some people went to a memorial in Brezov and to Moshe's maternal grandparents' house in Glinna. The Bar Or and Gamulka families retraced childhood memories. We returned to the location of Haim's house. His house had been destroyed during the war. There is a large garden and a small kitchen and an outhouse on the grounds. The lady of the house invited us to visit. She was out of town when we came on the first day. They own two neighboring plots of land, filled with flowers and vegetables. Suddenly, Haim looked at the front of the house and announced: "This is Bella Krychman's house!" Bella is Larry's cousin and lives in Montreal. Larry and his mother lived there in the ghetto (April-August 1942). We were invited to enter and Larry immediately found the room in which they slept. Nothing has really changed. At the front door we saw an outline of nails which must have anchored the *mezuzah*! The present owners are warm and friendly. They bought the property only 20 years ago. We returned to the hotel and I skimmed through a memorial book from Manievich. Rafi Shapira, one of our group members, was bringing it to the Historical Museum of Rovno on the following day. Manievich was a resort town closer to Kovel. I found two pictures of Devorah Burko, the daughter of Gedalyah Burko, Gitel's brother. Our daughter's middle name is Devorah – in her memory. Larry remembers her well. What a coincidence! If Rafi had not casually mentioned it, I would not have thought of looking through it.

Now, the impossible! As we sat in the tiny lobby of the hotel, a man approached and asked if anyone spoke Polish. Larry answered positively. The man lives near Warsaw and drives the Polish priest to visit the ten remaining Catholic families in Rokitno. He was born in Rokitno and left in 1945. This is when the Jews and the Poles left. His father worked at a Jewish bakery and the Gitelmans (friends of our family) were his neighbors. It turns out that he attended the same Russian language kindergarten as Larry. He actually used to speak Yiddish which he learned from his classmates. He and Larry reminisced about their teacher whose name they had both forgotten. They remembered the beautifully decorated large tree put up by the teacher for the New Year. What next comes to mind is the Russian soldier who came to entertain the children with magic tricks. He came only once and chose two boys for a special trick. He gave them a glass of milk to drink, but he then collected all the milk under their chins in a glass. The Polish man and Larry were those two boys!

The Polish man remembers the day of the massacre in the market square. He was swimming in the river when shots rang out. He ran home ducking the shots overhead.

We walked to the railroad tracks to look for the bridge over the river. It was where Larry swam in the summer and skated in the winter.

At the market square we tried to recreate the horrible day. Dafna, Haim's daughter began to run when Haim imitated the shouting woman. She quickly ran out of steam. We wondered how they all ran away on that fateful day. An adrenalin rush due to fear must have propelled them.

After dinner we sat outside on the porch. It is part of a café with music blaring and much dancing inside. A group of university students who are home for the summer was interested in the reason for our visit. They did know about the market square and other Holocaust events. They were impressed that we wanted to come and to bring our offspring and encouraged us to continue to do so.

On Day Five we split up. The Bar Or and Gamulka families once again felt the need to return to Okopi. This is not only the place where Larry and Haim had hidden, but it is also where Haim's mother and sister died of dysentery. Larry clearly remembers helping to bury them in the forest. Larissa, the teacher from Borovey, joined us. A local peasant and his family took us by horse and wagon into the forest. The peasant knows that there are some graves inside the forest. Haim and his family went deep into the woods and felt they have reached some closure. The Gamulkas remained behind since the ground was almost knee-deep in rain water.

Early that evening we attended a special ceremony to unveil a plaque put up at the entrance to the market square. It commemorates the events of August 26, 1942. The inscription is in Ukrainian and Hebrew. Speeches were made by Haim in Hebrew and Russian and by the present mayor of Rokitno. The youngest members of our group, Yonatan and Gal, placed flowers and did the actual unveiling. As we began our gathering, an intense rain began to fall. We felt the heavens were crying as our fallen are remembered.

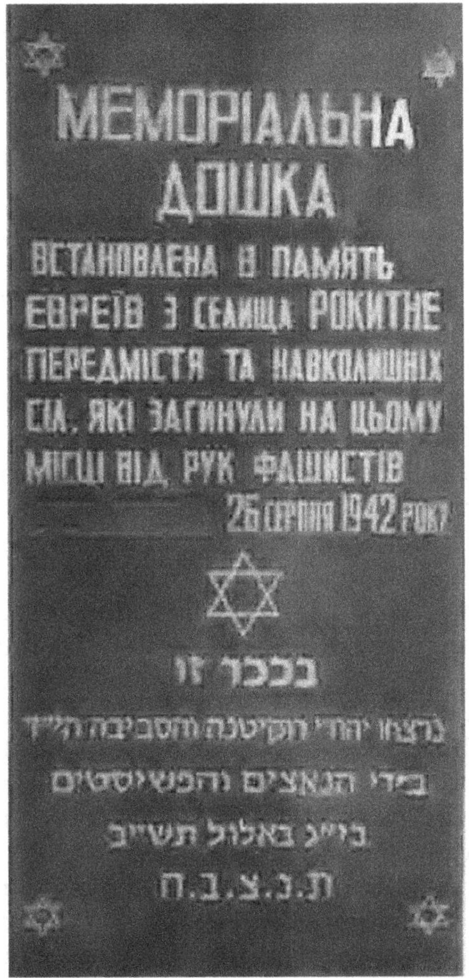

Fig. 2J
The memorial plaque of the massacre of the 26th August 1942, at the entrance to the Rokitno Market Square

(Hebrew translation:)

IN THIS MARKET SQUARE
The Jews of Rokitno and the surroundings,
may their blood be avenged
Were murdered by the Nazis and the Fascists
On 13th Elul, 5742
May their souls be bound up in the bond of life

We invited the mayor and his wife for dinner. We all spoke about the trip and its meaning to us. The vodka flowed as toasts were made.
Avi, our filmmaker, who is of Moroccan heritage, said he, at last, understood what the Holocaust is all about and what it means to be a Jew. He actually cried with Haim inside the forest earlier that day.

On Day Six we prepared to leave Rokitno, but we visited the cemetery on the way out. Nina promised to take care of Leah Burko's grave. She will also plant, in her garden, the seed sent to me by Lora Metelits. Lora's grandfather came from Rokitno and she was instrumental in putting out my English translation of the memorial book on the Internet. The grandfather had given her the original seed and she has planted it many times since. Two old peasant women spoke to us at the cemetery. They remembered the piles of Jewish bodies being trampled by pigs.
Before arriving at our hotel we visited Babi Yar. It is a grand memorial to those who were massacred in Kiev. There were at least 40 000 Jews thrown into the river and into ravines there. It represents the end of our attending memorials and visiting cemeteries- at least as a group.

On Day Seven, Larry, Dani and I left the group who stayed to tour Kiev. We were driven to Chernigov by Sergei, our friend Nat's grand-nephew. The reason for our visit is that Larry found out only a few years back that his father had died there. Yonah Gomulka was a soldier in the Soviet army and was taken prisoner by the Germans. When his unit was asked to identify the Jews, he and others stepped forward. They were immediately shot. Someone who did not step forward lived to tell the story. We visited the memorial to the partisans who died defending the town. There were two Jews among them. We then went to a memorial to the Jews who were massacred in a mass grave. Larry recited *El Maleh Rachamim* for his father and we lit a candle and felt some closure. We visited the old Jewish cemetery which is now being cleaned up and repaired. Prior to 1939, 40% of the population was Jews. We returned to the Jewish Community center where we met Semyon Bellman, the director. He spoke to us about his work and told us about the efforts to maintain Jewish life. They are so proud of their work. Since the fall of the Soviet Union many younger people have left for Israel. We saw the small synagogue which is used constantly. They are also preparing a memorial book to contain the names of all the Jews who were killed during the war. We gave him details about Larry's father. Larry felt he has finally buried his childhood!
We met in Haim and Haya's room to talk and to say good-bye. It was very difficult to let go. We have cried and laughed with the group for the past week. We hugged and we kissed and we promised to see each other again. As I write these words, we have been back for several weeks. We are happy that we traveled to Larry's childhood home and that we were able to see signs that Jews had once lived in this small town. When Larry speaks about his childhood, I truly understand and can visualize what he is describing. We know that we would return, even on our own, with other members of our family. It is our history!